# TELEVISION AND VIDEO SYSTEMS

# TELEVISION AND VIDEO SYSTEMS

## *Operation, Maintenance, Troubleshooting, and Repair*

Charles G. Buscombe

**PRENTICE HALL,** Englewood Cliffs, New Jersey 07632

**Library of Congress-In-Publication Data**

Buscombe, Charles G.
Television and video systems : operation, maintenance, troubleshooting, and repair / Charles G. Buscombe.
p. cm.
Includes index.
ISBN 0-13-903014-X
1. Television—Maintenance and repair. I. Title.
TK6630.B87 1990
621.388—dc20 89-8781
CIP

Editorial/production supervision and interior design: **Lillian Glennon**

Cover photograph courtesy of **Sencore News**
Manufacturing buyer: **Gina Brennan**



Printed in the United States of America

10 9 8 7 6 5 4 3 2 1

ISBN 0-13-903014-X

Prentice-Hall International (UK) Limited, *London*
Prentice-Hall of Australia Pty. Limited, *Sydney*
Prentice-Hall Canada Inc., *Toronto*
Prentice-Hall Hispanoamericana, S.A., *Mexico*
Prentice-Hall of India Private Limited, *New Delhi*
Prentice-Hall of Japan, Inc., *Tokyo*
Simon & Schuster Asia Pte. Ltd., *Singapore*
Editora Prentice-Hall do Brasil, Ltda., *Rio de Janeiro*

# Contents

# Preface

As the title suggests, this book is about video systems, specifically, the most widely used and popular electronic consumer products ever conceived and developed: television, TV/monitors, projection sets, and VCRs. It is written with two objectives: to help train future technicians, and to make life easier for technicians presently working in the field.

Such consumer products, whether for home entertainment or enlightenment, have become an important part of our culture and a way of life for many of us. Like it or not, that spells progress with a capital "P" and a multibillion-dollar enterprise that offers great promise for the future of those employed in this lucrative and rapidly expanding field. There are untold opportunities for would-be technicians who will one day be called upon to service and maintain such equipment.

As we all know, there have been rapid technological advances in recent years, so that even the most skilled technician is hard-pressed to keep up. Compared to yesteryear and its infancy, electronic servicing is now a different ballgame, where the untrained and unskilled are obliged to fall by the wayside, making room for the skilled tech to take his or her place in what is now rightfully considered a semiprofession.

With that in mind, this book was written in an effort to keep pace with rapid advancements and to serve the needs of the teacher, the student, and those practicing their chosen profession. Hopefully, it will do justice to each. As a prerequisite, it is assumed that the reader has been exposed to the fundamentals of electronics and although desirable, if not essential, has had some hands-on experience working with electronic circuits, solid-state devices, and test equipment.

Most teachers of electronics are on a seemingly endless quest for the ideal textbook. Of course, no book can be everything to everyone, but to you, the teacher, I would say, with all sincerity and humility, that this is a book that probably comes closest to serving your needs. I know only too well how difficult and frustrating it can be adapting a new text to an existing course of study. But as a classroom text, this is a book that you can work with and readily adapt to almost any curriculum and method of instruction.

For the most part, electronic basics have been omitted except in some instances, where a review of certain fundamentals seems necessary. Most chapters are in two parts, theory and troubleshooting. Block diagrams are used extensively, supported by numerous partial schematics and other illustrations. Theory for each type of equipment is presented in a logical and straightforward manner. To avoid overwhelming the beginning student with a lot of detail and confusing terms at the outset, each subject begins with simple descriptions and explanations, progressing gradually to the more complex. Engineering concepts and mathematics have all but been omitted in the presentations. Both you and your students should find the numerous questions on theory and troubleshooting at the end of each chapter provocative and stimulating, and extremely useful in promoting classroom discussions. There is also a full schematic of a late-model color TV set which serves as an exercise in schematic reading and circuit tracing. It is referred to in many of the chapters on TV.

It is an unfortunate fact of life that many graduate students are not yet ready to service sets and must first serve a period of on-the-job training before being able to cope. The reasons for this should be apparent to all. In the real world, theory is but a means towards an end. Most textbooks are heavy on theory and shortchange the practical, which in this author's opinion is a grave mistake, considering the objective. Hopefully, this book, which treats theory and troubleshooting with equal emphasis, will help shorten the transition from novice to expert.

And to you, the student technician—first let me congratulate you on your undertaking. I am sure that you have made a good choice. Of course, learning a new subject, with its dearth of information, and struggling with unfamiliar terminology is not always that easy. But let me put that to rest. As a one-time student myself, I can identify with you and your problems. So take heart. I assure you it will be all worthwhile. As for the book, which you will soon learn is not just another textbook, I know that you will find it a "readable" text containing a wealth of information that is of great benefit. And I firmly believe that it will find a permanent place near your service bench, where it will be used for reference long after graduation and for years to come. Good luck in your studies and all the best for a successful and profitable career.

And to you, the technician working at your profession—you should find this book most helpful in your day-to-day troubleshooting, particularly for the invaluable and much-needed information it contains on the latest advancements in TV technology, including projection sets, digital and HDTV, MTS/stereo, and VCRs. Indeed, it is truly a practical book, where the information you need is easy to get at and is presented in a form readily available for quick reference. No need to take time away from the bench to wade through a lot of extraneous material. Then there are the numerous troubleshooting flow drawings, covering all possible breakdowns and failures, common causes, and procedures.

The scope and content of the various chapters are described below. For further particulars, refer to the table of contents.

- *Chapter 1.* An introduction to television in general terms. TV as a system encompasses both broadcast stations and receivers; to understand one requires a knowledge of the other. Here, with the aid of a block diagram, we learn about the various signals being generated; the composite video signal; an introduction to color mixing principles; and a description of how images viewed by a camera are converted into electrical impulses, processed, and transmitted along with the sound signal.
- *Chapter 2.* The fundamentals of conventional television receivers, both monochrome (BW) and color. A block diagram treatment is used to show all the major stages and signal flow, with descriptions. Various kinds of picture tubes are illustrated and described, including receiver controls and their functions. Further information covers color basics and color mixing and how electronic impulses produce images in black and white and full color.
- *Chapter 3.* A tabular presentation of electronic components with descriptions, typical uses, common defects, and methods of testing. Emphasis is on PCBs (printed circuit boards), solid-state devices, and ICs in particular. Handling and testing precautions are also covered, and repair procedures are included where appropriate and warranted.
- *Chapter 4.* A description of all types of test equipment, their functions, and uses with illustrations. In addition to basic instruments, this includes all the modern and sophisticated multifunction testers found in most up-to-date and progressive service shops for repairing complex electronic equipment. Also included are common servicing aids, such as probes, special tools and accessories, chemical compounds, and the like.
- *Chapter 5.* An introduction to electronic troubleshooting and repair. The table of contents shows the variety of subjects covered, including procedures for testing and troubleshooting all types of circuits, devices, and equipment described in this book. Included are such topics as SMD (surface-mounted device) technology, scope tracing, and testing by signal injection and substitution. Additional information on troubleshooting specific circuits is presented in later chapters.
- *Chapter 6.* Power supplies. This is the first of 13 chapters that deal individually with specific stages and sections of television re-

ceivers. All types of primary and secondary power supplies and associated circuits are described, including those used in VCRs and other equipment. Also covered are voltage regulators, voltage distribution networks, hot chassis problems, and an introduction to startup/shutdown circuits. In addition to common defects and probable causes, the section on troubleshooting and repairs contains shortcut procedures for isolating B+ shorts and other overload conditions.

- *Chapter 7.* Functional descriptions of the vertical sweep section of TV, with emphasis on the countdown generator and complementary-symmetry output circuits. Includes descriptions of typical waveforms and voltages, the treatment of all common trouble symptoms with causes and procedures, and troubleshooting and repairs.
- *Chapter 8.* Generation and control of horizontal sweep. Typical circuits are described, including the countdown generator. Varactor control and other AFC (automatic frequency control) circuits are covered, including troubleshooting and repairs.
- *Chapter 9.* Functional descriptions of the sync stages and noise immunity systems. Typical circuits are presented, including integrating and differentiating of sync pulses. Troubleshooting and repairs.
- *Chapter 10.* Functional descriptions of horizontal driver, output and HV circuits. Secondary power supplies and other sweep-dependent circuits are fully explained. In the section on troubleshooting and repair the emphasis is on precautionary procedures to prevent destruction of the output transistor and other expensive components.
- *Chapter 11.* The purpose and need for startup/shutdown circuits. A functional description of the various systems is given, together with the common causes of shutdown. Testing and validating startup and shutdown functions are covered, together with troubleshooting and repairs.
- *Chapter 12.* Functional description of basic VHF and UHF tuners (channel selectors). Principles of heterodyning and frequency conversion and AFT (automatic fine tuning) are presented. Tuned circuit fundamentals and response curves are discussed, as is varactor control of pushbutton tuners. Cable-ready tuners, frequency synthesis and phase-locked-loop tuners, remote control systems, alignment and troubleshooting and repairs are all included.
- *Chapter 13.* Functional description of the video IF strip, detector, and AGC (automatic gain control) stages. IF response curves, narrowband and broadband color systems, and tank and trap circuits are additional concerns. The SAW filter and syncronous detector are described and their influence on picture quality. Typical AGC circuits are covered, along with troubleshooting, alignment, and repair.
- *Chapter 14.* Video amplifier stages of monochrome and color sets. Frequency compensation and video peaking are covered, as well as ceramic and comb filters and the sandcastle circuit. Troubleshooting and repair information is provided.
- *Chapter 15.* The chroma signal processing stages and more specifics on how BW and multicolor images are produced. Color fundamentals, phase angles, and vectors are discussed, and the combining of luminance/chroma signals. Bandwidth considerations are included, and demodulation and typical circuits are described. CRT matrixing, automatic chroma control (ACC), and the role of the output circuits that drive the three guns of the CRT are covered, in addition to troubleshooting, alignment, and repairs.
- *Chapter 16.* Chroma switching and color sync. The need for a subcarrier in the chroma demodulation process is explained along with various subcarrier generating circuits together with other aspects of color synchronization. The relationship between phase angles and color hues is further explained. Additional subjects are tint control circuits, the burst gate, color killer, and chroma switching functions. Detailed AFPC (automatic frequency and phase control) alignment procedures are given along with troubleshooting and repairs.
- *Chapter 17.* A follow-up of Chapter 2, where different types of CRTs were described. Topics covered include associated components and controls, operating conditions, voltages, and setup adjustments for BW and color sets. Convergence problems and typical adjustment procedures are included, together with CRT testing, restoration, handling, and replacement. Troubleshooting

and repair of related circuits and components are the final topics.

- *Chapter 18.* The TV circuits and components that process and reproduce sound. Functional descriptions of the sound stages of both monochrome and color sets are presented, including AM/FM fundamentals and comparisons. Demodulating the FM signal is described, together with typical circuits. Preemphasis, deemphasis, and frequency response considerations are also covered, as are complementary-symmetry output amplifiers. Speakers, crossover networks, impedance matching considerations, and stereo receivers are discussed. The MTS/stereo system is described, including functional operation of the DBX noise reduction system. Troubleshooting, alignment and repairs completes the chapter.
- *Chapter 19.* Digital Television. The principles of computer logic applied to television for producing special effects such as PIP (picture-in-picture), multichannel search and monitoring, and others. A brief treatment of binary logic fundamentals, including functions, symbols, devices, and circuitry, is also given. Analog and digital signal processing are covered, and also the subject of how special effects are produced. Additional topics include the following:

*HQ* (high quality) considerations. Picture resolution is defined and different means of accomplishment are discussed. Circuits used in TV sets, monitors and VCRs to enhance picture quality are described.

*HDTV* (high-definition TV). An insight into problems inherent in the present NTSC system of television broadcasting and reception and the urgent need for changes. Compatibility considerations, the magnitude of changeover conversion problems and the dilemma faced by designers, and possible solutions and alternatives are included.

*IDTV* (improved-definition TV). As an interim approach to true HDTV. The concept of double scanning is described in comparison to other systems in use. Troubleshooting and repair information is provided for each topic.

- *Chapter 20.* VCRs: the intermarriage of electromechanical devices and electronic processing circuitry. Next to television, its companion, the videocassette recorder is unquestionably the most popular consumer product today. Starting with a basic overview of the system, we study the theory of operation, the fundamentals of magnetic recording, the intricacies of electromechanical devices, and the electronics, with details on specific circuits used in all modes of operation. Information is given on HQ and super-VHS formats, hi-fi stereo, and the latest innovations, including digital circuitry and special effects featured in late-model VCRs.

- *Chapter 21.* VCR servicing. Presented here as a follow-up to Chapter 20 is all the information needed to learn to repair and maintain VCRs. Troubleshooting is presented in two ways: with flowcharts and an extensive listing of all possible trouble symptoms with probable causes (the meat of the subject) and procedures. Problems most often encountered are presented, including typical waveforms and voltages to expect at key checkpoints. In addition, flowcharts, where troubles are categorized as record or playback problems for both picture and sound, are given. Special emphasis is placed on servo control mechanisms and the various sensors that monitor and control operations. Procedures for cleaning play/record heads and other items in the tape path are described, together with common ailments and breakdowns. Troubleshooting, maintenance, and repairs are all covered.

- *Chapter 22.* Projection TV. Functional operation of the two systems, front and rear projection, is described. A tabular presentation is given of all major components and the purpose of each. Typical circuits are given, including information on cleaning and adjustment of the optical systems. Setup procedures for the light tubes (CRTs) and typical problems are additional topics. Correcting for raster distortion, and troubleshooting and repairs, completes the chapter.

**Charles G. Buscombe**

# Acknowledgments

I would like to thank the following publishers and companies, which so generously provided me with information and illustrations, for which I am extremely grateful: Sencore, General Electric, RCA, Mitsubishi, Toshiba, and Prentice-Hall. In particular, I wish to thank the following people for their advice and assistance in the planning of the book and for the material they provided: Greg Burnell, Tom Barrowcliff, Russell Souter, Walt Herrin, David Compton, Robert Young, and David Shoults, and my son, Gary.

Last, but certainly not least, thanks to my dear and loving wife, Beryl, for her patience and forebearance and the peace and quiet that prevailed most of the time during the writing effort.

**Charles G. Buscombe**

**To all aspiring electronic technicians,**
**students, and those presently engaged**
**in practicing their chosen profession**

# 1 The television system

A typical TV station consists of studios with their numerous facilities for generating and producing program material, live and from remote pickups, videotape, satellites, and so on. Also included is the transmitter and antenna system, which is often located at a remote site selected for maximum coverage. Pictures and sound signals are transmitted as high-frequency electromagnetic waves to the numerous TV receivers within range, as well as providing material to the ever-increasing cable (CATV) services. An understanding of the signals being generated at the studios and by the transmitting equipment can greatly aid in understanding what takes place in a receiver.

## 1-1 TELEVISION BROADCASTING FUNDAMENTALS

All TV stations generate and radiate high-frequency (RF) carrier waves. By a process called *modulation*, picture and sound information is superimposed on the carriers (there are two). In the process, *sidebands* of the carriers are produced, an upper and a lower sideband extending above and below the carrier frequencies by an amount determined by the ever-changing modulating frequencies. All information to be transmitted is contained in these sidebands.

A TV station has *two* transmitters, an amplitude-modulated (AM) transmitter for the video (picture) signals [together with synchronizing (sync) signals]; and a frequency-modulated (FM) transmitter for the sound signal. With AM, the carrier amplitude varies in accordance with the strength of the video and sync signals. With FM, the strength of the carrier remains constant and the carrier frequency changes with the audio. Low sound levels produce small variations of the RF carrier frequency, and strong audio produces large frequency variations in the RF carrier. A black-and-white station generates only a monochrome or *luminance* signal. A color broadcast contains both luminance and chroma information. At TV frequencies, propagation and good reception are generally limited to line-of-sight.

*Compatibility.* All American stations comply with the National Television Systems Committee (NTSC) regulations. This means that a color set can receive black-and-white (BW) broadcasts (in monochrome, of course), and a BW set can receive color broadcasts in black and white. This is accomplished by transmitting color information within the band of frequencies allocated for black and white.

## 1-2 SIDEBANDS, CHANNEL ALLOCATIONS, AND BANDWIDTH CONSIDERATIONS

There are two bands of frequencies allocated to TV: a "low" and a "high" VHF (very high frequency) band, and a UHF (ultrahigh frequency) band. The VHF band is split into two parts. Except for a gap between channels 6 and 7, the VHF band extends from 54 MHz (channel 2) to 216 MHz (channel 13). UHF stations (channels 14 through 83) use frequencies between 470 and 890 MHz. Other bands now available for channels receivable with a "cable-ready" tuner (from a CATV service) are the mid-band, superband, and hyperband.

Each station is assigned a 6-MHz range of frequencies, which, despite the insignificant number, is considerable. By comparison, an AM radio station requires only 10 kHz. All video, chroma, sync, and sound signals are transmitted within this 6-MHz bandpass (Figure 1-1). Note the off-centered video carrier frequency and the unequal upper and lower video sidebands, known as *vestigial sideband transmission*. This is done to reduce the transmitted bandwidth of the available frequencies allotted to TV. High video frequencies (from 0 Hz (the carrier) to about 4 MHz (4 million Hertz) on the upper sideband, but the lower sideband extends only about 1 MHz from the carrier. This means that the station puts out more signal for low video frequencies than it does for high frequencies. This is compensated for later at the receiver. In Figure 1-1, note the relatively narrow band of frequencies allocated for the sound signal, at the high end of the overall bandpass allocation. The picture and sound carriers are separated by 4.5 MHz. Also note the relative locations of the two adjacent channels, each extending from where the other leaves off (Figure 1-2).

Chroma information is transmitted along with the video within the same bandpass (Figure 1-1b), and is centered about 3.58 MHz above the video carrier. Chroma signals require their own carrier. The video and chroma center frequencies are separated by this amount. The chroma is transmitted as a double-sideband (DSB) suppressed carrier.

As with the video, the chroma, which is sandwiched within the video passband, has upper and lower sidebands known respectively as I and Q sidebands. Vestigial transmission is used, with the I sidebands containing more information than the Q sidebands (Figure 1-1b).

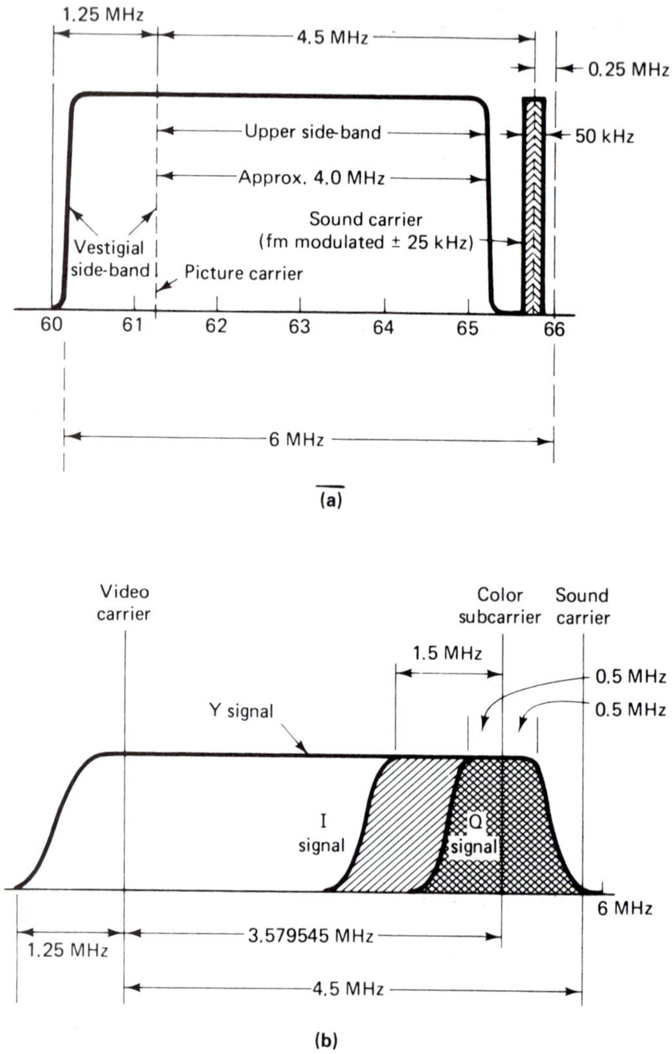


**FIG. 1-1** Frequency limits and vestigal sidebands. Video bandpass with I and Q sidebands added for color.

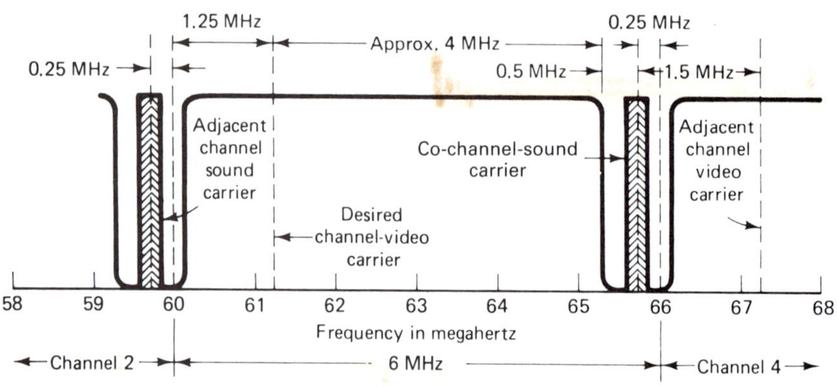


**FIG. 1-2** A portion of the VHF spectrum.

## 1-3 TELEVISION CAMERAS

Although there may be videotape and other sources, all video and chroma signals originate from a camera, which converts visual images into electrical impulses. A typical color camera contains three cathode ray tubes (CRTs), one for each of the three primary colors, red, green, and blue. Using a system of dichroic mirrors, lenses, and optical filters, each CRT receives an image corresponding to its primary color identity and any secondary (complementary) colors contained in that color.

A cross section of a typical camera tube is shown in Figure 1-3. The viewed image is projected onto a target plate or mosaic containing 1 million or more photosensitive particles. Each particle corresponds with the smallest element of a picture, sometimes referred to as a *pixel* (picture element).

A CRT comprises an electron "gun" with a heated cathode that emits electrons, and other elements that control the electron stream. The electrons are directed as a beam at the target plate. The beam is deflected vertically and horizontally simultaneously to produce what is called a *raster*. Beam deflection is accomplished by electromagnetic *yoke* coils surrounding the electron gun. The electron beam sequentially scans each picture element on the target, and as it does so, the target gives off secondary electrons representing the output signal. The strength of the beam and the CRT output varies in accordance with the brightness of each picture element being scanned. Video signals generated by

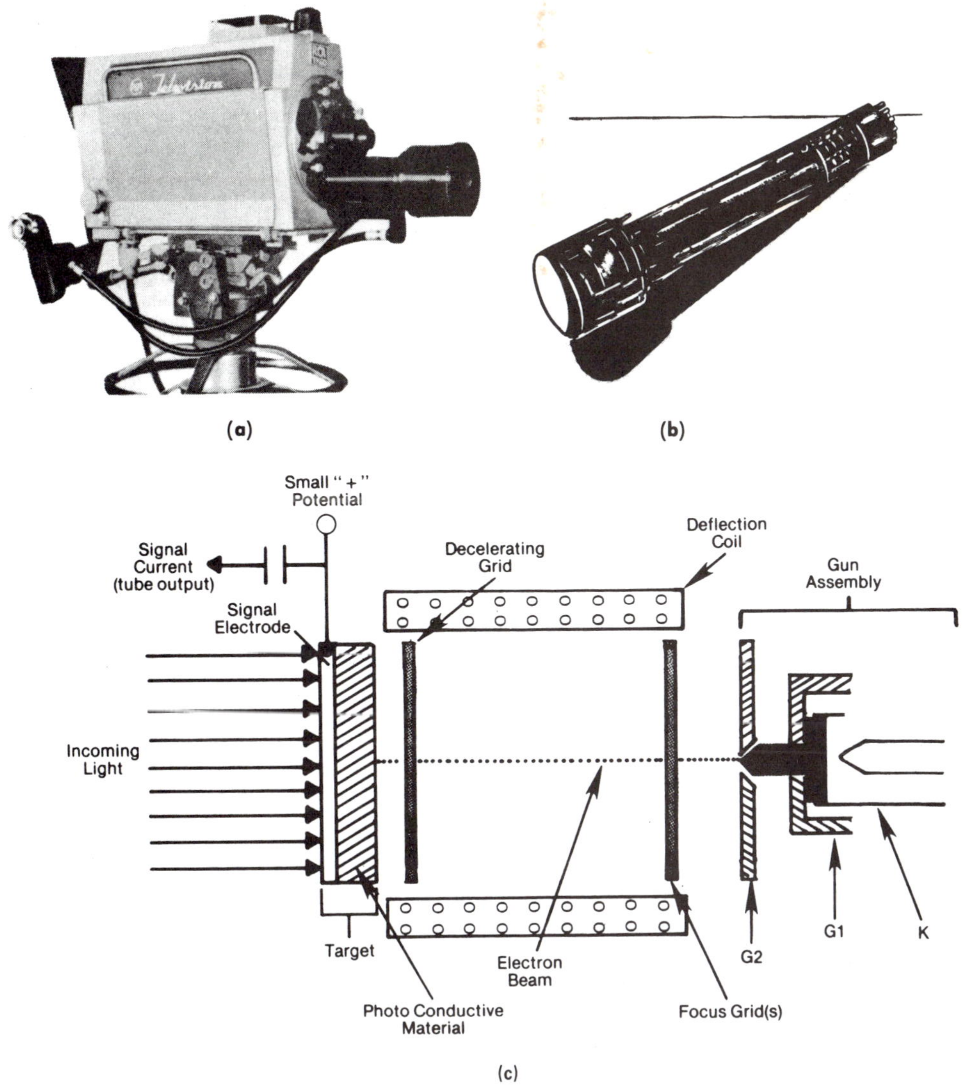


**FIG. 1-3** Typical TV camera tube. The magic of converting images into electrical impulses. (Courtesy of Sencore News).

each CRT are synchronized with the raster scanning.

## 1-4 BEAM SCANNING AND RASTER DEVELOPMENT

As an arbitrary starting point at a given moment in time, assume that the electron beam is directed toward the upper left side of the screen (Figure 1-4). Under the electromagnetic influence of the horizontal deflection yoke, the beam is made to move from left to right across the screen. At the same time, under the influence of the vertical yoke, it is pulled downward, producing a visible *scanning line* sloping downward to the right. At this point, the beam is deflected rapidly to the left side of the screen. This is called *horizontal beam retrace*. Retrace lines are blanked out and not seen by the viewer. When the beam reaches the left side of the screen, the screen becomes unblanked and another line is produced in the same manner as before until $262\frac{1}{2}$ lines have been scanned.

When the beam reaches the bottom of the screen, the magnetic influence of the vertical yoke reverses and the beam begins to move upward. During this *vertical retrace* interval (which is blanked out) the beam is still being influenced by the horizontal sweep (deflection) and continues to move upward in zigzag fashion until it reaches the top of the screen. This completes what is called the scanning of a *field*. At this point the vertical influence is reversed and the beam starts downward to scan a second field, as before. This time, because the scanning starts and stops midline (as indicated), the second scanning results in "odd" lines that are *interlaced* with the "even" lines of the first field. The result is a raster comprised of 525 lines (known as a *frame*) which effectively scans every picture element on the target plate.

The horizontal scanning rate for monochrome is 15,750 Hz/s. For color it is slightly lower, 15,734 Hz. The vertical sweep frequency is 60 Hz. Since there are two fields for each frame, the picture repetition rate is 30 per second—rapid enough to prevent flicker. By comparison, the frame rate for theater movies is only about 24 per second. At the receiver, a raster is developed on the picture tube in the same manner with scanning precisely synchronized to the station and with the video signals received, so images will be reproduced at their proper points and at the proper times on the screen.

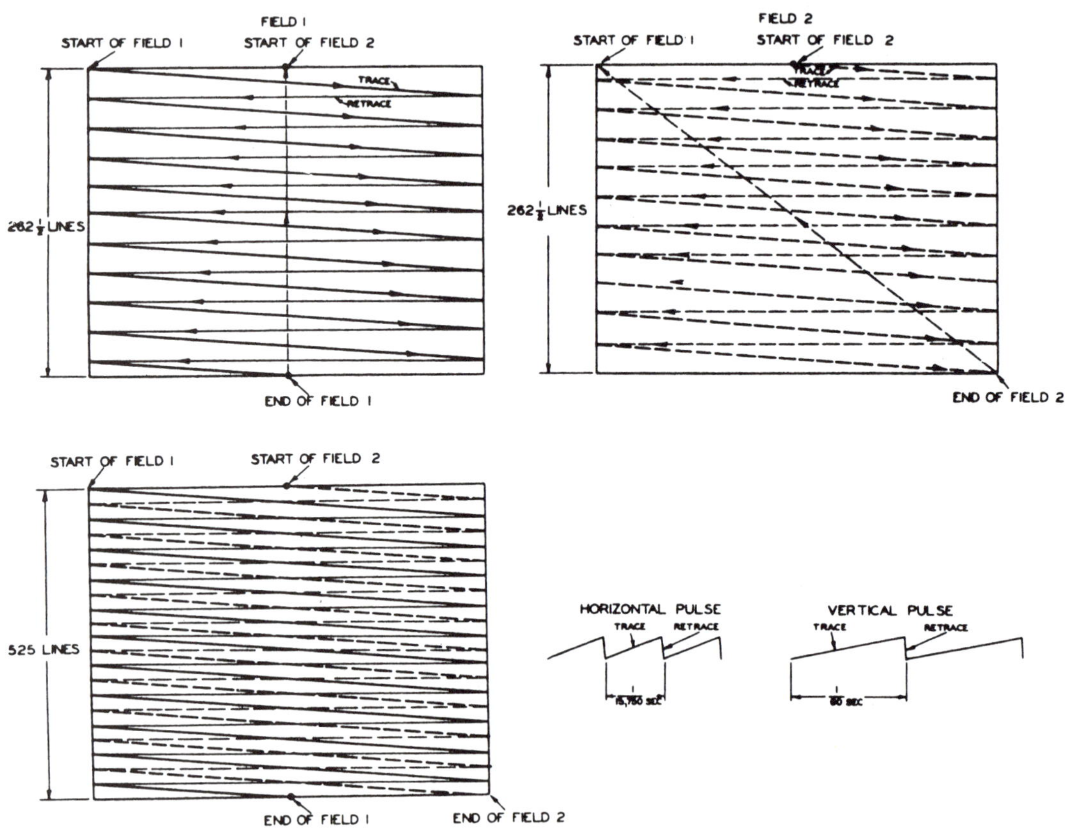


**FIG. 1-4** Interlaced scanning and raster development.

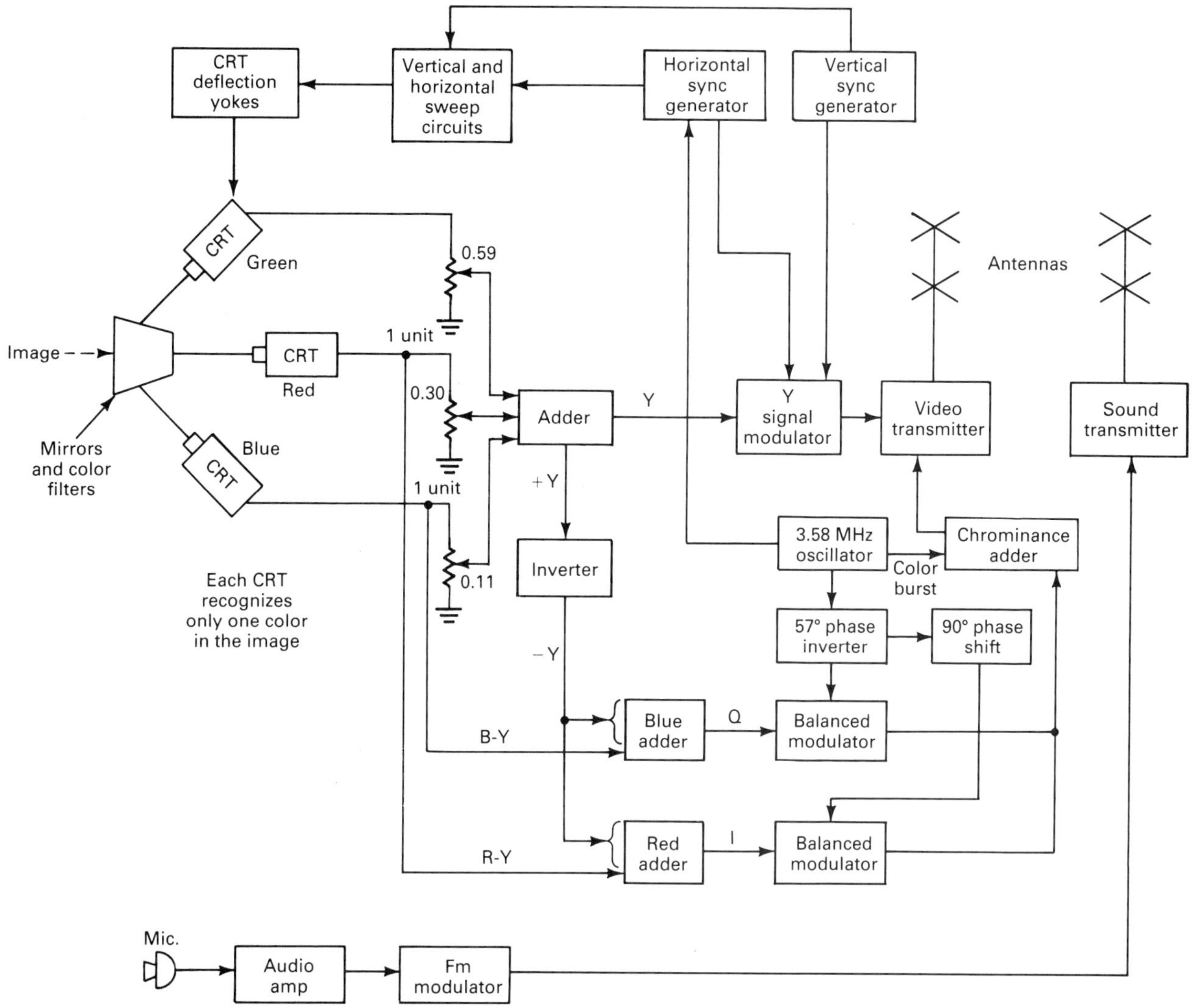


**FIG. 1-5** TV station block diagram. Note the three color levels for producing white.

A block diagram of a typical TV station functions is shown in Figure 1-5. The functions of each block are described briefly in Table 1-1.

### Synchronization

Note the vertical and horizontal sweep circuit blocks that supply the yoke with beam deflection currents (Figure 1-5). Each is supplied from a sweep generating stage. The sweep circuits are synchronized by pulses developed by sync generators, a sampling of which is transmitted.

## 1-5 COLOR MIXING

A mixture of red, green, and blue in the proportions 30% red, 59% green, and 11% blue produces white (the complete absence of color). The outputs of the three camera tubes are adjusted to these values and combined in an "adder" stage. The output of the adder is a black-and-white monochrome (Y signal) that modulates the transmitter and is transmitted along with other signals. Full output from the three camera tubes creates white. Zero output results in black (a dark screen).

To produce colors, samplings of the red and blue CRTs are fed to red and blue adders. The red adder receives a voltage representing an undiluted "pure" red, otherwise known as an R − Y (red minus white) voltage. The blue adder receives a voltage representing an undiluted or pure blue called a B − Y (blue minus white) voltage. These are sometimes referred to as *color difference signals*. Both adders also receive an inverted sampling of the Y signal voltage to establish the brightness levels of the colors. The output of the red adder, designated I (for "in phase"), feeds one of two "balanced" modulators. The blue adder output, designated Q (for "quadrature"), feeds the other modulator. Note

***TABLE 1-1***

Color TV station functions

| *Stage or Item* | *Function* | *Remarks* |
|---|---|---|
| Camera | Converts image into signal voltages | Monochrome camera has one CRT; typical color camera has three |
| Beam-splitter mirrors and filters | Projects color images to corresponding color-related CRT | Each CRT receives only images containing its primary and complementary colors |
| RGB CRTs | Produce signal voltages corresponding to their color-related functions | |
| CRT deflection yokes | Produce electromagnetic deflection of CRT electron beams | |
| Vertical and horizontal sweep circuits | Supply sweep current to yokes | Simultaneous vertical and horizontal deflection produces a raster |
| Vertical and horizontal sync generators | Produce sync pulses to control sweep circuits | Sync pulses are transmitted along with the video |
| Matrix | Converts camera outputs into I, Q, and Y signals | |
| Y signal modulator | Modulates the transmitter with luminance information | |
| Balanced modulators | Modulate the 3.58-MHz subcarrier oscillator with I and Q chroma information | Modulator chroma outputs feed the transmitter to modulate the RF carrier |
| Subcarrier oscillator | Produces a 3.58-MHz continuous-wave signal that is modulated by the chroma signals | A sampling of the oscillator signal (color burst) is combined with horizontal sync and transmitted |
| Phasing network | Develops two phase-shifted oscillator signals | The two out-of-phase subcarriers are modulated by corresponding I and Q chroma signals |
| Audio amplifier | Amplifies the audio signals from microphone or other audio source | |
| FM modulator | Frequency modulates the RF carrier developed by the sound transmitter | |

that there is no provision for producing and transmitting green or its complementary colors. Green is produced at the receiver as a mixture of red and blue.

To modulate or demodulate a signal requires an unmodulated continuous-wave (CW) carrier. In this case it is a subcarrier, at a frequency of 3.58 MHz. The balanced modulators separately phase modulate the same 3.58-MHz subcarrier, but remain separated from each other by a specific phase angle. As shown in Figure 1-5, these two signals are phase-shifted 57° and 90° relative to the subcarrier.

The actual subcarrier signal per se is not transmitted as such, and to provide color synchronization at the receiver a short burst sampling of the oscillator is transmitted as a part of each horizontal sync signal (Figure 1-5). The chroma outputs from the balanced modulators are combined in a chrominance adder stage, then fed to the transmitter, where they are multiplexed with the monochrome signal and readied for transmission.

## 1-6 COMPOSITE VIDEO SIGNAL

The signal that modulates the video transmitter is a complex mixture of video information (monochrome and chroma) plus numerous sync and blanking pulses (Figure 1-6). The video information is ever changing in frequency and amplitude, in accordance with brightness and color changes of the picture being televised. By comparison, the pulses are constant and repetitious. Figure 1-6 shows about five lines of video information. High-amplitude *blanking pulses* periodically interrupt the video to darken the CRT screen during vertical and horizontal retrace periods. Sync pulses are superimposed on the blanking pulses. Their function is to synchronize raster development with the video signals. In the figure, note the vertical blanking interval of relatively long duration. The sync pulses on the vertical blanking pedestal synchronize the horizontal sweep generator during the vertical retrace interval and provide sync for the vertical sweep. (More on this later.) Figure 1-6b shows an enlarged view of one horizontal sync pulse with a *color burst* on the back porch of the blanking pedestal. The burst is used to synchronize color on a color set but is ignored by BW receivers.

Note the callouts for events as they occur during the vertical blanking interval that follows each field. At point A, as the last line of picture information was scanned at the bottom of the screen, the sudden rise in blanking voltage darkens the screen.

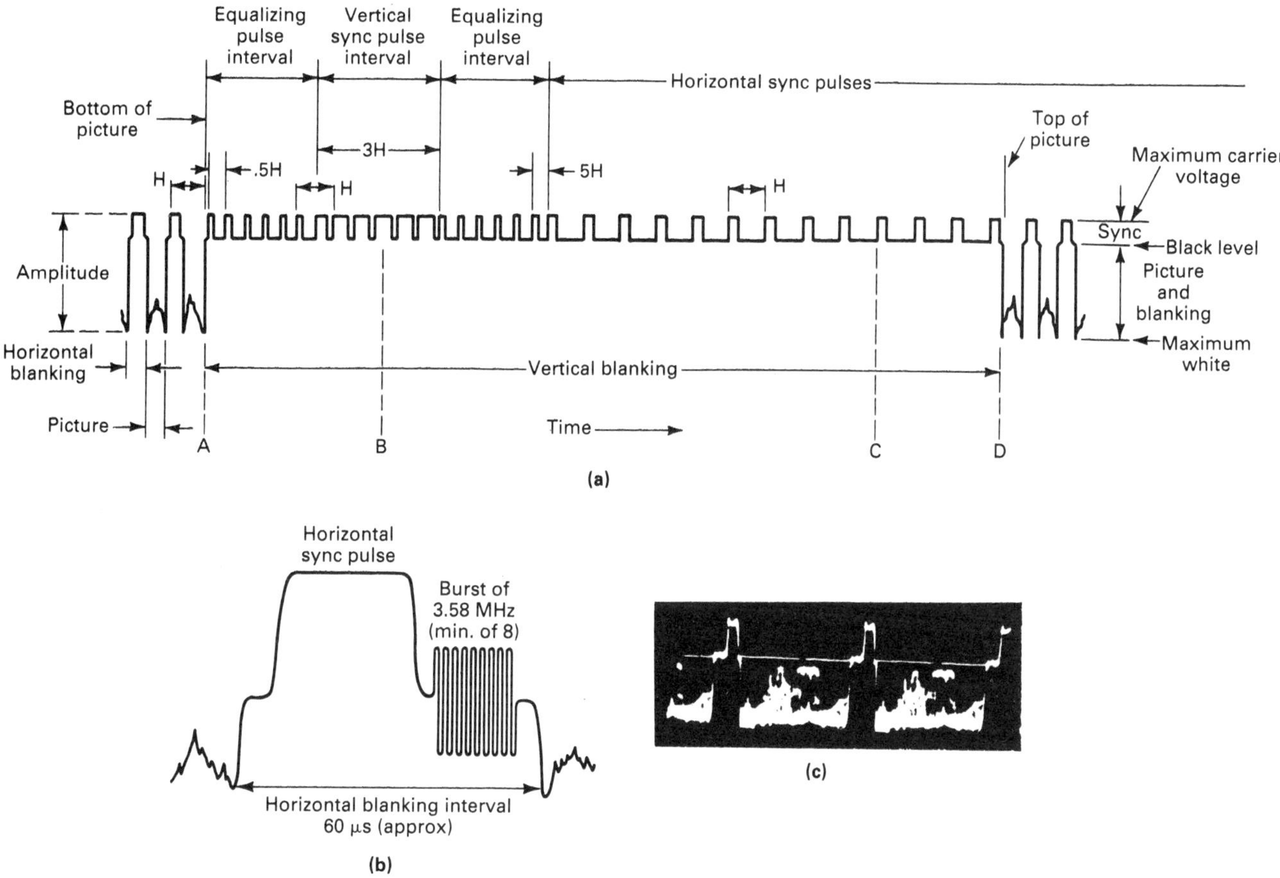


**Fig. 1-6** The composite video signal.

The beam is still moving *downward*. At point B, one of six vertical sync pulses triggers the vertical sweep and the beam starts moving up. Point C corresponds to the approximate time when the vertical trace reverses again and the beam moves downward to trace another $262\frac{1}{2}$-line field. At point D, vertical blanking ceases and the screen lights up as the first line of the picture is scanned near the top of the screen. All the serrations on the vertical blanking pulses control the *horizontal* sweep during vertical retrace. Some picture information is, of course, "lost" to the viewer during vertical and horizontal retrace periods when the screen is blanked out, but this is not noticeable because of the short duration.

## QUESTIONS

1. Name all the signals transmitted by a station within its 6-MHz bandpass allocation.
2. What is vestigial transmission, and what is its purpose?
3. Why does the video signal occupy so much of the bandpass of a TV station?
4. Why are channels allocated according to a station's geographic location and rated power?
5. Explain briefly how colors viewed by the camera CRTs are readied for transmission.
6. Why is the finest picture detail not transmitted in color?
7. Explain why the color subcarrier is needed and why it is not transmitted.
8. Do each camera's CRTs view all the colors in a picture? Explain.
9. What is the Y signal, and how is it produced?
10. Why is the color green not transmitted?
11. How are the I and Q color signals separated from each other at the output of the modulators?

# 2 Television receivers

This chapter serves as a brief introduction to TV receivers, both black and white and color. In the interests of brevity and simplicity at this point in the book, much of the information is presented in tabular form. A more detailed treatment of all subjects is provided, as appropriate, in later chapters.

## 2-1 RECEIVER FUNDAMENTALS

The stages of a typical BW receiver are shown in Figure 2-1, with arrows indicating signal flow for producing two outputs, a picture on the cathode ray tube (CRT) and sound from the speaker. Stage functions are described briefly in Table 2-1.

A basic TV set comprises several main functional areas, most of them interrelated: low- and high-voltage power supplies (PSs); vertical and horizontal sweep stages, for producing a raster; sync stages, for synchronizing raster scanning with the video signals received; and the video and sound signal stages, where the incoming signals are processed to drive the CRT and the speaker. Each block in the diagram may represent one or *several* stages having the same function.

Besides the numerous ac and dc voltages necessary to the operation of all TV circuitry, there are numerous signal voltages. Some signal voltages are received from the station, some are generated internally, and some are control signals used to control various receiver functions.

Signals are passed from one stage to another in each functional area in various ways: direct coupling (often referred to as *dc coupling*), capacity coupling (*ac coupling*) using capacitors, and transformer (*inductive*) coupling. Impedance matching is an important consideration in most cases, particularly in the efficient transfer of *power,* where more than voltages are involved: for example, driving power output transistors, deflection yokes, and the speaker—in fact, anywhere where inductances are used.

In addition to the usual components found in most electronic equipment (e.g., coils resistors and capacitors), modern TV sets contain a great many *solid-state* components: discrete components such as diodes and transistors, and ICs. In recent years, multifunction ICs have taken over almost completely.

## 2-2 MONOCHROME RECEIVER OPERATION

A raster is prerequisite to developing a picture. It is produced in the same manner as described for camera tubes in Chapter 1. Vertical and horizontal sweep circuits develop and supply sawtooth currents to the deflection yoke. The yoke produces electromagnetic fields, causing the CRT electron beam to sweep vertically and horizontally simultaneously to create the scanning lines. With a TV set, amplitude variations of the received video signal "intensity modulate" the CRT beam to create black-and-white images.

When the tuner is set to receive a given channel, the RF picture and sound signals for that channel are amplified and converted to lower (IF) carrier

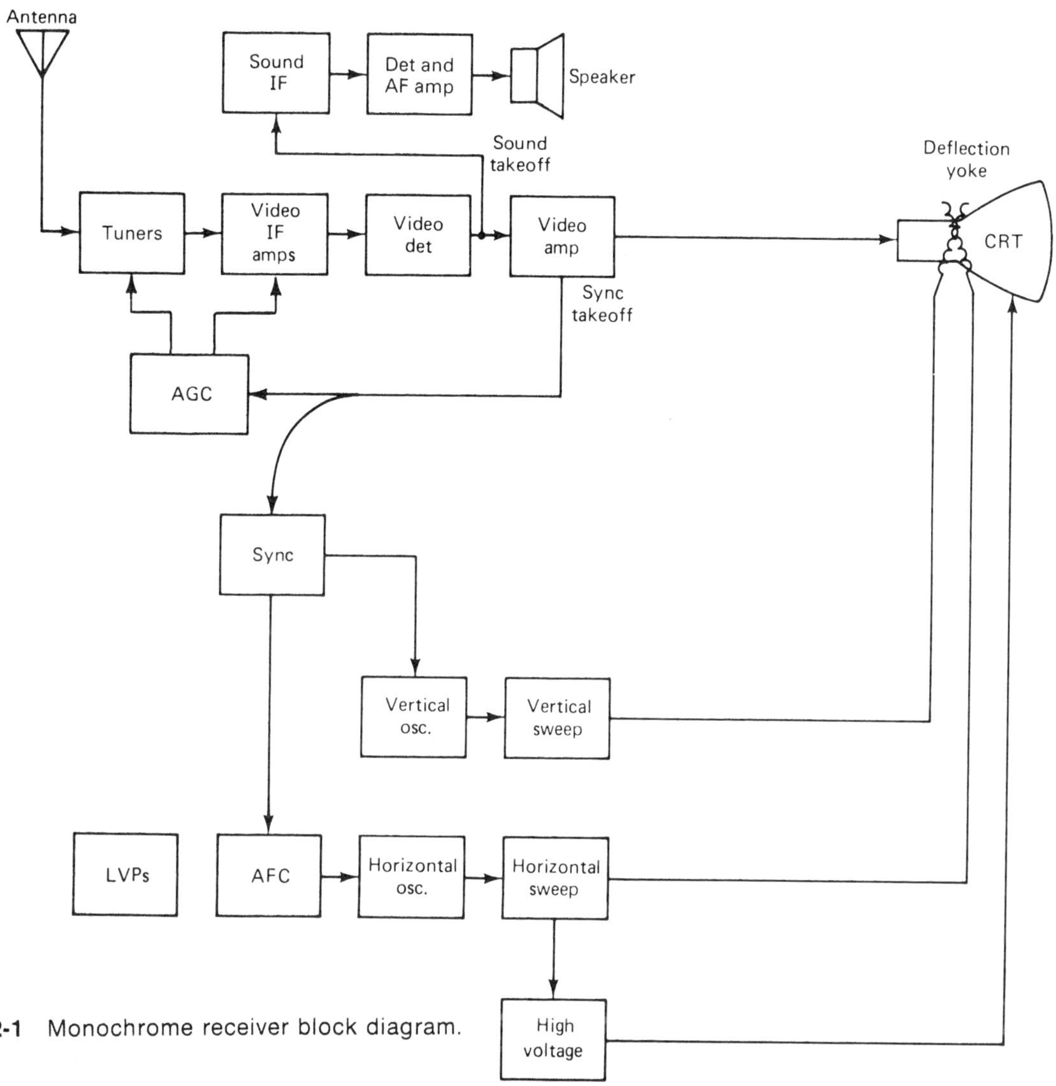


**FIG. 2-1** Monochrome receiver block diagram.

frequencies, 45.75 and 41.25 MHz, respectively. The two signals are further amplified by *fixed-tuned* IF amplifier stages. The video detector demodulates the video signal (recovers it from its carrier), and develops a 4.5-MHz signal from the heterodyne "beat" between the picture and sound IF carriers. This 4.5-MHz signal becomes the new sound IF carrier. The video output from the detector is further amplified to feed the picture tube.

The 4.5-MHz sound signal (extracted from any point after the video detector) of a BW set is amplified by a fixed-tuned IF section, demodulated, and further amplified at audio frequencies to drive the speaker. Picture and sound are maintained relatively constant by the AGC circuit, which regulates the gain of the RF and IF amplifiers.

Raster scanning is synchronized with the received video signals by sync pulses that control the vertical and horizontal sweep generators (oscillators). The hardest-worked circuit is the horizontal output stage, which develops the sweep, HV and focus voltages, and gating pulses, which key various circuits into conduction.

### User Controls

There are two kinds of control, user controls and service controls and adjusters. The former are described as listed below; the latter are described in later chapters.

- *Power switch:* to turn set on and off. Usually combined with volume control
- *Volume control:* as the name suggests
- *Tone control:* as the name suggests

***TABLE 2-1***

Monochrome receiver stage functions

| *Stage or Item* | *Function* | *Remarks* |
|---|---|---|
| Vertical sweep (vertical oscillator and amplifiers) | Generates and amplifies vertical deflection voltage | Vertical beam deflection of CRT to develop a raster (see Chapter 1) |
| Horizontal sweep (horizontal oscillator and amplifiers) | Generates and amplifies horizontal deflection voltage | Horizontal beam deflection of CRT to develop a raster |
| Sync | Amplifies and separates vertical and horizontal sync pulses from the video signal | To synchronize beam deflection with the video signal |
| Automatic frequency control (AFC) | Uses horizontal sync pulses to control the horizontal oscillator | For precise control of horizontal sync |
| High voltage (HV) | Produces CRT beam current | High voltage (HV) is developed from the horizontal output amplifier |
| Low-voltage power supply (LVPS) | Primary source of power for all stages | |
| Tuners (VHF and UHF) (the "front end") | Selects desired channel and convert signals from RF to IF | |
| Video IF strip | Amplifies IF signal from tuners | Fixed tuned to one frequency for both video and sound signals |
| Video detector (demodulator) | Recovers video signal from the IF carrier | |
| Video amplifiers | Amplifies the video signal | To intensity modulate the CRT beam current and create a picture image |
| Picture tube (CRT) | Converts video signals into images | |
| Sound IF strip | Amplifies sound IF signal coming from sound takeoff in video section | |
| Sound detector (demodulator) | Recovers audio signal from the frequency-modulated IF carrier | |
| Audio amplifiers | Amplifies signal to drive the speaker | |
| Speaker | Converts AF signal to audible sound | |
| Automatic gain control (AGC) | Maintains constant picture and sound levels | Regulates gain of RF-IF stages |

- *VHF channel selector (tuner):* to select the VHF channel desired
- *UHF channel selector:* to select the UHF channel desired
- *VHF and UHF fine tuners:* manual controls to compensate for oscillator drift
- *AFT overide switch:* to select automatic or manual fine-tuning modes
- *Contrast control:* varies video signal amplitude to control picture contrast
- *Brightness control:* varies CRT bias to control picture brightness
- *Focus control:* varies the voltage on the CRT focus grid to obtain proper beam focus
- *Height control:* varies raster height by controlling amplitude of the vertical sweep voltage
- *Vertical linearity:* varies shape of vertical waveform to obtain uniform spacing of scanning lines and proper pix proportions
- *Vertical hold control:* adjusts vertical sweep frequency to obtain vertical sync
- *Horizontal hold control:* adjusts horizontal sweep frequency to obtain horizontal sync
- *Width (horizontal size control):* varies amplitude of horizontal sweep voltage to obtain proper raster width
- *AGC threshold control:* adjusts receiver sensitivity in accordance with strength of received signal
- *Video peaking control:* sharpens fine picture details by increasing gain of the high video frequencies

## Monochrome CRT

A sketch of a typical BW CRT is shown in Figure 2-2. The components are described briefly in Table 2-2.

## Black and White CRT Operation

The negative electrons emitted from the heated cathode are attracted by positive charges on several elements in the gun and the high voltage applied (via

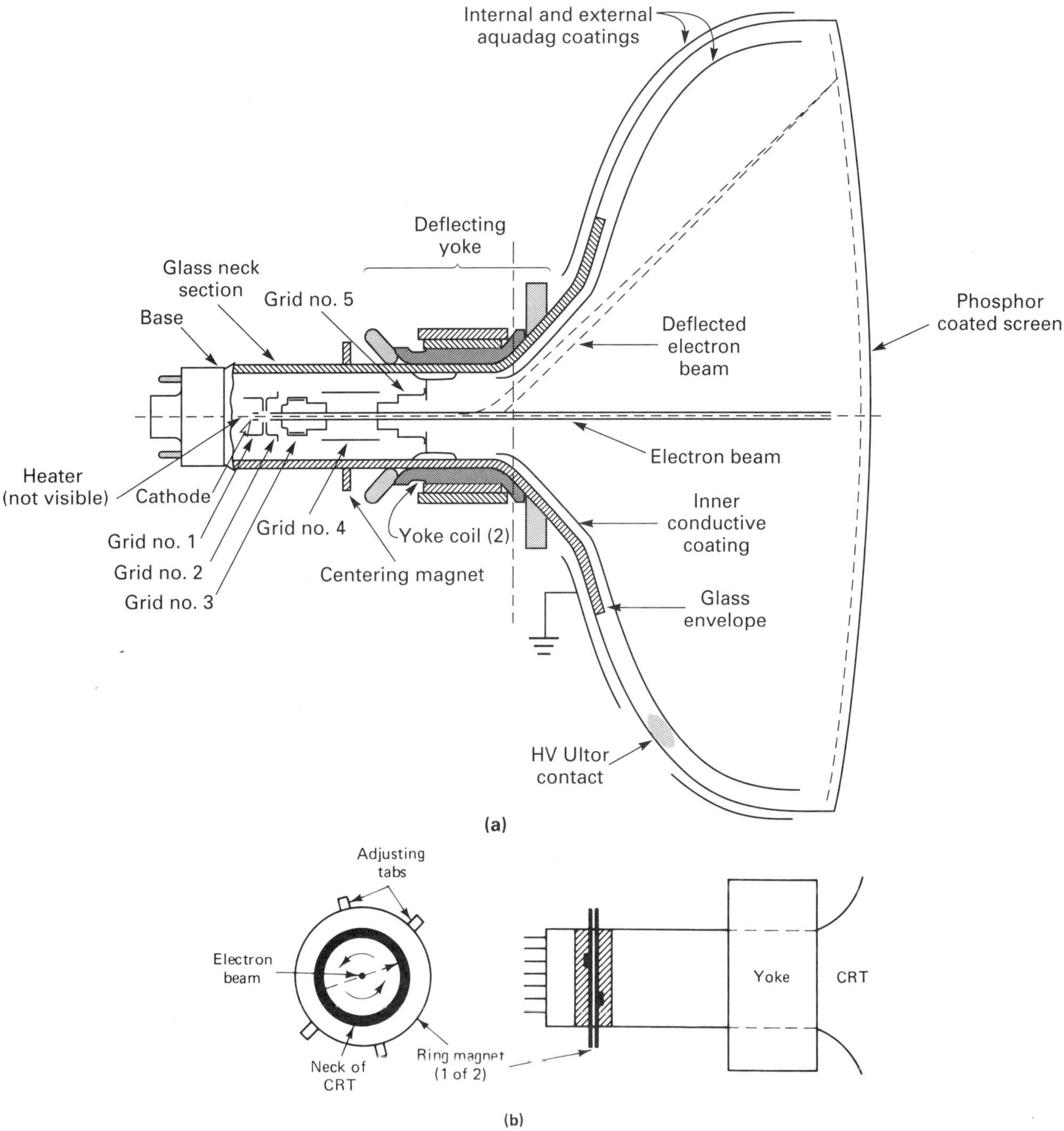


**FIG. 2-2** Monochrome CRT and beam deflector. Typical raster-centering ring. Centering magnets provide a fixed amount of offset to the electron beam.

the ultor contact) to the graphite (aquadag) coating on the inner surface of the bowl. Beam intensity (which determines brightness) is controlled by the grid-to-cathode bias. Because of mutual repulsion of the electrons, the beam tends to spread. The amount of voltage applied to other grids opposes the spread, causing the beam to strike the screen at a pinpoint, as required for good focusing. The magnetic centering ring (Figure 2-2) aims the beam in a straight line until it leaves the gun.

As it leaves the gun, the beam comes under the influence of the deflection yoke. As with current in a wire, the electron beam is surrounded by a circular magnetic field which reacts with the electromagnetic

***TABLE 2-2***

Monochrome CRT components

| *Unit or Element* | *Description and Location* | *Purpose* |
|---|---|---|
| Glass envelope | Has a high vacuum; the faceplate is coated on the inner surface with phosphor and reflective silver particles | The phosphor coating glows when struck by the electron beam. Silver deposits serve as an ion barrier and a mirror for increased light output. |
| Electron gun | A long, narrow neck containing the beam control elements | To generate and aim the electron beam; electrons are attracted to the high positive dc on the anode and accelerated by charges on various grids |
| Heater | Located near the tube base, inside, but insulated from the cathode; heated with low-voltage ac | To heat the electron-emitting cathode |
| Cathode | A metal sleeve surrounding the heater | Coated with an oxide to emit electrons when heated |
| Control grid (grid 1) | An open-ended cylindrical element just forward of the cathode | Bias and signal voltages applied between the grid and cathode control the beam current |
| Screen grid (grid 2) | A cylindrical element just forward of the control grid | Supplied with a positive dc voltage to accelerate the electron stream |
| Focus grid (grids 3 and 4) | Forward from and similar to the screen grid | Causes the beam to converge and focus at the faceplate screen surface |
| Deflection yoke | An external coil assembly located on the tube neck against the flared bowl of the CRT; consists of vertical and horizontal deflection coils | When supplied with vertical and horizontal sweep voltages, the electromagnetic flux generated deflects the beam in both directions to produce a raster |
| Beam centering ring | Adjustable, magnetized flat washers located on the CRT neck near the base | To move the beam up, down, and sideways to center raster on the screen |
| Ultor | A button contact on the side of the CRT bell; HV connection to an internal anode (aquadag graphite coating) | The ultor is well spaced from the grounded outer coating on the CRT |
| Anti-pincushion magnets | Two permanent magnets near the forward end of the electron gun; adjusted to overcome inward or outward bowing of raster edges | Used only with large BW CRT's. |

(EM) field of the yoke coils and the beam is deflected by the same attraction and repulsion principles as with an electric motor. The direction of motion (in this case, the beam) is determined by the direction of currents in the yoke coils, which is constantly changing. The *stronger* the currents, the greater the deflection and the bigger the raster.

### Developing a Black-and-White Picture

A raster is produced on the CRT in the same manner as described earlier for camera CRTs (Figure 2-2b). Simultaneous with raster development, the video and blanking pulses received (the composite video signal shown in Figure 2-6) are being applied to the control grid (or cathode). Variations of this signal voltage create changes in beam current. Voltage changes at the grid in a positive direction increase the electron flow, creating white picture images. A negative-going voltage at the cathode produces the same effect. Negative-going voltage changes at the grid (positive-going at the cathode) *decrease* beam current and brightness. Black is the result of beam current cutoff.

Figure 2-3 shows one line of picture information as it corresponds with the picture reproduced. Note the horizontal blanking pulses that reach the cutoff level, and the sync pulses that extend beyond, into the *blacker-than-black region.*

Frequency variations of the video signal determine the size of picture elements being reproduced during the period of each horizontal beam trace. Low video frequencies (from near 0 Hz to about 2 MHz) correspond with slow changes, producing relatively large objects during the short (53.3-μs) horizontal trace interval. High frequencies (from about 2 MHz to the upper limit of 4.2 MHz) represent rapid changes, permitting many variations in beam current (and brightness) to reproduce smaller objects. Fine picture detail (the pixels) are created by the highest video frequencies, between 1.5 and 4.2 MHz.

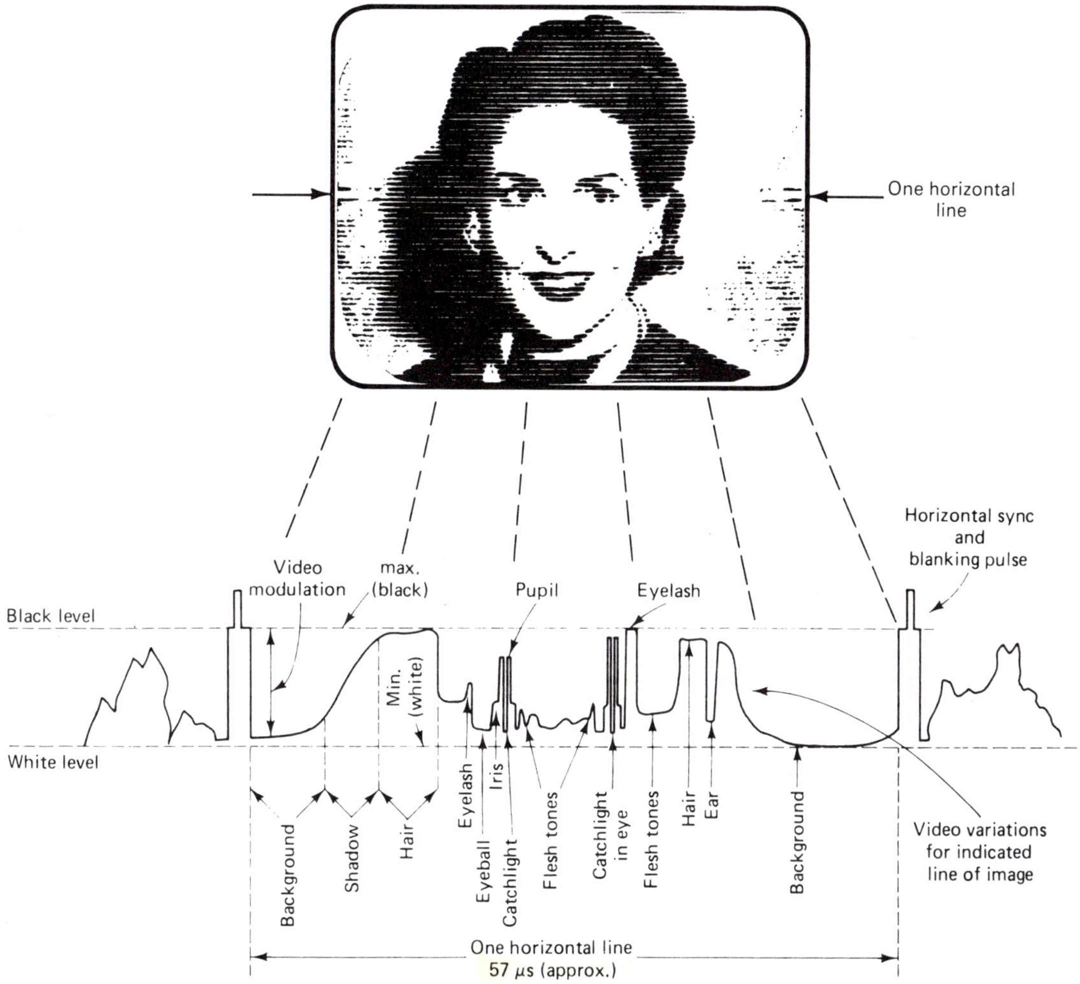


**FIG. 2-3** Video fluctuations and pix development. The short-duration pulses produce the fine details.

Resolution plays an important role in picture quality. Of the 525 lines transmitted, on older sets only about 330 lines actually contain picture information (count them). The rest are "lost" to the viewer, as explained earlier. Some modern sets are capable of 450-line resolution, which greatly enhances a picture and is especially desirable when used with a VCR (see Chapter 20).

To illustrate further how picture images are produced, consider the six examples shown in Figure 2-4a. These are produced by feeding different signal frequencies to a CRT or the video section of a receiver. Such displays are useful for signal tracing a set, for checking linearity, and so on. The number of bars or lines produced, and whether they are vertical or horizontal, depend on the relationship between the injected generator frequency and the vertical and horizontal sweep frequencies. Note the frequencies used in the examples; even multiples of either 60 or 15,750 Hz produce vertical or horizontal lines or bars; the higher the frequency, the greater the number of bars. Odd multiples of these frequencies produce unrecognizable out-of-sync conditions.

### Test Patterns

Test patterns are sometimes transmitted to check conditions at the station and to enable technicians to evaluate receiver performances. By viewing test patterns you can determine such things as the receiver bandpass, relative amplification of high and low video frequencies, and raster linearity.

## 2-3 COLOR RECEIVER OPERATION

The major stages and sections of a typical color set are shown in Figure 2-5. Most of the circuits are also found in monitors and VCRs. About half the number

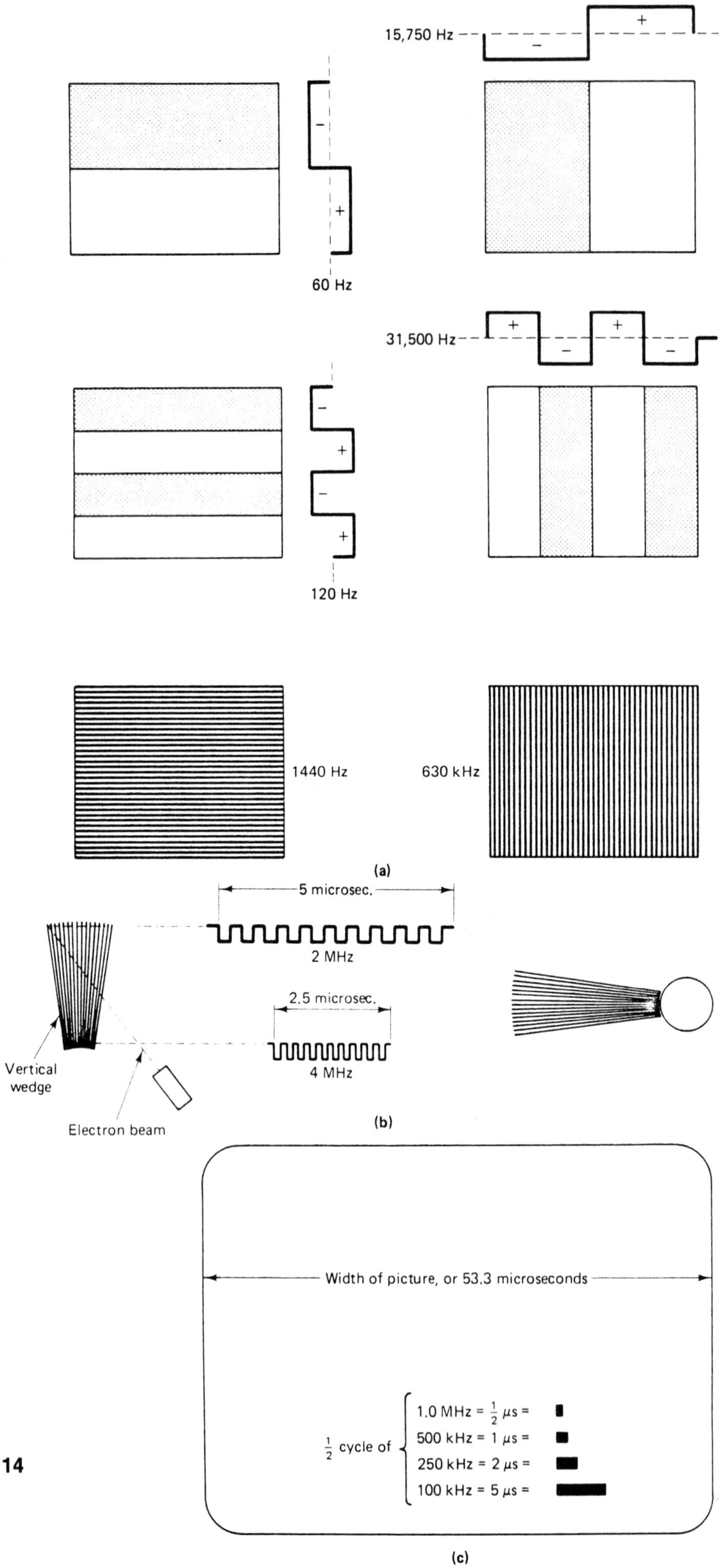


**FIG. 2-4** Bar patterns and resolution. Resolution can be determined by observing test pattern wedges. Image sizes vary with frequency.

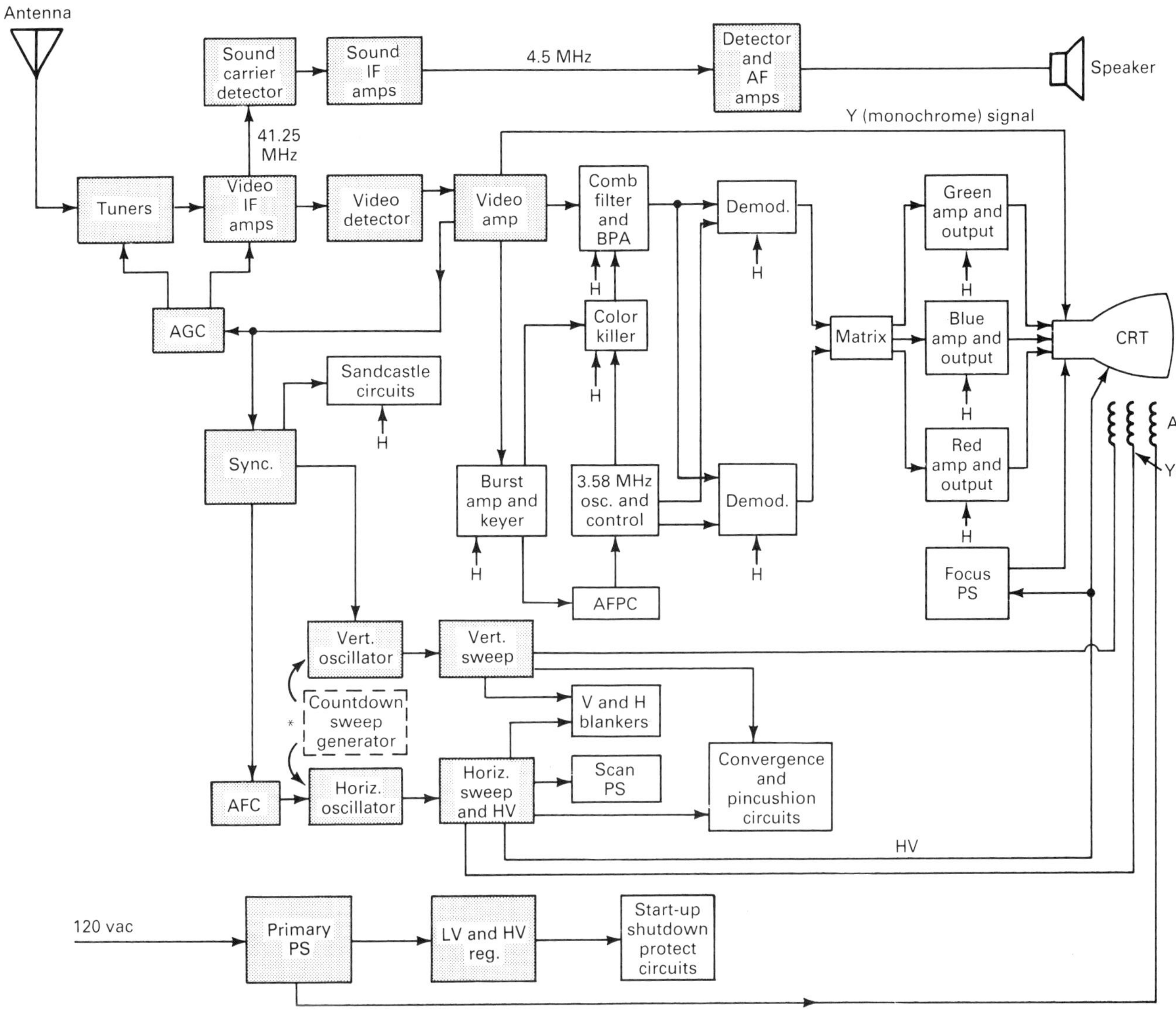


**FIG. 2-5** Color set block diagram. * Countdown CKT used in modern sets. ** H denotes horizontal gating pulses. Shaded blocks are also used in black and white sets.

of blocks (shaded for identification) perform the same or similar functions as those of their counterparts in a monochrome receiver. There are some differences, however. The sound takeoff is *ahead* of the video detector, in the IF strip. The sweep circuits are considerably more complex. The horizontal output stage, for example, has a greater role to perform in supplying dc (scan) power to most of the stages. HV and focus voltage requirements are generally greater for a color CRT. Note also the numerous stages that are gated (keyed on or off) by horizontal sync pulses. The complexity of color sets varies considerably, especially in the chroma circuitry and depending on the type of CRT used.

A typical color set also has a number of automatic functions, as described later. Table 2-3 provides an overview of all chroma-related stage functions. A more detailed description is upcoming. Refer to Figure 2-5 for the following general description of color receiver operation. [*Reminder:* Many of the stage functions (shaded blocks in the diagram) perform as in a BW set and will not be repeated at this time.]

### Sound

Unlike a BW set, the 41.25-MHz sound IF carrier is separated from the video in the last IF stage. The signal is then demodulated and converted to 4.5

***TABLE 2-3***

Color receiver stage functions

| *Stage or Item* | *Function* | *Remarks* |
|---|---|---|
| Primary power supply | Primary source of power for all stages | Older sets had one PS; modern sets (hot chassis types) are transformerless; one PS feeds the horizontal output stage, which in turn furnishes scan power to all stages |
| Startup/shutdown | Enables the horizontal sweep circuit to develop scan power; automatic shutdown of set for excessive HV or a horizontal output failure | As protection against harmful x-rays and component damage |
| Voltage regulators | Regulate and stabilize dc outputs of the LV and HV power supplies | |
| Horizontal output stage | Provides secondary dc scan power for most stages; horizontal gating (keying) pulses for numerous stages; sweep voltage for pincushion and convergence circuits; HV, focus voltage, and heater voltage for the CRT | In addition to supplying yoke with horizontal sweep power |
| Pincushion circuits | Prevent inward and outward bowing of raster edges | Vertical sweep voltage is introduced into the horizontal yoke and horizontal voltage into the vertical yoke |
| Convergence | Multicoil assembly on neck of CRT; to maintain proper beam convergence over the entire screen surface | Convergence coils are supplied with vertical and horizontal sweep voltages; permanent magnets are used for static convergence |
| Phase-locked-loop (PLL) countdown circuits | Digital system for generating precisely accurate and stable vertical and horizontal sweep voltages | Obviates the need for vertical and horizontal hold controls (no frequency drift) |
| Comb filter | Separates video and chroma signals from each other | For improved picture quality and reduced interference |
| SAW filter | Surface/acoustic-wave device | To improve the IF response |
| Bandpass amplifier (BPA) | Narrow-bandpass amplifier that separates chroma from luminance (Y) signal | Sometimes called the chroma IF strip |
| Sandcastle circuit | Synchronizes several receiver functions | See Chapter 15 |
| Color killer | On/off switching circuit to control the BPA | BPA is off when receiving BW programs; turned on when a color burst is recognized |
| Burst gate or amplifier | Keyed amplifier that feeds color burst to killer stage and the subcarrier generator | |
| Subcarrier oscillator or generator | Generates a 3.58-MHz CW signal required to demodulate the chroma signals | Oscillator is crystal controlled for frequency stability |
| Automatic frequency and phase control (AFPC) | Uses color burst to maintain proper frequency and phase of the subcarrier oscillator | To ensure proper colors and their occurrence relative to beam deflection |
| Chroma demodulators | Demodulate the I and Q color difference signals | Each demodulator is supplied with a specific phase of the 3.58-MHz signal |
| RGB chroma amplifiers | Amplify and feed red, green, and blue signals to the corresponding control grids of the CRT | *Note:* In Figure 1-5 the video (Y) signal drives the CRT cathodes, and matrixing (combining) of chroma and Y signals takes place in the CRT; many sets matrix in the demodulators or color output stages (pre-CRT matrixing) |
| Color CRT | Has three guns that direct corresponding RGB-related electron beams to the screen | Red, green, and blue screen phosphors are illuminated individually by the three beams in accordance with RGB signal variations |
| Automatic degaussing coils (ADG) | Externally surrounds the CRT faceplate; develop an ac magnetic field to ensure that CRT elements are not magnetized | Even weak magnetic fields result in misconvergence and color problems; the AGC is momentarily energized with each receiver turn-on |

MHz and amplified in an IF stage. The FM demodulator recovers the audio component, which is further amplified to drive the speaker.

### Video

After detection, the luminance and chroma signals are separated from each other by a sharply tuned filter or comb filter. The Y signal is amplified by several video stages, then fed either directly to the CRT or some preceding chroma stage, where it is combined with the chroma signal. The chroma signal is amplified by the narrowband BPA and fed to the chroma demodulators. The demodulators are also supplied with 3.58-MHz CW signals from the subcarrier generator, as required in the demodulation process.

In Figure 2-5, the video (Y) signal and the chroma are recombined at the CRT. In many sets, the Y signal is fed to the demodulators or chroma amplifiers. This is called pre-CRT matrixing, and is described in Chapter 15. Here the outputs of the two demodulators are combined in a matrix stage to produce three color-related signals. These RGB signals are then amplified individually to drive the three guns of the CRT.

To retrace our steps a bit, the 3.58-MHz CW subcarrier signal required for demodulation is generated by a crystal-controlled oscillator or another form of generating circuit. In Figure 2-5, a phase-shifting network provides two differently phased oscillator outputs to feed the demodulators. Some sets have three demodulators, which require three such outputs.

The subcarrier generator is frequency and phase locked to the received color burst, which is a sampling of the generator's counterpart at the station. The AFPC block performs this function. The color burst, which exists only when receiving a color program, is amplified by the keyed burst gate to feed the generator. The color burst also serves another function, to enable and disable the color killer, which in turn acts as a switch to turn on the BPA when a burst is sensed and to turn it off in the absence of a burst to prevent noise and other interference from degrading the picture during BW reception.

### Automatic Functions

- *Automatic channel selection:* as the name suggests
- *Instamatic control:* single-button control for color, tint, contrast, and brightness
- *Automatic fine tuning (AFT):* overides manual fine-tuning control
- *Automatic gain control (AGC):* see Table 2-1
- *Automatic degaussing (ADG):* to demagnetize CRT automatically
- *Automatic color control (ACC):* to maintain proper color intensity
- *Automatic tint control (ATC):* to maintain uniform color tinting
- *Color killer:* see Table 2-3
- *Automatic brightness limiter (ABL):* to protect the CRT from excessive beam current

### User Controls

In addition to the user controls listed in Section 2-2 for a monochrome set, the following are peculiar to a color receiver. Service-type controls and adjusters are covered in later chapters as appropriate.

- *Color or chroma control:* to obtain desired color saturation level
- *Hue or tint control:* to obtain proper colors in the picture

### Color CRT

Sketches of three types of color CRT are shown in Figures 2-6 to 2-9. They are described briefly in Table 2-4.

### Color CRT Operation

Basically, the operation of each of the three guns is the same as described for a monochrome CRT. Each gun corresponds with one of the three primary colors: red, green, and blue. To accommodate the additional elements, the neck of a color tube has a larger diameter than a BW CRT, and with the electron beams a greater distance from the yoke, the deflection sensitivity is reduced. This calls for increased sweep power. Also, because of the shadow mask or grill, which blocks some electrons, light-producing efficiency is reduced, which calls for higher beam currents, increased HV, and increased electron emitting capability of the cathodes. The three heaters are connected in parallel internally.

With proper adjustments, all three beams pass through each opening in the mask or grill to strike their corresponding color phosphors on the screen (see Figures 2-7 and 2-10). We view the impact

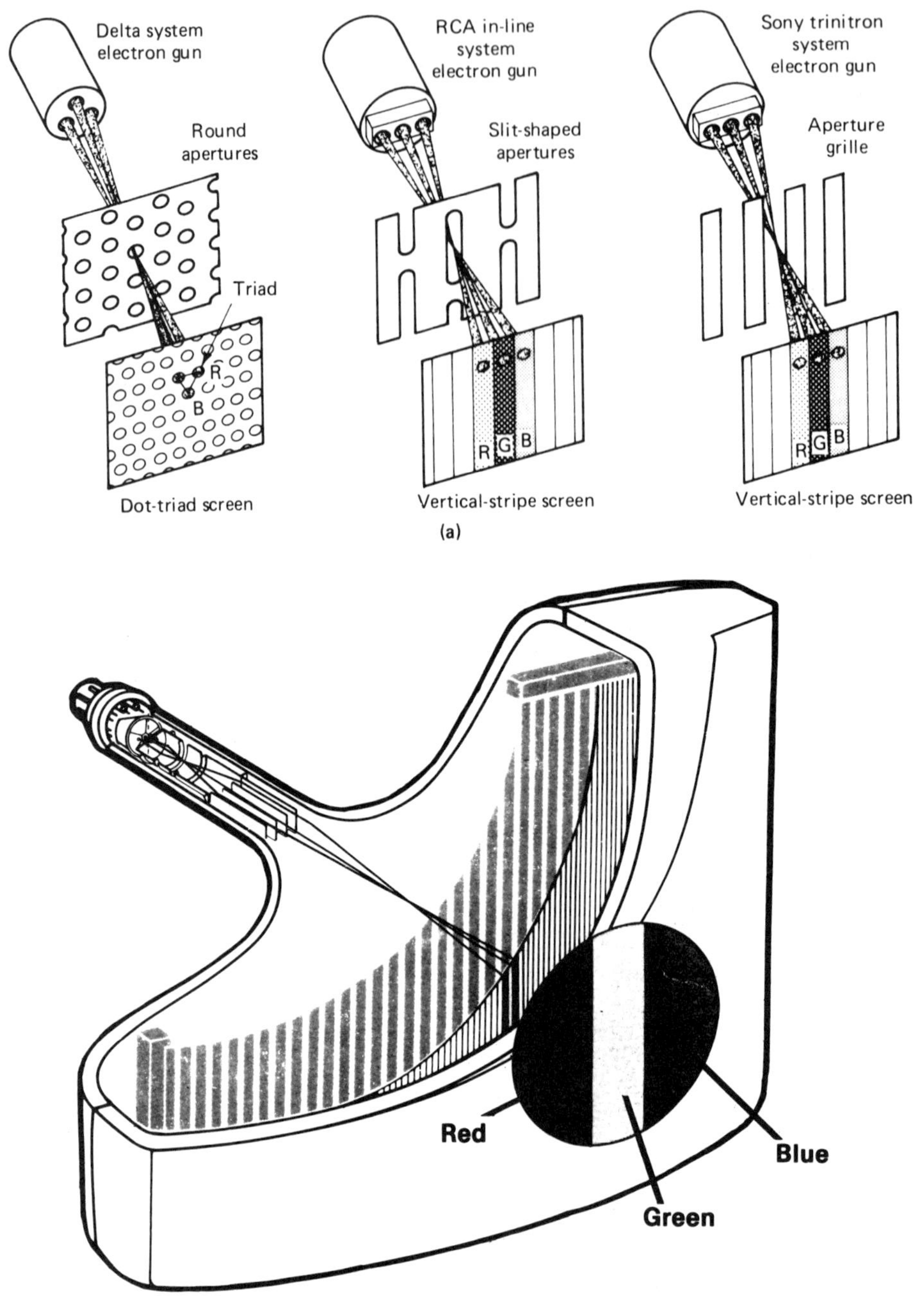


**FIG. 2-6** Color CRT's and beam aiming. To impact the proper phosphor dots or stripes requires accurate positioning of shadow mask or aperture grill and precise control of each electron beam. (Courtesy of Sencore News).

points as a mixture of the three primary colors (Figure 2-11). The individual colors in the mixture can be observed on close inspection with a magnifying glass.

In general, dc operating voltages and applied signal voltages are much greater than for a BW tube. Cutoff bias for a typical large-screen color CRT (to darken the screen) is about 100 V and the peak-to-peak level of the applied RGB signals is about the same amount. The three guns are individually controlled. In the setup procedure (Chapter 17), screen grid voltages are adjusted to produce a white raster. If only one gun is conducting, a single-color raster is produced. One or two weak guns result in a color-tinted raster.

Amplitude variations of the applied signals control the relative strength of the three beams at any given instant and therefore the colors viewed in

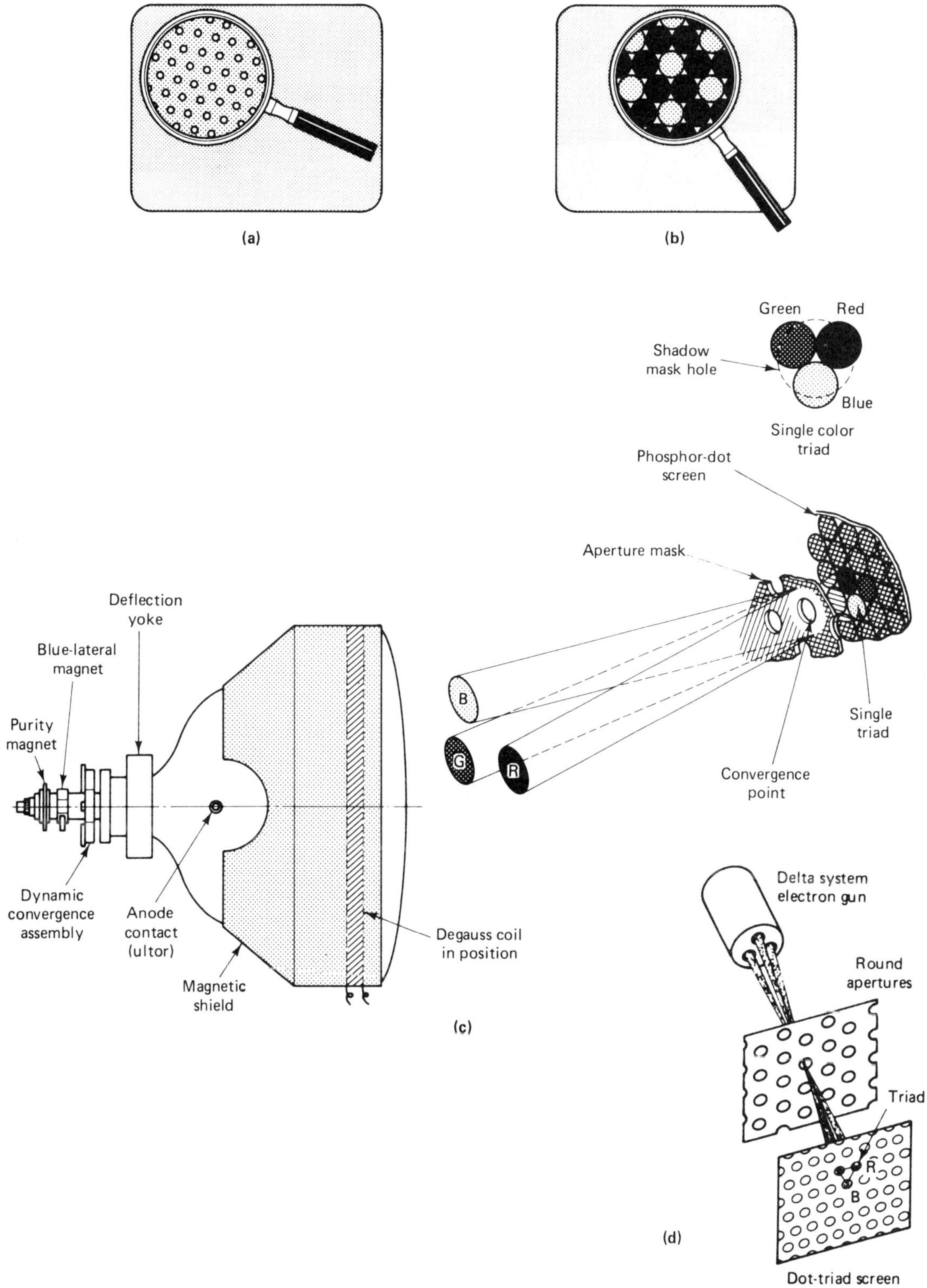


**FIG. 2-7** Delta CRT beam aiming. The shadow-mask (delta-type) CRT: (a) arrangement of aperture mask holes; (b) arrangement of phosphor dots; (c) alignment of guns, mask and phosphor dots (all three beams must converge to pass through each hole in the shadow mask to impact their respective color phosphors on the screen); (d) three electron gun assembly.

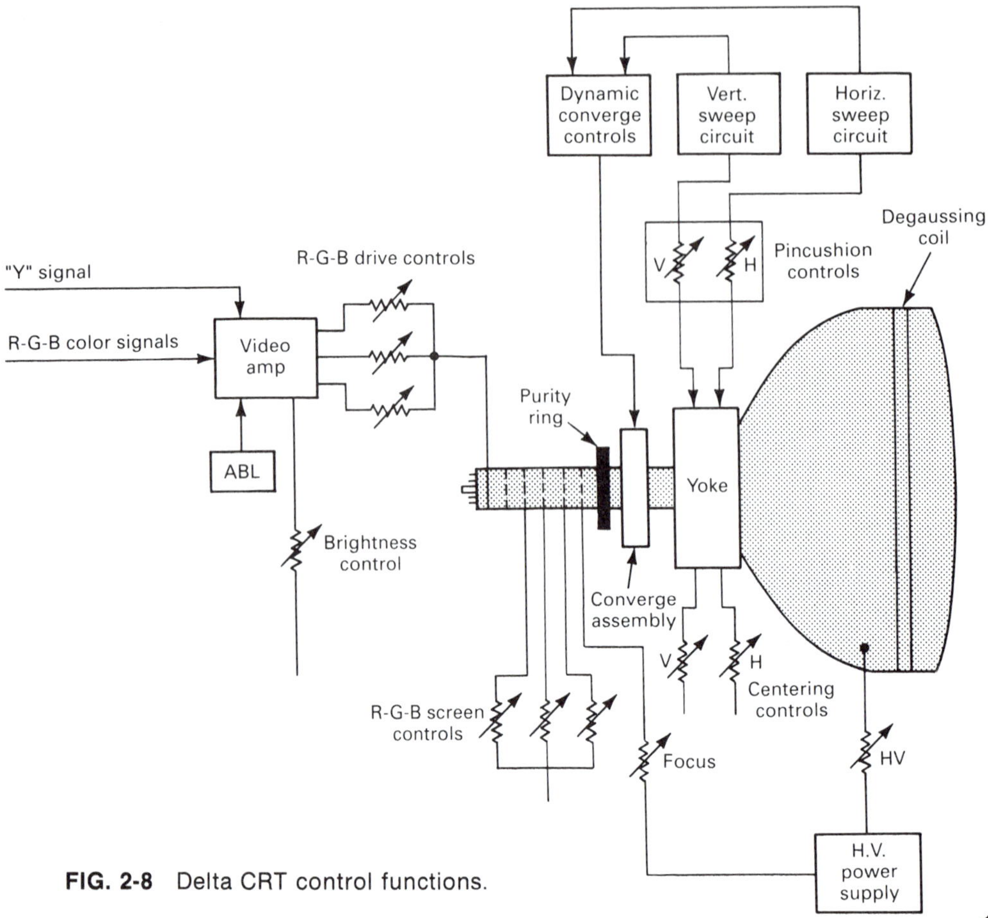


**FIG. 2-8** Delta CRT control functions.

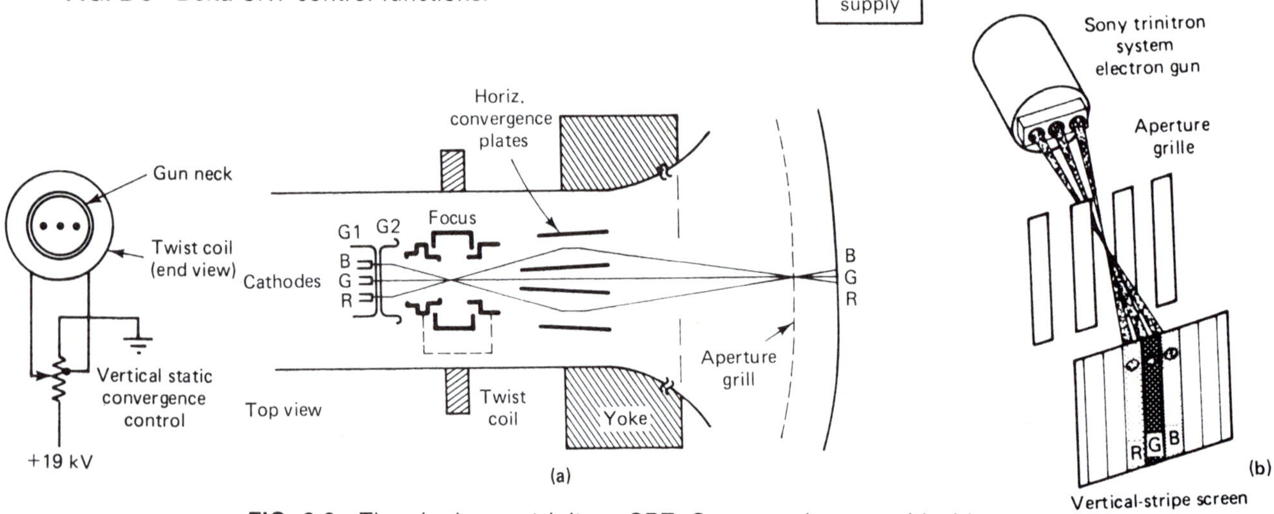


**FIG. 2-9** The single-gun trinitron CRT. Converge is easy with this type of CRT.

the image. Since each gun produces a single-color image, the three beams must be converged precisely to obtain a picture in perfect registry.

## Color Fundamentals

Every color has three characteristics: hue, saturation, and brightness. *Hue,* or *color* (used interchangeably), is the main characteristic that distinguishes one from the other (e.g., yellow, violet, orange, etc.). *Saturation* refers to the vividness or strength of a color as determined by the amount it is diluted by white light (e.g., pink is the dilution of a saturated red). *Brightness* is self-explanatory but should not be confused with saturation.

As explained previously, white is a mixture of the three primary colors in the proportions 30% red, 59% green, and 11% blue. All complementary colors

***TABLE 2-4***

Color CRT components

| *Unit or Element* | *Description and Location* | *Purpose* |
|---|---|---|
| | DELTA- OR SHADOW-MASK-TYPE CRT | |
| The CRT | Has three separate and identical electron guns (similar to a BW CRT) in a triangular configuration; screen has red, green, and blue phosphor dots arranged in groups of three (triads); an "aperture mask" (shadow mask) is positioned behind the coated screen | Tiny holes in the mask are precisely aligned to the center of each triad; the three beams converge and cross over in each hole to strike their corresponding color dots on the screen |
| EXTERNAL COMPONENTS | | |
| Deflection yoke | As for BW sets | |
| Convergence assembly | Consists of three sets of coils and adjustable permanent magnets; mounted on neck directly behind deflection yoke; dynamic adjusters may be separate or part of the assembly | Adjusts for proper convergence of the three beams |
| Blue lateral magnet | Small adjustable magnet behind convergence assembly | Adjusts blue beam laterally |
| Purity magnets | Adjustable magnetized "washers" (similar to centering magnets on BW CRTs) | Adjusts for proper beam landing on screen phosphor dots |
| Degaussing coil(s) | One large coil or several small ones that encircle the CRT near the faceplate | Supplied with ac to demagnetize the CRT |
| Shield plates | Metal covering around the CRT bowl (on some sets only) | To shield against electromagnetic and electrostatic influences |
| | TRIPLE-GUN, IN-LINE, APERTURE-GRILL CRT | |
| The CRT | Has three electron guns mounted side by side (in line); the three-color screen phosphors are arranged in alternate vertical stripes; a slotted aperture grill is positioned behind the coated screen | The three beams converge and cross over in each grill slot to strike their corresponding color stripes on the screen |
| EXTERNAL COMPONENTS | | |
| Deflection yoke | As for other CRTs | |
| Convergence coil assembly or adjustable magnet rings | Instead of a convergence coil assembly, most sets now use an adjustable permanent-magnet assembly | Ensures that each beam strikes its corresponding color phosphors |
| Twist coil | Small rotatable coil at the rear of the tube neck | Same function as the purity ring on a delta CRT; adjusted for proper beam landing on phosphor stripes |
| Degaussing coils | As for other color CRTs | |
| Spark gaps | Closely spaced gaps between grids, cathodes, and grounds; usually built into the CRT socket | Provide protection to receiver components in the event of arc-overs in the CRT |
| | SINGLE-GUN, APERTURE-GRILL CRT (TRINITRON) | |
| The CRT | Has three in-line cathodes, but single control and accelerating grids are common to all three beams; has built-in electrostatic convergence plates | Uses a slotted aperture grill and vertical stripes of color phosphors on the screen; this type of CRT has few convergence problems |
| EXTERNAL COMPONENTS | | |
| Uses a twist coil and/or adjustable ring magnets on the tube neck | | |

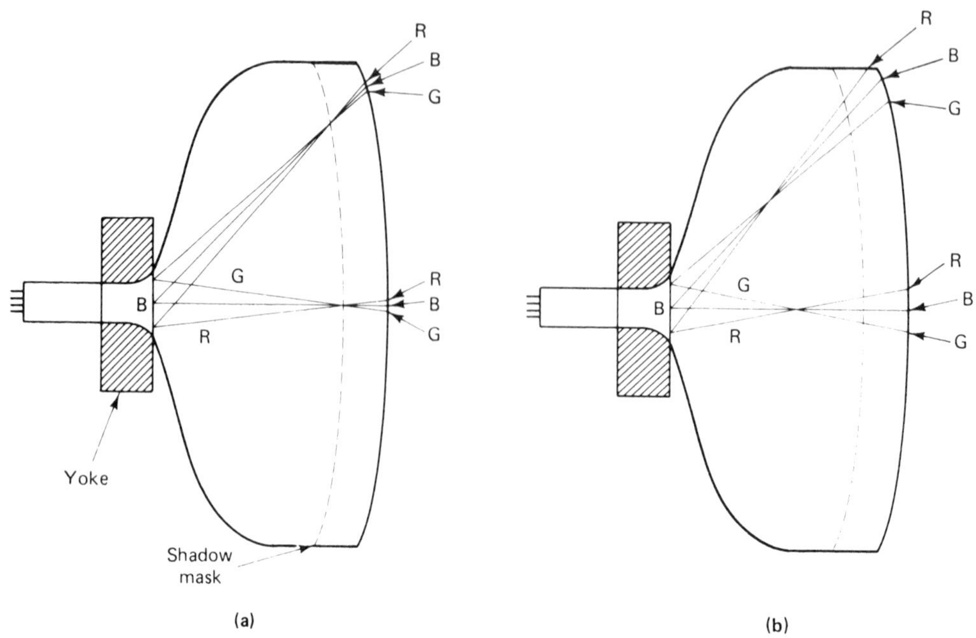


**FIG. 2-10** Convergence and beam landing problems. Perfect convergence is necessary for the beams to strike their proper phosphors. (CRT geometry and beam deflection exaggerated for clarity): (a) normal beam crossover, convergence, and landing; (b) misconvergence (beam crossover too soon).

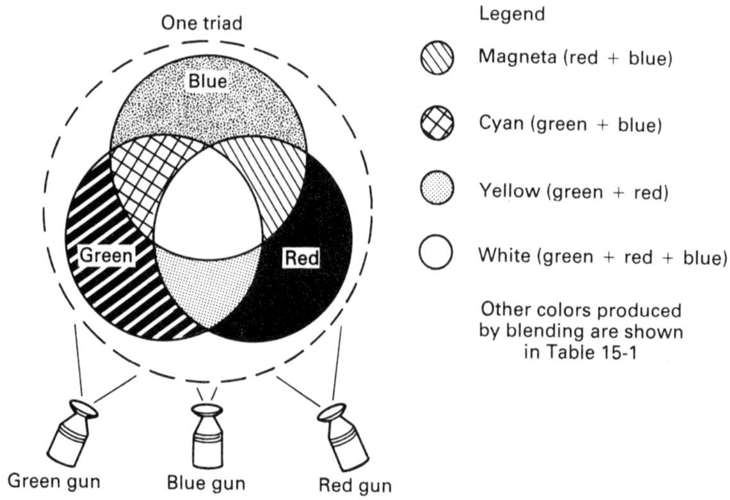


**FIG. 2-11** Delta CRT color mixing. A proportionate mix of the three primaries on each triad appears as white.

are produced by proportionate mixtures of two or three of the primaries (see Table 15-1). Black, of course, is represented by a dark screen (all CRT beams at cutoff). Gray is the mixture for white, but at reduced brightness.

One shortcoming of the human eye is its inability to discern color on very small objects, which is why chroma stages of a TV set have a limited frequency response and why we view extremely fine details of a picture only as black and white.

## CRT Setup Adjustments

Such adjustments are necessary after replacing a CRT, and may be required at other times to obtain a good color picture and a monochrome picture devoid of any color contamination. This calls for color purity adjustments (to obtain a white raster), drive adjustments for a good BW picture, and convergence adjustments for registration. Setup adjustments are given in Chapter 15.

## Producing a Color Picture

The main prerequisite in obtaining a good color picture is a white (or near-white) raster (indicating that all three guns and related circuits are in good shape). This is accomplished by a number of critical adjustments which are described later in detail. Assuming a white raster and that the color control has been turned off, a picture is viewed only in black and white; color contamination or color outlines on an image indicate the need for further adjustment.

With the color control turned up, chroma signals reaching the CRT create grid/cathode voltage variations on the three guns, varying the relative intensity of the beam currents to create color images in accordance with the position on the screen where the beams strike at any given instant. Simultaneously, the Y signal is influencing the intensity of all three beams to produce fine picture details and the amount of white in the mixture needed to create subtle variations of hue.

## Producing a Black-and-White Picture on a Color Set

Assuming proper adjustments, there should be a white or near-white raster. With the reception of a monochrome signal, the chroma signal path is interrupted by the killer stage in the absence of a color burst and the picture is developed by the Y signal only. With proper adjustment of the drive controls, each of the three guns is driven by the correct amount of color-related signal to produce white: hence a monochrome picture.

## QUESTIONS

1. Explain how intensity modulation of the CRT beam produces picture elements ranging from black to white.
2. Explain sequential scanning and how it relates to picture development.
3. Name four oscillators found in every color set, and their functions.
4. Why are two subcarriers required for the modulation and demodulation of a color signal?
5. State two functions of the color burst.
6. Why is a delay line required in the video amplifier section of a color set?
7. What is gray-scale tracking?
8. Explain interlaced scanning and why it is done.
9. A 525-line picture is transmitted but not all of them are usable. Explain.
10. Explain the basic differences between a delta CRT and an in-line CRT.
11. Briefly explain how the correct colors are displayed on a picture at the proper times.
12. What two functions are served by the Y signal?
13. Explain the need for three guns in a color CRT.
14. State the purpose of a shadow mask or aperture grill.
15. How are colors other than red, green, and blue produced on a CRT?
16. A good BW picture cannot be obtained on a color set if one or more of the guns are weak. Explain why.

# 3 Electronic components

In essence, components are fundamental to all things, both animate and inanimate. Whether we are dealing with a beautifully functioning machine each of whose parts depends on the other, the intricacies of a winged aircraft, the mysteries and wonders of the human body, or a sophisticated electronic device—the only real differences that make them unique and distinguishable from each other lie in the nature of the components and how they are assembled, joined, and interconnected, all working in harmony to achieve a specific goal. Although some of the components and devices used in electronic equipment are special items, most are common run-of-the-mill parts found on the shelves of Radio Shack or other jobbers (Figure 3-1). Table 3-1 lists most components along with their functions and other particulars. Most of those listed, unless otherwise specified, are for TV, although most can be found in other electronic equipment. Components used only in specialized equipment are described in later chapters. Following the table is a section devoted to the testing of such components. Related subjects are treated in Chapter 5.

## 3-1 FUNCTIONS AND USES OF ELECTRONIC COMPONENTS

Most of the components found in consumer electronic products are listed and briefly described in Table 3-1.

## 3-2 COMPONENT TESTING, SUBSTITUTION, AND REPAIR

Once again using the analogy of mechanical devices (and biological living organisms—ourselves), all component parts operate under conditions of *stress*, which leads to their eventual breakdown. With electronic devices, parts usually break down for one of three reasons: voltage or current overload, or extremes of temperature. Voltage overload causes the breakdown of capacitors, diodes, and transistors, to name a few. Current overload will damage or destroy resistors, transformers, and the like. High temperatures can hasten the demise of most parts.

Direct *substitution* of suspected components has long been an acceptable procedure. However, this approach is not applicable to *all* parts, particularly those in critical circuits where proper operation depends on impedance matching and other factors. In such cases, the substitute part should be identical to the original or have similar characteristics. Substitution is generally limited to standard off-the-shelf items such as resistors, capacitors, diodes, and transistors. An *RC* sub-box can be a useful bench item. Of course, only known-good parts are used for substitution.

In-circuit tests can often be made on certain components, but results are not always valid, and there is a danger of creating shorts (Figure 3-2). The rule is: When in doubt, remove or isolate the part and retest. As a final reminder, components such as FETS and ICs are sensitive to static charges and

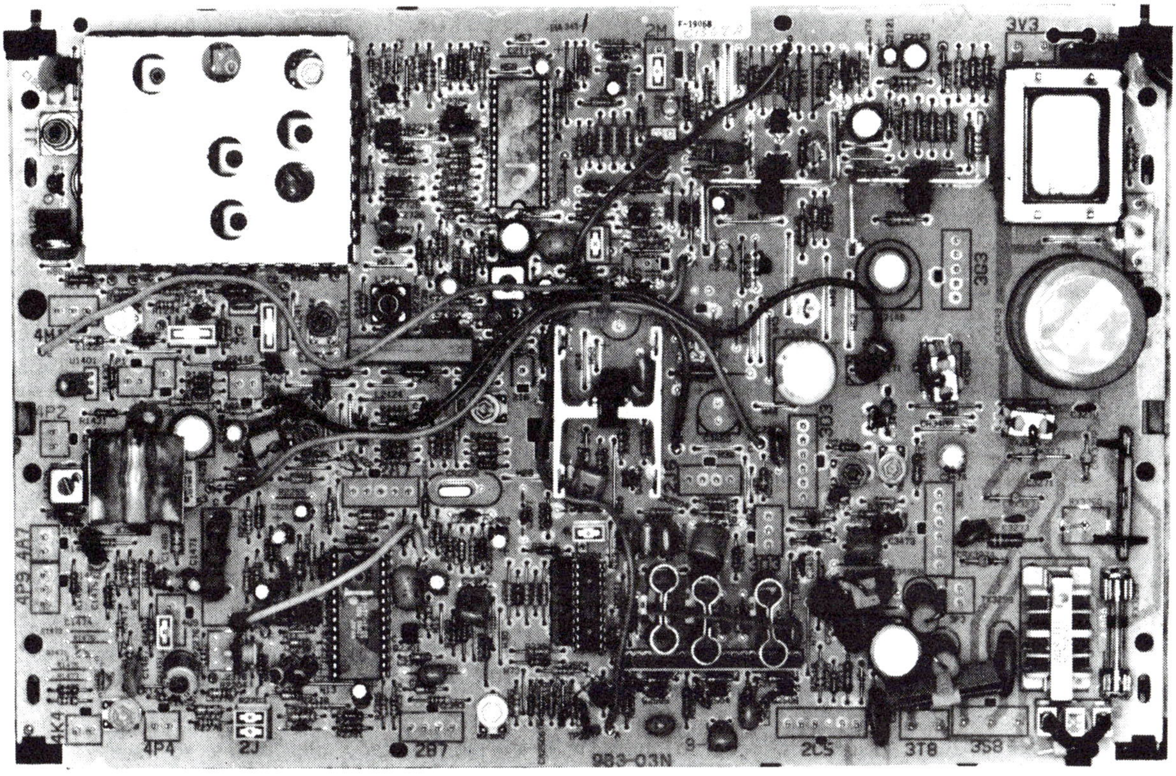

(a)

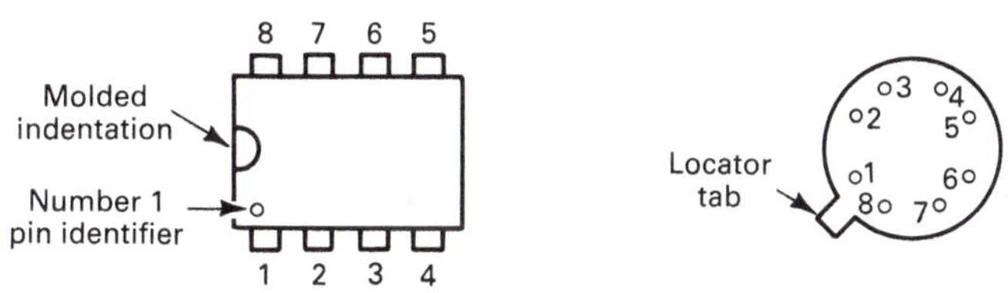


FIG. 3-1 Components on a typical TV circuit board. (a) a typical chassis with numerous ICs; (b) details of an IC (Courtesy of Zenith).

special precautions must be observed in testing and handling (see Chapter 5).

In the following paragraphs we describe the defects peculiar to each component listed in Table 3-1. Also included are suitable testing procedures for each. Depending on circumstances and available test equipment, alternative procedures are provided in some cases. Although the testing of some items requires specialized equipment, most tests can be performed with little more than a meter.

## 3-3 COMPONENT DEFECTS

*Resistors (Fixed).* A resistor may open up, change value, or become "noisy." Check with an ohmmeter, or for greater accuracy, an *RC* bridge. For in-circuit testing, make sure that no residual voltage is present, which invalidates the results. The resistor under test may also be shunted with other components, such as diodes and transistor junctions, coils, or other resistors that can influence the reading. Where a reading is suspect, try reversing the meter leads. If a resistor measures higher than its coded value, it is bad. For a low reading, isolate from the circuit and retest.

*Variable Resistors (Pots).* Pots may become open, or erratic and noisy. Measure total resistance between the two outer terminals and compare with the schematic. Connect a meter from one end to the center terminal (the wiper arm), noting how the resistance changes as the control is varied slowly. Repeat between the center lug and the other extreme terminal. Watch for any erratic or abrupt variations in the reading, and if they appear, try cleaning by applying contact cleaner where it can enter. Work the control until the cleaner evaporates. Persistence sometimes pays off, but if not, replace the control.

*LDRs.* Check with an ohmmeter while making changes in ambient lighting.

***TABLE 3-1***

Electronic components

| *Component* | *Function* | *Uses* |
|---|---|---|
| Resistors (fixed) | Reduce voltage or current; enable circuit decoupling and isolation; establish a time constant | In all electronic circuits |
| Variable resistors (rheostats and potentiometers) | Control of ac or dc voltages. Two types: rotary and slide-type pots | Most electronic equipment |
| Light-dependent resistor (LDR) | Resistance changes with light intensity | Where desired to control circuit functions with light variations |
| Thermistors | Changes resistance when subjected to temperature variations | In temperature-controlled circuits |
| Voltage-dependent resistor (VDR) or varistor | Changes resistance with voltage variations | In voltage-controlled circuits |
| Fusistor | A fusible limiting resistor | For limiting current and circuit protection |
| Capacitors (solid dielectric) | Pass ac and block dc currents; signal coupling, bypassing, and filters; tuned circuits | Radios, TVs, VCRs, etc. |
| Capacitors (electrolytic) | Power supply filtering; passing low-frequency signals | All electronic devices |
| Switches (all types) | For switching power, signals, or as function selectors, various types: mechanical, electro-mechanical, analog IC, etc. | All electronic devices |
| Circuit breakers (CB) | For current overload protection | In power circuits |
| Coils (air core) | Tuned circuits; reduce or limit high-frequency currents; high-pass filters | In high-frequency (RF or IF) equipment |
| Coils (iron core) | Same as above and PS filters | As above and PSs |
| Degaussing coil | Used on color TV sets and monitors to demagnetize the CRT | May be energized manually or automatically |
| Ceramic filters | Accept or reject a narrow band of RF signals | In TV sets, monitors, and VCRs |
| SAW filter | Sharply tuned RF-IF filter | To separate video and chroma signals in TV sets, monitors, and VCRs |
| Comb filter delay device | Acoustic device for delaying the chroma signal for separation from the video signal | Used in all modern TV sets, monitors, and VCRs to enhance picture quality |
| Transformers (air core) | Stage-to-stage signal coupling; Impedance matching | In high-frequency circuits |
| Transformers (iron core) | As above and for power transfer to increase or decrease voltage or current | In RF circuits if ceramic (powdered iron) core; and power circuits if laminated iron |
| HV flyback transformers | Develop high voltage at low current from horizontal sweep circuits | In TV sets and monitors to furnish HV to the CRT and drive the deflection yoke and other sweep-dependent circuits |
| Oscillating crystals | For frequency control of oscillators | In TV sets, monitors, and VCRs |
| Diodes | Solid-state devices for rectifying ac to dc; dc isolation; detection and limiting | As rectifiers in PSs; detectors in signal circuits, and for AFC control of generated signals |
| HV/focus voltage diode rectifiers | To rectify HV horizontal sweep pulses | To supply HV dc to a CRT; most sets now use either an IHVT (integrated HV transformer) with built-in rectifiers or a HV multiplier unit |
| Varactor diode (varicap) | Frequency and phase control of tuned circuits | Channel selection in TV and VCR tuners; horizontal sweep and chroma AFC circuits |
| Zener diodes | Dc voltage regulation | In low-voltage PSs |
| Light-emitting diodes (LEDs) | As panel indicator lights | As power-on and status indicators in digital logic equipment |
| Digital readout displays | Front-panel display of time, counts, levels, events, etc.; may use LEDs or LCDs (liquid crystal display) | Used on TV sets, VCRs, and other equipment |

**TABLE 1-1**

*(continued)*

| *Component* | *Function* | *Uses* |
|---|---|---|
| Transistors | Solid-state devices that perform the same functions as vacuum tubes in older equipment | As amplifiers, oscillators, etc.; small transistors are for weak signal voltages; large ones (with heat sinks) are power amplifiers |
| Field-effect transistors (FETs) | For amplifying weak RF signals where a high signal-to-noise ratio is desired | In TV/VCR tuners and preamps |
| Integrated-circuit (IC) "chips" | For performing combined multifunctions that previously required numerous discrete components | Used in most modern electronic equipment |
| SCRs and triacs | Power switching | Sweep and power circuits in TV sets and VCRs |
| Deflection yoke | To sweep or deflect the beam(s) of a CRT vertically and horizontally | Mounted on the neck of the CRT, where its coils produce an electromagnetic (EM) flux |
| Convergence yoke or adjustable magnets | Multicoil unit or system of magnets for converging the beams of a color CRT | Mounted on the neck of the tube just aft of the deflection yoke |
| Modules | Compact replaceable unit containing parts and wiring for one or more stages | Such units are either plug-in or interconnected with cables and connectors |
| Printed circuit boards (PCBs) | Thin boards or cards containing all components, including transistors and ICs for one or more stages; everything is interconnected with "printed" wiring. Employs surface mounted technology (SMT) with components on one side and wiring on reverse side. | Most PCBs are provided with edge connectors to facilitate installation and removal |

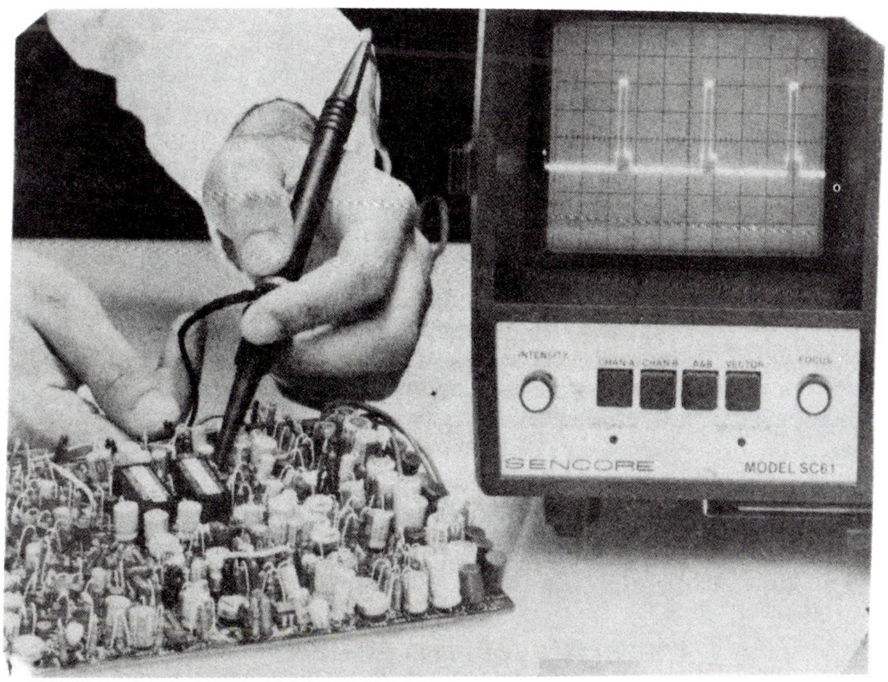


**FIG. 3-2** Component testing in hard-to-get-at places (Courtesy of Sencore News).

*Thermistors.* Alternately heat and cool, noting variations in resistance. For heating, use a hair dryer or direct application from a low-wattage soldering iron. To cool, use a coolant spray. When defective, a thermistor usually reads high. Check with the schematic.

*VDRs.* Connect in series with a limiting resistor and a current meter to a variable external PS. Monitor the voltage (across the VDR) and the current as the applied voltage is varied. Compute the resistance for different amounts of voltage.

*Fusistors.* Check with an ohmmeter. If defective, it will either be open or measure high.

*Capacitors (Paper, Ceramic, etc.).* May be shorted, leaky, open, or changed in value. Instruments made for the purpose can be real timesavers (see Figure 3-3). When testing in-circuit (with the power off and using a conventional ohmmeter, not a DMM), if the pointer kicks beyond the scale in either direction there is residual voltage which must be grounded out before proceeding. Cut one end loose from the circuit. A zero-ohms reading indicates that it is shorted. Low readings indicate leakage; the lower the reading, the greater the leakage. If there is no leakage, you get an initial reading that goes to infinity as the capacitor becomes charged by the meter battery. For small capacity values the time interval is short with a reading of infinity; for large values it may take several seconds to reach a high ohmic reading. If there is no initial deflection, either the value is very small or the capacitor is *open,* a common defect and one not easily determined. For a suspected open, the capacitor may be bridged with a similar unit while noting any changes in circuit operation. For a leaky or shorted capacitor, the suspect must be cut loose before making the substitution.

An ohmmeter test is not always infallible because of the low meter voltage. A more definitive test calls for a higher voltage. For bench testing, use an external PS adjusted to an amount not exceeding the rating of the capacitor under test. Connect a dc voltmeter and the capacitor in series across the PS output while noting the meter reaction at the moment contact is made. If the capacitor is okay, the meter will deflect as it becomes charged, then return to zero. As with ohmmeter testing, the time of charging depends on the capacitor value. A shorted capacitor will instantly indicate the full voltage of the PS. If leaky, the final readings will be somewhat less than the applied voltage. If open, there will be no meter reaction.

If no PS is available, use the voltage of the set being worked on. In most cases a capacitor will have voltage at one or both terminals, and if so, cut the end with no voltage loose from the circuit. Test as just described. As an alternative, where one end of a capacitor is grounded (or nearly so) and no voltage is applied, connect the meter between a B+ point and the loose end of the capacitor.

In lieu of a voltmeter, and provided that the voltage is 70 V or more, a small neon bulb can be used as an indicator. At the moment of making contact, a good capacitor will give one flash, then extinguish. If open, there will be no flash. If shorted, you get a constant bright glow. If leaky, the bulb may be dim or continue to flash. This test is not suitable for electrolytics, however, since they always have some leakage. To check the value of a capacitor, use a bridge analyzer.

*Electrolytics.* These may be open, shorted, leaky, or lose value if dehydrated. As described for solid dielectric capacitors, an ohmmeter or voltmeter test will indicate an open or shorted unit but is not too good for leakage testing. For a capacitor operating at 100 V dc or more, see if it can retain a charge for a reasonable length of time. Charge it from voltage of the correct polarity (and not exceeding its rating). Disconnect, and short out the terminals. A good capacitor will give a strong crackling spark several seconds (or minutes) after being charged.

A capacitor with high leakage will sometimes get warm and reduce the voltage when connected into a PS. If connected inadvertently across the ac power line, it can explode. One indication of a dried-up unit (which loses capacity) is a powdery residue around the terminals. A more reliable test for electrolytics is made with a bridge-type analyzer. Where one section of a multisection electrolytic checks bad, replace the entire unit.

*Switches.* Typical defects are physical damage and open or erratic contacts. When suspect, and depending on the type, examine for bent or broken contacts. Check with an ohmmeter on the *lowest* range. You should get a consistent reading of zero ohms each time the switch is operated. Many toggle switches become unreliable after a time; they either hang up or fail to short out. As with controls, clean using liberal amounts of cleaner, operating the switch while monitoring the meter. Unless the cleaner contains a lubricant, for exposed contacts apply a small amount of Vaseline to prevent wear. If necessary, replace the switch.

*Circuit Breakers.* These items do give trouble, especially when overworked. They may become open or unreliable. One indication is a circuit breaker (CB) that gets warm. The arcing from poor contacts will also produce staticky sounds from the speaker and flashes on a TV screen. After reset, an ohmmeter check at the terminals should indicate zero ohms. Anything more than that spells trouble. With the set operating, repeatedly tap the CB to see if it opens up and cuts off the power. Replacement with a CB of the same rating is the logical solution.

*Coils and Transformers (All Types).* Coils can become open, near-open (high resistance), grounded, or have shorted windings. An ohmmeter will quickly show up an open or grounded coil but not shorted windings where only a few turns are involved. A clue to a shorted winding (where the coil is part of a tuned circuit) is an increase in the resonant frequency. Broken or missing tuning slugs will have the same effect.

Shorted winding in power circuits (e.g., filament and power transformers, HOTs, and yokes) results in overheating and eventual burnouts. For yokes and flybacks, a ringing tester is an almost indispensible item. To test a filament or power transformer, operate it without a load (if necessary, all secondary leads disconnected). Check all secondary voltages. If it gets hot, or excessively warm and gives off a burned odor, and the output voltages are low, the transformer is shorted out. If there is no overheating, the trouble is elsewhere. Shorted rectifiers, filters, and regulators are good possibilities.

Transformer windings and other coils generally have low resistance, and a high reading makes them suspect. Frequently, it is due to corrosive action where leads are soldered to the windings. Watch closely for variations in resistance, and when energized, any indications of smoke or internal arcing. When suspected, try applying an overload voltage directly across the coil for a short time, followed by a recheck of the resistance. A bad connection will sometimes open up; if it is okay, no harm is done.

*Ceramic Filters.* These units are almost trouble-free, but when suspect and removed from the circuit, check for grounding or an open or shorted coil, as described previously. A clue to a bad filter is where it grounds out the signal or does not adequately reject the unwanted frequency.

*SAW Filter.* As with a ceramic filter, this device (see Figure 13-5) seldom gives trouble, and when it does, it either kills or weakens the signal. Unless treated with respect, the input/output transducers can shatter, and of course the tuned coils can go bad. Check the coil continuity and inspect for broken or missing core slugs.

*Comb Filter Delay Device.* This item is also relatively trouble-free. When suspect, inspect for damage and make the same general tests as for ceramic and SAW filters.

*Oscillating Crystals.* Trouble symptoms include the inability to stabilize the frequency of an oscillator, but breakdowns are rare. When suspect, the best test is substitution.

*Diodes (Most Types).* These become open, shorted, or leaky. Test in-circuit or out-of-circuit with an ohmmeter or a diode/transistor tester. On the R × 100 range of an ohmmeter a good diode will read roughly 20 Ω or less (in the forward direction) with the negative meter lead connected to the cathode. For the reverse direction, with meter leads transposed, the reading should be much higher. For PS rectifiers, 100 kΩ or so is typical; for small diodes used in signal circuits, it should be close to infinity. A low reading in the reverse direction indicates leakage. A high reading in the forward direction for a PS rectifier results in a voltage drop and poor regulation. A shorted diode will read 0 Ω in both directions, and infinity if open. To identify the terminals of an unmarked diode, compare readings with those taken on one that *is* marked.

*HV Stick-Type Rectifiers.* These may be open or leaky but not shorted. Ohmmeter testing is *meaningless*. Test by substitution while looking for an increase in HV or focus voltage under load (at full screen brightness). Another approach is connecting the rectifier to 100 to 200 V with a 50-kΩ load, while monitoring the load voltage. When reverse biased, the voltage across the load resistor should be negligible. With the leads reversed, the meter should indicate at least 50% of the PS voltage; the higher the better. Where rectifiers are enclosed in an encapsulated package and there is low output, they cannot be checked individually, and substitution or replacement is the only answer.

*Varactor Diodes (Varicaps).* A shorted varactor diode will usually disable an oscillator. If open or leaky, it will be ineffective in controlling frequency. Test as described for other signal circuit diodes. When reverse biased, no leakage can be tolerated. If in doubt, replace the diode.

*Zener Diodes.* Same defects and ohmmeter tests as for other diodes. A shorted zener will kill the B+; if leaky, it will reduce it. If open, there will be no regulation and the output will be excessive. To determine avalanche voltage and regulation efficiency, connect a zener series with a high-value limiting resistor to a variable dc PS, with the cathode connected to B+ (for reverse biasing). Vary the voltage, noting the level where conductance begins and the output voltage becomes stabilized.

*LEDs.* A LED can become open, shorted, leaky, or have a weak glow. Try an ohmmeter check, but results may be inconclusive. Substitute, comparing brightness levels when powered from a 3-V battery.

*Digital Readout Displays.* The display may be completely inoperative, or one or more segments may not be working. Using a small lamp, check the output of the driver amplifier, and when initiated, check at each segment that is not working properly. If there is little or no driver output, circuit problems are indicated. If the output is normal the display is defective.

*Transistors.* Like diodes, which they resemble, transistors become open, leaky, or shorted. Feel the transistor for possible overheating, in which case it has probably been damaged or destroyed, and possibly by some other defect. Test with an ohmmeter or diode/transistor tester, preferably out of the circuit. Instead of unnecessary desoldering and soldering on a PCB, which can damage components, isolate it for testing by cutting across the printed wiring at a convenient point. Restore the circuit later with a drop of solder or piece of wire.

Most sets today mark the B, E, and C terminals of a transistor on one or both sides of the PCB. To identify and test an *unmarked* transistor, proceed as follows. (*Note:* Actual readings may vary considerably, depending on the meter used and the ohms range selected.)

1. *Identifying unmarked terminals.* Take three ohmmeter readings with the meter connected arbitrarily to each pair of leads. The object is to get two readings the same, whether high or low. The common terminal for both readings will be the *base.* The other two will be the C and the E.
2. *Determine transistor type.* With the negative meter lead connected to the base, note whether the two equal readings are high or low. High readings (in megohms) identify it as an NPN type. Low readings (100 Ω or less on the ×100 range) means that it is a PNP. Readings will be reversed if meter leads are transposed.
3. *Identifying E and C terminals.* Ignoring the base terminal identified previously, a reading between the other two is normally in megohms, but depending on the meter leads, one reading is slightly less than the other. For a PNP type, the higher reading of the two is with the negative meter lead at the collector. With a PNP and the high reading, the negative meter lead connection is the emitter.
4. *Evaluation test.* On the lowest meter range, a reading of 0 Ω between any two terminals indicates a shorted junction. If infinity (on the megohm range), the junction *may be* open. (As stated earlier, readings between C and E on small-signal transistors are normally in megohms and can be mistaken for an open junction.)

With small transistors, as with diodes, a reversed-bias reading of less than 1 MΩ or so indicates serious leakage. For power transistors, a reading as low as 100 kΩ is generally acceptable. When in doubt, compare readings taken on a similar transistor that is known to be good. In the final analysis, substitute.

*FETs.* Fets, too, can become open, leaky, or shorted. In general, ohmmeter testing is performed in the same manner as for ordinary transistors—except for the need to observe handling precautions, as discussed in Chapter 5. They are extremely sensitive devices and can easily be damaged or destroyed by static charges and voltage surges. The gate junctions are particularly vulnerable, and readings of less than infinity at these points will greatly reduce the FET's effectiveness as a low-level low-noise amplifier.

*ICs.* Possible IC defects include shorts, leakage, and open circuits. Unfortunately, they cannot be tested per se, and checking their good/bad status follows a process of elimination:

1. Check voltages at all pins and compare with the schematic. Clues to look for are weak or missing voltages and voltages at pins where none should exist.
2. Check the input and output signals. As-

suming normal applied voltages, a normal input but no output usually means that the IC is bad.

3. Check for defects external to the IC. If there are no external defects, the IC is probably defective and must be replaced.

*SCRs and Triacs.* These become open, shorted, or leaky. Perform ohmmeter tests as for diodes and transistors. The reading from gate(s) to cathode (in both directions) should be roughly 1 kΩ; the other readings, close to infinity. To check the switching function, connect in a test circuit (Figure 3-3). With the switch closed, the indicator lamp should not light. With the switch open, the lamp should come on. If shorted, the lamp will be lit at all times. If open, the lamp will not light at either switch position.

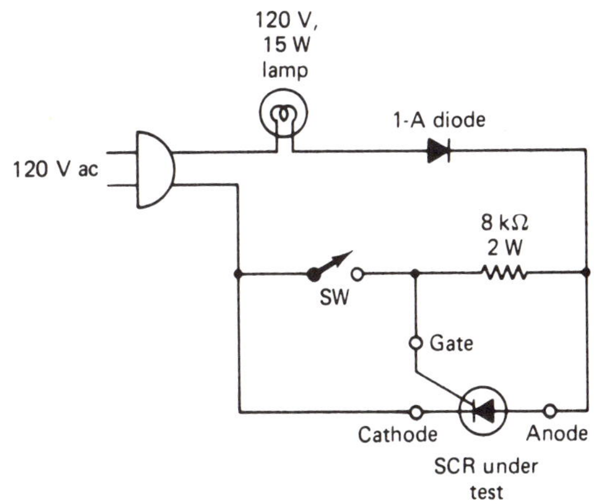


**FIG. 3-3** Simple SCR test circuit.

*Deflection Yokes.* These have the same kinds of defects and test procedures as for other coils. An open yoke causes a loss of deflection; a shorted yoke develops a keystone-shaped raster. With ohmmeter testing, each pair of coils should have the same resistance. Clues to shorted windings are overheating and internal arcing with smoke. For more definitive tests, use a flyback/yoke ringing type of tester (Figure 3-4).

*Convergence Yokes.* Defects include physical damage, bad coils, and weak magnet adjusters.

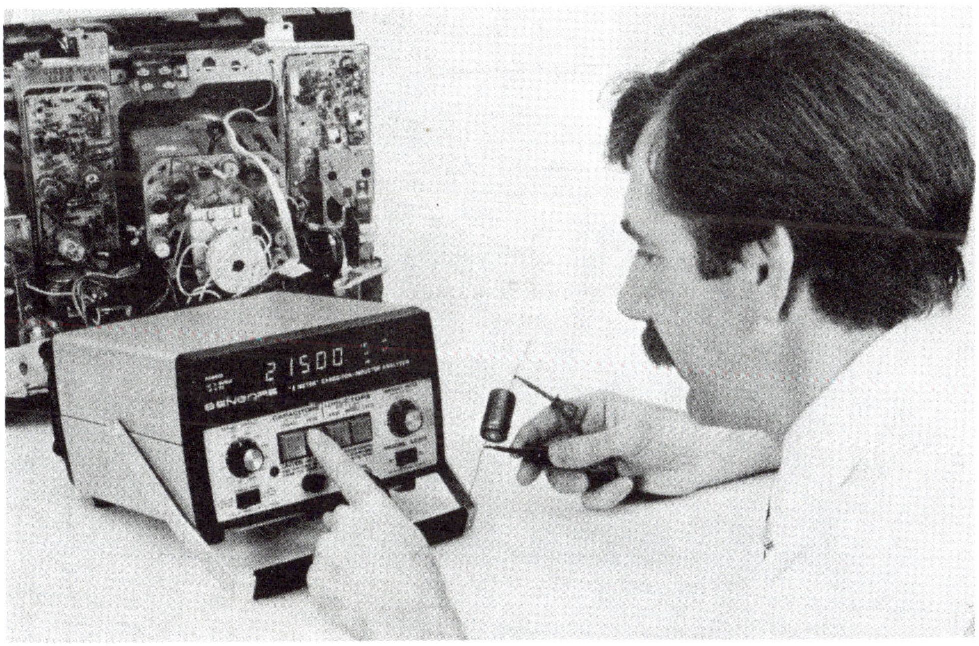

(a)

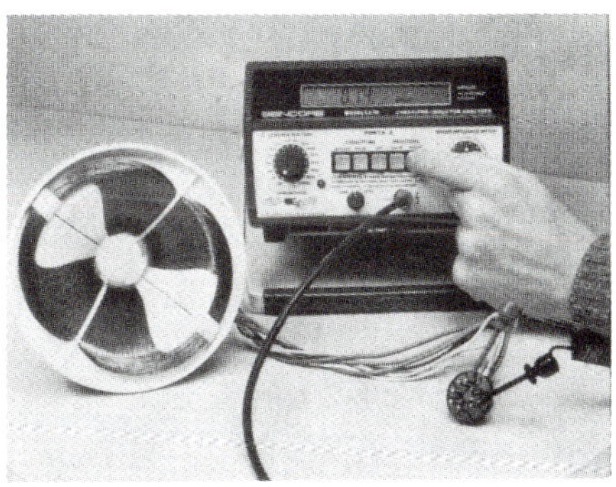

(b)

**FIG. 3-4** Capacitor and yoke testing. (a) testing a capacitor; (b) testing a deflection yoke (Courtesy of Sencore News).

Breakdowns are rare but can create convergence problems. Inspect for damage and missing or inoperative adjusters. Substitute suspected weak magnets. Check the continuity of all coils and their connecting leads.

*Modules.* Since there is no standardization, modules are tested individually using normal troubleshooting procedures. Check the integrity of the cables and connectors. If not repairable, they are usually replaced on an exchange basis.

*PCBs.* Besides component breakdowns, troubles peculiar to PCBs are intermittent edge connectors and hairline cracks in the printed wiring. For specifics, see Chapter 5.

## QUESTIONS

1. When testing a capacitor with a voltmeter and dc supply, explain the meter reaction if the unit is shorted, leaky, or open.
2. What are the possibilities when a tuned circuit will not resonate at the proper frequency?
3. Explain why an ohmmeter measurement across a diode or transistor junction depends on which way the leads are connected.
4. A resistor is connected in a circuit with solid-state components. State its probable condition when it measures (a) the coded value; (b) much less than coded; (c) much higher than coded.
5. Give a step-by-step procedure for identifying and testing an unknown transistor.
6. How would you proceed when an IC is suspected?
7. Shorted windings are suspected in a power transformer. State some symptoms and how you would proceed.
8. When you suspect that a capacitor is leaky or shorted, can you bridge it with a substitute? Explain.
9. What precautions must be followed in handling and testing a FET? Explain.
10. You should never trust an ohmmeter reading when it reads (a) 0 Ω on the megohm range; (b) infinity on the lowest range. Explain why in each case.

# 4 Test equipment and servicing aids

It is unfortunate that in a world of high-tech consumer products we still do not have that magical tester that will identify any and all defects at the touch of a button, or carried a step further and a few years into the future, robotics that will make the repair. But with new testers on the market and others on the drawing board, we are coming close.

Attempting to repair modern electronic equipment without suitable tools or instruments would be like working in the dark with your hands behind your back. Although most servicing jobs can be handled by an experienced technician with little more than a few basic instruments, modern sets and difficult problems require highly sophisticated testers (Figure 4-1). In the real world, lacking such equipment translates into wasted effort, frustration, headaches, and loss of income.

But we must crawl before we walk. It is suggested that the beginner start off modestly, acquiring only the essentials: a meter, an AF/RF signal generator, and an oscilloscope. More complex (and expensive) instruments can be purchased later as the need arises. Many instruments can be obtained secondhand at considerable savings. Some can be constructed from kits (e.g., Heathkits). Many servicing aids can be made up as do-it-yourself projects for next to nothing. As a further saving, the technician is encouraged to maintain and service his own equipment. Test equipment like other consumer products are subject to failure, and troubleshooting calls for the same general approach as for any electronic device.

In this chapter we describe briefly both simple and complex instruments, including those found in progressive service shops. Procedures for using them are provided in subsequent chapters.

## 4-1 TESTING FUNDAMENTALS

There are two main categories of test instruments: those used to localize troubles to a particular stage or section of a set, and those used to isolate a defect to the component level. Localizing troubles naturally comes first. In general, there are three ways of

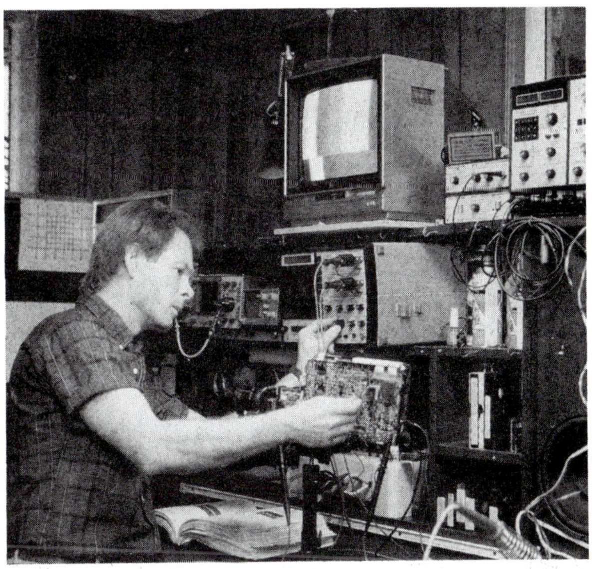

**FIG. 4-1** A well equipped repair shop. Good equipment makes servicing a pleasure. (Courtesy of Sencore News).

doing this: *voltage checking, signal tracing*, and *signal injection*. An accurate meter is required for checking ac and dc voltages. Signal tracing makes use of a scope or other indicator type of instrument to follow the progress of a received signal or one generated within the set, to the point where the signal becomes lost, weakened, or otherwise degraded.

With signal injection, a test generator substitutes for the weak or missing signal. It is injected at various points in a circuit to locate the point where the normal signal is lost or weakened and the injected signal takes over. With this method, the response may be observed on a TV screen, heard from a speaker, or indicated on a scope or a meter. Signal generators are also used for aligning tuned circuits. Isolating a defect usually calls for checking voltages applied to the troublesome stage and testing suspected components. Various instruments are available for checking components.

## 4-2 TEST EQUIPMENT

### RF Signal Generators

This type of generator is used to check high-frequency (RF-IF) stages. The output of most RF generators is quite low, generally less than 1 V rms, but strong enough to overload low-level stages, as in the tuner and IF preamps. One or two output attentuators are usually provided, which may be calibrated in millivolts or microvolts. When injecting a signal in a troublesome circuit, use the least amount of signal that gives an indication without overloading or creating distortion. Use approximately the same signal levels encountered at the same circuit points during normal receiver operation.

A typical generator (Figure 4-2) develops frequencies from about 500 kHz to approximately 30 MHz in several ranges. Higher frequencies make use of the harmonics of fundamentals generated by the lower frequencies. Dial calibration accuracy depends mainly on the cost and quality of the instrument. When aligning tuned circuits, the signal should be injected at some point ahead of the circuit being tuned, to prevent errors resulting from loading and detuning effects. Calibration accuracy is of prime importance. Check it periodically and prior to use. Allow a warm-up period for the frequency to stabilize.

Unless the instrument contains a dc blocking capacitor in series with its output, one should always be used to prevent damage to the attenuators and the receiver components. Most generators provide

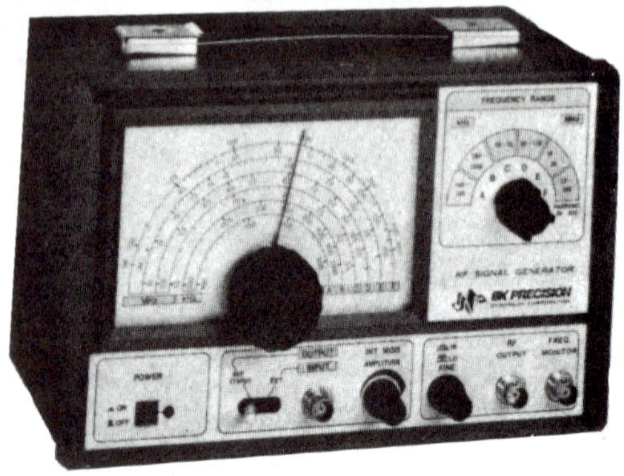

(a)

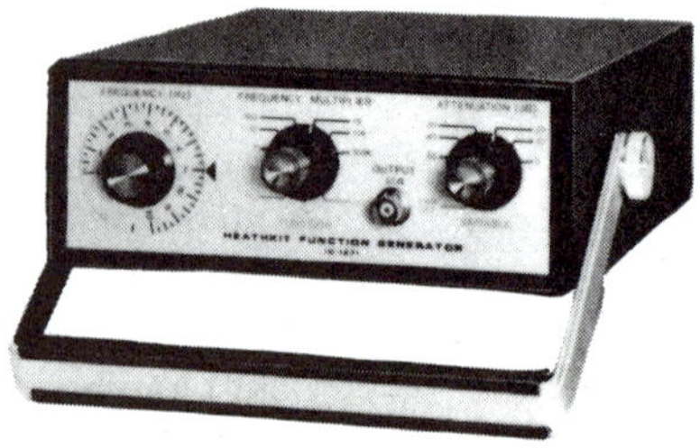

(b)

**FIG. 4-2** RF/AF signal generators. (a) A typical RF generator (B&K precision); (b) A function generator develops frequencies from zero $H_z$ well into the RF spectrum (Courtesy of the Heath Co).

unmodulated RF (CW) and modulated RF. A sampling of the modulating audio frequency (usually 400 Hz) is available for use in low-frequency circuits.

### Sweep Generators

The RF output of a sweep generator is *FM (frequency modulated)* at a 60-Hz sweep rate. It is used for checking and aligning tuned circuits where it sweeps a band of frequencies centered at the frequency of the main dial setting. The amount of sweep is adjustable from zero to about 30 MHz, in accordance with the bandpass of the tuned circuit being checked or aligned. When used with a scope, a *response curve* is produced. The shape of the curve and amplitude variations depend on the gain of the circuit under test for the frequencies being swept. For example, when checking or aligning an IF stage with a center frequency of 40 MHz and a bandpass of 5 MHz, the generator would be tuned to 40 MHz and the sweep set for approximately 10 to 15 MHz. To identify frequencies associated with various points on the curve, a *marker signal* (from an *accurate* RF generator) is introduced, which shows up as a small notch or blip on the curve. More on this in later chapters.

## Video Sweep Modulation Equipment

Video sweep modulation (VSM) is an alternative to regular sweep alignment. It is used to obtain the necessary flat-topped overall response of the very critical tuned circuits in the bandpass amplifier of a color set. The following items are required: sweep generator, marker generator, an absorption marker (calibrated adjustable wave trap), and an RF modulator, plus an oscilloscope. The modulator accepts the sweep and marker signals to produce a frequency-modulated AM signal which is fed to the receiver input. The resulting response curve as it appears on the scope has a center frequency marker of 45.75 MHz (the video IF carrier) and two additional markers of 3.08 and 4.08 MHz, as produced by the absorption marker.

## Noise Generators

Noise generators are inexpensive instruments that can be used as a backup to regular signal generators, particularly for signal injection to locate a dead stage in both low- and high-frequency circuits. A typical noise generator produces a signal rich in harmonics covering a wide range of frequencies. As an indicator in localizing troubles, it creates an interference pattern on a TV picture tube and/or a raspy sound from the speaker.

## Audio Generators

Unlike the low-level single frequency (400 Hz or 1 kHz) obtainable from an RF generator, a good AF generator provides continuous coverage from near 0 Hz to 50 kHz and up. A typical generator has a fairly high output, about 10 V peak to peak (p-p), consistent with normal signal levels found in video, audio, chroma, and sweep stages of TV, where it finds the greatest use. Most AF generators provide a variety of waveforms: rectangular, sine, and sawtooth. Typical uses include signal injection (substitution) and testing for stage gain and distortion in amplifiers.

## Dot/Crosshatch Pattern Generators

A dot/crosshatch pattern generator develops several frequencies for producing a variety of dot and line patterns which are displayed on the TV picture tube (Figure 4-3). Many color bar generators, described next, also produce these patterns. Such patterns are used for adjusting sweep linearity and beam convergence of a color set. The signal may be fed to either the antenna terminals or the IF strip.

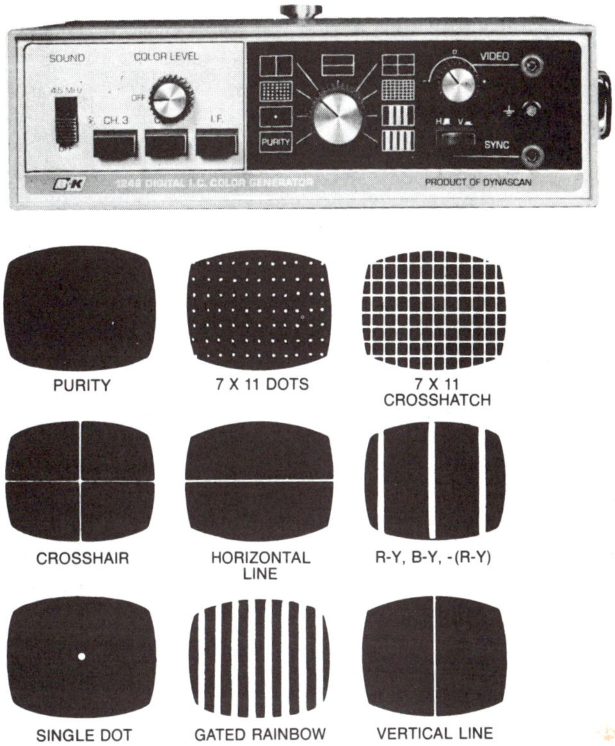


**FIG. 4-3** Dot/crosshatch/bar generator and display patterns. Such patterns serve as diagnostic aids and facilitate adjustments. (Courtesy of B/K Precision).

## Color Bar Generators

A color bar generator produces a number of color bars of different hues on the CRT of the set being worked on (see Figure 15-10). The appearance of the bars provides information on the development and processing of the various color signals produced by the receiver. If any colors are missing, this is a clue to the probable cause. It is also used in receiver setup adjustments, particularly for adjusting the range of a tint control. When fed to the antenna terminals or the IF strip of a properly operating receiver, a typical generator produces 10 bars, each a different color, ranging from yellow/orange, through red and blue, to green.

There are two kinds of color bar generators; the NTSC type and the so-called gated rainbow generator. An NTSC generator produces bars in their *true* colors (i.e., proper values of hue, saturation, and brightness). Although not quite as accurate, a rainbow generator is preferred by most technicians because of its lower cost.

A rainbow generator produces two kinds of signals, which heterodyne to create a third signal that produces the bars. Hue is a function of phase, and with the ever-changing phase relationship between the signal generated and the receiver subcarrier oscillator during each horizontal scan of the CRT beam, every 30° of shift produces a different-colored bar.

### Signal Tracers

There are various ways of tracing signals in a receiver, the oscilloscope providing the most useful information. In lieu of a scope, you can use an ac voltmeter, which is often okay for locating a weak or dead stage. An audio amplifier (or the one in the set being worked on) can also be used. For example, when its input is connected to various points in a vertical sweep circuit or a video or chroma amplifier, the presence of a signal is indicated by a raspy sound from the speaker. In conjunction with an amplifier-type demodulator probe, you can even trace through IF stages. Inexpensive signal tracers incorporate a high-gain amplifier, a meter, and a speaker.

### Stage or Video Analyzers

Instruments of this type have been around for a long time. A basic analyzer is used to check all stages and sections of a set by substitution. As such, it has a counterpart for practically every functional area of a receiver. It is especially useful for monitoring applied voltages and inputs and outputs simultaneously when there are intermittent problems.

Modern versions of this instrument can greatly reduce servicing time, but are quite expensive. One popular model that can be found in most well-equipped service shops is shown in Figure 4-4. This is a truly versatile multipurpose instrument that can check any and all circuits in a TV set or VCR by substitution. It contains numerous measuring instruments, except a scope. Its uses and capabilities include the following:

- Provides for tuner substitution with signal generator outputs for all VHF and UHF channels
- Provides a crystal-controlled 45.75-MHz IF signal for troubleshooting the IF strip, including stage gain testing, alignment, and the adjustment of synchronous detectors, a critical adjustment beyond the capabilities of many instruments
- Generates dot/crosshatch patterns for checking and adjusting linearity and convergence
- Generates gated-rainbow color bars for servicing chroma, comb filters, and video output circuits in TV and VCRs. It also provides for bar sweep alignment of the bandpass amplifier
- Generates a vertical interval reference (VIR) signal for dynamic testing of automatic station-controlled color circuits.
- Provides a ringing test for yokes and flyback transformers
- Has a 0- to 35-V regulated dc power supply for clamping and substitute checking of

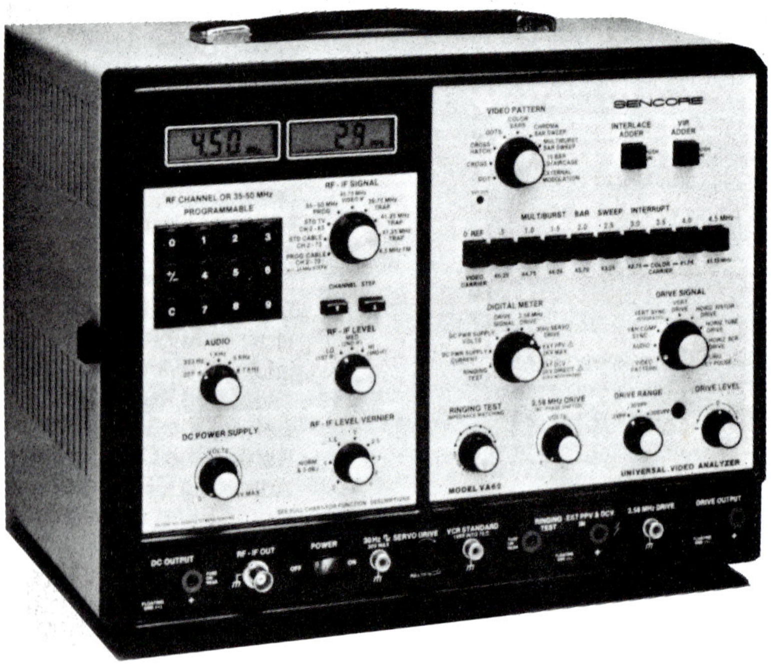


**FIG. 4-4** Stage substitute/video analyzer. Such instruments are indispensable to the busy technician (Courtesy of Sencore News).

AGC, AFT, ACC, and VCR servo loop circuits
- Contains a digital meter for accurate measurement of all dc voltages and currents as well as ac signal and pulse voltages encountered in most stages.

### MTS Stereo Analyzer

An instrument of this type is essential for checking the performance of TV and VCR stereo, particularly in the adjustment of decoders where it substitutes for all the signals transmitted by the station: the SAP pilot signals, and the composite stereo signal. Some models incorporate meters for dynamic load testing, power output and channel separation measurements.

### Frequency Counters

Using computer-type logic circuits, this instrument enables accurate frequency checks on all TV and VCR oscillators as well as PLL countdown circuits. It is especially useful for intermittents and suspected frequency drift. A typical counter will check frequencies from 10 Hz to 1 GHz with high sensitivity. Frequency is displayed on a digital readout. Some models can even check the crystals used in TV and VCRs.

### Capacitor and Inductor Analyzers

This is the modern version of an earlier instrument known as a CR bridge. It is used to measure the values of capacitors and coils of all kinds and to check their condition. A typical instrument will accurately measure capacitor values from 1.0 pF to 200,000 μF, and inductors from 1 μH to 10 or more Henries. Solid dielectric capacitors are checked for shorts and leakage at their rated voltage. A separate quality test is made on electrolytics. Inductors are checked by ringing, as described next.

### Flyback/Yoke Testers

Shorted windings in yokes and flybacks are very common, and even one shorted turn can have an adverse effect on circuit operation, causing overheating and eventual burnout. Unfortunately, because of the low resistance, an ohmmeter will not detect a few shorted turns. Substitution is okay, but nine times out of ten the substitute must be an exact replacement, and who can stock that many items? Testing can be done in two ways. Early model testers used the coil under test as part of a tuned circuit excited by a power oscillator operating at roughly 1500 Hz. Shorted windings increase the resonant frequency, indicating "bad" on a meter scale.

Modern instruments indicate the rate of decay (damped oscillations) when the coil is momentarily shock excited by a strong oscillatory current. This is called *ringing*. With a good inductor, oscillations continue for several cycles; with shorted turns, they quickly die out, as indicated by a decreasing cycle count on a digital readout (see Figure 3-4). Quick tests can be made in-circuit, but out-of-circuit test results are usually more valid. Ringing tests can also be performed with basic instruments by shunting the coil across a scope input and exciting it with a strong square-wave voltage from an AF generator.

### Diode/Transistor Testers

Ohmmeter checking of solid-state devices is okay but time consuming. Diode/transistor testers (Figure 4-5) can do it faster and better. A typical tester will identify the transistor type (NPN or PNP) and the terminal leads on diodes and transistors as well as checking their condition. Most can also check FETs and provide a gain check that can be useful for matching transistors in critical circuits.

Most testers can perform an in-circuit quick check with results indicated on a go/no-go meter scale. But because of the shunting effect of low-re-

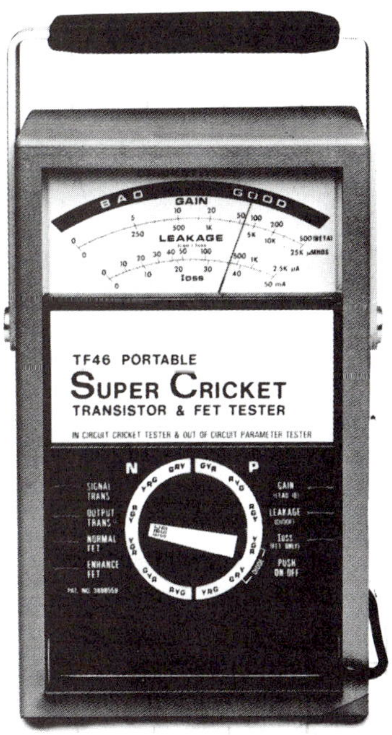


**FIG. 4-5** Typical transistor tester. (Courtesy of Sencore News). In-circuit testing with such instruments comes easy.

sistance circuit components—other diode and transistor junctions, in particular—results are not always conclusive. As for other components, the rule is: When in doubt, isolate or remove and recheck. Remove power prior to testing, and on live circuits, use only miniclips or a needlepoint probe to avoid shorting closely spaced connections.

## 4-3 *E, I,* AND *R* MEASURING INSTRUMENTS

Except for digital types, the basis of all meters is a current-indicating device called a *movement,* which consists of a small pivoted coil with a needle (pointer) attached. The coil is surrounded by a magnet and rotates in its magnetic field. Current or voltage being tested is applied to the coil to produce a magnetic flux that reacts with the flux of the magnet. Deflection is proportional to the strength of the coil current and is indicated on a calibrated scale. The earliest meter movements were relatively insensitive, requiring about 1 MA for full-scale deflection. A good meter today has a sensitivity of 50 μA.

Depending on how it is connected, such a meter movement can measure voltage, current, or resistance—all the factors to consider in any circuit. A meter that can perform all three functions is called a *multimeter* (Figure 4-6). Once considered essential in servicing, such instruments now have a limited use and have largely been superseded by digital meters. Single-function meters, still used to some extent, are described next.

### Current Meter

A sensitive movement can measure currents as low as a few microamperes. For higher currents (milliamperes or amperes), it must be shunted with a low-value *shunt resistor*. The lower the shunt resistance, the greater the extended range. Since the current through the meter coil is limited, any additional current being checked must be bypassed through the parallel-connected shunt. Most meters have several ranges, as selected with a switch. A typical shunt is generally about 1 Ω or less.

For checking current, the meter must be connected in *series with a load* and never across the voltage source. A mistake in connecting, a short in the circuit under test, or a shunt becoming open can instantly damage or destroy the movement. When connecting into a circuit, the positive side of the meter goes to the most positive point in the circuit under test. Always start with the highest current range, working down, as necessary, as testing progresses.

**FIG. 4-6** E, I and R measuring instruments. (a) BK precision; (b) VTVM Heath kit; (c) DMM Beckman. The old gives way to the new.

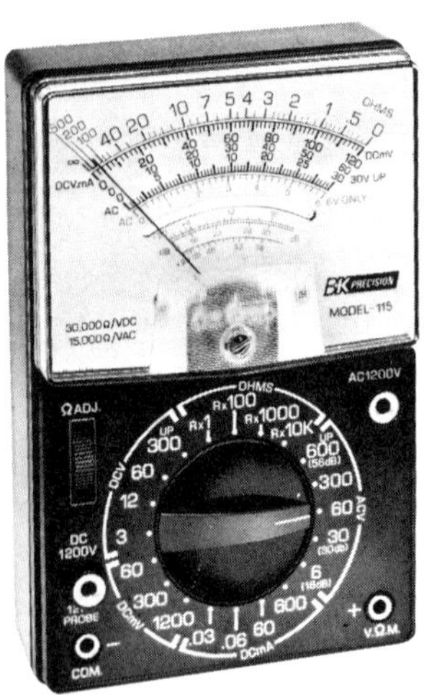


(a)

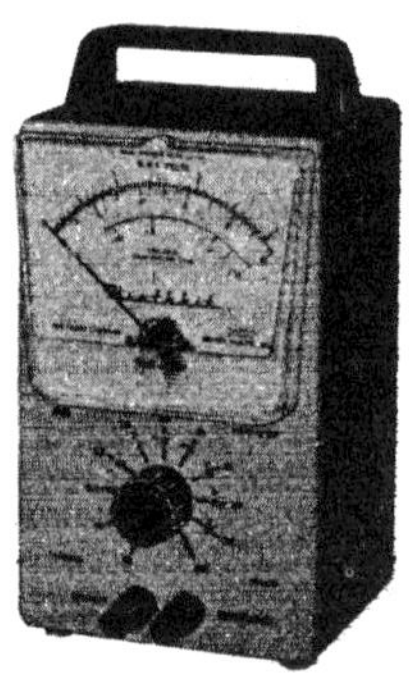

(b)

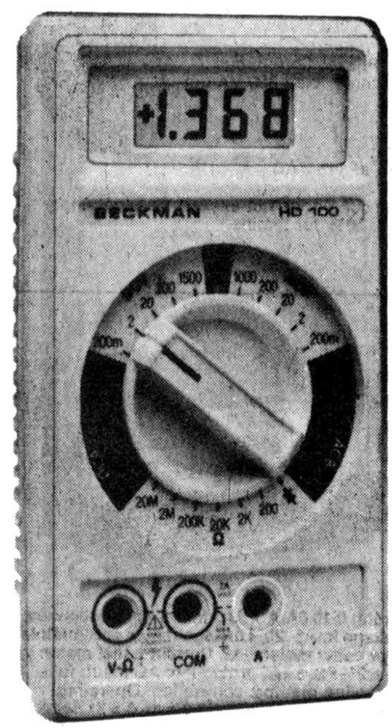


(c)

## Basic Voltmeter

A dc voltmeter is basically a current meter with a series-connected *multiplier* resistor. Unlike an ammeter shunt, a multiplier is a high resistance, usually several thousand ohms, depending on the movement sensitivity and the desired voltage range. The greater the multiplier resistance, the greater the voltage that can be measured, and the higher the sensitivity, the more resistance that is needed for any given range. An extreme example is the multiplier encased in the probe for checking HV in a TV set. It may measure hundreds of megohms.

Compared to a current meter, a voltmeter is connected across a circuit to measure the potential difference between two points; + to + and − to −. Start with the highest anticipated voltage range and work down. For solid-state circuits, the meter must be capable of measuring fractional voltages with great accuracy.

The accuracy of voltage measurements depends largely on circuit *loading*. The current required by the meter comes from the circuit under test, usually via one or more resistive components. This creates an unavoidable *IR* voltage drop, which reduces the meter reading accordingly. The lower the meter sensitivity (high current drain) and the greater the circuit resistance, the greater the *IR* drop and the measurement error—hence the need for a high-sensitivity movement. For checking ac voltages, the voltage under test must be converted to dc with a rectifier.

## Basic Ohmmeter

A simple ohmmeter consists of a battery and a current-limiting resistor connected in series with a meter movement. With the test leads connected together, and assuming that it has been *zero adjusted,* the meter will indicate 0 Ω on a calibrated scale. Any additional circuit resistance (a resistor being tested, for example) will reduce the deflection and give a corresponding higher ohms reading. The more sensitive the meter, the higher the values of resistors that can be measured.

Never take resistance readings on a live circuit. As with a current measuring meter, it can be destroyed instantly. Be aware that any residual voltage (with the set turned off) will change the reading drastically. Check the ohmmeter accuracy periodically against another meter or by measuring several resistors of known value. When in error, check the internal battery, especially when the meter will not zero set. (*Caution:* A dead or leaking battery will damage the instrument by corrosive action.)

## Volt/Ohmmeter (Multimeter)

Combination meters of this type (Figure 4-6) can still be found in most shops as a backup for making tests that do not require extreme accuracy. As with the current and ohmmeters just described, they can be destroyed by improper use. Attempting to check voltage when on a current or ohms range can be disastrous. *Double check* the function and range settings selected before taking a reading.

## Vacuum-Tube Voltmeter and Electronic Voltmeter

An electronic voltmeter (EVM) is a solid-state version of the once popular vacuum-tube voltmeter (VTVM) (Figure 4-6). With each type the meter movement is connected as one arm of a balanced bridge circuit. Both instruments are used to measure voltage and resistance with high accuracy. They have several advantages over a VOM. They are more sensitive, which enables them to measure higher resistor values, well into the megohms. Having a high input impedance (typically about 10 MΩ), they do not load the circuit being tested. This means very little current drain and increased accuracy when checking high-resistance circuits. They are less subject to overload damage than is a VOM. Meters of this type do not have a current-measuring capability.

## Digital Voltmeter and Digital Multimeter

The digital voltmeter (DVM) and its companion the digital multimeter (DMM) (Figure 4-6) are the choice of many technicians, and for good reason. Using logic circuits and a digital readout, they are highly accurate (about 0.1% for most functions); circuit loading is negligible; there is no need to switch ranges or try to interpret readings on the fine divisions of a meter scale; and they are protected against overload. Typical features include the following.

*Autoranging.* All functions and ranges are under microprocessor control. This means that voltage, current, and resistance ranges are selected automatically according to the values being checked. This can be a real timesaver.

*Extended Ranges.* These may be from 1 mV to 1999 V, ac or dc; current (ac or dc), 0.1 μA to 1999 mA; resistance, 0.001 Ω to 19.99 MΩ. Values are indicated on a three- or four-digit numeric display. Usually, three least-significant digits are displayed. *E, I,* and *R* values being tested are sampled continuously, with the decimal on the readout being relocated automatically with range changes. Dc polarity is also indicated. There are two basic types of meters: ac operated for bench use, and battery powered.

### Oscilloscope

Next to a meter, a scope is by far the most useful and versatile item for servicing TV sets and other electronic equipment. Uses include waveform analysis, signal tracing, peak-to-peak voltage measuring, stage gain checking, distortion tests, frequency measuring, and the alignment of tuned circuits. A well-designed scope with all the latest refinements is desirable (and often necessary) for checking and evaluating conditions in modern high-tech equipment, and a busy technician needs the best (Figure 4-7). For the novice, however, even a simple inexpensive scope is better than nothing for signal tracing and waveform analysis where extreme accuracy is not called for. The limitations of such a scope are less-than-perfect linearity of the horizontal trace; low vertical amplifier gain, which limits its usefulness in low-level stages; and poor frequency response of the vertical amplifiers. A functional drawing of a basic oscilloscope is shown in Figure 4-8. Following is a brief description.

The heart of any scope is the CRT. It functions much like a monochrome TV picture tube except for some differences. Each has an electron gun, which comprises a heater, cathode, and several grids. Whereas the beam on the TV picture tube is deflected electromagnetically, a scope uses electrostatic (ES) deflection. As shown in Figure 4-8, there are two sets of built-in deflection plates, one pair for vertical deflection, the other two for horizontal deflection. Voltages applied to the plates influence the beam as it travels to the screen.

A sawtooth generator is the source of voltage applied to the horizontal plates to sweep the beam horizontally. A sawtooth waveform is required for linear deflection and a rapid retrace. The sawtooth sweep frequency is adjusted in accordance with the frequency of the signal voltage being checked. Both coarse and fine frequency controls are provided. A basic scope has a frequency range from near zero to about 200 kHz.

The signal to be tested or evaluated is applied to the vertical plates via a high-gain amplifier. Simultaneous deflection of the beam vertically and horizontally traces out the waveform being checked. The number of cycles displayed is determined by

(a)

(b)

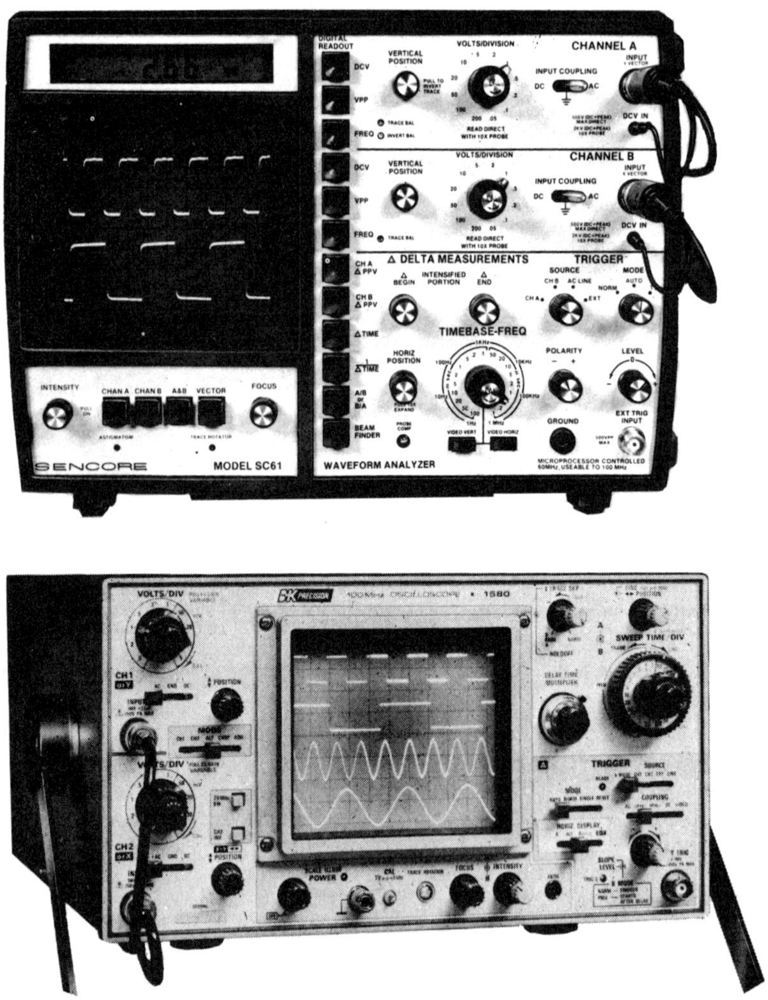


**FIG. 4-7** Typical modern oscilloscopes. (a) Courtesy of Sencore News; (b) A multi-trace triggered sweep CRO is a good investment (B&K Precision).

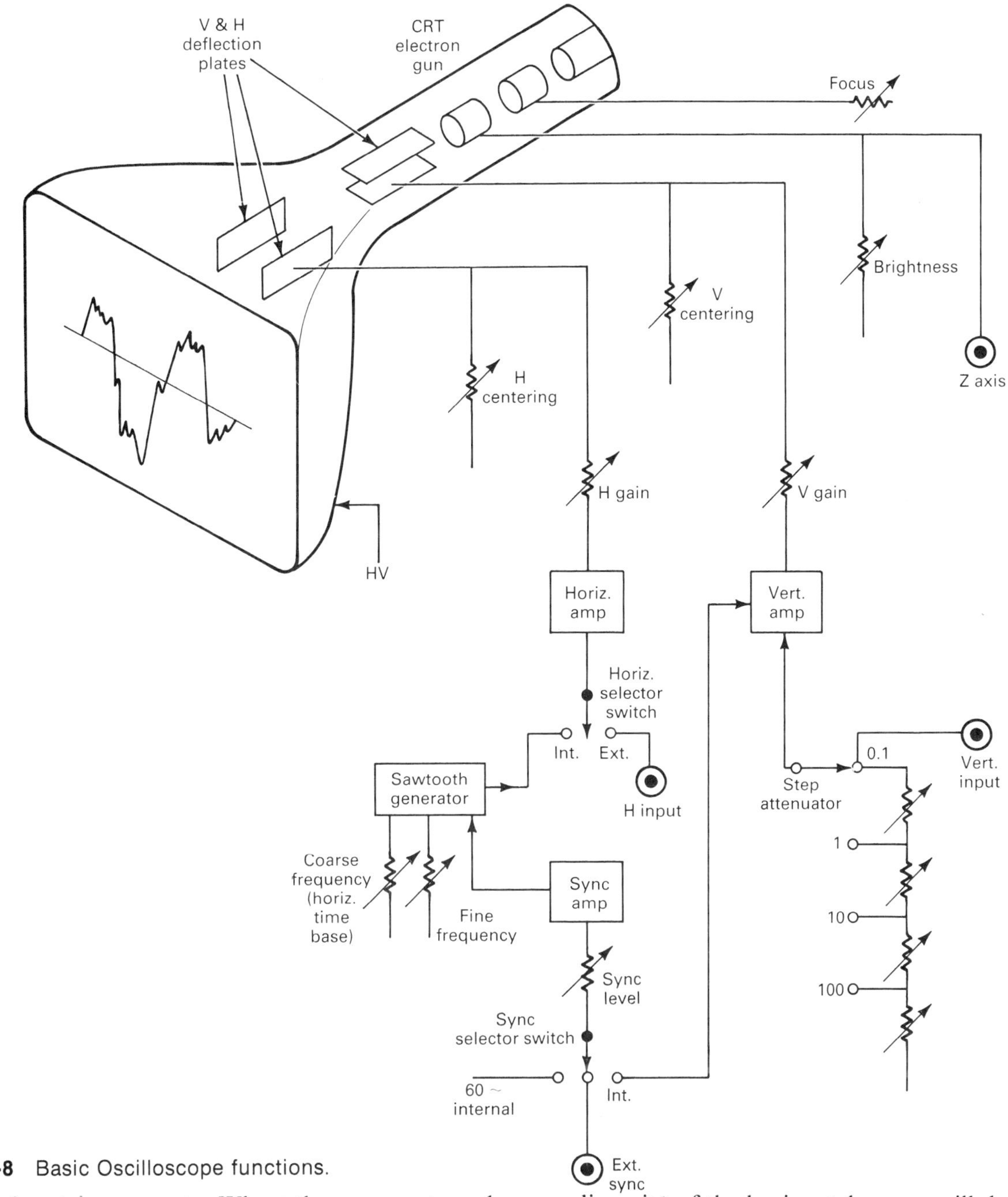


**FIG. 4-8** Basic Oscilloscope functions.

the horizontal sweep rate. Where the sweep rate and the frequency of the signal under test are equal, one cycle is displayed. To observe two cycles, the sweep rate must be reduced by one-half. For more cycles, the sweep rate must be reduced proportionately. The slower the horizontal beam trace, the more waves that can be traced out as the beam moves from left to right across the screen. Since most waveforms are repetitive, two or three cycles are all that is needed for observation. With one wave spread across the screen you can observe the maximum amount of detail. Only recurrent signals can be observed and analyzed. Nonrecurrent waveforms (e.g., a composite video signal) appear as a blur, as their frequency changes constantly. Any nonlinearity of the horizontal sweep will distort the display.

As with TV, the horizontal sweep and the applied signal must be synchronized. Without sync, the sawtooth generator is free-running and the waveform displayed will be unstable. Three alternative means of sync are provided as shown: INT (internal) using a sampling of the applied signal, 60 Hz (from the ac power line), or an external source. The sync level is adjustable.

To operate a scope (where nothing is observed on the screen), proceed as follows.

1. Start by adjusting the vertical and horizontal centering, brightness, and focus

controls at midposition, until some light appears. Readjust later as necessary when a trace appears. Avoid excessive brightness if there is only a dot or a thin line, which can burn the screen.

2. Adjust the horizontal gain control for a trace extending across the tube face.
3. Connect the signal to be checked to the vertical input terminal using shielded cable. Adjust the vertical gain control for the desired amount of vertical deflection.
4. Adjust the horizontal sweep frequency controls to obtain one or two waveforms.
5. Starting from zero, slowly increase the sync level until the display is locked in sync. Excessive sync can distort the waveform.

### Dual-Trace, Triggered Sweep Oscilloscope

Dual trace and a triggered sweep (Figure 4-7) are two features incorporated in all high-quality scopes to extend their usefulness. Dual trace makes it possible to display two different signals or ac voltages simultaneously. Among other things, triggered sweep provides a high degree of sync stability and lets you examine the most minute details on complex waveforms.

Uses for dual trace include simultaneous comparison of two signals, monitoring the input and output of an amplifier where there are intermittent problems, checking the balance of push-pull output amplifiers, and checking and measuring time intervals and durations of periodic pulses. A dual-trace scope has two identical vertical amplifier channels, each separately controlled. An electronic switch switches alternately from one input to the other to produce the two displays.

With a basic scope the horizontal is operating at all times. With triggered sweep, horizontal deflection is initiated "triggered on" by the signal or voltage being checked, and a display is obtained for only the time of horizontal trace. The screen is blanked out until the start of each cycle of the input signal. For the duration of each trace, a lockout circuit prevents noise and other interference from upsetting the sync. The improved sync stability ensures accurate measurements and observation of waveform details. Good triggering depends on the strength and polarity of the signal under test. With this type of scope, the horizontal sweep frequency control is called a *time base* control, and in addition to frequency, is calibrated for units of time.

The usefulness of a scope is enhanced by other features as follows: capability for expanding a display horizontally for better resolution of waveform details; digital readout for peak-to-peak measurements without having to count squares on a graticule; direct coupling in the vertical input circuit to permit measuring the dc component of an ac signal; polarity reversing switch to display a signal, either upright or inverted; and provisions for instantly generating fixed sweep frequencies for viewing commonly used signals such as vertical and horizontal sweep and color burst.

### CRT Checker

There is little need anymore for checking small radio and TV tubes, but a CRT checker is an almost indispensible instrument. A typical checker will check emission, and for leakage, shorts, and gas as indicated by good/bad markings on a meter scale. Some have a life expectancy test to see how fast the emission drops off when the heater voltage is reduced. Many testers today also have provisions for restoring a CRT (i.e., burning out shorts) and increasing the emission (rejuvenation) by removing "crud" buildup on the cathode. Most checkers have an extender cable (with adapters) for connecting to a CRT (see Figure 17-8). Some have a single meter; others have three meters for simultaneous checking and comparison of the emission of all guns of a color CRT.

## 4-4 SERVICING AIDS AND ACCESSORIES

In addition to test equipment, the serious technician requires most, if not all, of the items described below.

### Servicing Aids

- *DC power supply (variable and regulated):* temporary substitute for receiver dc voltages, as a bias box for clamping AGC and other circuits being checked, as a source of voltage for component testing, and so on.
- *Variable transformer (variac):* adjustable autotransformer for increasing or decreasing ac line voltage
- *Isolation transformer:* a 1:1 ratio trans-

former for isolating a receiver or test equipment from the ac power line, as required for servicing most modern hot chassis sets (Figure 4-9)

- *Field strength meter (FSM):* a sensitive RF indicator for surveying antenna sites; also for antenna orientation
- *Tuning wand:* pencil-sized tuning stick with a piece of ceramic core at one end and a piece of nonferrous material at the other end; used for checking the resonance of an RF tuned circuit
- *Picture tube degausser:* a large-diameter coil for demagnetizing a CRT; a discarded ADG coil from a TV set makes a suitable substitute
- *Picture tube brightener (filament booster):* small step-up transformer used to increase the emission of a weak CRT by raising the heater voltage
- *Tuner substitution unit (subber):* for substitute checking of a suspected bad tuner; tuners cannibalized from a discarded TV set can be used here
- *Test speaker:* temporary substitute for receiver speaker
- *C and R sub-box (decade box):* convenient assortment of resistors and capacitors for substitution testing
- *Neon bulb voltage indicator:* used with dc to check leakage of capacitors, and so on; checking for ac line voltage; for checking the high-amplitude pulse output of a horizontal sweep circuit
- *Walkie-talkies:* two required; for two-way communication during antenna installation and orientation

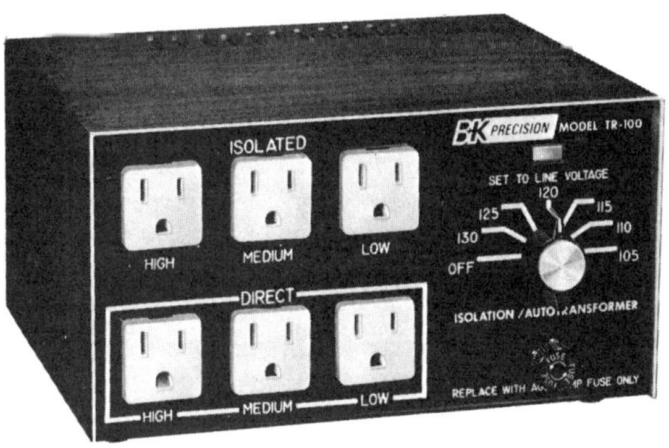


**FIG. 4-9** Typical isolation transformer. Such units are essential for servicing "hot chassis" sets (Courtesy of B & K Precision).

### Cables, Probes and Miscellaneous

- *Direct probes, low- and high-impedance probes:* for proper impedance matching when connecting test equipment to a receiver under test
- *Logic probes:* for signal tracing logic circuits (Figure 4-10)
- *Demodulator probes:* used with a scope, EVM, or signal tracer for tracing modulated RF signals (Figure 4-10); some probes have a built-in amplifier for increased sensitivity
- *HV probe:* high-value multiplier resistor encased in a well-insulated probe (Figure 4-10); used with a dc voltmeter for measuring the HV applied to a CRT
- *Needlepoint test probe:* for making positive contact with hard-to-get-at, closely spaced connections, or to puncture insulation for continuity testing
- *Minilock clip leads:* miniature clip-on connectors for contacting components and closely spaced terminals in confined areas
- *Clip leads and assorted jumper cables:* for temporary hookups
- *Spare cheater cords:* two sizes; for connecting a receiver to a power line
- *Alignment tools:* for adjusting tuned circuit slugs
- *VCR head demagnetizer:* to demagnetize VCR heads (Chapter 21)
- *VCR test and alignment tapes:* for accurate alignment of VCR adjusters
- *Soldering gun and iron; common hand tools:* medium- and high-wattage gun and 25- to 40-W soldering iron; low wattage needed for printed wiring and for working with solid-state components
- *Solder sucker and wicking braid:* For removing solder from PCBs, ICs, and so on
- *IC desoldering tip:* soldering iron attachment for simultaneous heating and desoldering of all IC pin contacts
- *Dip-type IC chip extractor tool:* spring-loaded tool for easy removal of IC when desoldering
- *Trouble light and dental mirror:* for viewing in dark, inaccessible areas
- *Large mirror with stand:* for making CRT setup adjustments
- *Illuminated magnifier:* for working on

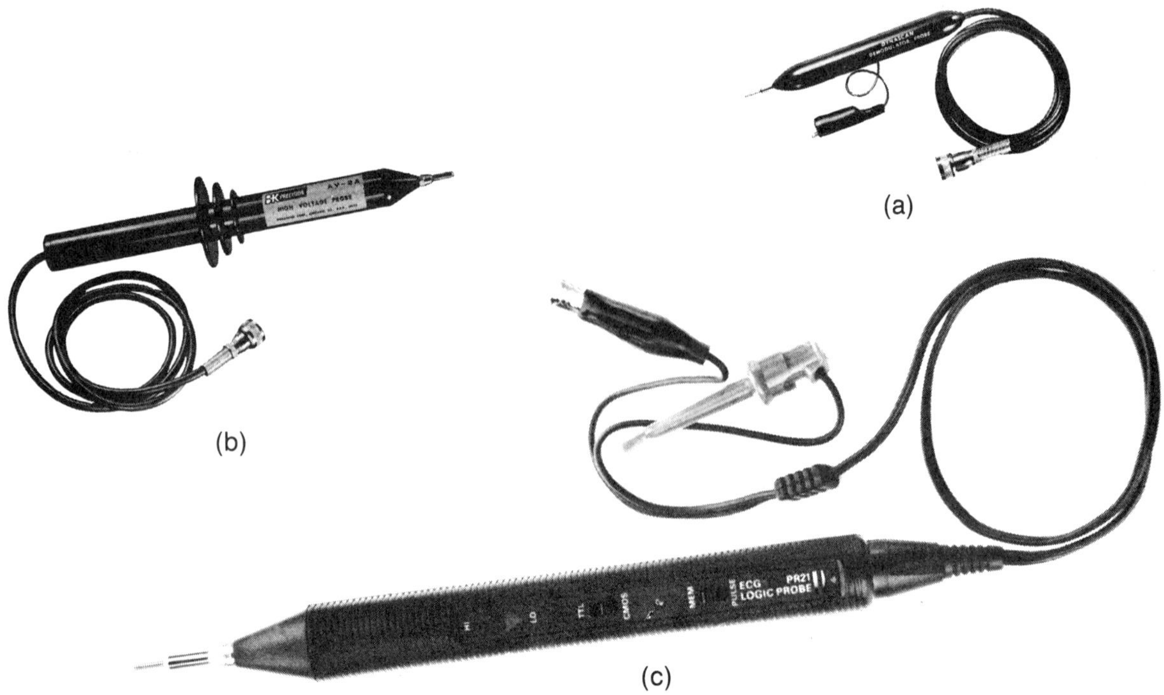

FIG. 4-10 Common Probe types: (a) demodulator probe; (b) HV probe (Courtesy of B & K Precision); (c) troubleshooting digital circuits comes easier with a logic probe (Courtesy of Phillips ECG).

PCBs, tuners, miniature components, and so on.

### Chemical Aids

- *Adhesives:* for repair of small parts
- *Lubricating oil and grease:* for switch-type tuners, dial drives, and other mechanisms
- *Contact cleaner:* to clean dirty/noisy controls and switches
- *Anticorona aerosol spray or dope:* to prevent corona discharge in HV circuits
- *Silicone grease:* to improve heat conduction from power transistors to their heat sink
- *Component cooler:* aerosol coolant spray for chilling suspected intermittent components

For others items, refer to jobber catalogs.

## QUESTIONS

1. Give two ways for restoring the emission of a weak picture tube.
2. Inaccurate readings result from using a low-sensitivity VOM to measure voltage in a high-resistance circuit. Explain.
3. A good-quality VOM is just as accurate as an electronic voltmeter for measuring battery voltages. Explain.
4. How would you remove shorts from a CRT?
5. Explain the uses of the following instruments: (a) dot/crosshatch generator; (b) color bar generator; (c) signal tracers and stage analyzers; (d) oscilloscope; (e) frequency counter; (f) digital meters.
6. When making an in-circuit test of a component, an ohmmeter needle deflects beyond full scale. State the probable reason and how you would proceed.
7. Explain the operation of a typical flyback/yoke tester.
8. Give a step-by-step procedure for using an ohmmeter to identify a transistor type, its terminals, and its condition.
9. The resistance of a diode or transistor junction checks either high or low, depending on the polarity of the meter leads. Explain.
10. How does the output of a sweep generator differ from that of an AM signal generator, and for what purpose is it used?
11. State some of the advantages of a high-quality modern oscilloscope over a basic inexpensive scope.

# 5 Basic troubleshooting and repair techniques

Servicing electronic equipment is a skill that comes with practice. At first, what should be a relatively simple problem can be a real challenge for the beginner. Later, when he or she acquires more knowledge and expertise, those kinds of problems become commonplace and routine, to be taken in stride. A successful technician has the ability to analyze and reason in a logical manner. After observing and studying symptoms and deliberating on the possibilities, the procedure in most cases is as follows: checking voltages, signal tracing, analyzing and interpreting waveforms, then zeroing in on the defect. The *sequence* of testing depends on circumstances, the nature of the complaint, and on the technician himself or herself (Figure 5-1).

In this chapter we cover a variety of topics, starting with practices as applied to video equipment in general. Although much of the material that follows is for TV, most of the procedures apply to other equipment as well. It is suggested that the procedures be read first to grasp the different concepts, then again later for a better understanding.

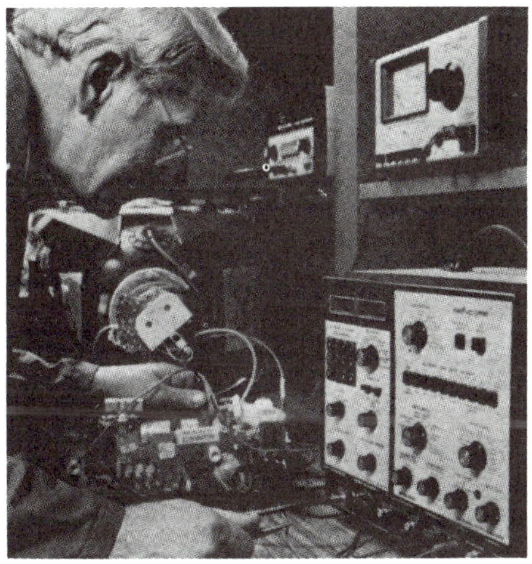

**FIG. 5-1** Deep concentration. (Courtesy of *Sencore News.*)

## 5-1 GOOD WORKMANSHIP AND SAFETY PRACTICES

The successful technician knows that good workmanship pays off and that sloppy and unsafe work habits create many problems. Most involve common sense: Avoid haywire hookups and connections; do good soldering; practice cleanliness; and above all, use common sense and discretion at all times. There are many potential safety hazards to be aware of constantly. Unfortunately, good safety practices are often disregarded or overlooked. Here are some reminders.

- *Electric shock.* Getting shocked too often should be a warning that you are getting careless. Keep one hand out of the way while working on live circuits. Do not trust the insulation on HV wires (e.g., the HV applied to a TV picture tube). Remember that a CRT can retain a charge for a very

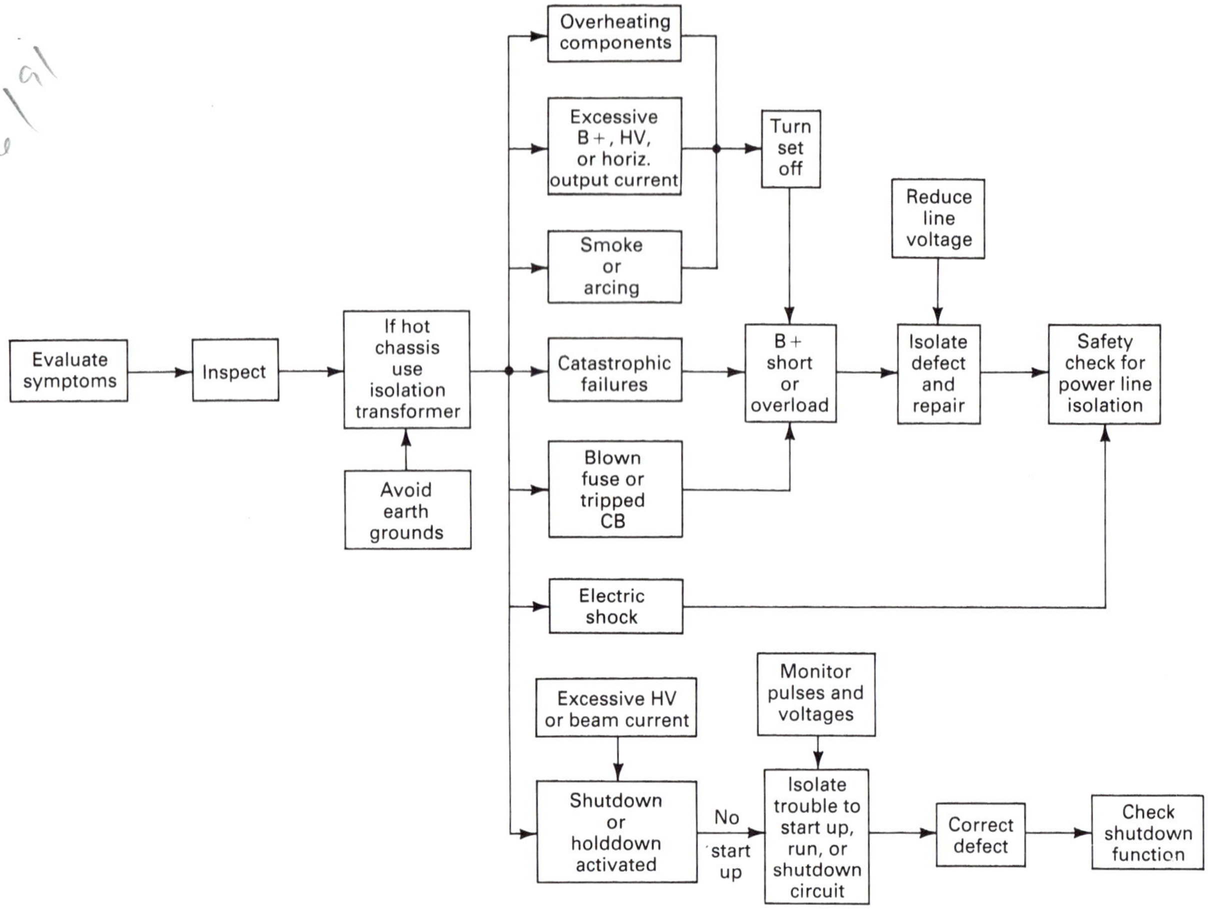


**FIG. 5-2** Troubleshooting hazardous conditions.

long time. Coming in contact with the ultor can be disastrous. On house calls, keep children away from the work area. Take special precautions when working with hot chassis equipment. Check the integrity of isolation components to make sure that the ac is not grounded to the chassis, and never defeat their purpose. Figure 5-2 shows other hazards and the procedures to follow.

- *Fire hazards.* Keep combustible materials clear of unattended equipment that is plugged in.
- *Burns.* Avoid contact with soldering irons and components that dissipate considerable heat: high-wattage resistors, power transistors, and so on.
- *Chemicals.* Ensure good ventilation when working with aerosol sprays, cleaning solvents, and so on. For eye irritation, flush immediately with cold water.
- *Bodily injuries.* Avoid strains. Lift heavy chassis and other items using thigh muscles, with loads close to the chest. On antenna or cable installations, be ever alert to the danger of falling off a roof or making contact with overhead power lines.
- *The x-ray hazard.* Make sure that all HV shields and baffles are in place. When working with TV, check for excessive HV. Where the set has an automatic shutdown circuit, never defeat its purpose, except briefly when testing (see Chapter 11).
- *Component damage.* Use common sense and be ever alert. At the first signs of smoke, arcing, overheating, or the odor of burning insulation, turn the equipment off immediately. Avoid creating shorts when probing or testing live circuits. Avoid probing with screwdrivers. Do not bridge capacitors or connect and disconnect instruments to or from FET or IC circuits with the power on. Treat delicate and sensitive parts with respect. Use an isolation transformer where equipment or testers have the power line connected to chassis. Make sure that all heat sinks are in place before applying power.

Never replace components with the power on. As an added precaution where the equipment contains sensitive and expensive components such as multifunction ICs, install a surge and spike protector at the wall outlet.

### Hot Chassis Hazards

"Hot" is actually a misnomer since it bears no relationship to temperature. The problem arises from the fact that one side of the ac power line is grounded, and by reference, the "live" side is considered hot. If anything earth grounded connects to the hot side of the line, it represents a direct short and blows fuses or circuit breakers, damages equipment, and sometimes starts fires. Fuses and circuit breakers offer some protection, but even with a blown fuse or tripped CB, the equipment may still be hot unless *unplugged*. It is an unfortunate fact of life that much of the electronic equipment today has a transformerless PS, with one side of the ac line tied to the chassis. Figure 5-3 shows several potentially hazardous conditions that result from this.

Figure 5-3a shows this with the ac line connected to the chassis of the TV set, VCR, or whatever. There is no problem, however, as long as the equipment does not make contact with an earth-grounded item such as a water pipe, gas range, or grounded antenna system. Figure 5-3b shows what can happen if the plug is reversed. There is now 120 V between the chassis and the water pipe, as shown. This is a potentially lethal situation since someone standing on wet ground or touching a grounded object will receive a severe shock. This can also occur when working on a supposedly dry patio cement slab. One attempt to prevent this is the use of *polarized plugs,* which can be inserted only one way. Also, power tools, lawn mowers, and other items are provided with a third-wire connection for grounding, or with a self-grounding three-prong plug.

Some equipment is designed with a *floating ground,* a ground return for the circuitry that is isolated from the chassis. As shown in Figure 5-3c, an *isolation network* connects from the floating ground to the chassis. A high-value resistor provides a path for dc and static impulses: a capacitor for passing high-frequency signal voltages. Never defeat its purpose. An alternative with some equipment is a chassis completely insulated from its cabinet, control knobs, and switches.

When repairing hot chassis equipment, an *iso-*

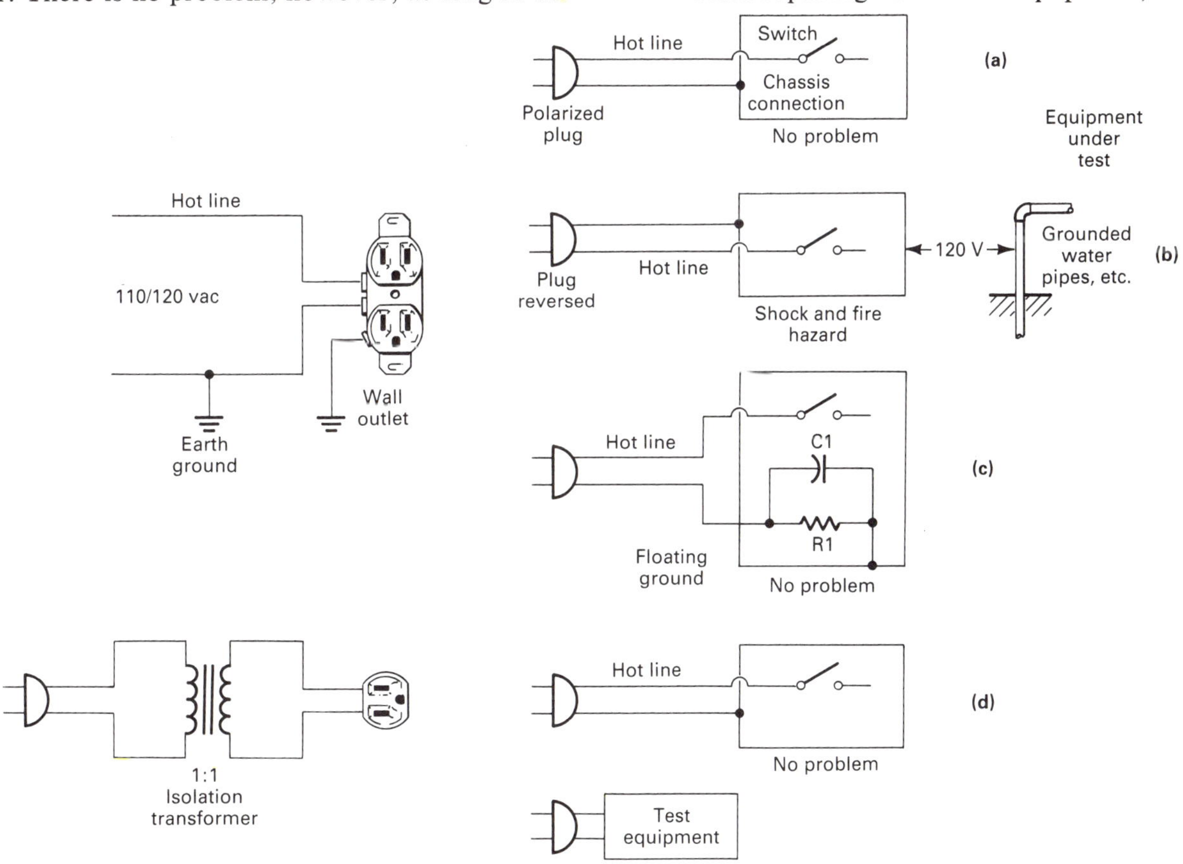


**FIG. 5-3** Power line and hot chassis hazards.

*lation transformer* should *always* be used to isolate the equipment under test from the grounded power line. This also applies to hot chassis test equipment. With this protection, no equipment damage results from inadvertently grounding the equipment. Lacking an isolation transformer, two power transformers may be used with their filament windings connected back to back.

### Soldering and Desoldering

Many troubles can be traced to imperfectly soldered connections, particularly on printed circuit boards, where cracks may develop in the printed wiring at junctions of large components that may be stressed during servicing. Another common problem is where the heating of high-wattage resistors melts pigtails loose from the wiring. Such defects are often intermittent and difficult to pinpoint.

Working with PCBs, transistors, ICs, and other miniaturized components requires a small-tipped, low-wattage (25 to 40 W) pencil-type soldering iron. Excessive heating can damage components and cause PCB wiring to peel away from the substrate. For less critical operations, use a higher-wattage iron or gun. Use only 60:40 rosin-core solder, *never* acid-core solder or pastes, which can cause corrosion, arcing, current leakage, and premature component breakdowns.

Tweezers are useful for holding small parts and wires when soldering. A "third-hand" clamp or jig can also be helpful and can serve as a heat sink to prevent damage by overheating of critical components.

Desoldering calls for special tools and techniques, especially when working with transistors and ICs, since heating must be maintained during removal. For ICs, special soldering iron tips are available to heat all pin connections simultaneously, to facilitate removal. Good lighting is required, as is the use of a magnifying lamp in some cases.

Some method is needed to remove solder while desoldering: a bulb or plunger-type suction "sipper," some tinned wicking braid to soak up the excess, and a stiff bristle brush for brushing away molten solder, being careful to avoid splattering, which can bridge and short out closely spaced contacts.

## 5-2 CHASSIS LAYOUT FAMILIARIZATION AND CIRCUIT TRACING

Do not be intimidated by the complex array of components when you encounter an unfamiliar piece of equipment. Start by identifying the main functional areas and stages with the aid of pictorial diagrams when available. When circuit tracing, do not be overwhelmed by the numerous parts tied to terminal junctions or printed wiring. Tracing older hand-wired equipment was relatively easy (except where wires were cabled and not coded). Tracing printed wiring on a PCB can be more difficult, and it is easy to go astray. Check against the schematic frequently to avoid being sidetracked into an unrelated circuit. Fortunately, most PCBs have the wiring and component identification markings stamped on the board.

Where there is uncertainty about wire terminations, check the continuity from one end to the other using the $\times 1$ ohmmeter range. A reading other than zero means an open circuit or that you have been sidetracked to an unrelated wire. In the absence of a proper schematic and other data, it is like working in the dark.

### Schematics and Other Technical Data

In some cases an experienced technician can get by without a schematic, but usually a proper diagram and other data can reduce servicing time and make life easier (Figure 5-4). With difficult problems, such information may be essential. Most service shops rely on manufacturer's data and Sam's PHOTOFACT and "VCRfacts" packets, available at some libraries and jobbers. Included are parts lists, voltage and resistance charts, pictorial diagrams, partial and overall schematics, alignment and adjustment procedures, and photos showing parts locations. Important waveforms and peak-to-peak voltages are usually indicated on the schematic. The polarity of all dc voltages is assumed to be positive unless marked otherwise.

In special instances where a schematic is not available, you may get by with a similar diagram from another year, model, and so on. In extreme cases, once a problem is localized you can make up your own partial diagram as you proceed with testing. This is not too difficult if the PCB is "road mapped" with suitable markings. File such sketches away, with pertinent comments, for future reference if needed.

A foldout at the back of the book shows a typical modern color TV set. As an aid to scope checking, note the small blocks with dark arrows indicating normal waveforms and peak-to-peak voltages at referenced key circuit points. In the legend, (H) indicates that the scope sweep frequency is adjusted for 15,750 Hz. With (V), the scope frequency is 60 Hz. Other blocks call out normal dc voltages. The diagram is referred to in later chapters as appropriate.

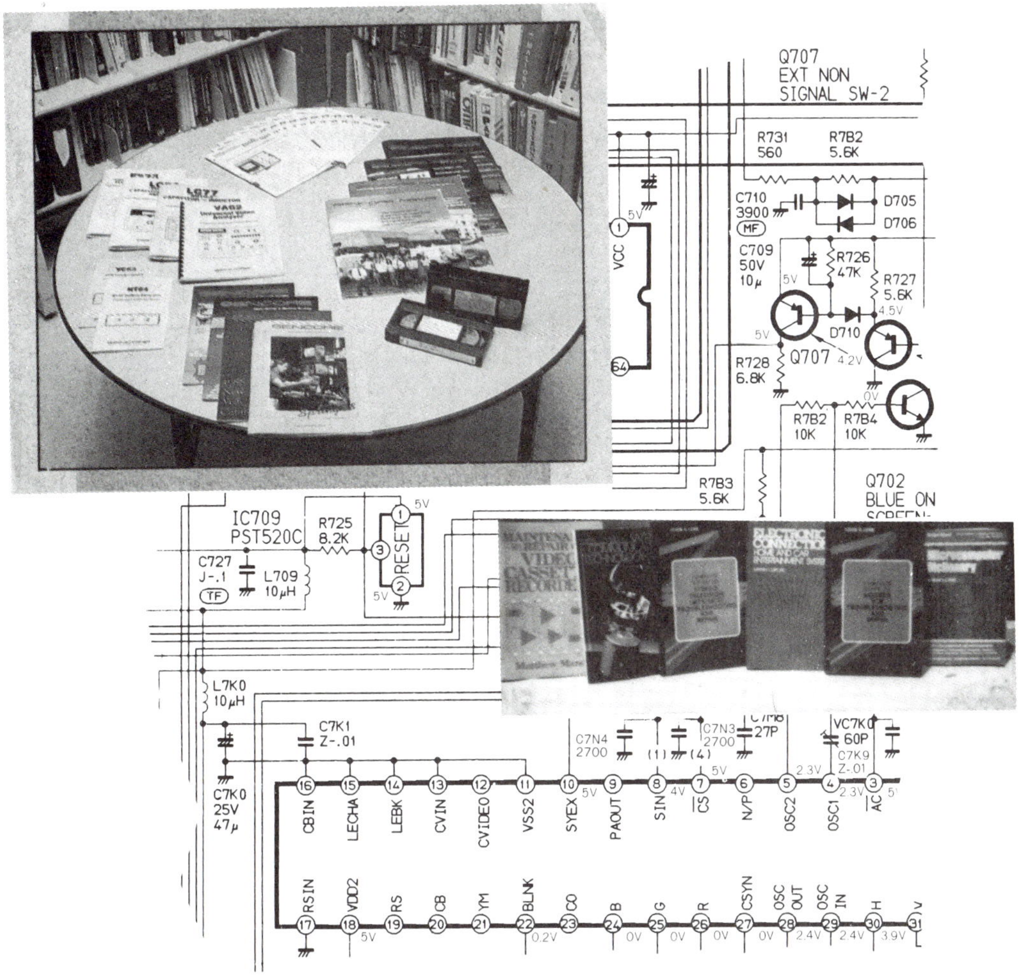


**FIG. 5-4** Schematics and other technical data. Authoritative books and a proper schematic are essential tools of the trade.

## 5-3 INSPECTION, SYMPTOM ANALYSIS, AND DIAGNOSIS

Start every job with a thorough inspection both *before* and after applying power. Look for obvious defects such as loose or disconnected connectors, broken or loose wires or components, bad soldering, damaged modules or PCBs, melted wax under transformers, and so on. With equipment turned on, check first for signs of overheating, burning, arcing, and so on, that caught in time might prevent further damage. For such conditions, remove the power immediately and do your thinking later. Make full use of all senses: touch, smell, sight, and hearing. Feel resistors, transistors, ICs, and transformers for possible overheating. Component overheating provides a good start for troubleshooting. This also applies to parts that should run warm but are cold to the touch.

Prior to testing, time spent observing and diagnosing symptoms is well worthwhile, and considerable analytical reasoning is needed to avoid the pitfalls of false starts and wasted effort. When diagnosing troubles, consider the relationship between the various stages in reference to an overall diagram of the equipment. Sometimes there are multiple symptoms which may or may not have a common cause. In such cases, treat the most urgent (priority 1) condition first.

### Typical Symptoms and Procedures

There are some general problems applicable to most electronic equipment, with the same or similar causes, and calling for the same general procedures (see Figure 5-5).

- *Completely dead.* Probable loss of primary power: ac, dc, or both. Check for damaged line cord, blown fuse or tripped circuit breaker, defective power switch, and so on. If there are signs of arcing, smoke, or over-

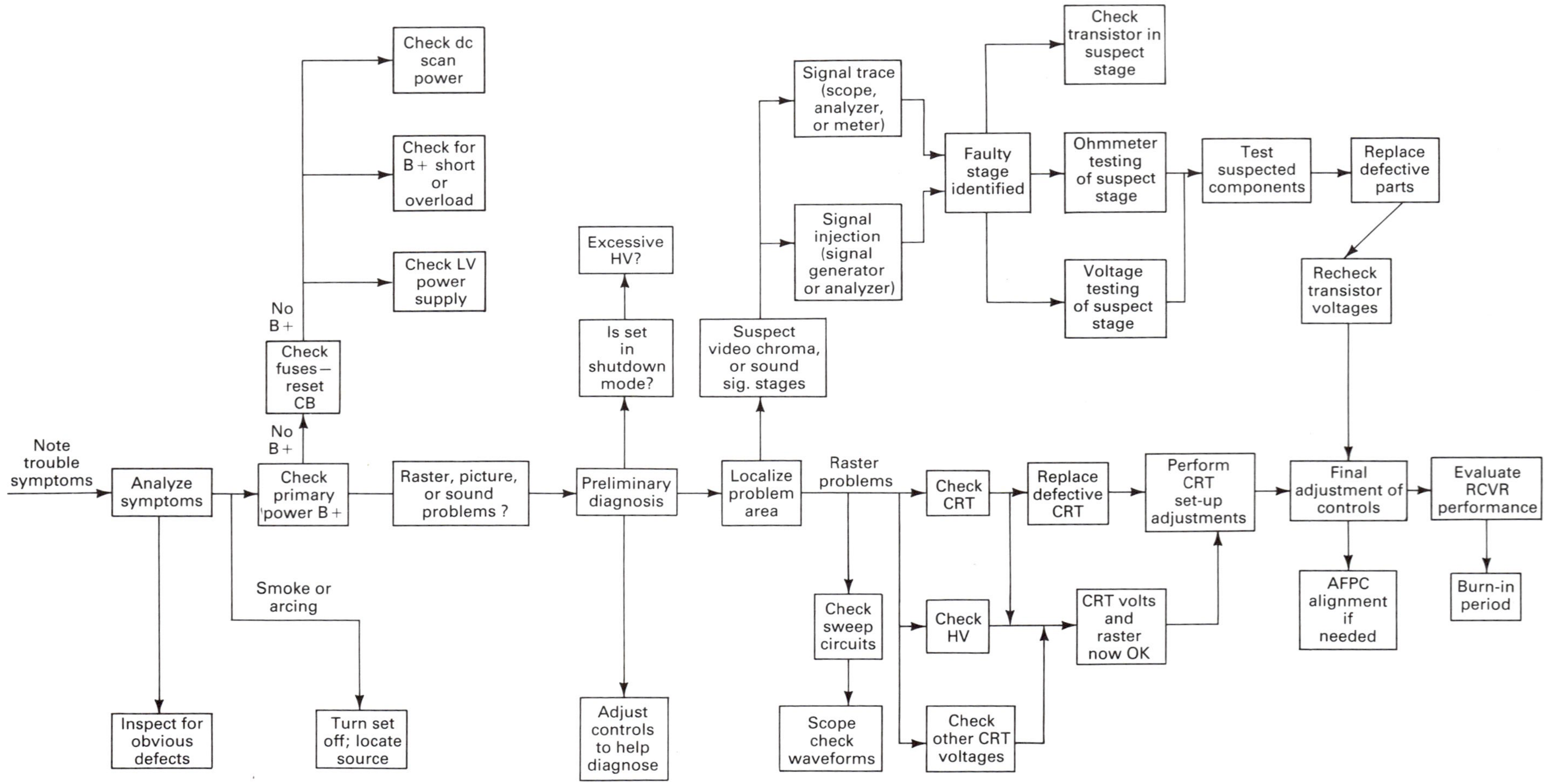


**FIG. 5-5** TV troubleshooting flow drawing.

heating, remove the power and check for a B+ short. The short may be near the source or far removed, such as a shorted bypass capacitor, diode, transistor, or IC.

- *One or several functions inoperative.* Assuming that there is dc power, make note of all functions not working. Analyze the system to determine possible causes. Check voltages, components, and all parts associated with the failure. Localize, then pinpoint the defect. Before replacing a defective part, check for others that may have caused the failure or resulted from it.

*After making repairs,* check all functions, make any necessary adjustments, and perform a burn-in check while monitoring for any unusual or intermittent conditions.

### Troubleshooting Modules and PCBs

Because of crowded and inaccessible components and printed wiring that is difficult to trace, working with these items can be tedious and time consuming. Because a board that uses SMT (surface-mounted technology) is generally translucent, components and wiring can be viewed from either side with the aid of a high-intensity lamp. Another aid is "road mapping," where components and wiring are marked onto the board, much like on a schematic (Figure 5-6).

Problems peculiar to PCBs are cracked or damaged boards, bad contacts at edge connectors, shorted PC wiring or connections caused by solder splashes when servicing, hairline cracks in the PC wiring, and broken soldered joints where large components such as electrolytics are soldered to the wiring. Rough handling is the usual cause of the latter.

An open circuit in a section of wiring is indicated when there is no continuity from one end to the other. To locate an invisible crack in the wiring, use an ohmmeter and needlepoint probe, making as many tests as needed to pinpoint the break. Bridge the gap with a drop of solder. It is more expedient in some cases to bridge the entire section from one end to the other with a length of hookup wire. This is the best procedure for intermittent problems. If necessary, inspect the board close up with a magnifying lamp and touch up all suspected connections.

If the B–C–E (base, collector, emitter) termi-

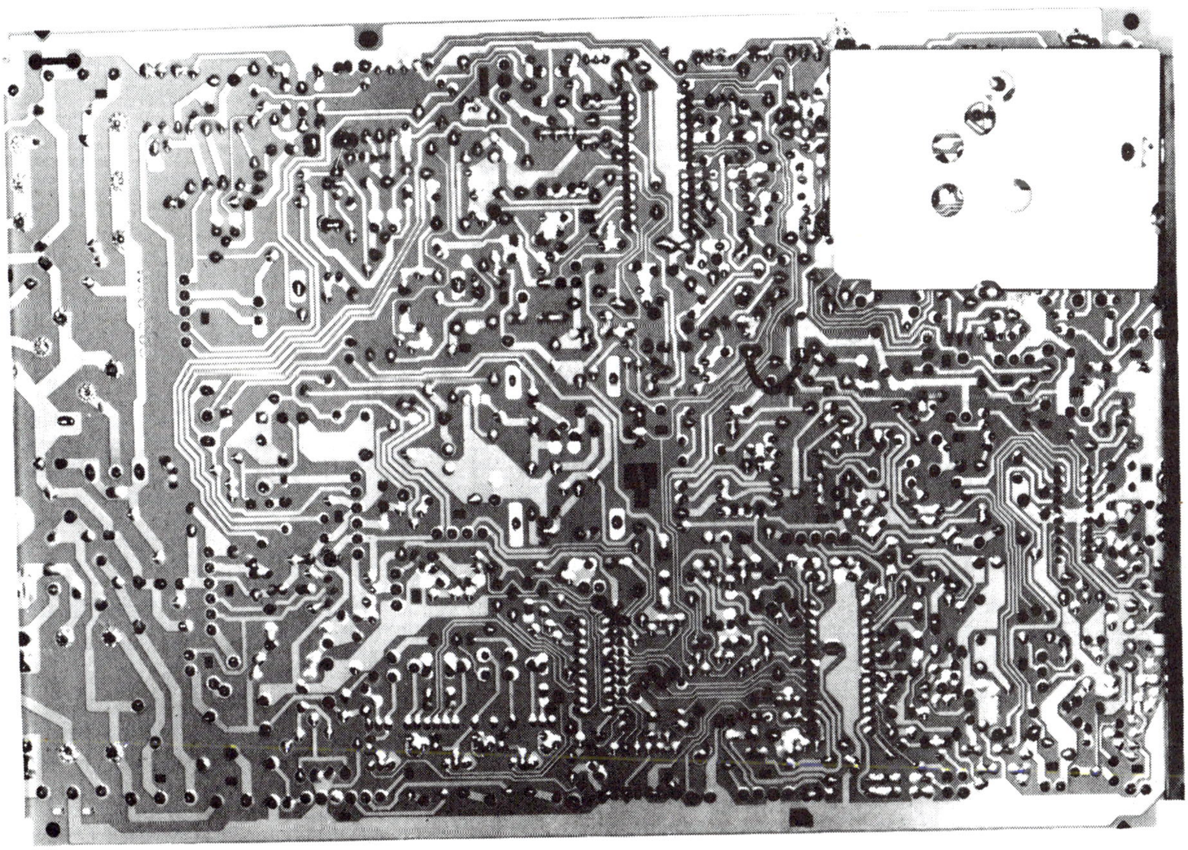

**FIG. 5-6** Wiring side of a typical PCB. (Courtesy of Zenith)

nals of a transistor are not clearly marked, identify them with a sketch before removal for testing or replacement. In confined areas it may be expedient to relocate a part being replaced, to the wiring side of the board. In some cases, clip out the bad component, leaving short stubs for soldering to the new part. It must be done rapidly, however, with minimum heat, or the stubs will melt loose from the wiring. If for any reason a module or PCB cannot be repaired in a reasonable amount of time, it is customary to replace it as a unit, on an exchange basis.

*Localizing the Problem.* This is the customary first step before attempting to pinpoint a defect. Considering the overall schematic and the nature of the problem, decide the most likely stages involved and plan your attack accordingly. The right decisions can save you time and money.

Verify that there is dc output from the power supply; if not, it is the logical place to start. Check dc operating voltages at transistors and ICs in suspected stages, and compare with the schematic.

Where signal amplifiers are suspect, signal trace stage by stage using a scope, EVM (on ac), or stage analyzer to determine where the signal is lost, weakened, or otherwise degraded (Figure 5-7). Check waveforms, peak-to-peak signal amplitudes, and gain of amplifiers compared to those indicated on the schematic.

An alternative procedure is known as *signal injection* (signal substitution), where an RF or AF generator is alternately fed through a blocking capacitor to the input and output of each suspected stage, noting the response on a scope or other indicator (Figure 5-8). When working downstream (in the direction of normal signal flow), the response normally gets weaker as fewer stages are involved. When proceeding upstream (toward the equipment inputs or signal source), the response level gets stronger since there are more stages following the point of injection.

With the injection method, avoid overloading with excessive signal, particularly high-gain, low-level (preamp) stages to prevent waveform distortion and other misleading indications. In general, low-level stages are tested with weak signals, and high-level (output) stages with stronger signals. With ICs, signal trace all inputs and outputs, being careful not to create shorts with the test prods.

*Waveform Analysis.* A scope is extremely useful for isolating troubles quickly. In reality, it is a *must* for troubleshooting modern, sophisticated equipment. Most schematics indicate normal waveforms and signal amplitudes at various points in a circuit. Some deviations from the waveshapes can be expected, depending on the scope used and other factors. It is a matter of interpretation and deciding on what deviations are significant and those that are not.

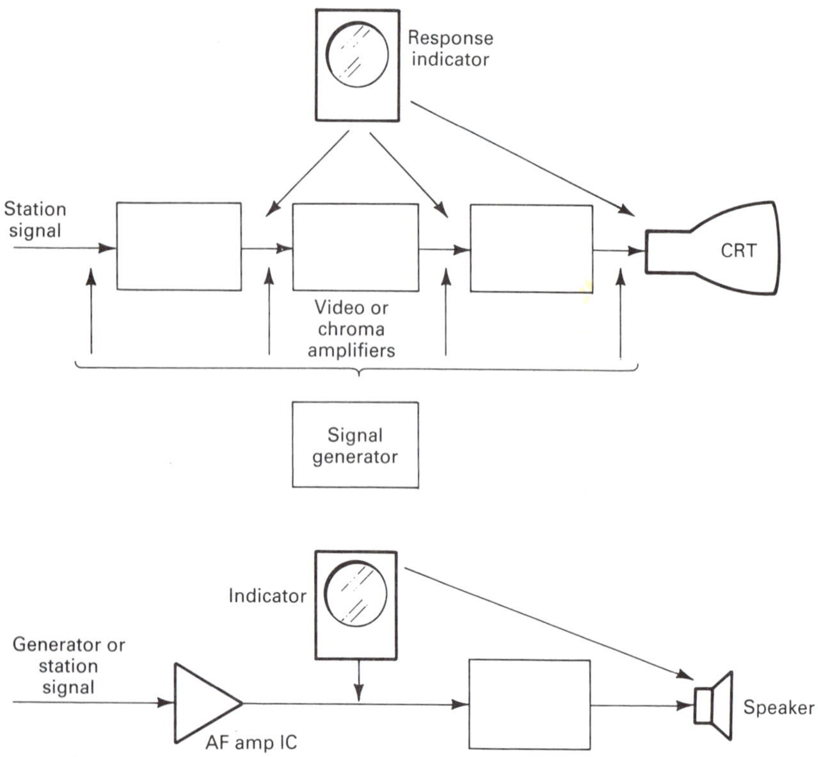


**FIG. 5-7** Localizing troubles by signal tracing or injection. Signal source may be a generator, stage analyzer, or station signal. The indicator may be a scope, stage analyzer, ac meter, speaker, or picture tube.

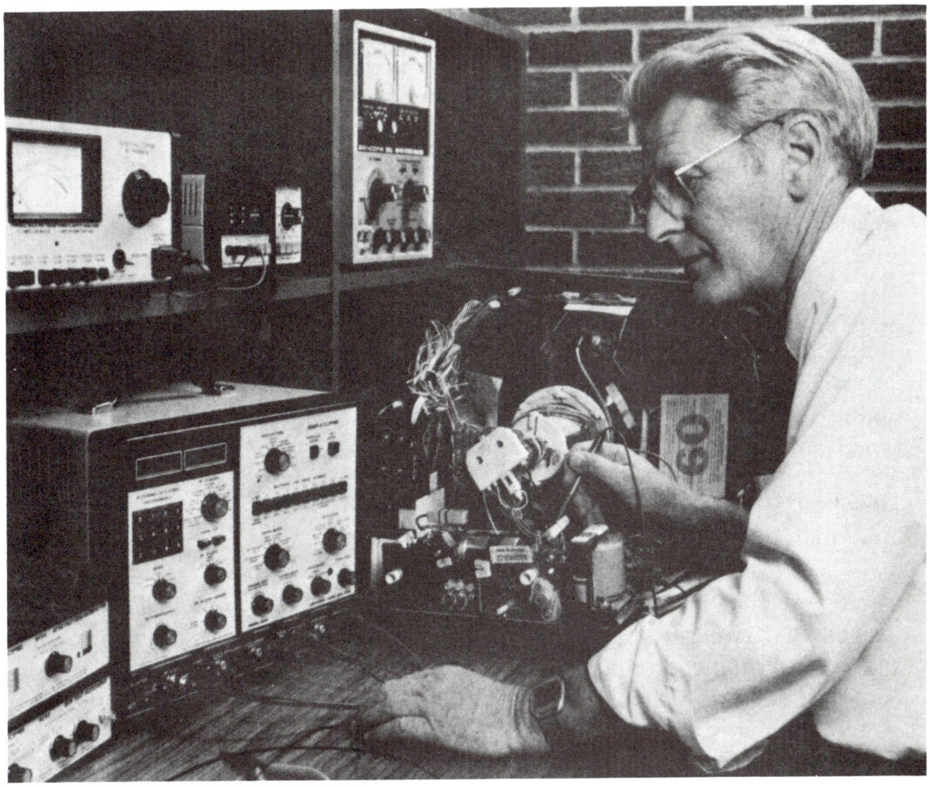

**FIG. 5-8** Localizing a defect with signal injection. Signal substitution can localize troubles fast. (Courtesy of *Sencore News*.)

A basic inexpensive scope is fine for most run-of-the-mill problems and distortion checking, but a dual-trace, triggered sweep scope with a wide bandpass (60 MHz) is preferred for viewing waveform details. Direct indication of peak-to-peak voltages is another advantage of scope tracing signals, but some tolerance can be expected from those shown on a schematic. To avoid overload distortion when a generator is the signal source, use the lowest practical amount of output. Compensate by increasing the vertical gain of the scope.

### Troubleshooting Power Supplies

Compared with other circuits, the basic primary PS is generally the easiest to troubleshoot. Typical problems are little or no dc output, poor regulation, overheating components, and hum. Loss of dc can be caused by loss of ac power up to the rectifiers; or a B+ short in the PS itself, at one of the many branch circuits, or at one of the loads (i.e., the numerous transistors and ICs that draw current). Low B+ can pose a more difficult problem because often the condition is marginal. For this problem, suspect such things as open or leaky rectifiers or the input filter, leaky or shorted capacitors in the branch circuits that distribute voltage to the various loads, or a transistor or IC drawing excessive current. An overheating resistor or other component is an obvious clue and a good place to start. Look for the defect at the load end (the end farthest from the voltage source). Where a transistor or IC is suspect, cut it loose to see if the overload is relieved and the voltage restored.

Poor regulation can be caused by a bad rectifier diode, excessive current drain, or a problem with the voltage regulator. A shorted zener is very common. For hum or other indication of poor filtering, look for an open or dried-up electrolytic. For more detailed procedures, refer to Chapter 6.

### Troubleshooting Voltage Regulators

Zener diodes and power transistors, the main items in voltage regulators, often become shorted, leaky, or burned open. If shorted, the B+ is killed; if leaky, the B+ is reduced; and if open, the voltage increases, endangering other components in a set. With sets having a shutdown circuit, some protection is provided. For more details and a method of checking regulation, refer to Chapter 6.

### Troubleshooting Amplifiers

All electronic consumer products contain one or more amplifiers: high- or low-frequency signal amplifiers, power output amplifiers, or dc voltage amplifiers. High-gain, low-level amplifiers are found primarily at the signal input stages. Power amplifiers usually provide some voltage gain, but their primary function is to develop signal power to drive devices such as transducers and speakers. Some amplifiers use only a single transistor, in some cases several. A multistage amplifier may be contained in a single IC, usually along with other, sometimes unrelated circuits.

Checking stage gain and signal flow can be done in two ways. One is signal tracing, where some input signal or internally generated signal is followed, stage by stage, from its source to its destination. A scope, ac meter, or stage analyzer is used. The other method is signal injection, using a suitable generator whose output corresponds with the signals normally present at those points in the equipment under test.

For low-frequency circuits an AF generator is used; an RF generator is used for high-frequency stages, particularly stages with tuned circuits. All amplifiers should provide some gain between input and output. If not, check further in that stage for the defect.

With the signal injection method, proper signal levels are important since too much can cause overloading and possible component damage. Where a stage is found to be weak or dead or is otherwise suspected, isolate the cause with dc voltage checks, resistance checking, checking transistors and other components, and making adjustments, as appropriate. Compare all voltages, waveforms, and signal levels with those shown on the schematic.

## Troubleshooting Oscillators

Unlike an amplifier, an oscillator generates its own signal, at some specific frequency depending on its purpose. Oscillations are produced using some means of in-phase feedback from output to input. An oscillator may be free-running or controlled by a crystal or some form of AFC circuit. Unless controlled in some manner, high-frequency oscillators are prone to frequency drift. Frequency instability may be caused by component defects, voltage variations, or temperature changes, particularly if critical heat-sensitive components are located near a heat source, such as a high-wattage resistor. A frequency counter is a good instrument for this kind of problem. If the oscillator has tuned stages, misalignment is another possibility.

An oscillator may be dead, weak, intermittent, or off frequency. Each condition calls for specific and appropriate testing procedures. Unfortunately, tests for a weak or dead oscillator are not always conclusive because of significant voltage changes between the oscillating and nonoscillating states. One method is to check for an ac generated voltage at the base or collector of the transistor or some corresponding terminal of an IC. Another method is watching for a slight change in collector voltage as a transistor is alternately enabled and disabled by bridging a capacitor from base or collector to ground. In a well-equipped shop the procedure is usually performed with a scope or stage analyzer. If the oscillator is proven faulty, follow conventional testing procedures to isolate the defect.

## Troubleshooting DC-Coupled Stages

With ac coupling between stages, a coupling capacitor or interstage transformer effectively blocks dc while permitting an ac signal to get through. With direct (dc) coupling, any dc at the output of one stage is passed on to the input of the next downstream stage, where it contributes to the biasing of the transistor or IC (Figure 5-9).

Dc coupling is generally used to prevent attenuation of low frequencies and where the dc component of a signal must be preserved. Such circuits are not easy to service and when a breakdown occurs, abnormal voltage conditions are passed along, and sometimes accentuated, to affect the operation of all downstream stages adversely. If a sensitive FET or IC is included in this loop, it is almost certain

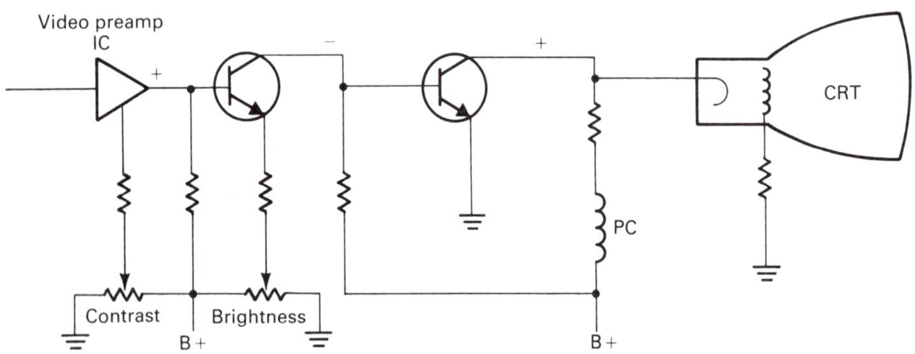


**FIG. 5-9** Typical dc-coupled amplifier. Note the signal polarities. Defects affecting transistor operating voltages are passed on to subsequent stages: in this case, creating changes in CRT bias and raster brightness.

to be destroyed. With ac, capacitive coupling, a shorted or leaky capacitor can create the same conditions.

Modern TV sets, VCRs, and stereo sets use dc control of volume, tone, and other functions. A small dc voltage, regulated by a potentiometer-type control, is used to bias a control transistor that may be directly coupled to other stages. Any defect creates voltage problems that are passed on stage by stage.

Should a defect occur in any one of several dc-coupled stages, all voltages are affected and the problem is in deciding which stage is at fault. One approach is to work upstream from the point where the abnormal voltages are first discovered until a stage is reached where voltages check normal. Except where there is heavy feedback, this usually identifies the troublesome stage. It can be helpful to break up the dc loop by isolating stages as appropriate. To supplement dc voltage checking, signal tracing can be used to pinpoint the problem. Where voltages on any given stage check out okay, chances are that all upstream stages are trouble-free.

### Troubleshooting Closed-Loop Circuits

A typical loop circuit embraces one or more interdependent stages where a portion of the output signal is fed back to the input stage via what is called a *feedback loop*. There are two kinds of feedback: positive or regenerative feedback, and negative, degenerative, or inverse feedback. Positive feedback is used in some oscillator circuits where the output signal is fed back in phase to reinforce the input signal and produce oscillations. Negative feedback is out of phase with the input. It is found mainly in audio amplifiers to reduce waveform distortion by cancellation, and for stability. This at the expense of stage gain.

AGC is another example of a closed-loop circuit, where AGC controls the stage gain and the signal level, in turn, varies the AGC voltage. Still another example is a digital logic circuit, as in a microprocessor-controlled PLL circuit for controlling a tuner oscillator.

To troubleshoot loop circuits, it is necessary to break the loop at some point so that each stage in the loop can be checked individually. This is usually done by signal injection working from the output back to the input. A defect may be found anywhere within the loop. Check all components within the loop. With negative feedback, an increase in the signal level can be expected when the loop is opened.

### DC Voltage Distribution

Resistors are used to reduce a power supply voltage to the amount required by a particular stage or component. There are two ways of doing this:

- *Series-dropping resistors*. With this method the *IR* drop depends on the resistor value and the amount of current drawn by the load. If there is no current, then, of course, there is no voltage drop, a basic rule to remember when troubleshooting. In this instance the same amount of voltage will be measured at both ends of the resistor.
- *Voltage divider*. This consists of two resistors tied together, one connected to B+ and the other to ground. The load is supplied from their junction. With no load (no current being drawn) the voltage is split between the two resistors in proportion to their values. When a transistor or other kind of load draws current from the junction, the voltage at the junction drops; the greater the current, the greater the voltage drop. The *bleeder current* through the grounded resistor is in effect wasted, but it does help in maintaining good voltage regulation. Where the bleeder section of a divider opens up, the voltage at the junction increases drastically. An increase in bleeder resistance raises the junction voltage but not as much. If the series resistor connected to B+ becomes open, voltage at the junction drops to zero.

### Isolating a B+ Short or Overload

A component breakdown in a voltage distribution network is a common problem but usually one of the easiest to troubleshoot. Where there is loss of voltage at a circuit point, check the temperatures of all associated resistors, gingerly (by touch), and other nearby components. A high-wattage resistor that runs cold is either open or there is no current flow, for whatever the reason. A low-wattage resistor that gets hot indicates a B+ short or a load drawing too much current. Check the resistance to ground at each end of all associated components. The short will be found at some circuit point that measures zero or some low value relative to ground.

An alternative method is by voltage checking at various points. The defect will be found at the point of lowest voltage reading. Where voltages are low but resistance checks to ground are high, chances are that some load is drawing excessive current. (*Reminder:* The cause of the problem may be found at a point far removed from the testing area.)

### Current Testing

When analyzing a problem it can be helpful to know the current drain of a transistor, PCB, or module; the branch current in a voltage distribution network; or the total current delivered by a power supply. In most cases current is determined by computation, using Ohm's law and the measured amount of voltage drop across the known value of any resistance in the circuit. Instead of relying on the coded tolerance of a resistor, accurately measure its value. Check the voltage across the resistor from one end to the other but not in reference to ground. Compute the current, $I = E/R$.

An alternative method of direct measuring of current with a conventional current meter is somewhat risky (for the meter) and the circuit must be broken into. (A digital type of DMM is the preferred instrument.) The procedure is to open the circuit at a convenient point and insert the meter *in series with the load*. Double check your connections and the meter polarity. Avoid haywire hookups. (An inadvertent short can destroy the meter.) Start with the highest meter range or a range consistent with the anticipated amount of current. If the meter reads backwards, reverse the leads. Remove power before disconnecting the meter.

### Isolating the Defect

There are numerous possible causes for most trouble symptoms: component breakdowns, a soldering or wiring problem, misadjusted controls, and so on. Some faults can be discovered by a thorough inspection. Others may require considerable testing, the results of each test hopefully providing more clues and information which eventually leads to a solution. Some tests may duplicate those made earlier when localizing the defect to a particular stage or section.

Seldom do you find only one defective component, because the original defect (the primary cause of breakdown) usually creates an overload that damages or destroys other parts. For example, a shorted capacitor, transistor, or IC may cause a resistor to burn up. It then becomes a question of cause and effect, and which caused which. In some cases a simple component failure can result in the *catastrophic destruction* of many parts, especially critical items such as FETs and ICs. Being aware of this possibility, always look for the *cause* before replacing components or they, too, may be destroyed. Fortunately, such catastrophic failures are the exception, not the rule.

Most defects can be isolated with voltage and ohmmeter testing in the suspected stage. An overheating resistor or other component, provides a good starting point. Otherwise, concentrate on a transistor or IC, prime focal points in most stages. With the power off, make an in-circuit test of the transistor, and if necessary, repeat the test with two of the three leads disconnected. Make ohmmeter tests between transistor and IC terminals relative to ground. Record your measurements and compare with the schematic. Measure and record the transistor and IC operating voltages and compare with the schematic. Investigate any abnormal readings. In some cases even slight discrepancies can be significant, especially critical bias voltages. Be careful not to create shorts with test prods or clip leads (Figure 5-10). Such shorts invariably compound

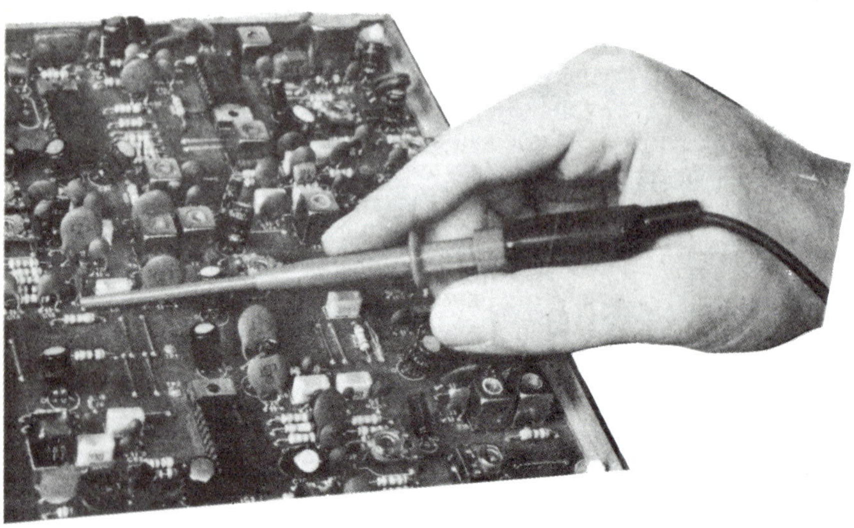

**FIG. 5-10** Isolating a defect in a large PCB. Proper probes are needed to prevent shorts. (Courtesy of *Sencore News.*)

your problem and destroy components. Study the schematic and check all components that could account for abnormal measurements. (*Reminder:* Where dc coupling is used between stages, the cause of a defect may be found several stages upstream from the point where abnormal conditions are discovered.) Where the condition of a component is in doubt, substitute, and as a last resort use the shotgun approach—replacing all small, inexpensive components that are possible suspects.

*Resistance Testing at Transistors, FETs, and ICs.* PHOTOFACT and "VCRfact" packets include resistance charts showing the normal resistance readings to expect at each transistor and IC terminal, in reference to ground. Such measurements in conjunction with voltage checks are a great help in troubleshooting. Before making any resistance tests, make sure that the power is off and the filters have been shorted out to remove any residual charge that will influence the readings. Record all measurements and compare with the chart or schematic. Study the schematic for possible defects that could account for abnormal readings. Lower-than-expected readings can be due to the shunting effect of diode and transistor junctions, or their counterparts in an IC. To check further, isolate the terminal and repeat the test. Try reversing meter leads and retest. (*Reminder:* The resistance of a good junction should be high for one reading and low for the other, with the leads reversed. Similarly, a resistor that measures higher than its coded value is bad.) For a low reading, one end must be cut loose (as with a solid-state device) and the test repeated. A 0 Ω reading indicates a direct short, or ground.

With PC boards, the easiest way to isolate is to cut across the printed wiring at an appropriate spot, rather than doing a lot of soldering and desoldering, which becomes messy and damages components and the printed circuit. Remember to resolder the break later by bridging the gap with a drop of solder or a short length of wire.

*Voltage Testing at Transistors, FETs, and ICs.* The dc operating voltages of solid-state devices are extremely critical, especially bias, where even *fractional* departures from specified amounts can significantly affect how well the device operates, if at all. This is why an *accurate, low-range* meter is required for taking measurements.

All readings should adhere closely to those specified on the schematic and should be recorded for later evaluation if need be. To prevent the devastating results of a short when touching closely spaced contacts, use only miniclips and hook-type or needlepoint probes.

The condition of solid-state components and their operating voltages are interdependent. If all voltages check normal, chances are that the device and its associated components are okay. On the other hand, abnormal voltages may be caused either by circuit disorders or by the device itself. Therefore, the testing or substitution of the device should come first. After replacing a bad device, all voltages will often return to normal.

In order to conduct, a transistor must be supplied with base and collector voltages of the correct polarity, with a small amount of forward bias. Polarity depends on the type of transistor, positive for an NPN device and negative for a PNP, as indicated by the middle letter.

Although voltages shown on a schematic are in reference to ground, true operating bias is measured between the base and the emitter. Bias is the difference between the two absolute values: the base-to-ground voltage and the emitter-to-ground voltage. Polarity is established by the greater of the two readings. For example, if base to ground checks 1.5 V positive, and emitter to ground is 0.1 V positive, the true B-to-E bias is +1.4 V. In this case the transistor must be an NPN type. As another example, if the B-to-E readings are −0.25 V and +0.03 V, respectively, the bias is −0.22 V (a PNP type). If there are no polarity markings on a schematic, a positive polarity is assumed.

Thus, after checking the integrity of a device, it is customary to take three measurements: B to ground, E to ground, and B to E, the latter being the most significant. For an abnormal bias reading, determine which of the three is off the most, and proceed accordingly. Table 5-1, in conjunction with Figure 5-11, shows probable cause for abnormal voltage readings. All measurements are with reference to ground.

*MOSFET Operating Voltages.* Great care must be exercised when checking MOSFET voltages since they can be destroyed instantly by discharging capacitors, creating arcs, shorts, and so on. A MOSFET is similar to a vacuum tube in many ways: the *source,* the electron emitter corresponding with the plate; the *gate* or gates, acting as control grids; and the *drain,* which functions as a plate or anode to attract and receive the electrons. Depending on the type, the gate(s) may require either a − or a + voltage relative to the source.

As with a transistor, the measured operating voltages depend on circuit conditions and the good/

**TABLE 5-1**

Abnormal transistor voltages

| *Transistor Terminal* | *Voltage High* | *Voltage Low* | *Zero Volts* |
|---|---|---|---|
| Collector | Shorted transistor, open L2 | Shorted transistor, too much forward bias, R2 may be open | Open transistor, open R3, shorted C2 |
| Base | R2 open | Shorted or leaky transistor, R1 value increased, R2 decreased, C1 leaky | B/C transistor short, R1 or L1 open, C1 shorted |
| Emitter | Open transistor R1 or L2 open, shorted C1 | C/E transistor leakage, leaky C2, R2 open | R3 open (no emitter current), C/E transistor short, shorted C2 |

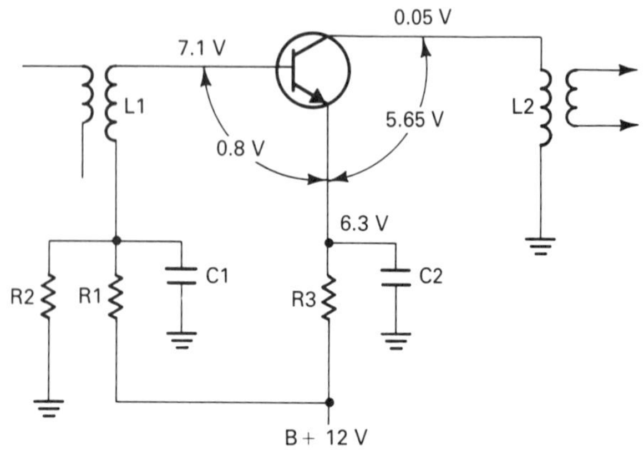


**FIG. 5-11** Typical transistor circuit. Normal operating voltages are indicated. Abnormal voltages are caused by a bad transistor or other component defects.

bad condition of the MOSFET itself. For example, loss of bias can result in no current flow and a high drain voltage equal to the supply. A common defect is shorts or leakage between the gates and other elements because of breakdown of the thin film of insulation used. To offset this possibility, some MOSFETs have built-in protective diodes shunted across the elements. In troubleshooting, record all three operating voltages and compare with the schematic. Although a MOSFET is usually the primary reason for a breakdown, check all associated components for other possibilities before making a replacement. (*Reminder:* MOSFETs require special handling precautions, as described later.)

*Voltage Checking at IC Terminals.* Abnormal voltages may be caused by either a defective IC or a fault external to the device. This *must* be considered before making a replacement. When suspect, measure and record voltage readings at all terminal pins. Compare with the schematic. Where a voltage is low or missing at some terminal, break the connection from the circuit by cutting across the printed wiring at some convenient point, and recheck to see if voltage is restored at the wiring side of the break. If it is, the IC is probably defective. If not, look elsewhere for the loss of voltage. Feel the ICs. If an IC runs hot, it is probably shorted out.

Check for the presence of voltage at some pin where there shouldn't be any. Again, the cause is either a bad IC or an external problem. As with FETs, ICs require special testing and handling precautions.

## MOS IC and MOSFET Handling Precautions

MOSFETS and MOS ICs (ICs containing FETs) are extremely sensitive devices that are easily damaged or destroyed by arcing, voltage spikes or surges, and even static electricity charges. Hence a number of precautions *must* be observed during handling, testing, or replacement. As protection against static charges, a new device generally comes packed in aluminum foil or conductive foam, which should not be removed until immediately prior to use. Once installed in a circuit, the device is somewhat protected against static. When working with these devices, observe the following precautions.

- Before handling the device or circuit board containing such items, discharge any static buildup on your body by touching the chassis. It is also wise to ground yourself through a high-value resistor during testing and repair, being careful not to create a shock hazard to yourself.
- Place PC boards containing such items on a metal surface after removal from a set or prior to installation.
- Avoid the use of Freon sprays, which generate static charges.
- Use only antistatic solder suckers.
- Use only a low-wattage soldering iron and

ground it. Avoid excessive heat when soldering.

- Avoid creating shorts or arcing, as by discharging capacitors or arcing the CRT HV. High-voltage corona discharges also pose a risk.
- Use only suitable meters and other test equipment, and ground them before use. Use a wrist strap as an added precaution.
- Do not store or ship the devices in plastic containers. Use only approved conductive foam or aluminum foil packets.

## 5-4 REPLACING ICs

Preventing damage to the IC, nearby components, and printed wiring requires considerable skill, patience, dexterity, and of course, the proper tools. If it is a MOS IC, observe the precautions described previously. To remove a suspected or defective IC, the connections must be heated while exerting some pulling force or leverage. Remove excess solder as you proceed, using braid, a sipper, or other device. Avoid overheating that might damage wiring or the IC in the event that it later proves to be okay and will be reinstalled. Special soldering iron tips are available that heat all terminals simultaneously. After removal, clear all holes in the substrate and remove excess solder. Avoid solder splashes.

Prior to installing a new IC, verify that there are no other defects that may damage or destroy the new item. Orient the new IC correctly relative to its notched end and align all pins with their respective holes, then gently press into place. Verify that all pins protrude on the wiring side of the board. Solder each terminal within 3 seconds or less using minimal heat.

## 5-5 INTERMITTENTS AND OTHER TOUGH DOGS

There can be great satisfaction in repairing equipment that others have given up on. If you are unlucky enough to encounter one of these monsters—and rest assured that eventually you will—start with a thorough inspection. Keep an eye open for the unusual and unexpected, and do not assume anything. Listen to the owner's complaints, but do not accept them as gospel.

When the equipment has been worked on recently, such things as wiring errors, wrong components, and poor soldering are commonplace. Check frequently against the schematic. When the going gets tough and each frustrating approach seems to lead nowhere, take a break—and maybe sleep on it. A clear head and a fresh start may be all that is needed. When you are really stuck, do not be too proud to seek help—from other technicians, factory field reps, or whomever. Finally, when all else fails, read the fine print in the service manual.

### Troubleshooting Intermittents

With most such troubles the equipment is probably in a supersensitive state where almost anything—the mere touch of a meter probe, or walking across the floor for example—is enough to restore operation or make it act up. Unless the symptoms remain long enough to permit testing, everything checks okay. You have two options: Monitor the key checkpoints in the suspected circuit while the set "cooks" on the bench, or a more aggressive approach, jump in and force the condition to develop. Until it does, signal tracing, voltage checking, or whatever is usually a waste of time. How you proceed should be determined by the nature of the problem. Most intermittents can be classified and treated as follows.

*Physical Disturbances.* This is where the equipment acts up when tapped, moved, or jarred. Connect monitoring equipment (voltmeter, scope, stage analyzer, counter, etc., as appropriate) to key checkpoints, such as the inputs and outputs of the suspected stage. Make a note of normal indications and readings, then any changes as they occur. Record such information for later evaluation. A dual-trace scope is useful for monitoring input and output signals simultaneously. Start by tapping the chassis and components using a suitable object such as a screwdriver handle. While reducing the intensity of the tapping, try to locate the most sensitive area. Using an *insulated* probe, gently probe components and wiring in the suspected area. If a PCB, gently press, twist, and bend the board slightly. Look for closely spaced wires or connections that may be shorting out or grounding. Watch for poorly soldered connections, particularly on a PCB. Touch-up any and all suspicious joints.

*Electrical Disturbances.* Some intermittents are related to voltage and/or current. When suspected, try increasing or decreasing power supply voltages with a variable transformer (variac) at the ac input. Starting with a low amount, gradually increase the line voltage while monitoring key circuit points. When a component is suspect, try applying an overvoltage or current overload directly to its terminals. If it is an expensive item, use discretion, to avoid damage. Replace any small component that is at all suspect. If symptoms can be made to show up, note any voltage or signal deviations from the norm, then continue with normal troubleshooting procedures.

*Thermal Disturbances.* The equipment may act up only after several minutes or hours of operation. In some cases the reverse is true. Observe and record voltages and signals at key checkpoints when the equipment is cold, then again after warm-up, when the symptoms appear. In some cases, symptoms cannot be created after removal from the cabinet to a cooler environment. Apply heat to suspected areas using a hair dryer or the equivalent. Try heating the entire unit by covering with a blanket or a box enclosure for a *short time,* in some cases with a low-wattage lamp as a heat source. (*Caution:* Avoid overheating and do not risk component damage by leaving equipment unattended.) Where a specific component is suspect, try heating its pigtails or other contacts directly with a soldering iron. If this has no effect, try cooling with coolant spray until frost appears. Try alternating between heat and cold.

## 5-6 TV TROUBLESHOOTING AND REPAIR FUNDAMENTALS

In addition to the information contained in Section 5-3, the following applies specifically to TV.

### Apprenticeship Training and Other Considerations

It is generally unwise to break into TV repairing full time, on a shoestring, without considerable expertise and business acumen. Better to start off slowly, working at a shop, making house calls and working with experienced technicians doing bench repairs. Concurrent with taking a course or on-the-job training, some people prefer to start doing repairs on their own in a modest way, part time—not in competition with established shops but as a means of gaining experience.

As a beginner or do-it-yourselfer, equipment needs are minimal: a combination volt/ohmmeter for resistance and voltage checking, a basic oscilloscope for signal tracing and waveform analysis, an AF/RF signal generator for locating a faulty stage, a soldering iron or gun, and a few common hand tools. The list will gradually expand with time and as needs arise.

*TV Recycling.* Many older sets are discarded because of too many defects entailing high labor costs or the need for expensive items such as a flyback or power transformer, a tuner, or a picture tube. In some cases the set was wrongly condemned and repairs may be minimal. For the novice, discarded receivers present a challenge and an excellent means of gaining experience. Even when not repairable, such sets provide an endless source of usable components: resistors, capacitors, and transistors, to name a few. Naturally, all such cannibalized parts must be tested prior to use. This, too, is part of the initiation.

Some component defects, such as an open coil or a PCB with a break in the PC wiring, can readily be repaired. Attempting to repair other items, however, may not be warranted considering labor time and reliability. Examples are defective speakers, yokes, flyback transformers, tuners, and a CRT that does not respond well to rejuvenation. For such items it is usually better to replace rather than repair. Tuners are generally replaced on an exchange basis.

### Typical Schematic Diagram

A proper schematic is just as important as having the right tools and test equipment. A schematic of a late-model color set appears as a foldout at the back of the book. The set has four multifunction ICs. The shaded areas represent critical components that require *exact replacement.* Most other components are off-the-shelf items. Normal waveforms with peak-to-peak voltages are shown on the adjoining page. They are referenced to small rectangular blocks at key checkpoints on the diagram. Circuit functions are described in later chapters.

### Service Adjustments and CRT Setup

Many TV troubles can be corrected with nothing more than simple adjustments, and how such adjustments affect picture and sound can be helpful in localizing and isolating defects. Adjusting controls indiscriminately, however, can compound problems, making diagnosis unnecessarily difficult. As a precaution, mark the control positions so that their settings can be restored if need be. Until the precise nature of the problem is known, never tamper with *tuned circuit* adjustments, since this is seldom required, and realignment calls for considerable know-how.

The quality of a picture, a color picture in particular, depends on the *proper* adjustment of controls and adjusters associated with the CRT. CRT setup is an involved procedure that can be overwhelmingly difficult for the novice but is relatively easy for the experienced technician. Certain basic touch-up adjustments can be made, however, by a knowledgeable person. After CRT replacement, a complete setup adjustment is required. The procedures are described in Chapter 17.

## Signal and Voltage Substitution

This method, sometimes called *signal snatching,* may be used in the absence of regular test equipment. In essence, one section of the receiver (or another set) is used to check a suspect stage by substitution. The speaker and/or picture tube serve as indicators. Some examples follow.

*Tuner Substitution.* The IF signal from the tuner of an operating set is fed to the IF input of the set being worked on. Simply transpose the interconnecting coax cables. Use caution if it is a hot chassis.

*Audio Stages for Signal Tracing.* The audio stages are used for checking video, chroma, and sweep stages. When fed to the first AF stage, signals from stages being checked produce a raspy sound from the speaker. No sound means a dead stage.

*Video Stage as a Signal Tracer.* The video stage is used for checking sound and sweep stages. The picture tube is the indicator. Signals from these stages produce a bar pattern on the CRT screen. The darkness of the bars is indicative of relative signal strength.

*Oscillator Substitution.* The oscillator output of a working set is substituted for a suspected oscillator (e.g., subcarrier and sweep oscillators).

*Using the Subcarrier Oscillator as a Signal Generator.* The accurate 3.58-MHz signal can be used for aligning traps, the BPA, and the burst gate of a troublesome set, and for checking calibration of a signal generator.

*Voltage Substitution.* Where there is a LV or HV power supply malfunction and there is a need to restore set operation before getting involved in what could become an unprofitable repair job, in some cases receiver operation can be restored by substituting voltages temporarily. For LVPS problems, a variable, regulated power supply is required. From the schematic, determine the normal value of B+ for that circuit point and adjust the external PS accordingly. Disconnect the main B+ output, and connect the substitute PS at that point. Voltage will drop under load when the set is turned on. Readjust the voltage to the proper amount. (*Caution:* The procedure entails certain risks, especially if it is a hot chassis. In this case use an isolation transformer and the proper ground connection.)

To substitute HV so that a raster and picture can be observed, borrow the HV from another set. First make sure that the substitute HV does not exceed the requirements of the set under test. Connect the chassis together with a jumper. Connect the HV wire of the substitute set to the CRT ultor of the receiver being worked on. (*Reminder:* A CRT holds a charge for a long time. To avoid being shocked, discharge it several times before handling.)

## Final Burn-In Checking

After repairs are completed, and prior to wrap-up and delivery, the repaired item should be operated on the bench for an hour or more. This provides time for any obscure, previously overlooked problems to show up. It is also a last-minute opportunity to evaluate performance critically and to make any adjustments that could improve operation. For equipment plagued with intermittent problems, the burn-in period should be a *must,* particularly if nothing definite was found or corrected. Sooner or later such problems are bound to reoccur, resulting in an unprofitable callback and some loss of prestige. Keep a checklist as a reminder.

For a TV set, examine the picture critically. Is the brightness and color up to par? Is it in perfect focus? If not done previously, measure the HV and if necessary adjust to the value specified. Is the color in perfect registry, with no indications of color fringing on a BW picture? If not, a slight touch-up of purity and convergence might be all that is needed.

Check the sync stability and reception on all channels. If the color sync is not all that it should be, touch up the AFPC. Make sure that all adjusters around the CRT are locked into position. If not already done, make the all-important safety leakage check for a power-line ground. Tap the chassis and do not be surprised if some new intermittent condition shows up, which it frequently does on older sets.

The list is endless, but a few reminders: a final adjustment of the AGC and killer threshold controls, and cleaning an erratic tuner or noisy control. The customer will appreciate it. Do not forget the power cord and possible arcing at the interlock. Wiggle the cord at both ends to see if the set cuts out.

With a VCR, operate all buttons one last time and try all modes. Are recordings up to par? Is the picture quality on playback all that it should be? Make sure that the tracking control is adjusted as well as all preset channel adjustments. If the head and tape path were not cleaned thoroughly, run a cleaning tape. For additional checklist items, refer to Chapter 21.

## QUESTIONS

1. Explain the procedure for checking a multistage amplifier by (a) signal tracing; (b) signal injection. What instruments may be used?
2. State four uses for an oscilloscope in servicing.
3. Explain how to locate a B+ short in a voltage distribution network if no schematic is available, using (a) an ohmmeter; (b) a voltmeter.
4. Explain by cause and effect where two or more components are found defective.
5. What trouble is indicated where (a) a high-wattage resistor runs cold; (b) a low-wattage resistor gets hot? Explain your reasoning.
6. When making an ohmmeter check on a set with the power off, the needle deflects off scale. What is wrong, and what would you do?
7. State the uses of (a) an AF signal generator; (b) an RF generator.
8. A transistor or IC should never be replaced without first checking for other defects. Explain.
9. Why do you get a different ohms reading across a diode or transistor junction when the meter leads are reversed?
10. What signal, voltage, and resistance conditions might lead you to suspect an IC? How would you proceed?
11. When progressing upstream through a multistage amplifier, should the response increase or decrease when using (a) a scope; (b) a signal generator? Explain.
12. Explain the general procedure for an intermittent problem.

# 6 Power supplies

All electronic equipment contains one or more primary power supplies that operate from the 120-V ac 60-Hz power line. Its purpose is to furnish the low dc voltages required by transistors, ICs, CRT electron guns, VCR motors and relays, panel indicator lights, and digital readouts. The PS reduces the 120-V ac line voltage to a lower value, which is then rectified [converted to pulsating dc (PDC)], filtered, regulated, and distributed to various circuits. Although most low-voltage power supplies (LVPS) are basically the same, there are some variations for special applications. This includes switching-type PSs; sweep-derived (scan) PSs, and their associated HV supply used by TV sets and monitors; switching-type power supplies similar to the latter type but driven from separate oscillator and driver circuits; and dc-to-dc converters used in battery-operated equipment.

## 6-1 POWER SUPPLY FUNDAMENTALS

Figure 6-1 shows the main functional areas of a typical, two-section LVPS. One section provides unregulated dc for circuits that are not too critical; the other section furnishes regulated dc for circuits that cannot tolerate voltage fluctuations.

The first block on the left comprises all ac circuitry ahead of the rectifiers: the ac power cord (line cord) or cheater cord (if a TV set), line fuses or circuit breakers (CBs), the power on/off switch, RF hash filters, and power and filament transformers when used. The 120 V ac goes through the power switch and a fuse or circuit breaker to the rectifier(s), either directly or via a transformer, if provided. The RF filter, consisting of one or two small coils and a capacitor, helps to prevent bursts of noise (hash) from entering the equipment via the back

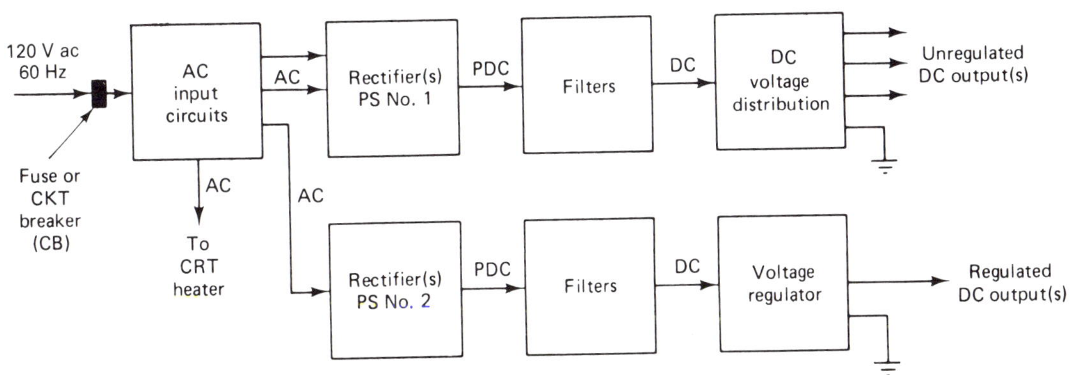


**FIG. 6-1** Typical LVPS block diagram.

door, as it were. The fuse or CB provides protection in the event of a short or overload. Instead of a conventional fuse, sometimes a *fusister* (fusible resistor) is used, which provides overload protection while limiting the initial current surge when the equipment is first turned on.

Good design calls for a transformer that isolates the equipment from the power line and provides either a step up or a step down in voltage. In the interest of economy, some modern equipment, TV sets in particular, are transformerless (i.e., the line voltage is rectified directly, and one side of the power line connects to chassis or a floating ground). This is known as a hot chassis design, and under certain conditions can be hazardous to both the user and the equipment itself. In most cases, a transformer will also have a heater winding to supply 6 V ac for such items as dial lights, and in older TV sets, to heat the CRT filament(s).

### Fuses and Circuit Breakers

These items offer protection against fire and component damage. Their job is to open the circuit in the event of a short or overload condition. Fuses are used at the ac input of most equipment, in the main B+ circuit, or both. Typical ratings are 2 to 3 A, depending on the equipment.

*Warning:* Never replace a fuse with a higher rating than specified and do not defeat its purpose, except temporarily in some cases, while testing. Some fuses (slo-blow) have a delay action, so they do not pop from momentary line surges. In an emergency during repairs, a piece of fine wire can be used. For example, No. 30 copper wire will melt open at about 10 A; No. 34 wire, at roughly 5 A. Vacuum-tube heater circuits are sometimes protected with a fuse link, a short length of fusible wire.

A circuit breaker consists of a thin bimetal strip with a heater element. A current overload causes the strip to bend, opening the circuit. When the overload is relieved, the CB can be reset at the press of a button. A tripped CB does not always indicate an overload since it itself may be defective. Lightly tapping will often show up a bad CB.

### Rectifiers

The rectifiers in the block diagram for PSs 1 and 2 are solid-state diodes, which, having a high back-to-front resistance ratio, pass current in one direction only. PSs may have either + or − dc outputs, or both, as determined by which way the diodes are connected. Figure 6-2 shows a number of rectifier configurations.

In circuit (a), a single diode is used, and connected as shown, has a + dc output. With this transformerless configuration, the rectifier rectifies the peak of the ac input, producing approximately 150 V with no load. When loaded, the value drops to about 130 V or so, depending on the load current. This is known as a *half-wave rectifier,* and rectifies only every half-cycle of the ac. The output is pulsating dc (PDC), whose ripples are somewhat difficult to filter out.

Circuit (b) has dual outputs, both + and −, as determined by the diode connections. They, too, are half-wave rectifiers.

Circuit (c) shows a *voltage multiplier,* in this case a doubler. Two diodes are used, in conjunction with two electrolytic input capacitors. The capacitors (C1 and C2) are alternately charged by alternate cycles of the ac via their corresponding diodes. The output (approximately 250 V) represents the sum of the series-aiding capacitor charges. This is a full-wave rectifier whose fluctuations are easier to filter out. Note that the negative end of one capacitor is not grounded.

Circuit (d) is a voltage tripler. During one alternation of the ac, C1 is charged (to 150 V) via D1. When the ac reverses, the line voltage, series aiding with the charge on C1, causes D2 to conduct, charging C2 to twice the line voltage (about 300 V). On the next alternation, the 300 V, aided by the line voltage, charges C3 to about 450 V (no load). With a load (the equipment connected and drawing current) the output typically drops to about 300 V or so. As with all voltage-multiplier circuits, the voltage under load is determined by capacitor values, the current drain, and the charging of the capacitors.

Circuit (e) represents a dual-output PS using a step-down power transformer. The negative PS utilizes both halves of the winding, with diodes D1 and D2 for full-wave rectification. The + PS uses this voltage series aiding with D3. Note the polarity of the diodes and filter capacitors.

Circuit (f) uses a bridge rectifier consisting of four diodes connected in a diamond configuration, as shown. The output is full wave without the need for a center-tapped winding. Two diodes conduct (in series) during alternate changes of the ac. For one half-cycle the current is through D1 and D4, and through D2 and D3 for the next reversal. The small-value capacitors across the diodes are to prevent radiation associated with silicon-type diodes and diode switching.

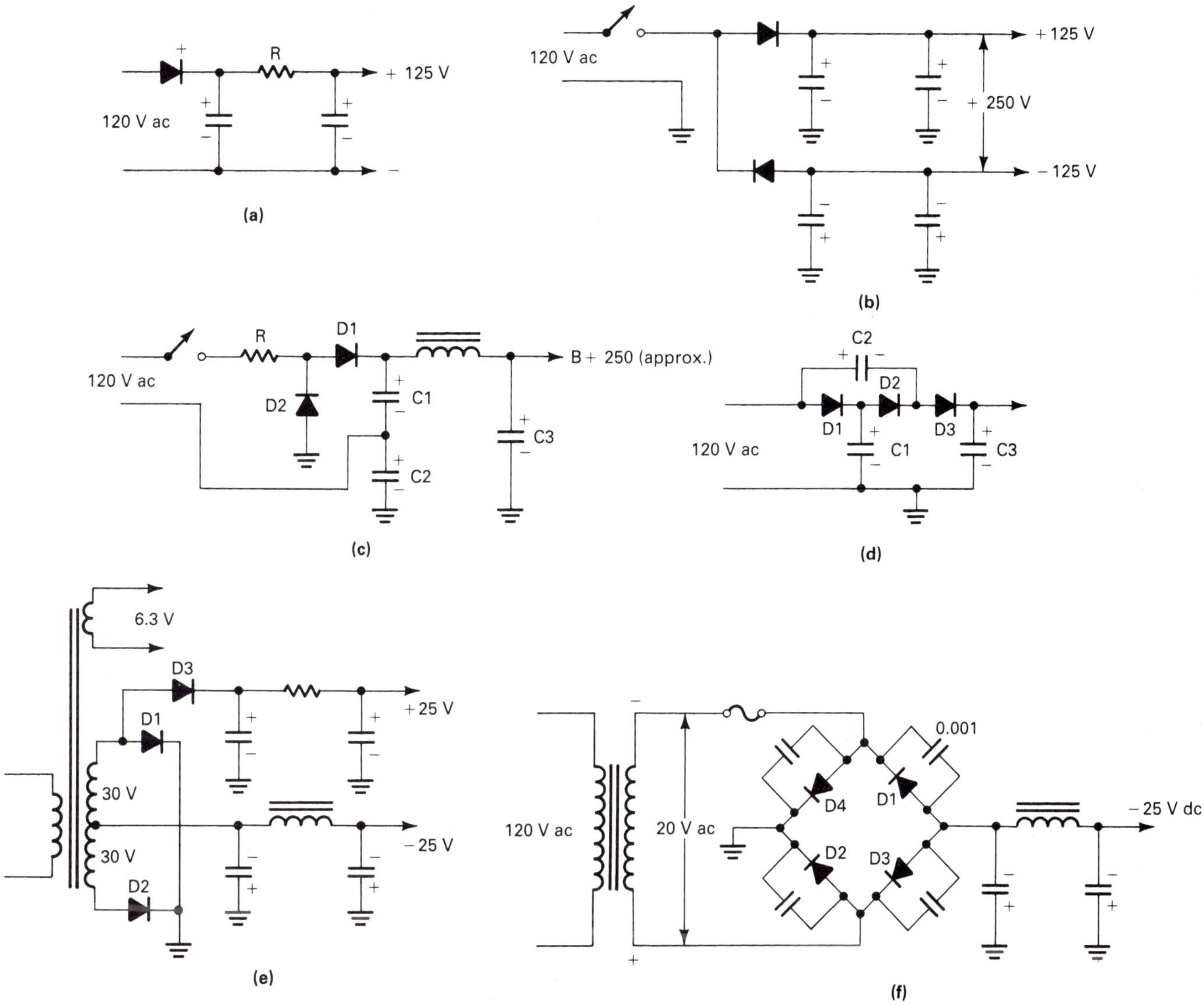


**FIG. 6-2** Rectifier configurations.

## 6-2 FILTERS

Filters are used to smooth out the fluctuations of the PDC (pulsating dc) current. High-value electrolytic-type capacitors are used in combination with either a choke coil or a resistor for noncritical circuits if the current requirements are low. In the foregoing circuits, the capacitor at the rectifier output is called the *input filter;* the one after the choke or filter resistor is the *output filter*. The former is responsible primarily for the amount of voltage output; the latter capacitor does most of the actual filtering. The filter choke or resistor tends to oppose variations of current. The capacitors charge at peak levels of voltage and discharge into the load circuit, the two working together to produce a relatively smooth output. Capacitor values range from about 10 to 2000 MF or greater. The greater the current demands, the greater the capacity that is needed to do the job.

### Active Power Filter

An active power filter (APF) is very effective in filtering out 60- or 120-Hz ripple voltage and any audio or sweep voltages that may be present. The latter effect greatly reduces problems of interstage coupling due to signals developed across the internal impedance of the PS, which is common to all stages. Two typical APF circuits are shown in Figure 6-3. For maximum effectiveness, conventional filter capacitors are also used in the circuits. In circuit (a), ripple voltages are reduced by cancellation. Any voltage fluctuations present at the output also appear across the filter driver transistor Q2, which am-

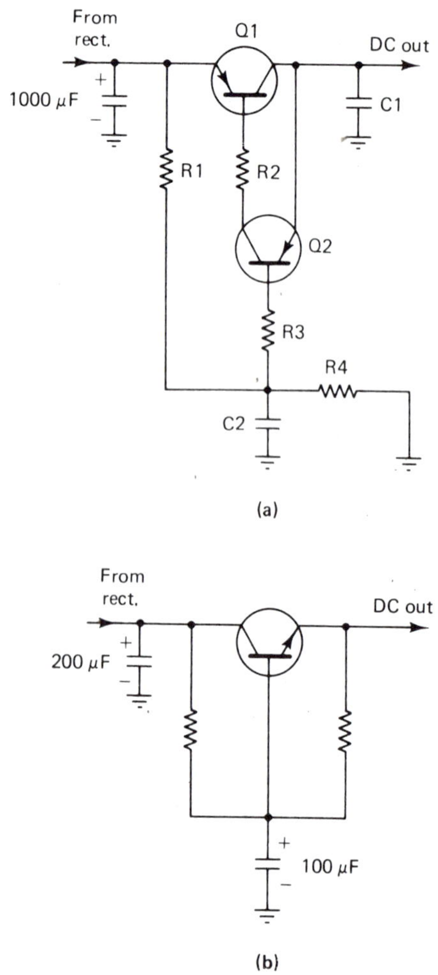


**FIG. 6-3** Active power filters.

plifies and inverts them. This ac voltage is applied to the base of Q1 (a power transistor) in phase with ripple voltage coming from the rectifiers. Being approximately equal in amplitude and opposite in polarity, they cancel out, resulting in pure dc at the output.

Circuit (b) uses a power transistor series with the output. Its action is similar to that of a voltage regulator. Any increases in transistor current (due to ripple fluctuations) produces an increase in reverse bias, decreasing the transistor conductance and reducing its output. Any valleys in the ripple voltage accomplish the reverse, thus smoothing out all fluctuations.

## 6-3 VOLTAGE REGULATORS

All electrical power sources have a certain amount of internal resistance across which an *IR* voltage drop is developed with current flow. The greater this resistance and/or the greater the current drawn by a load, the greater the voltage drop, resulting in a corresponding reduction in the available output voltage. Voltage regulation is defined as the difference between the no-load voltage and the voltage under load conditions (LV = NLV − *IR* drop). Ideally, 100% regulation would mean no variations whatsoever, a condition impossible to achieve.

A simple regulator circuit employing a zener diode is shown in Figure 6-4a. The zener, as with any diode, represents a high resistance when reverse biased. When its zener voltage (avalanche voltage) is exceeded, it conducts. The higher the voltage, the greater the conductance, and vice versa. The series resistor passes zener current in addition to the load current(s). When the zener conducts, the increased current through the resistor produces an increased *IR* drop, decreasing the output voltage accordingly. The reverse holds true if the voltage tends to drop, the reduced *IR* drop across the resistor causing the output to increase, and holding it relatively constant.

More complex circuits are used to stabilize the B+ furnished to critical transistor and IC stages. In

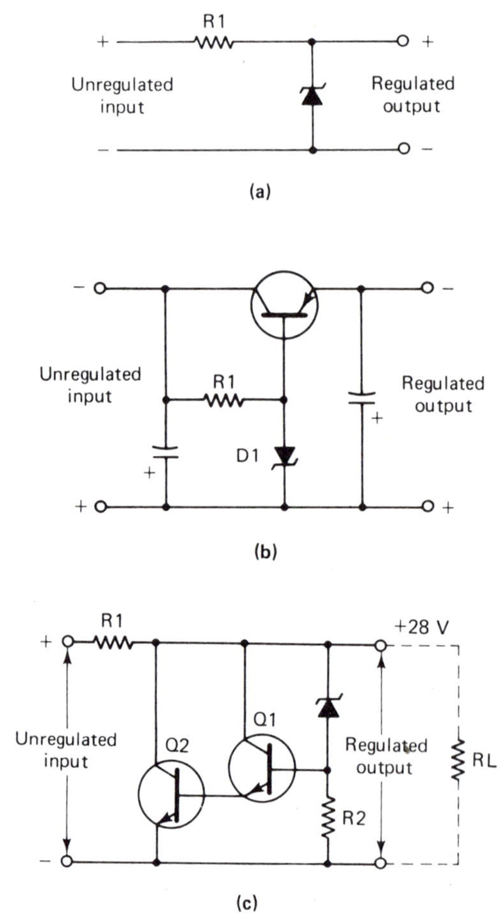


**FIG. 6-4** Dc voltage regulators.

some cases two circuits as in Figure 6-4a are connected in cascade for greater effectiveness. For even better control, transistors, are employed.

Figure 6-4b is called a series regulator. Notice the similarity to the APF of Figure 6-3. The series-connected power transistor (sometimes called a *pass transistor*) handles the full-load current, in this case a PNP type because it is a negative PS. The transistor, whose conductance changes with variations of input or output voltage, functions much like a variable resistor. The dc output is continuously compared with a reference voltage, the input voltage between the base and emitter of the transistor. The base voltage is held constant by the zener. If the reference voltage drops, the transistor conductance increases, passing more current to the load. If the voltage increases, conductance becomes less and the output drops.

Circuit (c) represents a shunt-type regulator circuit. Transistor Q2, connected in shunt, functions as a variable load. Transistor Q1 senses any changes in voltage to control the conductance of Q2. The zener stabilizes the base voltage of Q1. An increase in voltage represents an increased forward bias for Q1, producing a similar increase for Q2, increasing its conductance and the current through R1. The increased *IR* drop across R1 reduces the output voltage accordingly. The reverse holds true if the output voltage tends to decrease. Circuits (b) and (c) are used extensively to supply power to the horizontal output transistor of modern color sets. As such, they are called *HV regulators*.

## 6-4 DC VOLTAGE DISTRIBUTION

Every transistor and IC in any equipment must be supplied with a precise amount of dc voltage; and reducing the PS voltage to the proper values is done in two ways: (1) with series-dropping resistors and/or (2) with voltage dividers. The simple circuit shown in Figure 6-5 is an example of both methods. Here a transistor and an IC get their operating voltages from a 40-V power supply. The circuit has several branches and the current leaving the negative side of the PS divides; some electrons (25 mA) go through the C/E junction of the transistor.

Some current (12 mA) takes a path through the IC circuits. All currents recombine and return to the PS via the series-dropping resistor R1. This total current drain (approximately 37 mA) develops an *IR* voltage drop (10 V) across the resistor. The amount of voltage dropped (reduced) by a series-dropping resistor depends on the amount of load current and the value of resistance, in this case 272 Ω.

Because of the low resistance of the transformer winding (T1), there is very little voltage drop and the transistor collector is supplied with 28.1 V. Resistors R4 and R5 represent a voltage divider. Assuming negligible base current, the 30 V divides or splits in direct proportion to the two resistor values, the greatest amount (29 V) across the higher value (29 kΩ) and a lower amount (1 V) across the 1-kΩ resistor. This provides a +1-V forward bias for the transistor.

Resistors R2 and R3 constitute another voltage divider. The voltage split in this case is different, however, because of the current through R2 (approximately 2 mA) while neglecting the negligible bleeder current through R3. In this instance, the voltage split is *not* in proportion to the resistor values. Another, more complex example of a voltage distribution network is shown later, under troubleshooting.

### Primary Power Low-Voltage Power Supply

A typical TV circuit is shown in Figure 6-6. To degauss (demagnetize) a color picture tube, a large coil (or series of smaller coils) is mounted externally, around the periphery of the tube near the screen. It

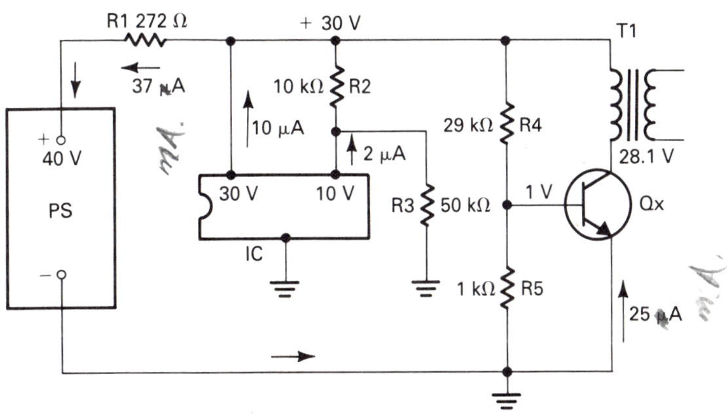


**FIG. 6-5** Simplified voltage distribution network.

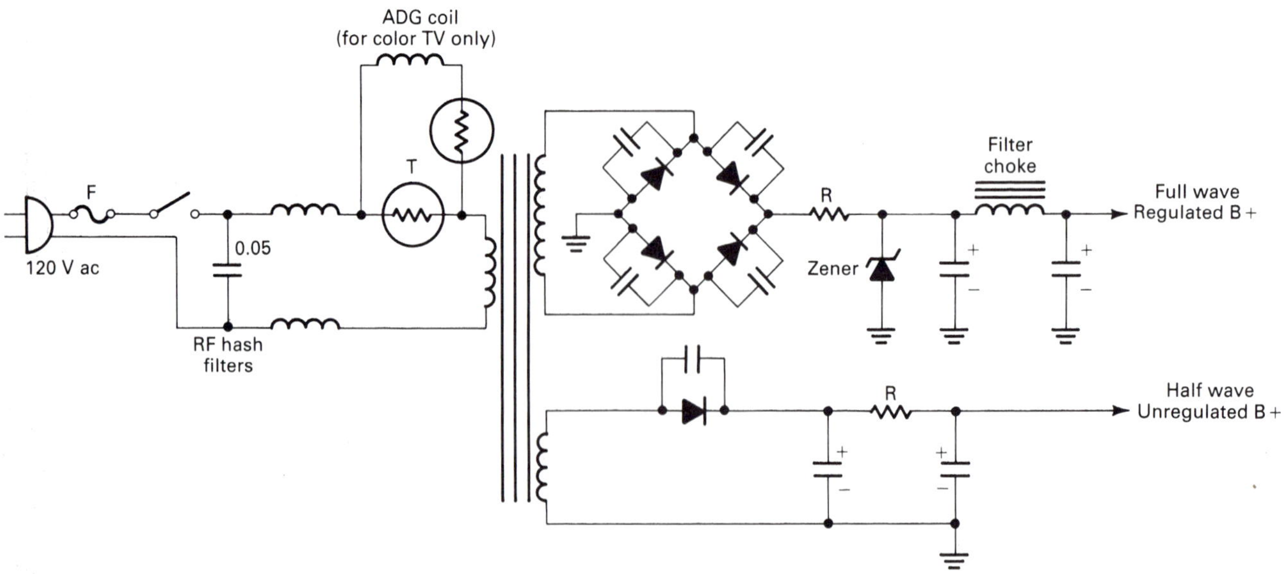


**FIG. 6-6** Typical dual-output TV power supply.

is connected in the ac input line. Each time the set is turned on, the coil is momentarily energized with ac. This is called *automatic degaussing* (ADG). One or two thermisters (varistors) are connected to the coil(s) as shown. From a cold start, when the resistance of the one is high and the other is low, current is shunted through the coil(s). In a few seconds, while heating, their resistances change, cutting off the coil current. Other sections of the PS are conventional, as described previously.

## High-Frequency Power Supply

All modern TV sets use what is called a *scan-derived,* flyback PS. With this system, most circuits get their dc operating voltages from the flyback transformer in the horizontal output stage. In addition to driving the deflection yoke and developing HV, there are several windings that furnish low voltages, at the high horizontal sweep frequency (15, 750 Hz) or 15,734 Hz). These voltages are then rectified, filtered, and distributed throughout the set. The advantages of this system are greater efficiency and fewer filtering problems than with 60- and 120-Hz power supplies. Because of the high ripple frequency, only low-value filter capacitors are required. With most sets, the CRT heater is also powered from one of these low-voltage windings. The regular 120-V ac 60-Hz PS is also needed to supply primary power for sweep circuit startup and for the high current requirements of the horizontal output transistor. Under overload or excessive HV conditions, a protective *shutdown circuit* automatically cuts off the power to disable the set (see Chapter 11).

## High-Voltage Power Supply

The HV winding on the flyback transformer develops a 15,734 Hz or 15,750-Hz HV pulse that is rectified to supply the HV and focus voltage requirements of the CRT. The HV winding on early-model sets developed about 50 kV p-p. To reduce breakdowns, the flyback transformer in modern sets produces a lower voltage (about 8 kV), which is then increased with a voltage tripler. More on this later.

## Switching-Type High-Frequency Power Supply

Many late-model color TV sets, VCRs, and some other equipment use a high-frequency power supply similar to but unrelated to the scan-derived PS. It has a separate oscillator that is synchronized to the horizontal sweep. It uses a separate high-frequency power transformer with a ferrite core to keep losses to a minimum. The rectified outputs from several low-voltage windings supply the dc requirements of most TV stages. As with scan power supplies, and because of the high ripple frequency, there is no need for large electrolytic filter capacitors. With this system the amplified oscillator voltage is switched on and off (by a power switching transistor) to excite the transformer. This results in a square-wave output.

## Low-Voltage Switched Power Supply

*Low-voltage* switching-type PSs are becoming increasingly popular. They have several advantages over other PSs: increased efficiency, small size, and

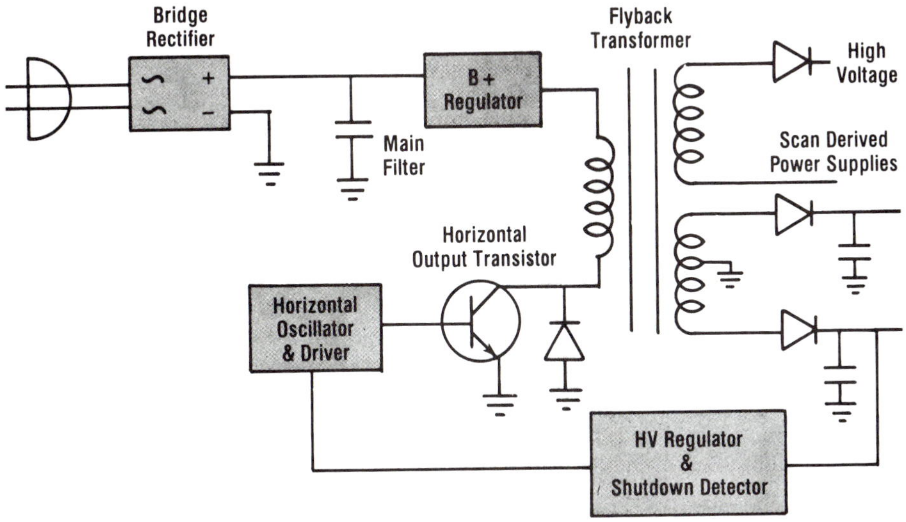


***The scan derived power supply for a television looks functionally similar to the switched mode power supply shown below.***

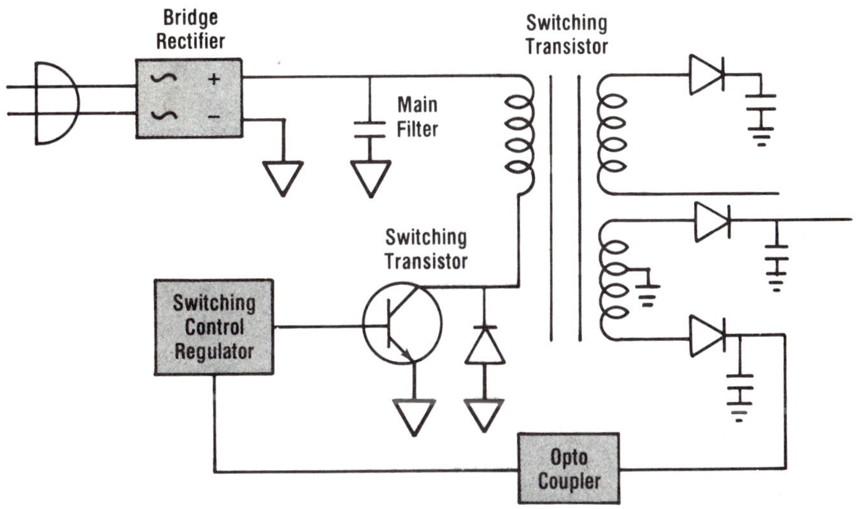


**FIG. 6-7** Basic switching mode power supply. The scan-derived power supply for a TV set (a) looks functionally similar to the switched mode power supply (b).

they operate over wide variations of load current. Some of these PSs operate with 60-Hz power. Used extensively in VCRs, they are switched on and off at the proper times under digital logic control (see Chapter 20).

In many respects one type of switched PS is similar to the conventional TV–HV flyback PS. In Figure 6-7, note the comparison. Both use a flyback transformer and both operate at a relatively high frequency. Both use a transistor to switch power on and off to the transformer, both have a damper diode to reduce the inductive kickback from the transformer, and both regulate the circuit operation to control the output voltage.

There are some differences, however. The switched mode PS is not restricted to 15,750 Hz for its operating frequency. Whereas a scan-derived PS varies the dc voltage, with the switching PS, either the frequency or width of the pulse may be changed. With the switching PS, the switching transistor is part of an oscillator circuit; with TV, oscillations originate from the horizontal sweep oscillator.

## DC-to-DC Converters

A dc-to-dc converter system is often used with battery-powered portable equipment, typically from a 12-V car battery. The 12 V supplies power to a flip-flop switching circuit that drives a transformer. The transformer outputs are rectified and filtered to furnish the amounts of dc required by the equipment. With this PS, the square-wave ripple component sometimes creates a filtering problem.

### Typical Low- and High-Voltage Power Supplies

The foldout schematic at the back of the book uses conventional circuits, with a few exceptions. This is a hot chassis set with one side of the power line tied to chassis ground. Note the varistor across the ac line for hash suppression, and the single "posistor" series with the degaussing coil. Also note that there are two fuses (instead of a CB): a 3-A fuse at the ac input and a 1-A fuse in the dc circuit. This PS uses a half-wave rectifier to develop 125 V. The item marked STR3125 is an IC that functions as a voltage regulator and error detector. The series-limiting resistor R802 is provided for surge protection. Since this is a hot chassis design, an isolation transformer is required when servicing.

High voltage, CRT focus voltage, and various scan-derived voltages are furnished by the flyback transformer, T444. Note the built-in HV rectifier diodes that reduce the possibility of corona arcing. This set uses a startup/shutdown circuit that senses excessive HV to disable the horizontal sweep circuit. More on this in Chapters 10 and 11.

## 6-5 TROUBLESHOOTING AND REPAIR

Breakdowns directly or indirectly associated with a basic LVPS are very common, but generally are the easiest to troubleshoot and repair. Typical trouble symptoms are no operation (dead equipment), hum problems, loss of one or more functions, overheating components, smoke, and arcing.

Regardless of the symptoms, start every job with a thorough inspection, first with the equipment turned off, then again with power applied. Look for the obvious: loose or broken wires, disengaged connectors, loose or damaged contacts, poor soldering, solder splashes, damaged components, and so on. With power on and relying on all four senses (sight, sound, smell, and touch), check for anything abnormal. Feel items such as resistors, diodes, transistors, and ICs for signs of overheating. Look for wax drippings under transformers. If there is smoke or arcing, turn the equipment off *immediately* while planning your next move.

B+ shorts are common: either grounded wiring or shorted components. A short at or close to the main dc bus will blow fuses, trip the CB, and in some cases damage or destroy components. Common causes are shorted filter capacitors, voltage regulators, ICs, and transistors. Determine and correct the cause *before* making a replacement.

Power supply shorts often cause resistors and other components to overheat and burn up. Determine both cause and effect. A good place to start is at the end of a component, where the lowest voltage and/or resistance is measured to ground. As testing progresses, frequently check with schematic to identify possible suspects. Where there is little or no B+ but resistance to ground checks high, some transistor or IC is probably drawing excessive current and loading the circuit. Determine what stage or components are involved, then isolate by cutting the B+ feed to see if the drain is relieved and the B+ restored.

With a TV set, note whether there is a power transformer; if not, it is probably a hot chassis type that requires an isolation transformer and special precautions to prevent electric shock and damage to components.

Check for heater glow in the neck of the CRT. This often provides a good clue from where to start. If the set is completely dead and no blown fuse or tripped CB, the automatic shutdown circuit may have been activated or the horizontal sweep circuit disabled, which kills all scan-derived voltages. A shorted pass transistor in the regulator that feeds the horizontal output transistor is a common cause of shutdown.

Typical trouble symptoms and conditions and probable causes and procedures are described next. See the troubleshooting flow diagram in Figure 6-8.

### Symptoms and Procedures

*Dead (Where Overload Conditions Are Present).* An overload condition may be indicated by a blown fuse or tripped CB, overheating components (resistors, diodes, transistors, transformers, ICs, etc.), and smoke. These are typical conditions resulting from a circuit or component *short* or excessive current drain due to other causes, such as too much forward bias on a power output transistor (thermal runaway). If no B+ at rectifier output, check for a shorted rectifier, zener diode, regulator transistor, or filter capacitor. Unless the fuse blows, the transformer will overheat and be damaged or destroyed. If the B+ is *low*, overheating components, but with no apparent short, look for a *leaky* capacitor or transistor junction or a transistor or IC that's drawing too much current. Rectifiers with a short life are not uncommon, as caused by any of the foregoing conditions. For an overheating power transformer, check for high line voltage, a short on the main B+, shorted input filter, shorted rectifier(s), or in some cases shorted windings in the

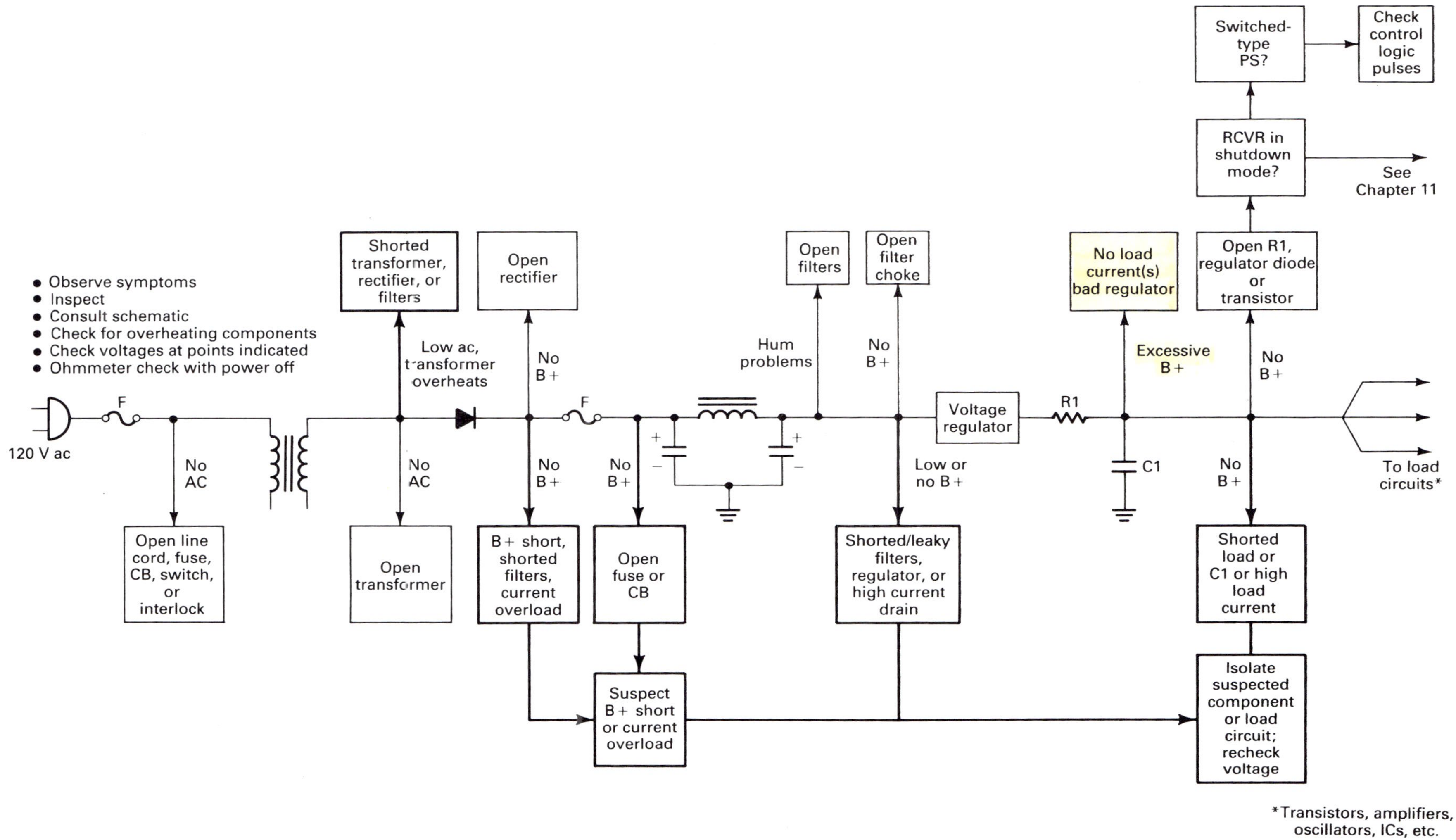


**FIG. 6-8** Primary PS troubleshooting flow drawing. Sequence of testing: left to right. Heavy lines indicate overload conditions with overheating components.

transformer itself. (*Reminder:* A too-high rated fuse will not protect a circuit.)

*Dead.* If *no* overload is evident and *no* B+, look for an *open* circuit. A high-wattage resistor that runs cold provides a good clue. If no ac up to the rectifiers, suspect a blown fuse, defective line cord or switch, or (rarely) an open transformer primary. A low-rated fuse may blow even when there are no circuit defects. If the ac is okay but no dc, check for open rectifier(s), a series-limiting resistor, or a filter choke, depending on at what point the voltage is lost. If an open component is found, chances are it was caused by a B+ short. Correct the cause before making a replacement. Where the same voltage is measured at both ends of a dropping resistor, it indicates the loss of current flow, for whatever reason.

*Dead.* If strange and confusing symptoms and test results, and the equipment was worked on recently, suspect that a man-made problem was introduced. Check with the schematic for possible wiring errors, wrong component values, wiring shorts, poor soldering, and so on.

*Low B+.* Possible causes are generally the same as for no B+ except to a lesser degree: for example, filters that leak but are not shorted, a dried-up input filter that has lost capacity, a leaky rectifier, a voltage-dropping resistor that has increased in value, or low line voltage. For the latter, try a booster transformer. Assuming the building wiring is adequate, contact the utility company.

*Excessive B+.* The usual cause is a nonoperating voltage regulator or one or more stages or components drawing little or no current. Localize, then determine the cause, which may be a bad transistor or IC that's not conducting, improper operating voltages, or an open circuit such as the bleeder resistor of a voltage divider.

*Fuse Blows or CB Trips When Chassis Is Grounded.* This is probably a hot chassis circuit. See if the *RC* isolation network has been defeated. Use an isolation transformer for the equipment and test instruments. As a safety measure, consider installing a (GFI) ground fault interrupter at the power source.

*Reversed Polarity.* If the power supply output voltage has reversed polarity, the rectifier(s) have probably been installed backward. If no schematic is available, observe the polarity of the filters.

*Hum and Ripple Problems.* This is generally a filtering problem caused by open electrolytics in the primary power supply or farther along in the voltage distribution network. Try to relate the problem to a particular circuit function. Use a scope or ac voltmeter to check the ac ripple component or any signal voltages present at all suspected filters. The one with the highest ac reading is probably open. While monitoring results, bridge all suspects with a substitute capacitor of the same voltage and capacity ratings. Avoid surges that can damage or destroy sensitive transistors and ICs. If only one section of a multiple capacitor checks bad, replace the entire unit. Observe correct polarity when replacing electrolytics. Open diodes in a bridge rectifier can also cause ripple problems.

*Audible Hum or Buzz.* May be caused by loose and vibrating power transformer laminations. Tighten screws, insert wedges, or apply cement or varnish.

*Arcing.* This can have serious consequences: destruction of components and a common cause of fires. Quickly locate the arcing site, then immediately remove power to prevent further damage. If arcing between closely spaced contacts, spread the connections. If on a PCB, remove any excess solder or solder splashes that may be responsible. Clean up any conductive residues in the circuitry. Look for small bits of loose hardware. If arcing is heard but not visible, it may be inside a component, such as a capacitor or transformer. Watch for wires with scraped or burned insulation.

*Catastrophic Failures.* This is where *many* components can be destroyed as a result of a single breakdown or an inadvertent short created by improper or careless servicing practices. Once it happens, all you can do is to replace the bad parts and look for and correct the cause before applying power. If the failure is due to carelessness, learn from your mistake.

*Intermittent Operation.* Power supply problems are seldom intermittent, but there are a few possibilities, such as poor soldering, particularly at a point where many wires come together, intermittent connections within a component, and perhaps most common of all, a hairline crack in a PC board.

To localize an intermittent condition, monitor power supply voltages at key circuit points while tapping and probing as necessary.

### Voltage Distribution Problems

Transistors and ICs must be supplied with dc operating voltages if they are to perform their functions as oscillators, amplifiers, or whatever. Figure 6-9 shows the voltage distribution network for a typical, hypothetical amplifier. The IC preamp is followed by three, direct-coupled stages using discrete transistors. (A later version would have *all* stages incorporated in a single IC.) The main purpose of the various resistors is to supply the IC and the transistor elements with specific amounts of voltage. The IC in this case is supplied from a regulated B+ source. The transistors are supplied with unregulated dc. The circuit uses both series-dropping resistors and voltage dividers. One voltage divider (resistors R1 and R2) reduces the B+ to the amount required by the IC. The IC current is carried via R1 and stabilized by the bleeder resistor R2. Voltage measured at the IC in reference to ground is the same amount that appears across R2. The bypass capacitor C1 provides a low-reactance path and ground return for signal voltages that might otherwise be developed across the resistors and the internal resistance of the power supply.

Voltages for the transistors are supplied from the voltage divider R3/R4. Another divider network, R5/R7, reduces the voltage further for transistor Q1. Capacitors C2 and C3 provide additional filtering, bypassing, and decoupling. Resistor R6 is the load resistor for Q1, across which its output signal is developed. The dc drop across R6/R7 also represents the forward bias for Q2. Bias for Q1 is provided by the voltage divider R10/R11. Resistor R8 is the load resistor for Q2. The emitter current of Q3 develops an *IR* drop across R9. Bias for Q3 is the difference between this voltage and the dc drop across R8. Bias voltage polarity is determined by which voltage is the greater.

With such a dc-coupled circuit, any malfunction will have an adverse effect on all voltages in the downstream stages. In servicing, try and localize the trouble to one stage by signal tracing and/or signal injection. Measure and record all voltages and compare them with those shown on the schematic. Component defects probably responsible for abnormal voltage readings are described next. It is assumed that there is dc output from the PS.

*No Voltage at TP-1; Resistor R1 Overheats.* The IC or C1 is shorted out.

*Low Voltage at TP-1.* Heavy current drain by the IC; leakage in the IC or C1.

*Excessive Voltage at TP-1.* Little or no current drawn by the IC. R2 open or increased in value.

*DC Voltage Exists at TP-3.* No voltage indicated on the schematic. Leakage in the IC or coupling capacitor is shorted or leaking.

*No Voltage at TP-2; R3 Overheats.* C2 is probably shorted, or the output transformer winding is grounded.

*Low Voltage at TP-2.* Heavy current drain by one or more transistors. C2 leaky. C3 leaking or shorted.

*Excessive Voltage at TP-2.* Little or no current drawn by the transistors. R4 open or increased in value.

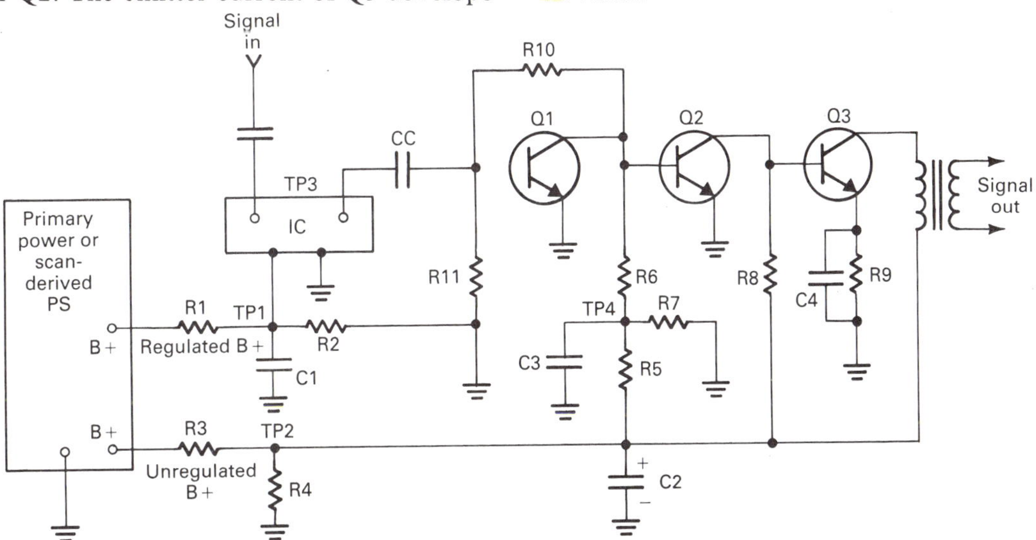


**FIG. 6-9** Typical voltage distribution system.

*No Voltage at TP-4 or Q1.* C2 or C3 shorted. R5 open. Q1 or Q2 shorted.

*Low Voltage at TP-4 and Q1.* Leaky Q1 or Q2 junction. C2 or C3 leaking. Value of R5 or R6 increased. Excessive Q1 current.

*Excessive Voltage at TP-4.* Little or no Q1 current. R7 open or increased.

*No Q1 Base Voltage.* Q1 shorted or R10 open.

*Low Q1 Base Voltage.* Q1 junction leaky. R10 value increased.

*Excessive Q1 Base Voltage.* R11 open or increased.

*No Q2 Collector Voltage.* Open R8. Shorted Q2 or Q3.

*Low Q2 Collector Voltage.* Q2 current excessive. Q2 or Q3 leaky. R8 value increased.

*Excessive Q2 Collector Voltage.* Little or no Q2 current.

*No Q3 Collector Voltage.* Open or grounded transformer primary. Shorted Q3.

*Low Q3 Collector Voltage.* Q3 or transformer leakage.

*No Q3 Emitter Voltage.* No Q3 current or C4 is shorted.

*Low Q3 Emitter Voltage.* Low Q3 current or leaky C4.

*High Emitter Voltage.* Q3 is shorted or R9 is open.

## Color TV Power Supplies

*Primary Power Supply.* In general, all the foregoing test and repair procedures apply to TV. With color sets, however, there is the ADG circuit to consider. ADG problems are rare and easily recognized as such. If suspected, monitor the ac voltage across the ADG coil as the set is switched on. There should be a momentary reading of ac, which drops to near zero after a few seconds. If it does not drop off and the coil is constantly energized, you see "whirls" of random color on the screen which interfere with the picture. Substitute or replace the series or shunt varistors.

Where there is picture degradation on a color set and the need to make frequent convergence adjustments, check for an open degaussing coil or a bad varistor. A completely dead set is a common problem with modern color sets, due to activation of the automatic shutdown circuit. If there is no sound or raster, check for dc output of the primary PS. If okay, troubleshoot the startup shutdown circuits as described in Chapter 11. If there is no B+ for startup, check the PS.

*Scan-Derived Power Supply.* If there is no heater glow in the neck of the CRT, no HV, and no dc output from any of the scan power supplies, troubleshoot the horizontal sweep circuit (Chapter 10). If there is no dc output from only one of the secondary power supplies, follow the same procedures as for a primary PS. Check the low-voltage, 15,750-Hz output from the appropriate winding of the flyback transformer. Check the rectifier(s) and filters. Check to see if stages supplied from the PS are shorting out the voltage or drawing too much current.

*High-Voltage Power Supply.* Assuming that there is output from the primary PS, if there is no sound or raster, either the horizontal sweep circuit is inoperative or the set is in the shutdown mode. If the set uses scan power and there is sound but no raster, check for HV at the CRT ultor. If there is normal HV but no raster, check for a bad CRT or problems with its operating voltages (Chapter 17). If no HV, check for HV pulsed output from the flyback transformer. Low output from shorted windings is common, but this loads the circuit, affecting all scan voltages. Check the HV rectifier(s) by substitution. Some sets have rectifiers built into the flyback. Other sets often use voltage triplers, which must be replaced as a unit. A shorted CRT can kill the HV and simulate troubles elsewhere. The CRT focus voltage may be supplied from the HV, or have its own rectifier, and can be checked separately. Picture and raster blooming is a symptom of poor HV regulation. This and HV troubleshooting procedures are discussed in Chapter 10.

*Switching-Type High-Frequency Power Supply.* Assuming that there is output from the primary PS but no output from the switching PS, check for oscillator voltage using a scope or DMM on a low ac voltage range. If there is no oscillator output, check the transistor and its operating voltages. If necessary, isolate the oscillator from other circuits that may be loading and killing the oscillations. If the oscillator output is normal, signal trace to the input of the switching transistor. Check this transistor, its operating voltages, and associated components as appropriate. Make the necessary repairs to obtain outputs from the various secondary windings of the transformer. Where there is little or no output from one of the supplies, proceed as described for the scan-type PS. If there is no transformer excitation and the cause is obscure, try driving it with a square-wave voltage from an audio signal generator. For troubleshooting a VCR-type 60-Hz switched PS, see Chapter 21.

### Battery-Operated Portable Equipment

For a dc-to-dc converter, troubleshooting is much the same as for a high-frequency switching-type PS. Check for oscillations, transformer excitation, and all voltages and components as appropriate to the circumstances.

Many small portable TV sets operate either from the power line or from an internal battery supply. To ensure a reasonably long battery life, all circuits are designed for low current drain. This includes the CRT filament, which on larger sets uses a considerable amount of power. Such sets usually have a built-in charging circuit. If the set operates okay from the power line but not from batteries, there is a good chance that the batteries are defective or in need of charging. Measure the battery voltage under load (with the set turned on). A battery problem is indicated where the voltage changes drastically between power turn-on and turn-off. Assuming that it is a rechargeable battery, recheck the load voltage after undergoing a recharge cycle. The charging circuit is a conventional PS, and when suspected, is checked accordingly.

## QUESTIONS

1. Explain why the output of a PS drops under load and the factors involved.
2. Why must the voltage rating of a filter capacitor be greater than the expected output voltage under load?
3. Which is more difficult to filter, a half- or full-wave PS? Explain why.
4. How would you use a multiwinding transformer to raise or lower the line voltage? Why must phasing be considered?
5. At what point does a zener diode start conducting, and for what purpose?
6. What is a scan-derived PS, and where and why is it used?
7. Using an example, define voltage regulation.
8. Explain the operation of a transistor-type voltage regulator.
9. Why is a no-load measurement of a battery or PS voltage almost meaningless?
10. Explain why an isolation transformer should always be used when servicing hot chassis equipment.
11. If the grounded bleeder resistor of a voltage-dividing network increases or opens up, the voltage at the junction of the resistors will increase. Explain why, and the component damage that may result.
12. What might you suspect where (a) a high-wattage resistor runs cold; (b) a low-wattage resistor overheats?
13. State the probable cause where the output of a PS has reversed polarity.
14. When ohms checking equipment with the power off, the meter pointer may deflect backwards or go full scale. Explain why and how you can prevent it.
15. Explain the procedure for locating a B+ short using (a) an ohmmeter; (b) a dc voltmeter.
16. How would you rate the condition of a resistor in a circuit if it measures (a) higher than its coded value; (b) less than its coded value? What would you do in each case?
17. Multiple troubles are quite common. Considering cause and effect, how would you proceed when you locate a bad component?
18. Catastrophic destruction of sensitive components is not uncommon. What precautions should you observe to avoid this when servicing equipment?
19. If there is no output from a PS but no signs of overload, would you suspect an open circuit or a short? Explain your reasoning.
20. State the probable cause of two shorted diodes in a bridge-type PS.
21. A PS has little or no output and the power transformer overheats. What would you suspect if (a) there is no overheating when certain secondary windings are cut loose from the circuit; (b) overheating continues when all secondary coil leads are disconnected?
22. State procedure if there is (a) no output from one of several scan derived PSs of a TV; (b) no HV and no output from any of the scan PSs? Explain your reasoning.

# 7 Vertical deflection circuits

This is the first of several chapters dealing specifically with TV receivers. Much of the detailed information presented here and in subsequent chapters is also applicable to VCR and computer monitors.

## 7-1 BEAM SCANNING AND RASTER DEVELOPMENT

Developing a raster on a TV or monitor picture tube is accomplished in the same manner as producing a raster on the camera CRTs at the station (Section 1-3). Under the electromagnetic influence of the deflection yoke, the electron beam(s) are deflected vertically and horizontally simultaneously to produce scanning lines that slope slightly downward to the right. In the process, picture images are produced by variations of beam intensity which are synchronized to the scanning.

Each top-to-bottom vertical scanning produces $262\frac{1}{2}$ horizontal lines, called a *field,* after which the beam is returned to the top of the screen. Following vertical retrace, another field comprising $262\frac{1}{2}$ lines is developed, with the lines *interlaced* with those of the preceding scanning. The resulting 525-line raster is called a *frame*. In practice, only about 480 of the lines are visible to the viewer. Some of the rest are blanked out at top and bottom of the screen; others are used up during vertical retrace. Although distinctly visible on a large screen, the lines are too closely spaced to be observed on a small screen. Scanning is very rapid, producing a frame (a complete picture) every $\frac{1}{30}$ of a second. The field scanning rate is 60 per second. Scanning continues uninterrupted, creating a picture with no noticeable flicker.

Picture quality depends in part on the spacing of the scanning lines. With upcoming state-of-the-art improvements, future sets will have approximately 1200 closely spaced lines for a greatly enhanced picture.

### Vertical Sweep Stages

The vertical sweep voltage is produced in one of two ways: in older sets, with an oscillator, and in most modern sets, using a digital-type countdown circuit. The terms *oscillator* and *sweep generator* are sometimes used interchangeably. The vertical sweep stages and their associated functions are shown in Figure 7-1. Note the alternative methods for generating the sweep voltage.

With one method, the vertical sweep originates with an oscillator that develops a 60-Hz voltage. To produce oscillations there must be some means of feedback, from output to input. In Figure 7-1 oscillations are developed and sustained by in-phase feedback from the output stage to the oscillator. Frequency is adjustable with the vertical hold control. The sync pulses received synchronize the oscillator with its counterpart in the station camera.

With the countdown system, the sweep voltage

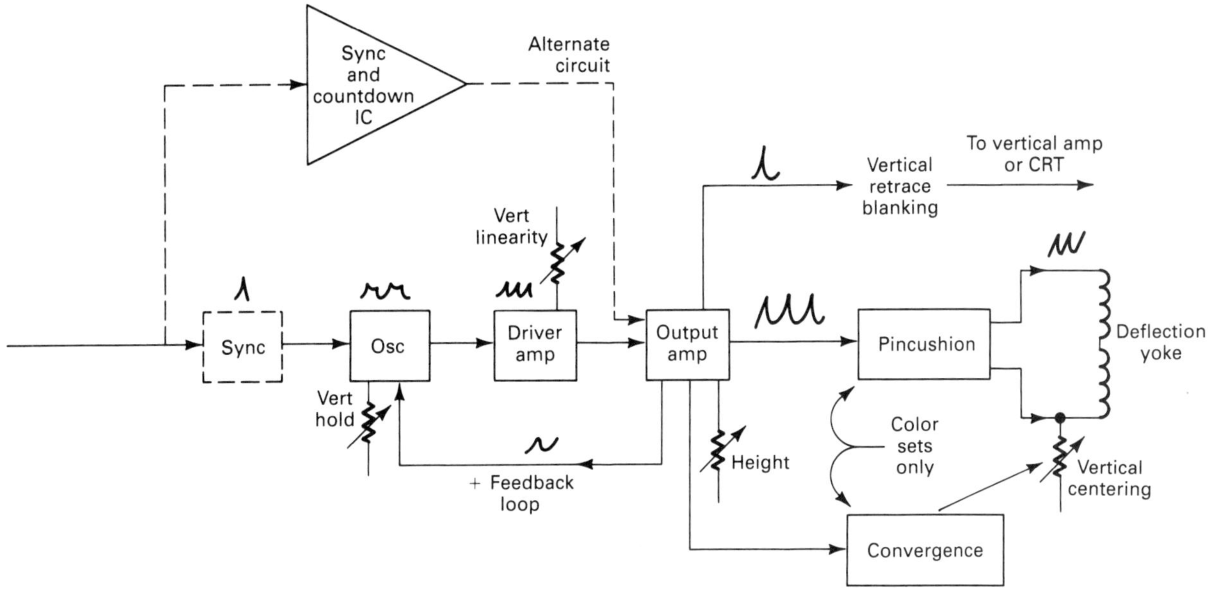


**FIG. 7-1** Vertical sweep stages. Except for the output amplifier, most functions in modern sets are performed by an IC.

is generated by a crystal-controlled oscillator whose relatively high frequency is subsequently reduced by one or more frequency dividers. Because of the inherent frequency stability, no front-panel controls are required. All functions are performed by a single IC. More on this later.

The driver amplifier (sometimes several stages) boosts the weak oscillator voltage, to drive the output stage. To ensure uniform spacing of the scanning lines and proper proportions of picture images, a linearity control may be provided to vary the shape of the sweep waveform. Drivers may be included in an IC or as separate discrete transistors. Sometimes a Darlington transistor is used as a predriver. The final driver is usually a medium-power type.

A power transistor is used in the output stage to develop sufficient sweep power to drive the yoke. A height control, found in any of the three stages, controls the amount of vertical deflection by controlling the sweep voltage amplitude. A sampling of the sweep voltage is used to darken the CRT screen during vertical retrace intervals. Without retrace blanking, retrace lines become visible. Some sets introduce a small amount of adjustable dc into the yoke to center the raster vertically.

On large-screen CRTs, the raster edges tend to bow inward or outward (pincushion effect). Monochrome sets use adjustable magnets to straighten the borders. Color sets accomplish this by feeding small amounts of vertical and horizontal sweep voltages into the yoke circuit. Similarly, sweep voltages are fed to a convergence yoke on the CRT neck to ensure that the colors produced by the three guns are in proper registry.

### Typical Vertical Oscillator Circuits

Figure 7-2 shows three basic circuits in common use. Circuit (a) is a multivibrator type of oscillator that uses two dc-coupled transistors. This is basically a conventional *RC*-coupled amplifier circuit with a feedback loop to sustain oscillations. Positive (in-phase) feedback is from the collector of one transistor back to the base input of the other. Frequency is controlled with variations of the B/E bias. Instead of a feedback loop, another type of circuit, called a common-emitter MV, uses the voltage developed across a resistor common to both transistors.

The third transistor (Q3) in Figure 7-2a functions as a sawtooth *waveshaper*. A sawtooth wave is required for linear beam deflection. When the transistor is turned off by the preceding stage, the waveshaping capacitor C charges from the B supply via the height control and its series resistor. During this charging period, the CRT beam is moving downward from top to bottom of the screen. When the oscillator becomes triggered by a sync pulse, Q3 is turned on, providing a low-resistance path to ground for discharge of the capacitor. Compared to the charging time, the discharge time is very short (see diagram), to ensure a rapid vertical retrace. Because of the nonlinear charging and discharging of the capacitor, only a portion of the curve is utilized, between the 37 and 63% levels, as shown. When the

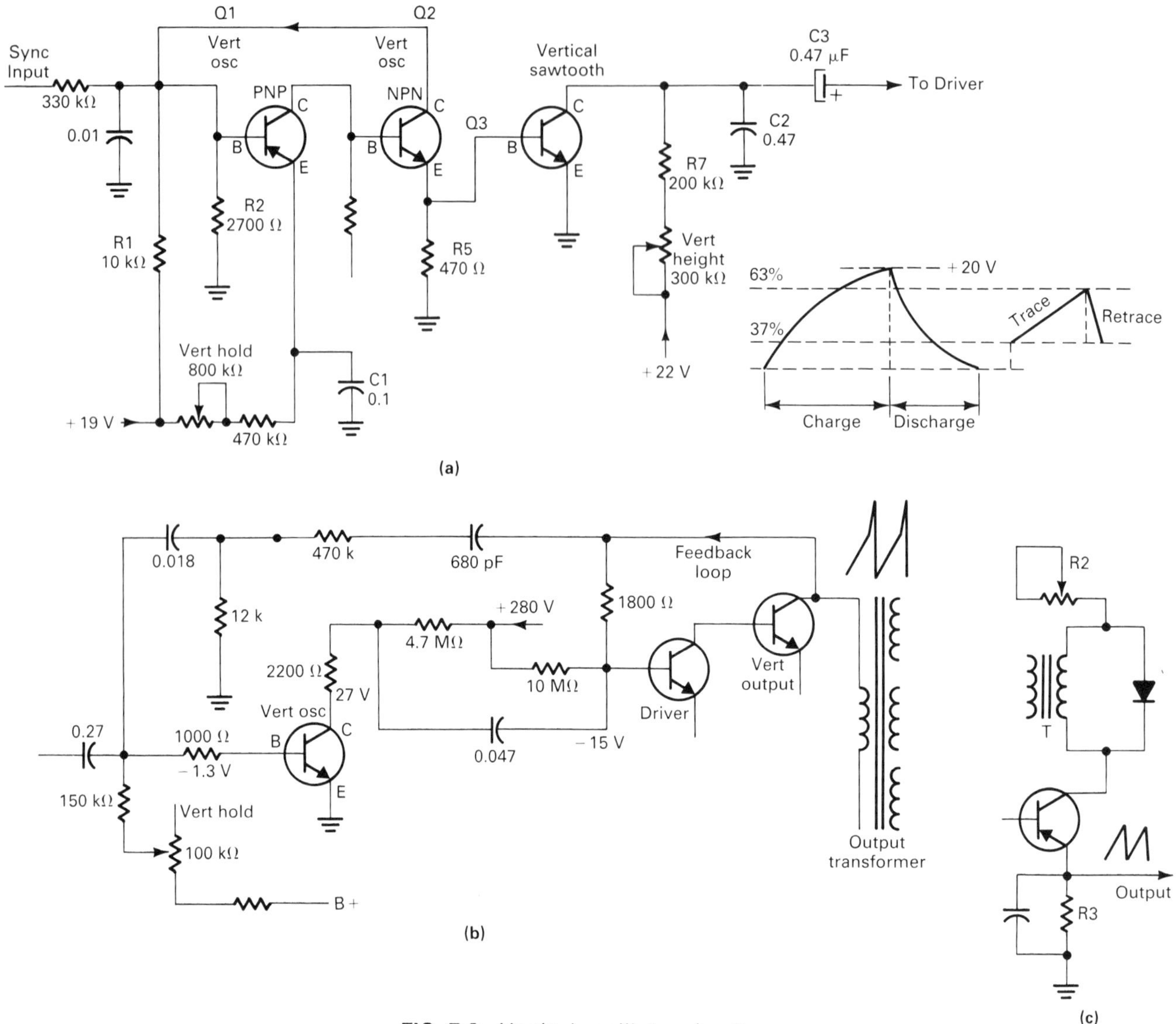


**FIG. 7-2** Vertical oscillator circuits.

oscillations reverse and the cycle is complete, Q3 is again turned off and the capacitor starts charging once more. The amount of charge buildup and the resulting amount of deflection depend on the *RC* time constant of the circuit, which is very critical. For example, the smaller the *R* and *C* values, the greater will be the sweep amplitude in the time alloted. But this at the expense of linearity since a larger portion of the charging curve will be utilized. However, loss of height and poor linearity can result from defects *anywhere* in the sweep circuit.

Figure 7-2b shows a multivibrator-type oscillator with feedback from the power output transistor back to the base input of the single-transistor oscillator. With this circuit, trouble in the output stage can result in a dead oscillator. Circuit (c) is called a *blocking oscillator*. Inductive feedback from collector to base is provided with a small transformer. Having a reverse bias, the transistor is in a nonconducting (blocked) state for relatively long periods. It is periodically turned on (unblocked) by the incoming sync pulses. The sweep voltage feeding the driver is taken from the emitter circuit.

### Countdown Sweep Generating System

This circuit as used in most modern sets generates both vertical and horizontal sweep voltages from a single crystal-controlled oscillator whose relatively high frequency is subsequently reduced with frequency *dividers* (Figure 7-3). The oscillator output of 503.5 kHz is reduced to 31,469 Hz by a divide-

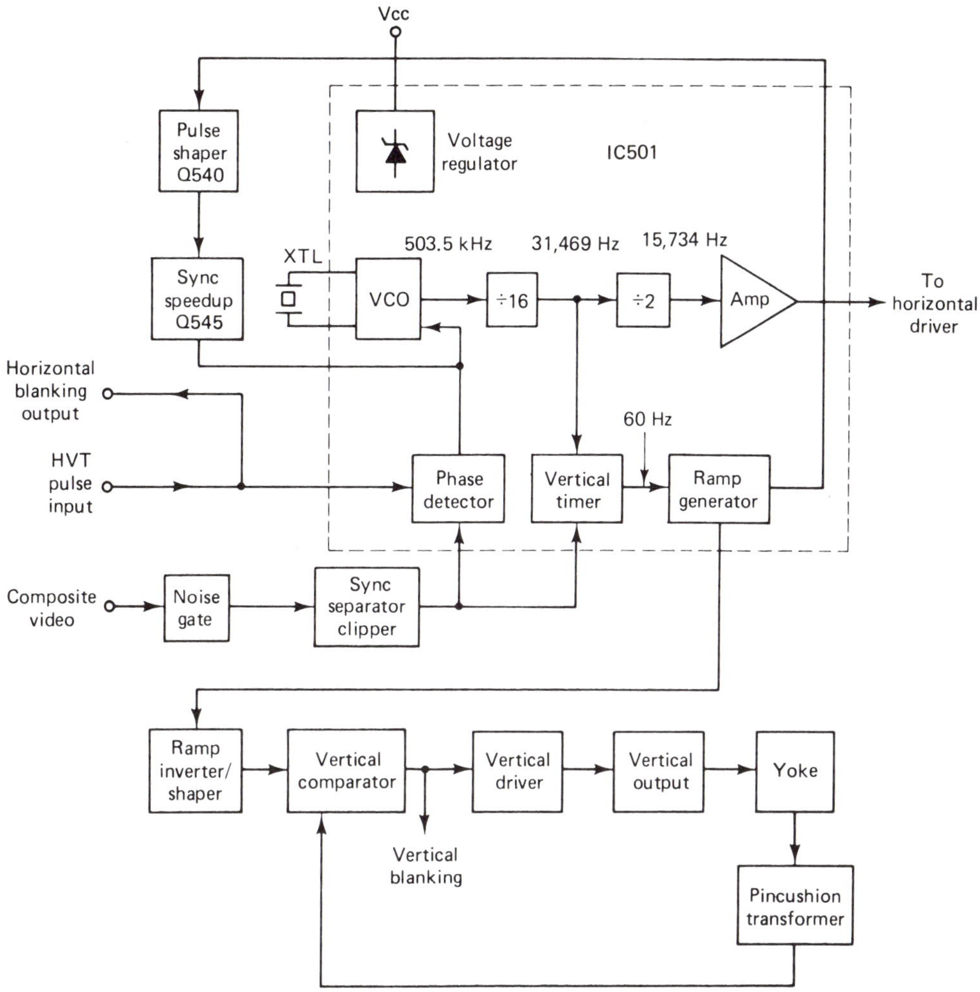


**FIG. 7-3** Countdown system. The countdown system is contained in IC501. Both vertical and horizontal sweep originates from a single oscillator. (Courtesy of General Electric.)

by-16 divider. A divide-by-2 divider further reduces the frequency by $\frac{1}{2}$ to provide the 15,734-Hz horizontal sweep voltage. The output of the 16 divider is also reduced to 59.94 Hz (approximately 60 Hz) by a vertical timer stage. The vertical sweep signal then goes through a number of waveshaping circuits, including a ramp generator to feed the vertical driver. Due to a high degree of frequency stability, this circuit obviates the need for vertical and horizontal hold controls. All functions are performed by a single IC.

## Synchronizing the Vertical Sweep

Developing picture images at precisely correct points on the screen relative to beam scanning at any given instant requires the vertical and horizontal sweep voltages to be synchronized with their counterparts at the TV station. This is accomplished with sync pulses that control the frequency *and phasing* of the generated sweep voltages relative to those at the station. After being separated from the video information, several vertical pulses are integrated into a single, sharply spiked pulse for triggering the oscillator.

In the absence of pulse control, an oscillator is in a free-running state and subject to frequency drift. Control is provided by the vertical sync pulses that are received as part of the composite video signal. In practice, the hold control is adjusted to the critical point where the sync pulses are able to trigger the oscillator.

Figure 7-4 illustrates how this is done. Sketch (a) shows the oscillator running slightly slow and the pulse arriving too late to take control. In (b), the pulse timing relative to the oscillator waveform is correct and the oscillator is triggered prematurely and thus under the control of the pulses. In (c), the

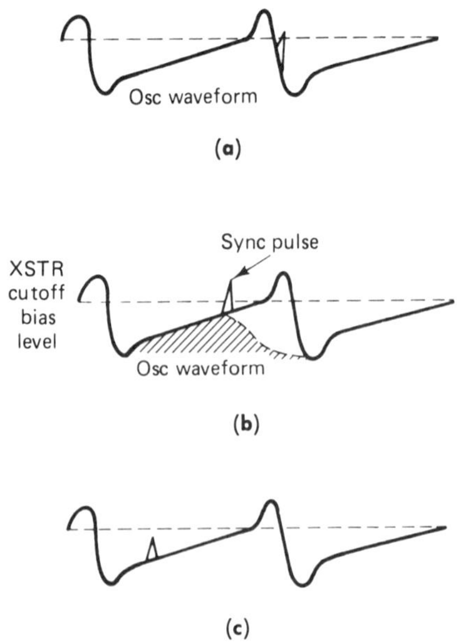


**FIG. 7-4** Oscillator triggering.

oscillator is running too fast and the pulse is not strong enough to reach the triggering level, resulting in loss of sync.

## 7-2 VERTICAL OUTPUT STAGE

Although voltage is required to produce a current flow, all inductances such as the deflection yoke are *current,* rather than voltage devices. To develop a sufficiently strong electromagnetic flux to deflect the CRT beam, especially on a large-screen tube, considerable sweep current is required, typically between 0.5 and 1 A. Voltage and current equates with *power,* necessitating the use of a *power amplifier* in the output stage. To obtain power output, a certain amount of drive power is also required, hence the need for a medium-power driver preceding the output transistor and the use of transformer rather than *R/C* coupling. To summarize, the following conditions must be satisfied:

1. The output amplifier must be capable of developing sufficient power to produce a raster that fills the screen vertically.
2. The output transistor must have adequate drive from the previous stage.
3. Sweep power must be efficiently transferred to the yoke (and convergence coils if a color set).

### Single-Ended Output Stage

A typical circuit for a small-screen monochrome set, including some alternate coupling methods, is shown in Figure 7-5. In this case a PNP transistor is used which is supplied from a negative voltage source. It is a conventional class A "common-emitter" amplifier biased to operate on the linear part of its curve. Note the input and output waveforms. With an input signal of 1 V p-p and an output of 50 V p-p, the voltage gain is 50. Maximum power transfer requires a 1:1 match between the transistor and the yoke. Hence a low-impedance yoke is used to match the low resistance of the transistor junction. Sometimes the two halves of the yoke are connected in parallel, sometimes in series. The shunting resistor is to suppress oscillations.

Because of its inductance, the yoke must be supplied with a voltage having a *trapezoidal* waveshape to produce a linear (sawtooth) current and linear beam deflection. The sharp spike on the wave-

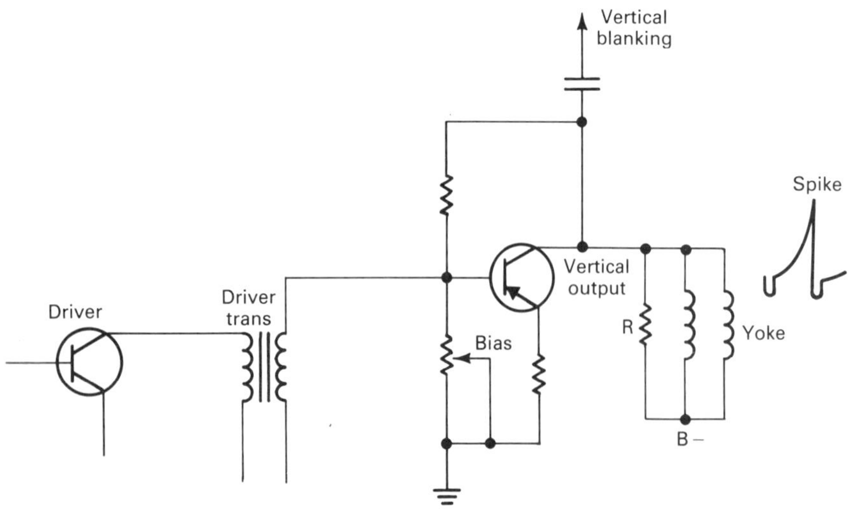


**FIG. 7-5** Single-ended vertical output circuit.

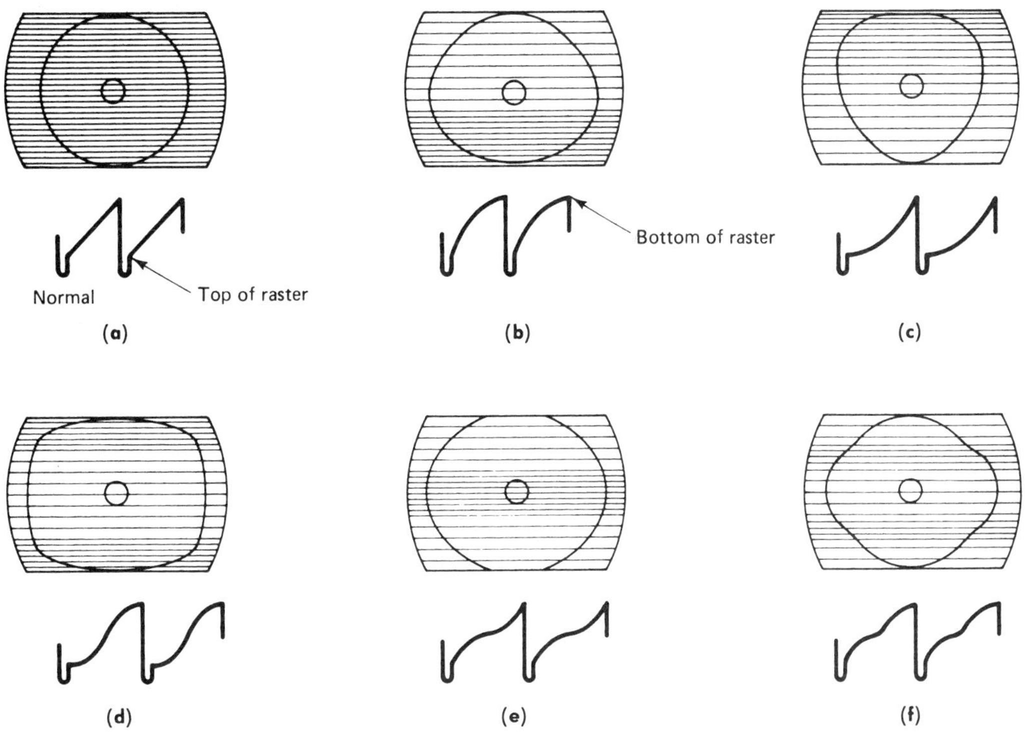

**FIG. 7-6** Waveshapes and vertical linearity.

form shown is the result of "shock excitation" of the yoke during the intervals of beam retrace. A sampling of the vertical sweep voltage is used to blank out (darken) the screen during vertical retrace intervals.

### Linearity

To obtain good linearity (normal picture proportions vertically), *current* in the yoke must increase at a linear rate, as produced by a linear sawtooth *current* waveform—regardless of the waveforms developed by the upstream vertical stages. Because of the yoke inductance, the applied sweep voltage must have a trapezoidal shape. Most schematics show the required waveforms. Figure 7-6 shows some examples of normal and abnormal waveshapes and their effects on raster and picture.

### Deflection Yoke

A yoke consists of two sets of coils, one set for vertical deflection, the other set for horizontal deflection of the CRT beam. There are two coils to each set: the vertical coils on the sides, the horizontal coils at top and bottom. A typical yoke configuration is shown in Figure 7-7. Since the need for horizontal deflection exceeds that of the vertical, the horizontal coils are positioned closest to the CRT neck for maximum influence on the electron beam(s).

The yoke has a low-loss ceramic (powdered iron) core. The diagram pictures a yoke for a large-screen BW set (note the adjustable pincushioning magnets); a color set yoke is similar but somewhat larger and wound with heavier wire. Yoke coils are sometimes shunted with built-in resistors to prevent "ringing" (i.e., sustained oscillations). In some cases there is also a thermistor or a voltage-dependent resistor (VDR) to maintain a constant amount of sweep, compensating for temperature and voltage variations.

Beam deflection follows the same principles that creates torque in an electric motor. Variations of sweep current produces a changing magnetic flux that interracts with the circular fields around the electron beam(s). Increases in vertical sweep current move the beam(s) from top to bottom of the screen; current reversals move it back to the top. Naturally, the stronger the current, the greater the deflection and raster height. Horizontal deflection is the same, but on a different plane.

The yoke is adjustable. It can be rotated to align the raster edges with the cabinet opening. It can also be moved back and forth along the neck. With a BW set it is positioned firmly against the CRT bowl. With a color set, its position is determined

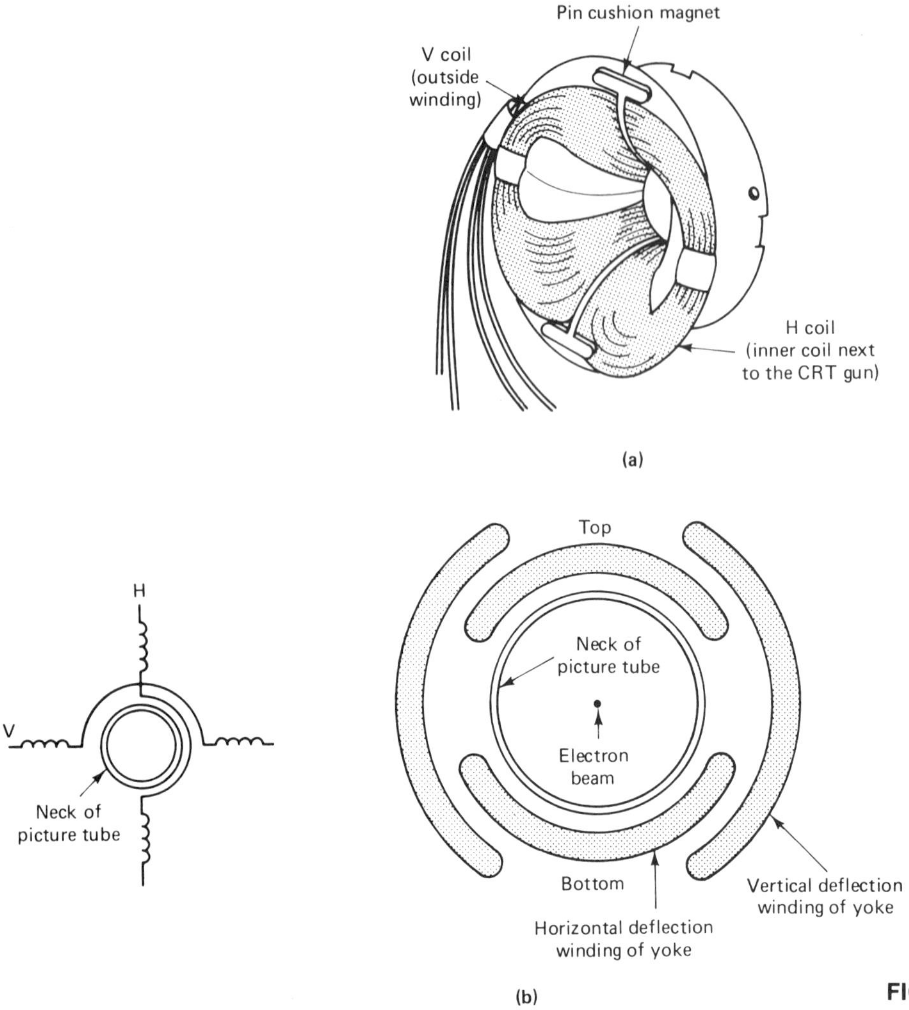


**FIG. 7-7** Typical deflection yoke.

experimentally while making setup adjustments. Wing nuts are provided to lock it in position.

## 7-3 COMPLEMENTARY-SYMMETRY OUTPUT AMPLIFIERS

There are several variations of this popular circuit, as shown in Figures 7-8 and 7-9. Each uses two power transistors operating in "push pull," conducting alternately, each taking over where the other leaves off and each providing one-half of the total sweep power. For optimum efficiency, the transistors operate either class AB or B, with current flow for only a portion of each cycle. The amount of current depends on several factors, such as the condition of the transistors, their operating voltages, especially the bias, and the amount of drive signal. Complementary-symmetry circuits are also used in audio output stages.

The circuit shown in Figure 7-8a uses unlike transistors, an NPN and a PNP, both operating in the emitter-follower configuration. They are supplied in series from a single B+ source, and for normal operation the voltage is split nearly equally between them. Capacitive coupling is used to feed the yoke and convergence coils and the pincushion circuit from the emitter junctions. A large-value capacitor is required because of the low (60-Hz) frequency, the low circuit impedance, and the relatively high yoke current requirements. Polarization is in accordance with the polarity of the B supply.

Circuit (b) also uses unlike transistors, but in this case they are supplied from two voltage sources of opposite polarity. This represents a zero dc voltage condition at the transistor junctions, thus permitting the yoke to be driven directly without a coupling capacitor. As in circuit (a), the two low-value emitter resistors are "fusible," to protect components in the event of an overload. One common problem with power transistors is *thermal run-*

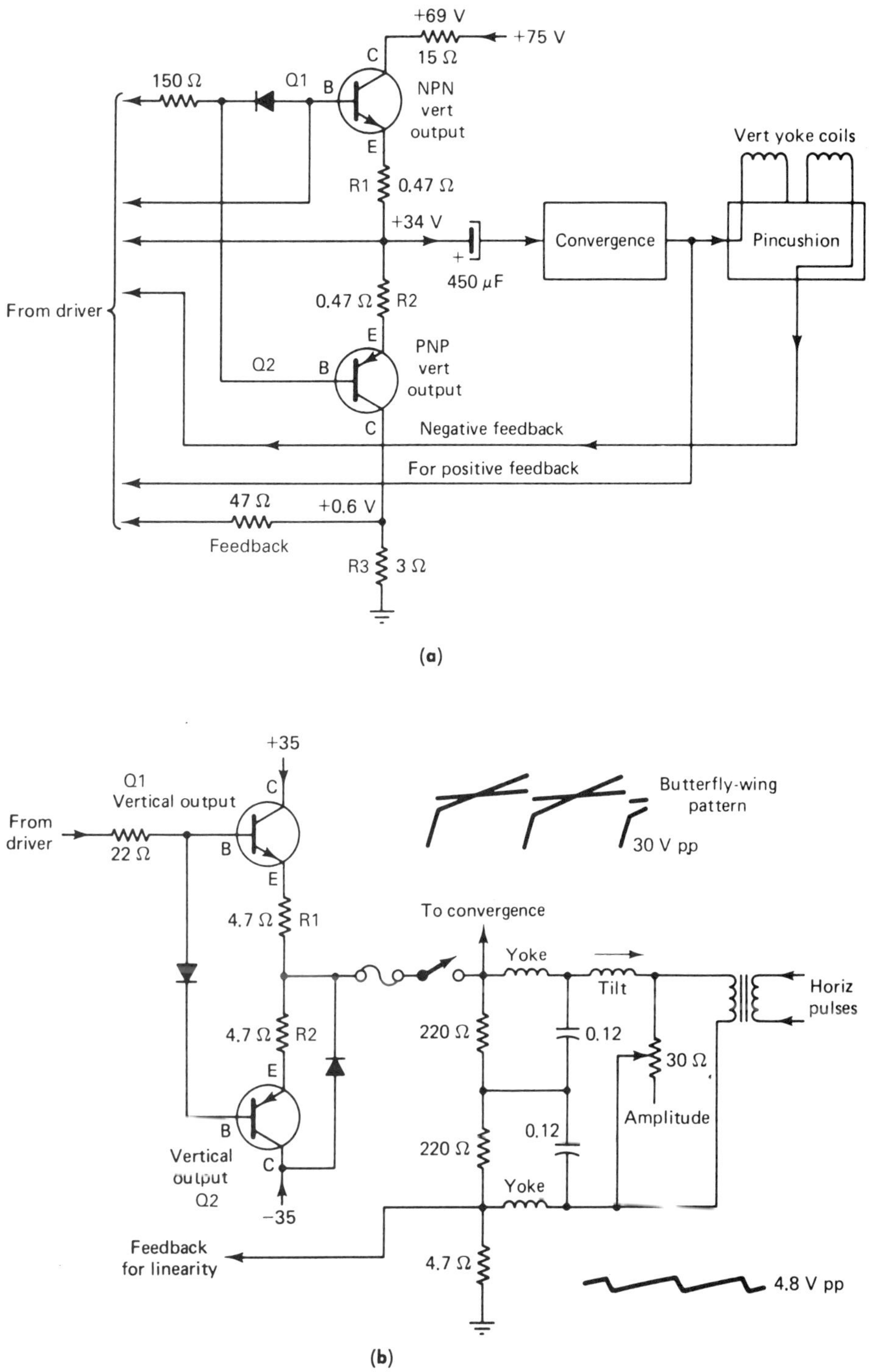


**FIG. 7-8** Complementary-symmetry output circuits.

*away,* a condition where incorrect operating voltages (particularly the bias) and junction leakage result in high current that progressively increases to damage or destroy the transistors and other components.

Except for the differences noted, operation of circuits a and b is almost identical. Initially, transistors Q1 are conducting due to a small forward bias and the Q2 transistors are turned off with reverse bias. The positive-going signal at the base of Q1 increases its conduction to supply sweep power to the yoke for scanning the upper half of the screen. When the increasing signal overcomes the bias on Q2, it starts conducting to furnish scan power for the bottom half of the raster. Transistor outputs combine at the junction of their emitters to drive the yoke.

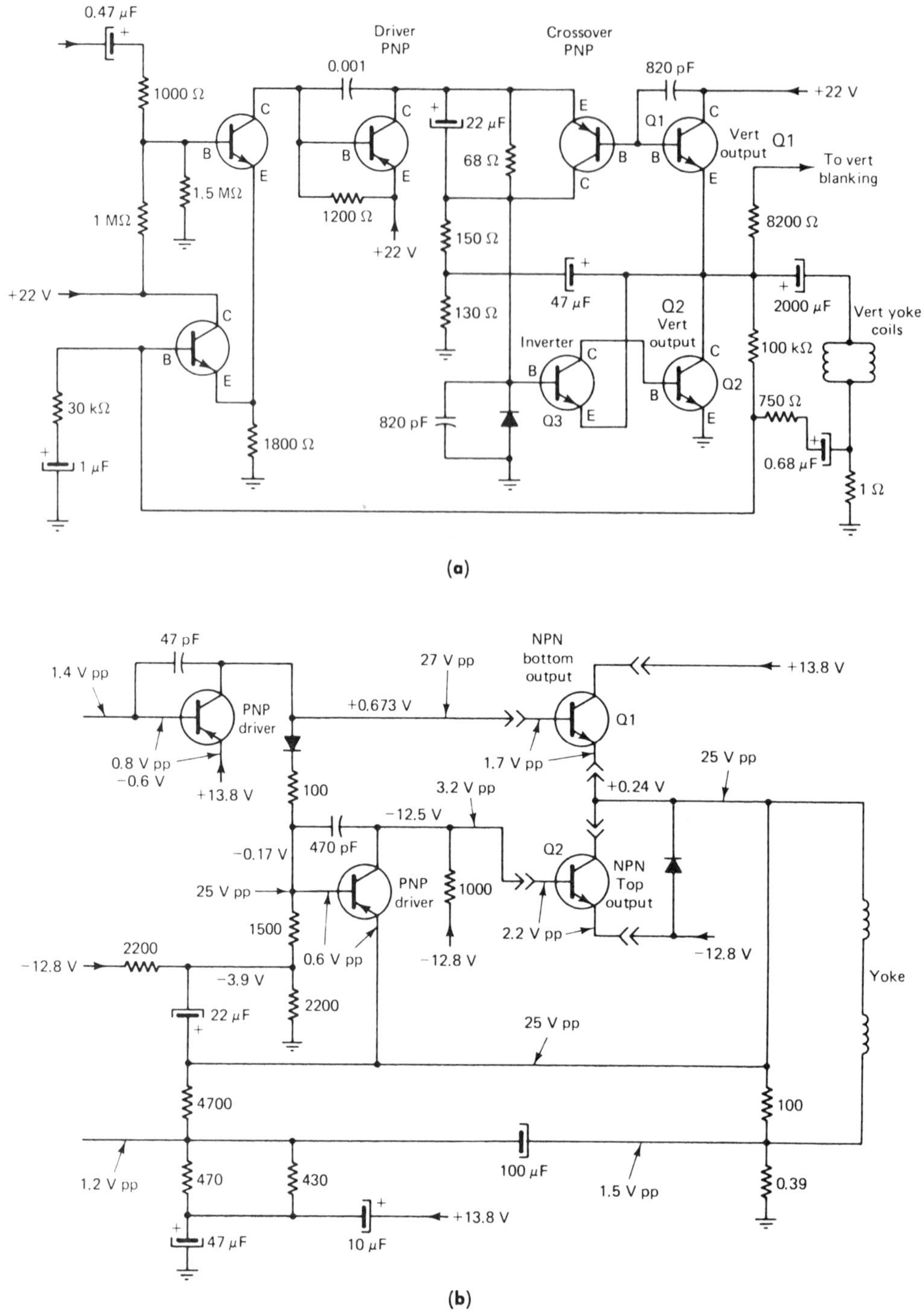


**FIG. 7-9** Quasi-complementary-symmetry circuits.

A problem peculiar to these circuits is *cross-over distortion,* which shows up as a notch at the center of the waveform and creates linearity problems midway down on the screen. The transistors normally conduct alternately, one taking over where the other leaves off. Problems occur if neither is conducting for a brief instant at the crossover point. Normally, this is prevented by introducing a small bias offset on one transistor, with a diode at the base inputs and the use of negative feedback. In some cases a trimpot is provided for critical adjustment of the bias. Insufficient forward bias reduces the amount of sweep; too much can result in thermal runaway.

### Quasi-Complementary-Symmetry Circuits

Two variations of this push-pull output amplifier are shown in Figure 7-9. Unlike the previous circuits described, these configurations use identical transistors (NPN types), one operating as an emitter follower, the other as a common-emitter amplifier. In circuit (a), both transistors are fed in series from one voltage source, each receiving one half the total. With dc at their junction, a blocking capacitor must be used to drive the yoke. Note its high value and the parallel yoke connections. Identical transistors must be driven with sweep voltages of opposite polarities. The phase inverter Q3 serves this function. A positive-going signal feeds Q1 directly, with an inverted (negative-going) signal driving Q2. Having different amounts of bias, the two transistors are alternately driven into conduction, Q2 providing the trace for the top half of the screen and Q1 for sweeping the bottom half. When both transistors are turned off, a self-induced kickback voltage in the yoke provides energy for beam retrace. Negative feedback is used to ensure equal drive to the two transistors.

Circuit (b) is supplied from two voltage sources of opposite polarities. With practically no dc at the junction of the transistors, the yoke can be driven directly with no need for a coupling capacitor. Here the yoke windings are in series. An inverter is required, which also functions as a driver amplifier.

*Raster Centering.* Any magnetic or electromagnetic influence will change the angle at which the CRT beam(s) strike the screen. With a BW set, this beam angle and the centering of the raster on the tube face are accomplished with a *centering ring*. This is a permanent-magnet device mounted on the rear of the electron gun. It consists of two flat, washer-like rings that are rotated one against the other.

A color set does it differently, by introducing a small amount of dc into the yoke coils. Normally, a yoke handles only the ac sweep voltage, and any dc current tends to develop flux that shifts the beam either up or down. Except for late-model sets that have no provision for centering, most sets use a potentiometer control for this purpose. The pot is usually fed from two low-voltage sources of opposite polarity. In some cases this reversible current is injected directly into the yoke circuit. Where there's direct coupling between the sweep stages and the yoke, this dc is applied to a driver stage, indirectly controlling the amount of dc current in the yoke.

*Other Vertical Sweep Functions.* In addition to furnishing sweep power for beam deflection, sweep voltage is also used for vertical retrace blanking and for color sets, providing vertical voltage to pincushion and convergence circuitry (see Chapter 17).

## 7-4 TYPICAL VERTICAL SWEEP CIRCUIT

In the foldout schematic, vertical sweep voltage is developed by the vertical oscillator (sawtooth generator) located in the large 42-pin multifunction IC (IC501). The free-running frequency is established by the *RC* time constant of capacitor C352 in conjunction with a number of resistors, including the hold control VR301. The sawtooth is developed by the on/off switching of two transistors in the IC. The oscillator is controlled by integrated sync pulses applied to pin 31. The oscillator signal is amplified by the vertical driver and exits via pin 26 to feed the vertical output amplifier in IC301 via pin 6. For heat dissipation, this power output IC is mounted on a heat sink. The output transistors are supplied with +24 V of scan power. The vertical sweep output at pin 2 of IC301 feeds the hot side of the yoke via a 1000-$\mu$F coupling capacitor, C353. Note the waveform and peak-to-peak voltage at WF15. Vertical blanking is fed from pin 8 of IC 301 to pin 22 of IC501, where it is superimposed on the chroma signal.

## 7-5 TROUBLESHOOTING AND REPAIR

Component breakdowns in deflection circuits are very common because of the high-amplitude sweep voltages and the high currents in the output stages. But fortunately, because of the multifunction ICs used in modern sets, there is little need for testing and replacing a lot of individual components. Due to the variety of vertical sweep trouble symptoms and the numerous possible causes, time spent analyzing each condition is well worthwhile. Depending on symptoms and circumstances, the general steps in troubleshooting (flowcharts, Figures 5-2 and 5-5) should be reviewed, followed by Figure 7-10, as a guide for specific problems.

Start with a thorough inspection, first with the set off, then with power applied while watching for anything obvious or unusual. With the help of the schematic and pictorial diagrams, locate and identify all components associated with the vertical sweep. Check for B+ at the main PS bus and the vertical branch circuits that supply transistors and ICs. Most modern sets use sweep-derived scan power, which means that a horizontal sweep defect can also disable the vertical stages, although it may not be immediately apparent since loss of HV means no raster.

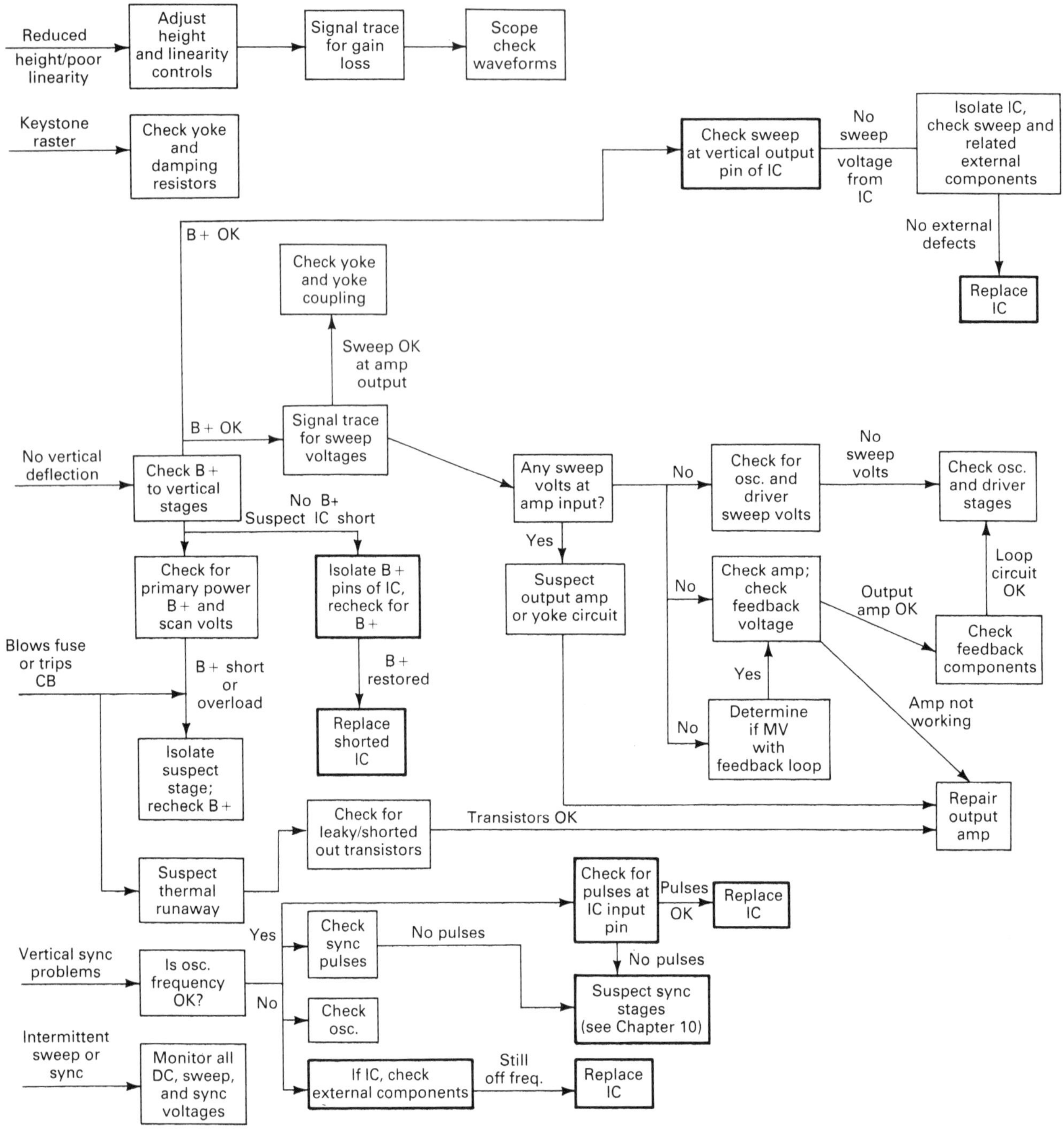


**FIG. 7-10** Vertical sweep troubleshooting flow drawing. The heavy black lines indicate ICs when used.

Where there is partial or complete loss of vertical sweep, attempt to localize the problem area by signal injection, signal tracing, or both. If the oscillator is functioning, follow its signal, stage by stage, using a scope, signal tracer, or a high-impedance ac voltmeter. Signal trace either upstream or downstream. With signal injection use an AF generator set for 60 Hz with a protective blocking capacitor (about 0.1 μF) series with the output cable. For complete loss of sweep (a bright horizontal line), turn down the brightness to avoid burning the screen.

Partial loss of raster height and other borderline conditions poses a more difficult troubleshooting problem. For such conditions a scope is the instrument of choice while making frequent references to waveforms shown on the schematic. Remember that waveshapes equate with linearity conditions, and amplitude with raster height.

If there is some form of raster, a preliminary adjustment of height, linearity, and the hold control can aid in analyzing the problem. Some interaction of controls can be expected, with some adjustments also affecting sync stability. Final adjustment of controls is made after repairs are completed.

### Localizing the Problem

The first objective is to localize the problem to one of four major areas: the sawtooth generating circuit (oscillator, switching, or countdown circuit), including the sync input; the buffer/driver stages; the power output amplifier; and the yoke circuit. Sweep-related circuits such as vertical blanking, raster centering, convergence, and pincushioning seldom give trouble.

*Oscillator, Switching, or Countdown Circuit.* A weak or dead sawtooth generator can be determined with a scope or ac voltmeter, preferably an EVM or DMM. For a multivibrator oscillator, with positive feedback from the output stage, first determine if the output amplifier is working (by signal substitution using a 60-Hz source with some *power* capability). If necessary, break into the feedback loop for further testing. The oscillator cannot function without sufficient feedback to sustain oscillations. Where the sweep signal originates from a switching or countdown circuit in an IC, check for sweep voltage at the appropriate IC pin. Refer to the schematic.

To achieve vertical sync, the sawtooth generator must be able to free run at the correct frequency before it can be locked in by the incoming sync pulses. Where a hold control is provided, it should be possible to roll the picture both up and down and to halt the roll momentarily at the approximate midsetting of the control. Oscillator circuits are extremely critical and the slightest defect can shift the frequency. If the frequency is okay but there is loss of sync, check for weak or missing pulses at the oscillator input or the sync input pin of an IC. Pulses must be of the proper amplitude and polarity to do their job. (Check with the schematic.) Touch the IC and if it is hot, it is probably shorted. But be absolutely certain that there are no external defects before considering replacement. Overlooked defects will inevitably result in destruction of the new unit when power is applied.

*Buffer/Drivers.* Most drivers operate as emitter followers to develop some drive *power* but little or no voltage gain. Check sweep voltage amplitude and waveshape at input and output and refer to the schematic. Where a driver defect is suspected, check the condition of the transistor or IC using voltage and resistance tests as appropriate. Because of its power dissipation, make sure that all heat sinks are in place. (*Reminder:* Do not be hasty in replacing transistors and ICs. If possible, first determine the *cause* of the failure and of any other breakdowns *resulting* from the failure.)

*Single-Ended Power Output Stage.* Check for sweep voltage (amplitude and waveshape) at input and output. Check the feedback loop if linearity or reduced height is the problem. Troubleshooting a single-ended stage is not too difficult but complementary-symmetry circuits can present a real challenge. Servicing such circuits is covered later in detail.

Since the output stage is supplied from the main primary power bus or secondary scan PSs, a B+ short or current overload will often blow a fuse, trip a circuit breaker, or destroy components. Where the transistor runs cold, determine why it is not conducting (e.g., the transistor is defective, there is an open collector or emitter circuit or a bias or drive problem). Transistor overheating (thermal runaway) is often a precursor of serious upcoming problems. Check for junction leakage, excessive forward bias, or inadequate heat sinking. Transistor leakage is very common, and incorrect operating voltages are often caused by the transistor itself. Make additional voltage checks with the transistor removed or isolated from the circuit. Check for a protective emitter circuit resistor that is burned open. When replacing an output transistor, use liberal amounts of silicone grease on both sides of insulator and be sure that the mounting screws are securely tightened. Where a current overload is suspected, it is a good idea to reduce the PS voltage and monitor the current to avoid further component damage. A low-wattage 110-V lamp in place of the line fuse or CB provides protection and gives a visual indication of relative current flow.

*Yoke Circuit.* Assuming normal sweep voltage at the amplifier output, check the sweep voltage at the yoke terminals. If low, and there is reduced raster height, check for a dried-up coupling capacitor (loss of capacity) or a shorted output transformer. For an off-center raster, check for dc at the yoke, where the cause may be a shorted or leaky coupling capacitor or an unbalanced output if it is a two-transistor circuit. Observe the correct polarity when replacing an electrolytic coupling capacitor.

For a keystone-shaped raster, suspect shorted yoke windings or, in rare cases, an open resistor across one yoke coil if they are in series. Check for shorted windings with a flyback/yoke tester or by substitution.

*Intermittent Sweep or Vertical Sync.* Monitor all dc, sweep, and pulse voltages while attempting to force the symptoms to appear (see Section 5-5).

### Burn-In Check

As a final step after making repairs, this should be a must, particularly with intermittent problems where the cause and remedies are at all in doubt. Also, an hour or more operating on the bench will often show up previously overlooked defects and provide a last-minute opportunity to make adjustments.

Troubleshooting procedures for specific vertical problems are described in the following paragraphs.

### Symptoms and Procedures

*Blows Fuse or Circuit Breaker Trips*

***Probable causes:*** Shorts or leakage in primary PS or voltage distribution network; shorts or leakage in transistors or ICs; excessive forward bias on driver or any power output transistors subject to thermal runaway.

With power off and capacitors drained, make a ohmmeter check from various B+ points to ground. A reading below a few hundred ohms indicates trouble. Follow procedures described in Section 5-2 to locate the short or leakage. When voltage checking, temporarily bridge a 110-V lamp across the blown fuse or CB to restore power, but avoid prolonged testing when there is an overload at the risk of further component damage. Try isolating suspected stages or components to see if the overload is relieved.

Feel transistors and ICs for possible overheating. Check transistors for junction leakage or shorts. Check bias in three ways: E to ground, B to ground, and B to E. The latter represents the true operating bias. Forward bias on an output transistor seldom exceeds 0.7 V, positive for an NPN type and negative for a PNP. Excessive forward bias results in overheating; too little bias prevents the transistor from conducting. For improper bias, suspect transistor leakage or shorts, defective voltage-dividing bias resistors, a shorted coupling capacitor from the previous stage, or other defects in upstream stages if direct coupling is used. Thermal runaway results in a gradual loss of raster height, variations in dc operating voltages, and component damage. (*Reminder: Before* replacing transistors, ICs, or other defective components, make sure that the breakdown was not the *result* of other circuit defects or the *cause* of component breakdowns yet to be discovered.)

*No Vertical Deflection.* (bright horizontal line across the center of the screen)

***Probable causes:*** Inoperative sweep generator, driver, or output stage; loss of B+ to vertical stages; open yoke; service switch defective or at wrong position.

Turn down the brightness to avoid burning the screen. Check for B voltage, and if missing, check for B+ shorts or an open voltage distribution resistor.

If there is B voltage, localize the trouble to one stage by signal tracing or signal injection. Once localized, check for a bad transistor, IC, or other component in that stage. Measure and evaluate the transistor and IC operating voltages compared with those specified on the schematic. Perform resistance tests from each IC and transistor terminal in reference to ground, and compare with the service data. Decide what defects could account for abnormal readings.

An open series-connected yoke coil, although rare, causes loss of sweep. Perform a continuity check. One open or shorted coil in a parallel connected yoke results in a keystoned raster. If the yoke is okay, and there is normal output from the amplifier(s) but partial or complete loss of sweep, suspect the coupling device: an open/dried-up coupling capacitor or defective transformer.

*Shrinking Raster Height.* (sometimes during receiver warmup)

***Probable causes:*** Thermal runaway in driver or output transistors; defective resistor or thermistor in output stage or yoke circuit; or poor dc voltage regulation.

If the output transistors overheat, check for the causes of thermal runaway, as described earlier. Monitor dc and sweep voltages during warm-up. Apply localized heat or cold to suspected components.

### Reduced Height and Poor Linearity

***Probable causes:*** Almost any defect in the sweep stages; in particular, suspect low B+, transistor or IC leakage, thermal runaway in driver or output stage, imbalance in complementary-symmetry output transistors, shorted windings in the output-stage coupling transformer where used, or feedback circuit defects.

Height and linearity problems often coexist. If sync stability is also impaired, suspect the sawtooth generating stage. If sync is ok, concentrate on the driver/output stages. Localize the trouble by signal tracing, signal injection or both. Compare waveshapes and p-p amplitudes at inputs and outputs with those shown on the schematic. Careful study and evaluation of waveform patterns often provides good clues. Some examples of waveforms, raster height, and linearity conditions are shown in Figure 7-11.

Drivers are emitter followers with a gain of unity, and any voltage gain indicates trouble in that stage. Low drive causes reduced beam deflection, and no drive results in a total loss of sweep. Where sweep voltage is lost or reduced at some point, try signal substitution and check for possible loading from defects in adjacent circuits. Isolate circuits for further testing. Where there is no output from a multivibrator oscillator that uses feedback from the driver or output stage, check these two stages *first* before investigating the oscillator input circuit. Make dc voltage and resistance checks in suspected stage. Common defects include bad diodes, transistors and ICs, defective resistors and capacitors, and dried-up yoke coupling capacitors.

*Other Linearity Problems.* (the picture may be stretched or compressed at the top, bottom, or center)

***Probable causes:*** Improperly adjusted height and linearity controls; most any sweep circuit defect, including low B+.

Adjust controls for uniform spacing of scanning lines or those produced by a bar/crosshatch signal generator. If the problem persists, scope check the waveforms at the input and output of each stage and compare with those shown on the schematic. Where some abnormal waveshapes are found, try checking the *current* waveform in the yoke, which *must be* a linear sawtooth. Break into the yoke circuit, inserting a 1- or 2-Ω high-wattage resistor. The scope display across the resistor should be a perfect sawtooth, as shown in Figure 7-11a. Note the linear rise in current and the rapid dropoff.

If the set has no linearity control, check the shape and amplitude of voltages in negative feedback loops and compare with the schematic. Such feedback voltages are quite critical and greatly affect height and linearity conditions. Break the loops and check all associated components.

### Raster Not Centered Vertically

***Probable causes:*** Vertical centering adjustment; dc leakage into yoke circuit; linearity problems; unbalanced output transistors if directly coupled to yoke.

What seems like a centering problem can be mistaken for other conditions: for example, excessive vertical blanking will darken the top portion of the screen, giving the appearance that the raster needs moving up. Poor linearity with crowding top or bottom can also add to the confusion since it gives the raster an off-center look. If in doubt, turn down the brightness and disable the vertical sweep to see if the horizontal trace is centered. Any dc current in yoke coils will offset the centering. This can be determined with a dc current or voltage check. This can occur if there is leakage in the amplifier-to-yoke coupling capacitor, or if directly coupled, an imbalance in the push-pull output transistors. A defective centering pot or its associated resistors can make the control ineffective. With a BW set, a weak centering ring is not uncommon.

### Deflection Problems for Top or Bottom Half of Screen (Push-Pull Amp)

***Probable causes:*** One output transistor not contributing its share of the sweep; unbalanced outputs; unbalanced input voltages from driver stages; a few shorted yoke windings with slight keystoning.

Determine from the schematic which output transistor is responsible for the portion of screen where there is little or no deflection. Concentrate on that circuit. Measure and record all dc operating voltages at suspect transistor. Typical values are shown in Figure 7-12. If there is an imbalance in circuits (a) and (c), the source voltage will not be split equally between the two transistors. This provides a clue to which circuit is at fault. An imbalance in circuits (b) and (d) results in some dc at the yoke where there should be none.

Feel both transistors, comparing their operating temperatures. Test the suspect transistor. If it's

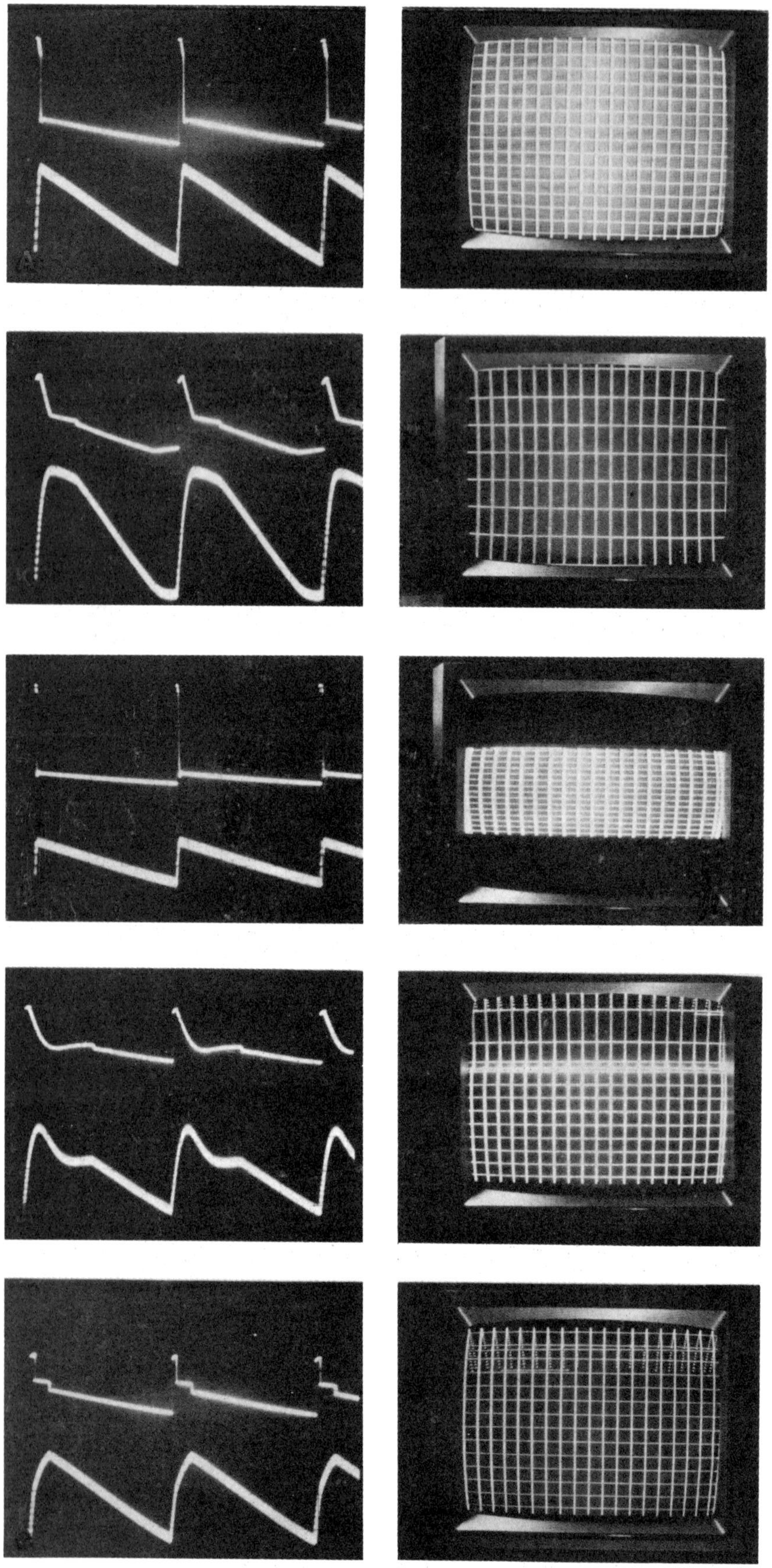

(a)

(b)

(c)

(d)

(e)

**FIG. 7-11** Waveforms and height and linearity conditions: (a) normal waveforms, normal deflection and linearity; (b) excessive height and stretched picture; (c) reduced height, good linearity; (d) stretched at the top with crossover distortion; (e) top foldover. Top displays: sweep voltage waveforms at amplifier output. Bottom displays: Yoke current waveforms.

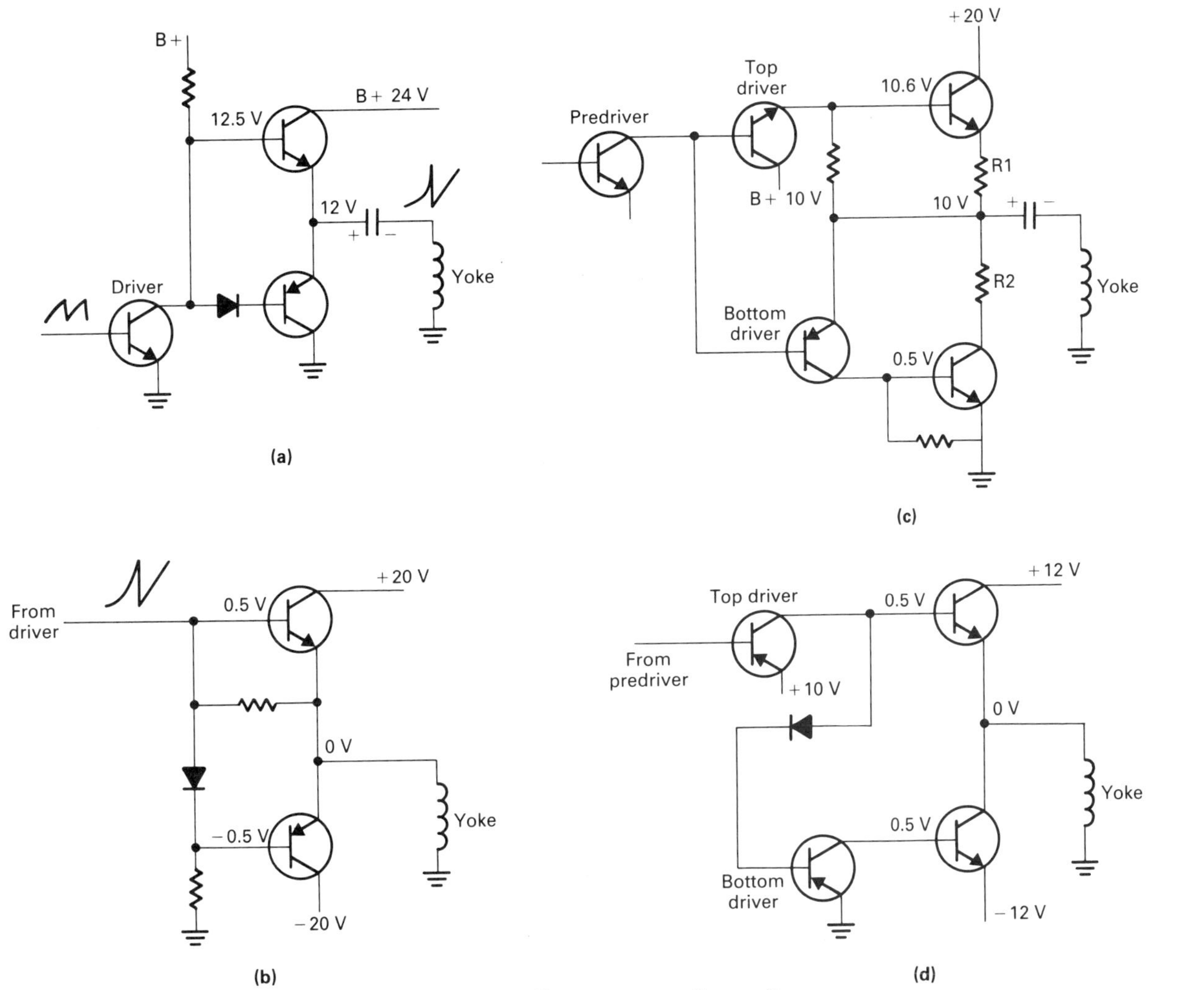


**FIG. 7-12** Push-pull output operating voltages.

overheating, there may be junction leakage. Check for excessive forward bias, and if so, check the bias emitter resistor and the bias voltage dividers. Check for a leaky coupling capacitor or, if dc coupling, a defect in the upstream driver stage. (*Reminder:* Bias is measured from base to emitter, not in reference to ground.) With silicone transistors the normal (no drive) forward bias is approximately 0.6 V, and any significant increase results in high current and overheating. Check with the schematic. Determine the current drain of each transistor by measuring and comparing the *IR* voltage drops across the emitter resistors. When subjected to overload, these low value resistors often open up or change value.

If the suspect transistor runs cold, it is not conducting; if slightly warm, it is conducting, but not enough. Assuming that the transistor checks okay, test for loss of collector voltage, an open circuit, loss of forward bias, or insufficient drive signal. Operating as a class AB or B amplifier (biased close to cutoff), the transistors require adequate drive signals to develop full output current. Scope check the input and output sweep voltages. At the inputs of the output transistors, their amplitudes should be nearly equal but of opposite polarity. If any discrepancies, check the phase inverter and check for possible loading by the output circuit. If necessary, remove or isolate the transistors and recheck the sweep voltages. Consult the schematic for proper waveforms and amplitudes. Typical examples are shown in Figure 7-11. (*Reminder:* In the absence of a drive signal a transistor will conduct, but there can be no sweep output.)

Some sets use a driver as one-half of a multivibrator oscillator, with positive feedback from the driver back to the oscillator input. This can create a servicing problem because there can be no driver input unless the oscillator is working and no oscillations if there is a driver defect. The trick is to break the feedback loop and troubleshoot each stage individually, starting with the driver.

Many late-model sets include the drivers and

output amplifiers in an IC (the foldout schematic, for example). In such cases, troubleshooting is limited to checking dc voltages, input and output sweep voltages, external defects, and if necessary, replacing the IC.

When one of two output transistors checks bad, they should *both* be replaced as a matched pair, even though one seems okay. Make sure that PNP and NPN types are not inadvertently installed in the wrong sockets. Make sure that the mica or plastic insulating wafers are not cracked, and use plenty of silicone grease on both insulators and transistors. Secure transistors firmly to their heat sinks. As a final step it is a good idea to recheck their operating voltages one more time, just to be sure.

### Dark Area at Top or Bottom of Screen

***Probable causes:*** There are several possibilities: raster off center vertically; poor linearity; reduced height; vertical blanking problems; unbalanced outputs from push-pull amplifiers; neck shadows.

With a centering problem, the top or bottom portion of the picture may be lost with a sharply defined black border at the other extreme, either top or bottom. If dark at both top and bottom, there is obviously a loss of height. A gradual shading, usually at the corners, is probably neck shadows. For this, adjust the yoke positioning, and for a BW set, the centering ring.

A gradual shading with a loss of picture across the top of the screen indicates *prolonged* vertical blanking due to a bad resistor or capacitor in the blanking circuit *RC* network or a defective blanking transistor if there is one. Unbalanced push-pull outputs, as described earlier, causes reduced deflection for the upper or lower halves of the raster.

### Bright Narrow Strip across Center of Screen

***Probable causes:*** A defect in the push-pull output stage as caused by incorrect bias (crossover notch distortion) or signal overdrive; picture foldover; a linearity problem or a bad CRT.

Crossover distortion occurs if both output transistors are conducting, or not conducting, at the time of crossover. The scanning lines may be expanded or compressed in this area. As shown in Figure 7-11, the crossover blip or notch can be seen readily with a scope display. Compare the operating voltages of both transistors with those called out on the schematic. The offset bias, in particular, is very critical. Check the dc at the common output of the two transistors for possible imbalance. Check all components at the base input circuits of both transistors, especially diodes for leakage.

Scope check and compare the signal drives at each transistor input. If considerably different in amplitude, check for defects in the drivers or phase inverter. Signal overdrive can also create crossover problems. Where the cause is elusive, try replacing both output transistors and the drivers—or the IC if one is used.

Where there is picture foldover on the bright horizontal line across the screen, and a possible linearity problem, localize the trouble by scope checking for abnormal waveshapes at all vertical stages. A bad picture tube can cause streaking, a similar condition. Try tapping the CRT neck or adding an isolation booster.

### Picture Foldover. (part of the picture is inverted, with overlap)

***Probable causes:*** Incorrect oscillator frequency or phasing; sawtooth-shaping circuit defect; extreme linearity problems in driver or output stage.

Foldover may be observed at either the top or bottom of the screen. Adjust vertical hold to see if one complete picture can be obtained, and if not, it is an oscillator problem. Check all voltages and components. A defective or wrong-value component in the *RC* sawtooth forming network can create this problem by extending the time of beam retrace. Scope check the sweep voltage in the output stage, comparing it with the sync rate.

### Edges of Raster Not Straight or Parallel with Mask Opening

***Probable causes:*** Anti-pincushioning defects or adjustments.

With BW sets, adjust positions of the pincushioning magnets near the bowl of the CRT. If ineffective, check for weak magnets. If necessary, remagnetize them. If a large-screen color set, try adjusting the pincushion controls in accordance with service manual instructions while observing a crosshatch pattern on the screen. If problems persist, check all pincushion circuit components, replacing any that are suspect or defective.

### Keystone-Shaped Raster

***Probable causes:*** Open or shorted yoke coils; an open damping resistor across one coil section.

A wedge-shaped raster occurs if both sections of the yoke do not produce equal amounts of deflection. Shorted windings is common, but an open coil is seldom found unless due to abuse or internal arcing. With a parallel hookup, one open or shorted coil results in keystoning; with a series connection an open coil results in a total loss of sweep. Shorted vertical coils produce a raster narrowed at the left or right sides. With shorted horizontal coils, the narrowing is at the top or bottom. Perform a continuity check, comparing the resistance of the two vertical yoke coils. They should be equal. The narrowed part of a wedge is directed toward the winding that is shorted.

Try removing the yoke from the tube neck leaving the connections intact. Turn brightness completely off to prevent burning the screen. Turn the set on for a short period while watching for internal arcing between windings. Remove the power and feel the coils. A coil with shorted windings will be noticeably warm.

Other tests can be made with a flyback/yoke tester as described in Chapter 4, or by ringing the yoke with an AF generator and a scope.

*Raster Breathing.* (scanning lines rhythmically expand and contract as a hum bar moves slowly up through the raster)

***Probable cause:*** Poor filtering of primary PS.

This is caused by the changing phase relationships between the ac power line and ripple voltage on the B+ feeds to the vertical sweep stages. Check for open or dried-up filters or an active power filter defect.

*Overheating Components.* (accompanied by vertical sweep problems)

***Probable causes:*** A B+ short or current overload.

For overheating resistors in the vertical stages, look for the short or overload at the end of the resistor that has the lowest voltage or resistance reading in reference to ground (see Section 5-2). The usual causes of an overheating transistor are a shorted or leaky junction, or excessive forward bias. The latter may be due to the transistor itself. For an overheating IC, suspect an internal short or the internal transistors are drawing excessive current, because the IC is defective, or due to external defects, which should be checked out before contemplating replacement.

*Vertical Retrace Lines on Picture.* (widely spaced, white sloping lines)

***Probable causes:*** Vertical blanking circuit defect; master brightness or RGB controls set too high; unstable vertical sync or improperly adjusted hold control; weak signal if an older set.

Retrace lines are normally blanked out by a differentiated sampling of the vertical sweep voltage applied directly or indirectly to the CRT. Scope check the blanking voltage, comparing p-p amplitude and polarity with that shown on the schematic. If blanking pulses are weak or missing, check for an open coupling capacitor or a defective resistor in the *RC* network. Check for an inoperative blanker transistor if there is one, and its circuit components. Check for insufficient negative bias on the CRT when the brightness is turned up. Trouble is indicated if the screen cannot be darkened with the brightness control turned down. The cause may be in any upstream stage that is dc coupled to the CRT. During CRT setup adjustments, try backing off on the master brightness and RGB controls.

*Burned-Out Emitter Resistors in Push-Pull Output Stage*

***Probable causes:*** Shorted or leaky power output transistors; shorted or grounded yoke if dc coupled from amplifier; excessive forward bias on transistors.

These low-value resistors (typically about 3 Ω) contribute to bias voltage and function as fuses in the event of an overload. Restore circuit operation with a temporary short across the open resistor(s), and after a short operating period, check transistors for overheating. Quickly check base and collector voltages, plus the drive voltage, then remove power. Check the transistors and if defective, replace as a matched pair. If bias voltage is still high, a driver circuit defect is the probable cause. Check the yoke circuit, and the coupling capacitor if there is one, for leakage. Replace the burned-out emitter resistors. Restore power, recheck all voltages, and monitor the transistors for possible overheating.

*Picture Inverted or Transposed Left to Right*

***Probable cause:*** Yoke is rotated or its connections reversed.

This can occur during servicing, especially when replacing a yoke. If rotated 180°, the picture will be inverted and transposed. If vertical yoke connections are reversed, the picture will only be inverted. If horizontal leads are reversed, the picture will be transposed, but this may not be immediately apparent until lettering appears on the screen.

*Power Output Transistors Have Short Life*

***Probable causes:*** Same as for thermal runaway. Also check the heat sink and for adequate ventilation.

*Yoke Ringing.* (wavy scanning lines and picture distortion on the left side of the screen)

***Probable cause:*** Crosstalk (horizontal sweep voltage induced from horizontal yoke into vertical yoke coils).

This problem occurs most commonly with series-connected yokes. Check for an open damping resistor after disconnecting one end from the coil, (the shunting effect of the low-resistance coil can result in a misinterpreted reading). If some loss of sweep amplitude can be tolerated, try reducing the resistor values. Try a different value of capacitor across the horizontal yoke.

*Poor Interlacing.* (pairing of scanning lines)

***Probable causes:*** Unstable vertical sawtooth generator; signal overdrive causing sync pulse compression or clipping; a B+ filtering problem; misadjusted vertical hold control.

Pairing means nonuniform spacing of the scanning lines. In extreme cases the lines developed by the odd and even line fields may overlap, reducing picture resolution by 50%. In less serious cases the line spacing may be nonuniform, sometimes accompanied by vertical jitter and a corresponding degradation of picture quality. It may be either a sync or a vertical sweep problem. Critically adjust the hold control to where the picture just starts to move upward. It should lock abruptly into sync. If it does not, scope check for weak sync pulses at the oscillator input. Weak pulses are often the result of clipping or compression in a video amplifier stage, as described in Chapter 14. A clue to this is where sync and interlacing problems occur only on the strongest channel received.

If the picture cannot be rolled in both directions, it is a problem of frequency drift or a hold control circuit defect. Monitor the oscillator output with a frequency counter if available. Troubleshoot the oscillator, or if an IC, replace it.

*Vertical Sync Problems.* (examples are picture roll, jitter, multiple pictures, split or divided picture, and critical hold control)

***Probable causes:*** Sawtooth generating circuit defect; weak or missing vertical sync pulses.

It should be possible to roll the pix up and down and stop the roll, at least momentarily, at the approximate midsetting of the hold control. If not, there is a frequency error, or drift, which calls for troubleshooting the oscillator, switching circuit, or the IC countdown circuit. (*Note:* With some older sets, because of circuit interactions, good sync lock-in depends on the relative settings of the height, linearity, and vertical peaking controls.) If there is a need to adjust the hold control frequently (especially if the picture locks in at one extreme setting), check for frequency drift with a counter. Alternately heat and cool all suspected frequency-related components. Junction leakage in an oscillator transistor is quite common; if suspected, try substitution or replacement. As an aid to localizing a fault, try signal substitution using an AF generator. If the hold control is erratic or overly critical, cleaning or replacement may be necessary.

Where the sawtooth generator produces a correct and stable frequency, but there is one or more symptoms of sync trouble, scope check for weak or missing pulses at the oscillator or IC input, and if necessary, upstream through the sync stages to their point of origin, the sync takeoff (see Chapter 9). If sync and sweep stages are contained in an IC, first determine if there are any external defects, then, if necessary, replace the IC.

*Vertical Convergence Problems.* (colors are not in registry)

***Probable causes:*** Improper CRT setup adjustments; defective adjusters or circuitry; weak magnets; defective convergence yoke or a bad CRT.

Assuming that the CRT is thoroughly degaussed and all adjustments have been attempted but good convergence is not obtained except perhaps near the center of the screen, suspect a *dynamic convergence* problem. Scope check for a proper parabolic-shaped vertical sweep voltage of the correct amplitude at all three vertical coils on the convergence assembly (refer to the schematic). If the voltage is okay, check for open or shorted windings.

If the parabolic voltage is weak, missing, or improperly shaped, scope trace it to its source, the vertical output stage. Troubleshoot all related circuitry, including the adjusters, replacing all suspected components. Reconverge as described in Chapter 17.

*Vertical Sweep IC Problems*

***Probable causes:*** Defective IC; an external defect; loss of B+ to the IC.

Where most or all sweep functions are performed by a multifunction IC, the IC itself is immediately suspect. But before considering replacement, rule out the possibility of defects *external* to the IC. Failure to do so can result in destruction of the new IC.

Depending on the symptoms, start by checking for B+ at the proper pin or pins (see the schematic). If there is little or no B+, there are three possibilities: no B+ coming from the PS, its being grounded out by the IC, or transistors in the IC are drawing excessive current. With the set off and after grounding out any residual circuit voltage, make an ohmmeter check from the B+ pin to ground. If reading is less than a few hundred ohms, open the circuit to isolate the IC from its voltage source. If source voltage is restored to normal, the IC is at fault.

Check for the presence of dc voltage on IC pins where there should be none. Such an unwanted voltage may be due to an external defect or the IC itself. Break the circuit to see if the voltage disappears. If it does not, the IC is bad.

Scope check for sweep voltage at the IC output pin. If weak or missing, break the circuit as a check for possible loading by defects in the external circuitry. If the sweep voltage output is okay and the output amplifiers are in the IC, check the yoke circuit. If discrete external transistors are used, troubleshoot the output circuit as described previously. If the IC is still suspect, replace it.

### *Vertical Sync IC Problems*

***Probable causes:*** Defective IC; loss of B supply voltage to sync circuits; sync circuit defects external to the IC.

Where sync circuits are contained in a multifunction IC, follow the same general troubleshooting procedure as described for sweep problems. Assuming that no dc voltage problems exist, scope check for sync pulses at the IC input pin. If pulses are weak or missing, make an ohmmeter check to see if they are grounded out by an internal defect. Break the circuit to see if normal pulses are coming from the sync stages, and if not, why. If no external defects are found and the sync problem persists, replace the IC.

### *Intermittent Vertical Sweep or Sync*

***Probable causes:*** Intermittent component defect; bad soldering; intermittent wiring shorts or open circuits (e.g., hairline cracks or solder splashes on a PCB).

Monitor dc, sweep, and sync voltages while attempting to make the trouble symptoms appear (see Section 5-5). For obscure and difficult problems (dogs) replace suspected components including ICs, and if warranted, even an entire module or IC mother board.

## QUESTIONS

1. Explain how a sawtooth wave is developed in an oscillator or switching circuit.
2. What points on a vertical sawtooth waveform correspond to the top and bottom of a raster?
3. With a sawtooth wave, there must be a linear increase in voltage followed by a rapid dropoff. Give the reason for each.
4. What are the advantages of a countdown sweep generating circuit over an oscillator?
5. Give some symptoms of an off-frequency vertical oscillator.
6. With excessive vertical retrace time, the lower part of a picture appears at the top of the screen. Explain.
7. What is crossover distortion with a push-pull output stage, and how is it normally prevented?
8. Explain why shorted yoke windings produce a keystone-shaped raster.
9. Explain the purposes of negative and positive feedback loops in a sweep circuit.
10. State three ways of feeding sweep voltage to the yoke.
11. Explain thermal runaway, giving several possible causes.
12. A scope display at the oscillator input could represent either sync pulses or sweep voltage. How would you determine which?
13. State probable causes of a dark strip across the top of the picture, if (a) the entire picture is visible; (b) the top portion of the picture is obliterated.
14. State several possible causes of an off-center raster.
15. Explain why output transistors draw more current when driven with a sweep voltage. Is there current flow in the absence of a drive signal? Explain.
16. How would you proceed where there is no sweep voltage developed by an oscillator that uses feedback from the output stage?
17. If only half a raster is produced on a set with a push-pull output stage, how would you proceed?
18. State some preliminary tests that should *always* be made prior to replacing a suspected IC.

# 8 Horizontal sweep generators and control circuits

In addition to its main function of developing horizontal deflection voltage for the picture tube, the horizontal section of a TV or monitor is called upon to perform a number of other functions: developing HV and focus voltage for the CRT, and for modern color sets, developing dc operating voltages for all circuits except the horizontal sweep generator and the output transistor. In this section we also furnish samplings of sweep voltage for horizontal blanking, anti-pincushioning, and convergence. As the hardest-working section of a set or monitor, it is understandably subject to the most breakdowns.

The simplified block diagram of Figure 8-1 gives an overview of the entire horizontal sweep section. Because of its complexity, in this chapter we deal only with the initial stages, the sweep voltage generator and its AFC control circuits. The drivers, output amplifier, and associated circuits are covered in Chapter 10.

## 8-1 HORIZONTAL SWEEP FUNDAMENTALS

The horizontal oscillator (or other type of sweep voltage generator) produces a 15,750- or 15,734-Hz voltage that is locked in frequency and phase with its counterpart in the cameras at the TV station. This is accomplished by horizontal sync pulses and AFC action to ensure that picture images are reproduced at their proper locations on the receiver or monitor screen. On late-model sets the sweep generator is part of a startup/shutdown system that disables the set in the event of an overload or hazardous condition.

The precisely controlled and synchronized generated voltage is amplified by driver amplifiers and a power output transistor to produce the necessary sweep *power* for beam deflection. The sweep voltage drives the horizontal windings of the deflection yoke, either directly from the output transistor, or inductively, via the flyback transformer. Sweep current in the yoke produces an electromagnetic flux that sweeps the beam horizontally across the screen.

As shown in Figure 8-1, there are other circuits supplied from the flyback transformer. This is the source of the HV and focus voltage for the CRT, and the sweep-derived scan voltages that furnish the dc operating voltages for most of the transistors and ICs in the equipment. Other "peripheral" circuits that utilize the sweep voltage include horizontal blanking, pincushion and convergence, and gating pulses for circuits that are keyed by the horizontal sweep.

## 8-2 SWEEP GENERATORS AND WAVESHAPING

Horizontal sweep voltage is produced in one of three ways: with a conventional oscillator, a countdown system, or by some form of electronic switching circuit. As with the vertical sweep section, a number of oscillator circuits have been, or are still being used, namely, variations of the multivibrator and

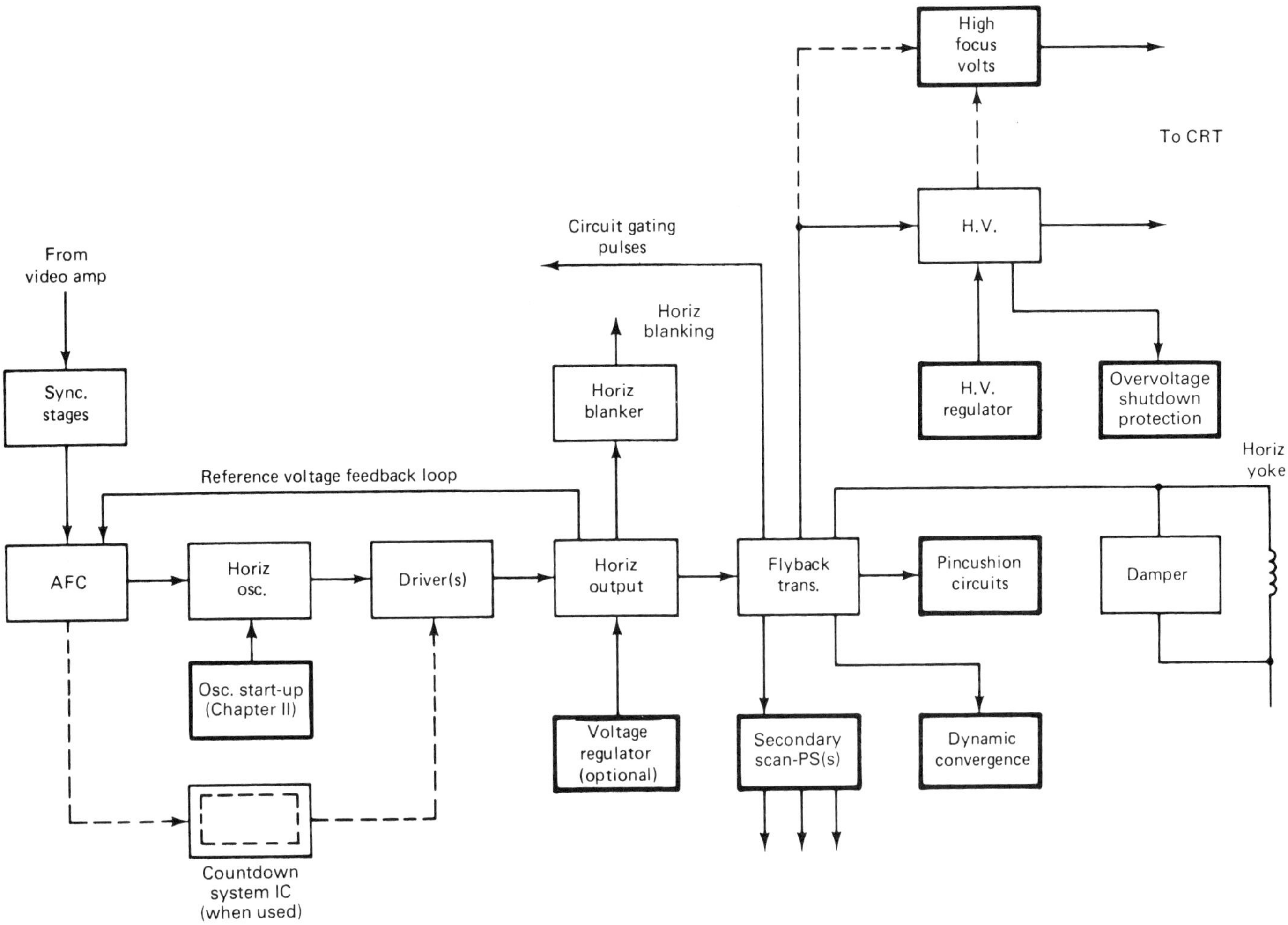


**FIG. 8-1** Horizontal sweep and sweep-related circuits. The heavy outlined blocks are for color sets only.

blocking oscillator circuits and sine-wave generators. One type of switching circuit (now out of favor) uses a pair of SCRs instead of the usual transistor. Most sets now use the countdown system, whose functions are performed by an IC.

Early-model sets traditionally used an oscillator with an *RC* circuit at its output for producing a linear sawtooth waveform, as described for the vertical sweep section (see Figure 7-11). With this system the linearity of the wave had to be preserved by all downstream stages to obtain linear deflection of the CRT beam. Modern sets still require a linear sawtooth *current* in the yoke, but upstream stages may develop a variety of voltage waveshapes.

The multivibrator and blocking oscillators used for horizontal sweep are similar to those used for generating a vertical sweep voltage (see Figure 7-2 and Section 7-1). The main difference is in the component values. When used as a horizontal oscillator, however, these circuits usually have a tuned coil in the collector circuit. It is called a sine-wave ringing or stabilizing coil. The name speaks for itself. It is shock excited to produce sinusoidal oscillations within itself, which tends to stabilize the frequency.

## 8-3 COUNTDOWN SYSTEM

As described in Section 7-1 and depicted in Figure 7-3, this system uses *one* oscillator to develop both the vertical and horizontal sweep voltages. With the frequency stability provided by a crystal oscillator there is no need for hold controls. Despite this, however, some form of AFC is still required, mainly to control horizontal phasing. Except for the crystal, most components are contained in an IC (see Figure 8-6).

## 8-4 RASTER SCANNING AND SYNCHRONIZATION

In order to reproduce a picture where each minute element of an image is positioned exactly as on the mosaic surface of the camera CRTs, each and every horizontal scanning line on the receiver CRT must be precisely synchronized with the camera scanning and the reception of video information. The vertical sweep generator is triggered *directly* by the received sync pulses, but because of its higher frequency, the horizontal sweep requires additional circuits (i.e., the AFC block shown in Figure 8-3). There are stringent requirements. The generated sweep signal must be stable and of the correct frequency, and *each cycle* of the generated voltage must be in phase with (precisely in step with) the sweep voltage generated in the cameras.

If the *frequency* is off, the picture on the screen (which may be barely recognizable) is broken up with a number of sloping bars. The greater the frequency error, the greater the number of bars. The direction of the slope is indicative of whether the sweep is too fast or too slow. A *phasing* error results in a picture split by a vertical black bar, with part of the picture of the even line fields on one side and the odd line fields on the other side. AFC systems are used to maintain proper phasing, but such systems cannot do their job unless the oscillator is running within a few cycles of the correct frequency.

### Pulse Train

The pulse train is a complex series of pulses for the purpose of maintaining uninterrupted control of the horizontal sweep during vertical retrace and to develop a sync pulse for triggering the vertical oscillator. At the completion of each horizontal trace of the CRT beam from left to right, and as the screen is momentarily darkened by the blanking pulse, a horizontal sync pulse initiates horizontal retrace to deflect the beam back to the left to begin another line. When the beam reaches the bottom of the screen after the scanning of a field, a vertical blanking pulse of relatively long duration is received. The vertical blanking interval, as it is sometimes called, has a number of serrations, as shown in Figure 8-2. Note the six equalizing pulses, followed by six vertical pulses, followed by six more equalizing pulses, and finally, a number of horizontal pulses.

The sequence of events is as follows: At point (A) on the diagram, the beam has just completed tracing out the last line of picture information at the bottom of the screen. The screen is blanked out for the duration of the vertical retrace, about 1250 μs. As the beam continues to move down, horizontal sync is maintained for the "unmodulated" scanning lines by every other equalizing pulse. Thus, with interlaced scanning, both odd and even line fields remain in sync at all times.

The next six pulses, wider than the first group, and commonly called *vertical* pulses, serve a dual function. As with the equalizing pulses, they control the horizontal for alternate fields. At the same time, they develop an accumulating voltage for triggering the vertical. How this is done is described in Chapter 9.

Depending on signal strength, the vertical oscillator may be triggered by any of the six vertical pulses, usually the second or third pulse, as represented by point (B) on the diagram. From the moment of vertical triggering, the beam starts moving upward. During the remaining time of vertical retrace, the horizontal oscillator is controlled by the next six equalizing pulses (for alternate fields), and finally, by 12 or so regular horizontal pulses. At some time during this final series of pulses [corresponding with point (C)], the vertical oscillator cycle is reversed and the beam starts moving downward. At point (D) the screen becomes unblanked, and the first line of picture information is scanned at the top.

## 8-5 AFC SYSTEMS

Three systems currently used to control the frequency and phase of the horizontal oscillator (or other type of sweep voltage generator) are (1) the phase detector, (2) reactance control, and (3) varactor control (Figure 8-3). Each circuit is supplied with two signals, a sampling of the generated sweep voltage (called a "reference" voltage) and the horizontal sync pulses transmitted by the station. The reference voltage, of a specific amplitude and polarity, may come from a driver stage or a tap on the flyback transformer. As shown in the diagram, the vertical and horizontal pulses coming from the sync stages are separated *from each other* by integrator

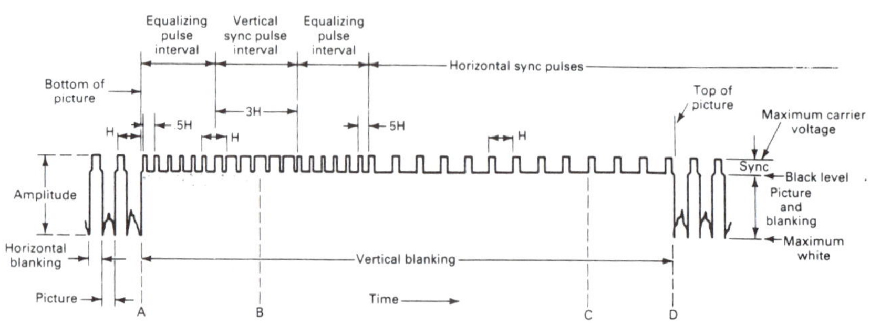


FIG. 8-2 Pulse train.

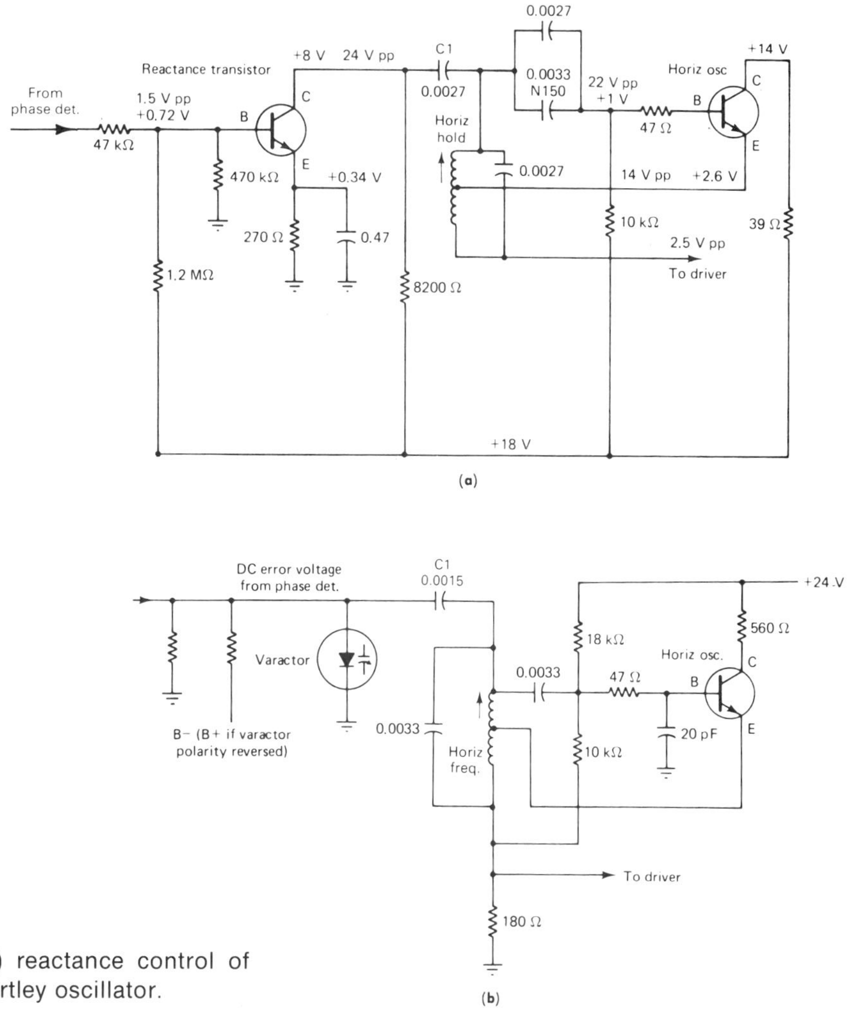


**FIG. 8-3** AFC control systems: (a) reactance control of oscillator; (b) varactor control of Hartley oscillator.

and differentiator networks, each having a specific *RC* time constant.

The phase detector compares the reference voltage with the sync pulses. If there is no frequency or phase error, no action is initiated or required. If there is a discrepancy, a dc error or correction voltage is developed. The correction voltage is applied directly to the oscillator, or via an intermediate dc error amplifier. This forces the oscillator to speed up or slow down until sync is regained. An antihunt *RC* network is often used to prevent the circuit from overreacting. Because of the close association between the oscillator and its control circuit, when troubleshooting, they are considered together.

### Phase Detectors

Three typical circuits are shown in Figure 8-4. Part (a) represents a simplified basic circuit with no frills. The two diodes, operating as a matched pair, are shunted by two equal-value load resistors. The diodes are connected back to back, in opposition. Incoming horizontal sync pulses are supplied to their junction. A reference pulse from the sweep circuit is applied to one diode. When an in-phase condition is sensed, the diodes conduct, developing equal and opposite dc voltages across the load resistors. The net voltage in reference to ground serves as a frequency-correcting voltage for the oscillator. The response to a fast- or slow-running oscillator is illustrated in Figure 8-5.

The circuit shown in Figure 8-4b uses a phase splitter (pulse inverter) to feed sync pulses of equal amplitudes and opposite polarities to the two diodes. Here the diodes are connected series aiding. With the feedback reference voltage fed to their common junction, the two diodes conduct in accordance with the instantaneous voltage received from two sources, the sweep circuit, and the sync. Where there is no oscillator phasing error, the equal and opposite voltages developed across the load resistors cancel out, with zero voltage at their junction.

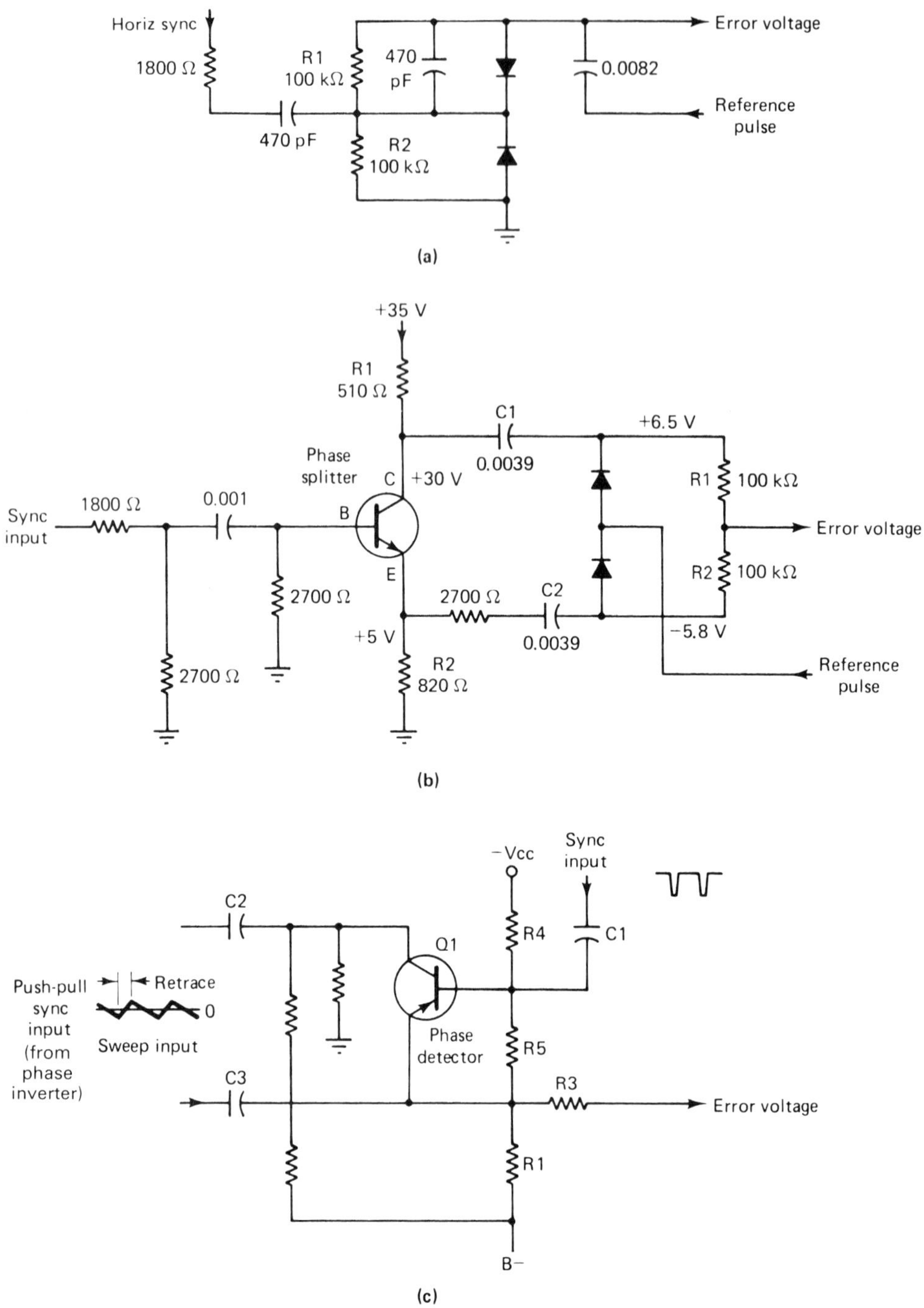


**FIG. 8-4** Basic phase detector circuits.

The result is no change in oscillator operation. A phase error causes one diode to conduct more than the other, unbalancing the circuit and supplying a positive or negative voltage to the oscillator. This forces it to slow down or speed up, as the case may be. Details of this are shown in Figure 8-5. Note the polarities and relative positions of the sync pulses and the reference voltage, things that determine which diode will conduct and by how much.

The circuit in Figure 8-4c uses a transistor in place of matched diodes. It is switched on and off in accordance with the instantaneous amounts of voltage at the three elements, which in turn are determined by the phase relationship between reference and pulse voltages. If the oscillator is running slow, increased conductance creates an increase in negative voltage developed across resistor R1 to speed it up. If the oscillator is running fast, con-

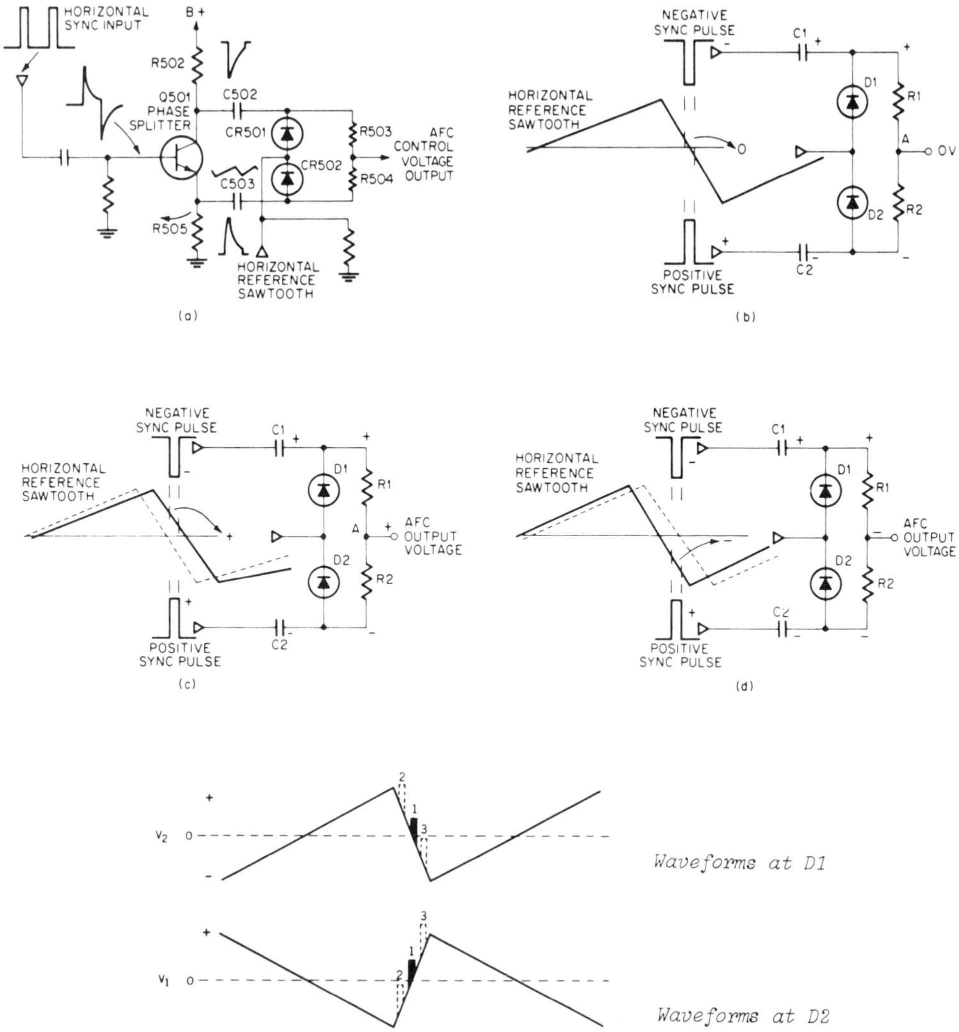


**FIG. 8-5** Phase detector operation. Conditions: (a, b) picture in sync; (c) oscillator frequency too low; (d) oscillator frequency too high.

ductance is decreased and the reduced error voltage produced slows it down. Resistor values establish the relative amounts of sync and reference voltage which are quite critical.

## Sine-Wave Oscillators

Both the reactance and the varactor AFC control systems are used with a sine-wave oscillator as shown in Figure 8-3. A sine-wave oscillator uses a tuned circuit consisting of an adjustable coil shunted with a low-value capacitor. It is sometimes called a Hartley oscillator and is readily identified by the tapped coil (an autotransformer), which provides for inductive feedback. When power is applied, the increasing transistor current produces an increasing magnetic flux, inducing an ac voltage in the upper section by transformer action. This voltage, which is in phase with the collector voltage, is coupled to the transistor base. When the transistor approaches cutoff or saturation, the decrease in current causes the flux to decrease, creating the opposite polarity of feedback voltage at the base. The ratio between the two coil sections establishes the amount of regenerative feedback, which must be sufficient to sustain oscillations. The frequency in this case is 15,734 Hz, the horizontal sweep rate. The frequency is adjustable with a coil tuning slug which serves as a master frequency or hold control.

*Reactance Control of Oscillator.* In Figure 8-3a a transistor is shunted across the oscillator tuned circuit, where it automatically controls the frequency and phase of the oscillations. The reactance control transistor, in series with the oscillator coupling capacitor, acts as a variable capacitive reactance in reference to the ground side of the circuit. A dc correction voltage from a phase detector produces changes in transistor conductance, simulated changes in reactance, and corresponding changes in oscillator frequency and phase.

*Varactor Control of Oscillator.* Figure 8-3b shows a typical circuit as used in most modern TV sets. Here a varactor diode is shunted across the oscillator tuned circuit. A varactor functions as a simulated capacitor whose value is governed by the amount of reverse bias applied, in this case, from a phase detector. If the oscillator is running fast, an increase in the applied reverse bias produces an increase in simulated capacitance, causing the oscillator to slow down. The reverse occurs if the oscillator is running slow. The dc control polarity determines which way the varactor is connected in the circuit. This method of control is also used in channel selectors and for other applications.

## 8-6 STARTUP/SHUTDOWN SYSTEM

To protect the user from hazardous x-ray radiation as produced by excessive high voltage, all modern TV receivers use a system that automatically disables the set if the HV supply for the picture tube becomes excessive for any reason. The system also protects against component damage under certain overload conditions. The oscillator (or drivers) normally get their B voltage from the primary power supply, then after receiver turn-on, from a sweep derived scan PS. When problems develop, the set is disabled by automatically removing the B voltage from the horizontal oscillator or drivers. With the loss of horizontal sweep voltage, no scan voltages are developed and the set goes dead. If there are no serious problems, after a brief period of 30 sec or so, an automatic startup circuit turns the set back on. When troubleshooting the system, an external voltage is used for temporary startup (kick-start) of the oscillator. Details of the system are covered in Chapter 11.

## 8-7 AFC/OSCILLATOR CIRCUITS OF THE FOLDOUT SCHEMATIC

All functions are performed by IC501. A conventional horizontal oscillator with phase detector AFC is used. The oscillator develops a frequency of approximately 31.5 kHz, which is subsequently reduced by a flip-flop circuit to the normal horizontal rate. The dc operating voltage is applied to pin 33 via the horizontal hold control VR401. This voltage comes from the primary power supply via a startup transistor Q403. The overvoltage shutdown circuit disables the driver. Sync pulses from the internal sync separator are applied to the AFC phase detector. A sweep reference voltage from the flyback transformer reaches the AFC circuit via pin 35. The external capacitor C402 is the sawtooth-forming capacitor. The oscillator drives a FF whose sawtooth output is applied to the driver internally.

## 8-8 TROUBLESHOOTING AND REPAIR

Older sets using discrete transistors and diodes for the oscillator and the AFC occasionally develop problems relating to these circuits, but for sets using ICs, such troubles are comparatively rare. Typical troubles associated with these stages include a dead set (because a dead oscillator results in loss of all sweep-derived PS voltages), reduced raster width, and partial or complete loss of horizontal sync, a condition that manifests itself in different ways. Major difficulties such as complete loss of sweep or sync are generally considered the easiest to troubleshoot and repair. Marginal complaints and intermittent troubles can be a greater challenge.

As with any TV problem, the first step is to analyze the symptoms and consider the plan of attack. This should be followed by inspection, first with the set off, then with power applied, while looking for anything abnormal, as described earlier. The next step is to localize the defect to a single stage or section by checking for dc operating voltages and scope checking for missing, weak, or degraded sweep waveforms at the input to the horizontal driver, comparing them with those shown on a schematic.

Where there is a raster, but loss of sync, scope trace for sync pulses at the input and output of the sync stages, up to the AFC circuit, which is usually a phase detector. If pulses are okay, check for a normal sweep reference voltage at the AFC. Check for a developed dc "correction voltage" of the proper amount and polarity, followed by other tests to be described later. Where the oscillator and AFC is contained in an IC, testing in general is limited to checking for applied B voltages, and scope checking for sync input pulses and sweep output voltage.

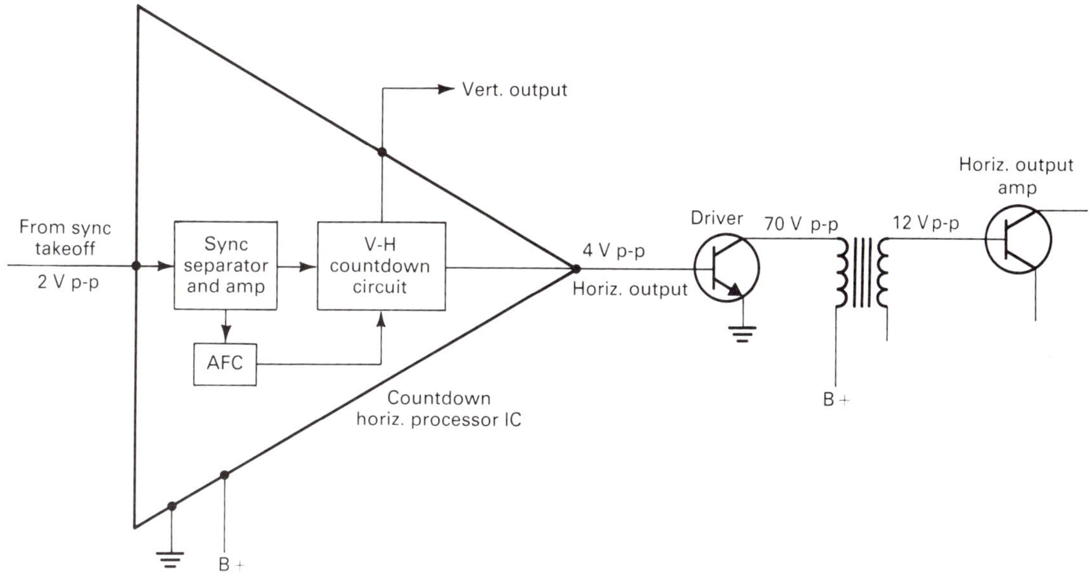


**FIG. 8-6** Troubleshooting the countdown system.

## Troubleshooting the Countdown System

Figure 8-6 illustrates the basic circuit with typical voltages to expect at key checkpoints. For details, see Chapters 5 and 7.

*Reminder:* When repairs are completed, a final burn-in check should be made for an hour or more.

Specific trouble symptoms and procedures pertaining to the oscillator/AFC circuits are covered in the following paragraphs. Troubles involving the drivers, horizontal output, and HV and yoke circuits are covered in Chapter 10. Figure 8-7 shows a troubleshooting flow drawing that can be used as a guide.

## Symptoms and Procedures

### *No Raster; No Sound*

***Probable causes:*** Receiver in shutdown mode; no B voltage output from primary PS; no sweep voltage output from horizontal oscillator.

Check for primary power B+ (see Chapter 6). If the set uses scan power, see if the sweep circuit is operating by checking for sweep voltage at the driver input; dc output from the scan PSs; and for HV. Determine if the shutdown circuit has been activated by checking for oscillator output, and if okay, perform a manual start-up as described in Chapter 11. If the set is not in the shutdown mode, and in the absence of run power from the scan PSs, use an external PS to operate the oscillator while testing. Adjust the voltage to the amount shown on the schematic. Check the oscillator transistor, its dc operating voltages, and all suspected components in the circuit. If trouble persists, isolate the oscillator from the AFC circuit. If the oscillator now operates, check the AFC circuit and its interface with the oscillator.

If the set uses an IC and there is no sweep output, check the applied B+ voltages and sweep-related external components. If still suspect, replace the IC. For intermittent loss of picture and sound, try tapping the chassis and components, probing the circuit, and so on, as described in Chapter 5.

### *No Raster; Sound Normal*

***Probable causes:*** If scan power is not used, loss of B+ feed to the oscillator, or a dead oscillator; where sweep derived scan power *is* used, and the oscillator is okay, suspect the HV dc circuit, the CRT, or its associated circuits.

Check for B+ to the oscillator. If no B+, check for an open or short in the voltage distribution network. There is obviously B+ on the main dc bus; otherwise, there would be no sound. If the set uses scan power, some of these PSs must be okay. Check the PS that feeds the sweep circuit. Suspect the CRT and its operating voltages, including the HV.

If the set *does not* use scan power and the oscillator is supplied with B+, concentrate on the oscillator if there is no sweep voltage at its output. Check the transistor and its operating voltages. Check all suspected oscillator components. For the possibility of loading by a faulty AFC circuit, isolate one from the other and repeat the oscillator tests.

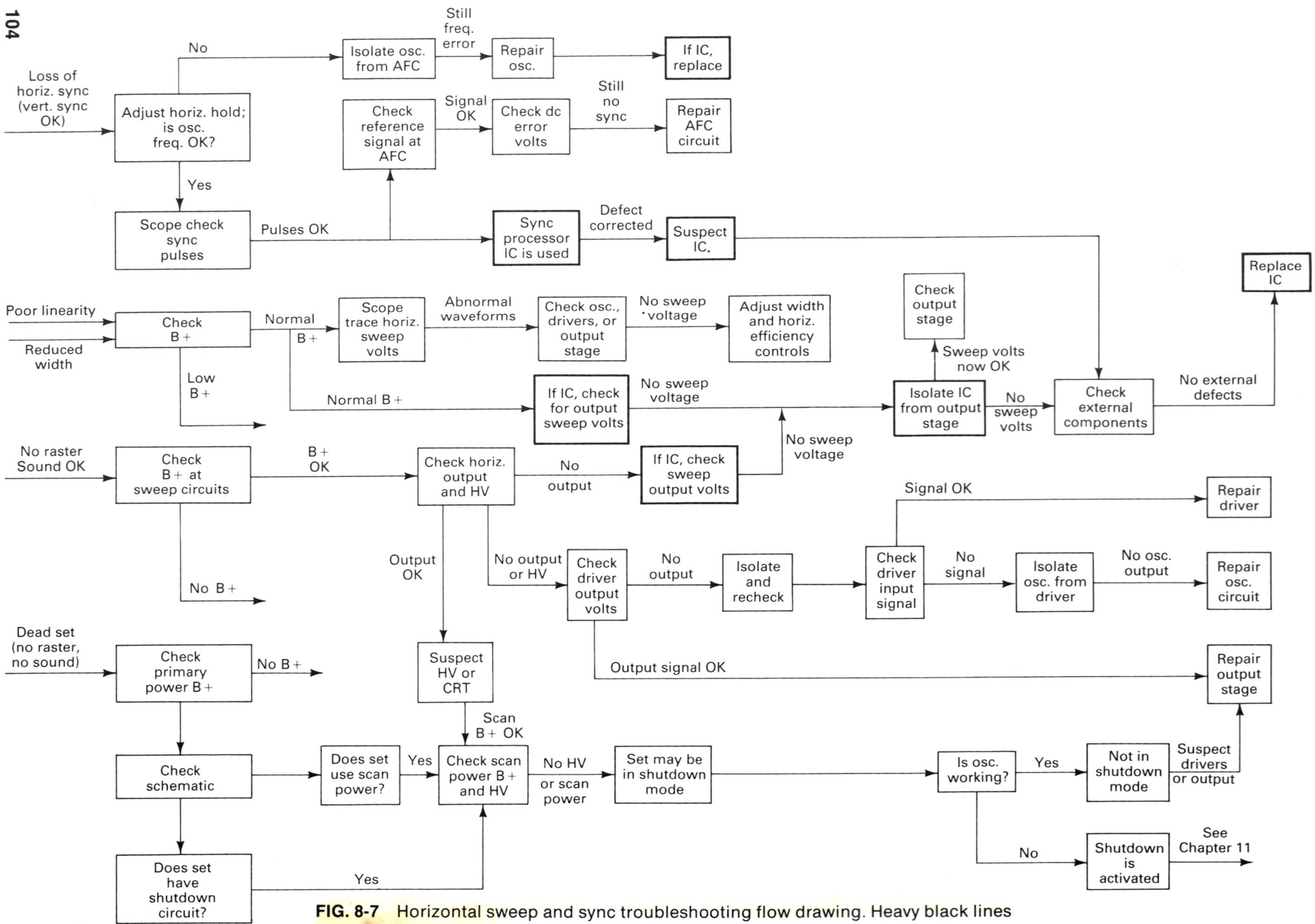


**FIG. 8-7** Horizontal sweep and sync troubleshooting flow drawing. Heavy black lines indicate IC when used.

*Reduced Horizontal Deflection.* (narrow raster)

***Probable causes:*** Low B+; low line voltage; excessive HV; weak oscillator; low output from a sweep processing IC.

Check for low line voltage and B+. If excessive HV, adjust to amount specified. Scope check the oscillator output and compare with the schematic. If the amplitude is low, the cause may be loading by the adjacent circuits, the AFC and driver stage, or a defect in the oscillator itself. Check for such things as leakage in the transistor, diodes, and capacitors. Look for resistors that have changed value. If adjacent circuits are suspected, isolate and repeat the tests. Where an IC is suspect, replace it.

*Poor Horizontal Linearity.* (picture is compressed or stretched horizontally)

***Probable causes:*** Sawtooth-forming circuit defects.

Scope check the sweep waveform at the oscillator output or input of the driver, and compare with the schematic. Check the transistor, its operating voltages, and all associated components that may be suspect. If necessary, isolate the oscillator from the AFC and driver circuits. Where a feedback loop is used, check waveform and components. If an IC is used and there's an improperly shaped waveform at the output, consider replacement after making preliminary tests as described earlier.

*Horizontal Foldover.* (portions of left or right sides of the picture are folded back on itself with images transposed)

***Probable causes:*** Too long a time constant in the waveshaping network, thus extending the horizontal retrace period; improper phasing between the CRT beam deflection and the sync pulses (an AFC sync problem).

Check all sawtooth-forming components. If an IC, consider replacement. Scope check the sync pulses at the phase detector input and if abnormal, refer to Chapter 9.

*Drive Bars.* (vertical bars appear on the left side of the picture)

***Probable causes:*** Excessive drive to output stage sometimes caused by oscillator "squegging" (generating multiple frequencies); an open sawtooth-forming capacitor.

Scope check oscillator waveform and compare with schematic. Check all sawtooth-generating components. If squegging is suspected, try adding ferrite beads on transistor leads.

*Horizontal Sync Problems.* (a variety of possible symptoms: picture tearing; split picture; multiple pictures; horizontal pulling; flag-waving; horizontal jitter)

***Probable causes (assuming that the vertical sync is okay):*** Defect in the oscillator or AFC circuits, or defective IC if used; missing or weak sync pulses from the sync stages; improper oscillator adjustments.

If complete loss of horizontal sync, where there's two or more pictures side by side, or the picture is broken up by a number of horizontal bars, it indicates that the oscillator is off frequency. The greater the number of bars, the greater the frequency error. It may be helpful to know whether the oscillator is running too fast or too slow. Where bars slope downward to the right, the frequency is too high; if sloping in the reverse direction, the opposite is true.

Try adjusting the frequency with the hold control and the slug-tuned coil if there is one. It should be possible to obtain bars sloping in both directions within range of the hold control. Normally, a picture should lock in at two or three bars. If the picture only syncs at one bar, the sync stability is only marginal. Try adjusting the ringing coil if one is provided.

If considerable adjusting is needed to obtain sync lock, chances are that it is compensating for defects that should be corrected to avoid future problems. One common possibility is shorted windings in the oscillator coil. The clue here is where the oscillator frequency is too high, (picture tearing with numerous bars) and tends to improve (bars become fewer) when the slug is entered into the coil.

Most any oscillator defect can alter the frequency, such as a bad transistor, leaky capacitors, resistor's changed value, incorrect dc operating voltages, shorted windings in an oscillator coil or transformer, broken or missing core slugs, and AFC circuit defects due to the close relationship that exists between the two stages. Also included is the input circuits of the next downstream stage, the driver. Each of the possibilities above should be checked out, and corrected, as described earlier. If there's an IC and it is suspected, make preliminary tests and, if necessary, replace it. (*Reminder:* An AFC circuit defect can change the oscillator frequency.) However, AFC problems usually affect the *phasing*, producing symptoms of picture bending or pulling, or a vertical black bar dividing the picture on the left side of the screen. When a malfunctioning AFC circuit is suspected, isolate or defeat its action, and check the two stages individually. *(Reminder:* Sync cannot be obtained unless the oscillator is capable of free-running at the correct frequency.)

Troubleshoot the AFC circuit as follows. First verify that there are normal sync pulses coming from the final sync stage, which is usually a sync separator. Normal amplitude is typically about 10 V p-p. If a scope check shows weak or missing pulses at the phase detector input, they may be grounded out or there is a defect upstream from this point. A common problem is sync compression as caused by signal overdrive, a video amplifier defect, or AGC troubles.

Where sync pulses are okay, scope check the reference voltage pulse coming from the flyback transformer. If weak or missing, check it back to its source. Check for a dc correction voltage at the phase detector output, and at the oscillator input, or other in-between stage. See if the correction voltage changes as it should as the oscillator coil is adjusted by a small amount. If the dc is weak, missing, or the wrong polarity, check the matched diodes or transistor, as applicable. Also check the equal-value load resistors. Check and compare the dc voltage drops across the resistors. This is extremely critical. Diodes and resistors should be replaced as a matched pair to avoid a circuit imbalance. If necessary, check other components in the phase detector, replacing any that are suspect.

Where a reactance or varactor-control circuit is used, and where the phase detector develops a normal dc correction voltage, check the reactance control transistor or varactor as applicable, and any other suspected components. Substitution is the best check for a varactor.

Where a sweep and sync processing IC is used, check for B+, scope check the sync pulse at the AFC input, and test external components as appropriate. If suspect, replace the IC.

After oscillator and/or AFC defects have been corrected, make final adjustments, as follows. Using jumpers, short out the ringing coil. Ground out the pulses at the AFC input. With the hold control at midsetting, adjust the oscillator coil slug to obtain a "floating" picture (i.e., where the picture momentarily stops drifting sideways). Remove the short from the coil. Adjust the ringing coil to regain a floating picture. Remove the ground from the AFC input. Make minor readjustments using the hold control. The picture should snap abruptly into sync when within a couple of bars of lock-in. If the ringing coil has little or no effect, check for shorted windings or a missing or broken core slug. (*Note:* Sometimes stability can be improved by experimentally changing the value of the resistor shunted across the ringing coil.) Check the sync stability. When switching channels, the picture should lock without hesitation.

*Squegging and Piecrusting.* Oscillator squegging produces a "Christmastree" effect, an overly bright jagged raster with streaking. For the "piecrust (geartooth) effect," a picture has jagged, sawtooth edges.

***Probable causes:*** Unstable or misadjusted oscillator; AFC defects.

Squegging indicates that the oscillator is simultaneously producing different frequencies, resulting in complete loss of sync. The high-amplitude pulses generated can destroy critical and sensitive components, ICs in particular.

As with an off-frequency oscillator, check all circuit components, including the transistor. Replace any that are suspect, particularly capacitors that show the slightest leakage. For the possibility of interaction from other circuits, try bridging B+ with a high-value filter capacitor, and/or by adding ferrite beads on critical leads. Try readjusting the ringing coil if there is one.

Piecrusting occurs if the oscillator cannot settle down to the correct frequency as sometimes caused by frequency drift or an antihunt network that is not doing its job. Check the stability of the dc correction voltage and if necessary, troubleshoot the phase detector. Try alternate heating and cooling of suspected components.

### Weak or Intermittent Sync

***Probable causes:*** Oscillator frequency drift; unstable AFC circuit; defective hold control; weak reception; interference.

Weak reception, interference, and unstable sync often go together. If possible, improve reception, overcome the interference, and the sync will probably improve. Clean or replace an erratic hold control. For oscillator frequency drift (where the hold control must be readjusted repeatedly) apply localized heat or cold to critical components. Check for a loose or cracked coil slug. Check the operation of the AFC as described previously. A defective varactor is quite common; try substitution. Procedures for intermittent troubles are described in Chapter 5.

## QUESTIONS

1. The vertical oscillator is triggered directly by sync pulses, but the horizontal oscillator requires an AFC stage. Explain why.
2. Explain why shorted windings in an oscillator coil raises its natural resonant frequency.
3. Explain the operation of a basic phase detector and how it controls the oscillator.
4. What is the approximate frequency of the oscillator (a) if there is a picture tearing with six bars sloping upward to the right; (b) if there are two complete pictures separated by a vertical black bar? (c) If several bars are sloping downward to the right, is the oscillator running fast or slow?
5. Explain the varactor method of oscillator control.
6. Identify all the pulses that control the horizontal oscillator during vertical retrace. Which ones trigger the vertical oscillator?
7. Why must the diodes and load resistors in a phase detector be matched precisely?
8. Where the oscillator is off frequency, how would you determine whether the trouble is with the oscillator or the AFC?
9. State two possible causes where the oscillator coil slug must be screwed fully into the coil to obtain sync.
10. State three tests for determining whether or not the oscillator is oscillating.

# 9 Sync stages

Sync pulses generated at the station control the vertical and horizontal sweep circuits in the cameras. These pulses are transmitted as part of the composite video signal. At the receiver(s), the composite signal (video information and pulses) that is present at the "sync takeoff" point in the video amplifiers is routed to the sync stages, where the pulses are stripped from the video by a sync separator or clipper stage. The vertical and horizontal pulses are then amplified and separated *from each other* to control their respective sweep generators. This method of control ensures that beam deflection at the receivers is constantly in step with beam deflection in the cameras. Beam synchronization is not to be confused with color sync, two completely unrelated functions.

Noise impulses can masquerade as sync pulses, creating problems of synchronization. To help maintain a stable sync condition, some sets include *noise immunity* circuits. Most modern receivers incorporate the sync stages in a multifunction IC.

## 9-1 SYNC SECTION

All stages involved with beam synchronization are shown in Figure 9-1. The AFC block, which also serves a sync function, was described in Chapter 8.

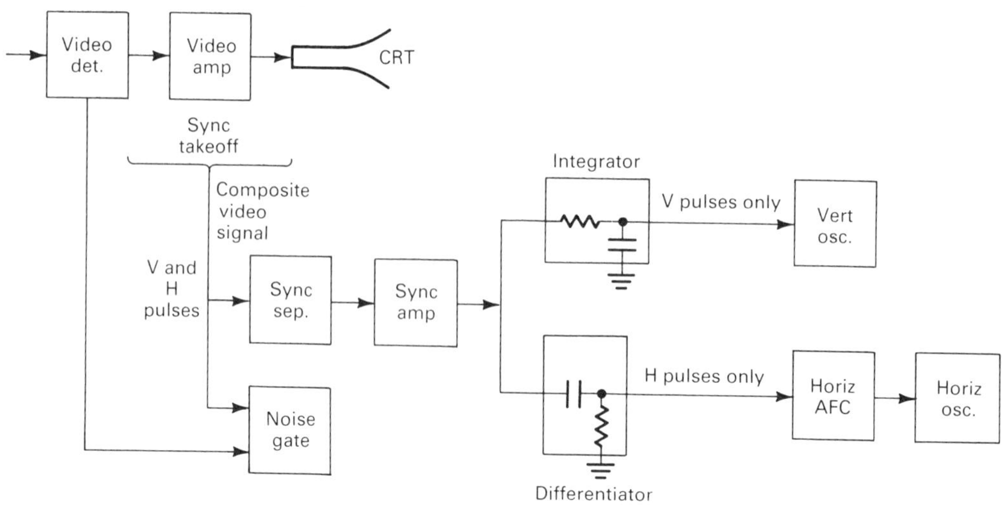


**FIG. 9-1** Sync and noise immunity block diagram.

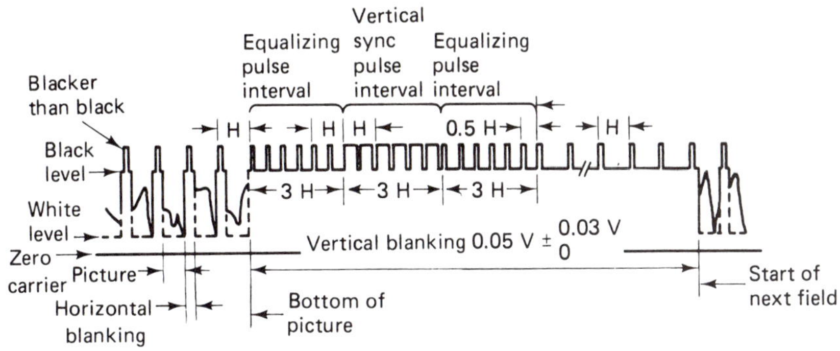


**FIG. 9-2** Composite video signal.

## 9-2 COMPOSITE VIDEO SIGNAL

This signal, generated by the station, is extremely complex. As shown in Figure 9-2, it contains the following: picture information, both monochrome and color; a color burst for synchronizing color reproduction; sync pulses for synchronizing vertical and horizontal deflection of the CRT beam; blanking pulses to darken the screen during vertical and horizontal retrace intervals; and in some cases additional signals for monitoring those transmitted and for automatic control of color fidelity at the receiver. In this chapter we are concerned only with the vertical and horizontal sync pulses.

As shown in the figure and described earlier, after each horizontal trace of the CRT beam, the screen is blanked out by a horizontal blanking pulse that biases the CRT to cutoff. A narrow horizontal sync pulse of short duration extends above the blanking level in what is referred to as the blacker-than-black region. During the horizontal retrace interval, this pulse controls the horizontal sweep generator. After beam retrace, the blanking pulse once more drops off to produce a visible beam trace for the next line of picture detail.

Following the scanning of each field, the video is interrupted by a vertical blanking pulse of relatively long duration, and the screen once more goes to black. Riding on the blanking pulse and extending above the blanking level is a *train of pulses* consisting of horizontal and *equalizing pulses,* used to control the horizontal sweep generator during the vertical retrace interval. Note the relative spacing and duration of the pulses, which will be explained later. The second group of six pulses to arrive are used to control vertical synchronization. Following vertical retrace, the blanking pulse drops off, the CRT beam is restored and the next line is scanned at the top of the screen. To do their job, sync pulses must represent at least 25% of the amplitude of the composite signal (see Figure 9-2).

### Hammerhead Display

Because the CRT is biased to cutoff and beyond, during the retrace intervals, sync and blanking pulses are normally not visible. But they *can* be made visible, as shown in Figure 9-3 by misadjusting the hold controls for an out-of-sync condition, and by turning up the brightness to prevent beam current cutoff. Although not illustrated to the same scale, in Figure 9-3a and b, the wide and faintly dark bars are produced as the beam is weakened, but not cut off, during the retrace intervals. The narrow *black* bars are produced by the sync pulses, which cut off the beam completely. Note the pulses, which correspond with the bars in Figure 9-3c and d. Sync pulses are permitted to reach the CRT but serve no useful purpose. The *hammerhead* near the middle of the vertical blanking bar is produced by the equalizing and vertical sync pulses shown in Figure 9-2. The hammerhead display is shown here for the purpose of illustration. When servicing a set, the relative darkness of the bars provides an indication of the pulse status, at least up to the point of sync takeoff. Pulses that are weak or missing appear little or no darker than the lighter blanking bars.

Figure 9-3c illustrates how part of the signal is observed on a scope with a blow-up of the horizontal blanking and sync pulses. Note the 8 to 10 cycles of color burst on the back porch. In Figure 9-3d, we see the pulses that occur during vertical blanking. Note the momentary "Vits" burst. It, too, is not visible to the viewer since it takes place beyond the top of the screen, which is still blanked out.

### Polarity Considerations

The composite video signal is ac with a dc component for reference. With a typical amplifier there is usually a 180° phase or polarity reversal between the input and output. If the video signal is applied to the CRT grid(s), it must have a negative-going polarity.

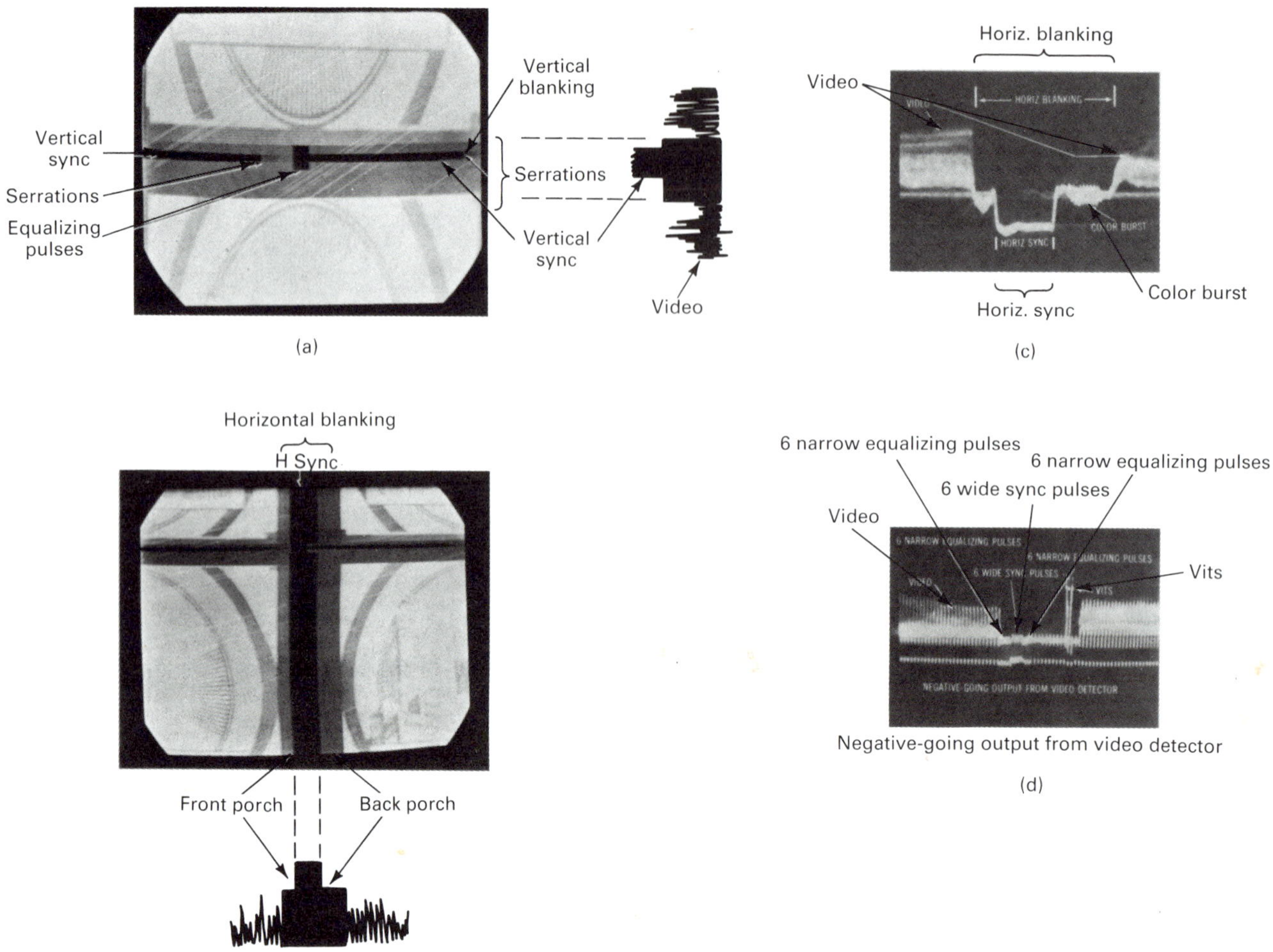


**FIG. 9-3** Hammerhead display.

If fed to the cathode(s), it must be positive-going. Certain troubles in the video section can reverse the normal polarity, resulting in a *negative picture* where black objects become white and white objects black. (Figure 9-4). This also shows up on a hammerhead display (Figure 9-3), where the sync and blanking bars show up white. If the defect creating this condition occurs ahead of the sync takeoff point, sync pulse polarities are also reversed, resulting in complete loss of sync. Pulse reversal can also take place in the sync stages.

The photo in Figure 9-4 was taken with the brightness turned up or the contrast level too low. At reduced brightness the vertical and horizontal sync bars become visible.

## Sync Takeoff Point

The *sync takeoff,* where some of the composite signal is routed to the sync stages, may be at any point in the video amplifier section. If at or near the detector output, more sync amplification is required compared to a takeoff point farther downstream near the CRT input. The composite signal is coupled to the first sync stage with a fairly low value of coupling capacitor, to avoid loading the video. Such loading can degrade the picture by creating a loss of fine detail.

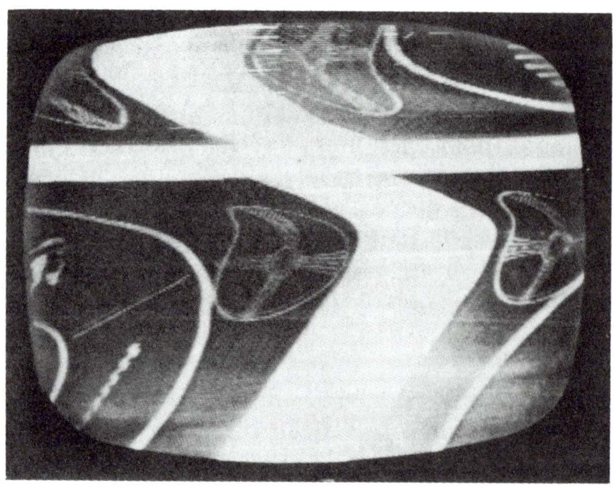

**FIG. 9-4** Negative picture. Signal polarity reversal also causes loss of sync.

### Sync Separator

The video signal must be stripped from the pulses to prevent it from upsetting the sync by randomly controlling the vertical and horizontal sweep generators. Either a diode or transistor can be used as a sync separator, as shown in Figure 9-5. In circuit (a), the diode is reverse biased by self-rectification of the input signal, which permits it to conduct only at the peaks of the signal (the pulses). In this case the signal has a positive-going polarity. If a negative polarity, the diode connections would be reversed. With a diode there is no reversal between input and output.

A transistor is used as a sync separator in circuit (b). It is prefered over a diode because it provides some amplification. Pulse clipping occurs in the B/E circuit; amplification takes place in the collector circuit. The B/E junction represents a diode that is reverse-biased to cutoff or beyond, as in circuit (a). Some bias is developed by the *IR* drop across the emitter resistor during conduction. But since a transistor cannot *bias itself* to cutoff, "excitation bias" is also provided by rectification of the signal input. Bias provided in this manner automatically adjusts to the signal level. In general, the greater the bias, the stronger the signal that is required for conduction. Although it results in some loss of gain, a high bias is desirable in order to clip the pulses completely and provide a "clean" output (Figure 9-6). Bias is determined largely by the *RC* time constant of the B/E circuit. With a short TC (low-value capacitors and resistors), conduction may be excessive, resulting in a video-contaminated output. It is a trade-off. With a long TC, conduction time is shortened, for a cleaner separation, but at the expense of amplification.

### Noise Immunity

Interference of various kinds (customarily called *noise*) produces a snowy or streaky picture, scratchy sounds from the speaker, and frequently upsets the sync. It can be a major problem in industrial areas where arcing occurs in motors and other electrical equipment. It also tends to be worse under adverse receiving conditions where a low signal-to-noise ratio increases the receiver sensitivity as the AGC loses control. As for remedies, whenever possible, interference of any kind should be reduced or eliminated at its *source*. A good antenna system also helps.

Many TV receivers (and other home entertainment equipment) use some form of noise-reducing

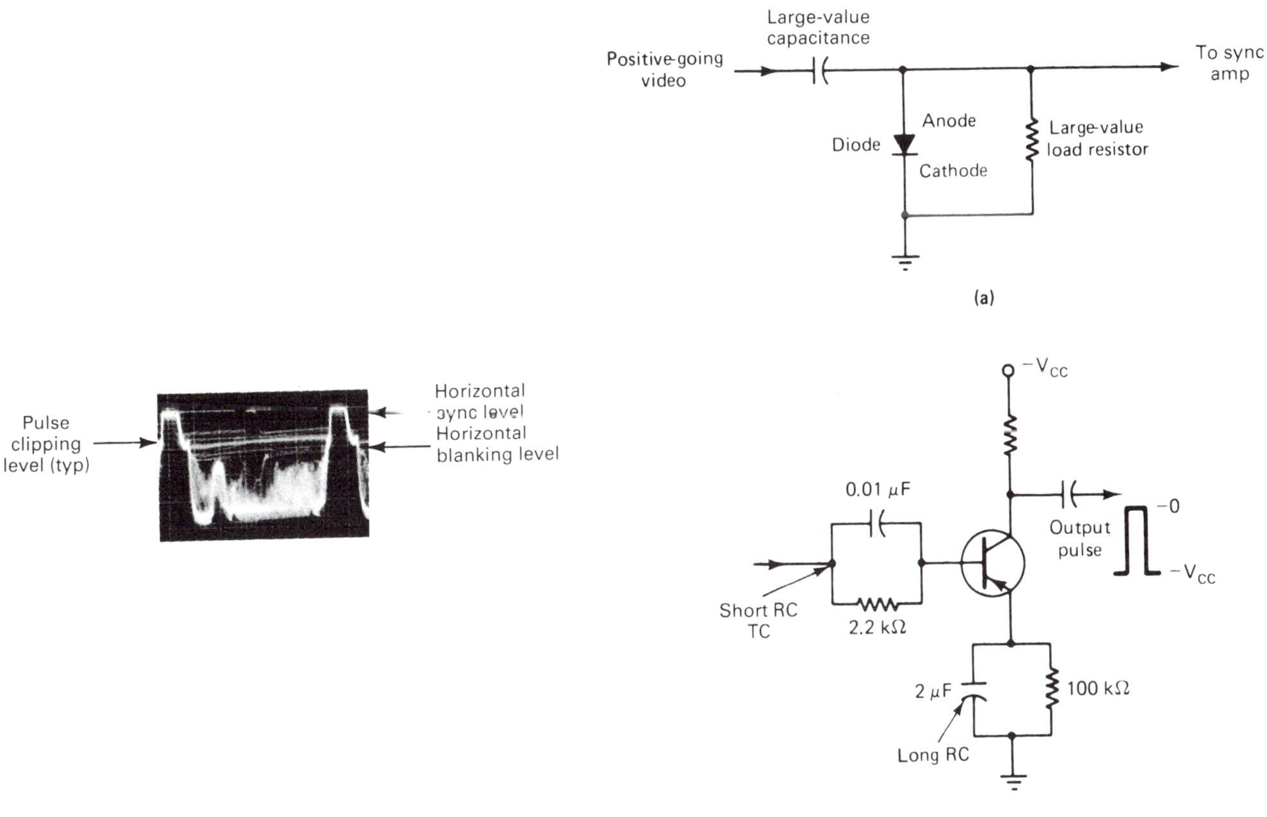


**FIG. 9-5** Sync separator circuits.

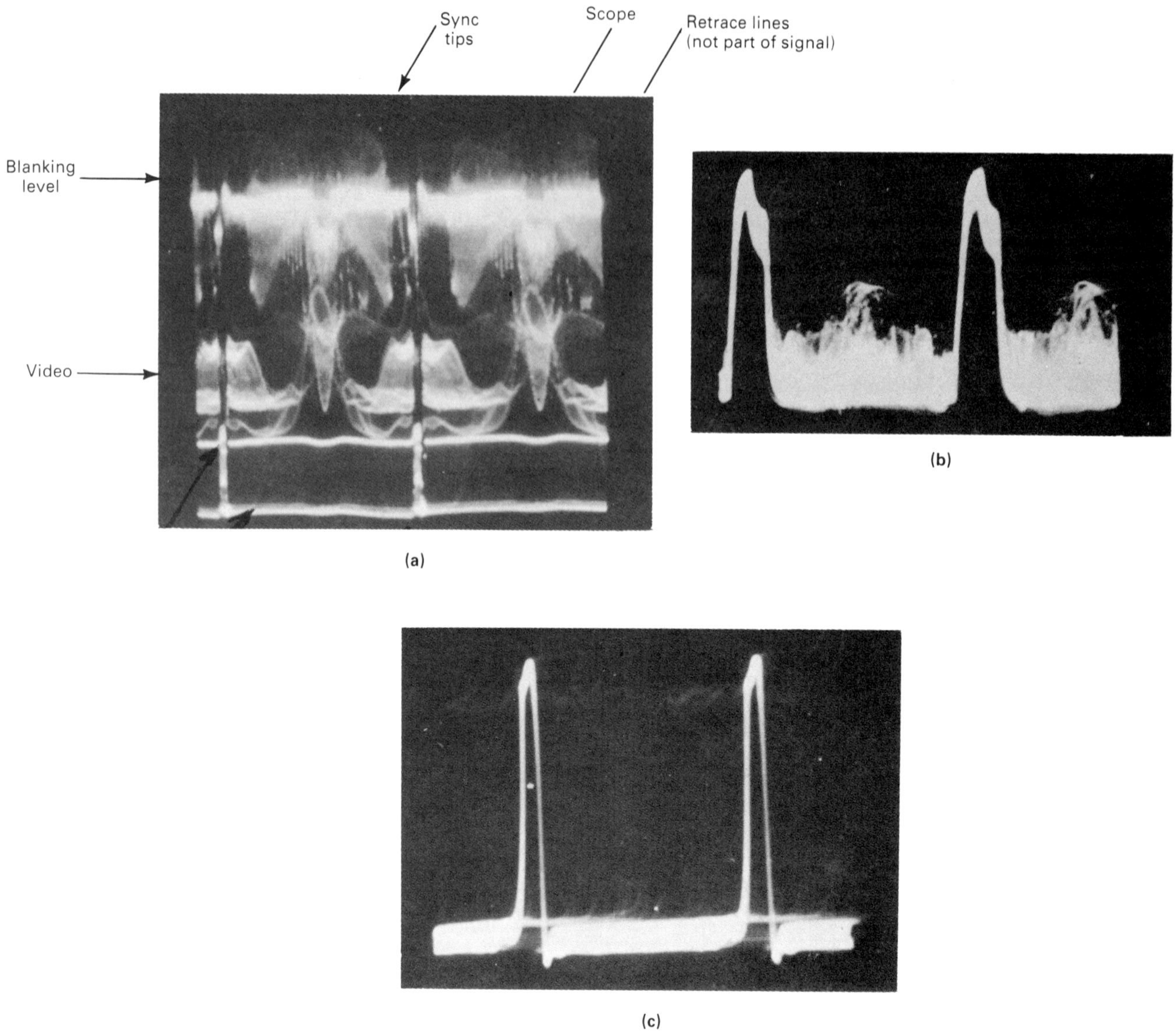


**FIG. 9-6** Scope waveform displays: (a) sync separator input; (b) sync takeoff; (c) sync separator output. Clean pulses are essential for stable sync.

circuit. The simple circuit shown in Figure 9-7a can be quite effective against "impulse noise" and other kinds of interference. Noise bursts stronger than the video signal are shorted to ground when the diode conducts. Diode polarity depends on the signal polarity at that point in the set. If warranted, this circuit can be added to any TV.

Most sets use a *noise-canceling circuit* such as shown in Figure 9-7b. In the absence of noise, transistor Q1 is biased to cutoff and the video reaches the next stage (the sync separator) via resistor R1. For low-intensity noise, Q1 amplifies and reverses the polarity of the noise voltage, which cancels out any noise in the signal at the collector. For high-intensity noise bursts, Q1 is driven to saturation, and both the noise and the signal are *momentarily* shorted to ground through the transistor junction.

Some sets use variations of those described, most operating on the principle that voltages of opposite polarity tend to cancel each other. In some cases a noise "threshold" control is provided.

## Sync Amplifiers

For optimum sync stability, many sets have one or more sync amplifiers to increase the pulse amplitude. Such amplifiers may precede or follow the sync separator. Since each stage creates a polarity

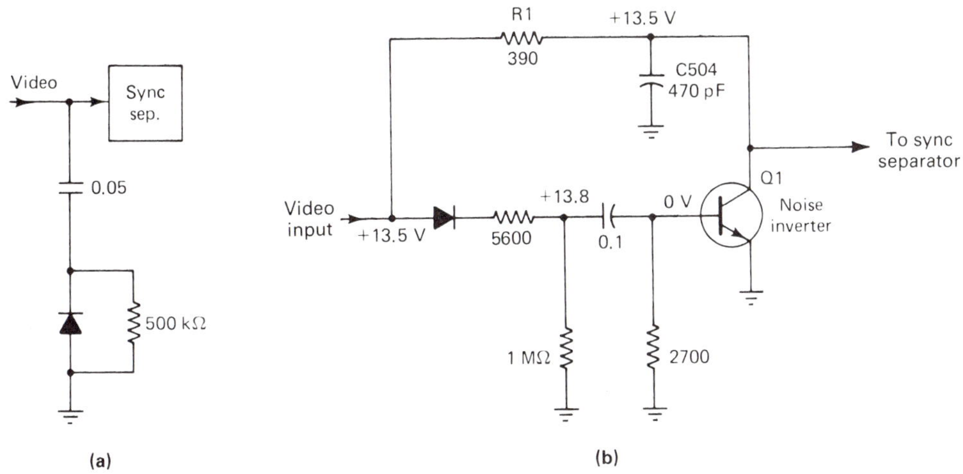


**FIG. 9-7** Noise immunity circuits.

reversal, it is essential that the pulse polarity be correct as it reaches the vertical oscillator and the AFC circuit. Some sets have "selective" amplifiers, one with a long time constant for handling vertical pulses only, the other with a short TC for the faster horizontal pulses.

Most sync amplifiers operate class A on the linear part of their curve. This calls for a small amount of forward bias and a fairly high collector voltage. The circuit is a basic *RC* coupled amplifier.

### Splitting the Pulses

After being separated from the video information, the vertical and horizontal pulses must be separated *from each other*. This is accomplished by two *RC* networks: an *integrator* network that passes only the vertical pulses and a *differentiating* network that passes only the horizontal pulses. The integrated vertical pulse is routed to the input of the vertical sweep generator and the differentiated horizontal pulses to the AFC input.

### Developing the Vertical Sync Pulse

As stated earlier, the vertical synchronizing pulse is developed by the six "wide" pulses that are part of the *train of pulses* riding on the vertical blanking pedestal (Figure 9-2). These pulses also function individually to control the horizontal sweep generator. The integrator is nothing more than a resistor and capacitor connected as shown in Figure 9-8. Relatively large values of *R* and *C* are used to obtain a long time constant, corresponding with the low vertical pulse rate of 60 Hz. Sometimes, for greater effectiveness, two or more integrators are connected in cascade, as shown.

*All* pulses (vertical, horizontal, and equalizing pulses) are present at the integrator input. Each of the first six equalizing pulses starts to charge capacitor C1, but because of the short duration of the pulses and the relatively long time between them, the voltage drops off as fast as it appears (Figure 9-8d). The next six vertical pulses are of longer duration, with a short time between them which causes an accumulative buildup of voltage on the capacitor. When viewed on a scope, the integrated pulses appear as a *single* sharply spiked pulse of short duration, as indicated.

The voltage buildup required to trigger the vertical oscillator normally occurs with the second or third pulse. For weak reception conditions it may take all six. If still not enough, the result is complete loss of vertical sync.

### Differentiated Horizontal Pulses

An *RC* network is required to shape the serrations of the horizontal pulse train of the vertical interval into usable sharply spiked pulses, and to reject the vertical sync pulses. The *R* and *C* components are connected as shown with low values for a short time constant. The differentiating action can be described as follows (see Figure 9-9). With the arrival of each pulse, the capacitor rapidly charges to the peak value of the pulse voltage. The relatively high charging current develops an *IR* voltage drop across the resistor, but *only while current is flowing*. This is the pulse voltage passed on to the horizontal phase detector.

When the capacitor becomes charged, current ceases and the voltage across the resistor gradually decays. With the low values used and the short TC, the rise time is almost instantaneous; the dropoff is more gradual but of no consequence since it is the leading edge of the pulse that does the controlling.

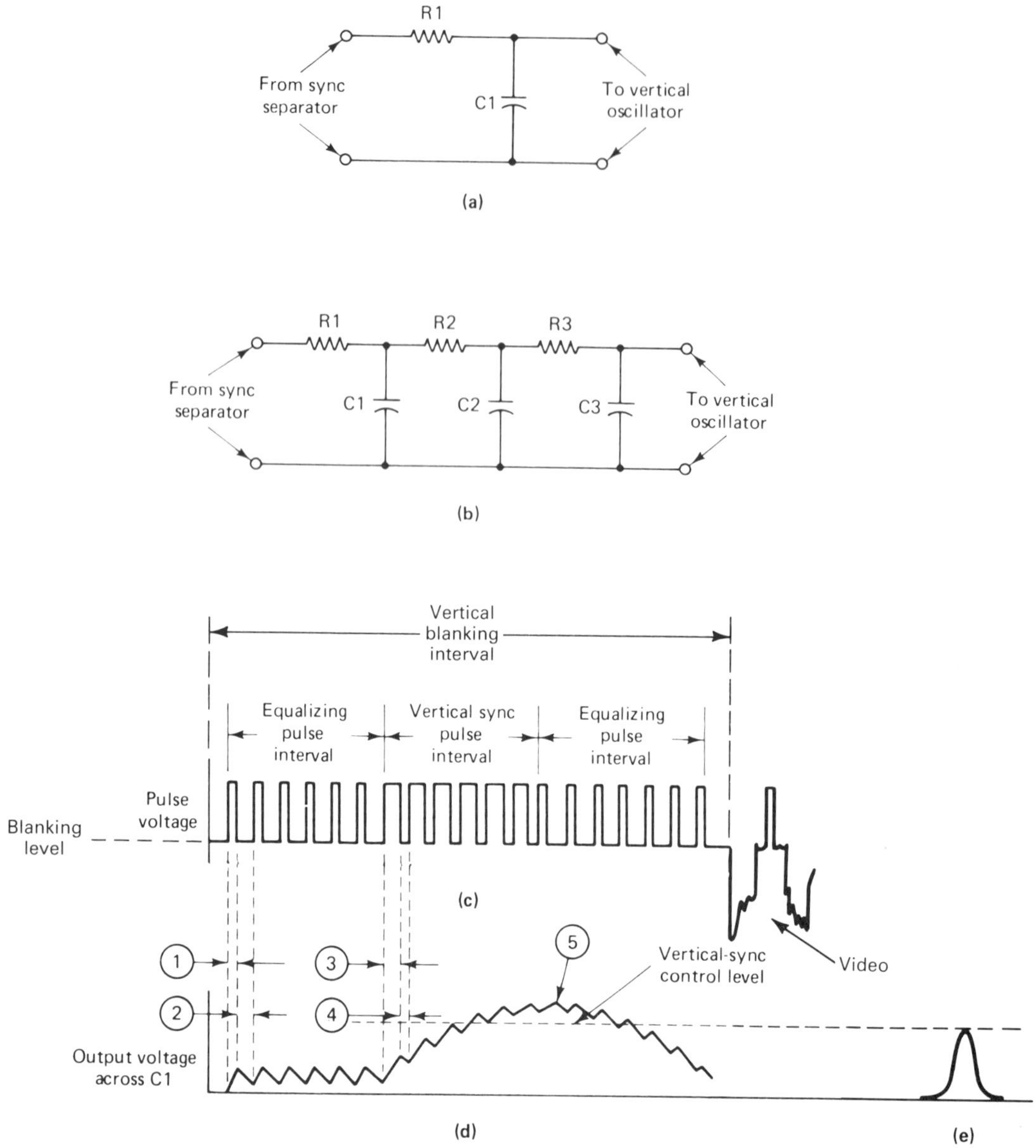


**FIG. 9-8** Integrated vertical sync pulse: (a) integrating circuit; (b) cascade integrating circuit; (c) vertical sync-pulse group; (d) output of integrating circuit; (e) as viewed on a scope.

In the time between pulses, the capacitor discharges through the resistor, developing a pulse of reversed polarity. These pulses serve no purpose since they occur during horizontal scan periods when the sweep generator is insensitive to change. (*Reminder:* With interlaced scanning, only *every other* pulse of the equalizing and vertical pulses is used for control of alternate fields.)

## 9-3 FOLDOUT SCHEMATIC SYNC FUNCTIONS

The sync takeoff from the video amplifier is at pin 7 of IC501. The composite signal is routed (in a roundabout way) to the sync separator via pins 38 and 39. The *R* and *C* components in the loop are to improve sync stability. Resistor R303 and capacitor C301 is the integrator network, which couples the output of the sync separator, via pin 37, to a "sync gate" that controls the vertical oscillator. The sync separator feeds horizontal pulses internally to the phase detector.

## 9-4 TROUBLESHOOTING AND REPAIR

Vertical sync problems were treated in Chapter 7, horizontal sync troubles in Chapter 9. This chapter is concerned only with the sync stages between the sync takeoff at the video amplifier and the input to the integrator and differentiating networks. A defect

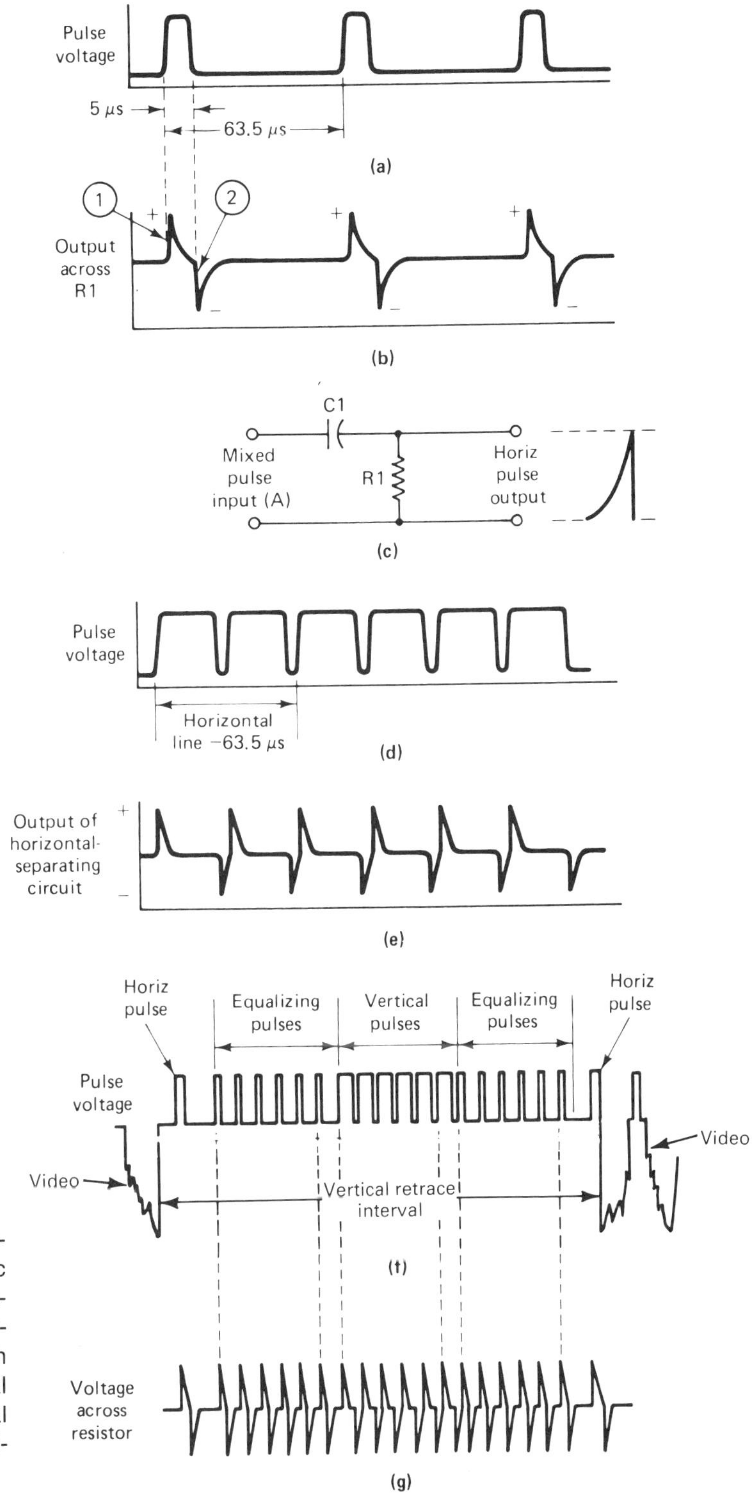


**FIG. 9-9** Differentiating the horizontal pulses: (a) horizontal sync pulses; (b) output of differentiating circuit; (c) differentiating circuit; (d) vertical-sync pulse with serrations; (e) output of horizontal differentiating circuit; (f) vertical pulse group; (g) output of horizontal-differentiating circuit.

in these stage affects *both* vertical *and* horizontal sync. Defects at or near the *RC* inputs normally affects only the vertical or horizontal, but not both.

Where there is a weak picture and poor sync, chances are that when the picture problems are corrected, the sync will also improve. For a weak picture with *snow,* it may be a tuner or AGC defect, an antenna problem, or the locale.

Troubles peculiar to the sync stages and suggested troubleshooting procedures are covered in the following paragraphs. The troubleshooting flow drawings of Figure 9-10 can be used as a guide.

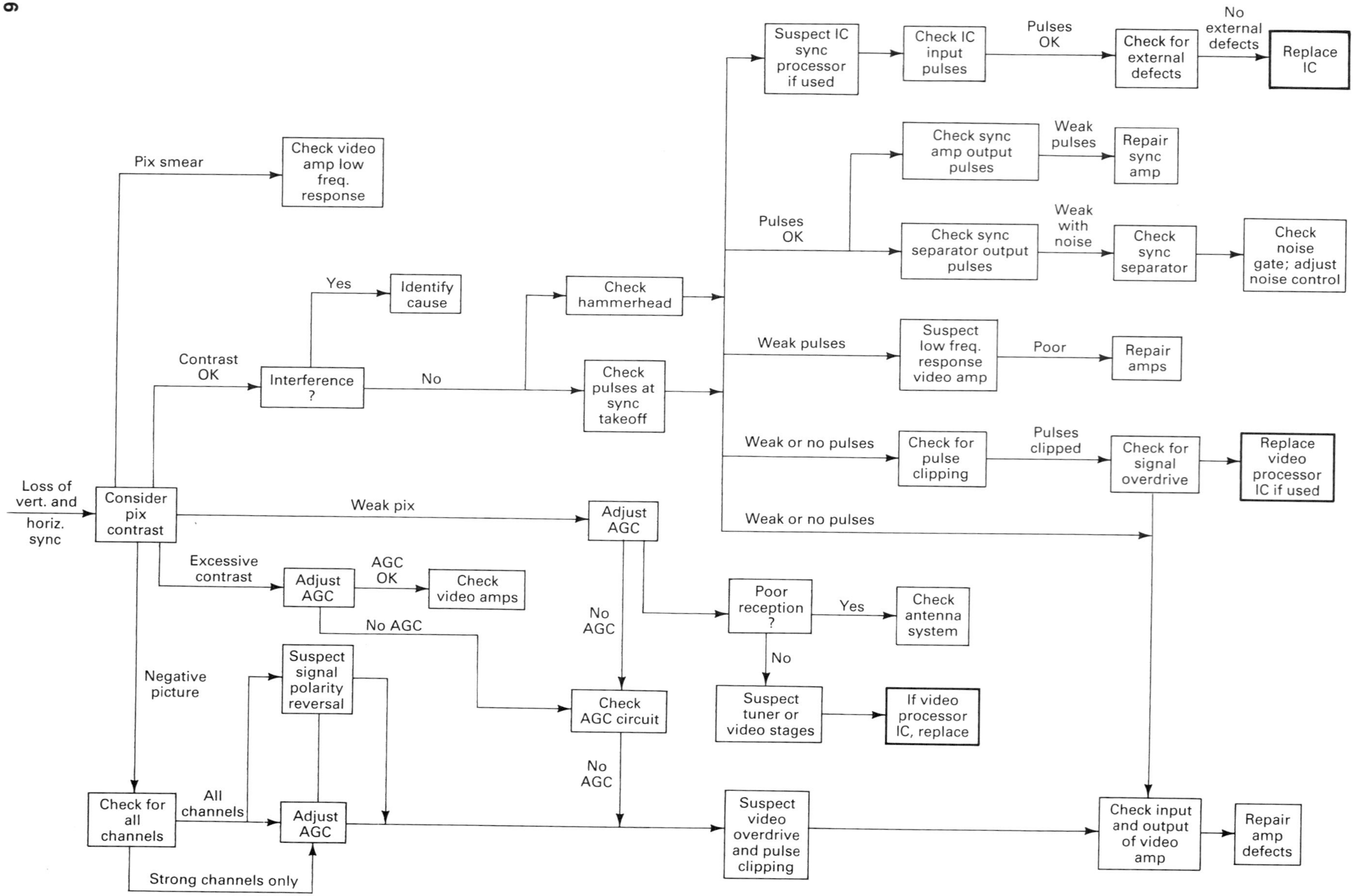


**Note: Heavy box outlines denote IC's when used**

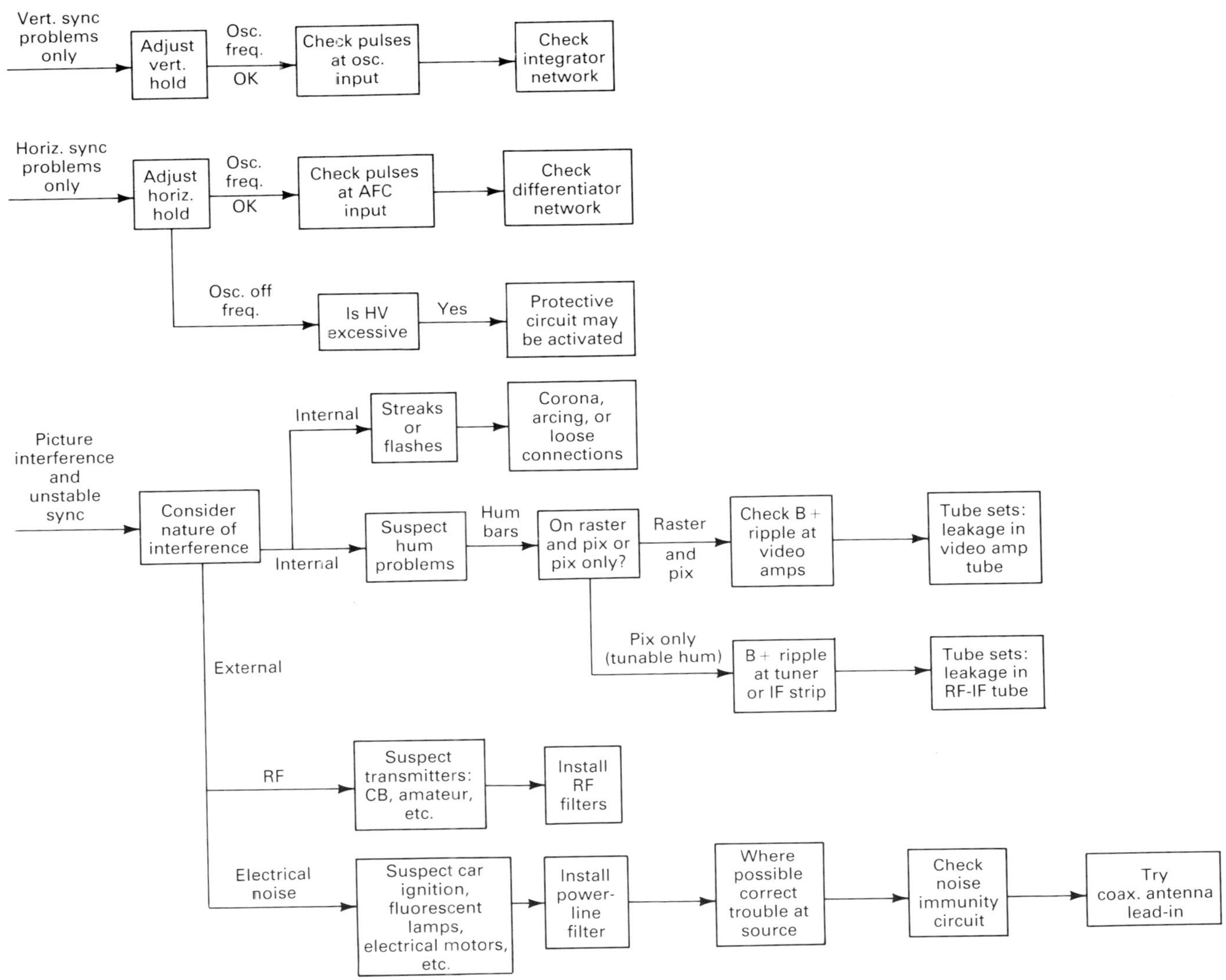


**FIG. 9-10** Sync troubleshooting flow drawing. The heavy box lines denote ICs when used. (page 1 of 2).

## Symptoms and Procedures

*Poor Vertical and Horizontal Sync.* Picture rolls and tears.

***Probable causes:*** Weak signal (if the picture contrast is also weak); pulse clipping or compression in video stages; defects in sync separator or amplifier stages; excessive noise or interference.

Scope check the composite signal at the sync takeoff point, for possible pulse clipping or compression. The pulses should be at least 25% of the total amplitude of the display, as shown in Figure 9-2. Depending on signal polarity and the scope used, the pulses may appear either upright or inverted.

Examine the hammerhead as described earlier and pictured in Figure 9-3. Misadjust the vertical hold until the blanking bar appears. Reduce the picture contrast and turn up the brightness until the bar is a light gray. The sync bar and hammerhead within the blanking bar should appear *black,* by comparison. A gray sync bar indicates weak pulses and no sync bar means that no pulses are getting through.

*Pulse Clipping and Compression.* If pulses are clipped or compressed at the sync takeoff (Figure 9-11), scope trace the signal upstream through the video stages to determine where the trouble first shows up. Common causes are signal overdrive due to poor AGC action, or a defect in a video stage that is unable to cope with even a normal signal level (see Chapters 13 and 14).

*Troubles in the Sync Stages.* If normal pulses at the sync takeoff point, scope check the input and output of the downstream sync stages (sync separator and amplifiers). Concentrate on the stage where the pulses are weakened or lost. Note whether the sync separator output is clean, with most or all the video removed. When the troublesome stage is found, check the transistor in that stage. Check its dc operating voltages, comparing with the schematic. Bias voltages are particularly critical, especially those at the sync separator. Typical voltages are shown in Figure 9-12. When switching channels, bias should normally vary from zero

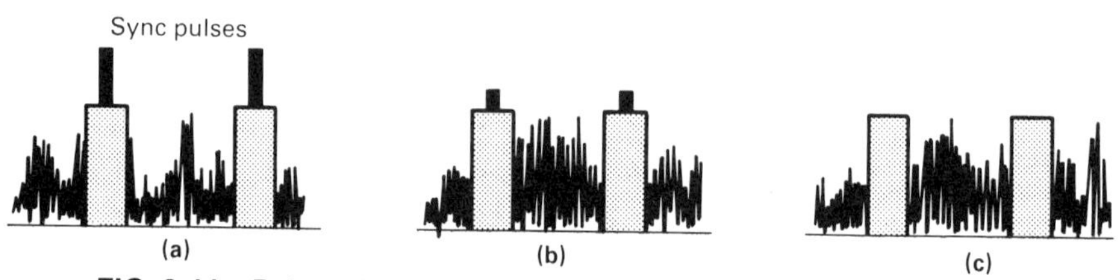


**FIG. 9-11** Pulse clipping and compression: (a) normal pulses (good sync); (b) pulse compression (unstable sync); (c) pulse clipping (complete loss of vertical and horizontal sync). Such problems usually occur in a video stage prior to the sync takeoff.

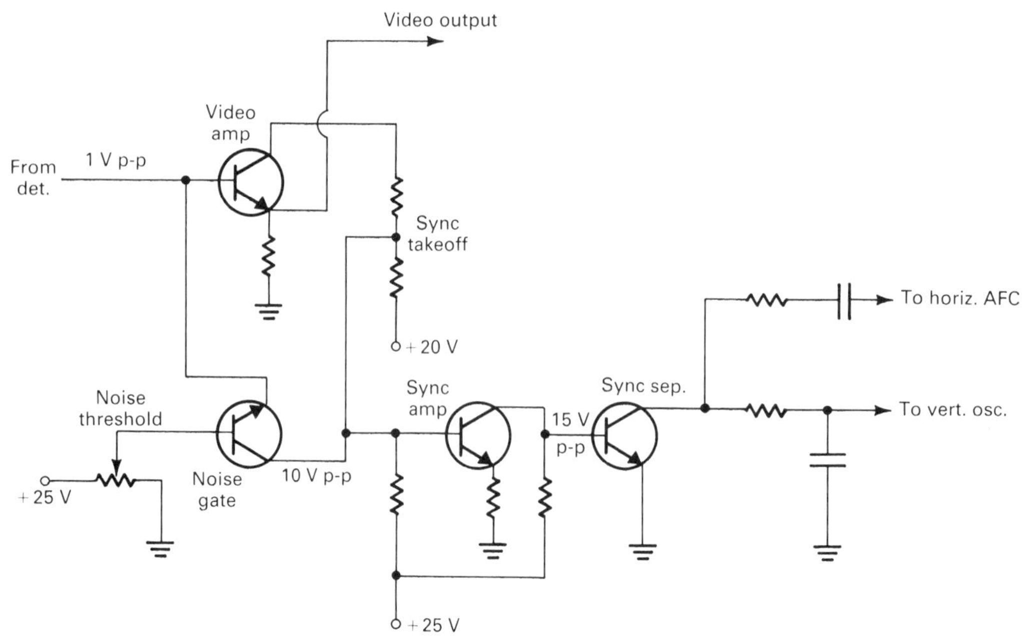


**FIG. 9-12** Typical sync stage voltages.

(off channel) to about 5 V with a strong signal. Check all suspected components. Where sync functions are performed by an IC, check dc and signal voltages at the appropriate pins. If no external defects are found, replace the IC.

### Poor Sync; Excessive Picture Contrast; (picture smearing)

***Probable causes:*** Misadjusted AGC threshold control; AGC defects; video signal overdrive.

Back off on the threshold control. If there are no changes in picture contrast, troubleshoot the AGC circuit (Chapter 13). Scope check for probable pulse clipping at the sync takeoff. Check for excessive signal at each video stage. If the levels are normal, check the stage where pulse clipping occurs. Common causes of signal overdrive are loss of AGC action, sharply peaked IF stages, and increased load resistor values in video amplifier stages.

### Loss of Sync and Negative Pictures. (black objects appear white, and white objects black)

***Probable causes:*** Signal polarity reversal somewhere between the video detector and the CRT input; reversed video detector diode.

As shown in Figure 9-4, the white blanking and sync bars indicates a reversed signal polarity at the CRT input. If the cause of the reversal is ahead of the sync takeoff, the sync pulses will also be reversed, as indicated on a scope. Signal overdrive is one possible cause. See if conditions improve when tuned to a weak station, by removing the antenna or backing off on the AGC control, if provided. In general, the same troubles that cause pulse clipping can also create this problem. Make sure that the detector diode has not been inadvertently connected backward during repairs. Check with the schematic.

### Weak Picture and Poor Sync

*Probable causes:* Anything that will weaken the signal (e.g., poor reception area, poor antenna installation, a weak stage between the antenna input and the sync takeoff, AGC defects, or misadjusted threshold control).

Locate and correct the cause of the weak signal and the sync will probably improve.

### Poor Sync and Noise Streaks on Picture

***Probable causes:*** Internal arcing; external impulse interference; improperly operating noise immunity circuit.

If arcing, locate and correct the cause. Corona arcing in the HV section and around the CRT is quite common. If interference from outside, try to locate the source and apply appropriate remedies. Try relocating the antenna and replacing ribbon-type lead-in with shielded coax cable.

Scope check all signals in the noise immunity circuit. Check the transistor(s) and dc operating voltages, comparing with the schematic. Replace all suspected components.

## QUESTIONS

1. Why is it necessary to strip the video from the pulses, and where does it take place?
2. What is the pulse train, and during what part of the raster scanning sequence does it arrive?
3. Explain how the integrated vertical sync pulse is developed.
4. Briefly explain how a transistor-type sync separator does its job.
5. Explain pulse compression and clipping, with several possible causes.
6. Explain the function of equalizing pulses in the pulse train.
7. Briefly explain how vertical and horizontal sync pulses are separated *from each other*.
8. What is a hammerhead display, and what information does it provide?
9. What is *clean* output from the sync separator?
10. Where would you check if there is (a) a normal picture and loss of sync; (b) a poor picture and loss of sync? Explain your reasoning.
11. No sync pulses are observed on a hammerhead display. What stages are suspect, and how would you proceed?
12. Explain how and under what conditions a negative picture is developed.
13. Where there is unstable sync and a scope shows considerable video at the output of the sync separator, how would you proceed?
14. What trouble symptoms would lead you to suspect (a) sync stages; (b) integrator network; (c) differentiator network and the AFC?

# 10 Horizontal drivers, output, and high voltage

The horizontal sweep voltage developed by the sweep generator is amplified by one or more driver stages, to drive the horizontal output amplifier. The output transistor drives the horizontal deflection yoke, either directly or from the horizontal output transformer (HOT), the flyback transformer. Besides contributing to horizontal beam deflection, sweep voltages from the output stage perform other functions, as shown in Figure 8-1: developing sweep-derived dc power supply voltages, including a boosted B+, and HV and focus voltage for the CRT; heater voltage for the CRT; energizing convergence and anti-pincushioning circuits; providing for horizontal retrace blanking; monitoring for hazardous overvoltage and overcurrent conditions (automatic shutdown); and furnishing gating pulses for keying numerous unrelated receiver functions to the horizontal sweep rate. With modern sets, most of these functions are performed by an IC.

## 10-1 DRIVER AMPLIFIERS

There may be one, two, or three such stages whose functions are twofold: to amplify the weak signal developed by the horizontal sweep generator and to provide sweep *power* to drive the output transistor. In some cases, driver amplifiers also contribute to waveshaping, since a *square wave* is usually required to switch the output transistor on and off. In most cases, the drivers furnish the sweep reference voltage for the AFC phase detector.

The driver transistor is transformer coupled to the output transistor. A typical driver transformer has a step-down ratio of approximately 10:1, to match the low impedance of the power transistor input circuit. A typical driver develops a sweep voltage of about 10 V p-p. For a BW set, with 100 V at the collector and drawing about 150 mA, this represents a drive power of around 15 W. For a color set, the drive power requirements are considerably higher.

### Output Stage

Figure 10-1 shows a basic output amplifier circuit as found in most BW sets. The transistor is biased close to cutoff for class B operation in the common-emitter configuration. With a drive voltage of 10 V p-p at its base and 900 V p-p developed at its output, the sweep voltage gain factor is about ×10. With 125 V at the collector and drawing approximately 200 mA, it represents about 25 W of sweep power. By comparison, the output transistor of a typical color set has a base current of nearly 100 mA, develops up to 5 kV p-p, and draws about 1.5 A for a power output of nearly 200 W, almost the total power consumption of an entire set. This is understandable since most circuits operate from scan power supplied by the horizontal output stage. Un-

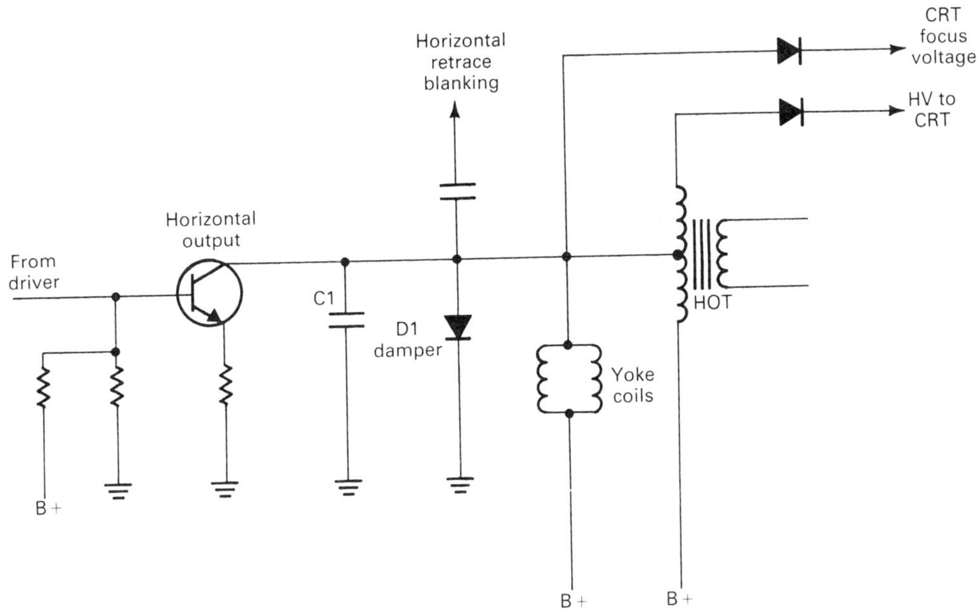


**FIG. 10-1** Basic horizontal output circuit of a black-and-white set.

like most circuits, however, the output stage gets *its* power directly from the primary power supply. Because of its high power consumption, and heat that must be dissipated, the output transistor is provided with a heat sink.

The output transistor operates as a switch, being turned on by the positive-going sweep voltage applied to its base. As its current increases, an increasing magnetic flux is developed in the yoke coils to deflect the CRT beam from left to right. Between cycles, the transistor is turned off (or nearly so), and the collapsing yoke flux results in horizontal retrace from right to left. The collapsing flux develops a self-induced voltage in the yoke coils, which is the source of energy for the first half of each horizontal trace. The second half of each trace is supplied by the output transistor. This action is shown in Figure 10-2. Normally, because of the high pulse voltage and its relatively high frequency, voltage measurements attempted at the output will result in meter or scope damage.

In Figure 10-2, the yoke and the flyback transformer are driven in parallel. In some cases the yoke is supplied from a secondary winding. Sometimes the yoke coils are wired in series, depending on impedance-matching considerations. For a typical BW set, the yoke current is about 4 A, and double that amount for a color set. The diode D1 (damper diode) damps out oscillations that occur during horizontal retrace intervals as the flux rapidly collapses around the yoke. Unless suppressed, such oscillations produce vertical "drive bars" on the left side of the screen. With older sets, the diode rectifies this voltage to develop a boosted B+ voltage, for use by other circuits. A sampling of the amplified sweep voltage is fed to the CRT (via dc-coupled video stages) for retrace blanking. Also shown is a diode that furnishes a rectified dc focus voltage to the CRT.

### Flyback Transformer

The *flyback transformer,* sometimes called the *horizontal output transformer* or simply HOT, transfers most of the sweep power to other circuits. As described in Chapter 3, it is a rather special transformer with several windings, each serving a different and specific function, including developing HV and focus voltage for the CRT. A flyback transformer, unlike those operated from the 60-Hz power line, has a ceramic (powdered iron) core (as with a yoke) to minimize losses due to the high sweep rate.

### Typical Color Set Output Stage

The circuit shown in Figure 10-3 is typical of that found in most modern color sets. Although higher power transistors are used, the driver and output transistor circuits are not too different from Figure 10-1. The yoke in this case is series connected with the anti-pincushion coils. The "trace capacitor"

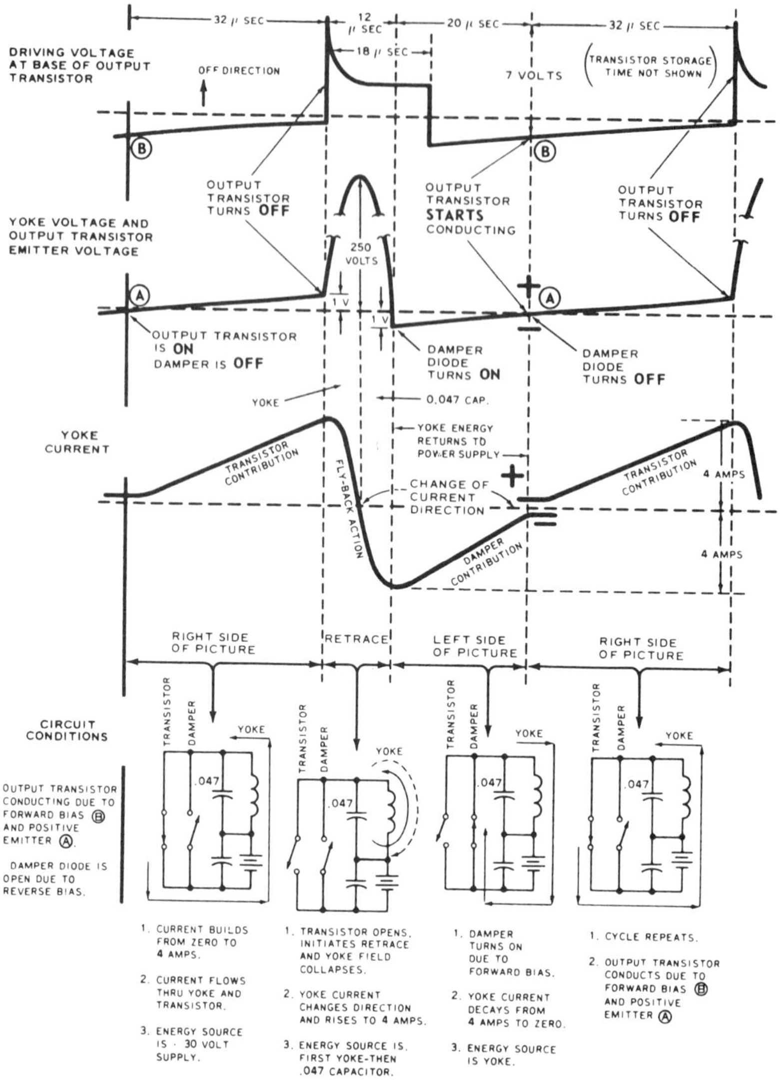


**FIG. 10-2** Developing the yoke current.

blocks the dc from the transistor collector, which would otherwise affect raster centering. Capacitor C1 (a "critical" component), sometimes called a *safety capacitor* (or retrace tuning capacitor), prevents the HV from reaching dangerous levels. There are usually two capacitors in parallel, so if one opens up there is still some protection. An open capacitor creates a dangerous increase in HV and can instantly destroy the transistor and damper and damage the flyback and other components. Note that B+ from the primary power voltage regulator gets to the transistor collector via the internal connections in the safety capacitor as pictured.

For improved efficiency, the flyback transformer shown here has two separated primary windings driven from the output transistor. There are numerous secondary windings. In addition to sweep-derived (scan) power supplies, one winding supplies heater voltage to the CRT filaments. Others furnish keying pulses for gating various circuit functions. This transformer is called an *integrated HV transformer* (IHVT) because it has the HV and focus voltage rectifiers built into the HV winding, which is split up into several coils to reduce the possibility of arc-over. The transformer is usually enclosed in a metal box to prevent radiations that can be picked up by the tuner and other circuits.

For optimum efficiency, the flyback, yoke, and associated circuits, lumped together, are made to resonate at approximately 70 kHz, the third harmonic of the horizontal sweep rate. The circled callouts on the diagram and the various sweep and dc operating voltages shown are considered later under troubleshooting.

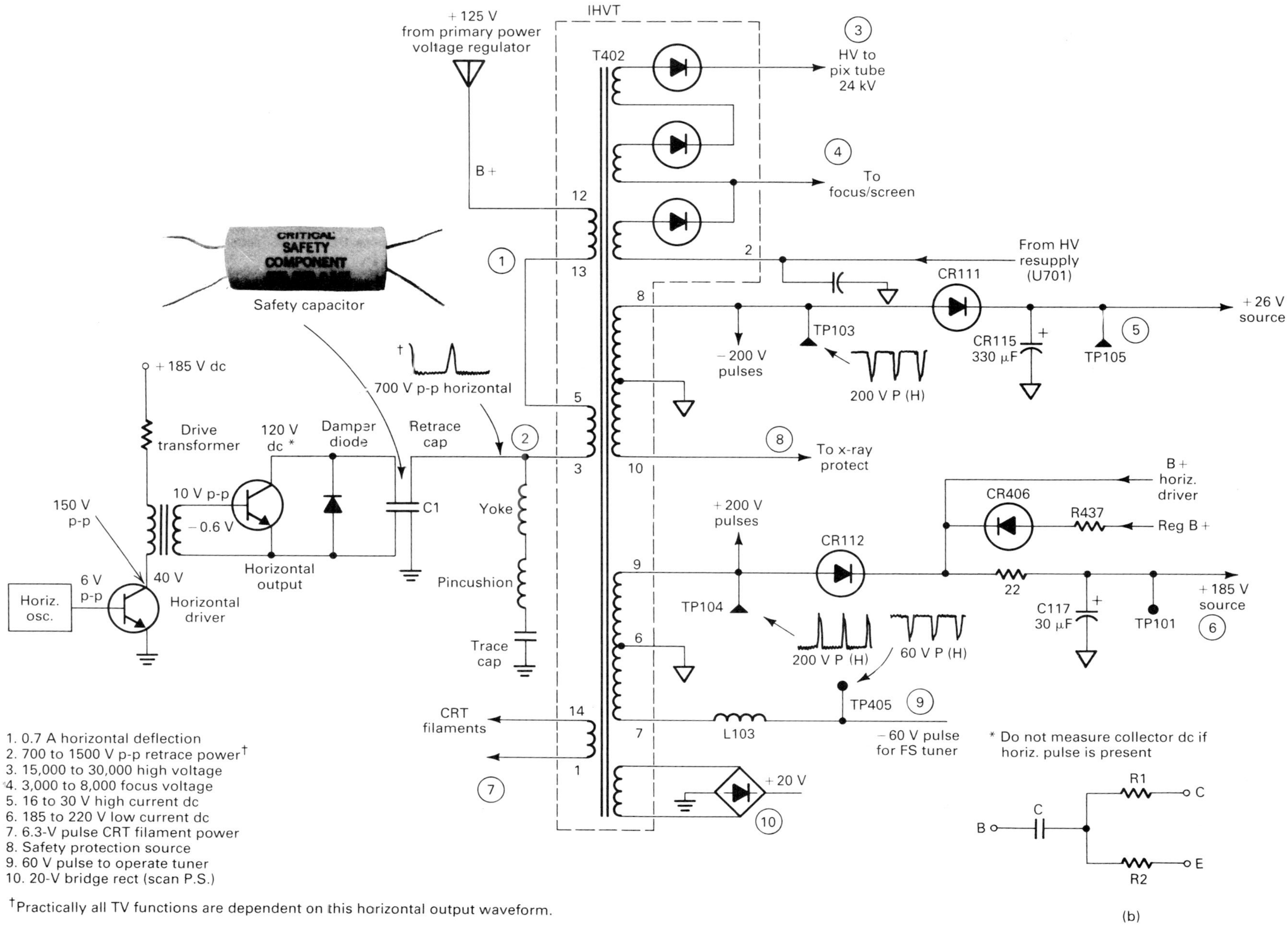


1. 0.7 A horizontal deflection
2. 700 to 1500 V p-p retrace power†
3. 15,000 to 30,000 high voltage
4. 3,000 to 8,000 focus voltage
5. 16 to 30 V high current dc
6. 185 to 220 V low current dc
7. 6.3-V pulse CRT filament power
8. Safety protection source
9. 60 V pulse to operate tuner
10. 20-V bridge rect (scan P.S.)

†Practically all TV functions are dependent on this horizontal output waveform.

**FIG. 10-3** Color set horizontal output functions.

## 10-2 SWEEP-DERIVED POWER SUPPLIES

With older sets, all B voltages were supplied directly from the 60-Hz primary power supply. For reduced power consumption (greater efficiency), and the need for less filtering, the dc operating voltages for all modern sets are obtained by rectifying the outputs of several windings of the flyback transformer. They are sometimes referred to as *secondary* or *scan power supplies*. They may deliver two or more different voltages of either polarity depending on circuit requirements. In some cases a single diode is used for half-wave rectification. The output polarity is determined by how it is connected. There may also be one or more bridge rectifiers for full-wave rectification as described in Chapter 6. Ultimately, of course, *all power* originates from the ac power line.

## 10-3 HV AND FOCUS VOLTAGE POWER SUPPLIES

A CRT requires a very high dc voltage to attract electrons from the heated cathode(s) to the "distant" screen. With BW sets, using medium-sized picture tubes, HV averages between 15 and 20 kV, to produce a beam current of a few hundred microamperes. By comparison, a large screen color set may require from 25 to 40 kV—or more in the case of projection receivers. The beam current of a typical 25-inch color set is about 1000 μA (1 mA) with the brightness turned up.

The HV coil(s) on a flyback transformer are wound with many thousands of turns of very fine wire. Heavy-gauge wire is not needed because of the low current. Early-model solid-state sets used a special stick-type rectifier which was essentially many diodes end on end (in series) to withstand the high peak-to-peak inverse voltage. Later sets employ a HV tripler unit consisting of several diodes and capacitors functioning as a voltage multiplier (Figure 10-4). With this unit, the input capacitor C1 becomes charged (to polarity as shown) as diode D1 rectifies the input pulse. Subsequently, there is a progressive buildup of voltage by the accumulating capacitor charges, each rectified by its associated diode. The last capacitor in the string becomes charged by the sum total of all capacitor charges. A tripler does not require too much voltage from the flyback transformer. In the figure, an 8-kV input produces an output of 25 kV. Many modern sets use an IHVT transformer with built-in rectifiers as described earlier (Figure 10-3). Early model sets provided some means for adjusting the HV; most modern sets do not. The HV does not require filtering, although the capacity represented by the inner and outer aquadag coatings of the CRT serve that purpose. The CRT is a very efficient capacitor and can store HV for very long periods. Hence the need for precautions when handling.

### Focus Voltage

Most color CRTs require a focus voltage between 4 and 6 kV. In some cases it is obtained by rectifying the high pulse voltage at the power transistor output

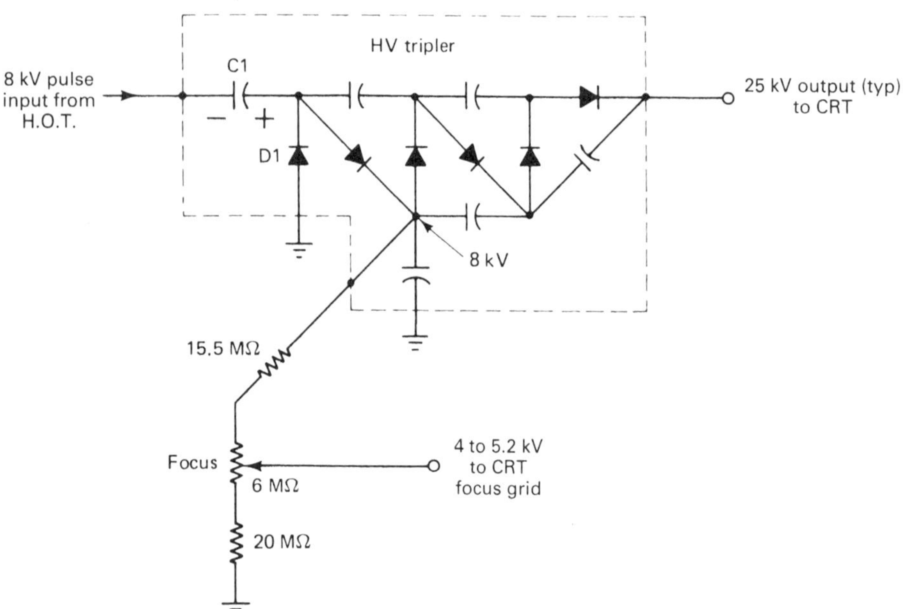


**FIG. 10-4** HV tripler circuit.

or from a separate winding on the flyback transformer. In Figure 10-4, it is obtained from the tripler unit. It is adjustable with a pot, as shown. Note the high-value resistors that are used.

### HV Arcing and Corona Prevention

At one time, HV arcing and corona discharge was a big problem, causing damage to components and sometimes starting fires. The problem has been largely overcome in modern sets with improved design, the use of more and better insulation, and "spark gaps" at critical points. As with lightning protection, a dangerously high voltage buildup will jump the gap and be safely conducted to ground. Since corona discharge usually emanates from sharp points, all such HV points must be rounded off and be well spaced from wiring and chassis ground.

### HV Regulation

The voltage output of any PS tends to drop under load because of the *IR* drop developed across its internal resistance. With a HV supply, the internal resistance is represented by the HV winding of the flyback transformer and the HV rectifier. The current, of course, is the beam current of the CRT, which is maximum when the brightness control is turned up. Amplitude variations of the video signal creates variations of beam current, resulting in unavoidable fluctuations of the HV unless it is regulated. Under adverse conditions, and when the brightness control is adjusted, voltage changes of 1 kV or more are not unusual. Such variations results in blooming and poor focus.

A raster and picture "blooms" (grows larger, and dimmer) with a reduction in HV, as when the brightness is turned up. This problem is alleviated by regulating the HV, which is usually done by regulating the B+ feed to the horizontal output transistor.

Some sets use a *saturable reactor* for HV regulation. This device is a transformer with several windings and a core that can readily be saturated. One winding carries the current of the output transistor. Another coil in conjunction with a capacitor forms what is called a *ferroresonant circuit,* which senses current changes. Such changes saturate the core by different amounts, changing the inductive reactance, and by transformer action creating desired changes to the transistor current. Where there is good regulation of the primary power supply, such a regulator is not required.

## 10-4 HORIZONTAL OUTPUT CIRCUIT VARIATIONS

The design of horizontal output and HV circuits always seems in a state of flux. Although such changes are too numerous to be described here, two representative circuits are described below.

### Dual Flyback System

This circuit uses a regular flyback transformer to develop sweep and other functions, and a similar transformer, operating from the sweep circuit, to produce the HV.

### SCR Sweep System

This system, which was popular a few years back, uses SCRs and diodes to develop horizontal sweep and HV. The circuit is shown in Figure 10-5. It is essentially a switching operation, with one SCR (SCR1) and its associated diode developing the hor-

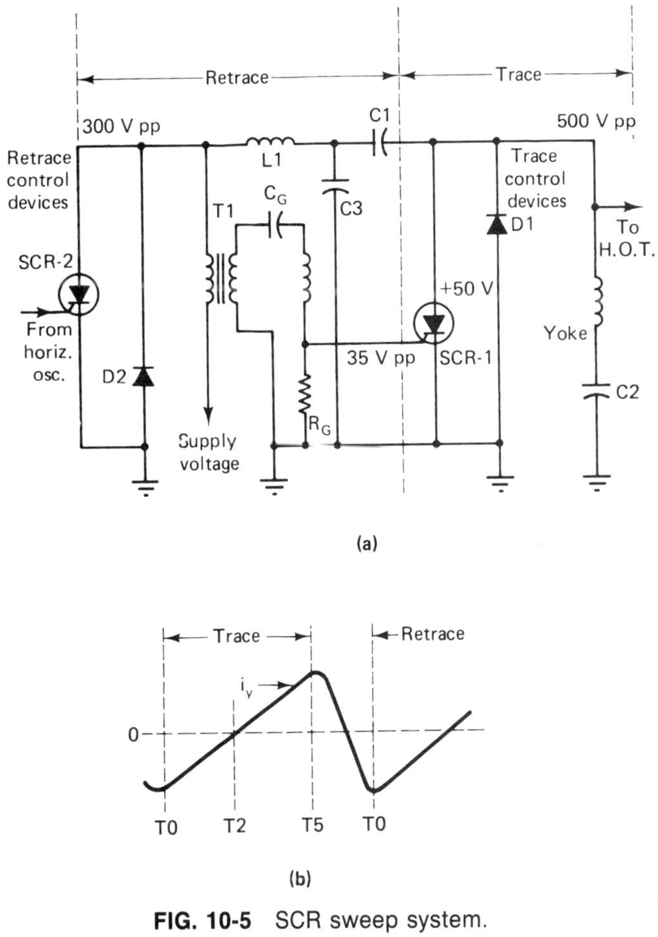


**FIG. 10-5** SCR sweep system.

izontal *trace,* and SCR2, in conjunction with its diode (D2) producing horizontal *retrace*. With each phase of the operation, the circuit is made to ring (oscillate) at a predetermined resonant frequency. The sweep voltage at the output of the trace circuit drives the flyback transformer. A variation of this circuit uses a transistor driver with a single high-power SCR in the output stage.

## 10-5 SWEEP- AND HV-RELATED CIRCUITS

There are several such circuits that are either dependent on the horizontal sweep and HV, or in other ways are associated with their operation. Horizontal retrace blanking and HV regulation as described earlier are two examples. Others are as follows.

### Horizontal Centering

Raster centering on a BW set is accomplished with a magnetic centering ring on the neck of the CRT. This method is not practical with color sets because of adverse affects on beam convergence. Most color sets inject a small amount of controlled dc into the yoke coils to offset the raster horizontally and vertically. The direction of current flow and the amount are adjustable.

### Width Control

Although late model sets dispense with this control, earlier models used various methods for controlling the amount of horizontal deflection. It can be done with a small adjustable coil either shunted across a portion of the flyback transformer or in series with the horizontal yoke.

### Automatic Brightness Limiting

Excessive beam current can damage the CRT. Different methods are used to limit the current to a safe value. Most ABL systems sense abnormal increases in HV or beam current to increase the bias on the CRT. For details, see Chapter 17.

### Pincushioning

Because of the curvature of the CRT screen, the ever-changing deflection angle of the beam(s), and the configuration of the yoke coils, the raster on a large CRT tends to bow outward or inward on the four sides. With a color set, correction is made by introducing some vertical sweep current into the horizontal yoke and some horizontal sweep current into the vertical yoke. The amplitude and waveshapes of these currents is adjusted to obtain straight raster edges. Anti-pincushioning circuitry is described in Chapter 17.

### Convergence

To obtain a white raster, a color-free monochrome picture, and a good-quality color picture, the three beams of a color CRT must be made to converge just before striking the screen. This is an extremely critical requirement involving a number of factors and adjustments that influence beam deflection and aiming.

Early-model color sets had a *convergence yoke assembly* mounted on the CRT neck immediately aft of the deflection yoke. Such a unit has three adjustable permanent magnets for adjusting beam convergence in the *center* areas of the screen. There are three electromagnets for developing a magnetic flux for convergence at the *edges* of the screen. Each set of coils is supplied with some vertical and horizontal sweep current. As with pincushioning, these currents are adjusted for a specific waveshape and amplitude. Interconnections of deflection yokes and pincushion and convergence circuits are shown in Figure 10-3. Most modern sets dispense with a convergence yoke and in its place use a number of adjustable ring magnets on the CRT neck for *static* convergence, and alter the twist and tilt of the deflection yoke (with wedges) to achieve *dynamic* convergence. More on this in Chapter 17.

### Overvoltage Protection (Startup/Shutdown System)

Excessive HV produces dangerous X-rays, and, as stated earlier, all sets must now have provisions for shutting down the receiver if the HV, for any reason, becomes excessive. A sensing circuit continuously monitors the HV, and if it increases beyond a predetermined level, a *shutdown circuit* is activated to disable the horizontal sweep generator or a driver. The resulting loss of sweep-derived voltages effectively disables all receiver stages with the exception of the primary PS. If the HV is only momentarily excessive, after a few seconds, the set operation will (or can be) restored. This is done with a *startup* circuit that restores B voltage to the oscillator or driver. Most shutdown circuits also protect against excessive *currents* that can damage or destroy components. Startup/shutdown circuits are described fully in Chapter 11.

## 10-6 FOLDOUT SCHEMATIC

The horizontal output, HV, and related circuits of the foldout schematic are typical of those found in most modern color sets. The output transistor is supplied with +125 V, which is regulated by module STR3125 in the primary PS. The sweep voltage exits IC501 at pin 24 and drives an external driver transistor (Q402). The output of the driver is coupled to the output transistor Q404 via a step-down driver transformer. Q404 has a built-in damper diode. Also note the parallel-connected critical safety capacitors. The sweep output of the transistor goes directly to the flyback transformer and the parallel connected yoke coils.

Horizontal blanking pulses from the flyback transformer are combined with vertical blanking pulses at the junction of diodes D204 and D205, amplified by video driver Q202, to drive the emitters of the RGB video output amplifiers. The blanking pulses superimposed on the video signals are fed to the three cathodes of the CRT, to darken the screen during retrace intervals.

The flyback transformer is the source of four sweep-derived PS voltages: +170, +125, +16.5, and +24 V, in addition to HV and focus voltages. Note that the transformer is an *exact replacement item,* as are other shaded areas and components on the diagram. The flyback transformer has built-in (integrated) HV rectifiers to develop 18 kV for the CRT anode. As with many modern sets, no HV adjuster is provided. Focus and screen controls feed lower dc voltages to the corresponding gun elements. Note the arc gaps tied to the gun elements. This set employs an adjustable PM unit for convergence, so there is no need for an interface with the sweep circuits.

The overvoltage circuit for protecting against x-rays consists of D402, D403, and the switching circuit within IC501. An overvoltage condition is monitored from pin 3 of the flyback through a rectifier circuit to develop 19 V of dc, which is then reduced by a voltage divider. This voltage is applied to pin 23 of the IC. If the voltage increases beyond the zener limits, the horizontal drive is turned off, to shut down the receiver.

## 10-7 TROUBLESHOOTING AND REPAIR

Horizontal sweep generator problems are covered in Chapter 8. Here we are concerned only with troubleshooting the drivers, the output stage and its associated circuits, and the HV section. Since this is the hardest-worked section of a set, this is where most breakdowns occur. The most common trouble symptoms are loss of HV (no raster), and loss of raster and sound because the shutdown circuit has been activated. There are numerous possible causes for both of these conditions. The question is: where to begin? For loss of HV, a good starting point is the horizontal output transistor (see the flow drawing, Figure 10-7). Results of the tests called for gets you started in the right direction; the detailed drawings that follow will aid in localizing the trouble, then isolating the defect. (*Reminder:* If the receiver employs a hot ground PS, it is *essential* to use an isolation transformer in the power line.)

Some preliminary tests should include a visual check for CRT heater glow. If a color set and the filaments are lit, it means that the sweep circuit is working, at least up to the flyback output. If there is no heater glow, it could be a burned-out filament or bad socket contact, but it usually means no output from the sweep circuit. The TV may be in the shutdown mode. Check for dc scan power voltages, and if there is none, check for the presence of a high-amplitude pulse voltage at the collector of the output transistor. A small neon bulb is good for this test. At the risk of damage, avoid using a meter or scope unless designed to withstand the high pulse voltages normally present. Avoid arc testing, which can damage or destroy sensitive diodes, transistors, and ICs. After removing power feel the output transistor. There is a good clue if it is running cold, or overheating. If the latter, turn the set off immediately.

If there is no sweep output, it is safe to check for dc collector voltage. If no dc, check back to its source, the voltage regulator and the primary power supply. If there is dc at the collector but little or no sweep pulse, suspect loss of drive, a bad output transistor, a shorted flyback transformer or yoke, or even a HV short in the CRT.

*Caution:* For troubles associated with the output stage, avoid destruction of the output transistor by operating the set at reduced line voltage until the problem is corrected.

In lieu of a variac, connect a 100-W bulb in place of the line fuse or CB, as a visual indicator. Another useful hint: Before replacing an output transistor when conditions are in doubt, install a substitute unit in its place. Such a temporary "dummy transistor," shown in Figure 10-3b, can be mounted on a discarded transistor base for easy installation. Measure voltages at all three pins, comparing with the schematic. Make sure that the forward bias is not excessive.

If there is no sound, HV, or CRT heater glow, check for B+ output from the primary power supply. If there is none, check for such things as a blown fuse, tripped circuit breaker, or defective line cord. If there are signs of overheating, check for a shorted rectifier or filter or other B+ grounding.

If the B+ is okay, there is either a sweep circuit defect (oscillator, driver, output stage, or flyback transformer), or the set is in the shutdown mode. One way to verify is to monitor HV and sound (with volume turned up) at the moment of receiver turn-on. A momentary burst of sound and a HV reading that quickly drops off indicates that the shutdown function is being activated. Attempt a manual "kick start," and if successful, it indicates a startup circuit defect. If no startup, the oscillator or driver is at fault. While monitoring for HV, temporarily defeat the shutdown circuit. If the HV is excessive, try reducing the line voltage pending the outcome of further tests. Determine and correct the cause, which may be a sweep circuit defect, a faulty voltage regulator, or the ABL circuit. If there is normal HV, the shutdown circuit is probably at fault. For details, see Chapter 11.

If no raster but the sweep output is okay, check for HV dc at the CRT ultor (Figure 10-6). If there is little or no HV, check for defects in the flyback HV winding, or a bad HV rectifier, or a tripler unit.

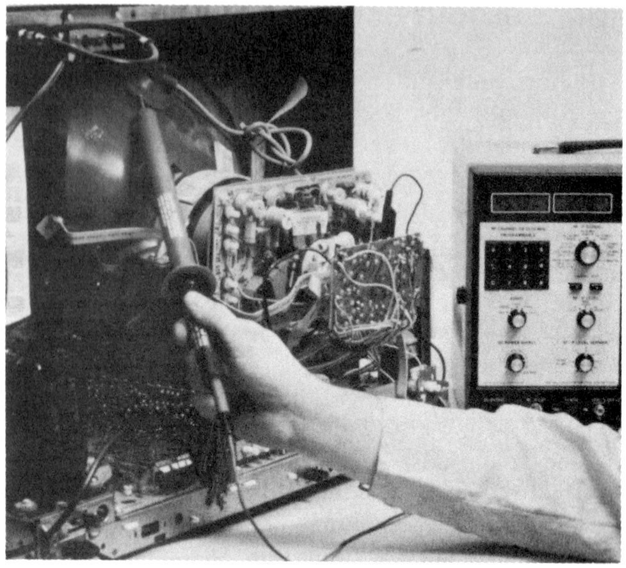

**FIG. 10-6** HV checking. (Courtesy of *Sencore News.*)

If no raster but the HV is okay, check for the loss of other CRT operating voltages, excessive CRT bias, or a bad CRT.

Common sweep-related trouble symptoms and procedures are described in the following paragraphs. As an aid, refer to the appropriate flow drawings (Figures 10-7 and 10-8).

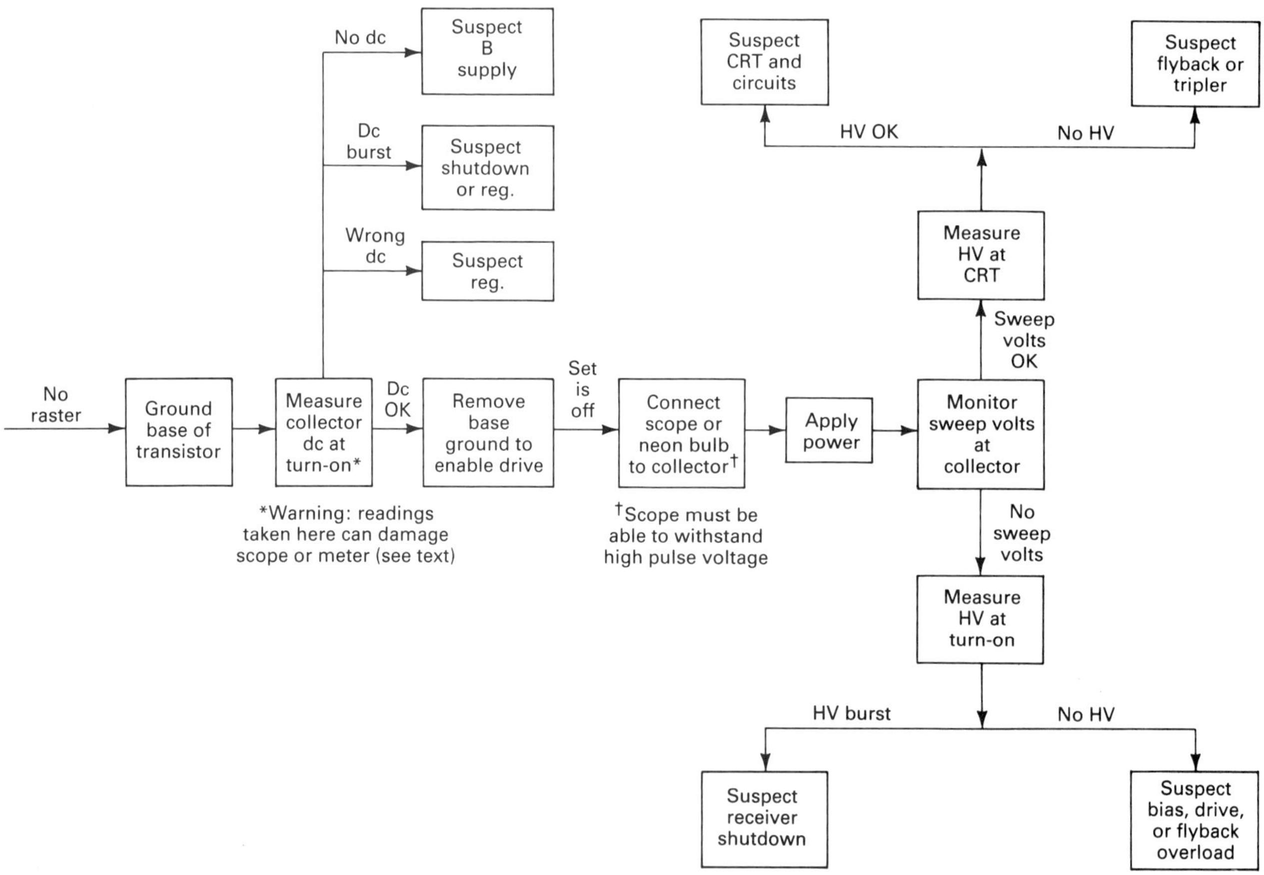


**FIG. 10-7** Preliminary testing of horizontal output and HV.

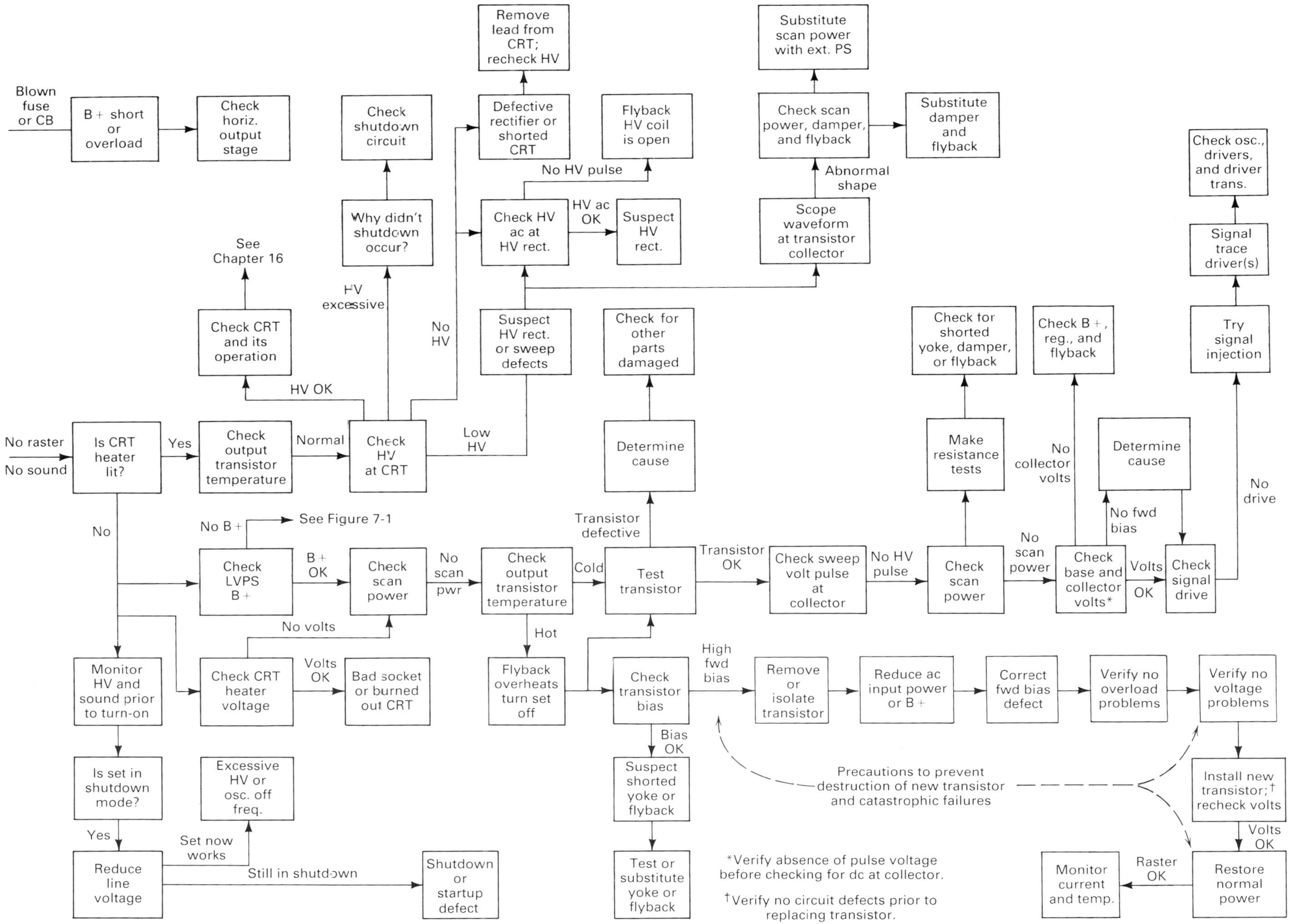


**FIG. 10-8** Horizontal output and HV troubleshooting.

## Symptoms and Procedures

### *Blown Fuse or Tripped Circuit Breaker*

***Probable causes:*** Short in primary PS; shorted power output transistor or damper diode; shorted flyback or yoke; shorted filter or bypass capacitor in voltage distribution network; excessive current drain or overload by driver or output transistor.

With the set off and after grounding out any residual voltage, make a resistance-to-ground check at various B+ circuit points. A reading less than about 5 kΩ usually means high leakage or a B+ short. Isolate the cause as described in Chapters 5 and 6.

Check current drain of the horizontal driver and output transistor. If excessive, troubleshoot these stages (as will be described later). When in doubt, try isolating these stages from B+ to see if the suspected overcurrent is relieved. Don't be tempted to use a higher-rated fuse and avoid resetting the CB more than twice since it can be damaged by overuse. A useful trick is to use a 100-W lamp in place of the fuse or CB until the problem has been resolved. The extent of an overload can be determined by the brightness of the lamp. "Normal" brightness varies with different sets.

### *No Sound; No Raster*

***Probable causes:*** Primary PS defect; horizontal sweep circuit defect; excessive HV or overcurrent activating the shutdown circuit; startup or shutdown circuit defects.

For each of these possibilities there are numerous possible causes. Each must be considered separately, as follows. Check for B+ at the primary PS. If none, proceed as described in Chapter 6. If there's voltage at the main bus, check for loss of dc at the output of a voltage regulator or a voltage distribution network that supplies both the sound and horizontal sweep stages.

If scan power is used, check for scan voltages and a CRT heater glow. If no scan power, the defect is either with the sweep stages or the receiver is in shutdown. If the latter is suspected, temporarily defeat its purpose (by examining the schematic) and check for excessive HV. If HV is okay, localize the trouble to one sweep stage by scope tracing or signal injection. Compare sweep voltage amplitudes and waveshapes with the schematic, particularly the drive voltage at the power stage input. Where there is little or no drive, and no "run power" is produced by the scan PSs, to operate the oscillator/driver stages, testing can be done using an external PS adjusted to the amount shown on the schematic. When the breakdown has been localized, check for B+ to that stage, and the transistor or IC operating voltages. Compare with the schematic. Check the transistor and all associated components. If an IC, check for external defects and if none, replace the IC.

*Note:* A scope used for checking the all-important waveform at the collector of the output transistor must be capable of withstanding voltages up to 1500 V p-p in some cases. If not, it is necessary to use a 100-to-1 high-voltage capacitor divider probe. A suitable 3-to-1 divider probe that can be made up consists of a 33-kΩ resistor series with a 68-kΩ resistor. The 33-kΩ unit goes to ground, the 68-kΩ to the transistor collector, and the junction of the two to the scope. When properly calibrated, a 500 V p-p display on the scope represents 1500 V p-p.

*Caution:* Remember to have the scope turned off when making connections, particularly the ground lead. As an alternative to using a divider probe, a waveform can be observed by bringing the scope probe close to, *but not touching,* the transistor. As a precaution cover the probe end with insulation.

Make a critical comparison of the pulse display at the transistor collector, with that shown on the schematic. Any deviations from the norm is indicative of subtle defects that can lead to an early breakdown of the transistor and other components. Such defects include a few shorted windings in the yoke, the flyback, or a cracked core; a shorted driver transformer; a leaky damper diode or safety capacitor; and oscillator timing circuit defects. The duty cycle of the pulse display is also important, and any abnormalities must be corrected to forestall early breakdowns.

*Caution:* An inadvertent short or ground can *instantly* destroy the expensive output transistor. Use extreme care when probing and taking measurements. Where the transistor is defective, do not be hasty in replacing it; the cause may still be present, and unless found and corrected, will destroy the new replacement. In addition, look for other bad components that may be the *result* rather than the *cause* of the breakdown. If it is not essential that the output stage be operating when making certain tests or repairs, as a precaution, disable or remove the transistor until the problem is corrected.

Make an accurate bias check on the output transistor, as measured between the base and the emitter. A forward bias of more than 0.6 V (the amount required to turn it on) can cause thermal runaway and destroy the transistor, the flyback transformer, and other components. (There is usually a low *reverse* bias.) Such an abnormal bias can be caused by a short or leakage in the transistor or a defective associated component. Check for overheating by touch (with power off), after several minutes of operation. Overcurrent often produces wax drippings under the flyback transformer, which may already be damaged.

If transistor runs cold, it is not conducting, and the cause may be a defective transistor, too much reverse bias, loss of drive, loss of dc collector voltage, or an open circuit (such as the flyback primary or an emitter circuit fuse or resistor). Check current by computation using the measured *IR* drop across a resistor in the emitter circuit or the "cold" end of the flyback transformer. For a color set the typical current drain is between 0.5 and 1.5 A. Loss of collector voltage can be due to a voltage regulator defect or an open flyback primary. If there are signs of overheating, the dc may be grounded out. The possibilities are: the transistor is shorted, there is a shorted damper diode or "safety capacitor," or there is a grounded coil in the flyback.

If there is B voltage at the collector but little or no pulse voltage (as indicated by a neon bulb or whatever), and loss of HV and scan voltages, suspect the following: loss of drive, circuit loading by a shorted scan PS, or shorted windings in the flyback or yoke. Shorted flyback or yoke coils will generally overheat. After several minutes of operation, remove power and feel the suspected coil for hot spots. Also check for arcing that may show up with reduced ambient lighting. Check for possible loading by a shorted scan PS.

An ohms check will sometimes reveal a shorted flyback or yoke, but the test is not valid if only a few windings are shorted out. In such cases, check by ringing with a flyback/yoke tester. In lieu of a tester, try the following. Disconnect the yoke. Check for pulse voltage at the transistor collector. Any increase indicates loading by a shorted yoke. Disconnect the flyback from the transistor collector terminal. Connect the primary of a substitute flyback (or a similar inductance) in place of the original (i.e., between the transistor and B+). Check for an amplified pulse voltage at the collector. Any improvement from previous tests indicates that the original flyback is shorted. (*Reminder:* When defective, always replace a flyback or yoke with an exact replacement.)

For the possibility of loading by a HV short in the CRT, simply remove the HV lead from the CRT ultor and see if sweep voltages are restored. If loss of sound and raster and no drive to the output stage, the set may be in the shutdown mode, either because of excessive HV or a malfunctioning shutdown circuit. For troubleshooting procedures, see Chapter 11.

*Summation.* Considering the importance of the subject, a recap seems appropriate at this time. The following is a summary of all factors relating to problems in the horizontal output stage, especially how to avoid destruction of the power transistor and other components while testing.

Where defects associated with the output transistor and the flyback are suspected, start by reducing the line voltage (with a variac) to about 30 V ac. Prepare to monitor the following: the drive voltage at the base terminal, the dc at the collector terminal, and the transistor current. (*Caution:* It is generally unwise to measure current *directly,* since a shorted transistor can instantly destroy the meter.) Determine current by the voltage drop across a resistor in the emitter or collector circuits. If the oscillator or driver operates from scan power, use an external PS adjusted to the amount shown on the schematic.

Slowly increase the line voltage to obtain about +70 V at the collector. The current reading should be about 50% of normal. No current can mean an open transistor junction or emitter resistor, or an open flyback. Low current can be caused by excessive bias or low drive. High current can be caused by excessive drive, a leaky output transistor, a bad flyback, or severe loading by a bad yoke or a defect in one of the scan PSs. For such possibilities, correct the problem *before* applying full line voltage.

Disable or remove the output transistor and temporarily restore normal line voltage. Measure the collector dc voltage. If excessive, suspect a voltage regulator defect such as a shorted "pass" transistor. Proceed as follows: While monitoring the dc collector voltage, gradually increase the line voltage starting at about 80 V ac. The dc should correspondingly increase, then level off. If it continues to increase with a higher-than-normal line voltage, the regulator is not doing its job. Voltage regulator troubleshooting is covered in Chapters 5 and 6.

Scope the drive signal. If there is little or no drive or an abnormal waveform, troubleshoot and repair the oscillator or driver *before* reinstalling the output transistor. If the drive is normal, reduce the line voltage again to about 30 V and install the transistor. If the current is high, check for flyback loading (e.g., a shorted yoke) or one of the scan PSs. Disconnect all flyback secondary circuits individually until the current drops to a reasonable amount. If the collector voltage is high (equal to the source voltage), check for an open transistor, emitter resistor, or insufficient drive signal.

Scope check the collector waveform. If it is of low amplitude or if there are indications of ringing on the baseline of the display, suspect a bad flyback or heavy loading. Check for a leaky damper diode or a leaky or open safety capacitor. (*Reminder:* An open safety capacitor will result in excessive HV and can instantly destroy the transistor and the damper, and damage the flyback and other components. *Do not* apply full power until the trouble is found and corrected.)

### SCR Sweep System Problems

***Probable causes:*** Defective SCRs and diodes in the switching circuits; other defects as described for the transistor sweep circuit.

Detailed troubleshooting of this not-too-popular system will not be given. The *general* approach to problems is as follows: If a blown fuse or tripped CB, check for a shorted SCR and/or diode in the *retrace* circuit, a shorted coupling capacitor, and an open circuit in the *trace* section (see Figure 10-5). If there is B voltage at the retrace circuit, check for a high ac pulse voltage at the anode of the retrace SCR. If little or no pulse, suspect a trace circuit defect or loss of signal drive from the oscillator. Check for drive voltage at the gate of the retrace SCR, which is normally about 10 V p-p. If there is no drive, inject a generator signal having a sharply spiked waveform. If the drive signal is reduced when connected, either the generator has insufficient output capability or the circuit is loaded by a shorted or leaky SCR, diode, or other associated component.

If the drive from the generator or receiver oscillator is normal, check for a triggering pulse at the gate of the trace SCR. If there is little or no pulse, it is either grounded out by the SCR or is lost in the coupling components. Scope trace the pulse from its source (the retrace SCR anode), the timing transformer, capacitor, and the coil. If the trigger pulse is normal, check for an amplified sweep voltage at the trace SCR anode. The waveshape is critical.

If there is no sweep voltage at the trace SCR, check all components in the trace circuit, particularly the SCR and diode. If the sweep voltage is weak, the prime suspects are a shorted flyback or yoke. An open in either of these circuits results in a high pulse voltage buildup that will quickly destroy the trace SCR and its diode.

### No Raster, Sound OK

***Probable causes:*** Loss of HV; defective CRT; loss of CRT operating voltages; excessive CRT bias.

For this condition, most of the possibilities just described for a dead set do not apply. Since there is sound, and assuming that the set uses scan power, everything must be okay up to the output of the flyback transformer. With a neon bulb, or checking for corona with an insulated screwdriver, check for high-amplitude pulse voltage from the HV coil of the flyback transformer. If little or no voltage indication, check for an open (or near open) HV winding, or HV rectifier if it is an IHVT. Where an external rectifier or tripler unit is used, and the high pulse voltage is okay at its input but there is little or no HV dc output, check for a bad rectifier, by substitution. (An ohmmeter check is not valid.) There is also a possibility that the HV is *grounded out* by a shorted CRT. To check, remove the HV lead from the CRT and see if HV is restored. When the HV is restored, and under load (with a bright raster), adjust to the amount specified on the schematic.

Where the HV is okay but there is no raster, test the CRT; and if that too is okay, check all CRT operating voltages. Record all readings and compare with the schematic.

### Raster, but No Sound

***Probable causes:*** Loss of B+ to the sound stages; defective sound stage or speaker.

If sound stages are supplied with B+ from a separate scan PS, refer to schematic and check for dc from that particular PS. If little or no dc, check for a defective rectifier, shorted filter capacitor, an open voltage dropping resistor, or in rare cases, an open flyback coil. A fusible resistor is often used with scan PSs as protection against a short in one of the load circuits supplied with scan power. Without protection, such conditions will overload the flyback transformer, increasing the transistor current to initiate a shutdown. For sound-stage defects, see Chapter 18.

### Small Raster. (reduced height and width)

***Probable causes:*** Low line voltage; low primary power B+; excessive HV.

For low B+ conditions, see Chapter 6. If the set uses scan power, check for reduced output from the horizontal sweep stages. Measure HV at the ultor with the brightness turned up. If greater than the amount specified, determine and correct the cause as explained earlier. If a control is provided, adjust as necessary. If the set has a shutdown circuit, determine why it did not activate (see Chapter 11). (*Note:* The greater the HV, the more difficult it becomes for the CRT beam to deflect. Conversely, *low HV* produces a *larger* raster.)

### Reduced Raster Width

***Probable causes:*** Low B+ feeding the horizontal sweep section; reduced output from the sweep stages; shorted flyback transformer.

Check B+ and compare with schematic. Check B+ output from each scan PS. Check for a weak sweep stage as described earlier. Many shorted windings in a flyback transformer will kill the HV; a partial short is a common cause of reduced width, but do not confuse with a keystone raster as caused by a bad yoke.

### HV Arcing

***Probable causes:*** Insulation breakdowns; excessive HV; Poor lead dress.

There are three kinds: arcing of the *HV dc, HV ac,* and *corona discharge* or leakage. Arcing of the HV *dc* is characterized by a loud cracking sound and is usually clearly visible. It may occur where a cracked or deteriorated HV lead is close to the chassis or other grounded item. The best remedy is a new lead. Attempts at repairs can result in a fire or damage to components in or near the arc path. Arcing can also occur around the CRT ultor if a loose terminal or accumulated dirt and grime on the glass. This area should be kept clean since even fingerprints can create a problem. (*Caution:* Avoid getting shocked. A CRT can retain a charge for a very long time.)

A newly installed CRT will sometimes arc inside, but this poses no problem and will usually subside after a short time when particles burn away. Arcing can also occur with poor grounding of the outer aquadag coating on the CRT. For this, relocate or tighten the grounding spring against the CRT bowl. If there is excessive HV, determine the cause, adjust, or if a late-model set, determine why automatic shutdown did not occur. One possible cause of excessive HV is an open or changed value of *safety capacitor* across the damper diode.

HV *ac* arcing can take place inside a flyback or yoke, or from the wiring between the transformer and an external HV rectifier or tripler unit. The arc site may not be visible except in a darkened room. Attempts at repairs are not advised and the items should be replaced. (*Reminder:* Arcing can destroy critical and sensitive components.)

A *corona discharge* occurs when air becomes ionized by HV. It is easily recognized by the sweetish smell of ozone and a faint hissing sound, and is quite common in areas of high humidity. It tends to emanate as a thin "streamer" from sharp HV points, and sometimes from the HV winding of the flyback transformer. For the latter, a new boot may be installed if the original has deteriorated. The location of weak corona can be difficult to pinpoint even in a dark room. A length of tubing can be helpful when used as a stethoscope probe. Once located, the remedy is obvious: increased spacing, rounding off any sharp points, or breaking up the discharge path with some good-quality insulation. In some cases, it helps to dress the HV wiring and/or apply an insulating film with an aerosol spray.

*Yoke Ringing.* (rippled scanning lines on the left side of the screen)

***Probable cause:*** Yoke shunting capacitor is open or wrong value.

Check schematic for proper value of yoke capacitor. Try substituting a slightly different value.

*Keystone Raster.* (trapezoidal distortion)

***Probable cause:*** Shorted yoke.

A shorted yoke can also load the horizontal output, reducing the HV and scan voltages, and in some cases initiating a shutdown. When suspected, check and compare the resistances of both horizontal coils; they should be equal. If not, confirm by removing the yoke from the CRT. With the yoke still connected and the *brightness turned down* (to prevent burning the screen), turn on the set. Carefully observe for signs of arcing within the coils. After a few minutes remove power and feel the coils (the innermost windings). A shorted coil will be warm to the touch.

For a faster and more conclusive test, use a flyback/yoke tester. If still in doubt, try substitution. With a substitute yoke, however, there may be reduced deflection because of a mismatch.

*Horizontal Linearity Problems.* (picture is stretched or compressed at the left, right, or center)

***Probable causes:*** Any defect in the sweep circuits that creates an abnormal waveshape; excessive drive; transistor leakage; defective damper diode or safety capacitor; in older sets, a misadjusted linearity control.

Check for adequate B+ and scope check all stages, comparing waveforms with those shown on the schematic. Where a negative feedback loop is used, check all associated components after breaking the loop. After trouble is localized, check the transistor in suspected stage, its operating voltages, and associated components. If an IC, and after checking for external defects, replace the IC.

*Blooming.* (Raster and picture expands and gets dimmer as the brightness is turned up)

***Probable causes:*** Excessive beam current; ineffective ABL circuit; insufficient CRT bias; poor HV regulation; misadjusted CRT screen grid controls.

If the screen cannot be darkened with brightness control, check for insufficient bias [measured between grid(s) and cathode(s)]. If bias problems, check grid and cathode voltages to ground and compare with schematic. The reading that is abnormal establishes which circuit is at fault (see Chapter 17).

Try backing off on the master brightness control if there is one, also the screen grid voltage controls; then readjust the tracking (see Chapter 17).

Check the HV regulation by monitoring the HV at the CRT ultor as the brightness control is varied. Some variations can be expected but should not exceed $\pm 1$ kV for a typical large-screen CRT. Check the resistance of the flyback HV coil. A high-resistance, near-open winding is not uncommon. If an IHVT type, the internal rectifiers may also be defective. Try substituting external rectifiers or the tripler, if used.

Check the regulation of the B+ feed to the horizontal output transistor. Check all regulator circuit components, particularly transistors, zener diodes, and SCRs. Replace any that are suspect. If low B+ at the output of the primary PS, check for weak rectifiers or increased resistor values (see Chapter 6). When warranted, try PS substitution using an external, well-regulated PS. Adjust to the amount specified on the schematic.

Check for excessive current drain of the horizontal output transistor. If excessive, troubleshoot the circuit as described previously. Check the operation of the ABL circuit. If suspected, check for excessive beam current at full brilliance. Replace all ABL critical components that may be suspect.

### Poor Focus

***Probable causes:*** *All* possibilities described for blooming; weak CRT; defects in focus voltage supply.

*Note:* A poor-quality picture is not necessarily a focus problem. Switch to a blank channel and closely examine the *raster*. The scanning lines should be sharply defined over most of the screen area. Ideally, good focus should be maintained over the full range of the brightness and other controls, although in some cases there is a trade-off. With poor focus, the lines become blurred and in extreme cases cannot be seen, resulting in loss of fine detail.

Start by adjusting the focus control and checking the CRT for emission and gas. If a color tube, compare the emissions of all three guns. Clues to a weak CRT include a milky appearance to white picture objects and a slowness in achieving full brightness during warm-up. Do not be hasty in making a replacement until all possible causes have been ruled out (see Chapter 17).

Check the focus voltage under load (with a medium-bright screen). If the voltage is low, try substituting the focus rectifier with one known to be good. Check for proper amount of HV as specified on the schematic. If abnormal, adjust or correct the cause as described previously. If the best focus is obtained at one extreme of the control, check all associated high-value (several megohms), high-wattage resistors. Where all else fails, try substituting with different values. If necessary, repeat all tests described for *blooming,* one of the more common causes of poor focus.

*Output Transistor Has a Short Life.* If receiver operation seems normal, it could be an intermittent condition creating increases in transistor current, periodic increases in line voltage, or a subtle defect associated with the output stage. Try monitoring the line voltage at times when power consumption in the community is lowest. Operate the set for lengthly periods on the bench while monitoring the sweep drive and output voltages, and the transistor dc operating voltages, particularly the bias. Even a *slight* increase in the normal forward bias can be significant. Monitor the transistor current with a low candlepower car bulb as a visual indicator in the emitter or collector circuit. Replace the transistor, the damper diode, and the safety capacitor even if they check out okay. This also applies to any suspected components in the voltage regulator, particularly if the B+ measures a little high.

### Intermittent Problems

***Probable causes:*** Most any intermittent defect, as described in Chapter 5.

Suggested procedures, depending on the symptoms, are as follows. If there is intermittent loss of sound and raster, the likely possibilities are a LVPS problem, intermittent HV, or shutdown circuit defects. Monitor the dc output of the primary PS, the

CRT for heater glow, and the sweep voltage at the input and output of the output transistor.

If an intermittent raster and the sound is okay, monitor the HV and the CRT operating voltages. Try tapping the neck of the CRT; an intermittent tube is not unusual. If the set does not use scan power, monitor the B+ to the horizontal sweep stages, the sweep voltage at the input and output of each stage, the HV, and the CRT.

## QUESTIONS

1. Name all functions performed by the horizontal output stage of a color set.
2. Under what conditions is the current flow from the HV power supply (a) maximum; (b) minimum; (c) fluctuating? Explain.
3. How is the HV regulated in a modern set?
4. What is good and poor voltage regulation? Give examples.
5. What is the purpose of the startup/shutdown circuit?
6. Explain blooming, listing several possible causes.
7. Explain how a damper is used to produce a B boost voltage.
8. If there is loss of drive, what happens to the current drain of an output transistor? Explain.
9. What is yoke ringing, and what purpose does it serve?
10. How would you determine if a dead set is in the shutdown mode; and if it is, how would you proceed?
11. Why are so many receiver functions affected by a loss of horizontal sweep?
12. A continuity check shows that the HV winding of a flyback transformer is open, yet the set still operates but with extreme blooming. Explain.
13. Under certain conditions you should never attempt to measure the dc at the output transistor collector. Explain.
14. If no HV, state two ways to determine if there is a high ac pulse voltage at the input to the HV rectifier.
15. What are the advantages of scan power over B voltage developed by a primary PS?
16. What circuits are suspect if the receiver is dead and there is (a) a visible glow to the CRT heater; (b) no glow? State your reasoning in each case.
17. State four possible causes of poor focus.
18. A set gives off the odor of ozone and there is a faint hissing sound. State the probable cause and how you would proceed.
19. Under overload conditions, a lamp in place of a fuse or CB serves a useful purpose. Explain.
20. Explain thermal runaway, stating causes and probable results.
21. Why is an ohmmeter check of a HV rectifier diode not valid, and what is the best test?
22. State three ways of checking for shorted windings in a flyback or yoke.
23. You lose the HV after replacing a HV rectifier. State two possible causes.
24. What would lead you to suspect a bad HV tripler, and how would you proceed?
25. How would you check the waveform at the horizontal output if no HV probe is available?
26. The expensive output transistor can be instantly destroyed by an inadvertent short. State several ways of protecting against it happening.
27. When is it necessary to use an isolation transformer? Explain.
28. Under what circumstances is it desirable to reduce the line voltage?
29. How does the power requirements of the output stage compare with the total power consumption of a modern transformerless set? Explain.
30. Testing for HV and beam current by arcing is not advisable with a solid-state receiver. Explain.
31. Special precautions are needed to scope the collector of the output transistor. Explain.
32. State four possible causes where there is dc at the output transistor collector but no amplified pulses.
33. Explain how the output transistor is able to conduct with a reverse bias.

# 11 Shutdown/startup systems

It has long been known that x-rays, developed by HV, are a potential health hazard, and the greater the voltage, the greater the hazard. Early TV receivers kept such emissions within limits by enclosing the HV section in a shielded cage. Although the HV developed by most sets has increased over the years, automatic shutdown circuits preclude the need for such extensive shielding. Protective shutdown circuits (sometimes called "hold-down" or "fail-safe" circuits) are mandatory in the design of all modern receivers.

The concept of a shutdown system is simple enough. When a dangerously high voltage is "sensed" or recognized, the shutdown circuit of most sets kills the horizontal sweep voltage. This results in a total loss of all scan power, including the HV, with a corresponding loss of both picture and sound. If the shutdown was caused by some momentary and nonhazardous condition such as a line surge, after a few seconds (if the condition no longer exists), a *startup* circuit restores the set to normal operation.

Besides protecting against x-rays, the system also acts like a fuse or safety valve, protecting against major component damage caused by voltage or current overloading. Such conditions are frequently the *cause* of the excessive HV which resulted in receiver shutdown. Unfortunately, however, such protection is not 100% because certain failures can *instantly* destroy sensitive components.

Troubleshooting a dead set that is in the shutdown mode poses a real problem for the service technician. There are two reasons for this. A set goes into shutdown instantly and without warning, with no opportunity to monitor voltages and circuit functions. Second, besides shutdown, there are numerous other possible causes for a dead set. Considering this, a technician must be thoroughly familiar with the horizontal output stage, and have a good understanding of shutdown and startup systems, before attempting a repair. In addition, he or she must follow a logical step-by-step procedure, not only to effect a repair, but to avoid further destruction of components while testing.

## 11-1 SYSTEM FUNDAMENTALS

The circuits that perform the shutdown/startup functions are shown in Figure 11-1. The system is comprised of four closed-circuit *loops*. One loop includes the primary PS (the source of *all* current), the voltage regulator that feeds the output transistor, and the transistor itself. Another loop embraces the flyback transformer (the source of sensing voltage), the sensing circuit, the shutdown circuit, and the stage being disabled, in this case the horizontal oscillator or one of the drivers. Another loop includes the primary PS (source of the startup voltage), the startup circuit, and the oscillator or driver. Another loop is represented by the *run power,* voltage developed by a scan PS to operate the oscillator or driver *after* the initial startup from the primary

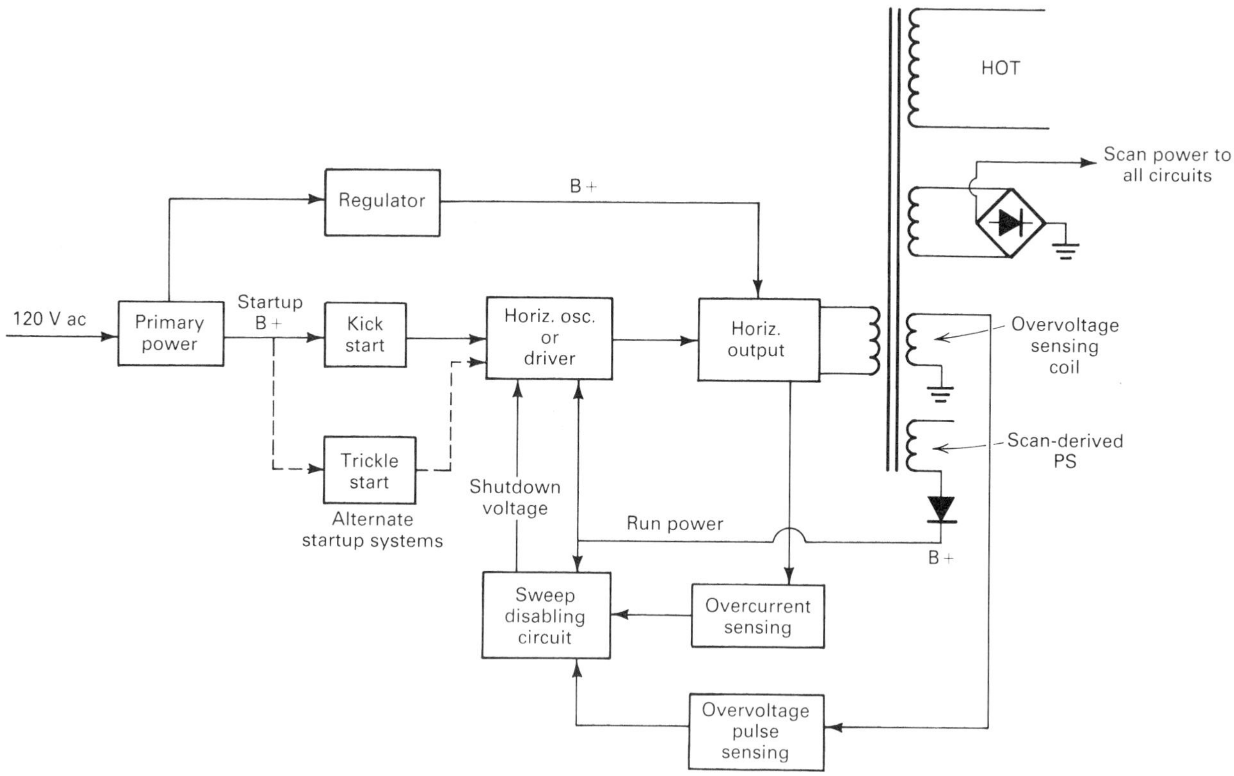


**FIG. 11-1** Startup/shutdown functions. Shutdown circuits offer protection against harmful x-rays and component damage.

power. Run power is used to reduce power consumption.

The loops are all interdependent and must all be operational to perform the various functions: (1) sensing a dangerous HV condition or an overvoltage or overcurrent situation in the output stage, and to initiate shutdown; (2) accomplishing receiver shutdown; and (3) performing the startup function. For example, if the sensing circuit is not working, the shutdown circuit will not be activated and a dangerous HV condition will prevail. The same is true if the shutdown circuit is not doing its job. If the startup circuit does not work, the set *remains* in shutdown indefinitely. Needless to say, a malfunctioning oscillator or driver cannot be started and a faulty output stage is incapable of developing run power even when startup *is* accomplished. A worst-case scenario is where the shutdown system fails to operate when a dangerous condition arises.

## 11-2 DISABLING AND STARTUP METHODS

### Disabling Methods

There are three systems used to disable a set automatically when an unsafe condition is detected: interrupting the horizontal drive to the output stage; removing B+ from the oscillator or driver; or upsetting the horizontal sync. Most sets interrupt the drive voltage, either by grounding, or by disabling the oscillator or driver in some manner. Some sets create a drastic change in oscillator frequency, so a picture cannot be observed; the frequency change also reduces the HV to a safe value.

Typical disabling circuits are shown in Figure 11-2. In circuit (a), the two zeners are normally not conducting because the trigger pulse from the flyback is weaker than their breakdown voltage. If the pulse becomes dangerously high (corresponding with excessive HV), the zeners conduct to trigger the SCR, which grounds out the B+ feed to the oscillator and the set shuts down. In circuit (b), a high pulse voltage from the flyback causes the zener to conduct, to trigger the SCR, which grounds out the sweep voltage at the base of the oscillator, to disable the set. *Sandcastle shutdown,* a system used by RCA and a few other sets, is another means of disabling a set, but it is not related to x-ray protection as described at this time.

### Startup Methods

There are two systems in common use: trickle start and kick start. Their names aptly describe how they operate.

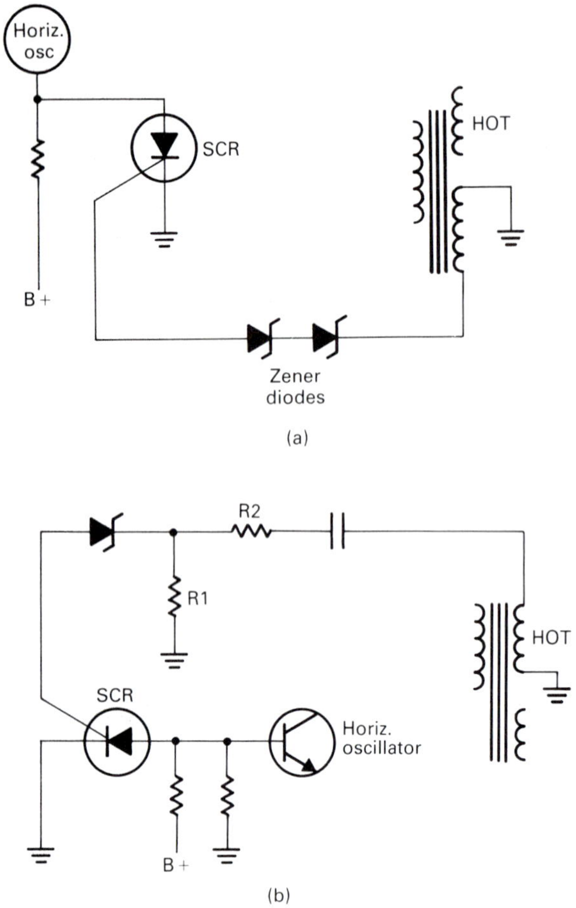


**FIG. 11-2** Basic shutdown circuits.

*Trickle Start.* This system, shown in Figure 11-3a, consists of little more than a diode and a high-value resistor series connected between the unregulated output of the primary PS and the horizontal oscillator. From a cold start, enough power trickles through to start the oscillator. When the output transistor receives the horizontal drive signal, scan-derived power from one of the flyback windings develops *run power*. Being stronger, the run power overrides the small amount of (trickle) start power, and henceforth, the oscillator and drivers continue to operate on run power only. The diode prevents a back flow of current after startup.

*Kick Start.* This system is slightly more complex than the trickle start. A basic circuit is shown in Figure 11-3b. The main item is a step-up start transformer supplied from the unregulated primary PS. From a cold start, a surge of current charges the series-connected, large-value capacitor. This one-time flow of current induces a voltage in the transformer secondary winding, which is then rectified and fed to the oscillator as a startup pulse. With the sweep circuits now operating, the oscillator and drivers continue to operate on scan power only. If the oscillator fails to start from the initial surge, a short time interval is required for the charge on the

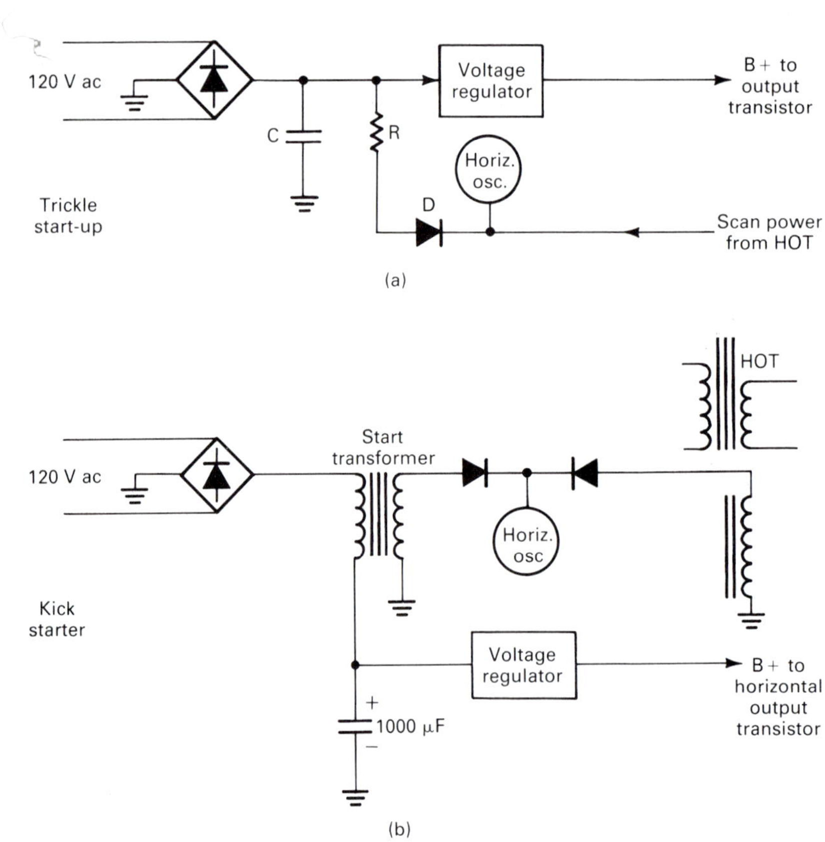


**FIG. 11-3** Horizontal startup systems: (a) trickle start; (b) kick start.

capacitor to leak away before another startup can take place.

## 11-3 SENSOR(S) OR SAFETY DETECTORS

Three methods are commonly used to sense a hazardous or abnormal condition: monitoring dc voltages; sensing a pulse from the flyback transformer; and monitoring the current of the horizontal output transistor. A sensor may have several inputs, enabling it to monitor several critical parameters simultaneously. Most sets monitor a pulse voltage developed by a secondary winding on the flyback. If a level detector senses an abnormally strong pulse, it means that the outputs from other windings are also high, and shutdown is initiated.

Some sets sense the regulated dc applied to the output transistor, the CRT beam current, and the CRT screen grid voltage. Any increase results in a shutdown. The output transistor current is usually monitored by sensing the voltage drop across a low-value, high-wattage resistor in its emitter circuit.

## 11-4 TYPICAL STARTUP/SHUTDOWN CIRCUIT

Following is a brief description of the system used in the GE foldout schematic at the back of the book. A pulse voltage from pin 3 of the flyback transformer is rectified by diode D403 to develop approximately 19 V dc, which is then reduced by the voltage divider R416/R417. The zener diode D402 is normally biased off. If the voltage at the zener rises above 16 V, it conducts and applies about 1.5 V to the switching circuit in IC501, via pin 23. This turns off the horizontal drive. The output at pin 24 is switched to zero, which kills the sweep and initiates shutdown. Terminals X and R are provided for checking the shutdown function. Note that all components indicated by shading are critical safety components.

The startup function is also performed by IC501, in conjunction with the "starter" transistor Q403. When power is applied to the set, a 12-V start voltage from Q403 is applied to pin 33. At this time D401 is on because the flyback is not developing 16.5 V dc. If the receiver is in shutdown, the startup is inhibited. When the oscillator starts up and scan voltages are produced, D401 is reverse biased to cutoff, and the sweep circuits are switched to run power.

## 11-5 TROUBLESHOOTING AND REPAIR

Like everything else, troubleshooting startup/shutdown problems can be difficult or relatively simple, depending on the expertise of the technician. But it is ironical that a system of such simplicity, which contributes nothing to picture and sound reproduction, can be the cause of much grief and frustration to the technician—following clues that lead nowhere, not to mention the power output transistors that may be inadvertently destroyed in the process—but such is the case, unless armed with a thorough knowledge of the system and a plan for systematic testing that is rigidly adhered to.

*Warning:* Most modern sets use the hot chassis design and it is *essential* to install a line isolation transformer *prior to* inserting the line plug. This also applies to test equipment since more than one item on the same outlet may defeat the isolation. Make certain that test equipment is well grounded; otherwise, *you* may complete the circuit. Failure to use an isolation transformer can result in component destruction and electric shock.

A defect in the sensing or shutdown circuits can initiate a "nuisance" shutdown in an otherwise normally operating receiver. This includes almost everything in the closed loops shown in Figures 11-2 and 11-3. The first thing is to determine whether or not the receiver *is* in the shutdown mode, since there are other things that can cause a dead set, such as loss of primary power, a defect in the B+ distribution network feeding the sound and horizontal sweep stages, a horizontal sweep defect, or a faulty startup circuit. After verifying that an isolation transformer is connected in the power line, check for dc output from the primary PS. If no B+, troubleshoot the PS as described in Chapter 6. As a servicing aid, refer to the troubleshooting flow drawing (Figure 11-4). (*Note:* When a set goes into shutdown, it may be necessary to wait 30 sec for the automatic startup to restore operation.)

### Test for Shutdown

Determine if the set is in the shutdown mode, as follows. Adjust volume control full on. Prepare to monitor the HV or output from one of the scan PSs. From a cold start, check for a momentary burst of sound and the production of scan voltages, which indicate that the shutdown has been activated. If there are no such indications, the receiver is *not* in the shutdown mode. Check for other possible causes

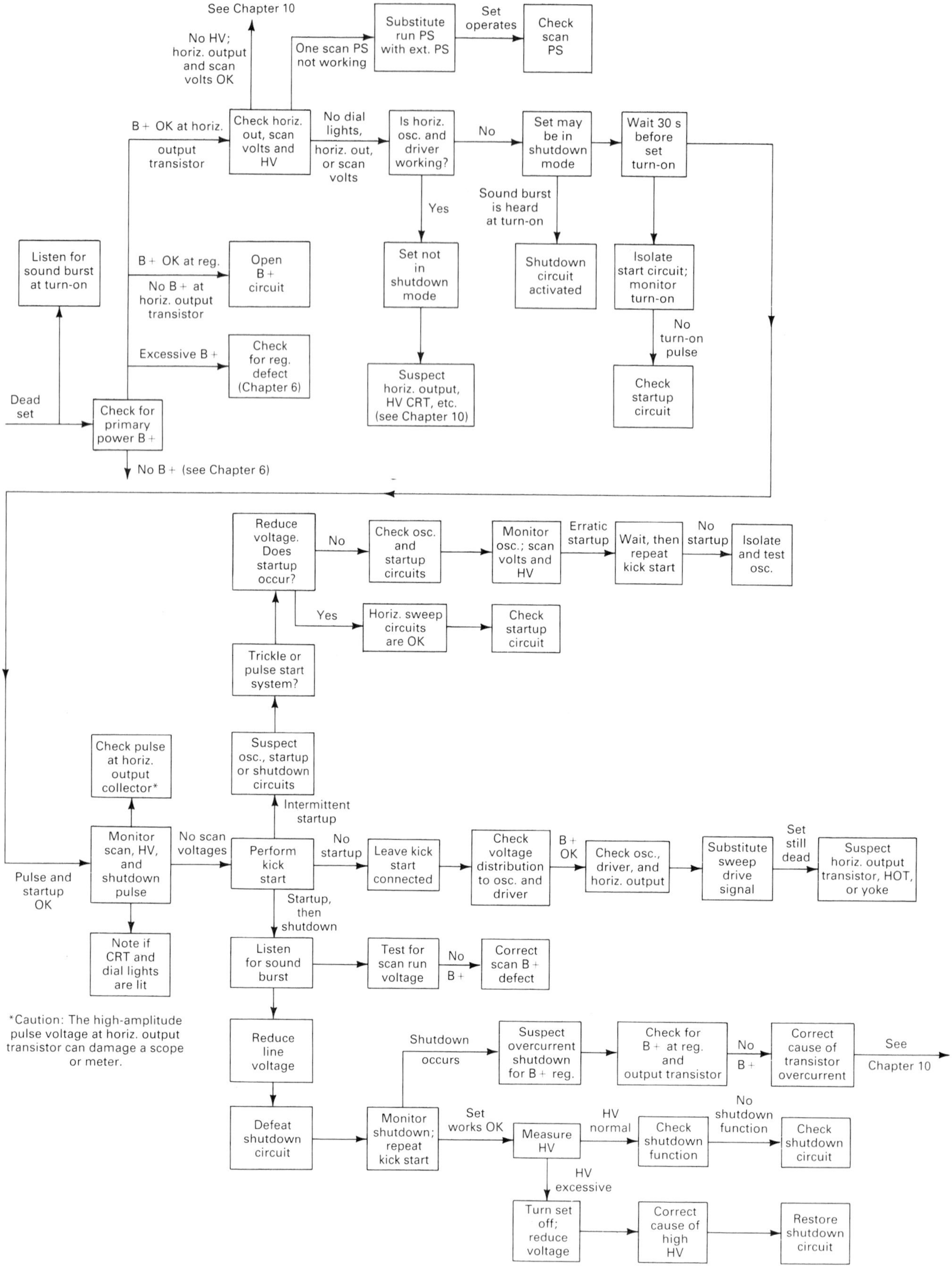


**FIG. 11-4** Startup/shutdown troubleshooting flow drawing.

of a dead set, such as loss of B+ or a horizontal sweep defect.

### Sandcastle Shutdown

As stated earlier, receivers employing a sandcastle circuit can go into shutdown if there is a defect in the sandcastle circuits or if the generated sandcastle signal is missing, low in amplitude, or has an abnormal waveshape. When this condition is suspected, scope check the signal, and if missing or abnormal, try to restore set operation using a substitute signal from a similar set, or as provided by a bar generator (Sencore). With the set operation restored, determine which receiver stage initiated the shutdown and make the necessary repairs.

### Shutdown Defeat

Receiver operation must be restored before any tests can be made. Depending on circumstances, one method is to *defeat* the shutdown function. This may be done by interrupting the sensing voltage at its source or by disabling the shutdown circuit in some manner. The method used depends on the circuit configuration of the set being worked on (refer to the schematic or to servicing notes).

*Warning:* Defeating the shutdown by disabling incurs certain risks since the cause(s) of shutdown probably still exist. All testing, after manually circumventing the shutdown function, should be done *rapidly* to avoid component damage. Turn the set off while considering the problem and contemplating the next moves. A better approach is to reduce the line voltage. This reduces the HV and overvoltage/overcurrent conditions to safe levels to permit further testing. In addition to the isolation transformer, connect a variac to the set as a means of changing the line voltage. Start with an input voltage of approximately 30 V ac.

### Preliminary Testing

There are numerous possible causes of shutdown and each must be considered separately. Most tests involve breaking one or more of the closed loops. Because of its complexity, no two technicians tackle the problem in the same manner. A suggested procedure follows. Check for primary power B+. Check for drive signal at the output transistor. If there is no drive, check the B+ feed to the oscillator and driver stages. If there is no B+, substitute, using an external PS adjusted for the proper amount as shown on the schematic. An alternative approach is to substitute the drive signal from a suitable generator, adjusted for 15.34 kH at the proper level.

### Checking the Output Stage

The collector of the horizontal output transistor is a logical focal point for checking the status of this stage and the numerous conditions affecting its operation. After a few minutes of operation, turn the set off and feel the transistor. If cold, it obviously is not conducting and the possibilities are: a bad transistor, excessive reverse bias, an open collector or emitter circuit, or no dc collector voltage. Although these conditions result in a dead set, they are not, however, causes of shutdown. If the transistor is warm to the touch, it *is* conducting. This means that the transistor is probably okay and is being supplied with collector voltage. If the transistor is overheating (thermal runaway), it is obviously conducting too much and the set should be turned off *immediately* to prevent component damage.

High transistor current can initiate a shutdown, and there are several possible causes, as outlined previously. To verify a suspected current overload, measure and monitor the voltage drop across an emitter or collector circuit resistor. A low-candle-power car bulb may also be *inserted* as a visual aid to indicate current changes as testing progresses. A direct-reading current meter can also be used, but with caution, since an inadvertent short, a haywire hookup, or a shorted transistor can instantly destroy the meter.

*Note:* To avoid component damage by the high current, make the following tests quickly, then remove the power.

Check the transistor. Measure the B-to-E bias voltage and compare with the schematic. Insufficient reverse bias (or too much forward bias) can be caused by transistor leakage or a failure in an adjoining circuit. Check for ac drive voltage and the sweep voltage waveform at the transistor base.

Adjust for a line voltage of 30 V ac. Continue to monitor the drive, the dc collector voltage, and the collector–emitter current. Slowly increase the line voltage until the collector voltage is about 70 V dc. Current should be about 50% of normal. Causes of *no* current are: an open emitter or collector circuit, a bad transistor, too much reverse bias, or no B+ at the collector. For the latter, check for an open flyback primary. Check for B+ back to the source, the primary PS, and the voltage regulator. An open

E-to-C junction in the regulator pass transistor is quite common. But before making a replacement, check further for the cause.

*Low* collector current can be caused by excessive reverse bias, low drive, a bad transistor, or low collector voltage. (*Reminder:* Take into account that the set is operating at reduced line voltage.) Low collector *voltage* can be caused by low primary power B +, a faulty voltage regulator, or because of high transistor current drain.

If current exceeds the norm by more than 50% (at the reduced line voltage), check for excessive drive, transistor leakage, excessive loading by shorted windings in the yoke or flyback, or a short or heavy drain from one of the scan PSs. To see what is loading the output stage (while monitoring the current), try disconnecting the yoke and, one by one, all suspected scan PS loads. Do *not* restore normal line voltage until such defects have been corrected.

If no defects are revealed by the tests thus far, *disable* or *remove the output transistor* and raise the line voltage back to normal. Measure the dc collector voltage. If excessive (considering that there is no current flow, i.e., no load on the primary PS), check for a shorted pass transistor in the voltage regulator, and if okay, check its ability to regulate, as follows. Vary the line voltage starting at about 80 V. Increased line voltage should produce a corresponding increase in dc. At some point, however, the dc should remain constant regardless of further increases in ac. Besides the pass transistor, zener diodes in LVPS regulators often break down.

If the scope shows little or no drive or an abnormal waveform, suspect an oscillator or driver defect. Shorted windings in a driver transformer are not uncommon and can greatly reduce the drive. If a suitable signal generator is available, disable the driver and inject a 15,734-Hz signal at the base of the output transistor. Correct all problems *before* reinstalling the transistor.

If there is normal drive at the transistor input, reduce the line voltage again to about 30 V ac, *then* reinstall the transistor. Using a scope that can handle high-amplitude pulses, check the waveform at the collector and compare with schematic. A low-amplitude output or an improper waveform (Figure 10-3) can be caused by any of the abnormal conditions previously described. The most common defects are: loading by one of the flyback "secondary" circuits, a shorted yoke, or flyback; or an open or leaky damper diode or safety capacitor. (*Reminder:* An open diode or its associated safety capacitor can raise the HV by several thousand volts. Unless the shutdown circuit is working, this can instantly destroy the transistor and damage the flyback. Do *not* restore normal line voltage until such defects are corrected.)

### Random Causes of Shutdown

As with circuit defects, random, sharply spiked line impulses or surges can initiate shutdown. Such events, however, are generally infrequent and momentary, and the automatic turn-on restores normal set operation. If a continuing problem, contact the local utility or install a line filter. For intermittent troubles, see Chapter 5.

### Failure to Shut Down

Where there is excessive HV and/or current overloads in the output stage, both the set user and the receiver components are at risk if the shutdown circuit fails to do its job. This can happen if the shutdown circuit has been disabled or is malfunctioning for any reason. Troubleshooting procedures for such conditions are described in the following paragraphs.

### Sensor Circuit Problems

Problems with safety detectors (sensors) can cause a set to go into shutdown when there is no need; they can also fail to initiate shutdown if and when a hazardous condition arises. Troubleshooting procedures for the different sensing methods are described below.

*Pulse Sensing Problems.* Most pulse sensing systems employ diodes and/or transistors functioning as level detectors to sense any increase in the flyback output, which corresponds to a dangerous HV condition. A defect in a sensing circuit can do one of two things, depending on the nature of the defect. By producing an erroneous signal, it can initiate a shutdown in a normally operating set, or if a hazardous condition develops, it can fail to initiate shutdown.

No testing can be done if the set is in shutdown. Restore operation by either defeating the shutdown, or preferably, by reducing the line voltage as described earlier. To see if there is a "nuisance" shutdown created by a malfunctioning sensor or shutdown circuit, break the loop by interrupting the "command" signal from the sensor to the shutdown circuit or by disabling the latter. Refer to the schematic for the best way of doing this. If shutdown is now averted and the set operates okay, troubleshoot the suspected shutdown circuit. Restore all circuits that were opened or disabled.

Where there is a dangerous condition and the set fails to go into shutdown, measure the pulse voltage developed by the pulse winding on the flyback, and compare with the schematic. The reading will naturally be low because of the defect that caused the shutdown and because of the reduced line voltage. If there is no pulse output but there is output from one or more scan PSs, check for an open pulse winding or some defect that is grounding out the voltage, such as a shorted zener or transistor in the level-detecting circuit. If the sweep circuit is completely dead with no scan outputs, make the tests described previously. *Note:* Where the sensing and shutdown functions are performed by an IC, verify the presence of B+ at the proper pins, and the absence of dc at pins where none should exist. If there are no external defects, replace the IC.

If there is pulse voltage, restore the normal line voltage. Measure the pulse amplitude and compare with the schematic. Check for a correct dc voltage at the sensor circuit output. If there is little or no dc, check all associated components, in particular the diodes and transistors, for shorts or leakage. If the pulse amplitude from the flyback is excessive, make tests as described earlier. After the cause of the excessive voltage is found and corrected, again measure the pulse voltage and the HV at the CRT. If a control is provided, adjust the HV to the amount specified. Validate the shutdown function by deliberately increasing the HV by momentarily raising the line voltage to about 130 V. If shutdown does not occur, power down immediately.

*DC Voltage Sensing Problems.* Examine the schematic to determine what voltage(s) are being monitored. Defeat the shutdown and at normal line voltage make *rapid* tests to see which of these voltages are excessive. Reduce the line voltage and troubleshoot the circuits involved. If the regulated B+ is monitored by the sensor, and checks high, suspect the regulator pass transistor or its associated zener. If a sensed scan PS checks high, perform tests described earlier. For excessive CRT beam current, suspect excessive HV, insufficient CRT bias, excessive CRT operating voltages, or an ABL defect (see Chapter 17).

For an unintentional shutdown when receiver operation is normal, disable the sensor or shutdown circuits as described previously. Reconnect any loop circuits that were broken. If set operation is restored, repair the troublesome shutdown circuit. After the defect has been corrected, validate the shutdown function as described later.

*DC Current Sensing Problems.* At reduced line voltage, check conditions that indicate excessive current drawn by the output transistor: for example, overheating of the transistor and flyback transformer, and little or no scan voltages or HV. Perform the tests described earlier. Where shutdown occurs and there are no indications of overload and the set works okay at reduced line voltage, interrupt the sensor/shutdown loop as described previously. Troubleshoot the faulty sensor or shutdown circuit as applicable. After repairs are made, reconnect the interrupted shutdown voltage. Validate the shutdown function.

### Shutdown Circuit Malfunctions

As with the safety detector circuits, a defect here can also fail to initiate shutdown when a problem arises. It can also initiate an unintentional shutdown when receiver operation is normal. At normal line voltage, measure the HV and scan voltages and compare with schematic. If excessive, and the set is not in shutdown, determine the reason. Ascertain that the sensing circuit is developing a proper command voltage.

Where a shutdown circuit defect is the suspected *cause* of shutdown, examine the schematic to determine the method used for shutdown. Start by establishing that the sensor output is not excessive. Try disconnecting the sensor voltage while monitoring the drive at the output transistor. Try defeating the shutdown circuit to see if set operation is restored. Test all components in the shutdown circuit, replacing any that are suspect.

### Failure to Start Up

The startup circuit initiates a power-turn-on sequence each time the set is switched on. It also restores power automatically if there is a temporary shutdown caused by line surges and the like. Besides normal output from the primary PS, the criteria for a successful startup includes (1) a trouble-free oscillator capable of being started by a momentary voltage impulse, (2) a startup circuit to produce this voltage, and (3) development of a run voltage to sustain the oscillator after startup. The run voltage is a scan-derived voltage that depends on proper operation of the entire horizontal sweep circuit. Failure of any element in this "loop" results in no startup. This includes a B+ voltage that may be slightly under par, or where the oscillator is slightly off frequency.

For a dead set, the first step, as described earlier, is to determine if the set is in shutdown. If it is not in the shutdown mode, check for B+ and the operation of the horizontal sweep stages. If it is in the shutdown mode, attempt to restore operation by reducing the line voltage. If unsuccessful, determine if the oscillator is working by scoping its output or the input to the driver. If there is no oscillator output, try a kick start.

### Manual Kick Start

With this procedure, an external PS is used as a substitute for the normal startup voltage, which may be absent or too weak to do the job. Adjust PS output to the value of the run voltage shown on the schematic. With the set switched off, connect the PS to a suitable B+ point at the oscillator or the startup circuit. Switch the set on. If receiver operation is restored, the start circuit is at fault. If it is not restored, the oscillator stage is at fault. Service the oscillator using an external source of B+. While troubleshooting the oscillator it is a good idea to disable or remove the output transistor to prevent destruction by an inadvertent short. After repairs are completed, disconnect the external PS to see if the automatic startup will restore set operation.

### Startup Circuit Testing

Determine from the schematic what type of start circuit is used, trickle or kick start. Verify that there is adequate output from the primary PS.

*Trickle-Start System (Figure 11-3a).* Check for a startup voltage at the moment of set turn-on. If low, or absent, check for circuit loading due to an oscillator defect, particularly if it is in an IC. Isolate the oscillator and recheck for voltage. Check the two critical components, the high-value resistor and its series-connected diode. The resistor may be open or increased in value. The diode may be open, shorted, or leaky. If in doubt, substitute. Some circuits employ an SCR for switching from startup to run power. Test the SCR, and if suspect, replace it.

*Kick-Start System (Fig. 11-3b).* Check for a momentary startup voltage at the moment of set turn-on. If weak or missing, check for possible loading by an oscillator defect. Check for a momentary ac pulse from the transformer output. If the ac is okay, suspect the diode D1. If there is no ac, one of the transformer windings may be open. If there is low ac, there may be shorted turns. The best suspect is the electrolytic series with the transformer primary. It may be shorted, leaky, open, or reduced in value. Any of these conditions calls for replacement. If shorted, the high current could have damaged the transformer. Substitute the capacitor and repeat the voltage check. (*Reminder:* Wait at least 30 sec for the capacitor to discharge before each voltage check.)

### Startup, Then Shutdown

This condition is evident when there is a characteristic crackle of HV accompanied by a "put-put" or "tick-tick" sound, followed immediately by shutdown. This indicates that the startup circuit and the sweep circuits were working, at least long enough to develop scan (run) voltage, before a defect initiated shutdown. Shutdown problems inhibit a successful startup and may be due to the sensing of a dangerous condition, insufficient run voltage, or a nuisance shutdown brought about by a too-sensitive level detector (sensor) or a defect in the shutdown circuit itself.

### Intermittent Startup or Shutdown

An intermittent or unstable startup or shutdown condition can be a real headache, and the worst of all worlds. This is because some critical measurements may deviate very little from the norm. Typical causes are a borderline B supply, slight defects in the start circuit that prevent developing a normal start voltage, a critical sensor circuit, critical oscillator, and a low run voltage that is incapable of sustaining operation. As described earlier, there are many possible causes for the latter condition.

Begin with systematic step-by-step checks to localize the problem to a particular loop of the system. In follow-up testing, critically evaluate all measurements. In some cases even slight discrepancies from normal voltages or waveforms can be significant.

### Shutdown Validation

When all repairs are completed, confirm that any circuits disabled have been restored. Deliberately create a shutdown condition by *momentarily* raising all receiver voltages by increasing the line voltage to about 130 V for a few seconds to see if shutdown occurs as it should. If it does, wait 30 sec or more. If working properly, automatic startup will restore set operation.

## QUESTIONS

1. State two reasons for the use of shutdown circuits.
2. Briefly explain the operation of a typical shutdown circuit.
3. Explain two systems for accomplishing automatic startup.
4. Name three methods used to sense a hazardous condition that results in shutdown.
5. Explain why startup/shutdown problems can be difficult to troubleshoot.
6. How would you determine whether a dead set was the result of shutdown?
7. How would you proceed if you decide that a set is in the shutdown mode?
8. Why is it risky to defeat the shutdown circuit in order to proceed with testing? What is an alternative procedure?
9. Most sets initiate shutdown by disabling the horizontal drive. Explain.
10. What is a kick start, and how and why is it accomplished?
11. Explain why a shorted transistor or SCR in the primary PS regulator can result in shutdown.
12. Explain three ways in which loading of the output stage can result in shutdown. How would you check out each possibility?
13. The horizontal oscillator and driver stages normally operate on scan power, which is lost when a set goes into shutdown. How would you proceed to check these two stages if suspect?
14. A scope shows no drive signal at the output stage. What might you suspect: (a) shutdown; (b) a faulty oscillator or driver; (c) loss of primary power; (d) any or all of the above?
15. Explain the operation of two kinds of startup systems.
16. State two ways to prevent destruction of the output transistor when testing for the cause of shutdown.
17. Name four defects that can result in shutdown and how to test for each.
18. The damper diode and safety capacitor are critical components. Explain why.
19. Explain why an output-stage defect affects the operation of *all* stages except the primary PS.
20. If set is in shutdown, give two ways to enable the oscillator/drivers to restore set operation so that tests can be made.
21. Where loading by one of the flyback secondary circuits is suspected as the cause of shutdown, how would you proceed?
22. Shorted windings in a flyback or yoke cause an increase in the transistor current. Explain why.
23. What is the only transistor supplied directly from the primary PS? Explain.
24. Give several possible causes where the B voltage output from the voltage regulator is (a) low; (b) high; (c) zero.

# 12 Tuners and remote controls

The evolution of tuners (channel selectors) over the years has been marked by many changes and innovations. Gone is the noisy, erratic tuner with its ancient channel-changing knob that was forever slipping or falling off. In its place a new and better system has evolved. Now we can change channels at the push of a button, and from the far side of the room can tune directly to cable channels and see the channel number we are watching displayed on the screen.

Although it is often more expedient to replace rather than repair a defective tuner, there are still times when repairs are warranted. Being faced with such problems requires a thorough understanding of all types of tuners, the defects that occur, and the appropriate procedures.

## 12-1 TUNER FUNDAMENTALS

The purpose of a TV tuner (sometimes called a *channel selector* or *front end*) is to select and amplify the picture and sound RF signals and convert them to lower, intermediate frequencies (IFs). Every modern set has two tuners, one for receiving VHF stations and one for UHF. A separate UHF tuner is required because special techniques are necessary to process ultrahigh frequencies, and because of the wide frequency band allocated to UHF. Each station requires 6 MHz of the available spectrum, which means 420 MHz for the 70 UHF channels as compared to 72 MHz for the 12 VHF stations. Tuners used in BW and color sets are basically the same.

A typical tuner has three stages: an RF stage, a mixer (sometimes called a frequency converter), and an oscillator. Besides transistors, each stage has one or more tuned circuits. The RF stage selects and amplifies the picture and sound signals contained within the 6-MHz bandpass. The mixer provides some amplification for the same band of frequencies, but its main function is to develop the IF signals. The oscillator generates its own signal, an unmodulated continuous-wave (CW) signal, required for the mixing process. Each stage has its own tuned circuit. The RF and mixer tuned circuits resonate at the frequency of the desired station. The oscillator tuned circuit determines the frequency of the generated oscillations and therefore the developed IF frequencies, to establish which station is received.

The various functions performed by a VHF and UHF tuner are shown in Figure 12-1. The VHF signals enter the tuner via a small impedance-matching device called a *balun*. A balun can match a 300-Ω ribbon-type transmission line to a 75-Ω tuner input, or the reverse if a 75-Ω coax cable is used. Some tuners have one or more *wave traps* or filters in the input circuit to combat interference, such as from FM stations and the like. The next block in the signal path is the first of several tuned circuits which resonate to the frequency of the selected channel. The next block is the RF amplifier, which may be a transistor or a FET. A FET provides a high signal-to-noise ratio, an important consideration for a snow-free picture, especially in a weak-signal area. The gain of an RF stage is controlled by AGC (see Chapter 13).

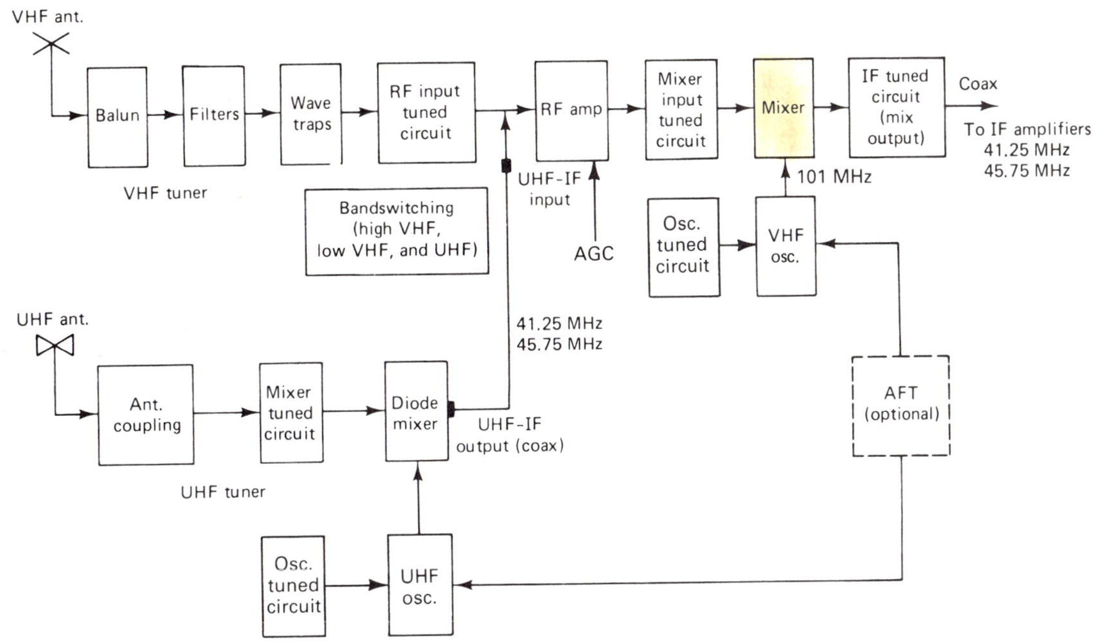


**FIG. 12-1** VHF/UHF tuner functions.

From the RF stage, the selected station signal goes through another tuned circuit and then to the mixer. Like the RF amplifier, either a transistor or a FET may be used. An unmodulated RF signal from a local oscillator is injected into the mixer, where it combines with the received signals to produce corresponding IF signals. More on this later. As indicated, the oscillator has its own tuned circuit, which is tuned higher in frequency than the other tuned circuits.

The IF signals produced by the mixing process are resonated by another tuned circuit then fed to the IF strip, either directly or via an IF preamp stage located on the tuner.

The simplified UHF tuner in the block diagram has no RF stage. The received signals go through a UHF tuned circuit to the mixer. The mixer here is a simple diode. Most tuners now use FETs for high gain and low noise. As for VHF reception, a local oscillator develops an unmodulated RF signal which is coupled to the mixer to produce the IF signals.

Instead of going directly to the IF strip, however, the IF signals are fed to the RF stage of the VHF tuner. For UHF reception with the channel selector at the UHF position, a *changeover switch* disables the VHF oscillator, and the RF and mixer stages function as broadband untuned *IF* amplifiers, providing additional gain for the UHF signals. Most switch-type VHF tuners have a changeover switch at the rear for oscillator disabling when the selector is at the UHF position.

The AFT (automatic fine tuning) controls the VHF and UHF oscillators to ensure the development of the proper IF frequencies in the event of drift. When properly adjusted, it obviates the need for a manual fine tuner.

## 12-2 DEVELOPING THE IF SIGNALS

The oscillator signal heterodynes (mixes with) the signals in the mixer. The resulting *beat signals* are the IF carriers. When tuned to any given station, the one oscillator signal combines with the two RF carriers to produce two IF carriers. Although the RF carrier frequencies are different for each station received, the IF frequencies are constantly maintained at fixed frequencies: 41.25 MHz for the sound and 45.75 MHz for the picture. These signals are passed on to the IF stages for further amplification. Like the RF/mixer stages, the IF section has a wide bandwidth to pass both the picture and sound signals. Each IF carrier is the numerical difference between the oscillator signal and the corresponding RF carrier. As described in Chapter 1, the RF carriers have a frequency separation of 4.5 MHz; the same separation is maintained at IF frequencies after conversion. For example, channel 2 transmits a picture carrier of 55.25 MHz and a sound carrier of 59.75 MHz. When channel 2 is selected, the oscillator produces a 101-MHz signal, which mixes with the picture RF carrier to produce the 45.75-MHz picture IF carrier. The same oscillator signal also combines with the sound RF carrier to develop the 41.25-MHz sound IF carrier. Stated differently, for any station received, the oscillator frequency is always higher than the two RF carriers by the amount of the IFs. The same picture and sound information contained in the RF sidebands is also contained in the IF sidebands.

In reference to the figure, note the UHF tuner that develops the IFs in the same manner. Note the frequency relationship between the generated oscillator signal and the station RF carrier frequencies to produce the established IF frequencies.

### Oscillator Tracking

The oscillator must always track with the received carriers by the correct amount, and for each station selected, its frequency must be *precisely* correct. If in error, it produces IF signals not matched to the fixed-tuned IF section, resulting in either poor or no reception. If the frequency error is great, it can result in receiving some station other than the one intended. If the oscillator frequency is off by 5 MHz, for example, the IFs will be off by the same amount, an error inconsistent with the IF amplifier tuning.

### Automatic Fine Tuning

Frequency drift is a common problem with high-frequency oscillators, and the higher the frequency, the greater the tendency to drift. This is why early-model sets had a manual fine tuner. With an automatic fine tuning (AFT) system the correct oscillator frequency is controlled automatically.

The basic AFT system is shown in Figure 12-2. It functions much like the AFC systems described in Chapter 8 for controlling the horizontal sweep oscillator. The discriminator circuit here is tuned to 45.75 MHz, the picture IF frequency. The discriminator is supplied with a sampling of the signal in the video IF strip. This signal reflects the accuracy of the tuner oscillator and its ability to produce an accurate IF frequency. The discriminator compares *its* resonant frequency with that of the developed IF signal. If there is a frequency error, a dc error voltage is produced and applied to the tuner oscillator, forcing it to slow down or speed up as the case may be. To use the manual fine tuner, a front-panel *defeat switch* grounds out the error voltage, as shown.

Instead of the tuning methods with AFT control described previously, most current-model sets use a digital *phase-locked-loop* system for channel selection. More on this later.

## 12-3 TUNED CIRCUIT FUNDAMENTALS

A tuned circuit responds to a specific frequency, making it possible to select a desired station from the multiplicity of signals present at the receiver input. Besides the tuner, such circuits are found in

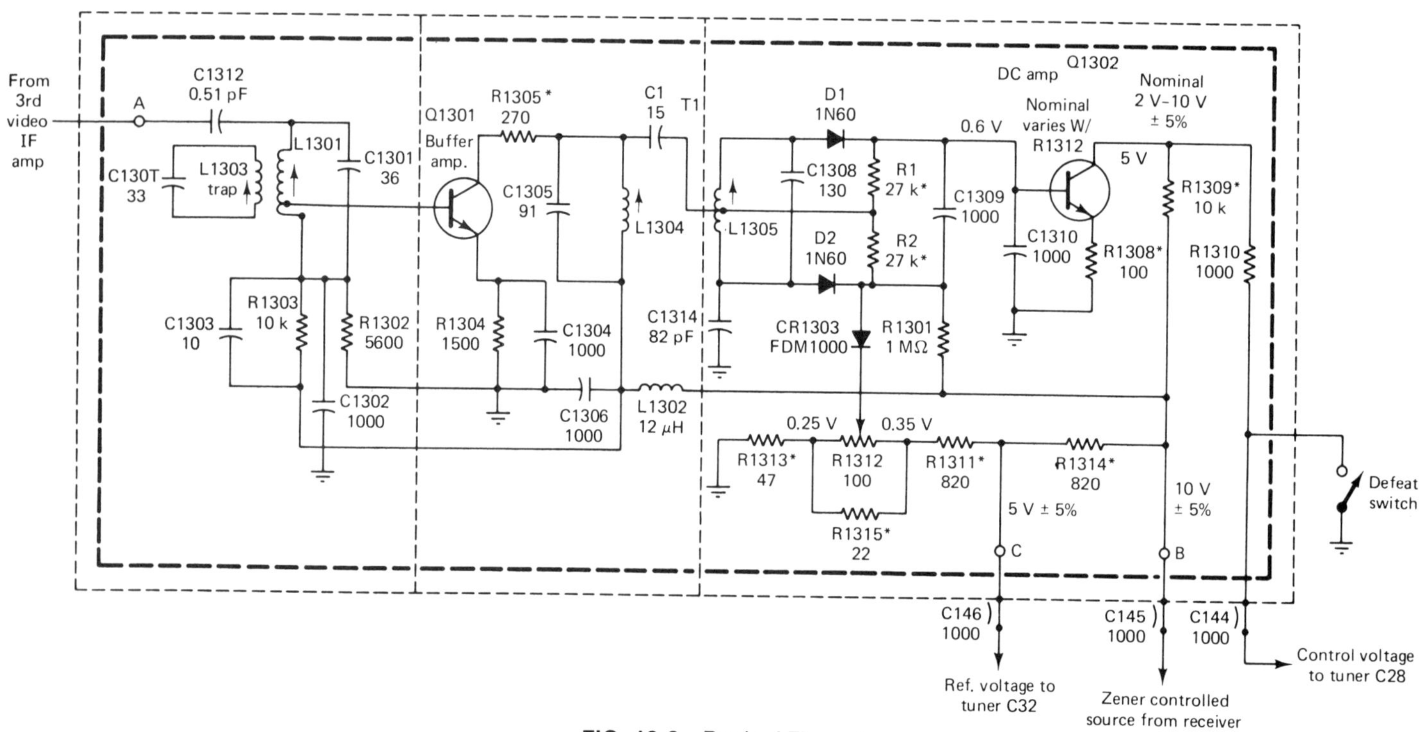


**FIG. 12-2** Basic AFT system.

all downstream signal stages to either accept or reject certain frequencies in accordance with their function and how they are connected. A tuned circuit is nothing more than a combination of inductance and capacitance that is "resonant" to a specific frequency. The resonant frequency of such a combination is dependent on the values of inductance and capacity.

### Inductance

Every coil possesses the property called *inductance,* designated by the symbol *L*. The inductance of a coil (or an inductor, as it is sometimes called) depends on the number of windings, its physical dimensions, and the type of core if one is used. For example, a large coil of many windings with an iron core would have a high inductance. On the other hand, a small coil of few windings with no core would have a small inductance. The basic unit is the *Henry;* smaller and more practical units are the milliHenry (mH) and the microHenry (μH). When used in a tuned circuit, the inductance is adjustable by means of a threaded core or "slug." A powdered iron core increases the inductance; a nonferrous core such as brass or copper does the opposite.

Like a resistor in a dc circuit, a coil opposes the flow of an *ac* current in accordance with its inductance and the frequency of the ac. This is called *inductive reactance*. A coil also has impedance (Z), a combination of reactance and ohmic resistance. The higher the inductance and/or frequency, the greater the opposition and the lower the current. Because of the high frequency of RF and IF signals, the coils used in a tuner are very small. At the other extreme, the inductance of a filter choke in a 60-Hz PS is quite large. Iron-core coils are most efficient since they increase inductance without an increase in resistance as when adding more windings.

### Capacitance

A basic capacitor consists of two or more conducting materials separated by an insulator or nonconductor. The basic unit is the *Farad;* Smaller and more practical units are the microFarad (μF) and the picoFarad (pF). *Capacitance* (designated *C*) is based on the total surface area of the conducting medium, the spacing between them, and the type and thickness of the insulating material, commonly called the *dielectric*. A capacitor having numerous conducting "plates" with their large surface area in close proximity to the dielectric would have a high capacity, or capacitance. The opposite would be true for a small capacitor. So-called "fixed" or solid dielectric capacitors, including electrolytic types, are found in every stage of a TV set. Capacitors used in tuned circuits are very small and sometimes adjustable.

A capacitor has the ability to store voltage, and in effect, to pass an ac current while blocking dc. The amount of ac current flow is governed by the *capacitive reactance* of the capacitor, which in turn is dependent on the capacitance and the frequency of the ac. The larger the capacitance and the higher the frequency, the lower the reactance, the greater the current flow, and vice versa.

### Resonant Circuits

Any coil and capacitor in combination is "resonant" to some specific frequency. The resonant frequency is determined by the relative values of *L* and *C*. Large values of *L* and *C* lower the resonant frequency. Small values such as those in TV tuners raise the frequency. The only capacitance used in some high-frequency tuned circuits is the distributed capacity of the coil windings and associated wiring.

There are two kinds of resonant circuits, series and parallel, as shown in Figure 12-3. A coil and capacitor in *series* has low opposition to signals at its resonant frequency. An example is the tuned circuit shown in Figure 12-3b. This so-called "acceptor circuit" also functions as a *wave trap*. With its low impedance at resonance, a desired signal is passed with ease from the antenna to the transistor. Unwanted signals above and below resonance are rejected, due to the high off-resonance impedance.

A tuned circuit with a coil and capacitor in *parallel* has a *high impedance* to signals at its resonant frequency. Figure 12-3a depicts such a circuit. A high signal voltage developed across its high impedance at resonance is passed on to the transistor. Unwanted off-resonant signals are rejected by the low impedance of the circuit. The example shown in Figure 12-3c uses both series and parallel resonant circuits, both functioning as wave traps. The parallel circuit rejects the undesired signal and the series circuit, in effect, short circuits it to ground.

### Tuning Methods

As stated earlier, tuning can be accomplished with variations of *L* or *C*. Early-model sets used small trimmer capacitors or variable air-tuned capacitors, which are still used in many UHF tuners. Most tuned circuits are resonated with an adjustable iron core. The more core within the coil, the greater the inductance and the lower the frequency. The opposite is true for a nonferrous core. Spreading or

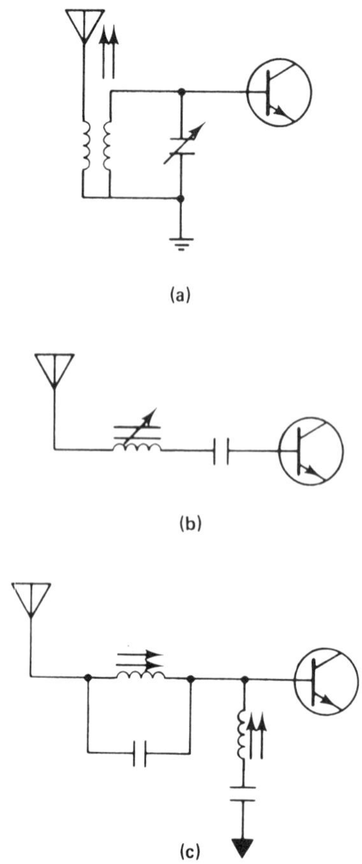

FIG. 12-3 Basic series- and parallel-resonant circuit applications: (a) high impedance at resonance and maximum signal feeding the transistor; (b) low impedance to resonant frequency and maximum rejection of signals off resonance; (c) series- and parallel-resonant circuits used as wave traps.

compressing coil turns is another means of creating small changes in frequency. Channel selectors in modern receivers use varactor diodes. A varactor simulates a variable capacitor, creating small, precisely controlled variations in capacitance when a specific amount of dc voltage is applied.

Channel selection with UHF tuners is accomplished with *tuned lines* because conventional coils have too much inductance for use at ultrahigh frequencies. A tuned line is basically a short length of transmission line (sometimes called a *stub*), terminated in a short circuit. As such, it behaves as an inductance. By shunting the line with a capacitor, it can be made to resonate within the UHF tuning range. Early-model tuners used continuously variable capacitors; currently, UHF tuners use varactors. Tuning is extremely critical at UHF frequencies and with capacitive tuning requires a high step-down gear ratio or a planetary drive. Modern tuners of this type have a 70-position detent to facilitate channel selection.

## 12-4 SELECTIVITY AND BANDPASS CONSIDERATIONS

Selectivity refers to the "sharpness" of a tuned circuit, that is, how well or how poorly a receiver selects desired signals while rejecting all others. *Bandpass* refers to how narrow or how wide a band of frequencies can be processed or handled. An unmodulated RF carrier represents only one frequency. The modulation frequencies in the sidebands extend well beyond the carrier, and receiving them requires an adequate passband. The 6-MHz bandpass requirements of a TV signal necessitate the use of broadband circuits having a wide bandpass, as shown in Figure 12-4. By comparison, an AM radio station requires only a narrow 10-kHz band of frequencies. Unfortunately, a high degree of selectivity and a wide bandpass do not go hand in hand, and one must be sacrificed for the other.

A wide bandpass can be achieved in several ways, all at the expense of selectivity and signal amplification. One method is to reduce the $Q$ factor by shunting a tuned circuit with low values of swamping resistance. In the IF strip, sometimes the tuned circuits are staggered, each to a slightly different frequency. Overcoupling is another means of obtaining a wide bandpass. More on this later.

## 12-5 RESPONSE CURVES

A *response curve* is a way of depicting the bandpass of a circuit and the relative signal gain that can be expected for various frequencies. Bandpass is judged at the 63% level. Typical front-end response curves are shown in Figure 12-4. Curve (a) is an ideal but unrealistic curve, impossible to obtain. Such a curve would represent equal amplification to all frequencies within the bandpass. Actual curves obtained are shown in Figure 12-4b and c. One is a double-humped response, the other a so-called haystack curve. Both provide a fair amount of gain for signals within the upper portion of the curve, but a rapid dropoff at the extremes. Note that the 6-MHz bandpass is at the 50% level. Signals represented at the bottom of the curve receive no amplification. Also note the relative locations of the adjacent channels: the sound carrier for the next lower channel on the one side and the picture carrier of the next

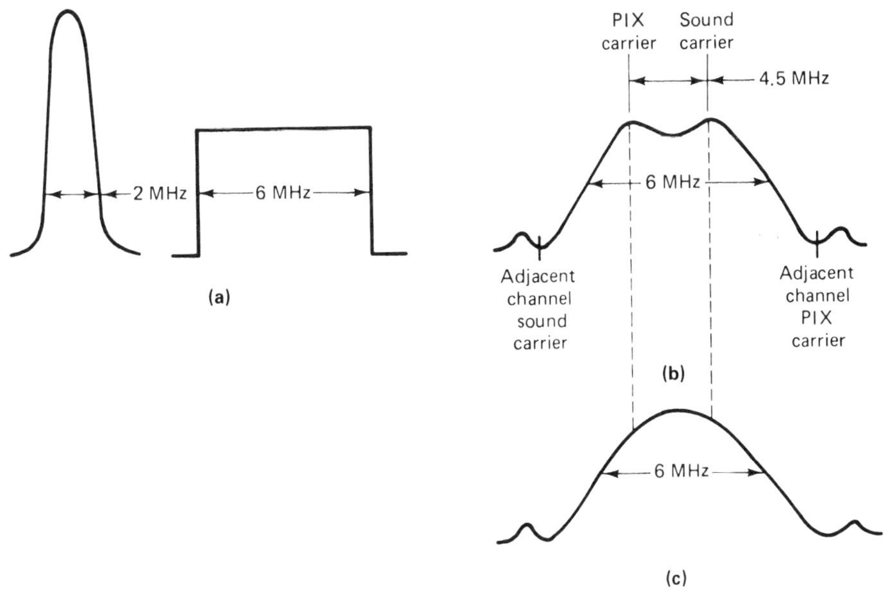


**FIG. 12-4** Front-end response curves: (a) ideal response; (b) double-humped response; (c) haystack curve. A wide bandpass is required to pass all the sound and picture information of a TV signal.

higher channel on the other side of the curve. If this were the curve for channel 2, the center frequency (57 MHz) would be at the middle, with points representing 54 and 60 MHz at the extremes, as indicated.

If the tuner bandpass is too narrow, the high modulation frequencies (those extending farthest from the carrier) would be lost or greatly attenuated. If the bandpass is too wide, the result is poor selectivity and interference from the adjacent channels. Adjacent channel traps are located in the IF strip to reduce this possibility.

## 12-6 CHANNEL-SELECTING SYSTEMS

There have been many changes in tuner design over the years, particularly in the method used for channel selection. Some early-model sets used an *inductuner,* a continuously variable inductance with a sliding roller making contact with silver-plated coil windings as the coil is rotated. For many years switch and drum tuners were in vogue. A typical switch-type tuner consists of a ganged multicontact rotary switch with a series of small coils connected between the contacts of each switch "wafer." Each tuner stage, RF mixer, and oscillator uses a similar arrangement. As the switch is rotated, more coils are added or subtracted. For channel 2 (the lowest-frequency channel), all coils are in series for maximum inductance. At the other extreme (channel 13), all coils except one are removed from the circuit.

With a drum tuner, removable clip-in coils (one for each channel) are mounted around the periphery of a rotatable drum. Each coil makes contact with corresponding stationary contacts when the drum is rotated to the desired channel position. Unlike the switch/wafer tuner, each coil is an independent tuned circuit. As with most tuners, some form of mechanical *detent* is provided to ensure that switch contacting corresponds exactly with the channel markings on the tuning knob. Wafer and drum tuners have one problem in common: noisy and erratic contacts due to dirt, oxidation, and wear.

### Varactor Tuners

Instead of the troublesome switching systems found in "mechanical" tuners, the tuners in most modern sets are "electronic," in the sense that tuning is accomplished with varactor diodes. As described earlier, a varactor tunes a circuit by simulating a variable capacitor. As each channel is selected (by pushbutton or PLL control), a precise amount of dc voltage (called the *tuning voltage*) is applied to the varactors to resonate the tuned circuits to the selected channel frequencies. Besides being small and relatively trouble-free, a varactor tuner can be located anywhere in the set since there are no front-panel selector knobs to turn (Figure 12-5).

### Pushbutton Channel Selection

Most modern sets use pushbutton control. For VHF, a typical basic control panel may have 12 pushbutton switches, one for each channel. Most current models, however, have a keyboard with numerals zero through 9, as on VCRs and for telephone

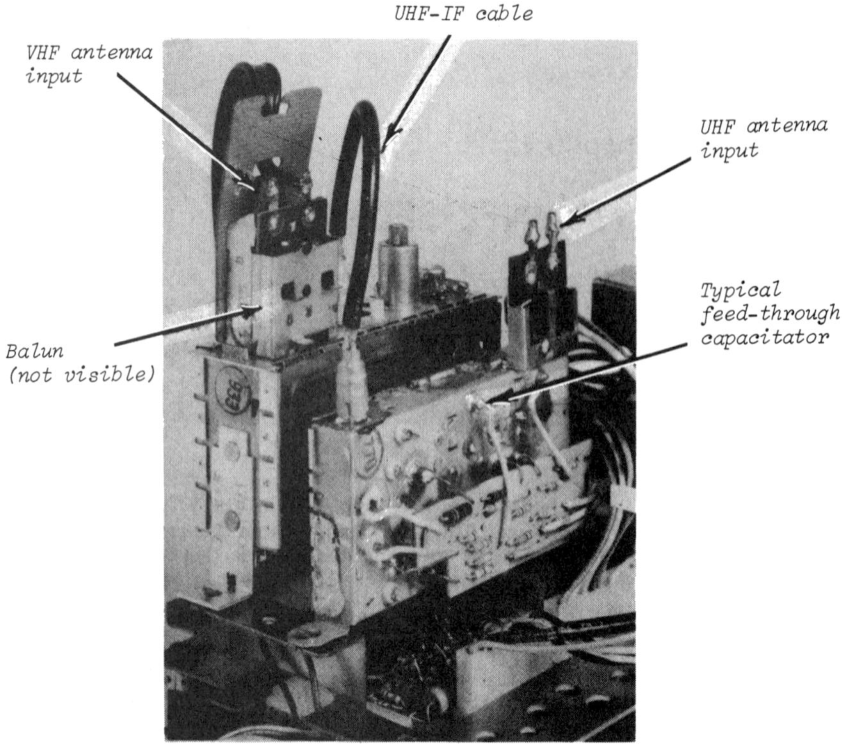


**FIG. 12-5** Typical varactor tuners.

dialing. For double-digit channel numbers you press two buttons. One recent-model TV uses a light-touch membrane keyboard now used extensively at store checkout counters. Sets using remote control require only two buttons for channel selection.

The simplified drawing of Figure 12-6 shows a basic pushbutton tuning system using varactors. Transistors and FETs are omitted for simplicity. Each tuner stage has its own set of coils and associated varactors. Trimmer capacitors across the coils are factory adjusted to resonate at the approximate channel frequencies. The varactors produce the necessary small frequency variations, corresponding with the amount of dc tuning voltage applied. The tuning voltage is supplied from a regulated PS. Twelve potentiometers, one for each

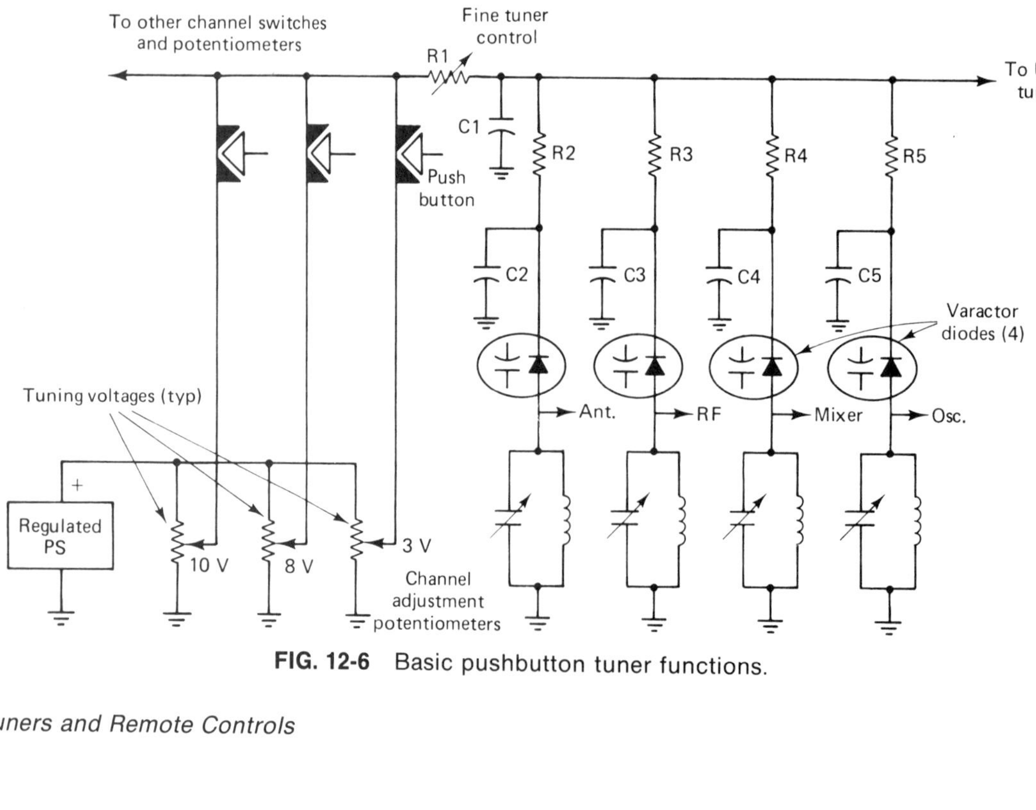


**FIG. 12-6** Basic pushbutton tuner functions.

channel, supplies a preset amount of voltage to all varactors when the appropriate channel button is pressed. Channel selection is instantaneous. A fine-tuning pot is provided to compensate for oscillator drift.

Because of the wide frequency gap between "low band" channel 6 and "high band" channel 7, additional varactor-tuned bandswitching circuits are required for the changeover. Thus each pushbutton switch does two things: It selects a specific amount of tuning voltage from one of the preset pots, and it selects a bandswitching voltage corresponding with one of three bands, high VHF, low VHF, or UHF. The UHF version of this tuner employs the same system of channel selection. The main difference is the use of *tuned lines* instead of the conventional VHF coils shown in the figure.

### VHF Varactor Tuner

The schematic of a typical VHF varactor tuner is shown in Figure 12-7. FETs are used in the RF and mixer stages. The four varactors are identified as TD1 through TD4. Note the complex array of traps and filters at the antenna input. The box at the right shows the amounts of voltage required for channel selection and bandswitching. AGC is applied to one gate of the FET in the RF stage. Note the connector at the mixer input that receives the IF signal from the UHF tuner. The IF output from the VHF tuner is taken from a buffer (preamp) transistor to feed the video IF strip.

### UHF Tuner

A basic UHF tuner, shown in Figure 12-8, employs tuned lines in the resonant circuits. There are four such lines or stubs: one at the antenna input, the others for tuning the RF, mixer, and oscillator stages. Each line, except the mixer, is shunted with a small trimmer capacitor and tuned with a varactor. The dc tuning voltage is applied to the three varactors via the tuned lines. Prior to the use of varactors, UHF tuners employed a three-gang variable capacitor with a gear-reduction drive for channel selection.

From the antenna input the signal is coupled to the first tuned line via a small hairpin loop. The three stages are compartmented with small windows (openings) in the separating baffles, for signal transfer between stages. The mixer here is a diode; similar tuners may use a transistor or a FET. From the mixer, the developed IF signal is resonated to 45 MHz by a conventional slug-tuned coil, amplified by a FET IF preamp, tuned again, then routed to the VHF tuner via a short length of coax.

## 12-7 PHASE-LOCKED-LOOP SYSTEM

The phase-locked-loop (PLL) system of channel selection (sometimes called frequency synthesizing or random-access tuning) is a digital system that uses computer-type logic. It can be likened to the countdown circuit described in Chapter 7. The PLL system, however, is considerably more complex since it must be capable of controlling *many* different frequencies. The basic system is shown in Figure 12-9. It differs from a countdown system in several ways; for example, the oscillator here (the tuner oscillator) is called a *VCO* (voltage-controlled oscillator). Instead of a phase detector there is a *frequency comparator* which essentially performs the same function. Instead of using sync pulses as a frequency reference, the reference signal here is developed by a crystal-controlled *reference oscillator*.

All logic functions are performed by ICs and a typical set may use anywhere from 1 to 10 such units. Conventional varactor tuners are used in a PLL system with one minor difference—the need to extract oscillator sampling signals, the feedback loops to the logic circuits.

### Tuner Oscillator

The PLL system develops a dc *tuning voltage,* which is supplied to all varactors in the VHF and UHF tuners. This voltage causes the RF and mixer varactors to tune these circuits to whatever channel is selected. The voltage controlled oscillator (VCO) varactors tune their circuits to develop the proper frequency needed to produce the correct picture and sound IFs. Although the RF/mixer circuits resonate to the channel frequency selected, it is the VCO oscillator that determines the station that will be received. A sampling of the CW signal developed by the VHF and UHF oscillators is supplied to the comparator via two feedback loops, for continuous monitoring. The frequency of the tuner oscillator outputs is *reduced by frequency dividers* before reaching the comparator.

### Reference Oscillator

This crystal-controlled oscillator develops an accurate reference signal which feeds the comparator via a *reference loop*. The oscillator frequency is usually about 4 MHz, depending on receiver design. This feedback loop also has two or more dividers to

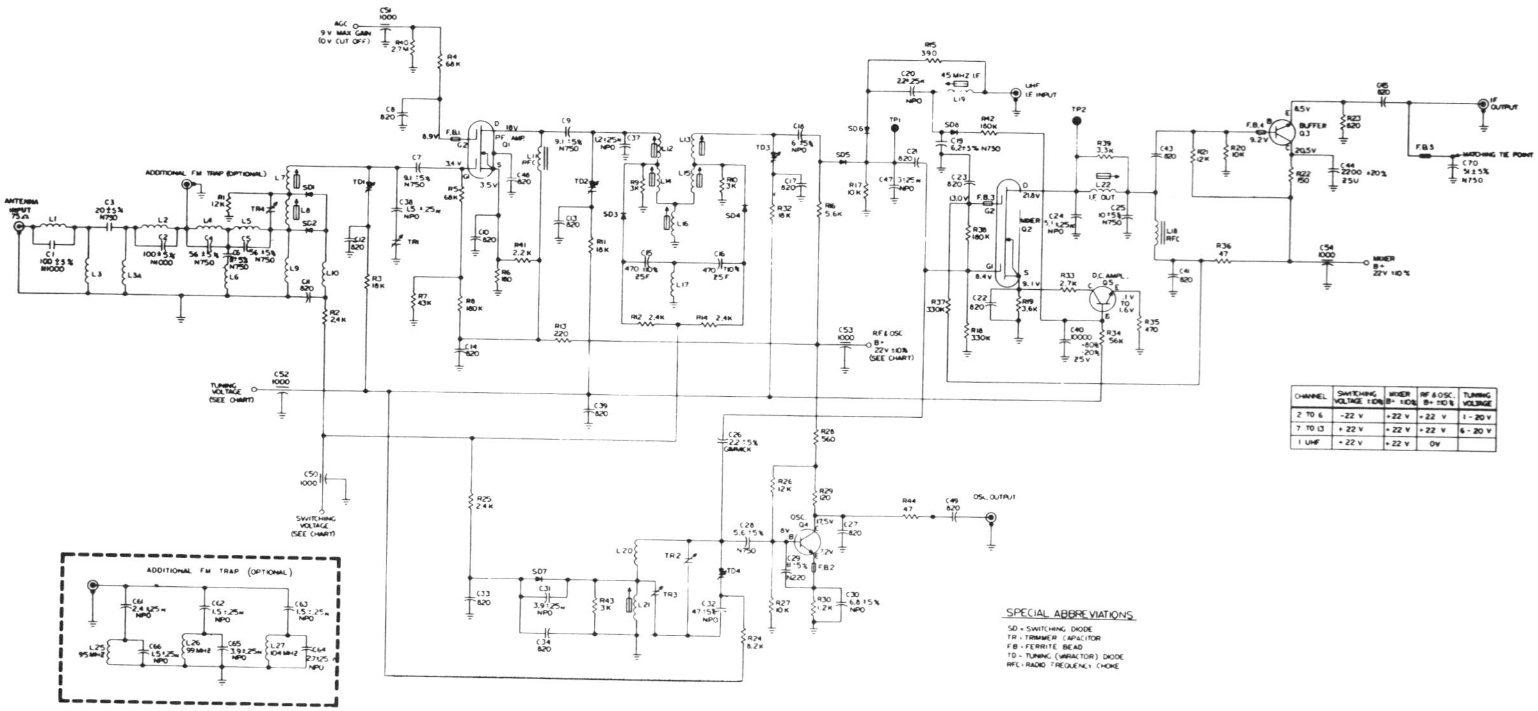


**FIG. 12-7** VHF varactor tuner schematic. FETs are used in the RF/mixer stages for low noise and high gain. Channel selection is accomplished by changing the dc tuning voltage.

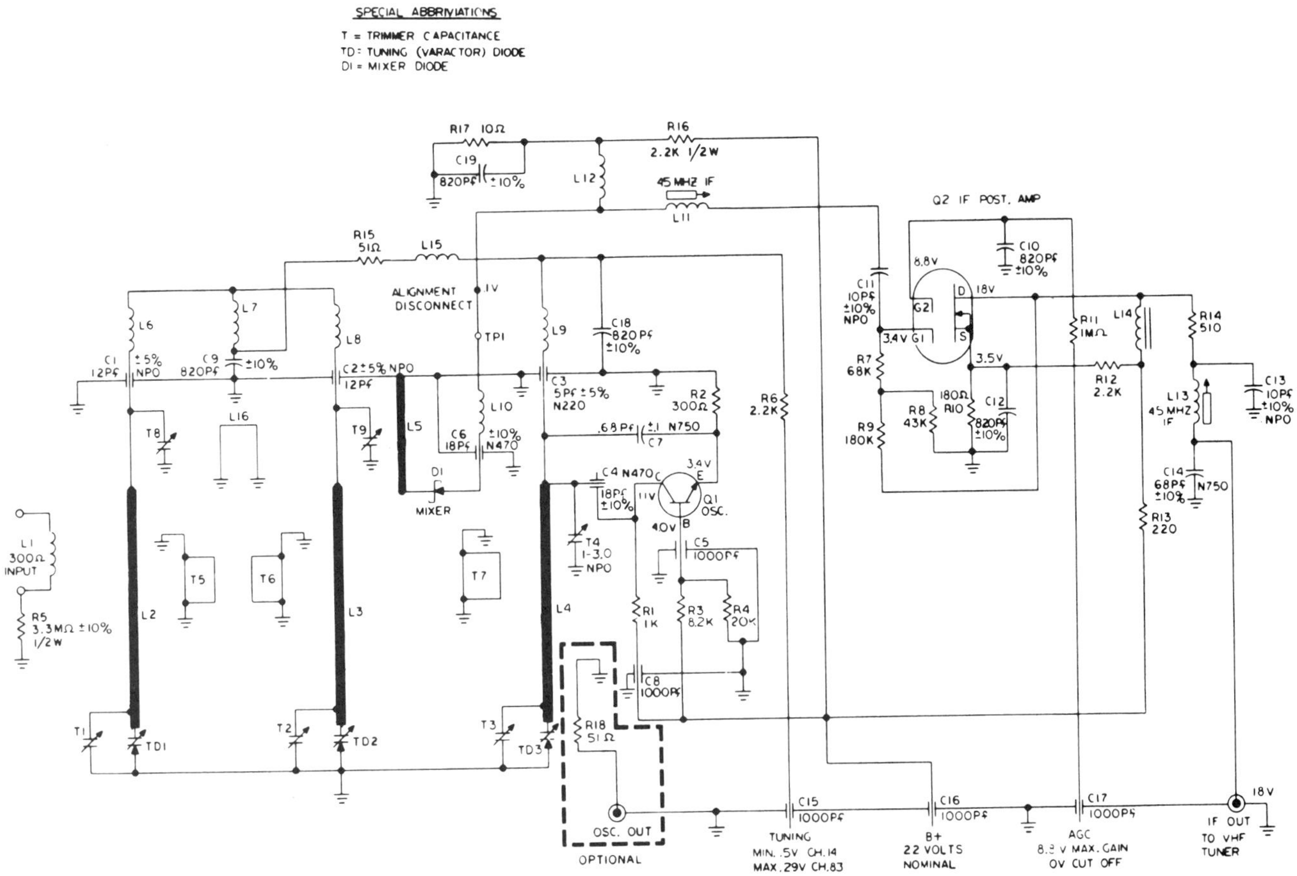


**FIG. 12-8** Basic UHF varactor tuner. Black sections are the four tuned lines. Specific amounts of tuning voltage (5 to 29 V) applied to varactors via the tuned lines determines which channels are selected.

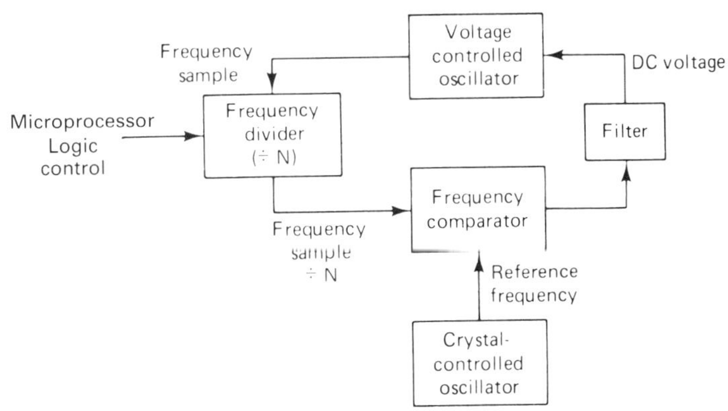


**FIG. 12-9** Basic PLL system.

reduce the frequency to a value suitable for comparison with that generated by the VCO.

### Frequency Divider

A divider is actually a frequency *counter* that uses digital logic to reduce the frequency of a signal by some predetermined amount. The dividing factor is called the *divide-by ratio*. Some dividers have a fixed ratio; others are programmable by a microprocessor for different ratios when required. The purpose of the dividers is to establish a 1:1 frequency relationship between the two signals supplied to the comparator *when the VCO frequency is correct* for the station channel selected. The multiplicity of divide-by factors makes it possible to obtain the necessary VCO frequencies for the reception of all VHF and UHF stations.

## Frequency Comparator

As shown in Figure 12-9, the comparator has two inputs. The frequency used is arbitrarily chosen *for comparison only* and varies for different sets. Based on the comparison, a dc *tuning voltage* is produced and fed to the oscillator of the VHF or UHF tuner as appropriate. If the VCO frequency is incorrect for the channel selected, the tuning voltage forces it to speed up or slow down until a 1:1 comparison is made. Once locked on a frequency, the VCO frequency is as accurate and stable as that of the crystal-controlled reference oscillator.

## Filter

This low-pass filter integrates the pulsed output of the comparator and filters out any fluctuations to produce a pure dc tuning voltage. Tuning voltages vary from near zero to about 30 V: the low values for the low channels and the higher voltages for the high channels. Whereas other varactor tuners require precise voltages for each selected channel, the amount of voltage with the PLL system is not critical because the tuner responds to polarity changes and variations, not to actual amounts.

## Digital Display Readout

Channel numbers are displayed on an LCD, LED, or a fluorescent readout unit (Figure 12-10). In many late-model sets the readout appears momentarily on the screen along with other information, such as real time. With a digital readout, each digit is made up from seven "segments" arranged in various patterns as selected individually by driver amplifiers.

## Functional Operation

To demonstrate the operation of a PLL system, let's look at a reference oscillator frequency of 4 MHz; if a divide-by-200 divider is used, the reference frequency at the comparator will be 0.02 MHz (20 kHz). The comparator will sense any difference between this frequency and that of the VCO after it too has been reduced. If a frequency difference is detected, a developed dc error voltage forces the VCO to change until a *matching* 20-kHz feedback signal exists at the comparator input. When the two comparator inputs are identical (in frequency and phase), the system becomes stabilized, with the VCO developing the correct frequency for the channel selected.

The foregoing example assumes fixed dividing factors, which means that the VCO can be locked to only *one* frequency. Different channels require different divide-by factors. This is accomplished with a microprocessor-controlled *programmable divider*. An additional divider called a *prescaler* may be used to relate the VCO frequency to one of three bands—the low or high VHF channels, or UHF—in order to produce an appropriate *bandswitching voltage*.

## Typical PLL Tuning System

A block diagram for a late-model (GE) set is shown in Figure 12-10. Note the programmable dividers used in both loops. The reference oscillator signal goes through two dividers to reach the comparator, where the resultant frequency is as indicated. Note that this frequency is peculiar to one particular receiver and remains the same regardless of the channel selected. To obtain frequency lock on the VCO, it must be matched by an identical frequency from the VCO feedback loop.

In the VCO loop, its signal goes through three dividers to reach the comparator. This represents a total dividing factor of 103,424 to produce the proper comparison frequency at the comparator input. If the VCO frequency changes, it creates a corresponding change in the comparison frequency, and a dc error voltage forces a change in the VCO until the two signals at the comparator are identical.

## Keyboard Control

When pressed (see Figure 12-10), each button develops a binary-coded-decimal (BCD) voltage corresponding to the channel selected. This BCD signal is recognized by the microprocessor, which selects the proper programmable dividers for bandswitching and receiving the selected channel. Signals are also developed to drive the proper segments of the channel number readout display.

## Up/Down Search Functions

When a channel selector arrow button on the keyboard is pressed, channels are momentarily previewed, in succession, from low to high channels, or vice versa, in accordance with the direction of the button arrow. The user can program a memory for instantly selecting several preferred channels. The sound is muted when scanning through undesired stations. With some sets, this memory is volatile and the programmed information is lost when

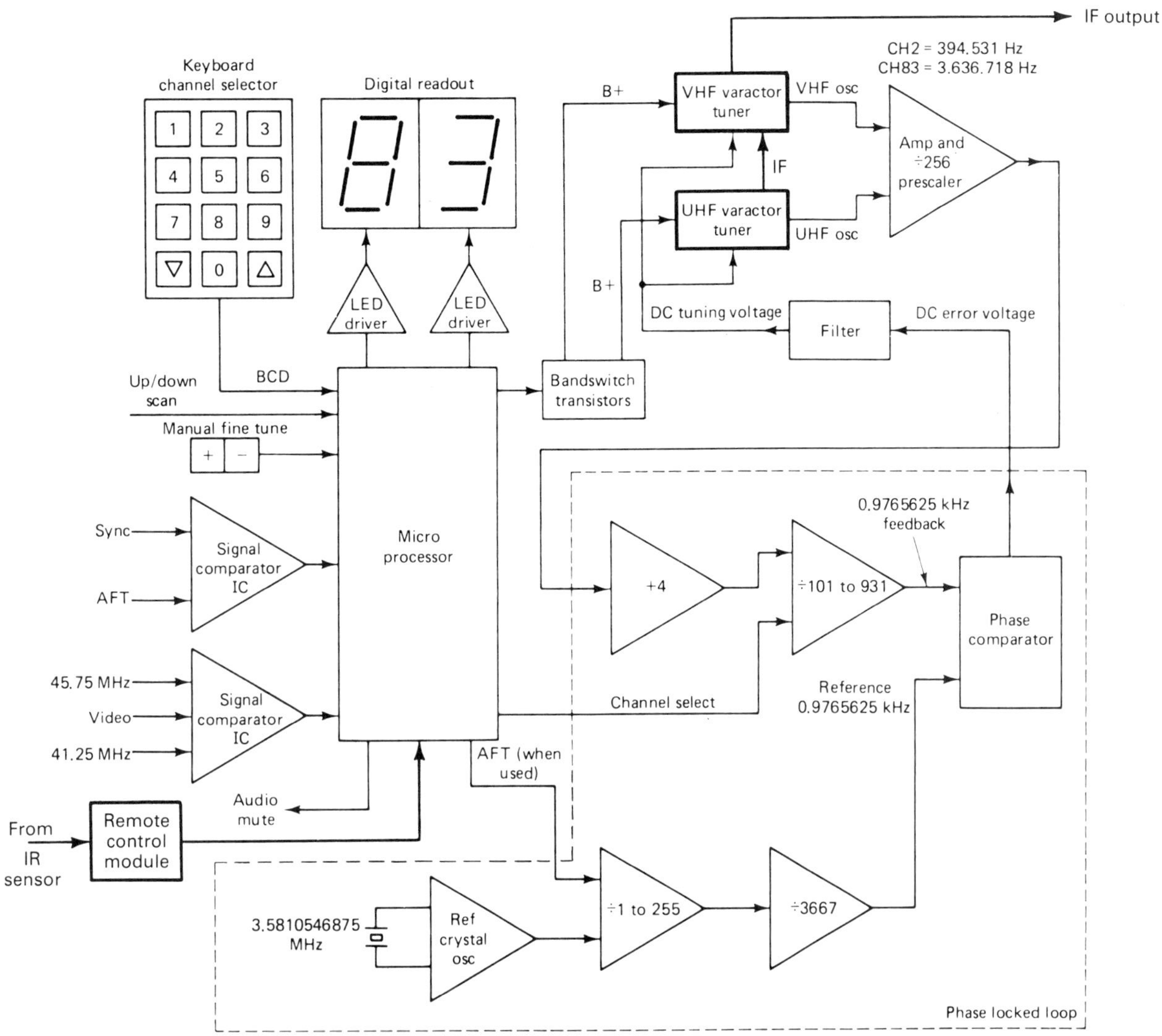


**FIG. 12-10** Typical PLL system. All PLL functions are performed by one or more ICs. (Courtesy of General Electric.)

the set is unplugged. In addition to the up/down *search mode* for selecting channels, most sets also provide for random-access tuning, direct channel selection from the keyboard. Many sets also have arrow buttons that function as an up and down volume control.

## Power Turn-On

When plugged in and switched off, some of the circuits in modern PLL sets remain in a standby mode and retain the memory of the last channel selected as well as other control settings. When the POWER-ON button is pressed, all circuits become energized by the switching action of a digitally controlled latching relay or triac. The reverse occurs when the button is pressed a second time, and the set reverts to standby.

## Cable-Ready Tuners

Virtually all PLL tuners are now considered *cable ready,* which means that they are able to receive CATV signals after they have been converted to frequencies in three CATV-UHF bands. A cable-ready tuner has the capability to receive up to 150 channels as supplied by local CATV services. Besides the standard VHF and UHF channels, this includes 9 midband channels, 14 superband channels, and 23 hyperband channels. The relative positions of these channels in the CATV frequency spectrum are shown in Figure 12-11. A decoder is required for "scrambled" signals. This is not to be confused with the converter box normally used for CATV reception. With a cable ready tuner, a converter box is required only when receiving special "pay to see" channels.

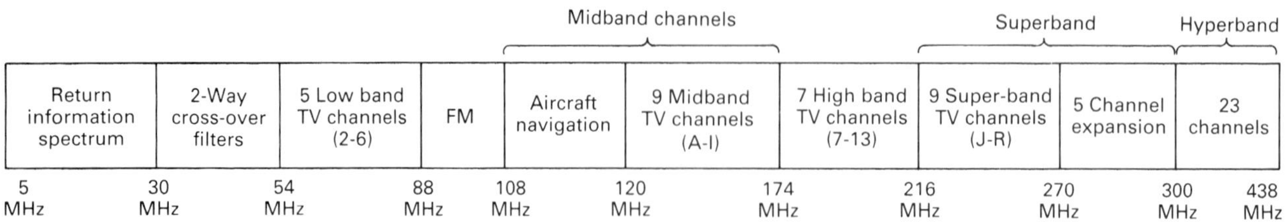


**FIG. 12-11** CATV system frequency spectrum.

## 12-8 REMOTE CONTROL SYSTEMS

Remote controls have long been popular for controlling TV receivers, changing channels, regulating volume, and other functions. Now they are almost an indispensible convenience for controlling other equipment, such as VCRs, cable boxes, and satellite receivers. A remote control system consists of a hand-held transmitter, a sensing device on the equipment being controlled, and the necessary electromechanical devices or electronic circuitry to perform the functions initiated by the transmitter unit.

Various mediums have been used to convey commands from the transmitter to the receiver. Early-model TV sets used an *acoustic* system, where ultrasonic waves produced by a mechanical transmitter or a multifrequency oscillator were picked up by a *transducer,* a kind of high-frequency microphone. Different "tones" initiated the various functions: receiver turn-on, channel selection, and volume control. Later models performed other functions, such as brightness, contrast, and color control. Selection is made by passing the signals from the transducer through a number of tuned filters. The functions are performed by small motors with reduction gear trains.

Another system of remote control used RF frequencies in the range 300 to 400 kHz. Buttons on the battery-operated transmitter initiate various modulation frequencies, each relating to a specific function to be performed. At the receiver, the signals are picked up by a ferrite rod antenna, detected, amplified, and filtered according to the desired function.

Currently, most remote controls use *infrared* (IR) as the means of communication between the transmitter and the equipment being controlled. The battery-operated transmitter contains the same binary logic circuits as used in the receiver for initiating and processing the various commands. A 33-kHz crystal-controlled oscillator is encoded with BCD signals from the keyboard. The signals are emitted (by a LED) as a series of invisible light pulses in the infrared spectrum.

At the receiver, the infrared carrier is detected by a light-sensitive diode, then demodulated to recover the coded signals representing the various command functions. This includes bandswitching and tuning voltages, and signals to activate the channel number readouts, the same as initiated by corresponding buttons on the receiver proper (see Figure 12-10). Universal IR transmitter units are now available for controlling virtually all late-model TVs, cable boxes, and VCRs.

## 12-9 TUNERS OF THE FOLDOUT SCHEMATIC

The VHF tuner here is a basic mechanical type. The UHF tuner uses a variable capacitor for channel selection. A small "antenna board" routes the VHF and UHF signals (via RC isolation networks) to the balun assembly. The balun provides a 300- to 75-Ω impedance match. Note the protective spark gaps. The VHF tuner gets its B voltage from a 16.5-V bus. The UHF tuner B+ comes from the VHF tuner. Only the VHF tuner is controlled by AGC. Both tuners use AFT control. A short length of coax feeds the UHF-IF signal to the VHF tuner. Both signals are fed via coax from the VHF tuner output to J101, the input to the IF strip. As is customary with most schematics, internal circuitry is not shown.

## 12-10 TUNER TROUBLESHOOTING AND REPAIRS

A major tuner defect normally calls for replacement on an exchange basis; there are times, however, when minor repairs might be attempted if the technician has the know-how, the time, and the inclination. The novice, too, can learn and profit from the experience. Tuner repairs require considerable patience and the use of proper tools when working in confined spaces. The minimum requirements include small cutters and needle-nose pliers, tweezers, trouble light, magnifying lens or combination light, an assortment of probes, and a low-wattage soldering iron. The following paragraphs deal with typical tuner-related problems and suggested troubleshooting procedures. The troubleshooting flow drawings (Figures 12-12 to 12-15) should also prove helpful.

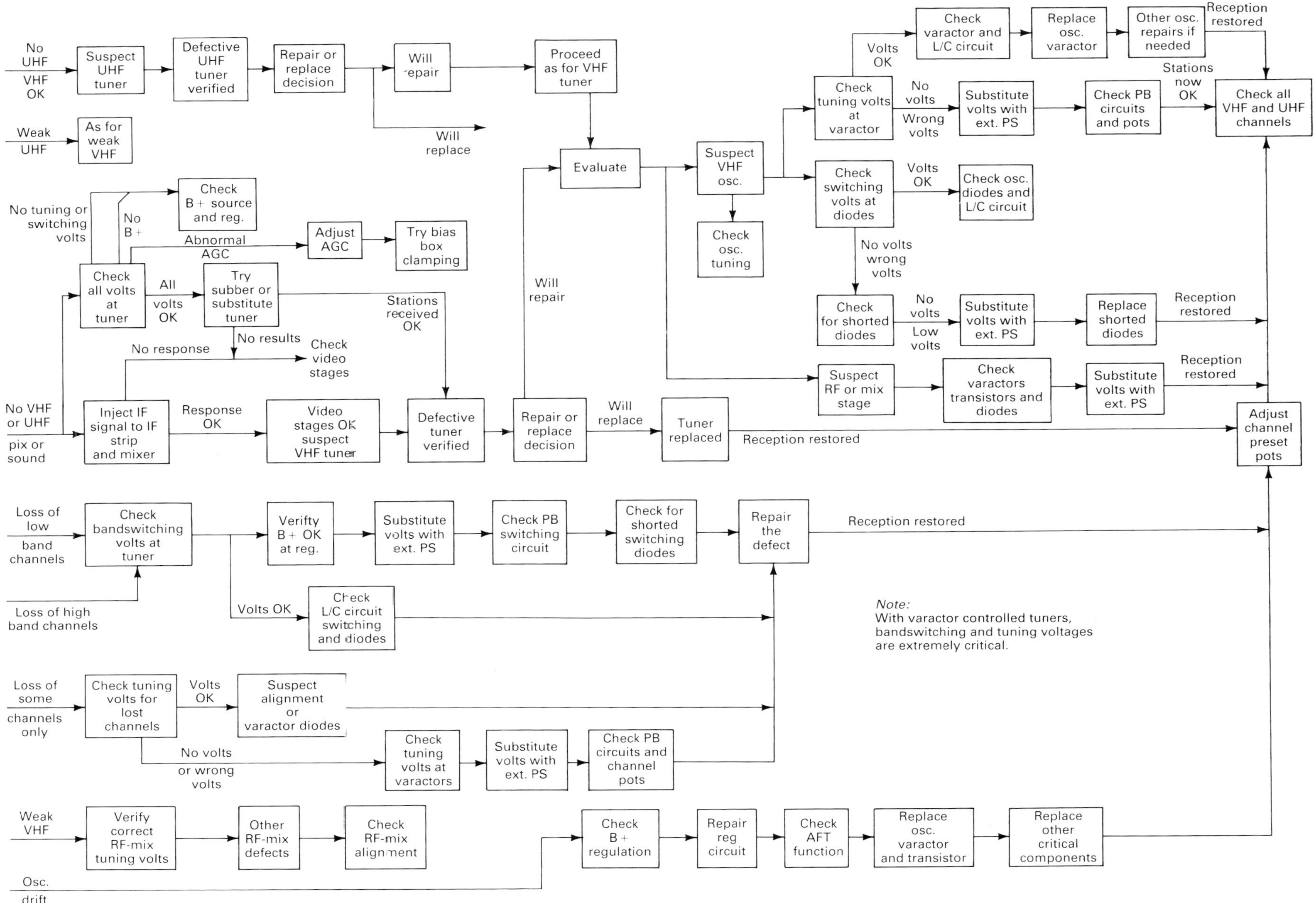


**FIG. 12-12** PB/varactor troubleshooting flow drawing.

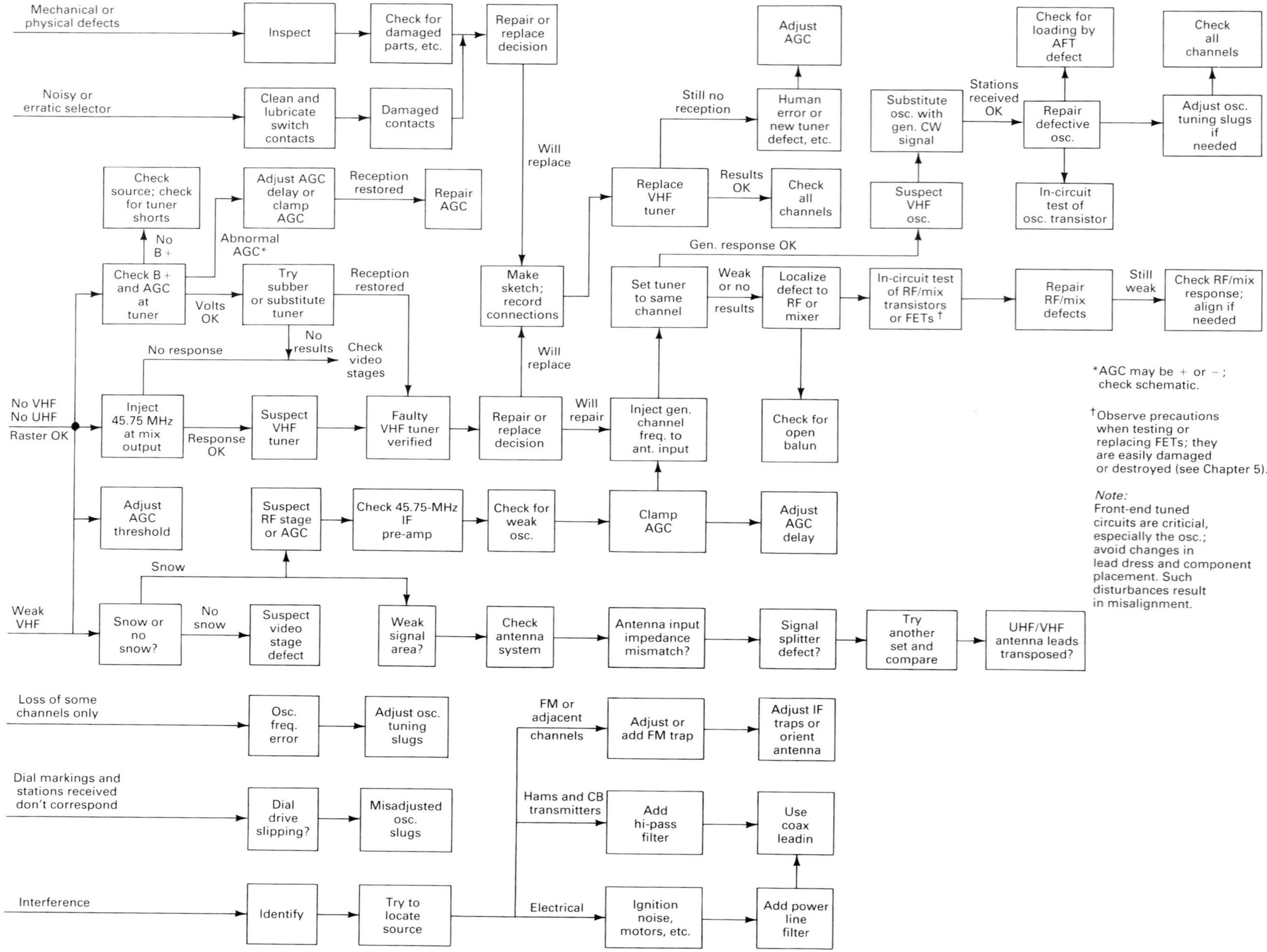


**FIG. 12-13** VHF tuner troubleshooting flow drawing.

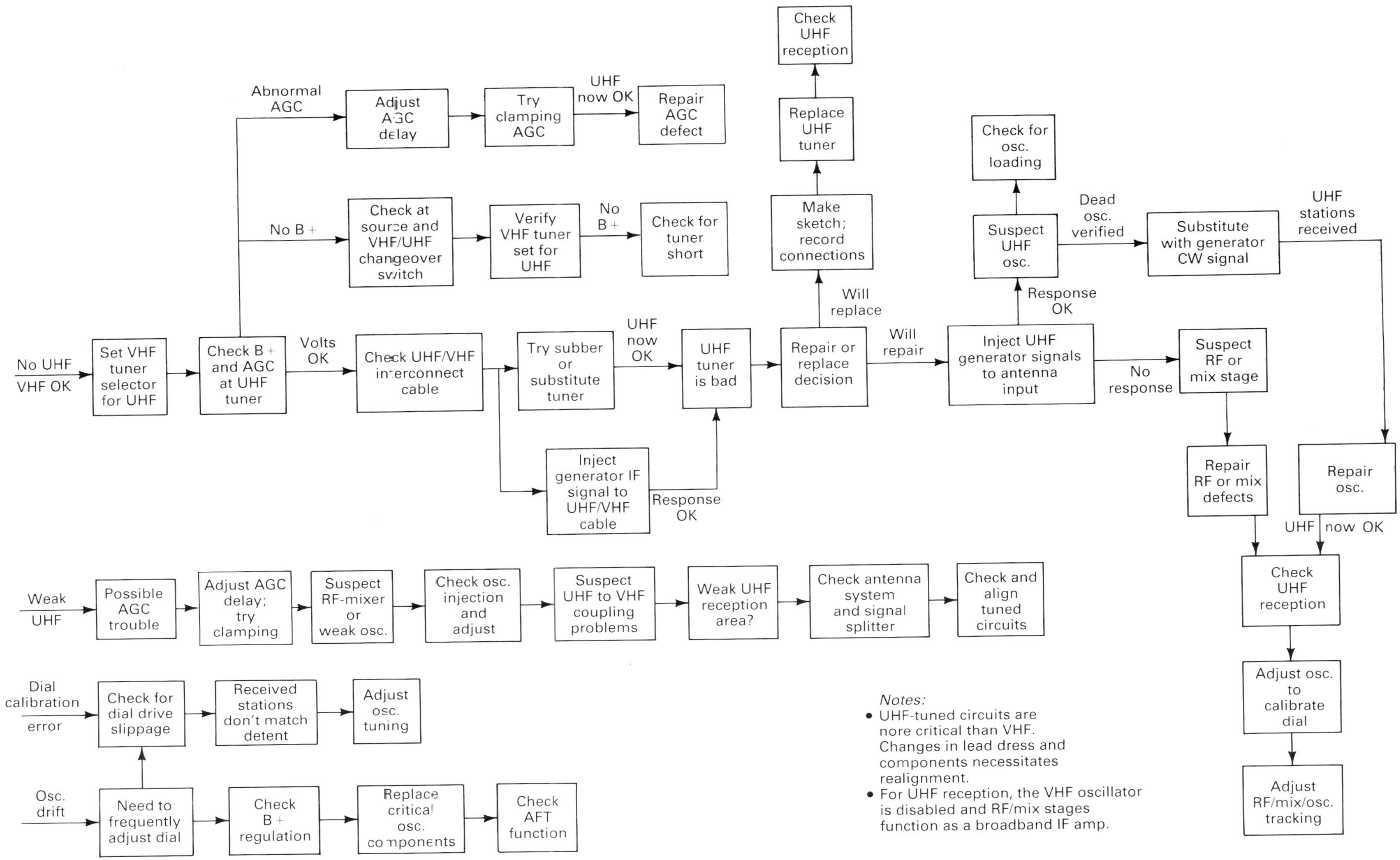


**FIG. 12-14** UHF tuner troubleshooting flow drawing.

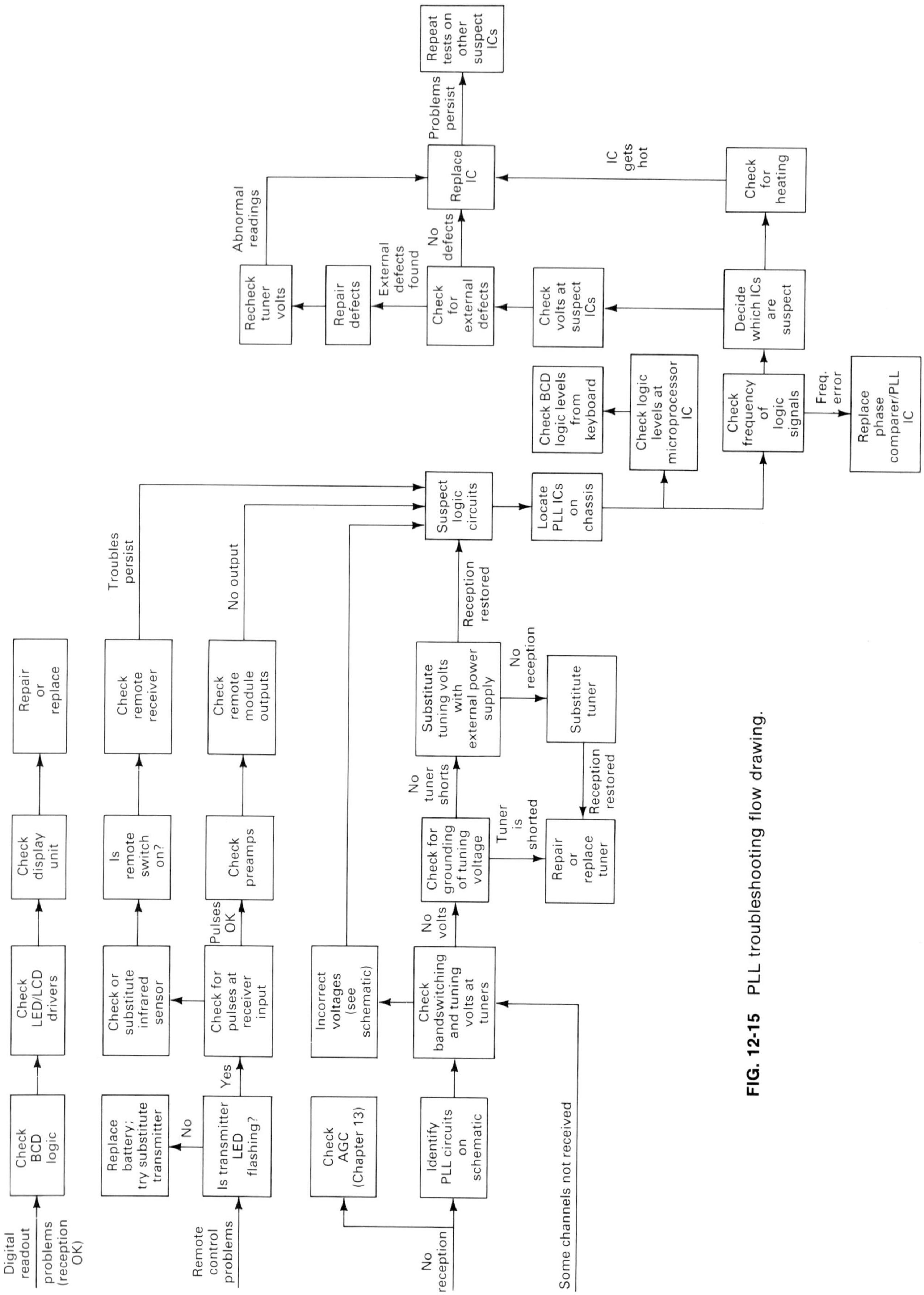


**FIG. 12-15** PLL troubleshooting flow drawing.

Specific procedures of course depends on the type of tuner being worked on. The first paragraphs deal with mechanical types (wafer/switch and drum) tuners. Following that, troubles with varactor tuners (including the PLL type) are discussed.

## Symptoms and Procedures

### *No VHF or UHF Reception.* (Raster ok)

***Probable causes:*** Defective VHF tuner; loss of tuner B+; AGC problems; a defect in the video IF strip between the tuner and the sound takeoff; problems with TV–VCR–CATV interconnecting cables or switching (check out this possibility before proceeding).

A VHF tuner must be operational to receive UHF so do not be concerned with UHF at this time. Start by adjusting the AGC control if there is one. Misadjustment or an AGC defect can block both picture and sound. For AGC problems, see Chapter 13.

Check for B+ at the tuner. If there is no B+, check for a defect in the voltage distribution network, a defective VHF/UHF changeover switch, or a B+ short in the tuner. For the latter possibility, check the resistance to ground, or break the circuit to see if B+ is restored.

Try signal injection. Feed a modulated 45.75-MHz signal to the first IF stage or to the tuner end of the coax. If the IF strip and subsequent stages are okay, you should get a bar pattern on the picture tube. The darkness of the bars is indicative of signal strength. If little or no indication, troubleshoot the IF strip (see Chapter 13). In lieu of signal injection, a *high-gain* scope can sometimes be used (with an amplifier type demodulator probe) for signal tracing the tuner, but signal levels are extremely low.

Check the integrity of the IF preamp stage on the tuner, if there is one, by feeding the 45.75-MHz signal to the mixer output. If the signal gets through, the IF strip is okay and the tuner is at fault. Substitute for the tuner using a subber, as described in Chapter 4, or a similar tuner type. (A tuner salvaged from a discarded TV set can easily be adapted for this purpose.) Assuming that the substitute has its own B supply, simply transfer the antenna leads and move the interconnecting coax from the receiver tuner to the output of the substitute tuner.

If the tuner is proven defective, decide whether to replace or attempt a repair. If the decision is to replace, *be warned.* A high percentage of those received by a repair depot *are not defective!* Make certain before jumping to conclusions. Where replacement *is* warranted, *prior to removal,* make sketches, and record all connections rather than trusting to memory.

To troubleshoot a dead tuner, inject some VHF channel frequency to the antenna terminals. Set the tuner to the corresponding channel. If there is no indication on the CRT, the oscillator is probably at fault. Try substitution, injecting a CW signal of the proper frequency into the mixer stage to see if reception can be restored. The frequency used will be the selected video RF carrier plus 45.75 MHz.

For a dead oscillator, check the transistor, preferably without removal, because any disturbance of the circuit will upset the tuning. Check all operating voltages and compare with the schematic. Check the other components, replacing any that are suspect.

If no signal continuity through the RF or mixer stages, repeat the tests described for the oscillator. Be careful to avoid shorts while testing, particularly where FETs are used. If the signal is lost in the IF preamp, isolate the defect by injecting a 45.75-MHz signal.

When reception is restored, check all VHF and UHF channels. Check the operation of the AFT defeat switch where used. With the AFT switched off, touch-up the oscillator adjustments for individual channels, where necessary. If the AFT is working, there should be no change when it is switched back on. Check the lock-in range by misadjusting the fine tuner in both directions. If necessary, make further touch-up adjustments or troubleshoot the AFT circuit, as appropriate.

### *Weak VHF Reception*

***Probable causes:*** Tuner defects; misalignment of RF/mixer tuned circuits; AGC troubles; poor reception area; antenna problems; defects in downstream IF stages between the tuner and the sound takeoff; IF misalignment.

Check antenna orientation. Make sure that the VHF/UHF antenna leads are not transposed. Try adjusting the AGC control if provided. If the weak picture is accompanied by *snow,* and it is not a problem with the antenna system or a poor location, suspect AGC troubles or an RF stage defect. For a weak picture without snow, suspect the downstream stages.

Measure the AGC voltage on and off channel and compare with the schematic. Extremely small deviations from the norm can be significant. Try clamping with an adjustable external PS, but do not exceed the amount specified, especially where an easily destroyed FET is used. Try adjusting the RF

AGC delay control if provided. For AGC troubles, refer to Chapter 13. Troubleshoot the RF/mixer stages as described earlier, but do not attempt alignment unless justified. It is seldom required unless components have been replaced or the adjustments tampered with. Where a weak IF stage is suspected, use signal injection or scope trace to check and compare stage gains, as described in Chapter 13.

### Loss of Some Channels Only

***Probable causes:*** Oscillator circuit defects; oscillator misalignment; damaged oscillator coils; dirty or damaged channel selector contacts.

If erratic or noisy when switching channels, check for damaged or misaligned contacts. Clean and lubricate. Inspect for damaged coils, loose or missing tuning slugs, and so on. Make sure that oscillator slugs are adjusted with the channel selector knob at the proper setting. A poor location or an antenna problem (including an impedance mismatch) are other possibilities to investigate.

### Stations Received Do Not Coincide with Channel Indicators

***Probable causes:*** Drive slippage; faulty detent; oscillator misadjustment.

Inspect. Replace or repair damaged mechanisms. Adjust individual channel slugs.

### *Oscillator Drift.* (It is necessary to adjust the fine tuner frequently)

***Probable causes:*** Defective or unstable oscillator components; loose coils or adjusting slugs; ineffective AFT circuit.

Inspect for loose parts. Replace the oscillator transistor. Try alternate heating and cooling of critical oscillator components and replace any that are suspect. (*Reminder:* Any disturbance of the oscillator circuit necessitates realignment, particularly on the high channels.) Check the AFT action as described earlier: but do not expect the AFT to cope with *drastic* variations of the oscillator frequency.

### AFT Malfunctions

***Probable causes:*** AFT circuit defect or misalignment.

Check the AFT action and lock-in range as described earlier. If there is no excessive oscillator drift, check for a balanced condition in the AFT discriminator. If the output error voltage is greater than $\pm 1$ V, with the AFT switched off, check the load resistors and diodes, which should be replaced as a matched pair. If an IC is used and no external defects are found, replace it. If necessary, touch-up the AFT adjustments at 45.75 MHz. If a signal generator is used, its frequency calibration must correspond *precisely* with the alignment of the IF strip.

### VHF Tuner Misalignment

***Probable causes:*** Tuned circuit defects; disturbance of component placement and lead dress when making repairs; indiscriminate tampering with adjustments.

Except for an occasional need to touch-up the oscillator adjustments, alignment is seldom required unless the circuit has been disturbed. Alignment procedures vary among sets. The following procedures are general. Refer to Sam's PHOTOFACTS or manufacturer's service data for specifics.

With AFT switched off and the fine tuner at midsetting, individually adjust oscillator slug(s) at the front of the tuner until the desired channels are received at the correct dial markings. Do not touch the fine tuner during this operation. With proper adjustment, it should be possible to receive all channels without using the fine tuner. Make sure that all channels received correspond with the dial settings. (*Reminder:* Although the RF/mixer stages are tuned to station frequencies, it is the *oscillator* that determines which channel is received regardless of RF/mixer alignment.)

The RF and mixer stages are adjusted for a 6-MHz bandpass centered at midfrequency for each channel selected (e.g., 57 MHz for channel 2). Because of their wide bandpass, these circuits are considerably less critical than the oscillator, but if too far off, can result in weak reception on some channels (particularly sound and color) and interference from adjacent channels.

The RF/mixer adjustment slugs are nonmagnetic (brass or copper) and screwing them into a coil raises the resonant frequency. This is the opposite effect compared to powdered-iron oscillator slugs. A *tuning wand,* described in Chapter 4, can be useful here for *evaluating* alignment conditions before any alignment is attempted. Changes noted when bringing the slugs near a coil indicates whether more or less inductance is required to obtain resonance.

There are several alternate methods of alignment, depending on equipment availability. Before starting, it is a good idea to disable the oscillator to prevent interference and misleading indications.

An *accurate* RF generator may be used, adjusting each tuned circuit for a peak reading on a scope or meter connected at some downstream point. In another method, called *sweep alignment,* a sweep generator sweeps the bandpass of the tuned circuit(s), producing a response curve on a scope. Important frequencies are identified and positioned on the curve, with *markers* produced by a marker generator. The procedure is carried out in two steps, first obtaining a response to *evaluate* alignment conditions, followed by actual alignment if required (see Chapter 13).

Another method is called *bar sweep alignment.* This fast and accurate method uses special equipment (Sencore, Chapter 4). For procedures, refer to the instruction manual.

*No UHF Reception.* (VHF okay)

***Probable causes:*** Defective UHF tuner; loss of B+ or abnormal AGC; open or shorted coax between the two tuners.

With the VHF tuner set for UHF reception (between channels 2 and 13 on the dial), check for B+ at the UHF tuner. No B voltage may be due to an open dropping resistor or a defective changeover switch. Check the UHF AGC voltage both on and off channel and compare with the schematic. Adjust the delay control if there is one, or try clamping with an external B supply to the amount shown on schematic. Check the continuity of the interconnecting coax. Make sure that it is firmly seated in the connectors at each end. Depending on the test results, try substitution using a subber or another tuner, as described for the VHF tuner.

If tuner is proven defective, decide whether to repair or replace. If the latter, and prior to removal, record all connections to avoid confusion when making replacement at a later time.

When repairs are attempted, start by injecting a UHF signal (corresponding to the tuner channel markings), to the antenna input terminals. Note whether a bar pattern response is obtained on the pix tube. Check the oscillator function by a small dc voltage indication at the mixer input. For a suspected dead oscillator try using an unmodulated generator signal (as a substitute) to see if reception can be restored.

After the trouble has been localized, test the transistor or FET in the bad stage, preferably without removal to avoid circuit disturbances and component damage. (*Reminder:* Component placement and lead dress in UHF tuners is *extremely critical* and *any* disturbance will have an adverse effect on tuner operation and alignment.)

Check voltages and compare with schematic. Check other components, replacing any that are suspect. For obscure problems and as a last resort, replace FETs and transistors even if they check ok. When the trouble is corrected, check reception at both extremes of the dial. Verify the calibration corresponds with the channel number markings or readouts.

*Weak UHF Reception.* (VHF okay)

***Probable causes:*** Weak RF, mixer or, oscillator stage; AGC problems; misalignment of tuned circuits; antenna problems; poor location for receiving UHF.

For a weak picture with snow, check the antenna orientation. Try a substitute antenna. Make sure that the antenna input leads are not transposed—a human error that happens frequently. Check AGC and B voltages. Even slight departures from the norm can be significant. Where a frequency conversion problem is suspected, try a generator as a substitute for the oscillator. Use a low-level output to avoid damaging FETs and transistors. Try a slight repositioning of hairpin loops used for interstage coupling at baffle windows.

*Dial Calibration Errors*

***Probable causes:*** Slipping dial drive or knob; defective detent; oscillator misadjustment.

Assuming no slippage or mechanical problems, when stations are not received at the proper points on the dial, it is usually due to misalignment. For an older set, some calibration error can be expected and tolerated. If warranted, adjust the oscillator trimmers by a *small* amount. If necessary to correct a tracking error, "knife" the outer tuning capacitor plates in small increments by bending.

As a final step, touch-up the RF/mixer adjustments for maximum picture contrast (minimum snow) at the high end of the dial.

### Varactor Tuner Repairs

Many of the troubles and procedures described for drum and switch tuners also apply to varactor tuners. The main differences are problems involving the channel selector keyboard and the generation of bandswitching and tuning voltages.

### Troubleshooting Basic Pushbutton Tuners

A typical pushbutton varactor tuner such as shown in Figure 12-16 is not too difficult to service. The biggest problem in some cases is locating it in a

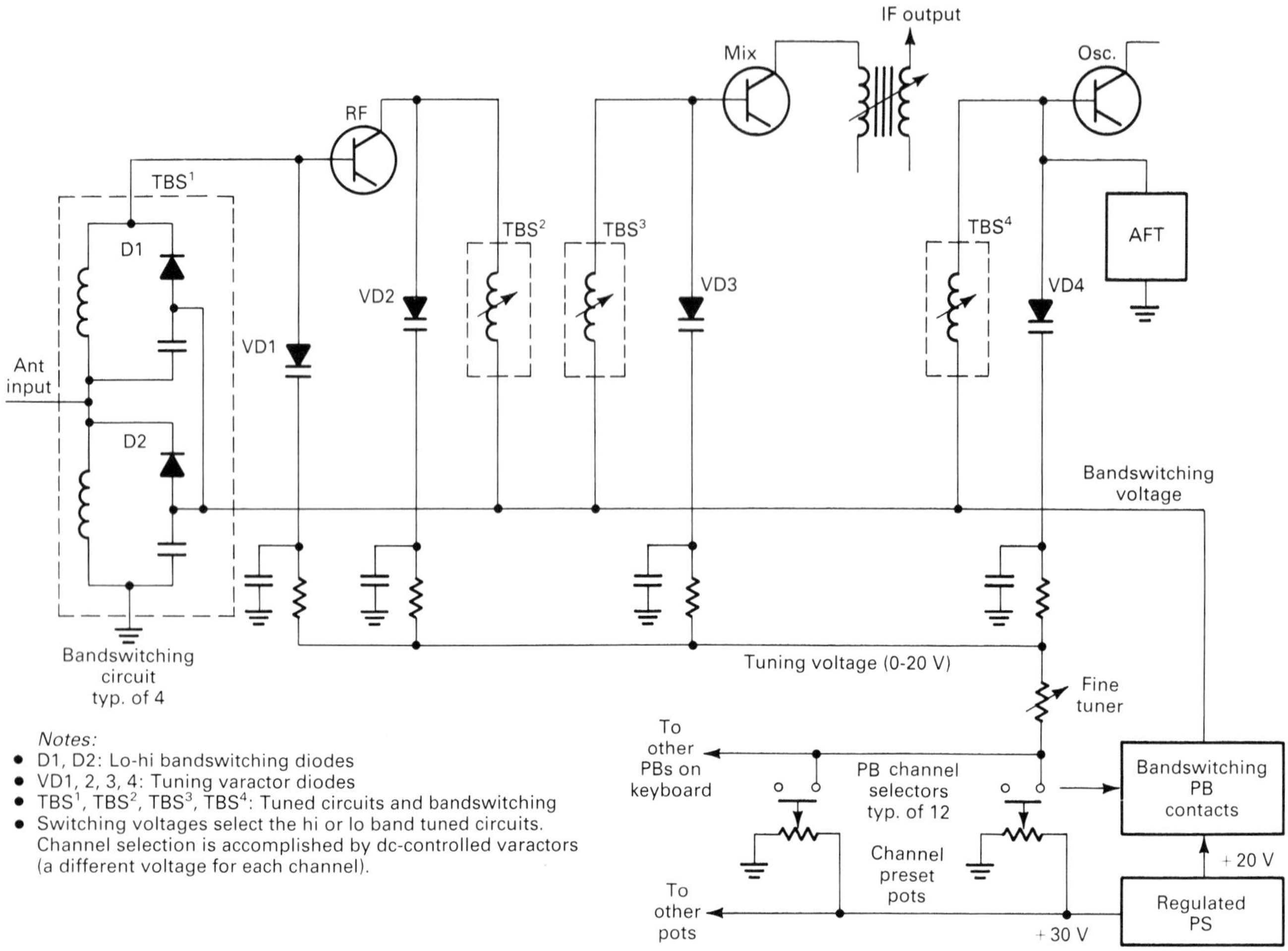


**FIG. 12-16** Troubleshooting the PB/varactor tuner.

crowded chassis and gaining access to its connections. Common trouble symptoms and suggested procedures are as follows.

### *No VHF or UHF Reception.* (raster okay)

***Probable causes:*** Defective VHF tuner; B+ or AGC problems; improper or missing bandswitching or tuning voltage at the VHF tuner; defective IF strip.

Verify the integrity of the IF preamp and the IF strip by injecting a modulated 45.75-MHz signal. Because UHF reception is dependent on the proper operation of the VHF tuner, it is assumed that the latter is at fault. The following tests therefore apply only to the VHF tuner.

Check B+ and AGC at the VHF tuner. Check for the tuning voltage, which usually varies from about 1.5 V for channel 2 up to 30 V or so for channel 13. Refer to the schematic for exact amounts. If no tuning voltage, check back through the fine tuner, the channel selector button assembly, and the channel adjusting pots, to the voltage regulator. Since all of the channels are out, the latter is the prime suspect. Troubleshoot it as described in Chapter 6.

Check for the dc bandswitching voltage, which is typically about 20 V. Here again the regulator is a good suspect. Loss of tuning and switching voltages, however, are often caused by a tuner short. Make ohmmeter checks to ground, and/or break the circuit to see if the voltage is restored on the supply line. Try using a regulated external PS adjusted to the proper voltage(s), as specified, to see if reception can be restored. Do not exceed the amounts called for, and adjust the PS *before* connecting to the circuit. If an internal defect is suspected, try a substitute tuner or subber. If the tuner is to be replaced, sketch and record all connections prior to removal. Terminal identities and interconnections are shown in Figure 12-17.

Tuner repairs are best made when removed from the chassis and using a substitute PS. Bad var-

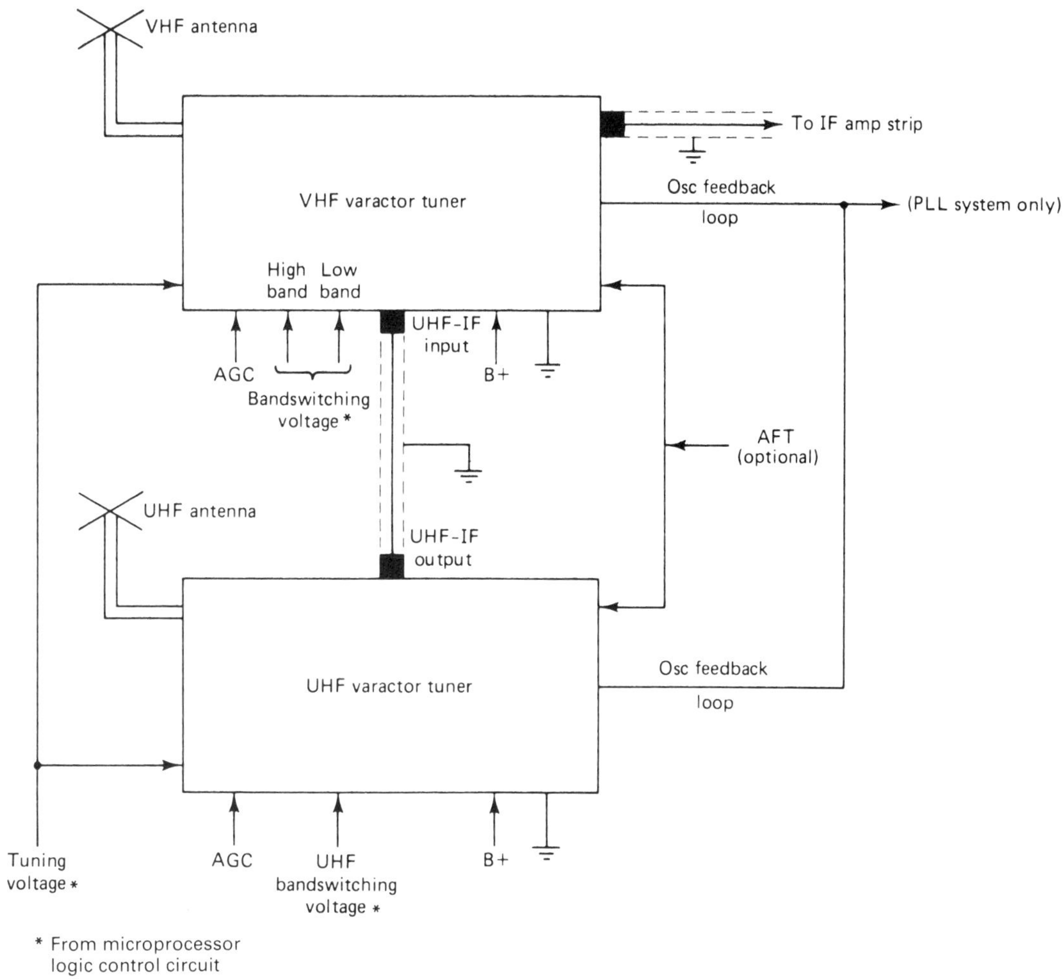


**FIG. 12-17** Tuner inputs and outputs. Tuning voltages are critical; refer to the schematic.

actors, FETs, and B+ shorts are very common. For a low ohms reading at the tuning voltage or bandswitching voltage terminal, localize the short or leakage to a particular stage or voltage-dropping network by making additional resistance checks to ground. The point of lowest resistance will be the trouble site. Disconnect suspected capacitors, varactors, and FETs until the short or leakage is relieved and the bad component identified.

For troubles other than missing or abnormal voltages, proceed as described for other tuner types. After the troubles have been corrected, adjust the individual channel pots for the stations desired.

### *Weak Reception*

***Probable causes:*** Same possibilities as described earlier; incorrect tuning voltages.

Although the same tuning voltage is applied simultaneously to all varactors, a short or leakage in an RF or mixer stage may not prevent the oscillator from operating, but will detune the "signal" stages. Measure and compare the voltages at each varactor. The point of lowest voltage identifies the defective component. Make in-circuit tests of the FET, the varactor, and associated capacitors.

### *Loss of High-Band, Low-Band, or UHF Channels.* (some channels received okay)

***Probable causes:*** Defects affecting one band only, such as missing or abnormal switching voltages.

Check bandswitching voltage associated with the nonoperating band. If voltage is missing or abnormal, check the source, the keyboard switching, and if necessary, the related switching diodes and tuned circuit components associated with the troublesome band.

### *Loss of Some Channels Only*

***Probable causes:*** Channel selector pots defective or misadjusted; defective pushbutton switches.

Monitor the oscillator tuning voltage for troublesome channel(s) as pot(s) are adjusted. Clean or replace bad control pots; if necessary, replace the entire assembly. If keyboard switching problems are suspected, check with an ohmmeter. If erratic, clean or replace.

### *Oscillator Drift*

***Probable causes:*** Bad oscillator transistor, varactor, or associated components; poor voltage regulation; AFT problems; erratic fine tuner control pot.

Check for poor voltage regulation; if necessary, repair the regulator. Check the AFT action as described earlier. Repair if needed. Clean or replace a noisy fine tuner. Alternately heat and cool suspected oscillator components. If trouble persists, replace the oscillator transistor and varactor and other critical components.

### *No UHF Reception.* (VHF okay).

***Probable causes:*** Open or shorted UHF to VHF coax; B+ or AGC problems; defective UHF tuner; missing or abnormal bandswitching or UHF tuning voltages.

Follow the same general procedures as for the loss of VHF reception. Avoid any unecessary disturbance of the critical circuitry. When repairs are completed, check the reception for all channels, making touch-up adjustments of the tuned circuits if warranted.

### *Weak UHF Reception*

***Probable causes:*** Same as for mechanical UHF tuners.

## 12-11 ELECTRONIC PLL SYSTEM TROUBLESHOOTING AND REPAIR

Troubleshooting is performed on a *systems* level, and since all functions are performed by ICs, a different approach is used compared to other methods of channel selection. Despite its complexity, however, the system is not too difficult to service. It is mostly a matter of correctly analyzing a problem, localizing the trouble to a particular functional area, then replacing the ICs that are faulty. The following troubleshooting procedures are general. Specifics vary with different sets and depend in part on which functions are performed by ICs and which are not.

### Tuners

Typical defects and troubleshooting procedures are the same as for varactor tuners described earlier, with one exception. With a PLL system, the *amount* of tuning voltage measured at the tuner is not too critical since it is the *frequencies* that are compared. Start by analyzing the problem and symptoms, noting which functions are impaired. Measure and record all voltages at the tuner connections, and compare with the schematic. If a counter is available, check the frequencies at the feedback loops as different channels are selected. Record such information for future reference. Examine the schematic and decide which ICs are possible suspects if one or more voltages are weak or missing, or the feedback frequency is incorrect. A microprocessor IC is usually a prime suspect since it controls most of the PLL functions.

### Logic Circuits

Locate and identify the suspected ICs. Feel each one. An IC that is hot is probably shorted. But do not be hasty in making a replacement. There is a better-than-even chance that it was caused by defects external to the IC or in another IC.

Make resistance and voltage checks at all pins of a suspected IC, and compare with the schematic. If an abnormal voltage is measured at one or more pins, or if there is voltage where none should exist, isolate those pins from the external circuitry, and recheck. Loading due to an internal short will reduce or kill the voltage at the terminals. A voltage reading at some "no voltage point" may be caused by an IC defect or by defects in the external circuit. If the latter, correct the cause before replacing the IC.

Check all input and output logic levels at the IC pins and compare with the schematic. Except where all functions are performed by a single IC, it is sometimes possible to check logic pulses at IC interfaces. A *logic probe* is an almost indispensible instrument for quickly tracing on/off digital pulses. A scope can also be employed, but a probe is faster and handier to use. Where a logic voltage is weak or missing at an IC input, check to its source or suspect that it is grounded out by a short in the IC.

If there is little or no output from the IC, it may be lost internally or grounded out by the external circuit. Make follow-up ohmmeter checks. If the IC is considered defective and no external defects are discovered, replace it. If trouble symptoms persist, follow the same procedure with other suspected ICs until normal operation is restored.

### Keyboard Problems

Using a scope or logic probe, check for BCD pulses as each button is pressed. If pulses are missing or abnormal, check the voltage source and the channel switching.

### Channel Readout Problems

If the set operates okay but there is an abnormal or missing readout of channel numbers, suspect the microprocessor, the driver amplifiers, the BCD-to-numeric decoders, or the LED or LCD readout assembly, as applicable. If one or more segments of a display is faulty, suspect the corresponding readout unit or its circuitry. Weak readouts are not uncommon and are usually caused by low voltage.

## 12-12 REMOTE CONTROLS TROUBLESHOOTING AND REPAIR

Typical problems are no control of one or more functions, or loss of sensitivity, making it necessary to operate the transmitter close to the receiver. Troubleshooting involves several items in the system: the transmitter, the receiver unit, and the devices or electronics that carry out the actions. Make sure that the receiver is plugged in and operating properly and that the unit in the receiver is turned on. Troubleshooting procedures depend, of course, on the type of system used.

### Acoustic System

Inspect the mechanical transmitter for damage. Typical defects are broken or missing springs, deterioration of rod support gaskets, and rods touching the case. Check the hammer impacts as each button is triggered. Try a substitute transmitter if one is available. Repair or replace as appropriate.

Using a meter or CRO, check for a *momentary* voltage at the microphone on the receiver as each transmitter button is pressed. If there is no indication and assuming that the transmitter is ok, the microphone is suspect. Try a substitute if available.

Signal trace the received pulses through the high-gain amplifiers, and the tuned filters—but they seldom go bad or require adjustment. Where some but not all functions are working, check the corresponding tone filters and the motors that carry out the action. Motors sometimes seize up, but most defects are mechanical.

### Modulated RF Carrier System

The most common trouble is a weak battery in the transmitter unit. Using a fresh battery, gain access to the circuit and check for ac voltage at the output transducer (speaker unit) as each button is pressed. Unlike the acoustic system, the reading should be constant. If there is no output, check the oscillator transistor and associated components. If only some buttons produce an output, try cleaning the switch contacts.

Check for signal voltage at the receiver input, and if none, suspect the receiver unit or a weak transmitter. If misalignment is suspected where some functions do not operate, try adjusting the corresponding tuned circuits while holding the transmitter close to the set.

### Infrared System

A weak battery in the transmitter is common. The clue is a dark or dimly lit LED or loss of sensitivity with the need to operate the transmitter close to the receiver. The flicker rate of the LED provides an indication of which functions, if any, are being initiated. A bad transmitter is normally replaced, but if repairs are attempted, troubleshoot as described for the corresponding logic circuits in the receiver.

If the transmitter is working, check for pulse voltage at the pickup sensor in the receiver. Try a new sensor diode. If troubles persist, troubleshoot the logic circuits as described earlier.

## QUESTIONS

1. Why is it possible to locate a varactor tuner anywhere in the chassis?
2. Explain the relationship between amplification, bandpass, and selectivity in an RF stage.

3. Explain the purpose of each of the three tuner stages.
4. Using a numeric example, explain frequency conversion from RF to IF.
5. Briefly explain the operation of an IR remote control system.
6. Explain the operation of the PLL system of tuning.
7. What three bands are selected by the bandswitching circuit?
8. What is oscillator drift, and what tuner control is used to compensate?
9. Explain why tuned lines are used for tuning UHF frequencies.
10. The oscillator is much more critical than the RF/mixer stages. Explain why.
11. Why do most tuners now use FETs in the RF/Mixer and IF preamp stages in preference to transistors?
12. Show with examples how series and parallel tuned circuits can be used as acceptor or rejector circuits.
13. Why must a tuner pass such a wide band of frequencies, and what is the probable effect of a narrowed bandpass? Explain.
14. What is the effect on the resonant frequency of a tuned circuit if (a) L is increased; (b) C is decreased; (d) both *L* and *C* are increased?
15. Why must the oscillator frequency change when switching channels?
16. Briefly explain the operation of an AFT circuit.
17. What are the advantages of PLL tuning over that of all other systems?
18. Explain varactor tuning.
19. Which tuner is suspect if there is (a) no UHF reception; (b) no VHF or UHF? Explain why in each case.
20. What is the function of a subber, and when is it used?
21. Explain the purpose of a logic probe.

# 13 Video IF detector, and AGC

At the tuner, the video and sound signals were converted from RF to IF; that is, the frequency of the video RF carrier (of the station received) was reduced to 45.75 MHz and the sound RF carrier to 41.25 MHz. Except for the lower carrier frequencies, the information contained in the sidebands (video, chroma, sync, and sound) remained unchanged.

The video and sound signals are amplified by an *IF preamp,* then routed via low-impedance coax to the video IF amplifiers, commonly referred to as the video IF strip. The amplified video (including the chroma and sync signals) is then passed on to the video detector, as shown in Figure 13-1. The sound signal is separated from the video at a point called the *sound takeoff.* For a color set, the sound takeoff is usually at the last IF stage. For BW sets, it may be anywhere between the detector and the CRT.

The function of the video detector is to *demodulate* the video signal, that is, to extract or recover the sideband information from the carrier. The AGC automatically regulates the gain and sensitivity of the receiver in accordance with the strength of the signals received.

## 13-1 IF STRIP

The IF strip is a three- or four-stage broadband tuned amplifier designed to handle the picture and sound IF carriers plus all the information contained

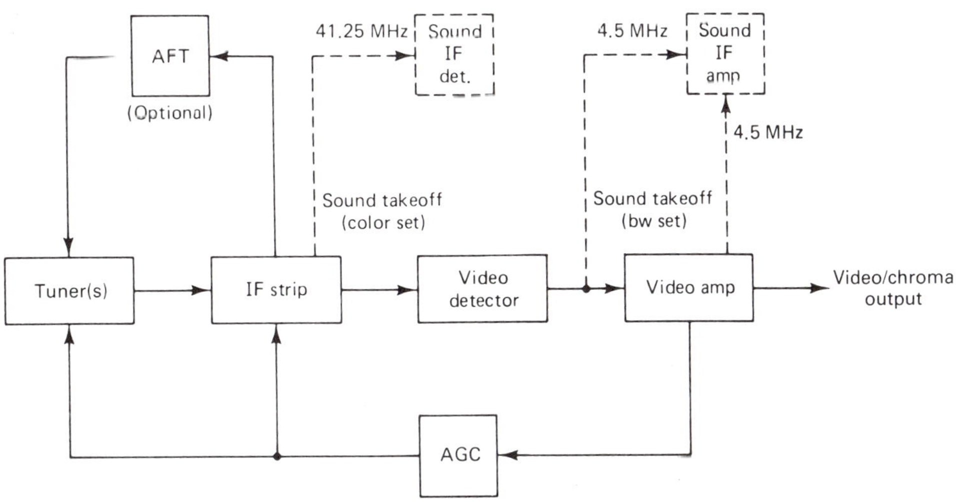


**FIG. 13-1** Basic block diagram.

in their sidebands. This includes video, sync, and color signals, plus the sound; each signal is represented by a band of frequencies. Like the tuner, this requires a wide bandpass, typically around 4 MHz for a color set. Modern sets incorporate the IF strip with other circuits in a multifunction IC.

### IF Amplification

The IF strip provides most of the signal amplification for the entire set. It is also responsible for rejecting unwanted signals that get through the broadband tuner stages. A typical IF stage has a gain factor of about 20 db, which for three stages provides an overall gain just under 10,000. Thus a 1-mV input signal, for example, would be increased to about 8 V at the detector. Most sets have a high-gain preamp ahead of the IF strip.

### Tuning

Tuned circuits are an important part of the IF strip. Their function is twofold; to accept the band of frequencies associated with the picture and sound IF carriers of the selected station, and to reject all others. With some sets the tuning takes place between each IF stage. Where an IC is used, the tuned circuits are ahead of the IF amplifiers. Late-model sets have a minimum of tuned circuits.

### Video Frequencies and Bandwidth Requirements

A brief review of the subject seems appropriate at this time. The video frequencies that make up a picture are contained in the sidebands of the carrier: in this case, the 45.75-MHz IF carrier. There are two sidebands, the upper sideband on the high-frequency side of the carrier, and the lower sideband on the low-frequency side. The low modulation frequencies (those that produce large picture objects and sync pulses) are close to the carrier. The modulation frequency *at* the carrier is 0 Hz. High video frequencies (frequencies that produce the fine picture detail) are those farthest from the carrier. Good picture resolution requires a bandpass of that amount. With vestigial sideband transmission as described in Chapter 1, the two sidebands are not equal.

The bandwidth requirement for the IF strip is largely determined by the size of the picture tube. A wide bandpass is unnecessary with a small CRT, but for a large tube, a wide bandpass is required to accommodate the highest frequencies that correspond with the finest picture detail. A small-screen set is designed to handle only frequencies in the range 2 to 3 MHz, and a bandpass of that amount is adequate. On the other hand, for a large screen with more numerous and widely spaced elements, greater bandwidth is required, up to a maximum of 4.2 MHz, the upper limit of the transmitted video. This compares with the 6-MHz passband of the tuner. The bandwidth of the IF strip is established by the degree of coupling between the IF stages and the alignment of the tuned circuits.

A bandpass wider than necessary reduces selectivity, increasing the possibility of interference, and also reduces stage gain. A narrowed bandpass provides more gain but reduces the amount of detail that can be observed.

### IF Response Curves

As described in Chapter 12, a response curve is a convenient way of showing the relative gain for different frequencies within the bandpass of an amplifier. Like the RF/mixer stages in the tuner, the IF strip also has a wide bandpass in order to handle the widely separated carriers and the wide range of frequencies contained in their sidebands. The curve for a typical large-screen BW set is shown in Figure 13-2a. The curve represents the relative gain for different frequencies. The baseline corresponds to zero amplification. The width of the curve (at the 50% level) is established by the highest video frequency to be passed, in this case, 4 MHz. By comparison, curve (b) is for a small-screen set. With a small screen, a 2-MHz bandpass is adequate to obtain sufficient picture detail. A narrow bandpass also provides for greater amplification, so fewer stages are required.

*Frequency Markers.* In Figure 13-2a, a marker representing the picture carrier (designated P) is at the 50% level on the high-frequency side of the curve. This corresponds with a video frequency of 0 Hz. The highest video frequencies are represented by a point exactly opposite—in the example, a video frequency of 4 MHz. All in-between video frequencies near the top of the curve receive good amplification, with those around 2 MHz, the center of the response, receiving the most amplification.

*Adjacent Channel Markers.* If a tuner has poor selectivity and is unable to reject interference from strong adjacent channels, its oscillator may heterodyne with adjacent channel signals, producing IF frequencies that may be received along with the

P, 45.75-MHz pix carrier marker
S, 41.25-MHz sound carrier marker
C, 42.17-MHz color subcarrier marker
U-S, upper color sideband marker (42.67 MHz)
L-S, 41.67-MHz lower color sideband marker
A-P, adjacent channel pix carrier marker
A-S, adjacent channel sound carrier marker

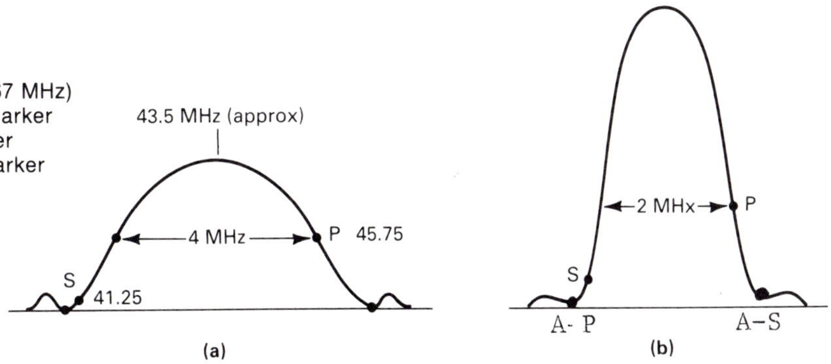


**FIG. 13-2** Black-and-white set's IF response curves: (a) large-screen set; (b) small-screen set.

desired signals. Adjacent channel traps tuned to these frequencies are incorporated in the IF strip to overcome this possibility. In Figure 13-2a, adjacent channel frequencies are shown as markers on the baseline, beyond the limits of the curve on both sides; the sound carrier of the next-higher channel on the one side, and the video carrier of the next-lower channel on the opposite side (see Figure 1-2). An excessively wide bandpass would encompass these frequencies, resulting in interference. The same thing can happen if the traps are misadjusted. Adjacent channel video traps are tuned to 39.75 MHz, adjacent channel sound traps to 47.25 MHz.

*Vestigial Sideband Compensation.* The portion of the curve extending from the carrier down to the baseline represents the upper vestigial sideband. The decreasing gain for these frequencies offsets the high gain for the frequencies of the lower sideband.

The 41.25-MHz sound IF carrier (designated S) is indicated by a marker near the baseline and barely within the limits of the curve. Typically, this marker is at the approximate 5% level, just high enough to receive *some* amplification but not enough to create problems of "intercarrier buzz" that results from the beat between the two carriers.

The markers shown assumes that a station is properly tuned in with the tuner oscillator developing a correct frequency. If there is a frequency error (as by misadjusting the fine tuner), all markers take up different positions on the curve, causing degradation of both picture and sound. If the fine tuner adjustment is far off, there may be total loss of picture and/or sound.

*Color Receiver Response Curves.* Because of the chroma information, a color set requires a somewhat wider bandwidth, as shown in Figure 13-3a. Note that the chroma signals are contained within the same bandpass as the monochrome video signals. The color carrier (subcarrier), which is 3.58 MHz from the video carrier, is represented by point C on the low-frequency side of the curve. As with the video, chroma sidebands extend on both sides of the subcarrier, the chroma frequencies from 0 to 1.5 MHz receiving high amplification, and frequencies from 0 to 0.5 MHz in the lower (vestigial) sideband receiving less gain to compensate for the high gain of the upper sideband frequencies.

### Broadband and Narrowband Color

The 3.58-MHz color subcarrier at the station is modulated by I signals, frequencies from 0 to 1.5 MHz in the lower sideband, and Q signals extending only to 0.5 MHz in the upper sideband. The carrier is removed and the full I sideband is transmitted but only a "vestige" of the Q sideband. As with vestigial transmission of the video signals, this must be compensated for by proper alignment of the IF strip.

Although the full 1.5 MHz of the lower sideband is transmitted, for reasons of economy, most receivers now utilize only 0.5 MHz of *both* side-

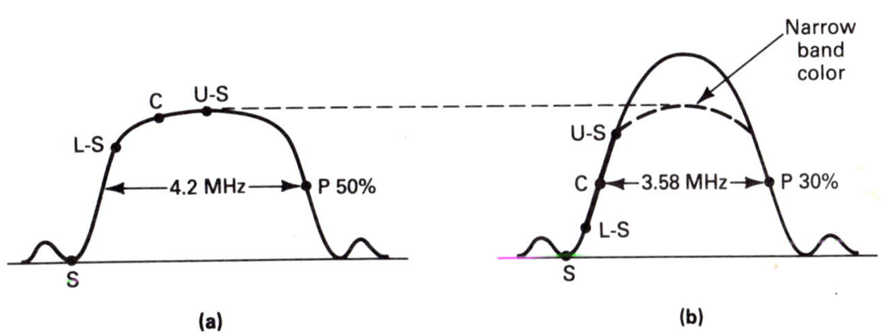


**FIG. 13-3** Color set response curves.

bands. Color sets are designed and aligned to obtain either a broadband or narrowband response.

*Broadband Color.* A typical broadband response curve is shown in Figure 13-3a. Note the ideal bandpass of 4.2 MHz, which is needed for high resolution and fine detail on large-screen sets. A trade-off is some reduction in stage gain. Chroma markers located near the top of the curve assure high gain for the color signals, including those contained in the lower sideband.

*Narrowband Color.* This curve (Figure 13-3b) is aptly called a *haystack* response. It represents a bandwidth slightly narrower than for broadband color, with the chroma subcarrier located well down on the low-frequency slope. Note that the highest frequencies of the lower sideband are close to the baseline, where they receive very little amplification. This is no detriment, however, since fine picture details (corresponding with the high frequencies in the chroma sidebands) are *not reproduced in color.* Attenuation of the high-frequency color signals is partly compensated for in the bandpass amplifier at the input to the chroma stages. This low-cost system has one shortcoming: reduced gain for low frequencies close to the subcarrier, which can cause unstable color sync under conditions of weak and noisy reception.

### Tanks and Traps

The tuned circuits at the input and output of each IF stage function as "loads" across which the signal voltage is developed. They are sometimes refered to as "tank" circuits, to differentiate from the tuned "traps" also used in the IF strip. Some examples of each are shown in the simplified drawing of Figure 13-4. Both series and parallel resonant traps are included, which function as described in Chapter 12. The series resonant traps at the input to Q2 have a low impedance at resonance to shunt any 39.75-MHz adjacent channel video signal or 47.25-MHz sound signals to ground. The parallel resonant trap that couples the signal to Q3 has a high impedance at resonance to reject unwanted signals. Frequencies above and below resonance get through unopposed. Transformer T1 in the Q3 stage performs a dual function. The primary winding serves as the transistor load and the secondary winding in conjunction with a capacitor acts as an absorption trap. Such a trap absorbs energy at its resonant frequency from the tank circuit.

A very effective trap (as found in most modern sets) is shown at the output of Q4. It is called a *bridged-T trap,* sometimes referred to as a *notch filter,* for obvious reasons. The arrangement has an extremely sharp rejection response as determined by the $Q$ of the coil and the value of the notch resistor.

A receiver has additional traps, which will be discussed later. Some examples are ceramic and SAW filters, the 41.25-MHz sound takeoff trap in the IF strip of a color set, the 4.5-MHz sound takeoff trap in the video amplifier of a BW set, and numerous other traps in the video and chroma amplifiers. The sound takeoff traps have two functions: to accept the sound signal for the sound IF stages and to prevent it being passed on to the video section. Sound reaching the CRT shows up as *sound bar* interference. Video in the sound produces a characteristic *buzz* in the speaker.

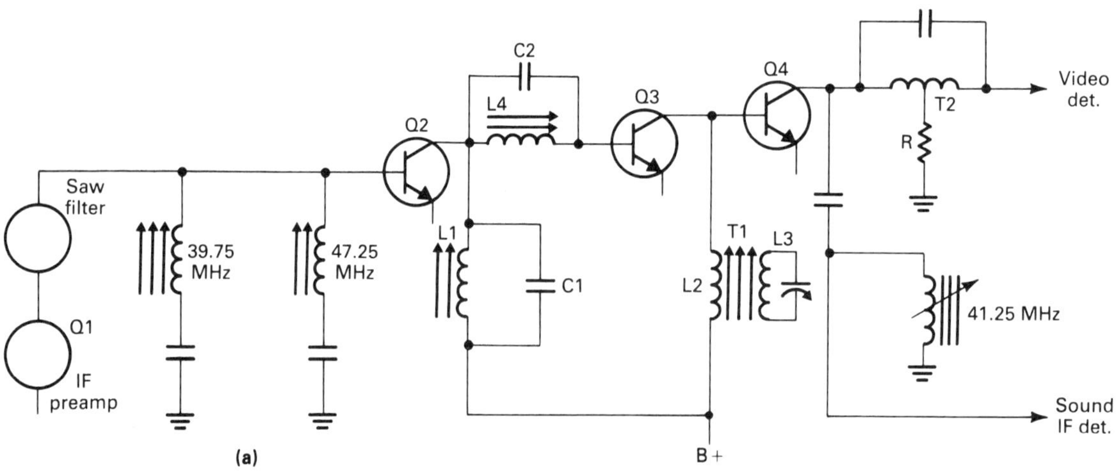


**FIG. 13-4** IF tuned circuits. A tuned circuit can be used to accept or reject a signal at its resonant frequency.

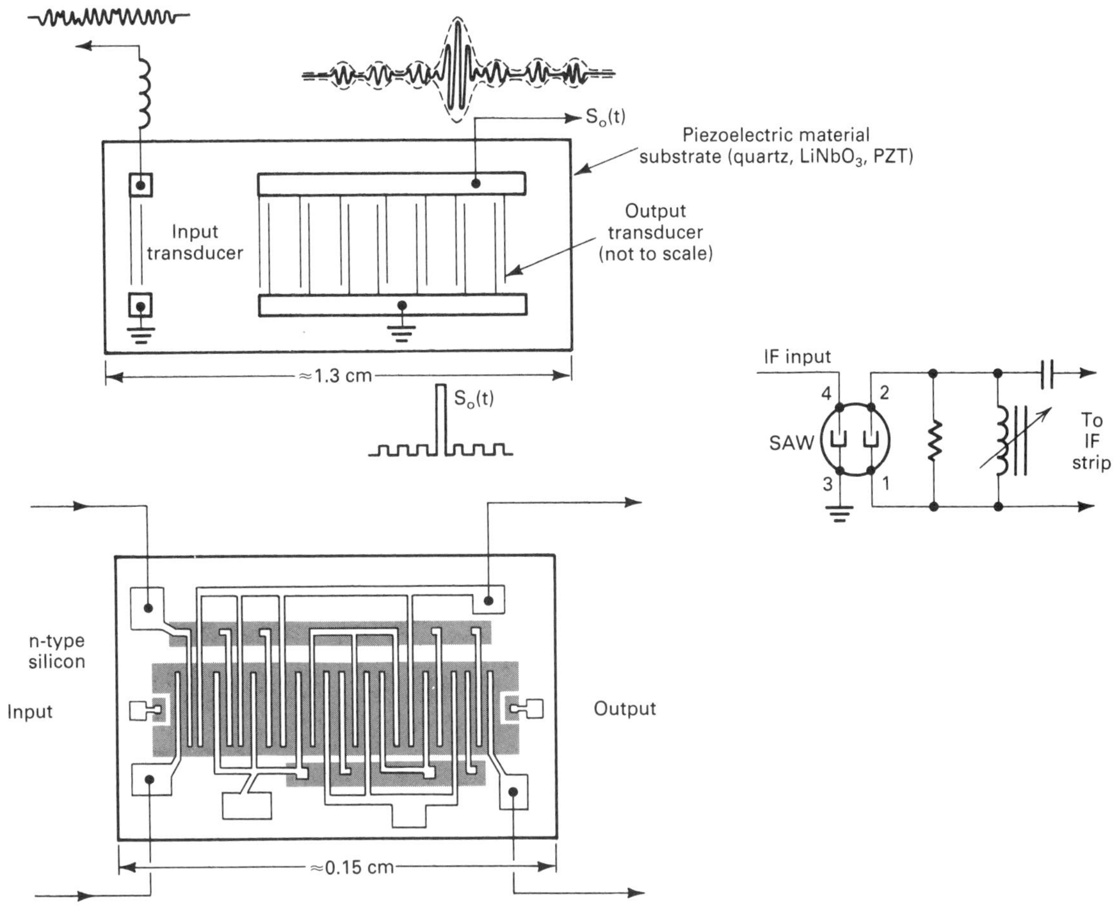


**FIG. 13-5** SAW filter. The lengths of the "fingers" tune the SAW filter. (Courtesy of *Sencore News*.)

## SAW Filters

A *surface acoustic wave* filter (commonly abbreviated as SAW and sometimes called a *crystal transducer*) is a unique acoustic device that accomplishes everything previously done by conventional *LC* circuits in the video IF strip. It provides for tuning, bandwidth, and waveshaping, as well as rejecting interference from adjacent channels. The device (as shown in Figure 13-5) consists of a piezoelectric quartz substrate on which are mounted a number of metal projections of different lengths, called "fingers." An acoustic wave generated in the crystal "echoes" back and forth across the substrate, inducing a voltage across the fingers and an external load resistor. Tuning (which never changes) is determined by the lengths and spacing of the fingers which respond to 10 different frequencies. The device has a wide bandpass, providing maximum gain at 44.5 MHz but an overall insertion loss of 20 dB: hence the need for a high-gain preamp. In a receiver, the SAW filter is located between the preamp and the input to the IF amplifiers contained in an IC (see the foldout schematic). An adjustable or fixed-tuned circuit is connected at its output for impedance matching. Tuning of the coil is critical to achieve maximum effectiveness and minimum insertion loss. Sometimes a tuned trap may be used in the preceding IF preamp stage.

## Coupling Methods

Bandwidth is determined by the *Q* factor (a figure of merit for the tuned circuits), their alignment, and the degree of coupling between the stages. Tight coupling and the use of low-*Q* circuits that are heavily loaded increases bandwidth but reduces stage gain. Loose coupling and high-*Q* circuits narrow the bandwidth and increase selectivity and signal amplification. Figure 13-6 shows different methods of coupling in use, as a means of obtaining the desired bandwidth as a trade-off for stage gain.

In circuit (a), impedance coupling is used between stages, and the high-*Q* coils are *stagger tuned,*

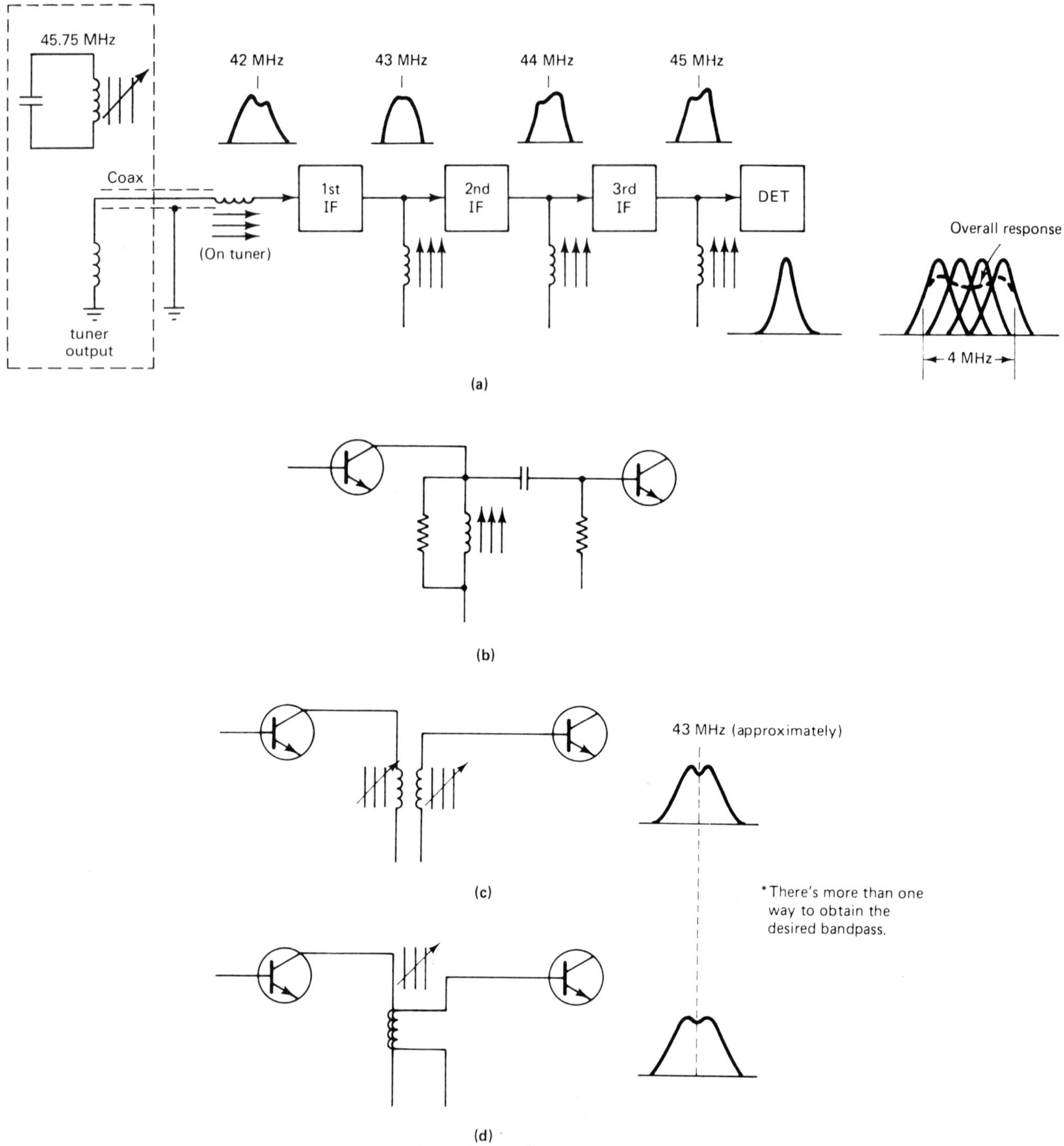


**FIG. 13-6** IF coupling and bandpass systems: (a) stagger tuning; (b) impedance coupling; (c) overcoupled transformer; (d) overcoupled bifilar transformer.

each to a different frequency within the passband. The coils may be shunted with small capacitors or rely on the distributed capacity of the windings to obtain resonance. The response of a single tuned circuit is relatively narrow, as shown, but when staggered and overlapped, the overall bandwith is widened. The greater the frequency difference between the resonance of individual stages, the greater the overall bandwidth. Note the low-impedance link coupling from the tuner to the preamp stage.

In circuit (b), the coil $Q$ is reduced by loading with a "swamping" resistor for an increase in bandwidth.

Circuit (c) uses double-tuned, overcoupled transformers. The tightly coupled windings increases the bandpass as indicated. The tuned circuits may be staggered or all adjusted to the same center frequency of approximately 43 MHz. When adjusted to one frequency it is called *synchronous tuning*.

Circuit (d) uses a *bifilar* transformer. With this transformer, primary and secondary coils are closely interwound to achieve maximum overcoupling. With such tight coupling, one core slug tunes both coils.

## 13-2 VIDEO DETECTOR

A basic detector, shown in Figure 13-7, is nothing more than a half-wave rectifier that changes the amplitude-modulated IF signal into a unidirectional current. The rectified current develops a signal voltage across the load resistor, RL in the diagram. A typical value is about 5 kΩ. This voltage has two components, ac and dc, that can be measured with either type of meter. The output signal polarity may be either positive or negative, depending on which way the diode is connected. In the example, the signal is "negative going."

The signal is constantly changing in both frequency and amplitude. These signal fluctuations represent the FM sound and the AM variations of video, chroma, and sync pulses. The detector produces an additional signal, a 4.5-MHz signal as a result of the beat between the 41.25-MHz sound IF and the 45.75-MHz video IF. Later, with the AM removed, it serves as a 4.5-MHz carrier for the FM sound. Figure 13-7 includes a scope display of the video and sync pulses as they appear at the detector output and at all downstream stages up to the CRT input. The output signal voltage is approximately one-half of the p-p voltage of the IF input. The actual amount depends, of course, on the strength of the signal received, ranging from about 2 V for a weak station to 10 V or so for a strong station.

Two small coils designated PC in the diagram are called *peaking coils*. Their function is to increase the level of the high video frequencies that produce fine picture details. The two FB items are *ferrite*

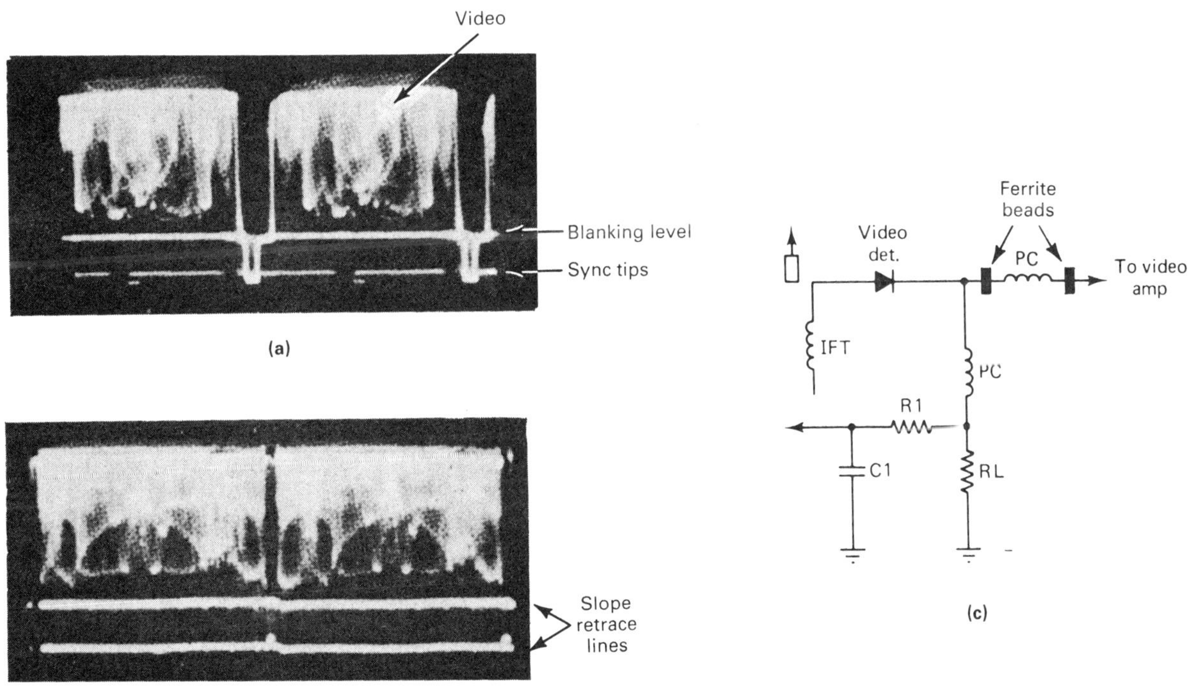


(b)

**FIG. 13-7** Video detector and its output signal: (a) CRO sweep frequency is 7875 Hz, to show two lines of video with horizontal sync pulses; (b) with CRO sweep set for 30 Hz, to show two complete fields of video and the (compressed) vertical blanking and sync pulses; (c) basic DET and AGC.

*beads*. They are used to prevent oscillations at harmonics of the 45.75-MHz IF signal. Unless suppressed, such signals may be radiated and picked up by the tuner, where they show up as "tweet" interference on the picture tube. Unless the detector is in an IC, all related components are enclosed in a shield can to prevent radiation.

The circuit as shown performs a dual function. The dc component developed across the load resistor is a source of AGC voltage to control the gain of the RF/IF stages. Components R1/C1 filter out IF and video amplitude variations. More on AGC later.

### Video Peaking

An important consideration in receiver design is the preservation of the high video frequencies, which if lost or attenuated cause a loss of fine picture detail. The problem begins with the detector and must be considered in all subsequent stages. In general, the higher the impedance of a circuit, the greater the bypassing of high frequencies to ground. Thus capacity effects, as in the case of lead dressing, must be kept to a minimum. The choice of load resistor is another consideration. It is a trade-off. A high-value resistor develops maximum output, but the increased circuit impedance causes attenuation of high frequencies. A low-value RL reduces the high-frequency loss but at the expense of signal voltage.

The peaking coils mentioned earlier are tiny coils, self-resonant to frequencies in the range 3 to 4 MHz. They are used to increase the high-frequency output of the detector and subsequent video stages.

Some receivers have a *peaking control,* a front-panel user control, a pot sometimes connected across a peaking coil to vary the amount of peaking desired. This tends to enhance a picture on the screen by emphasizing the fine detail to sharpen or "crispen" an image. It is particularly effective on old washed-out movies.

Carried to an extreme, overpeaking can result in video oscillations (*ringing*). Ringing of the high video frequencies can produce ghostlike images around fine picture details. Such ghosting is tunable (with the fine tuner) as distinguished from true ghosts produced by multipath reception or an antenna system mismatch.

### Synchronous Detector

Because of its advantages over a basic diode detector, this popular circuit is used in practically all late-model sets as a video detector, AFT demodulator, chroma demodulator, and sound detector. As a video detector, it produces a better-quality picture with less interference than is possible with a diode. All synchronous picture functions are performed by an IC (see Figure 13-8).

Some shortcomings of a diode detector are: no gain, nonlinear detection at low signal levels, and beat interference. It also detects extraneous signals, particularly those from adjacent channels. A synchronous detector overcomes all of these shortcomings. It detects the weakest signals that a diode overlooks. It is a linear detector with the added advantage of amplification. It disregards all signals other than those synchronized to the 45.75-MHz carrier (which minimizes the number of traps needed in the IF strip). Although the IC itself cannot be serviced, an understanding of the functions can help in isolating defects in the external components and alignment.

Figure 13-8a shows a simplified version of a synchronous detector. There are three functional circuits: a *reference amplifier* (known also as a *carrier generator*), a *differential amplifier,* and a *synchronous demodulator*. The carrier generator produces a signal synchronized with the 45.75-MHz station signal developed by the tuner. The generator has two square-wave outputs of opposite polarities, arbitrarily designated A and B. A tuned circuit (L1/C1) shunts the two outputs to maintain the proper phase relationships. Alignment of this circuit is crucial to proper circuit operation. Amplitudes are limited by the two diodes. The generator outputs are alternately in and out of phase with the station signal.

The differential amplifier (Q5/Q6) amplifies the signal from the IF strip to produce two outputs, 180° apart in phase. Transistor Q7 maintains a constant current. The station signal from the IF strip drives the differential amplifier and functions as a synchronizing signal for the generator.

The demodulator consists of four switching transistors (Q1, Q2, Q3, Q4) as four arms in a bridge configuration. Demodulator switching is alternately controlled from two sources feeding opposite arms of the bridge: the A and B outputs of the generator and the two outputs of the differential amplifier. The bridge operates as a full-wave rectifier developing a demodulated output for each half-cycle of the video IF carrier, to drive the downstream video amplifiers.

The circuit produces an output *only* for signals that are synchronized with the IF carrier, which prevents detection of any signals other than those of the station selected. Adjacent channel signals, for example, are out of phase with the carrier and there-

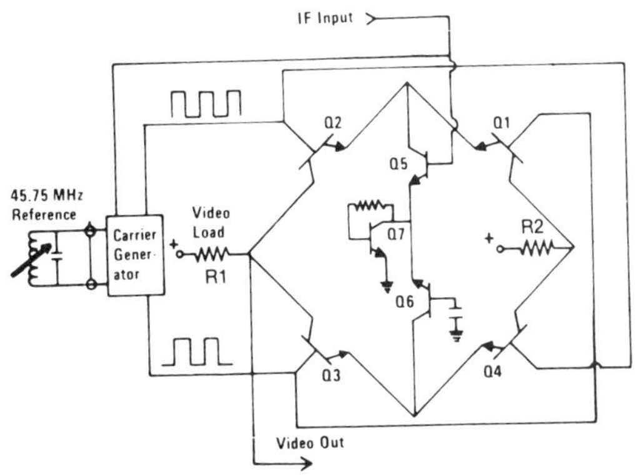


(a)

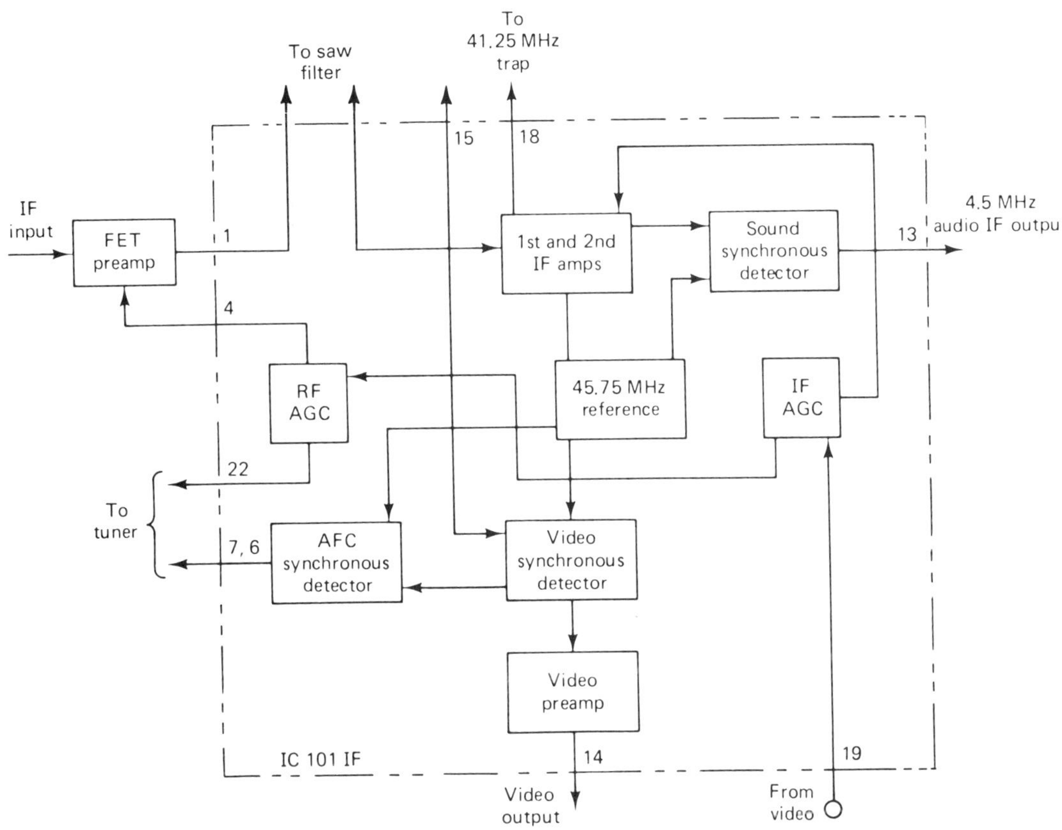


(b)

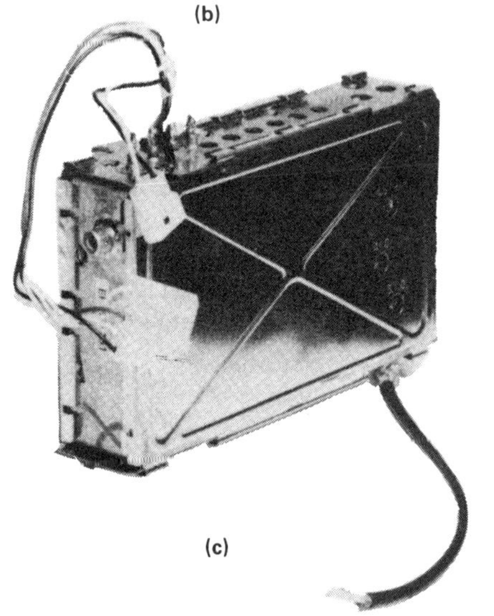

(c)

**FIG. 13-8** Synchronous detector: (a) typical synchronous DET; (b) three synchronous detectors and other functions are performed by this one IC; (c) tuned circuits and other components are contained in the module.

fore produce no output. The output consists only of the composite video signal of the desired station plus a 4.5-MHz beat signal.

## 13-3 AGC

A TV set must be able to operate under adverse receiving conditions, where signal levels from the antenna may be as low as 100 μV or so in a fringe area, to as much as 300 MV or more in areas close to the station. Weak signals, of course, produce weak snowy pictures. Unless controlled, excessively strong signals create problems of video overload. The earliest sets had no AGC and were troubled with these conditions. Receiver sensitivity and gain was controlled manually (but not very well) with the contrast control.

AGC is a simple enough concept patterned after the AVC used in all radio receivers. Ideally, it maintains uniform picture contrast, color intensity, and sound levels over a wide range of signal inputs. An AGC circuit rectifies the IF carrier to develop a dc bias voltage for controlling the gain of transistors or FETs in the RF stage of the tuner and two or more IF stages (Figure 13-9). It is a good example of a closed-loop circuit: the AGC voltage dependent on the signal input level and the signal strength dependent on the AGC. The amount of control bias developed is proportional to the strength of the signal received: low bias voltage when reception is weak and a greater bias to reduce the amplification of stronger signals.

The basic detector (Figure 13-7) can also develop AGC. A negative dc voltage (proportional to signal strength) is developed across the load resistor RL. The filter components R1/C1 smooth out the IF and video fluctuations, and the pure dc is routed as a control voltage to the RF/IF stages, as shown in Figure 13-9. However, this basic circuit has many drawbacks and is seldom used. Many sets use a system called *keyed AGC*.

### Keyed AGC

This method of developing an AGC voltage has many advantages over the basic circuit just described. It is relatively insensitive to noise. For a given signal input it produces a greater voltage, as required for controlling strong stations. It is fast acting because of a short time constant. This greatly reduces the annoying problem of "airplane flutter," rapid fluctuations of the picture caused by multipath reception of in and out-of-phase signals reflected from low-flying aircraft.

There are numerous variations of keyed AGC. One simplified version is shown in Figure 13-10. The heart of the circuit is a transistor called a *keyer* or AGC gate that produces the AGC voltage when it conducts. The keyer is "gated" into conduction by either a horizontal sync pulse or a sweep pulse supplied by a winding on the flyback transformer. AGC is not developed continuously, only during periods of conduction, which correspond to periods of horizontal beam deflection. When nonconducting (during horizontal retrace intervals) no AGC is developed; voltage comes from the discharge of capacitors and at such times the AGC and receiver operation is not influenced by such things as noise and signal fading. When these do occur it is not noticeable since the screen is blanked out during those periods.

The keyer is supplied with two kinds of "signal" voltage: sweep voltage, as stated previously, and a sampling of horizontal sync pulses whose sync tips correspond to the strength of the received signal. The keyer is normally biased off and is made to conduct *only* when both signals are present, that is, for the brief periods when the received sync pulses and the gating pulses from the sweep circuit occur simultaneously. If one or the other is weak or missing, of the wrong polarity, or if the timing is off, no AGC is produced.

In Figure 13-10, note the negative-going voltage supplied by the flyback transformer. The amount is quite critical. It is fed to the transistor emitter via a diode called a *pulse gate*. The composite video signal (the source of sync pulses) is applied to the transistor base from a video stage. The critical point at which the transistor can be turned on is established by the setting of a *threshold control*. At one extreme, a high reverse bias prevents conduction and the development of an AGC voltage. At the other extreme, the transistor is not keyed and develops a continuous AGC output, defeating the purpose of the entire concept. This is called an *overactive keyer*.

### Amplified AGC

A dc amplifier is sometimes used where the developed AGC voltage is too low to control strong signals adequately. As a *dc* amplifier, direct coupling must be used between the source and the stages being controlled. A typical amplifier is normally biased off with a reverse bias of approximately 0.2 V. The transistor is turned on by a forward-going

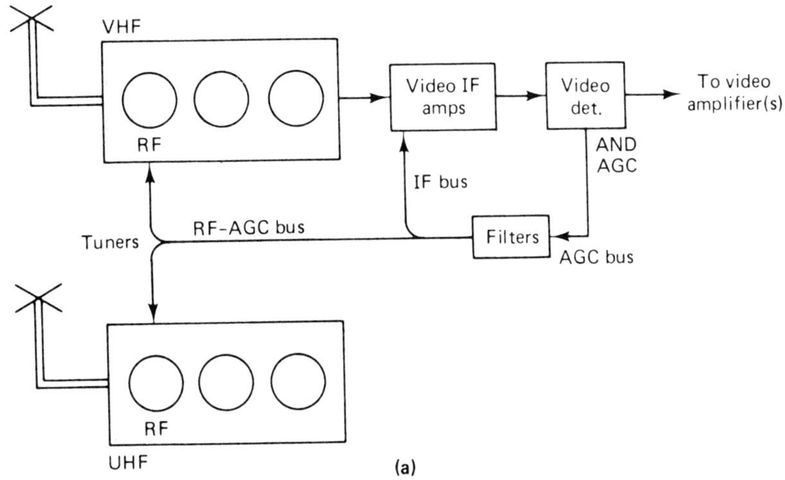


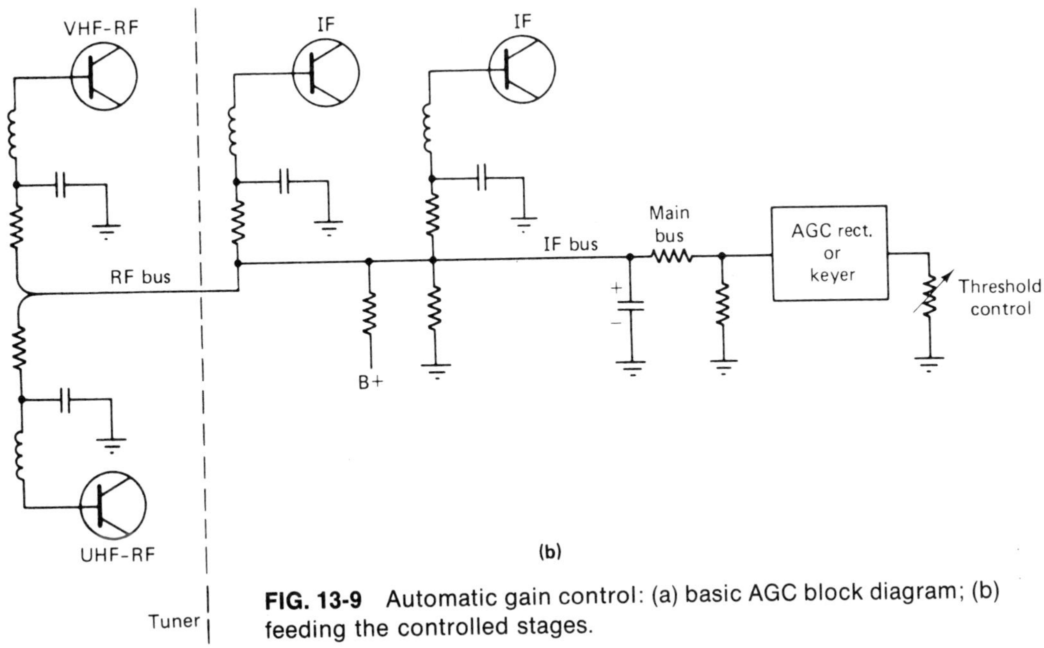


**FIG. 13-9** Automatic gain control: (a) basic AGC block diagram; (b) feeding the controlled stages.

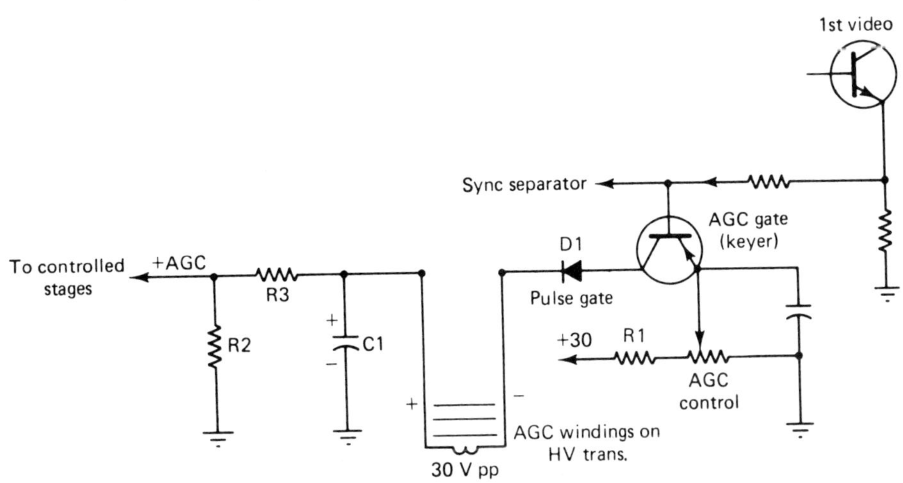


**FIG. 13-10** Basic keyed AGC circuit with simplified keyer circuit.

input voltage. Polarity depends on the type of transistor used. The voltage gain is about ×3. For increased gain, a Darlington-type transistor may be used. Factors to be considered are: the polarity of the source voltage, the polarity required for control of the RF and IF transistors, and whether or not a polarity reversal takes place between the input and output of the amplifier.

### Controlling Transistor Gain

For maximum amplification and high sensitivity to weak signals, a transistor must operate with a precise amount of forward bias. This is of particular importance in the tuner and IF strip, where signal levels are low and even fractional variations from the norm can have a significant and adverse affect on stage gain. The optimum *no-signal bias* is provided by a voltage divider and sometimes with a resistor in the emitter circuit. Polarity is determined by the type of transistor: negative for a PNP and positive for an NPN. An interesting aspect of a transistor is that it can be controlled by either an increase or a decrease in forward bias. There are two systems in use. Where gain is reduced by *increasing* the bias, it is called *forward AGC*. Where gain is reduced by *decreasing* the forward bias, it is called *reverse AGC*. This is not to be confused with reverse *bias,* since there is no change in polarity. Some sets use forward AGC, some use reverse AGC, and some use a combination of each for controlling the RF stage and the IF strip.

Forward AGC makes use of the saturation characteristics of a transistor. If bias is increased in a forward direction, a linear reduction in gain occurs as saturation is approached. Reverse AGC uses the cutoff characteristics and is preferred by most manufacturers. If the forward bias is decreased, the operation approaches cutoff where the gain drops to zero.

AGC may be applied to either the base or the emitter of a transistor. Polarity is determined by which element is being controlled and by the type of transistor. These things become apparent by examining a schematic. For example, if AGC is positive-going and it feeds the base of a PNP, a reverse AGC system is used.

Modern receivers use FETs in the RF/IF stages. With a dual-gate FET, one gate receives the signal and the other gate is AGC controlled to vary the source-to-drain current. The typical no-signal bias is in the range 5 to 10 V. Reverse AGC is commonly used for gain reduction. Cutoff occurs at about 5 V of reversed polarity.

### AGC Voltage Distribution

Figure 13-9b shows the AGC voltage distribution for a typical receiver. Note the numerous *RC* networks that function as filters and provide isolation and decoupling between the stages being controlled. Also note that the AGC divides: one "bus" supplying the two IF stages, the other bus supplying AGC to the two tuners. Resistors R1/R2 constitute a voltage divider to provide the transistors with the proper amount of no-signal bias required for maximum sensitivity and gain. When a signal is received, the AGC developed either adds to or subtracts from this voltage, depending on whether forward or reverse AGC is employed.

*RF versus IF Gain Control.* To prevent video overload, the gain of the IF stages must be controlled at all times, particularly when strong signals are received. The RF stage must also be controlled to prevent overdriving the mixer. For weak signal reception, however, the RF stage must operate wide open for maximum sensitivity, to obtain a high signal-to-noise ratio with minimum snow on the picture. This is accomplished by delaying the application of AGC to the tuners until the signal received has reached a reasonably high level.

*Delayed AGC.* There are several methods used to delay AGC control of the RF stages in the two tuners. One system uses a *clamping diode*. During weak signal reception (and when tuned off channel) the diode is forward biased into conduction to *clamp* the RF bus until the signal is strong enough to overcome the clamping voltage. At that point, the diode becomes reverse biased and the AGC takes over. A *delay control* is usually provided to establish the threshold level. It is adjusted for minimum snow on the picture.

## 13-4 FOLDOUT SCHEMATIC

The IF signal from the tuner is amplified by the preamp Q101, then applied to the SAW filter. Coil L103 at the filter output is resonant to the IF center frequency (44.5 MHz) for maximum gain, but the coil is not adjustable. R107 is a damping resistor. From the filter the signal goes through coupling capacitor C104 to pin 16 of the IC. The IC contains three IF amplifiers that are controlled internally by AGC developed by the basic detector. AGC is routed to the tuners via the AGC delay control VR123. Reverse AGC is used for the IF and RF stages. The IC also contains a synchronous AFT detector. The AFT error voltage is applied to the tuner from pin 5. AFT tuning is accomplished with coil L171.

## 13-5 TROUBLESHOOTING AND REPAIR

The video IF, detector, and AGC circuits seldom give trouble, particularly with modern sets, where these functions are performed by an IC. When defects do occur, it's usually a breakdown external to the IC. Here we are concerned with locating and correcting such defects. Many older-model sets using discrete components and individual stages are still around and require servicing. Some of the procedures in the following paragraphs apply to them also. Some information on aligning tuned circuits is provided, although with the increasing use of SAW filters, misalignment is no longer the problem it once was. Troubles peculiar to these stages are covered in the following paragraphs. The same symptoms, however, can be caused by defects in other stages. As an aid, refer to the troubleshooting flow drawings (Figures 13-11 and 13-12).

### Symptoms and Procedures

*No Picture or Sound.* (raster okay)

***Probable causes:*** IF or detector stage defects; excessive AGC; misadjusted AGC threshold control. (*Reminder:* Defects upstream from the sound takeoff affects both picture and sound. Defects downstream from the takeoff point affects only the picture.)

Localize the trouble to one stage by *signal tracing* or *signal injection*. As an *indicator,* use a scope, an ac meter, or the bar pattern on the CRT. In signal tracing the *station signal* through the IF strip, a demodulator probe must be used with the scope. It is not required for scope checking signals at the detector output or beyond. For signal injection, tune the generator to 45.75 MHz or some frequency within the IF bandpass. With the modulation turned on, you should get a bar pattern on the CRT. The darkness of the bars is indicative of signal strength. Periodically reduce generator output to lighten the bars. With signal injection and progressing stage by stage toward the tuner, the response should get stronger. Conversely, a weaker response can be expected when progressing downstream toward the CRT. The opposite is true when scope tracing the *station* signal. If signal is lost in the SAW filter, check it for shorts or other damage. Replace it if suspect.

If no stage defect is discovered, check the AGC voltage and compare with the schematic. Try adjusting the threshold control if there is one. When the faulty stage is located, check the transistor or FET operating voltages, the transistor or FET, and associated components, usually in that order. For a detector problem, test or substitute the diode.

Where an IC is used, tune to a channel and scope check the station signal at the input/output pins. As an alternative, try signal injection. Use a low signal level to avoid damage to transistors and FETs. If signal is not getting through the IC, check for loss of B voltage. If little or no B+, break the circuit and recheck. Loss of B+ may be due to a breakdown in the voltage distribution or a short in the IC. Check with an ohmmeter. If the B+ is okay, check the AGC output to the tuner. If an internal IC breakdown is suspected, check for external defects that might be the cause. If a synchronous detector is used, check the alignment of the external phasing coil. If no external defects are found, replace the IC.

*Weak Picture.* (poor contrast)

***Probable causes:*** IF detector or AGC defect; IF or synchronous detector misalignment.

Scope trace the station signal or use signal injection to locate a weak stage. If the picture is snowy, suspect the preamp or the SAW filter. If there is poor picture contrast but no snow, concentrate on the downstream stages. At the faulty stage, check for low B+ or abnormal AGC voltage. Compare with the schematic. Test or substitute the transistor or FET and other suspected components. Adjust the AGC threshold control if provided. If an IC is used, check for external defects as described earlier, and if none, replace the IC.

Suspect misalignment if tuned circuit adjustments have been tampered with or components replaced. Misalignment, however, is the last thing to consider. Alignment procedures are described later.

*Video Overload.* (poor sync, excessive contrast, buzz in sound)

***Probable causes:*** AGC problems; IF misalignment.

Abnormal or no AGC voltage is a common cause. Check AGC at the source, the bus, and other key points. Compare readings with the schematic when tuned to different stations. See if AGC varies as it should when the fine tuner is adjusted. Sharply peaked tuned circuits is another possible cause of overload, but do not realign unless justified.

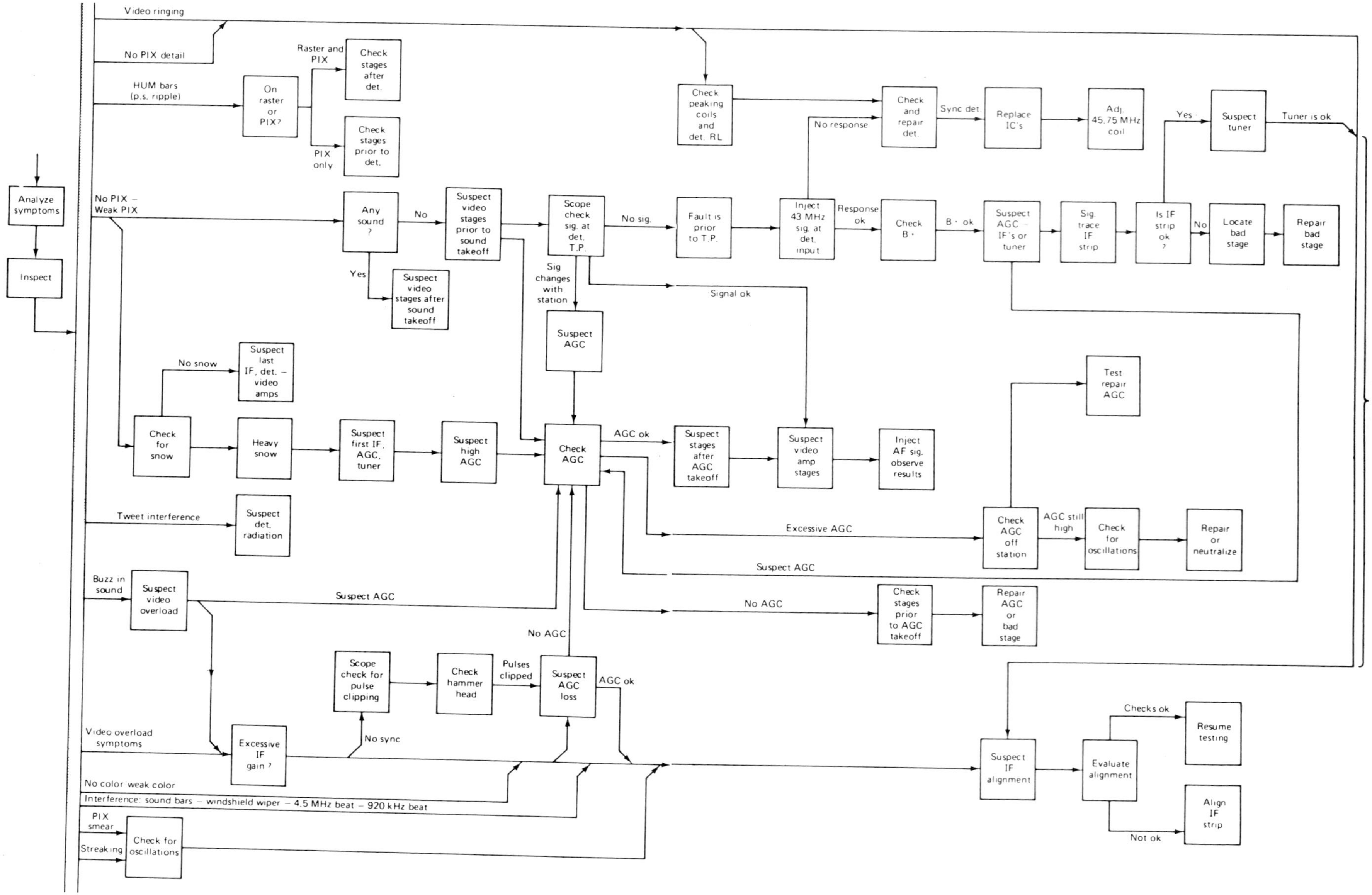


**FIG. 13-11** Video IF and detector troubleshooting flow drawing.

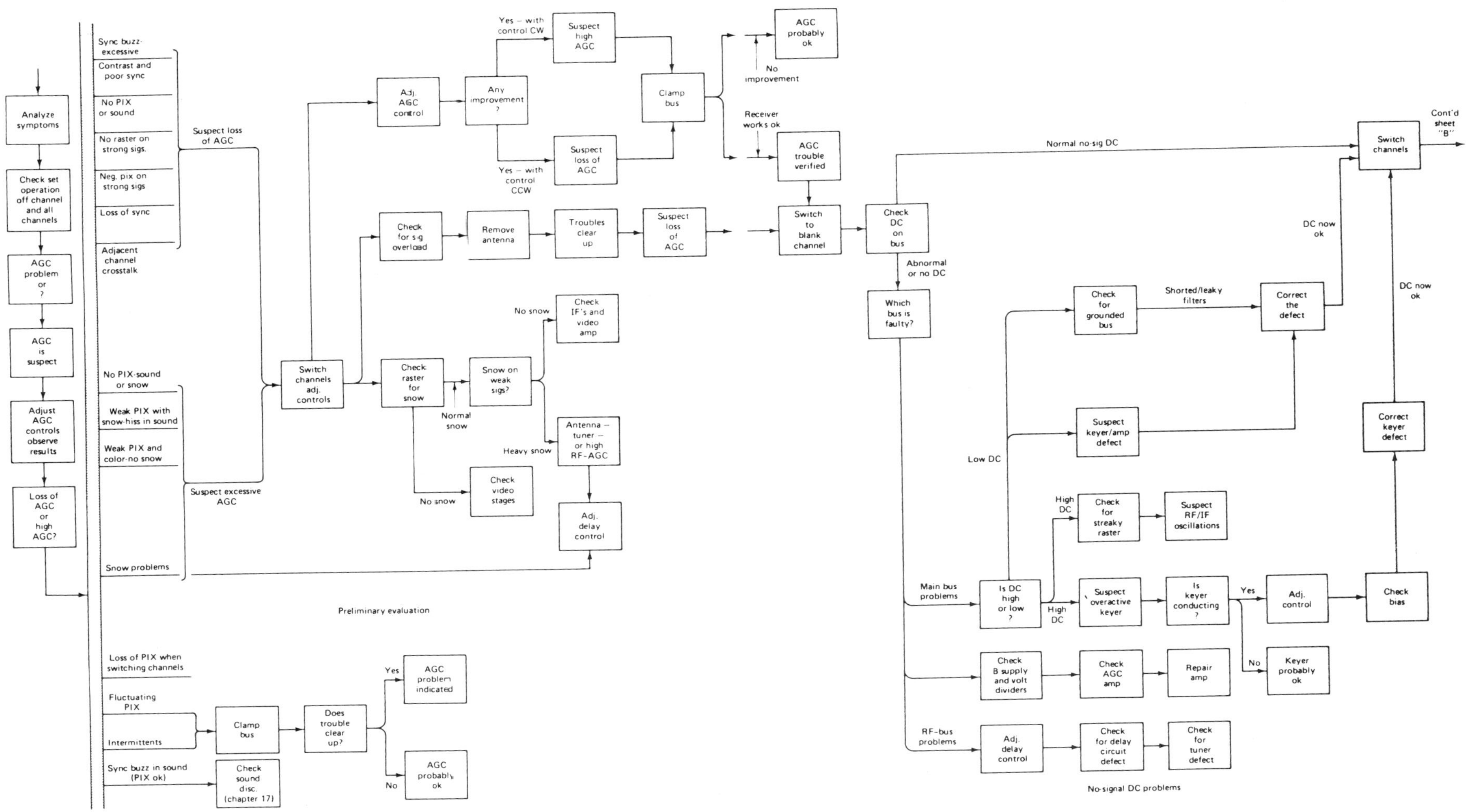


FIG. 13-12 AGC troubleshooting flow diagram.

(*Continued*)

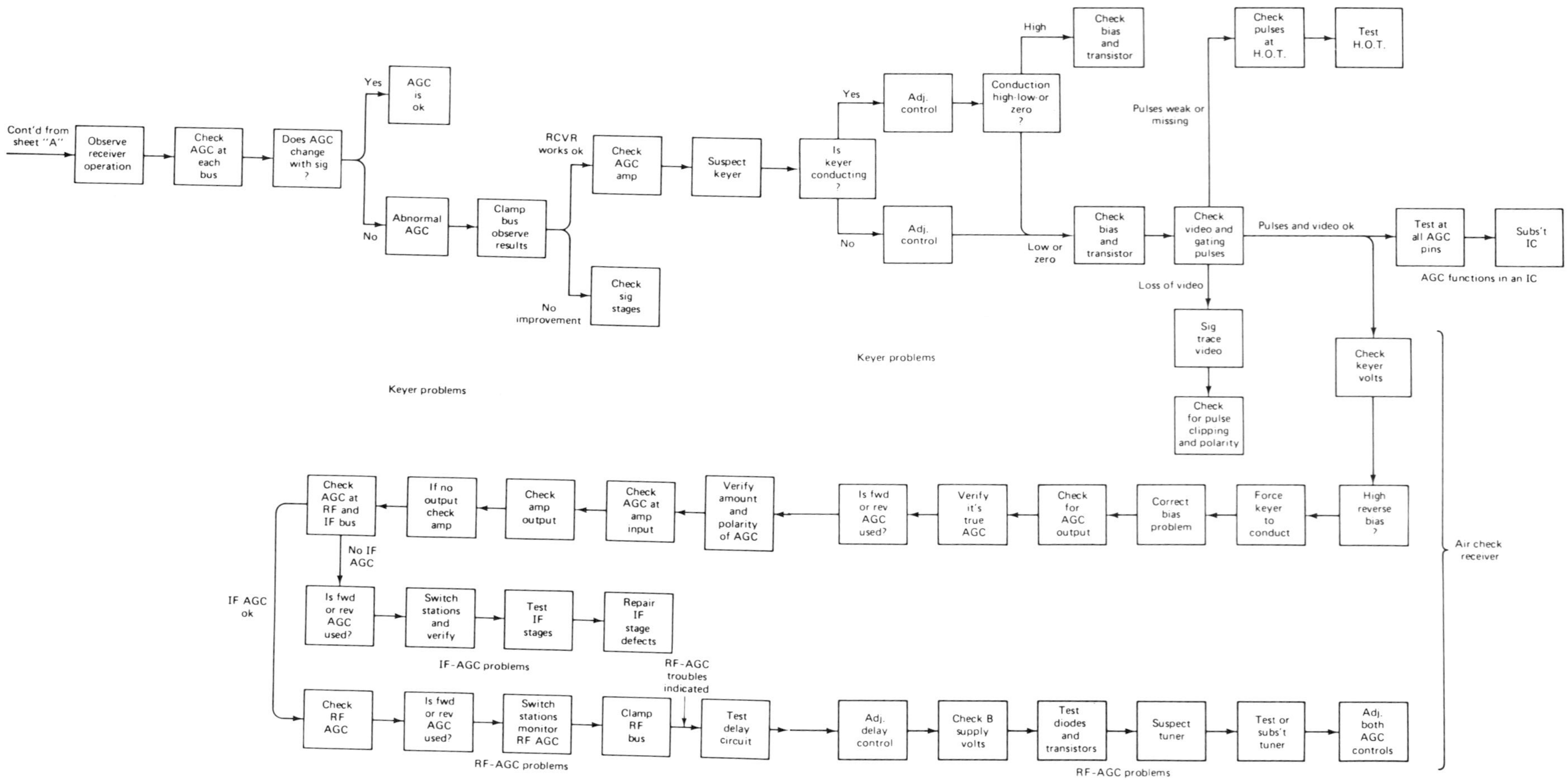


**FIG. 13-12** (*continued*)

*IF Oscillations.* (streaky picture, noise in sound, critical fine tuner)

***Probable causes:*** Misalignment; interstage coupling, poor lead dress, or missing beads on critical leads; open or bad grounds.

Oscillations are evident if there is considerable ac output from the detector when tuned to a blank channel. To localize, observe and listen for "birdies" when touching various components. Check all grounds and security of baffle plates and other shielding. Check coax from the tuner to the IF input, making sure that it is grounded at both ends. If warranted, realign or neutralize a troublesome stage, and if necessary, add ferrite beads to critical wires.

*Adjacent Channel Interference.* (windshield wiper effect)

***Probable causes:*** Defective or misadjusted traps; mixer overdrive due to loss of RF-AGC; defective SAW filter; defective or misaligned synchronous detector.

Test each trap and replace if suspect. Adjust traps using an *accurate* signal generator. Make sure that the adjustments do not affect the overall response. Test or replace the SAW filter. Check the AGC voltage at the tuner(s) and compare with the schematic. If suspect, check components in the synchronous detector. Touch-up the alignment if required. If interference persists, try orienting the antenna.

*Hum Bars on Picture.* (wide, dark, horizontal bars)

***Probable cause:*** 60-Hz hum modulation of the video signal.

Check for poor filtering of dc power feeding the IF strip (see Chapter 6). Check on and off channel. If there are bars on the raster only, when tuned off channel, the trouble is downstream from the detector. If bars are present only when receiving a station, check for excessive PS ripple at the IF strip.

*Tweet Interference.* (wavy lines on the picture)

***Probable cause:*** Radiation from IF strip or detector that is picked up by the tuner.

Check for oscillations. Check lead dressing. Make sure that the detector shield can is properly secured and grounded. Add ferrite beads to critical wires as needed. Try relocating antenna lead-in wires, and if coax, check its grounding.

*Pix Flutter.* (fluctuating contrast)

***Probable causes:*** Wobbly antenna mast; loose antenna elements; airplane flutter due to a keyed-AGC defect.

Correct the antenna defects. Check the AGC on the IF bus when switching on and off channels and by adjusting the fine tuner. If there is improper AGC voltage, check for a defect on the AGC distribution circuit or at the controlled IF transistors or FETs. A leaky transistor or FET can upset the AGC action. If there is abnormal AGC voltage at the keyer, check the keyer transistor and associated components, replacing any that are suspect.

*Overpeaking.* (video ringing or tunable ghosts on fine picture details)

***Probable causes:*** IF oscillations; overpeaked IFs; peaking circuit defects.

Check IFs for oscillations or misalignment. Check peaking control and associated components. If trouble persists, try shorting out one of the peaking coils.

### IF Alignment

Realignment of the IF tuned circuits is seldom required unless disturbed by hit-and-miss adjustments, altering the lead dress or replacing closely associated components. Even then, do not be too hasty, because many defects can emulate the symptoms of misalignment and they should be considered first. The cardinal rule is: Do not tamper with the adjustments until conditions of alignment have been *evaluated.* Failing to proceed with caution, you can end up with a picture worse than when you started.

*Preliminary Steps, Remarks, and Precautions.* Whether for evaluation, or actual realignment, an *accurate* signal generator is a *must.* Without it, you are wasting your time. Besides a signal generator, some type of indicator is required, either a scope or a meter. Depending on equipment availability, there are three methods that can be used. The procedures described here are of a general nature. For specific instructions, refer to manufacturer's service data or Sams Photofacts.

1. Examine the schematic and the chassis to locate and identify all the IF tuned circuits. Note the frequency assigned to each.
2. If it is a hot chassis receiver, use an isolation transformer but do not operate test equipment from the same transformer.

3. Use a blocking capacitor series with the signal generator cable as a precaution against damage to the generator and the receiver.
4. To prevent station signals and other interference from influencing the indicator response, disconnect or short out the antenna input; switch to a blank channel, and if necessary, disable the tuner oscillator. Turn off fluorescent lights in the area.
5. As a precaution against shocks, disable the HV.
6. Defeat the IF-AGC by clamping the bus. Use a well-filtered PS adjusted for the amount and polarity indicated on the schematic.
7. Accurate alignment is impossible if there is instability from regeneration or oscillations. With staggered tuning it can be caused by coils sharply peaked to the same frequency. Unfortunately, misalignment can be either the *cause* or the *result* of such instabilities. These problems may clear up as alignment progresses.
8. Signal overdrive can result in false and misleading indications. Use the lowest possible output from the signal generator and the most sensitive range on the scope or meter.

The different alignment methods are described below.

*AM Signal Generator Method.* Connect a meter or scope as an indicator to the output of the video detector, or as an alternative, a dc meter can be used to monitor changes in AGC voltage. Connect the modulated RF generator to the input of the video IF preamp. Adjust the generator to the approximate center of the IF bandpass (about 43 MHz). You should get an indication on the meter or scope, or a sound bar display on the receiver CRT. Vary the generator tuning and check for corresponding variations on the indicator. With the indicator at maximum sensitivity, reduce the generator output to obtain a barely perceptible indication. These are the conditions for greatest accuracy.

*Slowly* tune the generator over the IF bandpass, noting the peaks and dips that correspond with the assigned frequencies of the various tank and trap circuits. Check frequently against the schematic, noting and recording any departures from the results expected.

If realignment is necessary, adjust the traps first. With the generator set for the proper trap frequency(s), adjust each trap individually to obtain a dip (lowest indication or "null") on the scope or meter. Trap adjustments are extremely critical.

With the generator set to the specified frequencies, adjust the tank circuits individually for a peak indication. Repeat all adjustments at least twice, alternately dipping the traps and peaking the tanks until there are no further interactions. All final adjustments must be performed accurately and precisely.

An alternative procedure is to adjust each stage individually. Inject the generator signal at the input of the stage preceding the one to be aligned (to prevent loading the tuned circuit). Connect the meter or scope (with a demodulator probe) to the output of the stage being adjusted. Critically adjust all traps and tanks as described previously.

If the set uses an IC, a SAW filter, and a synchronous detector that requires adjusting, the detector should be tuned first before adjusting the filter coils. The only tuned circuits in the IF strip are a trap in the preamp stage and two "matching coils" at the input and output of the filter. The trap is nulled in the normal manner at its specified frequency. The SAW filter has a broadband response and is not adjusted to a particular frequency. One method is to switch off the channel and adjust the coil(s) for maximum background noise, snow on the screen, and AGC voltage.

Where one or more adjustments have little or no effect, there are two possibilities: a tuned circuit defect, or adjustments are being made at the wrong frequencies (i.e., incorrectly identified). Recheck the schematic to identify the tuned circuits and to verify their *proper* assigned frequencies. Where a defect is suspected, check for a cracked or missing core slug or for the possibility of shorted windings. Shorted turns *raises* the frequency of a tuned circuit.

*Sweep Alignment Method.* With sweep alignment, a response curve is displayed on a scope. Conditions of alignment (or misalignment) can be instantly determined by the location of frequency markers produced by an accurately calibrated *marker generator*. This is an accurate method when performed properly, but it is time consuming and requires special equipment. The equipment needs are a scope, a sweep generator, and a marker generator.

A sweep generator (as described in Chapter 4) produces an FM signal that "sweeps" over a band of frequencies centered at the frequency of the generator dial setting. The amount of sweep is adjustable from zero to about 30 MHz. The sweep is sinusoidal at a 60-Hz rate. A sampling of the sweep voltage is used by the scope for horizontal beam deflection, instead of its own internal sweep-generating circuit, which is disabled

With the equipment connected as in Figure 13-13, the marker generator disconnected or turned off, and the sweep generator tuned to 43 HMz (the approximate center of the IF bandpass), a response curve should appear on the scope. Center the curve on the screen using the generator tuning dial. Vary the amount of sweep in accordance with the anticipated bandwidth of the IF strip, usually about 4 or 5 HMz. If there is too little sweep, only the upper midportion of the curve will be displayed. Too much sweep covers more than the IF bandpass, resulting in a narrowed display that is difficult to work with.

Turn on the marker generator. When tuned to 43 MHz, a "blip" should appear at the top center of the curve. If it does not, change the generator frequency temporarily. Do not be concerned if the two generators don't agree. Accuracy is dependent only on the marker generator calibration. Vary the generator output until the marker is *barely visible*. Too much marker signal distorts the curve. If too little, it may not be visible on the slopes of the curve.

To evaluate alignment conditions, alternately tune the generator to significant frequencies, noting their locations on the curve. Marker frequencies and their proper locations are shown in Figure 13-3. The bandwidth of the IF strip is determined by markers located on opposite sides of the curve at the 50% level. For example, for a correctly aligned IF strip with a 4-MHz bandwidth, the marker frequencies would be 41.25 and 45.75 MHz. Check with the ser-

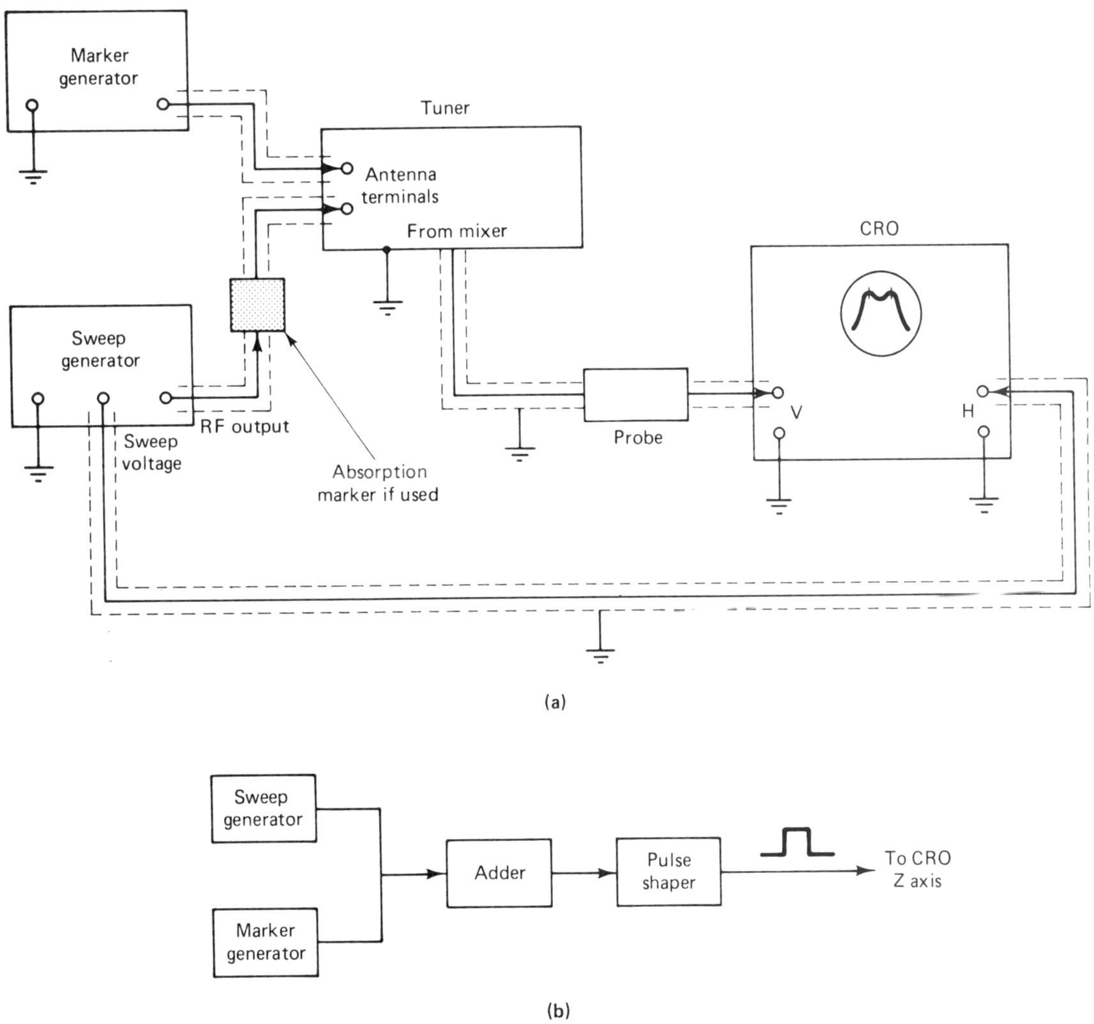


**FIG. 13-13** Sweep alignment setup: (a) the marker and sweep generators are usually combined in one instrument; (b) postinjection (intensity) marker system.

vice literature for the proper response for a particular receiver (i.e., wideband color or narrowband color with a "haystack" shape). Note the marker locations in Figure 13-3.

If the markers do not appear where they should and if the bandpass is too wide or too narrow, the IF strip requires realignment. Start by adjusting the adjacent channel *traps* until their markers are correctly positioned on the baseline just beyond the IF bandpass on both sides of the curve. Alternately adjust the IF *tank circuits* until all markers are correctly positioned and a normal bandpass is obtained. Normally, because of interactions, all adjustments must be performed more than once.

*Bar Sweep Alignment Method.* This fast and accurate method of alignment requires specialized equipment, a waveform analyzer (Sencore), described in Chapter 4. Procedures are beyond the scope of this book. Refer to the instrument instruction manual.

*Synchronous Detector Alignment.* Adjustment of the 45.75-MHz reference coil (Figure 13-8) is extremely critical and is best made with the bar sweep equipment just described. An alternative procedure uses the station signal. Randomly adjust the coil until a picture is received. This setting is approximately midway between the two settings where the picture is lost. This represents about two full turns of the coil slug. Refine the adjustment by *slowly* turning the slug in small increments in opposite directions while observing the picture. Adjust for maximum contrast and best picture quality. Check the results on other channels. If the picture drops out or the quality is impaired, make touch-up adjustments as necessary.

## QUESTIONS

1. Use of a SAW filter eliminates the need for most of the tuned circuits in the video IF strip. Explain.
2. Describe the advantages of a synchronous detector over a basic diode detector.
3. Too little or too much bias on an IF transistor will weaken or kill the signal. Explain.
4. Picture and color are adversely affected by misadjusted tuned circuits in the IF strip. Explain.
5. Explain why IF traps must be critically and accurately adjusted to their proper frequencies.
6. Why does a large-screen color set require a wider bandpass than a BW or color set with a small CRT?
7. For good color, markers representing the color sidebands must be positioned on a linear portion of the IF response. Explain why.
8. State possible causes where there is little or no effect when adjusting an IF tuned circuit.
9. Considering the loss of high chroma frequencies, why are most modern sets adjusted for narrowband color?
10. Briefly explain the operation of a synchronous detector.
11. Explain the significance of an IF response curve and its marker locations.
12. Name and explain several types of traps in common use.
13. Explain how vestigial sideband transmission is compensated for by proper alignment of the video IF strip.
14. Explain the operation of a keyed AGC system, giving the advantages over a basic AGC circuit.
15. Explain delayed AGC and why it improves the reception of weak signals.
16. Explain forward and reverse AGC.
17. What design considerations determine the bandpass of a video IF strip?
18. State the effect of an IF bandpass that is (a) too narrow; (b) too wide.
19. Explain why the marker for the sound IF carrier is located at a low level barely within the bandpass of the IF strip.
20. Explain the need for high-frequency compensation and the use of peaking coils. What is the effect on the picture if the high frequencies are lost or attenuated?
21. Why is the video detector circuit sometimes enclosed in a shield can?
22. Explain the 4.5-MHz sound IF carrier and where and how it is produced.
23. What would you suspect where a high AGC voltage is measured when tuned to a blank channel?
24. What is a bifilar coupling transformer, and why is it used?
25. What is meant by clamping the AGC bus, and why is it done?
26. Explain how a response curve is produced with the sweep method of alignment.
27. Where the symptoms are normal sound but no picture, what stages are suspect if it is (a) a BW set; (b) a color set? Explain.
28. All repairs should be made prior to aligning tuned circuits. Explain.
29. Where there is a normal IF signal at the input to an IC, but no output, how would you proceed?

# 14 Video amplifiers

Good picture contrast requires a signal strong enough to drive the CRT between the two extremes of *saturation* (to produce white images) and beam current cutoff for black images and a dark screen. The term *drive* refers to the amount of signal needed to produce the required changes in beam current. Drive requirements vary, depending on the size of the CRT. The amount of drive needed for a 19-inch BW tube, for example, is about 40 V p-p. For a 25-inch color set it is twice that amount. The low output of the video detector is boosted to these high levels in the video amplifier.

Video amplitude is adjusted with the contrast control. A weak signal equates with poor contrast between light and dark images. Weak signals cannot be compensated for by adjusting the controls, even with the contrast control full on. Turning up the brightness makes white images stand out, but black appears as gray; turning down the brightness produces black but no whites. For a color set, a weak signal produces weak color, with the same effects as just described.

In addition to amplification, an important consideration is *frequency response*. Low frequencies produce large objects, and high frequencies produce the fine picture detail. This requires an amplifier with a frequency response reasonably "flat," from about 20 Hz to 2 or 3 MHz for a BW set and up to 4.2 MHz for a color set.

Still another factor to consider is signal *polarity,* which is established at the detector. It must be negative-going when feeding the CRT grid and positive-going when driving the cathode. A reversed polarity produces a "negative" picture (as in photography), where blacks appear white and white images are black.

Practically all sets now use a *large-scale integration* (LSI) 28-pin IC chip (or its equivalent) which combines the functions of luminance and chrominance. A defect in this IC usually results in a dark screen.

## 14-1 BASIC VIDEO AMPLIFIER

A BW set video amplifier and its associated functions are shown in the simplified block diagram of Figure 14-1. These same functions (plus others) also apply to a color set, although the latter (to be described later) is considerably more complex. A typical amplifier has three dc-coupled voltage amplifier stages followed by a medium-power output stage to drive the CRT. They are usually contained in a multifunction IC. The signal may be applied to either the cathode or the control grid of the CRT.

Note the various takeoff points from the video amplifier: for example, the sync pulses which are routed to the sync stages and also used for the development of AGC. Other functions associated with the video amplifier and the CRT input are described in the following paragraphs.

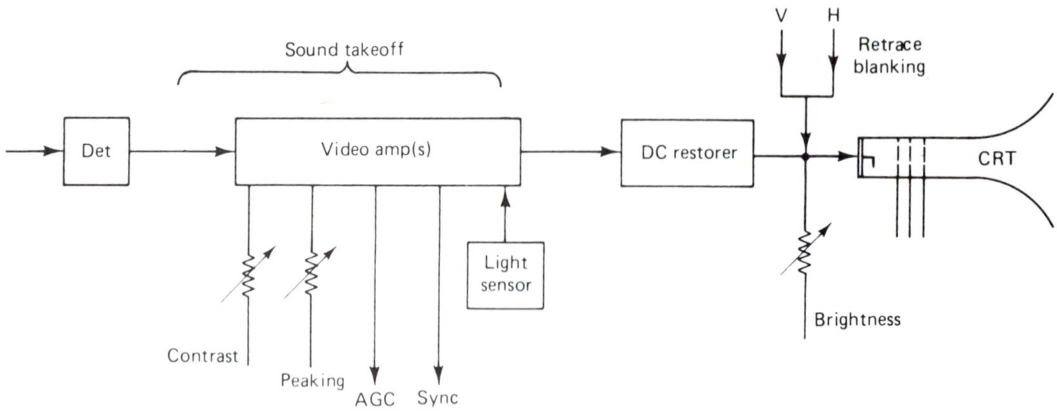


**FIG. 14-1** Black-and-white set block diagram.

### Blanking Pulses

Vertical and horizontal blanking pulses from the sweep circuits are shown here applied to the CRT cathode along with the video signal. As with the video, pulse polarity is positive. Current practice is to inject these pulses at some low-level point in the video amplifier.

### Sound Takeoff

With a BW set, the sound signal is separated from the composite signal at some point between the video detector and the CRT input. The 4.5-MHz beat signal developed at the detector is the new FM carrier for the audio contained in its sidebands. A 4.5-MHz tuned circuit at the takeoff point serves a dual purpose: It accepts the sound signal and passes it on to the sound IF stages; it also functions as a trap to prevent audio from reaching the CRT via the video amplifier stages.

### Composite Video Signal

The composite *monochrome* signal (Figure 13-7) consists of video information, blanking, and sync pulses. Pulse amplitude is constant and reflects the strength of the carrier. When there is motion on the screen, the amplitude and frequency of the video information are constantly changing in accordance with the lightness and darkness and the *size* of the images being produced. Blanking pulses darken the screen by overbiasing the CRT to cutoff during periods of vertical and horizontal retrace. Sync pulses are permitted to reach the CRT input, but serve no useful purpose this far downstream.

### Controlling CRT Brightness

The brightness of an off-channel raster (and picture images) is determined by the amount of CRT beam current. High current produces white on the screen; low current creates various shades of gray. The absence of current results in a dark screen, equivalent to black images in a picture. The amount of beam current in turn is governed by the amount of grid-to-cathode bias. A high negative bias reduces current; less bias causes an increase in current. For a typical BW CRT the cutoff bias is about −30 V. For a large-screen color CRT, by comparison, the cutoff bias is about 100 V. Bias is controlled by the brightness control. Too much bias [as when the brightness control is turned down (CCW)] results in dark images or if carried to extreme, no visible raster. Too little bias [brightness turned up (CW)] does the opposite, an overly bright raster and picture, where objects that should be black appear in various shades of gray. Although bias and brightness control are subjects concerning the picture tube, they are treated at this time because of their close association with the video amplifier.

As with any vacuum tube, bias can be produced in several ways: by applying a negative voltage to the control grid, applying a positive voltage to the cathode, or a combination of both. If the latter, the true operating bias is the difference between the two voltages as measured between grid and cathode. For example, with +25 V on the grid and +40 V on the cathode, the operating bias is −15 V. In addition to a "user" control, some sets have a "master brightness" control (see Chapter 17). It is a service adjustment, used to establish limits on the front-panel control and to compensate for reduced emission if and when it occurs.

Most modern sets use dc coupling between the detector and the CRT input, making it possible to control brightness (and contrast) at some point in the video amplifier. As might be expected, it adds to the problems of troubleshooting.

*Control Stage.* Modern sets control brightness and contrast by controlling the bias of a transistor (or IC) in a dc-coupled video amplifier (see Chapter 17). Such control originates from a *control stage,* a high-gain stage where small bias changes create significant changes in collector current. It is frequently several stages upstream from the CRT input. Small dc voltage variations produced by the brightness control produce corresponding changes in dc at each point up to the CRT. Except for an emitter-follower stage, there is a polarity reversal between the input and output of each transistor, culminating in the correct polarity at the CRT grid or cathode, as the case may be. For example, with 180° reversal at each of three stages, a negative-going signal from the detector produces a positive signal at the CRT cathode.

Picture contrast can be controlled in the same manner. Formerly, a contrast control consisted of a pot, functioning as a variable voltage divider for the signal. With dc control there is no need for shielding the leads to the control since the circuit is at ground potential as far as the signal is concerned.

*Automatic Brightness Control.* This is a feature found on some sets for regulating brightness automatically in accordance with ambient room lighting. A photosensitive LDR (light-dependent resistor) is mounted on the cabinet, where it senses changes in ambient brightness. It is connected in the biasing circuit of one of the dc-coupled amplifier stages (Chapter 17). For bright surroundings, the resistance of the LDR is low, indirectly (via a dc control stage) reducing the CRT bias and increasing the screen brightness. Conversely, in a dark room, the LDR resistance increases and the beam current and the screen brightness is reduced.

### DC Restoration

The video signal developed by the station cameras has a dc "reference level" that must be maintained to develop the proper brightness level, consistent with the scene being televised. If this dc reference is lost, dark scenes will appear brighter than normal, with a loss of black images. Bright scenes will darken accordingly (Figure 14-2).

If a receiver uses ac coupling between the detector and the CRT, the dc level is lost and must be restored. This may be accomplished with a diode connected across the CRT input. The diode rectifies the peak values of the video signal to produce a dc voltage corresponding with average levels of scene brightness. Where direct (dc) coupling is used between stages, the dc level is never lost, so there is no problem.

### Frequency Response

The ideal video amplifier would provide equal amplification for all frequencies from near 0 Hz to 4 MHz or better. Since the response of any amplifier tends to fall off at the extremes of low and high frequencies, some form of frequency compensation is required. Loss of low frequencies results in picture smear, poor contrast for large objects, and unstable sync. Loss of high frequencies causes a loss of fine detail.

*High-Frequency Compensation.* To prevent attenuation of high video frequencies, the "distributed capacity" of a circuit must be kept to a minimum. It is also important that the circuit impedance be kept as low as practical. As in the video detector, peaking coils are used at the output of each stage to increase stage gain for frequencies in the range 3 to 4 MHz. With ICs, a frequency-selective negative feedback loop is sometimes used. Video peaking, as described earlier, offers another means of emphasizing the high frequencies in an effort to crispen the fine details of a picture.

*Low-Frequency Compensation.* For low reactance to low frequencies, the values of coupling capacitors, when used, must be as large as possible. This also holds true for bypass capacitors. Low-frequency compensating networks can also be used in the collector circuit of each transistor. With such a circuit, the load impedance is increased for low frequencies, for increased amplification. With extensive use of dc coupling between discrete transistors, and since the advent of ICs, loss of low frequencies is no longer the problem that it once was.

### Retrace Blanking

Figure 14-1 shows the vertical and horizontal blanking pulses applied directly to the CRT along with the video. Since this requires pulses of high amplitude, most sets inject the pulses at some low-level upstream stage. In some cases the two kinds of pulses are injected at different points: for example, positive vertical pulses fed to the cathode and negative horizontal pulses to the control grid.

## 14-2 THE COLOR SET

A block diagram showing the video amplifier section of a color set, along with its interfacing circuits, appears in Figure 14-3. Note the additional stages and

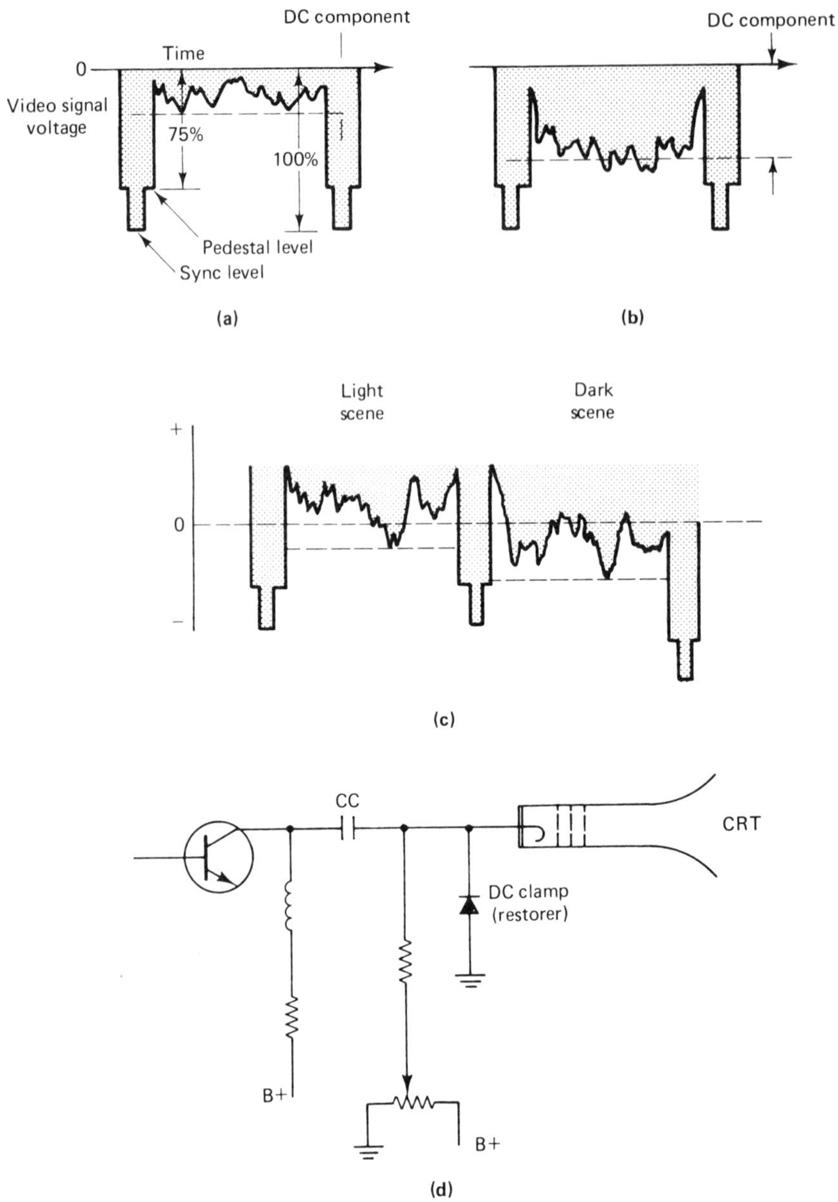


**FIG. 14-2** Dc restoration is required when the transmitted dc level is blocked with a capacitor.

circuits not found in a BW set (Figure 14-1). These are: the comb filter, the delay line (an item in the video amplifier), and the *sandcastle* and *ABL* circuits. Of special significance is the block representing all the chroma-related circuits, which is treated in Chapters 15 and 16. Note the alternate points of chroma takeoff (where chroma information is separated from the video) and where they recombine later in a video output stage to drive the CRT simultaneously. The inputs/outputs of the amplifier itself and the associated control functions are essentially the same as for a BW set, except that here the "combined" vertical and horizontal blanking pulses are applied to an early video stage.

## Composite Video Signal

The composite video signal developed by the station for color programming is not too different from the signal developed for monochrome transmission. One difference is the *color burst,* which is added onto the "back porch" of each horizontal blanking pulse (Figure 1-6), for the purpose of controlling color sync. Although not shown in the diagram, the lines of video information are *interleaved with* the phase-modulated chroma signals, which will subsequently be separated at the input of the video amplifier. When receiving a color broadcast, the video signal (the Y or monochrome signal) serves two pur-

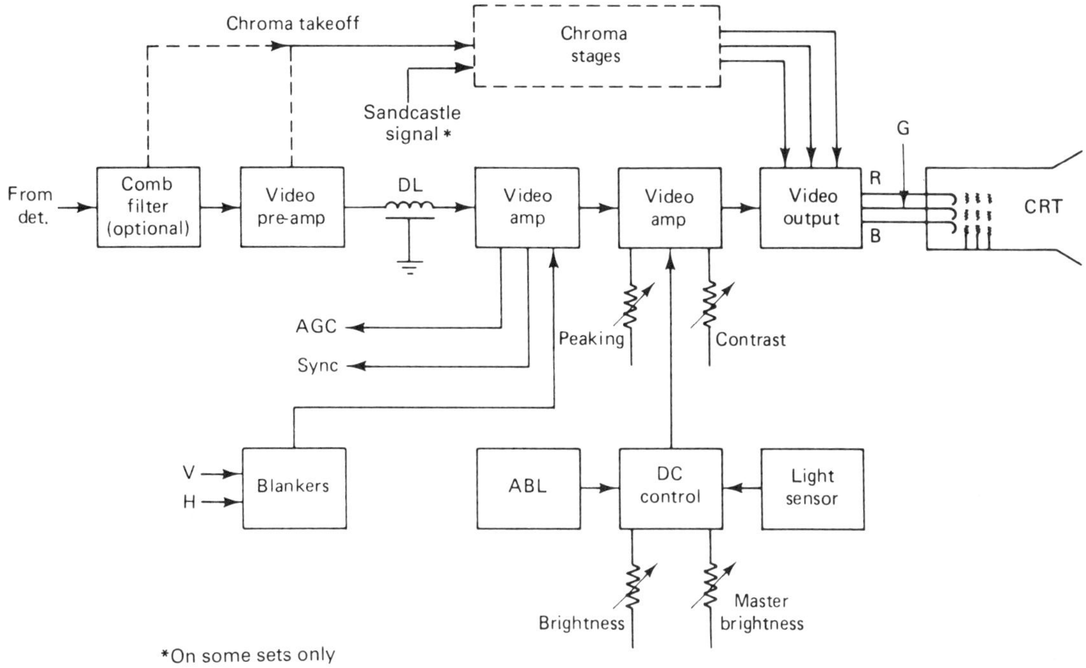


**FIG. 14-3** Color set video amplifier and related functions.

poses: It provides luminance information to establish the brightness levels of colors, and it produces the fine picture details that are too small to be shown in color.

For a color broadcast, many stations also transmit the VIR and VITS signals described earlier, for the purpose of monitoring the color quality of transmissions. Signal flow from the video detector to the CRT input is described next.

## Comb Filter

This circuit (found in practically all modern color TV sets, monitors, and VCRs) contributes greatly to the overall quality of a picture. It is used to separate the video (luminance) and chroma signals one from the other at the point of chroma takeoff shown in Figure 14-3. Formerly this was accomplished with a narrowband, 3.58-MHz tuned circuit. Prior to the use of a comb filter and because of the "interleaving" of video and chroma within the same IF bandpass, *complete* separation of these signals was not possible. This results in video getting into the chroma stages and color information reaching the video stages, creating problems in both instances. With more complete separation, the bandpass of the video amplifier can be expanded for improved resolution of fine picture details. As a bonus, more of the fine detail can be reproduced *in color*.

A comb filter (Figure 14-4) consists of several stages, for adding and subtracting (canceling) signals, plus a *delay device*. A typical delay device con-

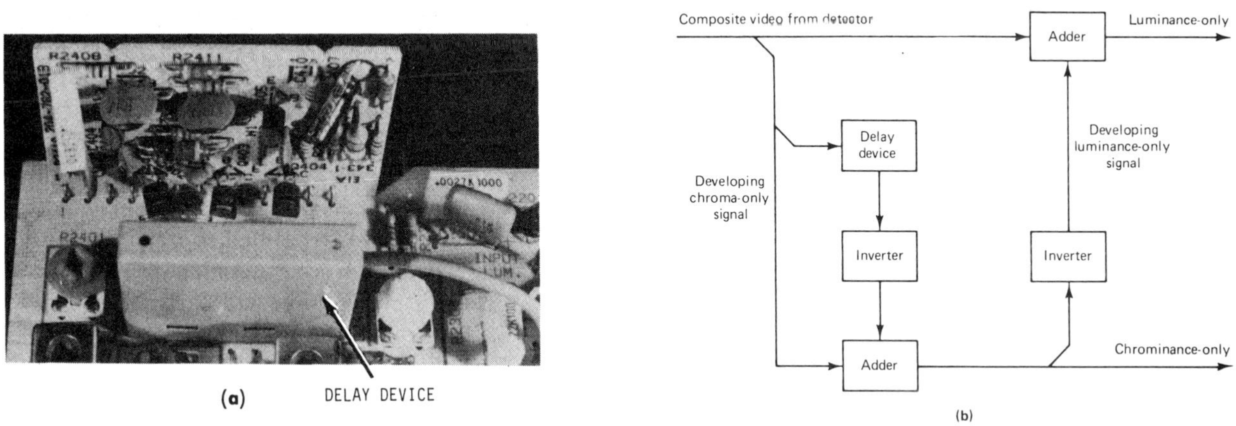


**FIG. 14-4** Comb filter. A comb filter ensures good separation of chroma and video.

sists of a glass enclosure with a transducer (speaker) device at one end to convert electrical pulses into acoustic waves. A microphone unit at the other end converts the sound waves back to electrical pulses. Separation of the signals involves a process called *combing*. The incoming signal splits into two paths: one path for the "luminance only" signal, a second path for the "chrominance only" signal. The purpose of the delay device is to delay a sampling of the luminance signal by approximately 1 μs, corresponding with the scanning of one line of pix information. The amount of delay is established by the time taken for the wave to traverse the glass enclosure. With the proper phase relationships, chroma from one circuit cancels the chroma in the other circuit, resulting in a chroma-free video signal to pass on to the video amplifier. At the same time, the "delayed" luminance signals of alternate scanning lines cancel each other to produce a chroma-only signal that is routed to the chroma stages.

### Sandcastle Circuit

The sandcastle circuit (RCA) is an all-encompassing master control circuit for synchronizing the major functions performed by the luminance/chrominance IC now found in most receivers. The circuit generates a special *sandcastle signal*, a combination of three signals: a flyback pulse, a delayed horizontal sync pulse, and a vertical pulse. The three pulses are combined outside the IC. Inside the IC, they separate, the flyback pulse providing horizontal blanking for the IC output signals, the delayed sync pulse separating the color burst from the horizontal blanking pedestal, and the vertical pulse providing vertical blanking.

A defect in the multifunction IC normally results in a dark screen. The same thing occurs for a missing or abnormal sandcastle signal. The amplitude and waveshape of a sandcastle signal is crucial to circuit operation. Fortunately, the sandcastle circuit itself seldom gives trouble, but when it does, it creates a real servicing headache. Symptoms include loss of raster, picture, video, color, or sync: together or in combination.

### Delay Line

This item (not to be confused with a comb filter delay device) is contained in the video amplifier section of all color sets. It is a special type of coil (a short length of coax in older sets) that delays the video signal by approximately 1 μs. This ensures that video and corresponding color signals reach the CRT at the same instant. Without such a delay, and since the two signals take different routes, the video would arrive first and the chroma a split-second later. The result would be an out-of-registry, ghost-like picture. To prevent ringing, and reflections that create standing waves, the delay line is terminated at both ends with an impedance-matching resistor.

### Video Amplifier

The video amplifier of a *color set* is sometimes called the luminance or Y amplifier, as noted in Figure 1-5. A typical receiver has four stages: using discrete transistors, an IC, or both. The configuration shown in Figure 14-3 has an additional stage, a medium-power video output stage that handles both video and chroma signals. In late-model sets the output transistors are incorporated in the IC along with the signal voltage amplifiers.

For monochrome reception, the color set video amplifier does the same job as its counterpart in a BW set, that is, amplifying the full range of frequencies that produces a picture in BW. For color reception, the amplifier is the source of signal that produces the smallest picture images and provides the necessary brightness to all colors.

As in the IF strip, the video amplifier contains *traps*, but for a different purpose. There are usually one or two 4.5-MHz traps to remove the 4.5-MHz intercarrier beat developed at the detector between the video and sound IF carriers. Some sets also have a 3.5-MHz trap at the point of chroma takeoff. Bridged-T traps are used in some cases; currently, most sets use the more efficient and sharply resonant *ceramic filters*.

In Figure 14-3, note the three inputs and outputs at the video output stage, where *matrixing* of the video and chroma signals takes place. With this configuration, the signals driving the three guns of the CRT contain both luminance and color information. With some sets, video and chroma signals *separately* drive different elements of the CRT. More on this later.

### Drive Controls

Many (but not all) sets provide three of these controls to establish the proper amount of video drive, individually to the three guns of the CRT. They are service adjustments used for *gray-scale tracking*, which is part of the CRT setup procedures, to be described later. The controls are identified in accordance with the guns being controlled; red drive, green drive, and blue drive. Their proper adjustment assures the brightest possible highlights in a picture and uniform brightness for all settings of the brightness control.

### Brightness Control

With a color set, raster brightness is controlled by changing the bias of all three guns of the CRT simultaneously. The same methods can be used as for a BW set: directly controlling the bias at the CRT input, or indirectly via a *dc control stage* in the dc-coupled video amplifier. Modern sets employ the latter method, sometimes in conjunction with a master brightness control, as described earlier. Adjusting the brightness control typically causes a bias change from near zero to about − 100 V to produce beam current cutoff, a dark screen, and black images.

### Automatic Brightness Limiter Circuit

The automatic brightness limiter (ABL) (Figure 14-3) is used to limit the CRT beam current. Excessive current, sometimes as much as 1 A or more, can damage the tube and create problems such as blooming and defocusing. The usual causes of high current are excessive HV or screen grid voltage, or loss of bias.

There are numerous variations, but a typical ABL circuit senses changes in beam current by monitoring the current directly or a corresponding voltage developed across a resistor in the HV return circuit. Where an abnormally high current is sensed, the ABL circuit develops a small dc voltage, which applied to the dc control stage in the video amplifier, increases the CRT bias to reduce the current to a safe value.

## 14-3 FOLDOUT SCHEMATIC

The negative-going signal from the video detector exits IC101 via pin 12 and is routed via the 4.5-MHz ceramic filter Z201 (which removes the intercarrier beat) to pin 6 of IC501. This set uses a narrowband (3.5-MHz) tuned circuit in lieu of a comb filter at the chroma takeoff. From pin 7, the signal goes through the delay line X201 to pin 4 and a contrast amplifier in the IC. The contrast control (a dc control of the dc-coupled amplifier) ties in at pin 5. High-frequency peaking components C201 and R209 connect to pin 2. The video signal exits IC501 from pin 22 and is routed via discrete driver amplifier Q202 and the service switch SW201 to the emitters of the three video output transistors, Q501, Q502, Q503. Note the blue and red drive controls. (There is no need for a green drive control.)

CRT brightness is controlled by the two series-connected brightness controls that tie into pins 40 and 41. The beam currents of the three CRT guns are adjusted and balanced individually by the red, green, and blue bias adjusters in the emitter circuits of the output transistors. The voltage across R208 (near the bottom of the diagram) is monitored for ABL control of beam current and brightness.

Sync and chroma takeoff is from pin 7 of IC501. Blanking pulses are applied to the output transistors from pins 19, 20, and 21. AGC takeoff is from the ceramic filter to pin 12 of IC101.

## 14-4 TROUBLESHOOTING AND REPAIR

Trouble symptoms associated with the video amplifier and its interfacing circuits are many and varied. This includes loss of raster; a weak or color-contaminated raster; weak pix or no pix; and color picture problems; problems with the sync, AGC, and sound. After considering the symptoms, the nature of the problem, and which circuits may be at fault, decide on a course of action. Study the schematic. Make a preliminary inspection, looking for obvious defects while identifying and locating stages and components that may relate to the problem.

Perform initial testing as suggested by the symptoms in an effort to localize the trouble to a particular area: for example, the CRT, the amplifier, or any of the associated circuits. This includes voltage tests at the CRT if there is a raster problem, and signal tracing if a picture problem.

If there is loss of picture or a weak picture but the raster is okay, use either signal tracing or signal injection to identify the bad stage (or IC). Check for the presence of a normal signal at the amplifier input, and if okay, scope check the input and output of each stage, progressing toward the CRT. For signal injection, use an AF generator (or the 400-Hz modulation of an RF generator) to obtain a bar pattern on the CRT or a display on a scope. Using either method, proceed either upstream or downstream, as appropriate.

Once the problem has been localized, isolate the defect with voltage, resistance, and component testing. As stated previously, this can be difficult with dc-coupled amplifiers since the defect may be several stages upstream from the point where abnormal conditions are first observed. (For procedures in troubleshooting direct-coupled amplifiers, refer to Chapter 5.) Where set uses an IC, check for the possibility of external defects, and if none, replace the IC. For defects relating to the CRT, refer to Chapter 17.

Trouble symptoms and procedures are described in the following pages. As an aid, refer to the flow drawings (Figures 14-5 and 14-6) as appropriate. There are three categories: *raster problems, BW picture problems* (assuming a normal raster), and *color picture problems* (assuming a normal BW picture). For convenience, both BW and color sets are considered under each heading. Depending on the type of set, use the information and procedures that are applicable. (*Reminder:* A BW picture is dependent of a normal raster, and a normal BW picture is necessary to produce a good color picture.)

## Raster Problems

### *No Raster or Dim Raster.* (sound ok)

***Probable causes:*** Defective CRT or conditions affecting its operation; excessive CRT bias caused by a defect in the dc-coupled video amplifier; sandcastle circuit defect; defective luminance/chroma IC.

Check the CRT and its operating voltages as described in Chapter 17.

If the video amplifier is dc-coupled and there is excessive CRT bias, look for a defect in one of the stages. High or low transistor current is a common cause. (*Reminder:* An abnormal dc voltage in any of the stages affects all voltages up to the CRT.) Where the amplifier is ac-coupled to the CRT, a leaky or shorted coupling capacitor will affect the CRT bias in the same manner. Where the sandcastle circuit is suspect, scope the sandcastle signal and compare with the schematic. Substitute for the sandcastle signal to see if raster returns. Where a multifunction luminance/chrominance IC is used and after checking for external defects, replace the IC.

### *Excessive Brightness*

***Probable causes:*** Short or leakage in CRT or abnormal voltage conditions affecting its operation; insufficient CRT bias caused by a defect in the dc-coupled video amplifier.

For amplifier defects that affect the bias, proceed as described for no raster or dim raster.

### *Hum Bars.* (one or two light or dark horizontal bars)

***Probable cause:*** Poor filtering of LVPS.

If bars are present on a picture *and* the off-channel raster, check the filtering of the B supply feeding the video amplifier. Poor filtering can also upset the sync. If bars are indistinct, misadjust the vertical hold to make them roll. For hum bars on the picture but not on the raster, check the filtering of the B+ feeding the tuner and IF strip.

### *Shading at Top of Screen*

***Probable causes:*** Neck shadows; hum bars; raster centering; excessive blanking pulses.

For conditions relating to CRT setup adjustments, refer to other chapters as applicable. Scope check the blanking pulses at the CRT input and refer to the schematic. If excessive, check for an *RC* defect in the pulse feed from the sweep circuits or the blanker circuit.

## Picture Problems

### *No Pix or Weak Picture.* (raster okay)

***Probable causes:*** Loss of signal between the tuner and the CRT; AGC defect; sandcastle defect.

Signal trace or use signal injection to locate the faulty stage. If a BW set and the sound is okay, the trouble is between the sound takeoff and the CRT. If no sound or picture, check the stages upstream from the sound takeoff. The delay line is usually accessible and makes a good starting point.

If a color set and the sound is okay, suspect the SAW filter, the detector, the comb filter, or any of the video amplifier stages; if there is no sound, suspect the tuner or IF strip. If there is a weak picture with snow, suspect the upstream stages. A weak picture without snow usually means a video amplifier defect. Check for excessive AGC that may be blocking the signal at some stage.

With a color set, a sandcastle defect can cause loss of picture. Disable the circuit or try overriding the sandcastle signal to see if the picture is restored. Where an IC is used and there is signal input but no output and no external defects, replace the IC.

### *Video Overload.* (picture smear, excessive contrast and color, buzz in sound, loss of fine picture, detail, unstable sync, etc.)

***Probable causes:*** AGC defect; video amplifier defect.

Check the AGC at the IF strip and compare with the schematic. On a strong station, scope check for video overload and pulse clipping at various points in the video amplifier. When localized, check

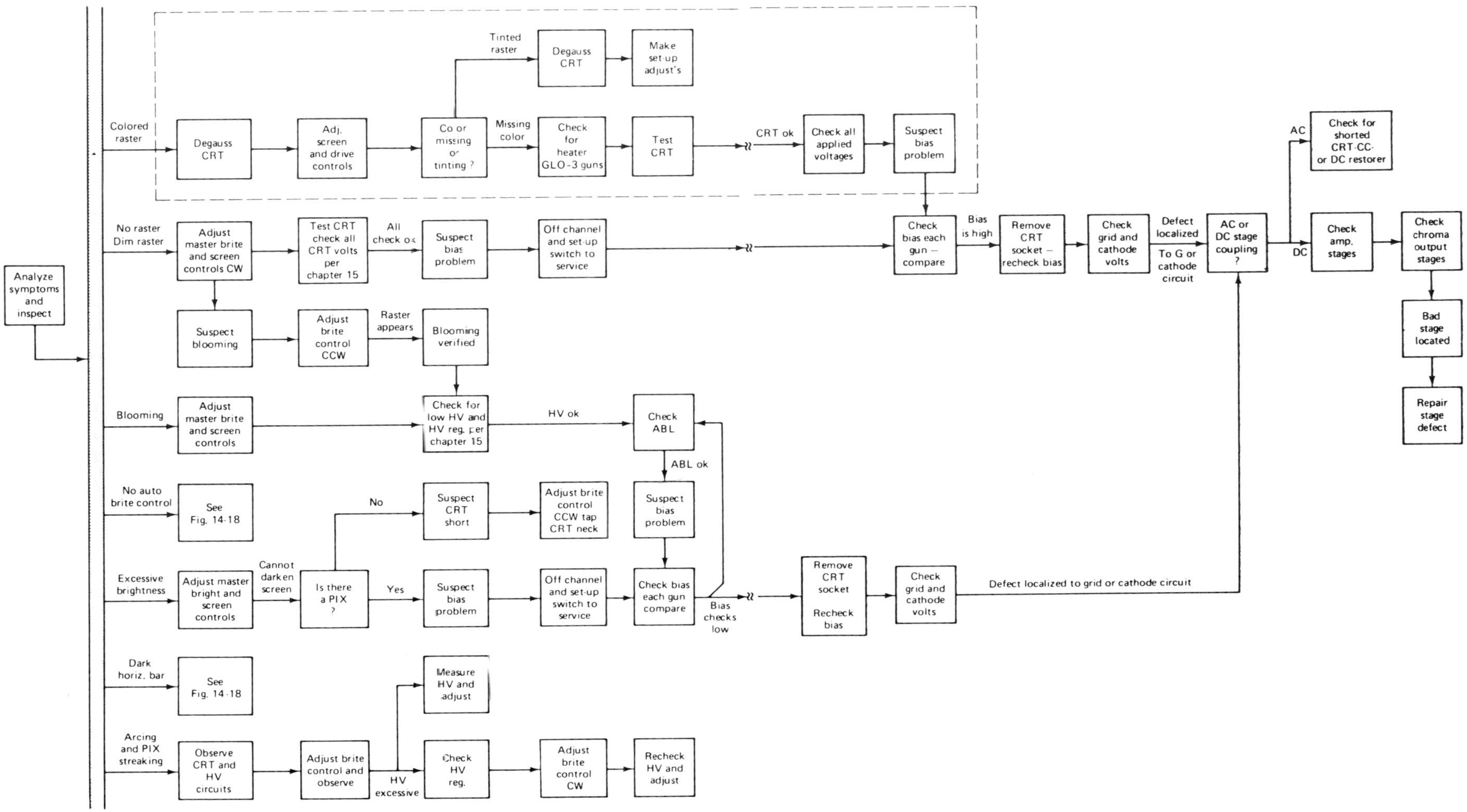


**FIG. 14-5** Troubleshooting color set raster problems.

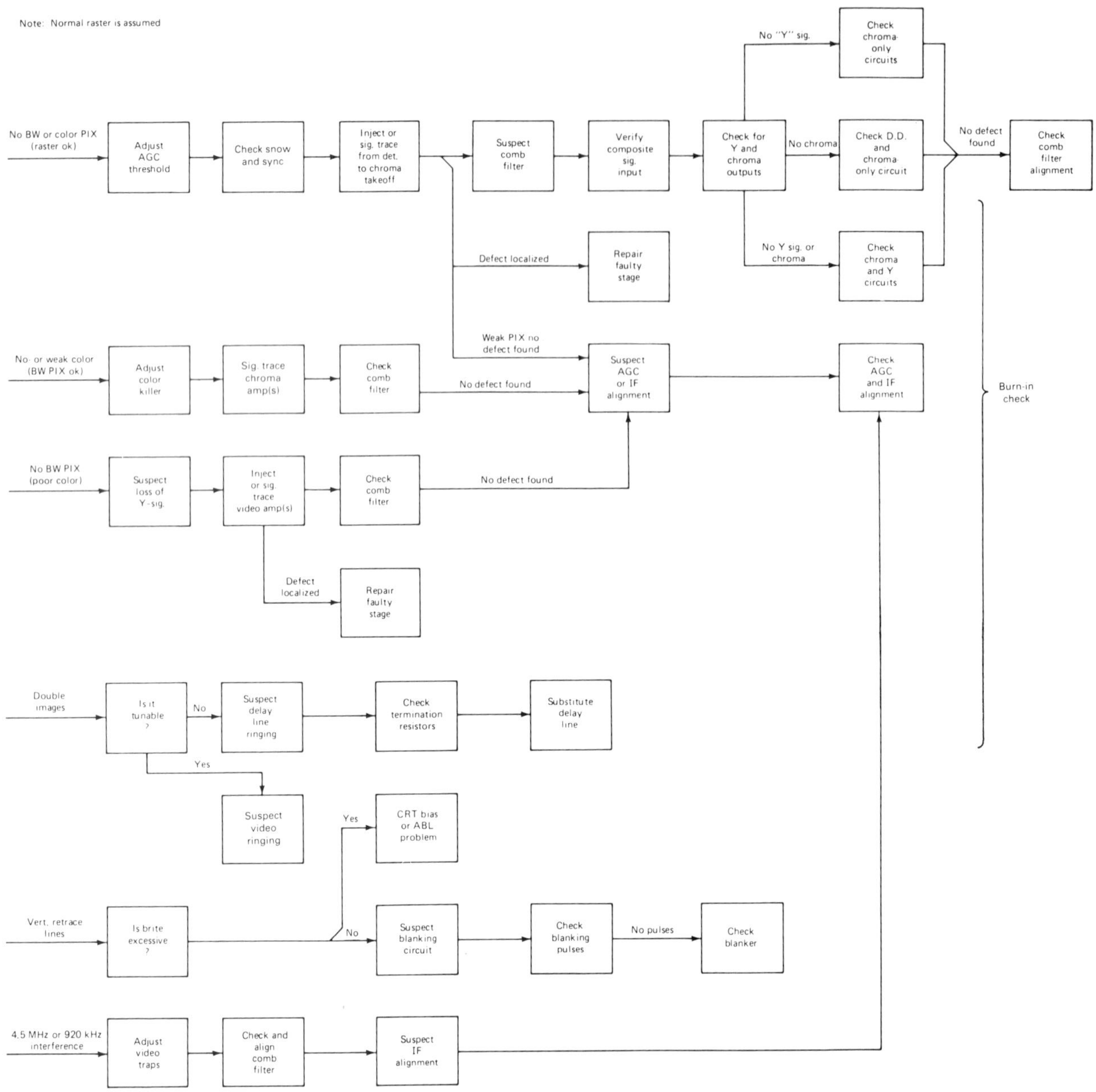


**FIG. 14-6** Troubleshooting color set picture problems.

the transistor, its operating voltages, and associated components. The cause may be upstream from the point where overloading occurs. If an IC and no external defects, replace it.

*4.5-MHz or 920-kHz Beat Interference.* (picture has grainy or wormy appearance)

***Probable causes:*** Video IF misalignment; misaligned 4.5- or 3.58-MHz traps.

Check for IF misalignment. Using an *accurate* signal generator, adjust the traps in the video amplifier. A ceramic filter, when used, operates in conjunction with a resonant circuit, but it is not adjustable.

*Harsh Color Picture; No Fine Detail; No BW Picture.*

***Probable causes:*** Loss of video signal in the video amplifier or comb filter; misadjusted comb filter (the clue to this defect is the absence of a BW picture during monochrome reception or with color control turned down).

Scope trace or use signal injection to localize the trouble where the signal is lost. Correct the defect, or if an IC with no external defects, replace it. Check the inputs and outputs of the comb filter and adjust if necessary. Such adjustments are extremely critical and should be attempted only with the proper equipment.

A *weak* video signal results in a weak BW picture, loss of fine detail, and some loss of color brilliance.

*BW and Color Picture Not in Registry.* (ghost effect, imperfect overlap of images)

***Probable causes:*** Improper CRT setup; misconvergence; delay-line defect.

If necessary, perform a CRT setup (see Chapter 17). Check the signal at the input and output of the delay line in the video amplifier. Check the DL, and if suspect, replace it. Check the impedance-matching resistors at the input and output of DL. With dc coupling, an open or grounded DL can also affect the raster itself.

*Picture Smear and Unstable Sync.* (large horizontal objects lack contrast)

***Probable cause:*** Poor low-frequency response of the video amplifier.

Check the frequency response with an AF generator and scope; use a low-level signal to avoid overload and damage to components. Try to localize the problem to one stage. Check for open or dried-up coupling or bypass capacitors.

*Loss of Fine Detail*

***Probable causes:*** Dim raster, poor focus, or blooming; improper CRT setup adjustments; video overpeaking or ringing; impedance mismatch in antenna system; poor high-frequency response of video amplifier.

Check the CRT and conditions affecting its operation. If necessary, perform a CRT setup. Scope check for excessive peaking or high-frequency ringing in video amplifier. Check for loss of high frequencies in the detector or video amplifier. Check components in high-frequency compensating networks.

## QUESTIONS

1. What are the advantages of dc coupling in a video amplifier as compared to the use of coupling capacitors?
2. What is the result of reversed signal polarity at the CRT input? Give two possible causes.
3. Explain how brightness is controlled from a video amplifier stage.
4. What is the delay line, and why is it needed?
5. Loss of the Y signal in the video amplifier causes loss of a BW picture and produces a harsh color picture lacking in fine detail. Explain.
6. Explain the need for dc restoration when ac coupling is used between the detector and the CRT.
7. Explain the need for low- and high-frequency compensation and how it is accomplished.
8. What is the effect on a picture where the video amplifier has (a) poor high-frequency response; (b) poor low-frequency response? Explain.
9. Poor low-frequency response can result in unstable sync. Explain.
10. Explain the purpose and operation of a comb filter and how it contributes to good picture quality.
11. Explain how video peaking can enhance the fine detail resolution of some images.
12. Explain the purpose of drive controls at the output of the video amplifier.
13. A large-screen set must have a better high-frequency response than a small-screen set. Explain why, giving approximate figures for each.
14. What is the purpose of a 4.5-MHz trap in the video amplifier of (a) a BW set; (b) a color set?
15. Explain why a defect in a direct-coupled amplifier can affect the off-channel raster.
16. Explain the operation of an automatic brightness control circuit using an LDR.
17. Where is the sound takeoff in (a) a color set; (b) a BW set? (c) Where and how are the 41.25- and 4.5-MHz sound carriers developed?
18. As the brightness control is turned up, an increase in video is required to develop black images. Explain.
19. What condition in the video amplifier can cause the BW and color images to be out of registry?
20. Explain some causes and results of video overdrive.
21. A defect anywhere in a dc-coupled video amplifier can influence the raster. Explain why and how would you proceed for such problems.
22. Luminance signals go as high as 4.2 MHz, but chroma signals are limited to 1.5 MHz. Explain.

# 15 Chroma signal processing

Of the many and diverse functions performed by a TV, perhaps none are more complex than those shown in Figure 15-1, where each block plays an essential role in the development of a color picture. Modern sets combine all these functions in a single IC, as indicated on the foldout schematic. There are three main functional areas, indicated by dashed lines; chroma signal stages, color sync, and chroma switching. In this chapter we are concerned with the processing of the chroma signal and combining it with the video signal to produce a color picture. With modern sets, all video and chroma processing is performed by a single multifunction IC.

Other blocks play an equally important role. Those shown for color sync include a subcarrier signal generator which produces the 3.58-MHz CW signal required to demodulate the chroma signals. The generator utilizes the received color burst for synchronizing with its counterpart at the station. This is necessary in order to produce the proper colors at their proper places on the picture image. The area identified as chroma switching includes a burst-sensing circuit to activate the chroma stages only when a color program is being received. Chroma switching and color sync functions are treated in Chapter 16.

## 15-1 CHROMA SYSTEM FUNDAMENTALS

Chroma and video signals are separated from each other at the chroma takeoff point indicated in Figure 15-1. Separation is accomplished with either a comb filter or a narrowband tuned circuit adjusted to the subcarrier frequency of 3.58 MHz. With most of the video signal suppressed, the chroma signal goes to a *bandpass amplifier* (BPA), a tuned, narrowband IF stage that amplifies only the sideband frequencies of the station's 3.58-MHz subcarrier. Color intensity is controlled here with the user *color control.* The chroma IF signal then goes to the chroma demodulators, where it is demodulated to produce three color-related signals. A carrier is needed in the demodulation process. This is supplied by the subcarrier generator, substituting for the subcarrier signal that was not transmitted.

The three outputs from the demodulators are discrete signals corresponding to the three primary colors, red, green, and blue. These signals are further amplified by three color-related output stages.

The video (Y) signal is combined (matrixed) with the chroma signals in one of three ways as indicated: at the demodulators, the output amplifiers, or the CRT. Each color signal is then used to "intensity modulate" its corresponding, color-related beam of the CRT.

Two identical images are produced on the screen: one created by the video signal and another produced in color. With the proper setup adjustments, the images precisely overlap and appear as one.

Specific colors developed by the demodulators depend on the phase relationship between the chroma signals and the subcarrier signal generated at any given instant. Thus to reproduce the original colors as viewed by the camera, and since each color

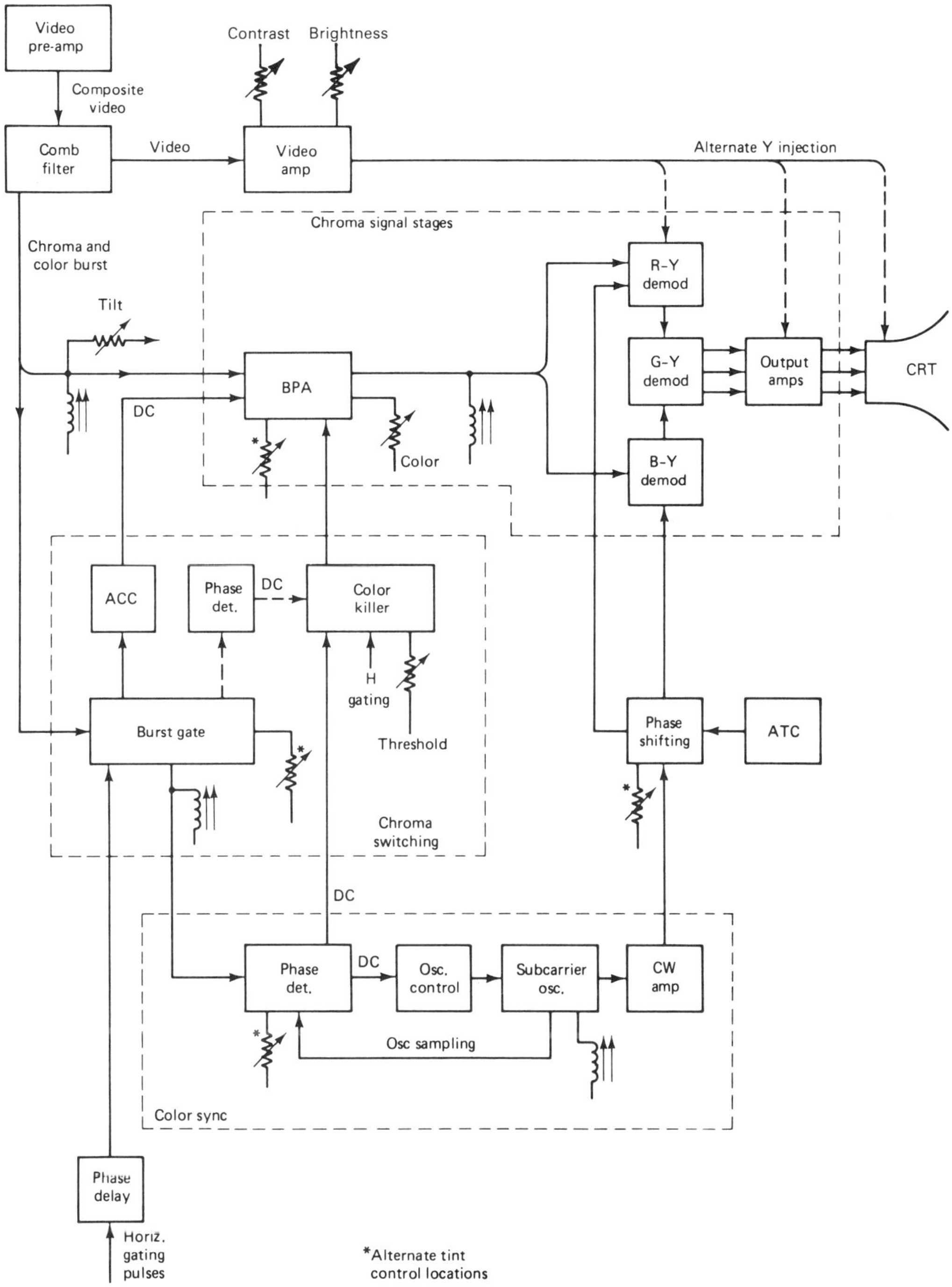


**FIG. 15-1** Chroma processing stages.

corresponds to a specific phase angle, the subcarrier generator must be locked in frequency and phase with its counterpart at the station. This is accomplished by sampling the received *color burst* that reflects the signal developed by the station subcarrier generator. More on this later.

To prevent interference from reaching the CRT via the chroma signal path when receiving a BW program, it is desirable that the chroma stages be disabled at such times. Since the color burst is present only when receiving color, it provides a means of automatically switching the BPA on and off. Color switching is accomplished with a *color killer* that enables the BPA when a burst signal is recognized by the *burst gate,* and disables the BPA when receiving BW. More detailed coverage of chroma signal processing and how a color picture is produced is provided in the following paragraphs.

### Chroma Takeoff

Most sets now use a comb filter (described in Chapter 14) for separating the video and chroma signals and routing them to their respective circuits. Earlier sets and some current inexpensive models use a tuned circuit (sometimes called a filter) peaked at 3.5 MHz, the subcarrier frequency. This circuit has a narrow bandpass, between 1 and 2 MHz, depending on the set. Its purpose is to pass only the I and Q sidebands up to about 1.5 MHz, the upper limit of the I sideband. Frequencies between 1.5 and 4.2 MHz (the video signals) are rejected. Both takeoff systems are sometimes used for more complete separation.

In some cases (for practical and economic reasons) the bandwidth, and the bandpass of the following PBA stage is limited to 1.0 MHz. Although frequencies up to 1.5 MHz are transmitted, those above 1 MHz are not considered essential since they produce only the most minute details of a picture, many of which are not reproduced in color. It is a trade-off between manufacturing cost and picture quality. The increased use of comb filters, however, makes it possible and worthwhile to strive for those hitherto obscure details.

### High-Frequency Roll-Off Compensation

Figure 15-2a shows a typical response curve of the *video* IF strip. The 42.17-MHz marker represents the chroma subcarrier, which is 3.58 MHz removed from the video IF carrier of 45.75 MHz. The 41.67- and 42.67-MHz markers correspond with the upper and lower chroma sideband limits. With *wideband alignment,* as depicted, the chroma sidebands are well down on the curve, where they receive very little amplification. This *roll-off* of high frequencies is compensated for in the alignment of the chroma takeoff circuit and the BPA tuned circuits that follow. This produces a response as shown in Figure 15-2b, where the circuits are peaked to the lower sideband frequency for increased amplification of these frequencies. An overall response curve is shown in Figure 15-1c. This is a double-humped response centered at 3.58 MHz which corresponds

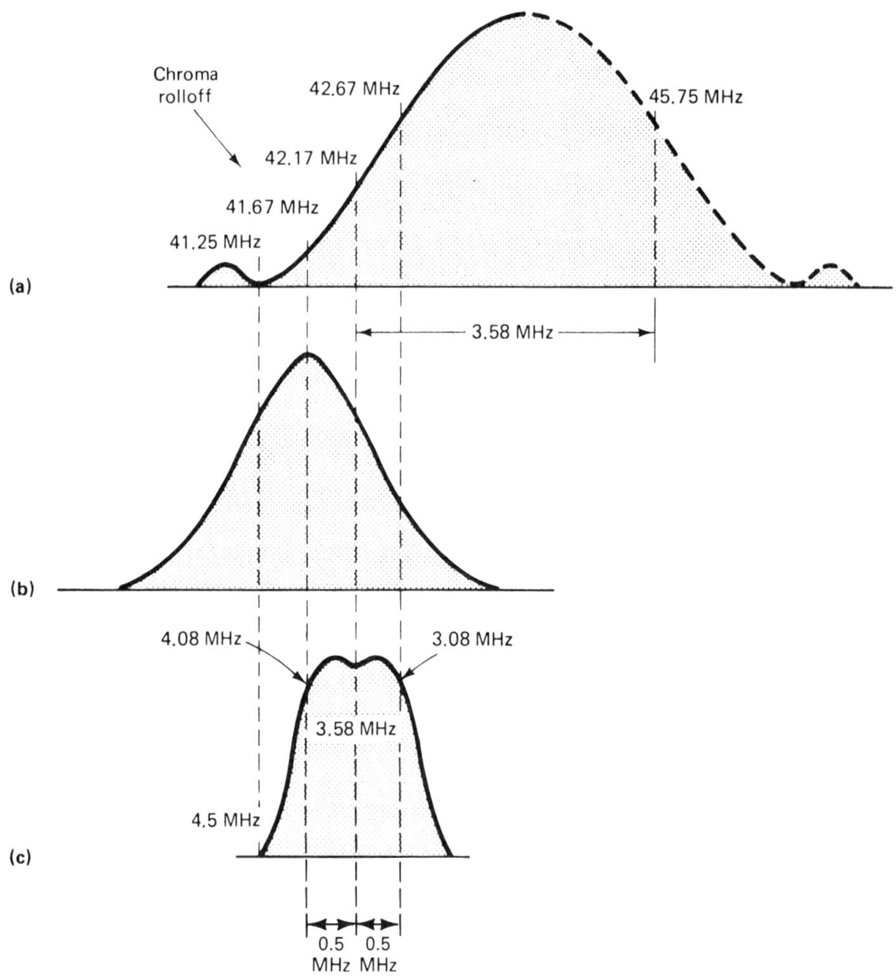


**FIG. 15-2** High-frequency roll-off compensation: (a) video IF amplifier response; (b) chroma takeoff circuit response compensates for roll-off in video IF strip; (c) resultant narrowband BPA response.

with the subcarrier marker frequency in curve (a). The bandpass of the resultant curve is from 3.08 to 4.08 MHz, a total bandwidth of 1 MHz. Because of the curve dropoff, the extreme frequencies from 4.08 to 4.5 MHz receive minimal amplification. The *tilt* control shown in Figure 15-1 adjusts the amount of tilt or slope of the curve and hence the rate of dropoff.

### Bandpass Amplifier

A typical bandpass amplifier (BPA) consists of four tuned stages with an overall gain of about 50×. It is a narrowband IF amplifier resonant to 3.58 MHz, the chroma subcarrier frequency. An overall response is shown in Figure 15-2c. The signals being amplified are the high-frequency I and Q sidebands of the 3.58-MHz chroma subcarrier, which has yet to be demodulated. As mentioned earlier, chroma gain is controlled here with the color control. In the absence of a color burst, the BPA is disabled by the color killer (Figure 15-1), which applies a reverse bias to the BPA output transistor. Some sets also disable the BPA during retrace intervals (with horizontal gating pulses) to ensure that color bursts, sync pulses, and noise do not reach the CRT at such times.

*Broadband and Narrowband Color.* Early-model sets utilized the full 1.5 MHz of the transmitted I sideband. Considering the 0.5 MHz for the Q sideband, this required a 2-MHz bandpass for the BPA. Frequencies above 0.5 MHz are no longer deemed essential since the tiny picture details they produce are not viewed in color. For cost-effectiveness, modern sets limit the chroma bandpass to 1 MHz. This is accomplished in the alignment of the chroma takeoff and BPA tuned circuits.

*Automatic Chroma Control.* The automatic chroma control (ACC) circuit also interfaces with the BPA to control its gain in accordance with the strength of the signal received, using the color burst as a reference. It functions much like AGC, to maintain a constant level of color saturation. Color levels are similarly controlled by the VIR signal with sets designed to process it. More on ACC in Chapter 16.

## 15-2 COLOR FUNDAMENTALS

From the PBA, the chroma signals are routed to the chroma demodulators, which converts them into three color-related signals required by the CRT. A color TV makes use of three *primary colors,* red, green, and blue, to produce images in color and black and white. To understand the operation of the demodulators fully requires a knowledge of color principles, phase angles, and vectors. Understanding color mixtures in particular can be very helpful in troubleshooting. A review of these topics seems appropriate at this time.

Every color has three characteristics: *hue, saturation,* and *brightness. Hue* is the identity of a color that distinguishes it from all others, such as red, yellow, or gold. *Saturation* is the intensity of a color. For example, a color may be described as deep, rich, vivid, or pale, according to how much it is diluted with white light (e.g., pale blue, dark blue, etc.). In the absence of white, a color is considered to be "pure" or fully saturated. *Brightness* refers to the amount of light that is absorbed or reflected by a color. A color may be extremely bright, barely visible, or any level in between while retaining its identity as a color.

*All* colors are derived from the three primary colors. White light is a mixture of the three primaries in the following proportions: 30% red, 59% green, and 11% blue. In other words, white light as we observe it is a combination of all colors of the spectrum.

Mixtures of these colors in various combinations and proportions produce secondary or *complementary* colors, as shown in Table 15-1. An *equal* mix of R and G, for example, produces yellow. The color produced by an *unequal* mixture depends on which color is dominant. Take red and green, for example. If R is dominant, we get a reddish yellow (orange).

A complementary color is identified by the colors that produce it; for example, yellow is the complement of R and G. Various shades of gray are produced by a mix of colors at different brightness levels. Black of course is the total absence of light.

An interesting characteristic of the human eye is its inability to discern color on tiny particles or images. This is why TV design is generally not concerned with chroma frequencies higher than 1 or 1.5 MHz. Higher frequencies produce images that are viewed only in black and white.

## 15-3 CHROMA SIGNAL DEVELOPMENT (AT THE STATION)

As described in Chapter 1, a typical camera contains three camera CRTs, each identified in accordance with one of the three primary colors. Although all three cameras view the same image, each camera "sees" and recognizes only its corresponding color in the image, including complementary colors containing its primary color. Each CRT produces an output corresponding with the strength of the color viewed. To obtain pure color information, the Y signal (luminance) is subtracted from each color. These are *saturated* colors with outputs designated R − Y, G − Y, and B − Y, respectively. R − Y, for example, means pure red minus the Y (brightness) component, which has yet to be added. Each signal is used to phase modulate a balanced modulator, as shown in Figure 1-5.

An RF carrier is required to modulate a signal. This carrier is produced by an unmodulated (CW) subcarrier oscillator operating at 3.58 MHz. The oscillator signal is supplied to the modulators, each at a different and specific phase angle relative to the original subcarrier.

In the modulation process at the station, the output of the modulator contains the R − Y information in the I sideband of the subcarrier; the output of the Q modulator contains the B − Y information in the Q sideband. Hereafter, the two signals are considered as two distinct signals, separated in phase and transmitted as such. Since the oscillator signals applied to the modulators are 90° apart, the sidebands produced are also separated by that amount. Green is not transmitted as a separate signal. It is developed at the receiver as a combination of the other two colors.

A proportionate output of each camera is combined to produce the Y or luminance signal, which is used to modulate a separate modulator. The chroma and luminance signals are then combined (matrixed) and transmitted all within the same bandpass.

At the receiver, chroma and luminance signals are recombined to produce images of the same colors and brightness as those viewed by the camera.

### Phase Angles and Vectors

The output of the station modulators is constantly changing in amplitude and phase. Amplitude corresponds to the intensity of colors. Phase corresponds with hue, the identity of a color. The colors produced for different phase angles during one complete cycle of the subcarrier reference oscillator are shown in Figure 15-3. For convenience, the vectors all indicate the same amplitude.

## 15-4 RECEIVER DEMODULATORS

The function of the demodulators is the reverse of that performed by the station modulators. Whereas the modulators superimpose the chroma information on the subcarrier, the demodulators recover the color signals from their respective carriers.

A typical chroma demodulator *system* (sometimes called a synchronous demodulator) consists of either two or three demodulators operating independently, separately, or together. Diodes have been used in the past; modern sets use either discrete transistors or demodulator circuits in a multifunction IC. A two-transistor demodulator circuit is shown in Figure 15-4. In this circuit they are arbitrarily called X and Z demodulators.

Chroma signals from the BPA are applied in parallel to the base of each transistor. Subcarrier oscillator voltage (at a specific phase angle) is applied to the emitter of each transistor. The only difference between the two demodulators is the phase of the subcarrier voltage applied to each of the transistors. Signals at the demodulator outputs are changing in amplitude in accordance with phase

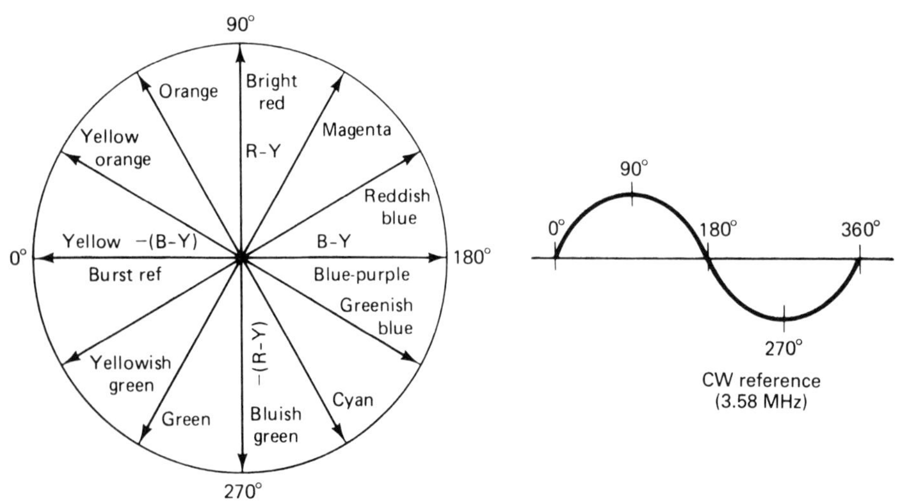


**FIG. 15-3** Phase angles and chroma vectors.

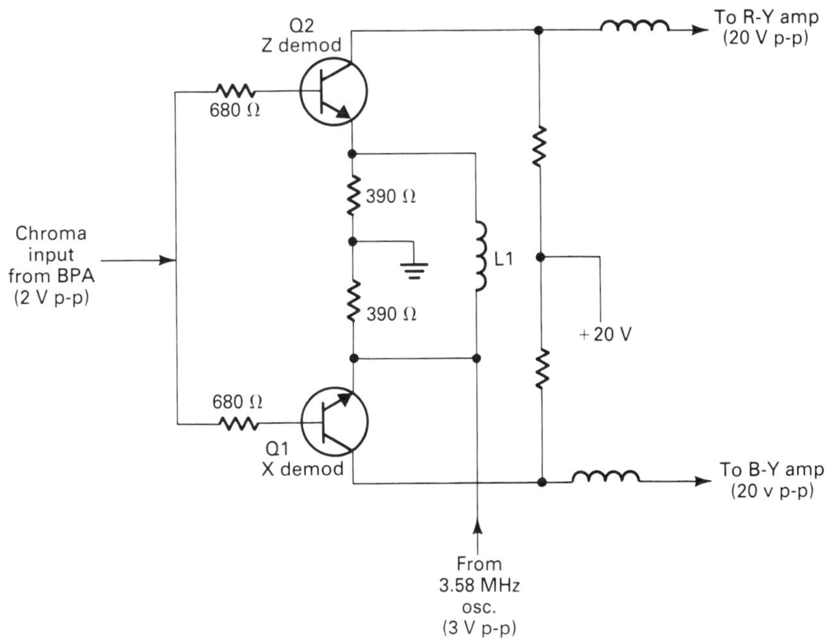


**FIG. 15-4** Simplified X-Z demodulation circuit.

variations of the input signals, which in turn correspond with the colors viewed by the camera. There are several systems of demodulation, although each operates on the same principles using the same basic circuit.

At the station, I and Q sidebands are produced using phase angles with a separation of 90°. Demodulators in current use employ different phase angles as established by the phasing networks between the subcarrier oscillator and each demodulator. The system used in each receiver design is determined by cost and by which colors need emphasizing because of variations in the light-producing efficiencies of the CRT screen phosphors used.

### Demodulator Operating Conditions

A small forward bias (measured between B and E) is required to make a transistor conduct. Polarity depends on the transistor type: positive for an NPN and negative for a PNP. With voltage applied to *both* elements, bias is the difference between the two. With a demodulator, the base voltage is the applied chroma signal and the emitter voltage is furnished by the subcarrier oscillator. For a PNP transistor the chroma at the base is negative-going and the oscillator voltage applied to the E is positive. For an NPN transistor, conditions are reversed. Each transistor is made to conduct or not conduct according to the instantaneous voltage at each element at any given instant.

The B-to-E voltage at each transistor is constantly changing in accordance with the instantaneous values of the two applied voltages. The chroma at the base is changing with amplitude variations of the different color signals. The voltage at the emitter is changing with sinusoidal variations of the oscillator voltage. The transistor will conduct *only* when both voltages are present and of sufficient amplitude at any given instant. If one or the other is weak or missing, the transistor cannot conduct and produce an output. In effect, the chroma is being periodically sampled and the transistors turned on and off by the oscillator voltage with each cycle reversal.

When a demodulator transistor conducts, it produces an output corresponding with one of the three primary colors. When two or three of the transistors conduct, a complementary color is produced. The amplitude of a demodulator output varies in accordance with the color intensity.

*Producing and Reproducing Colors.* When the red CRT in the station camera sees its color (or a red complementary color) in an image, the R − Y modulator produces an output corresponding with the color red. At the receiver (if the oscillator is locked in sync) the R − Y demodulator is made to conduct, producing a red output to drive the red gun of the CRT. If no output from the blue and green camera CRTs at that instant, the picture element struck by the CRT beam will be reproduced in red. Similarly, when the blue CRT in the camera sees its color in an image, the B − Y modulator produces an output corresponding with the color blue. At the receiver, the B − Y demodulator conducts to produce a blue signal to drive the blue gun of the CRT, and we see the picture element as blue.

Only one color can be seen by the camera and reproduced by the picture tube at any given instant. When a *complementary* color is seen by the camera, the primary colors contained in the mixture are viewed by *two* or *three* of the CRTs to produce outputs corresponding with the amounts of each color present in the mixture. At such times, the associated modulators develop outputs in accordance with the mixture. At the receiver, the corresponding demodulators conduct to produce outputs to drive two or three guns of the CRT simultaneously, and the picture element is reproduced in the same color as seen by the camera: for example, the color purple, when the red and blue beams are operating and the green gun is turned off.

When the camera sees white in an image, all three CRTs produce an output to modulate the subcarrier with proportionate mixtures of all three primary colors. At the receiver, each demodulator produces an output of the same proportions, to drive the three guns of the CRT to reproduce the picture element in white.

The brightness of each color reproduced at any instant is established by the amplitude of the luminance (video) signal that *simultaneously* varies the beam intensities of all three guns of the CRT. Picture images are produced in *black* at such times when there is zero output from the camera CRTs, when none of the demodulators are turned on, and when each of the picture tube guns are biased to cutoff.

## Demodulator Systems

There are several systems in use, based on the number of demodulators (two or three) and the choice of phase angles, both of which are design options. A demodulator can operate on any two axes that represent different phase angles, typically between 50 and 130°. With a two-transistor demodulator, the color green (and its complementaries) is produced by combining the R − Y and B − Y signals in an output amplifier that drives the CRT. With three demodulators, these two signals are mixed in the demodulators to produce a voltage corresponding with green. A three-transistor demodulator requires three outputs from the subcarrier oscillator, each of a different phase. With a two-transistor system, the chroma is sampled twice during one complete cycle of the oscillator output. For a three-transistor demodulator, the chroma is sampled three times during each oscillator cycle.

There are also high-level and low-level demodulators. A high-level demodulator (currently the most popular) is at some high-level point near the CRT input. A low-level demodulator is several stages upstream from the CRT. The names of the demodulators are I and Q, (R − Y) (B − Y), (R − Y) (G − Y), (R − Y) (G − Y) (B − Y), X − Z, and RGB. The operation of these systems can best be understood in reference to the "phasor" diagram of Figure 15-5.

Each vector represents a particular color, operating condition, and phase angle relative to the subcarrier oscillator signal. For the oscillator, the reference signal is 0°, as indicated. Vector lengths correspond with relative amplitudes for comparison. As stated earlier, phase angles are chosen by the set manufacturer to emphasize certain colors.

*I and Q Demodulators* (early model sets only) As indicated in Figure 15-5, the I demodulator operates at 57°; the Q demodulator, in quadrature, at 147°. The +I operating point corresponds with a slightly orangish red, commonly referred to as "flesh" color, one that can readily be identified. The +Q point relates to a color approximately midway between magenta and blue.

*(R − Y) (B − Y) Demodulator.* The R − Y axis, which corresponds to a reddish purple or magenta, is at 90°. The B − Y axis, corresponding with a purplish tinted blue, is in quadrature at 180°.

*(R − Y) (G − Y).* Here the color blue is produced by a mixture of red and green in a downstream B − Y amplifier. Typical angles used are 120° (magenta) and 270° (a greenish cyan).

*(R − Y) (G − Y) (B − Y).* This system uses three demodulators, to produce all three primary colors. Three outputs from the oscillator are required. Typical phase angles employed are 0° (a near yellow), 120° (magenta), and 270° (greenish cyan).

*X − Z Demodulator.* This is a commonly used two-transistor system. Typical angles are 119.9° (reddish magenta), and 63° removed, at 182.9° (a bluish magenta). Green is obtained by a mixture of R − Y and B − Y signals in a G − Y amplifier.

*RGB Demodulator.* This is another three-transistor demodulator, the outputs of which represent the three primary colors for driving the CRT. The phase angles are 76.5° (red), 299.9° (green), and 192° (blue) (see Figure 15-6).

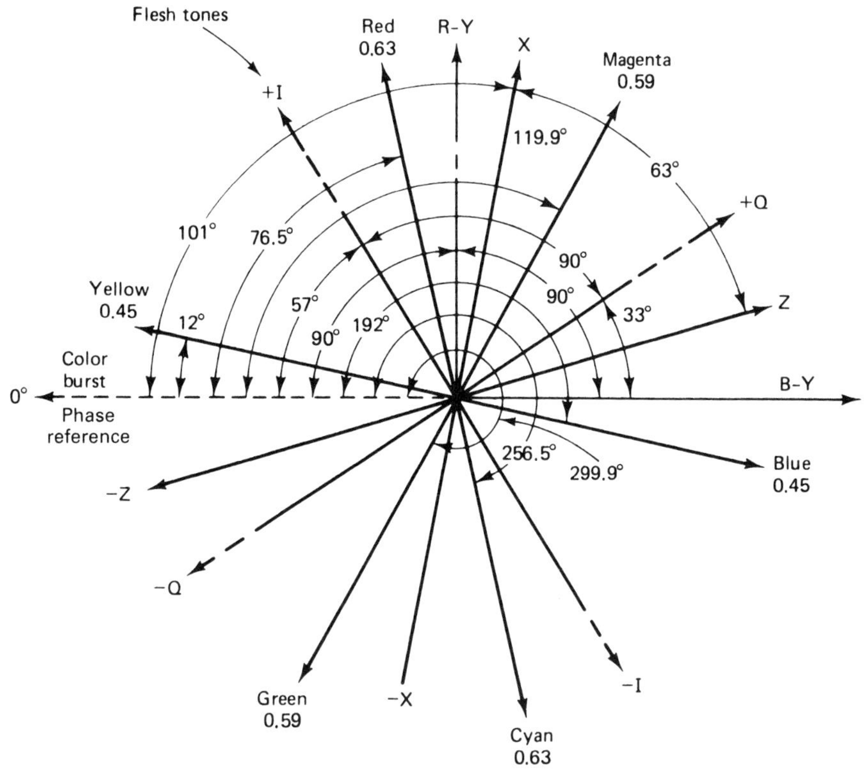


**FIG. 15-5** Color phase diagram. Demodulation axes are chosen to emphasize certain colors.

Demodulation axes are chosen to emphasize certain colors.

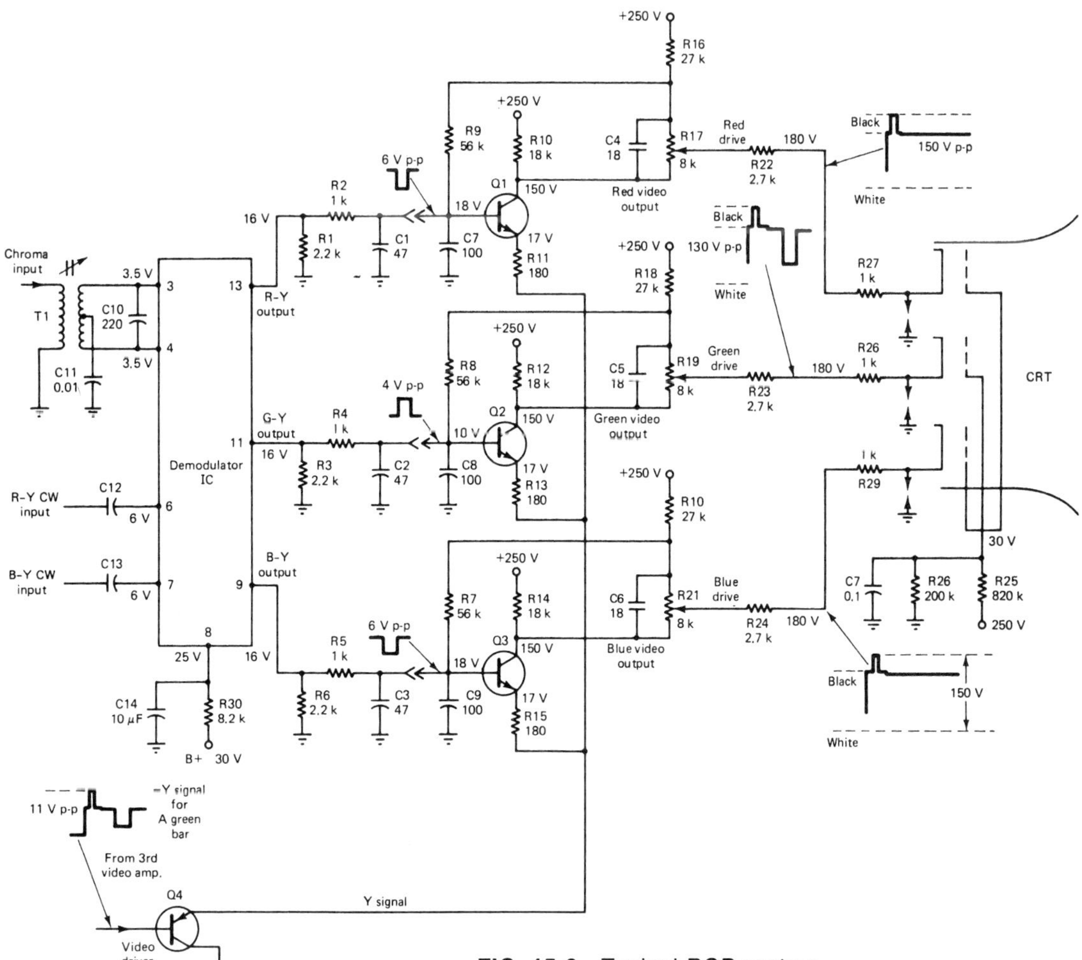


**FIG. 15-6** Typical RGB system.

## 15-5 TINT CONTROL

Most sets provide a manual tint control so that the user can vary colors slightly according to his or her preference. Colors are not always true for any number of reasons: camera problems where one or more CRTs are aging or improperly matched, transmission problems, subcarrier oscillator drift, or other defects in the receiver. As explained previously, hue and phase are intimately related, and the slightest change in the phasing of a chroma signal or the oscillator outputs can produce significant changes in color. The control is usually adjusted by observing skin tones during a high-quality telecast.

As indicated in Figure 15-1, color tint may be controlled in different circuits: the burst gate, the subcarrier oscillator phase control circuit, or in one of the oscillator phase-shifting networks.

### Automatic Tint Control (ATC)

Although many users still prefer to adjust colors to their own liking (with the manual tint control), most modern sets incorporate an ATC circuit that automatically performs this function. This is accomplished in a typical circuit by a slight shift in phasing of one of the oscillator outputs. A defeat switch is usually provided for switching to manual control.

## 15-6 MATRIXING AND CHROMA OUTPUT CIRCUITS

The CRT must be driven by two kinds of signals: RGB color signals and the video (luminance or Y) signal. In the absence of color signals, images are produced in black and white. Without the video signal, the images produced by the chroma-only signals appear harsh and unnatural and completely lacking in detail.

The chroma and luminance signals may be combined (matrixed) in several ways: in the demodulators, in the video or chroma output amplifiers, or by the CRT itself. If matrixing occurs in the CRT, it is called *CRT matrixing*. If it takes place upstream from the CRT, it is called *pre-CRT matrixing*—the system used in most modern sets.

### CRT Matrixing

A block diagram is shown in Figure 15-7. The video signal drives all three guns of the CRT simultaneously. With cathode drive as shown, signal polarity is positive-going, where increases in signal level causes a reduction in beam currents. For a normal setting of the brightness control (CRT bias), the signal must be strong enough to drive the CRT between the extremes of saturation and beam current cutoff. The drive controls individually adjust the drive to the three guns. Note the protective spark gaps connected to the CRT elements.

Red, green, and blue color-related signals individually drive the control grids of the three guns. Signal polarity is negative. The intensity of each of the three beams is made to vary in accordance with video applied to the cathodes and the color signals at the grids. White is produced by a 30%–59%–11% mix of the three colors. Pure colors are produced when single guns are being driven. Complementary colors are produced when two or three guns are driven at various levels of intensity.

### Pre-CRT Matrixing

With this method, matrixing may take place in the demodulators or the output amplifiers. Figure 15-8 shows a typical configuration. Note that only the CRT cathodes are driven and the control grids are at ground potential as far as the signals are concerned. With this circuit, each of the three matrix amplifiers are supplied with video and chroma signals. Note the three drive controls to individually adjust the amounts of Y signal to each amplifier. Other circuits have these controls at the CRT inputs. Outputs from the matrix amplifiers are voltages corresponding to the three primary colors. The three driver amplifiers use medium-power transistors to develop sufficient drive for the three CRT guns. Signal levels at the inputs to the power stages are about 2 V p-p; and at their outputs (CRT inputs) around 125 V p-p. Figure 15-8 shows a typical three-stage RGB output circuit where matrixing takes place in the transistors.

## 15-7 REPRODUCING BW AND COLOR IMAGES

To develop a BW picture from a *monochrome* telecast (on a color set), the chroma stages are disabled and the three guns of the CRT are driven *only* by the video signal. Each gun is supplied with a proportionate amount of signal to produce a white image. By examining the screen with a magnifying lens, all three primary color phosphors can readily be seen. From a distance, however, the eye interprets the mixture as white. Unless the three guns are properly adjusted, one or two beams will pre-

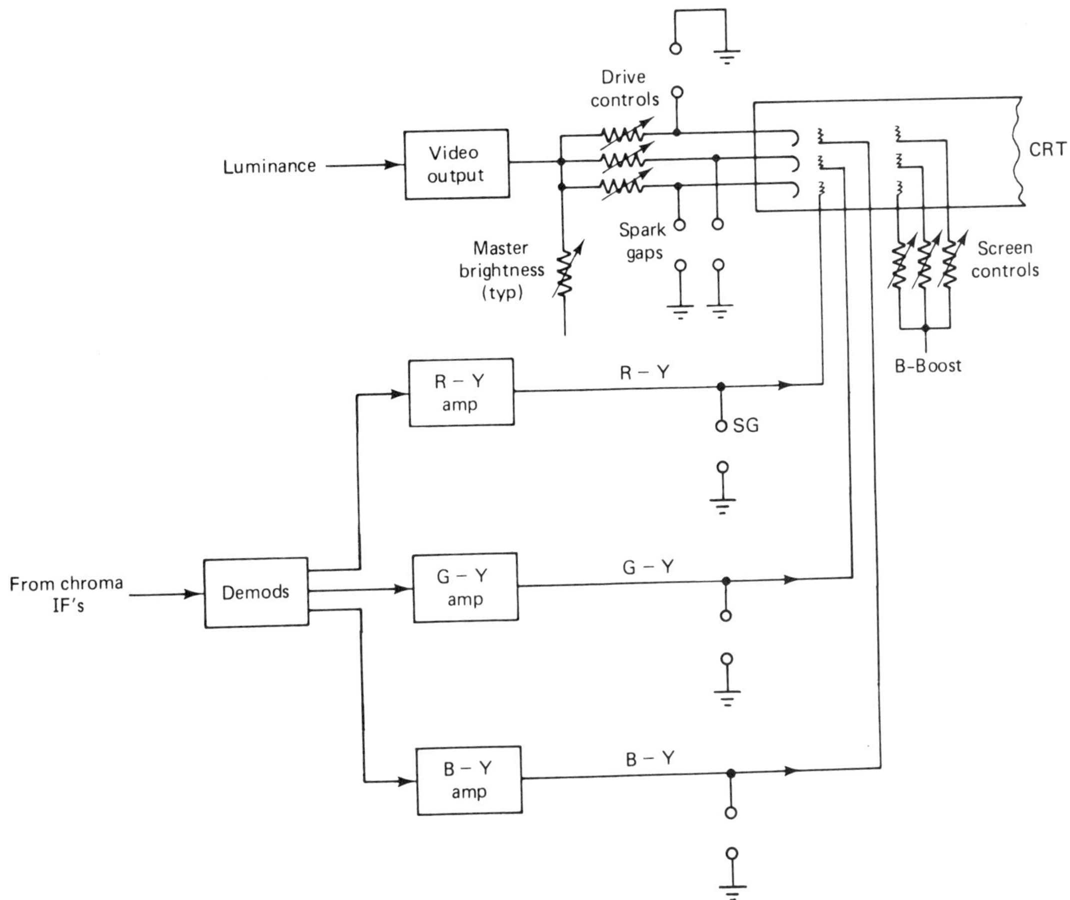


**FIG. 15-7** CRT matrixing system. Variations of beam current are created by the positive-going Y signal and the negative-going chroma signals.

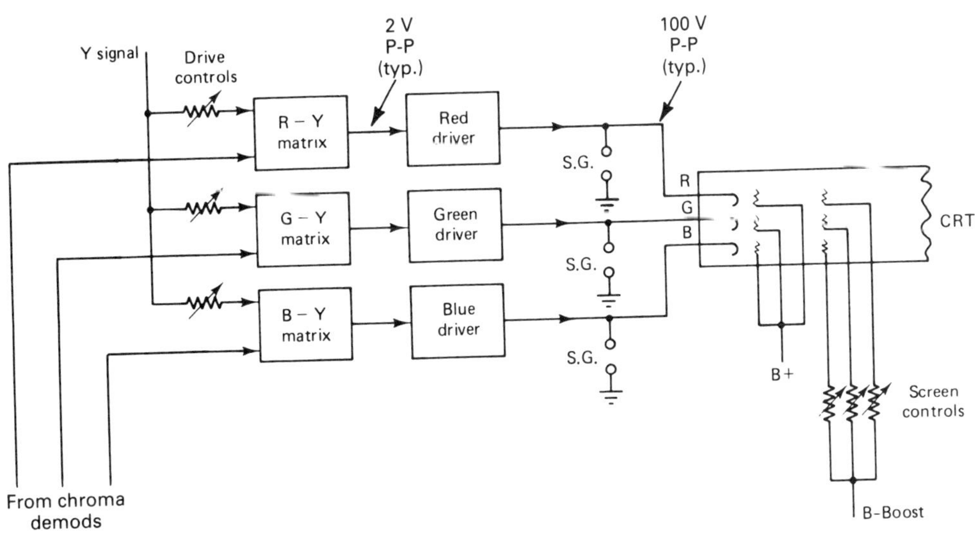


**FIG. 15-8** Pre-CRT matrixing.

dominate and the BW image will have a color-tinted background.

To produce a color picture, the chroma stages are turned on and the CRT is driven by both video and chroma signals. Voltage variations from the RGB output amplifiers produce corresponding variations in the intensity of the three beams, to produce proper colors at the beams' impact points on the screen. Images in BW are superimposed over the color images as a means of reproducing fine picture details and to provide brightness to the color images.

Figure 15-9 shows the different colors produced in accordance with the signals driving the three guns. With cathode drive, the guns are turned off by a positive-going signal, and conductance occurs during the negative-half cycles. This is clearly evident in the two upper examples. More on this in Chapter 16.

## 15-8 FOLDOUT SCHEMATIC

The composite video signal from pin 7 of IC 501 is tuned by L501/C502 to 3.58 MHz (the chroma take-off) for a bandpass of 0.5 MHz. The chroma signal reenters the IC at pin 9 to be amplified. Gain of the first BPA amplifier is controlled by ACC. Gain of

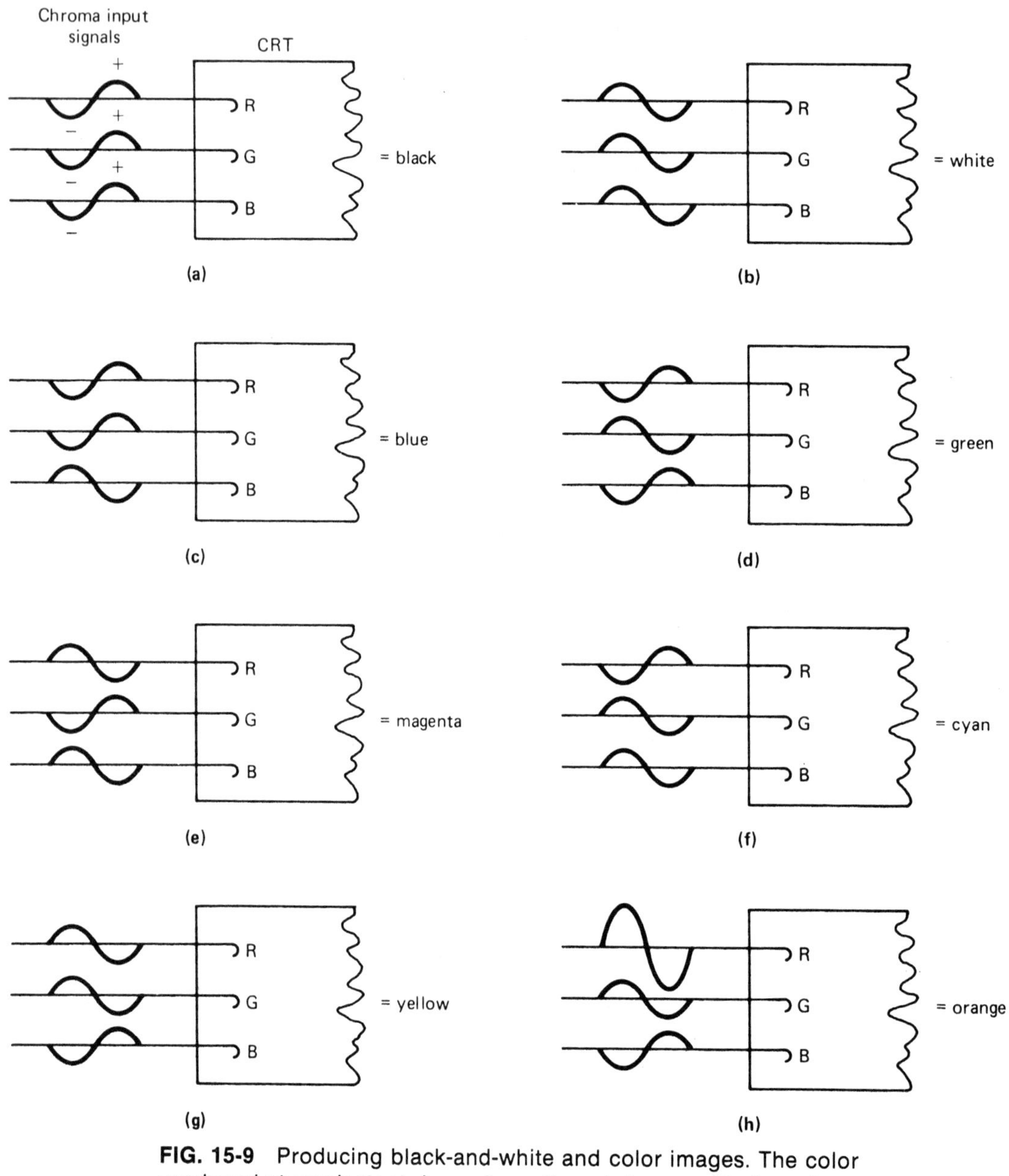


**FIG. 15-9** Producing black-and-white and color images. The color produced at any instant depends on the relative amplitude and polarity of signal drive to each of the three guns.

the second amplifier is controlled by the color control. The amplified chroma signal is routed to the synchronous demodulators via pins 14, 12, and C503. VR501 controls the chroma level to the demodulator inputs. Tint control is accomplished by variations of oscillator phase using VR507 at pin 8. The subcarrier oscillator crystal ties to the IC at pins 16 and 17. As can be seen, all circuits associated with demodulation and matrixing are internal. From the matrix, voltages corresponding with the three primary colors are routed from pins 19, 20, and 21 to three external power amplifiers and from there to the CRT inputs. Beam currents of the individual guns are controlled by pots in the emitter circuits of the power output transistors. As in many cases, there are only two drive controls. Red and blue drive is adjusted relative to the fixed drive of the green amplifier.

## 15-9 TROUBLESHOOTING AND REPAIR

There are four "conditions" to consider in troubleshooting these stages and each must be considered separately and *in the proper order:* the *raster,* the *BW picture, color picture,* and *color sync.* A bright, uncontaminated raster is prerequisite to obtaining a good picture, and a good color picture cannot be produced without a normal color-free BW picture and stable sync conditions. All four conditions are interrelated. For example, troubles in dc-coupled amplifiers can result in a color-tinted raster, with an adverse affect on both a BW and a color picture. Even slight variations from normal phase angles (a sync problem) will drastically affect the hues produced on a color picture.

Here we are concerned with troubleshooting all stages that process and synchronize the chroma signals. Raster problems were dealt with in earlier chapters; BW picture problems in Chapter 14. Color sync problems are considered in Chapter 16.

Start by evaluating the symptoms. Study the schematic and decide what stages and circuits are probably involved. Identify these circuits in the chassis while making a cursory inspection for obvious defects and other clues. Plan your approach to the problem and which tests to make first. Hopefully, the test results will get you off on the right track. Localize the fault by voltage checking, signal injection, or scoping waveforms of the signals received and those generated within the set. Work upstream or downstream as indicated by circumstances. As testing progresses, step back occasionally or take a break to rethink the problem. It is awfully easy to make an erroneous diagnosis and get sidetracked to a dead end that leads nowhere. Keep an open mind and be ready to change direction when conditions warrant.

As with the video stages, dc coupling complicates troubleshooting. Follow procedures outlined in Chapter 5. Where a multifunction IC is used, make sure that there are no external defects before making a replacement. Such defects can *instantly* destroy the new part.

When repairs are completed, operate the set on the bench for a reasonable burn-in period. This is a time when subtle abnormalities often show up, and a time to evaluate the set operation critically. Judge the picture quality on a good live program or preferably, with a color bar pattern.

### Troubleshooting with Color Bars

As stated previously, a keyed rainbow generator as described in Chapter 4 is preferred by most technicians to develop the bar pattern shown in Figure 15-10. With such a display, you can instantly evalu-

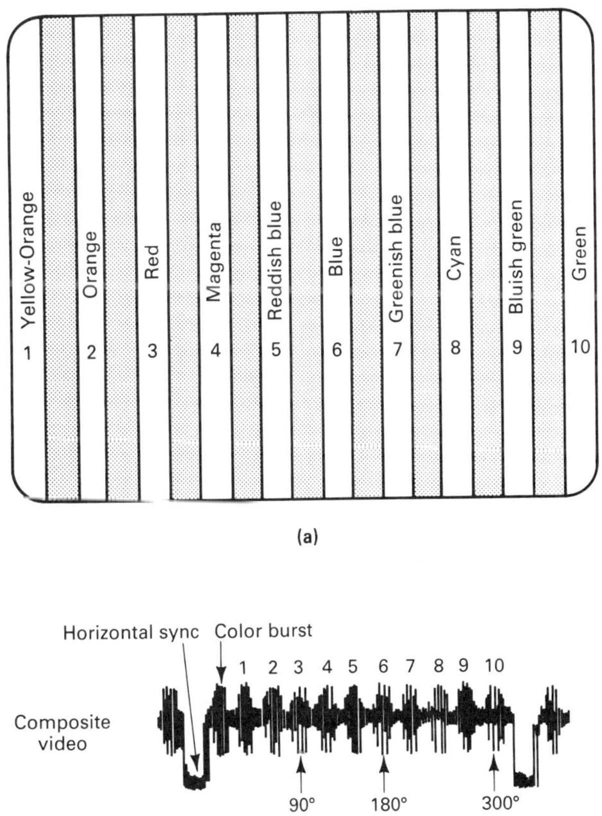


**FIG. 15-10** Generating a keyed rainbow pattern. A bar pattern is the fastest way to diagnose color problems.

ate all conditions that contribute to color development. For example, by noting which colors are missing, you can pinpoint which circuit is responsible, the particular demodulator or the phased output from the subcarrier generator. Similarly, if some colors are weak or overemphasized, you can identify the chroma output stage or CRT gun that is responsible. Incorrect colors due to misalignment can readily be detected and corrected for with an AFPC touch-up. The pattern is especially useful in adjusting color tint.

Symptoms and procedures are considered in the following paragraphs. As a quick-reference aid, refer to the troubleshooting flow drawings, as applicable (Figure 15-11).

### Symptoms and Procedures

*No BW or Color Picture.* (sound and raster okay)

***Probable cause:*** Loss of signal in some stage between the sound takeoff and the CRT (see Chapter 14).

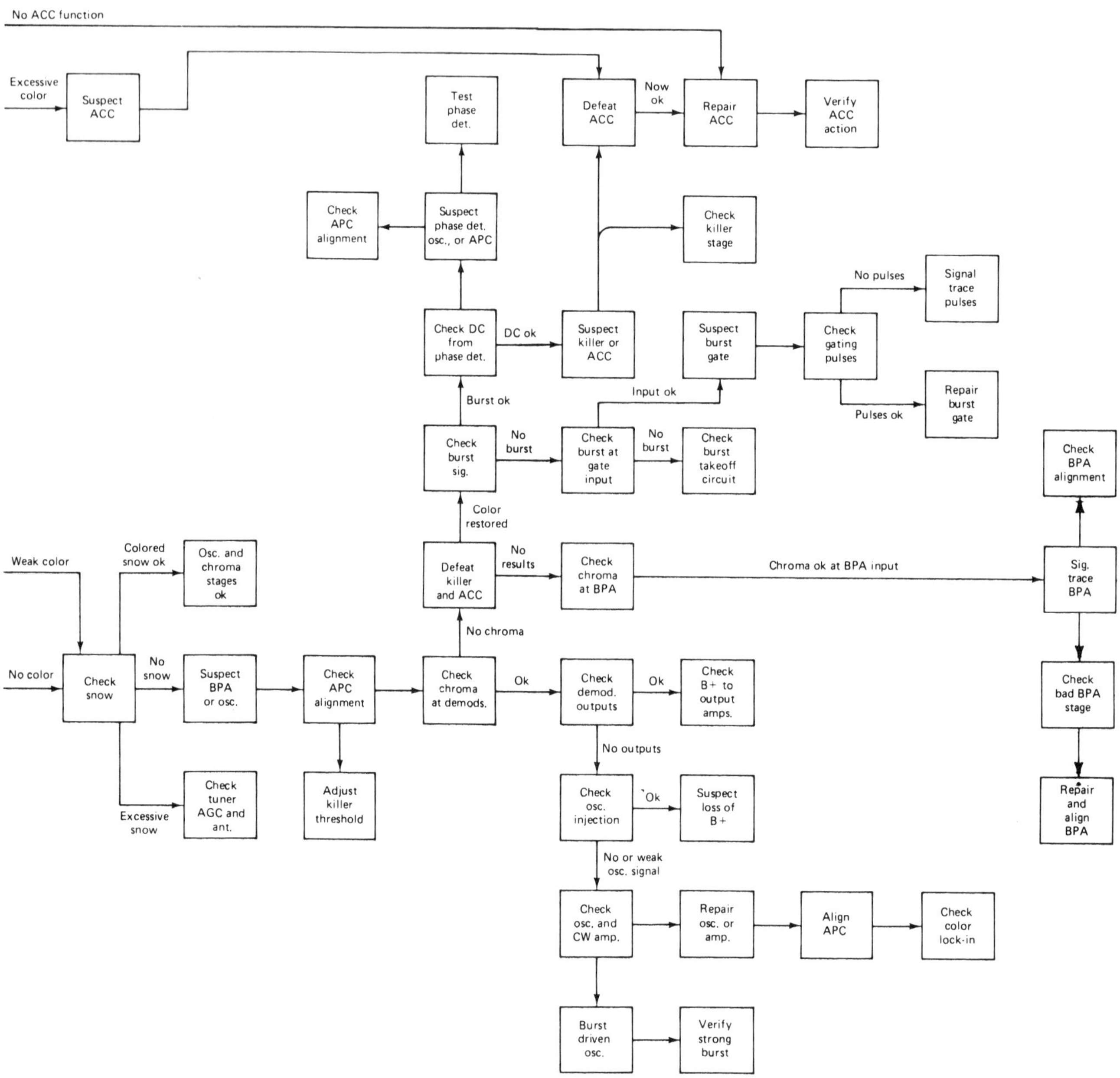


**FIG. 15-11** Troubleshooting flow drawing: color problems.

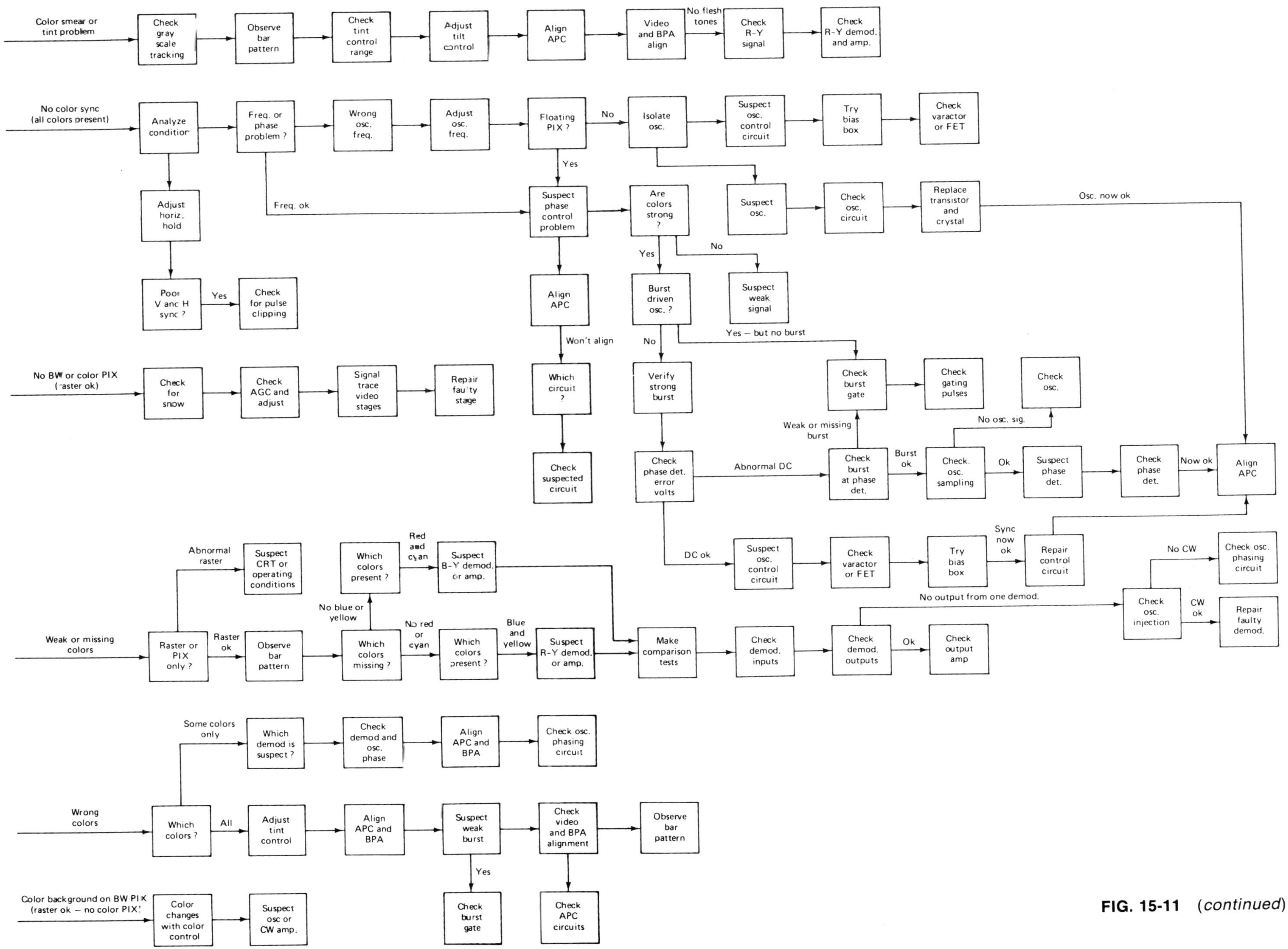


**FIG. 15-11** *(continued)*

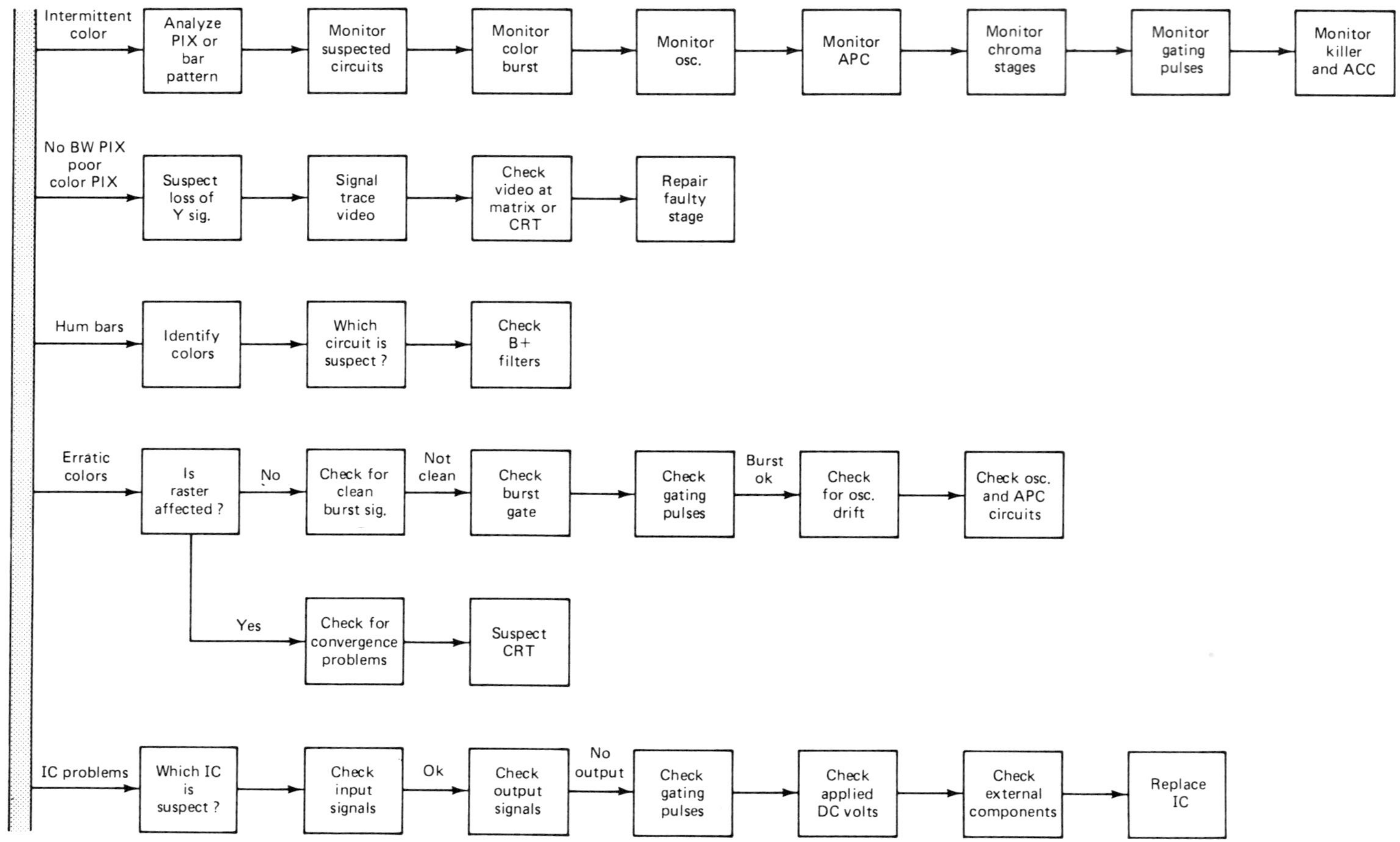


FIG. 15-11 (*continued*)

*No BW Picture; Harsh Color Picture and No Details.*

***Probable causes:*** Loss of video signal between the chroma takeoff and video output stage or the CRT; comb filter defect.

Signal trace video stages. Scope the Y signal at comb filter output and compare with schematic. If an IC is used, check input/output signals. If no output and no external defects, replace the IC.

*No Color or Weak Color Picture.* (BW Picture okay)

***Probable causes:*** There are numerous possible causes: dead subcarrier oscillator; loss of chroma signal in BPA; weak or missing burst signal from burst gate; ACC or killer stage defects; misadjusted killer threshold control; comb filter defect; misaligned video IF strip, BPA, burst gate, comb filter, or subcarrier oscillator; defective video/chroma IC; sandcastle circuit defect; demodulator defect; ACC circuit defect. *Note:* Strong confetti on the screen but no color indicates the oscillator is working.

*Killer Threshold Adjustment (If Provided).* This can be a critical adjustment, especially under weak signal conditions. Switch off the channel to obtain a "snowy" raster. Turn the control full on, then back off to the point where the "confetti" barely disappears. Check for strong color on all channels. If the control is turned up too far, the color may be okay but with color "fringing" on a BW picture because the BPA is operating wide open at all times. If the control is set too low, the color picture will be lost or weakened. Where control is ineffective, check for a killer circuit defect.

*Signal Tracing.* Signal trace the station signal from the chroma takeoff, through the demodulators and chroma output circuits, up to the CRT input. Compare waveforms with those shown on the schematic. A color bar pattern (Figure 15-10) can be helpful here. An alternative procedure calls for observing and analyzing a "daisy petal" display on a *vectorscope*. If using signal injection (Figure 15-12), tune the generator to 3.58 MHz. Monitor the signal levels by observing the bar pattern on the CRT or indications on a meter or scope. Where a signal is lost in the BPA and no defects are found, check the adjustment of the killer threshold and check to see if BPA is being enabled by the killer. If not, check for a weak or missing color burst. For problems of *weak* color, suspect a weak signal condition rather than total loss of signal.

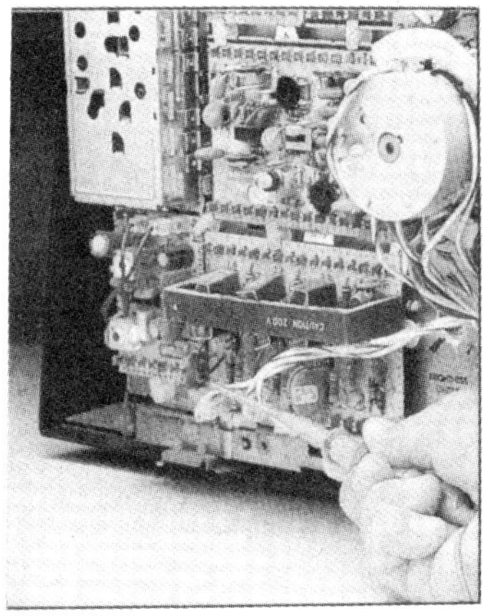

**FIG. 15-12** Signal injection at chroma output stage. Signal substitution is a good way to isolate a defect. (Courtesy of *Sencore News.*)

Where a sandcastle is used, scope check the sandcastle signal and compare with the schematic. If a missing or abnormal waveform, test for a circuit defect.

If there is a normal signal at the demodulator inputs but no chroma outputs, check for loss of B+ at this point or another defect affecting the operation of both or all three demodulators. Check for loss of the injected oscillator signals. Check for abnormal operation of the ACC circuit.

*Note:* The following procedures are general. For specific procedures, refer to the receiver service manual.

*Alignment.* If BPA or comb filter misalignment is suspected, touch-up the adjustments, including the tuned circuit at the demodulator input, and the tilt control if there is one. To avoid loading and detuning effects, inject a signal at least one stage upstream from the tuned stages, and the indicator one or more stages downstream. These adjustments are critical. Use a minimal signal level and scope or other indicator set for highest sensitivity. It is a good idea to defeat the ACC function and disable the AGC using an overide bias from an external PS. If there are any 4.5-MHz sound traps in the BPA or 3.58-MHz traps at the demodulator outputs, null them at this time.

Alternative methods of alignment are sweep alignment, as described earlier, or the use of bar sweep equipment. The procedures for bar sweep alignment can be obtained from Sencore. Video sweep modulation (VSM) is another method often used. With this method, the signal is injected at either the antenna input or some point ahead of the video IF strip to obtain an "overall" response curve. For narrowband color, the desired response is shown in Figure 15-2. In lieu of a generator marker signal (whose accuracy may be questionable), there is usually enough coupling from the 3.58-MHz oscillator to mark the center of the response. If not, connect a clip lead to the oscillator and bring it near the tuned circuits. Where problems persist, check for possible misalignment of the video IF strip. If an IC is used and no external defects, replace it.

For problems associated with the subcarrier oscillator and color sync stages, including AFPC alignment, refer to Chapter 16.

*Some Colors Missing from Picture.* (raster and BW picture okay)

***Probable causes:*** One demodulator defective or not receiving CW signal of proper phase from the oscillator; a defect in one of three chroma output stages, where such a defect does not affect the CRT input voltages. (*Note:* Since the raster and BW picture are normal, there is no reason to suspect a bad CRT or improper setup adjustments.)

From the color mixing chart (Table 15-1), determine which colors are missing, then troubleshoot the corresponding demodulator or output amplifier. A transistor breakdown is the most common cause. For an output stage defect, also look for heat-damaged resistors. For oscillator phasing problems, refer to Chapter 16.

*Some Colors Weak.* (normal raster)

***Probable causes:*** Low output from one demodulator or one output stage, as often caused by transistor *leakage;* one oscillator output weak as from a phasing network defect; misalignment of video IF strip or BPA.

From the color mixture chart, determine which circuit to suspect. Scope check and compare the outputs from demodulators and output amplifiers. Concentrate on a circuit with low output. Compare the voltage levels of the two- or three-oscillator outputs. Their amplitudes should be nearly equal. Check the alignment of the video strip and BPA. When suspect, make touch-up adjustments only as necessary and as a last step.

***TABLE 15-1***

Color mixing

| *Color Mixture* | *Color Obtained* |
|---|---|
| R + G | Yellow |
| R + B | Purple |
| G + B | Cyan |
| R + G + B | White or gray |
| R + yellow | Reddish yellow (orange) |
| R + purple | Reddish purple (magenta or brown) |
| R + cyan | Deep violet |
| G + yellow | Yellowish green |
| G + purple | Bluish green (turquoise) |
| G + cyan | Greenish blue |
| B + yellow | Bluish green |
| B + purple | Deep purple |
| B + cyan | Light purple |
| R + white | Pink |
| G + white | Pale green |
| B + white | Light blue |

*Wrong Colors.* (raster and BW picture okay)

***Probable causes:*** Defect in one demodulator or one output stage; oscillator phasing error; misaligned BPA, comb filter, or tilt control at chroma takeoff; ATC circuit defect.

Adjust tint control while observing skin tones. If conditions improve somewhat, an AFPC alignment is probably required (see Chapter 16). Check operation of the ATC circuit. If a color bar generator is used, check for the presence of all colors and their relative positions on the bar pattern.

If all colors are wrong, check the phasing of both outputs of oscillator. If only some colors are wrong, suspect the corresponding oscillator phase or demodulator. Scope check the burst signal and compare with the schematic. Check the alignment of the burst tuned circuits. If problems persist, check alignment of the chroma takeoff circuits and the BPA. Adjust only as necessary.

*Excessive Color*

***Probable causes:*** ACC circuit defect; video IF misalignment.

Try backing off on the killer threshold control if provided. Scope signal levels through the chroma stages and compare with schematic. A likely suspect is the ACC circuit if the BPA gain is excessive. If the IF strip is too sharply peaked, the chroma markers may be too high on the response curve.

*Fuzzy Indistinct Colors.* (raster and BW picture okay)

***Probable causes:*** Misalignment of comb filter, BPA, or IF strip; misadjusted tilt control at chroma takeoff.

Check alignment of the tuned circuits and adjust as needed. Make sure that the color markers are correctly positioned on the IF and BPA response curves. Critically adjust the tilt control. Where improper CRT setup adjustments are suspected, refer to Chapter 17.

*920-kHz Beat Interference.* (grainy lines on the picture)

***Probable causes:*** Misalignment of video IF strip, BPA, or traps; defective ceramic filter in chroma stages.

This kind of interference is caused by the beat between the 4.5-MHz sound IF carrier and the 3.58-MHz subcarrier oscillator. Check to see that the 41.25-MHz sound IF carrier is not too high on the overall IF response curve. Check the BPA alignment. Critically adjust all tuned traps. If the ceramic filter is suspect, replace it.

*Colored Hum Bar on Picture.* (raster okay)

***Probable cause:*** Poor filtering of dc supply to chroma stages.

Do not mistake this for poor color sync. Note the color of the hum bar and check for ripple on dc feeding the corresponding color circuits.

*Intermittent Color.* (BW picture okay)

***Probable causes:*** *Any* abnormal condition or defect that can cause loss of color can be intermittent (a common problem).

Monitor all chroma checkpoints, including the burst gate and oscillator while watching for the condition to develop. Check for poor soldering on chroma PCBs. If difficult to pinpoint the cause, localize the defect and replace any components that are suspect. Intermittent ICs are quite common. A weak color burst is another possibility, especially where a burst-driven oscillator is used. If nothing concrete is discovered, give the set a prolonged burn-in bench check while making every effort to force it to act up.

## QUESTIONS

1. State two ways of separating video and chroma at the chroma takeoff.
2. Why is it necessary to drive all three guns of the CRT with color signals to obtain a BW picture?
3. Define (a) a primary color; (b) a complementary color.
4. Explain broadband and narrowband color.
5. Explain the purpose of the subcarrier generator.
6. How do demodulators distinguish between the I and Q signals?
7. Explain the difference between the input and output signals of a demodulator.
8. Why is it desirable to disable the BPA when receiving a monochrome program?
9. Chroma frequencies up to 1.5 MHz are transmitted for the I sideband, yet most receivers only use frequencies up to 0.5 MHz. Explain.
10. How is the color green and its complementaries produced since no green signal is transmitted?
11. What is the essential difference between the various kinds of demodulators?
12. Why is the bandpass of the BPA limited to 1 MHz?
13. Briefly explain how a BW picture is developed on a color set.
14. Briefly explain how a color picture is developed.
15. Explain CRT matrixing and pre-CRT matrixing.
16. Describe two functions of the Y signal in the development of a color picture.
17. What is a fully saturated color?
18. To obtain proper colors, the phase of the subcarrier oscillator outputs must be controlled precisely. How is it done?
19. A bright "uncontaminated" raster is essential to the development of a normal BW or color picture. A good color-free BW picture is prerequisite to obtaining a good color picture. Explain why in each case.
20. What is meant by high and low-level demodulation?
21. Explain how proper alignment of the BPA and chroma takeoff circuits compensates for chroma roll-off in the video IF strip.
22. Explain why a dead subcarrier oscillator causes loss of color.

# 16 Chroma switching and color sync

The block diagram of Figure 15-1 shows the interrelationship between all chroma processing stages. As described in Chapter 15, the blocks enclosed at the top of the drawing develop the various color signals used to drive the CRT. The color sync stages are shown at the bottom, and the chroma switching and ACC stages are shown near the middle of the drawing. In this chapter we are concerned only with the switching and synchronizing functions (not to be confused with beam deflection sync).

## 16-1 COLOR SYNC AND SWITCHING STAGE FUNCTIONS

The hue of a color is determined by the instantaneous phase relationship between the subcarrier oscillator and the chroma sidebands. To obtain the correct colors, the subcarrier oscillator must be precisely synchronized with its counterpart at the station. This is accomplished with the color burst, an 8- to 10-cycle sampling of the station subcarrier signal. A color burst is part of the composite video signal received, where it exists on the back porch of each horizontal blanking pulse (Figure 1-6). The subcarrier itself is not transmitted.

As shown in Figure 15-1, the chroma signal is separated from the video (chrominance) signal by a comb filter or a tuned circuit with a narrow bandpass. The video signal is amplified, then matrixed at some downstream point with the chroma signal, where it serves two purposes; producing fine picture details (that are not reproduced in color), and restoring the brightness component to the colors. Depending on the set, matrixing may take place at one of three alternate points as indicated on the drawing.

The chroma signal reaches the CRT by a separate route, via the bandpass amplifier stages, the demodulators, and the output amplifiers as shown. At the chroma takeoff point, the chroma signal, sync, and blanking pulses are also fed to the burst gate. Its primary function is to remove everything except the color burst and supply a "clean" amplified burst to the subcarrier phase detector, which in turn controls the subcarrier oscillator.

As explained earlier, an unmodulated (CW) "carrier" signal is required for the chroma demodulation process. This signal is furnished by the subcarrier oscillator (sometimes refered to as a "generator"). Each demodulator requires a signal of a specific phase angle as described earlier. This is accomplished with a simple *RC* phase-shifting network. The manually controlled pot shown on the diagram enables the user to vary the phase of the signal and the tint of the colors to suit his or her preference. The ATC (automatic tint control) block does just what its name implies. Note the four alternate locations for a tint control.

The subcarrier phase detector compares the frequency and phase of the generated subcarrier with that of the color burst, which corresponds to the station signal. If frequency and phase are correct, the proper colors will be produced at the correct places on the CRT image. If there is a frequency or phase error, a dc correction voltage is developed to speed up or slow down the oscillator until color sync is restored. All the sync-related stages contain tuned circuits whose adjustments are crucial. They are commonly referred to as the AFPC (automatic frequency and phase control) circuits.

A frequency error results in complete loss of color sync. A large phase error produces wrong colors and floating bars called the *barber-pole effect*. A small phase shift alters the tint. Loss of the phased input to one of the demodulators causes the colors produced by that modulator to be missing from the image. With a dead oscillator, of course, you get no color since its signal is needed to turn on the demodulators.

The burst signal also controls a switching function, to enable the BPA to pass the chroma signal when receiving a color program, and to disable it when receiving a monochrome telecast. The object here is to prevent degradation of a BW picture by interference generated in the chroma stages. When the presence of a color burst is sensed, a phase detector develops a dc voltage that is applied to the killer stage. The killer circuit, in turn, uses this voltage to switch on the BPA. If there is no burst, the BPA is switched off. The killer is gated by the horizontal sweep so that it conducts only for the duration of the horizontal retrace. The BPA and the burst gate are similarly enabled and disabled by gating pulses for the same reason. Note that the killer has a threshold control, a manual service adjustment to establish the level at which the killer takes control.

The burst signal serves one additional purpose, automatic color control (ACC). The ACC block translates the amplitude of the burst into a dc voltage for controlling the gain of the BPA and hence the degree of color saturation. When a monochrome set is receiving a color program and having no color-processing circuits, it simply ignores the color burst and the chroma signals, to produce a picture only in BW.

## 16-2 SUBCARRIER OSCILLATOR

There are three kinds of circuits in common use: (1) basic feedback oscillator, (2) burst-driven oscillator, and (3) crystal ringing subcarrier generator. Although different in operation, they all have a common purpose—to develop a stable 3.58-MHz CW signal to control the conductance of the color demodulators. For frequency stability, each type of oscillator is crystal controlled. Phasing is controlled by the AFPC circuits in conjunction with the color burst.

### Oscillating Crystals

An oscillating crystal as used in TV sets, VCRs, and monitors consists of a thin wafer of quartz sandwiched between two metal plates which serve as terminals. When connected into an RF-generating circuit, the crystal is made to vibrate at the RF frequency, and in so doing, stabilizes the frequency to a high degree. Its ability to oscillate is called the *piezoelectric effect*. The natural vibratory rate of a crystal depends on several factors, particularly its thickness. The thinner the crystal, the higher the frequency. Extremely high frequencies are controlled with frequency-multiplying circuits or harmonics of the crystal frequency. Without such control, an oscillator is said to be *free-running* and subject to frequency drift. The crystal in a subcarrier oscillator operates at its fundamental frequency of 3.58 MHz. Crystals are hermetically sealed in a small packet and seldom give trouble.

### Basic Subcarrier Oscillator

Figure 16-1a shows a typical circuit. Oscillations are developed and sustained with positive feedback from voltage developed across R731 in the emitter circuit, through C727 to the transistor base. The emitter circuit resistors provide a small amount of forward bias for oscillator startup. The CW amplifier increases the weak oscillations to about 10 V p-p, the amount required by the demodulators. The oscillator frequency is established by the varactor and crystal and resonated by a tuned transformer at the amplifier output. The crystal (as part of the AFC control circuit) takes over its stabilizing function when the oscillator is tuned within a few cycles of its natural frequency. More on this later.

### Burst-Driven Oscillator

The burst-driven oscillator (Figure 16-1b) is also known as an *injection locked oscillator*. Unlike the circuit just described, this oscillator is crystal controlled *only* when a color burst is received; at other times it is free running. A *Colpitts circuit* is used where feedback voltage is developed from a capacitive voltage divider in the tuned circuit (C270 and C560) that establishes the frequency. This oscillator produces sufficient voltage to drive the demodulators without additional amplification.

When a color burst is received, it causes the

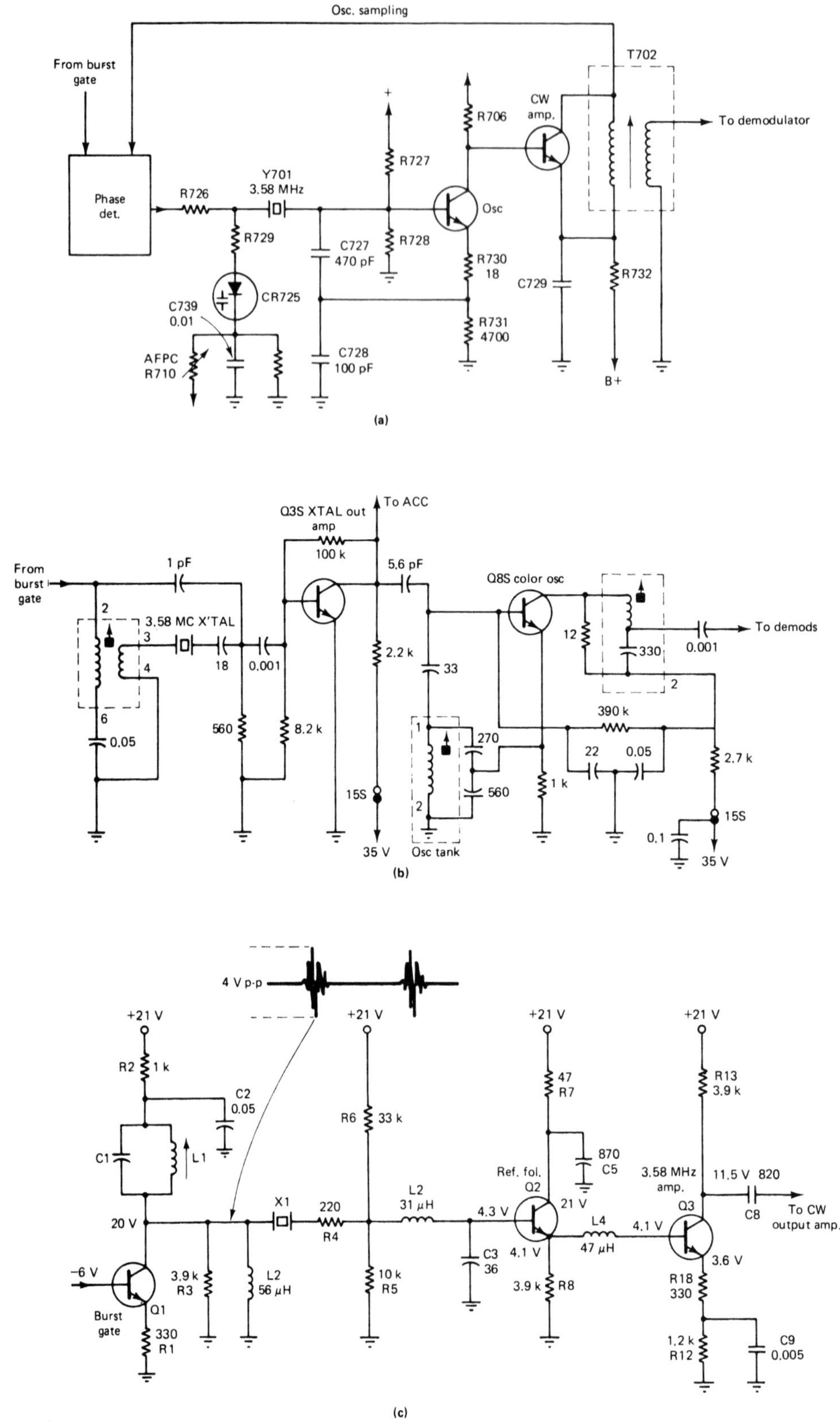


**FIG. 16-1** Subcarrier generating and control circuits.

crystal to ring or vibrate at a multiple of its natural resonant frequency, thus stabilizing the oscillator in both frequency and phase. The ringing voltage is amplified by Q38 before being applied to the oscillator. An advantage of this circuit is that there is no need for additional AFPC control. It has one shortcoming, however, a tendency to be unstable under weak or noisy receiving conditions due to its dependence on the strength of the color burst.

### Crystal Ringing Subcarrier Generator

A typical crystal ringing circuit is shown in Figure 16-1c. This is not an oscillator per se, hence the change in name. The received color burst causes the crystal to ring at the subcarrier frequency. Because of its high *Q,* the crystal continues to oscillate and produce a voltage during the interval *between color bursts* (i.e., during horizontal retrace periods). Because of weak oscillations, at least two stages of amplification are needed to drive the demodulators. The only tuned circuit is the one at the burst gate output. No color killer is required with this circuit. When receiving BW, the absence of a burst signal means a dead oscillator, and without it, there can be no output from the demodulators and no interference to pass on to the CRT. Although a weak or missing burst creates problems, with this circuit there can be no loss of color *sync* because there is no possibility of frequency drift.

## 16-3 PHASE SHIFTING AND COLOR VECTORS

At the station, a different oscillator phase was required by each modulator to produce the I and Q sideband frequencies. Similarly, at the receiver, each demodulator requires a different phase to produce outputs corresponding with two or three of the primary colors. As shown in Figure 15-1, phase shifting takes place between the output of the subcarrier generator and the CW inputs to the demodulators. It is accomplished with simple LCR networks. Adding inductance in a circuit causes the current to lag the voltage. The opposite is true for capacitance. The angle of lead or lag depends on component values. A transformer may also be used to obtain a 180° shift between the opposite ends of its winding.

The signal feeding each demodulator must be phase shifted by a different and specific amount. Thus, when the oscillator is synchronized to the burst signal (by the AFPC circuitry), each demodulator is made to conduct at slightly different times relative to the color burst, and by different amounts, to demodulate and recover signals corresponding with a particular color and its complementaries. Stated differently, as each demodulator samples the chroma input, it is turned on and off and its output made to vary in accordance with the ever-changing amplitude and polarity of the subcarrier signal as it cycles through 360°. Component values in phase networks are critical, and any defects will have an adverse effect on the colors produced by the associated demodulator.

Although a receiver can employ the same phase angles used by the station, most sets are designed for different angles to emphasize certain color tints or to compensate for variations of light-producing efficiencies of the CRT screen phosphors. Note the phase angles for the different types of demodulators shown in Figure 15-3. In most cases they are chosen to emphasize red or near-red to obtain good skin tones.

## 16-4 BURST GATE

The purpose of the burst gate (sometimes called an amplifier) is to develop a strong, "clean" color burst to feed the subcarrier phase detector. The 8 to 10 cycles of each burst are used by the AFPC system to control the subcarrier oscillator in both frequency *and phase*. The signal at the gate input consists of chroma information, blanking, and sync pulses. The color burst rides on the back porch of each horizontal blanking pulse. To achieve good color sync, a strong "noise-free" burst is *essential*. Noise bursts and other interference can upset color sync. Unwanted signals are rejected in two ways: by permitting the transistor to conduct for only brief periods (the duration of the burst signal) and by restricting the bandpass.

The burst transistor is triggered into conduction by sharply spiked horizontal sweep pulses, usually obtained from the flyback transformer. Bandpass is limited to about 0.5 MHz by a tuned transformer that couples the color burst from the burst gate to the AFPC circuitry. The transformer is critically tuned to 3.58 MHz.

A typical circuit is shown in Figure 16-2. Under no-signal conditions, the transistor is biased beyond cutoff by resistors in the base and emitter circuits. It is pulsed into conduction only when a burst signal is received. Note the waveforms at the gate input —

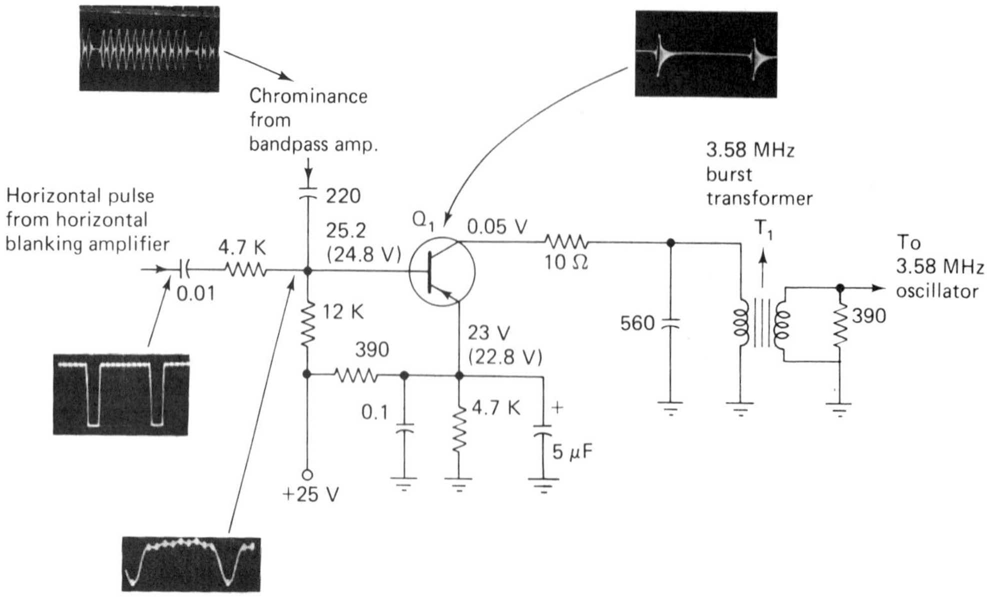


**FIG. 16-2** Typical burst gate. One requirement for good color sync is a strong, noise-free color burst.

the chroma and sync pulses which must be rejected. Also note the clean color burst at the gate output.

## 16-5 COLOR KILLER

This stage senses the presence of a color burst to enable the BPA during reception of a color program. For monochrome reception (when there is no color burst), the killer disables the BPA to prevent interference from reaching the CRT via the chroma stages. The circuit in Figure 16-3 shows how a dc voltage developed by the phase detector controls the killer transistor, which in turn controls the BPA. Note the threshold control, which establishes the level at which the transistor conducts and performs its switching function. The adjustment procedure is described in Chapter 15.

## 16-6 AUTOMATIC COLOR CONTROL

The automatic color control (ACC) circuit helps to maintain a uniform level of color in compensation for variations in the strength of the signal received. Its operation can be compared to that of AGC, raising the color level on weak signals and lowering it on the strong signals. As shown in Figure 15-1, it monitors the color burst from the burst gate, translating changes in amplitude into dc bias control of the gain of the BPA. As with AGC, some circuits incorporate a delay function to prevent color variations on very weak signals.

## 16-7 SUBCARRIER OSCILLATOR CONTROL

It is not enough that the oscillator generate the correct frequency; it must also be locked in phase with the subcarrier generator at the station. Figure 16-1 shows different systems of control.

### Varactor Control

With varactor control (Figure 16-1a), the color burst from the burst gate is applied to a conventional two-diode phase detector along with a sampling of the 3.58-MHz signal developed by the oscillator. The high-$Q$ crystal and the varactor diode function together as a resonant circuit, the crystal controlling frequency, and the varactor, the oscillator phase, in the same manner as described for controlling a horizontal sweep oscillator (Chapter 8). Phase variations are sensed by the phase detector to produce a small dc error voltage. This dc voltage creates small simulated capacity variations in the varactor to force the oscillator back into step. The AFPC pot establishes the correct amount of reverse bias for optimum control.

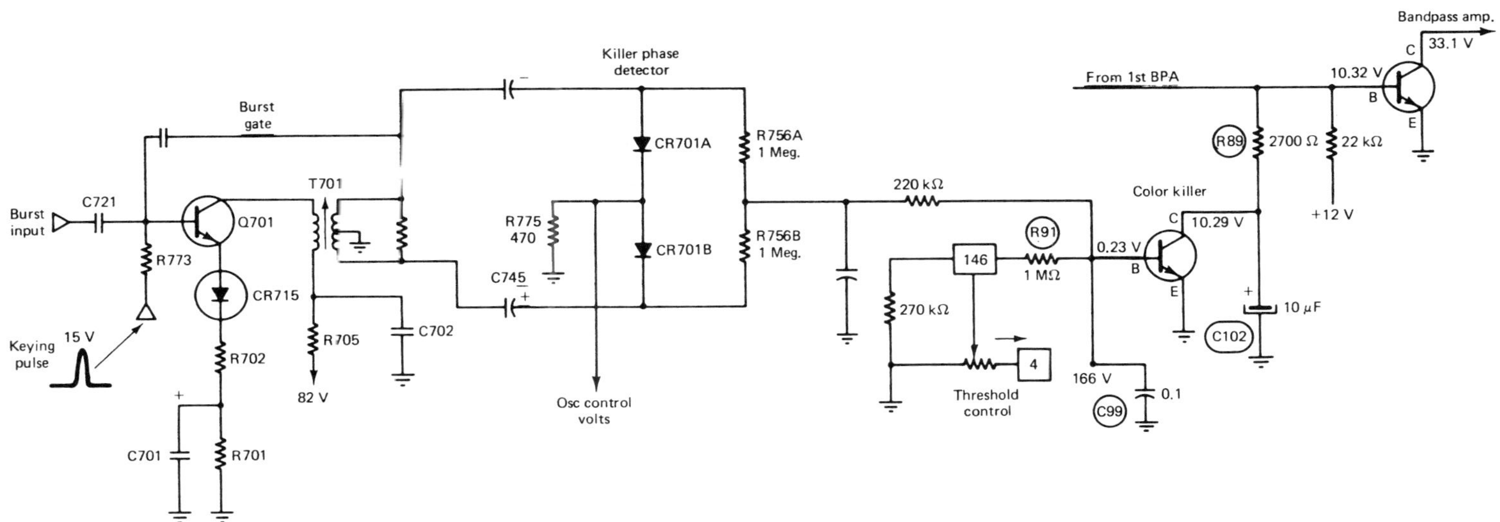


**FIG. 16-3** Color killer and chroma switching. The chroma (BPA) is switched off by the killer in the absence of a color burst.

### Burst-Driven Oscillator Control

In the burst-driven oscillator configuration (Figure 16-1b), the color burst is amplified by the step-up of the tuned circuit to make the crystal ring at the correct frequency and phase. No additional AFPC circuits are required. Color sync, however, is totally dependent on the strength of the burst signal, with possible loss of stability in weak signal areas.

### Crystal-Ringing Generator Control

With crystal-ringing generator control (Figure 16-1c), no phase detector or varactor is required. Color sync is automatically correct at all times because the color burst itself takes the place of the subcarrier signal. As with the circuit described previously, sync stability is dependent on a strong signal.

For optimum color sync, the tuned circuits of *all* AFPC systems must be aligned accurately and critically. This includes those in the burst gate, the phase detector, and the oscillator, AFPC alignment procedures are presented later under troubleshooting.

## 16-8 FOLDOUT SCHEMATIC

Most chroma and synchronizing functions are performed by IC501. From the chroma takeoff point (pin 7), the signal goes through C501 to a tuned circuit (L501/C502) resonant to 3.58 MHz with a bandpass of 0.5 MHz, then back to the IC at pin 9, to be amplified by the first and second amplifiers. The gain of the first amplifier is controlled by ACC action. The color control controls the gain of the second amplifier. The ACC detector provides bias for the first amplifier in accordance with signal strength. Further processing of the chroma signal was described in Chapter 15.

The color control (VR501) varies the amount of chroma signal to the demodulators. Tint control is accomplished at pin 8 by VR507. The dc voltage at pin 8 controls the phase of the subcarrier oscillator signal. The crystal (X555) connects to the oscillator at pins 16 and 17. The color killer connection at pin 13 provides a voltage to cut off the second chroma amplifier during BW reception.

The color oscillator is locked into the phase of the burst signal by the APC circuit. The APC circuit compares the VCO output and burst phase to produce the 3.58-MHz subcarrier and provides PLL control of the VCO by the comparator output. (The PLL function is described in Chapter 12.) The burst signal is extracted from the demodulator input of pin 14. An APC loop filter connects to pin 15. When no color signal is received, the chroma amplifier is cut off by a bias voltage applied from the color killer (CK) circuit.

## 16-9 TROUBLESHOOTING AND REPAIR

Color sync and switching problems, with appropriate procedures, are described in Chapter 15. Also refer to the troubleshooting flow drawings of Figure 15-11.

### AFPC Alignment

Proper alignment of all tuned circuits associated with the burst gate, the subcarrier oscillator, and its AFC circuits is crucial to the development of a good color picture. This is not to be confused with CRT setup adjustments (Chapter 17) or alignment of the chroma signal stages (Chapter 15).

The symptoms of AFPC misalignment are many: loss of all color, loss of some colors, unstable color sync, and so on. Faced with the problem of a mediocre color picture or marginal sync, the technician is strongly advised to consider realignment, particularly when no defects can be found. It is surprising how often a few simple touch-up adjustments are all that is needed. The adjustments to be made are listed below, including a general alignment procedure. For specifics, refer to the receiver service instructions.

#### *AFPC Adjustments*

- *Burst transformer:* tuned transformer at the output of the burst gate; must resonate at 3.58 MHz to obtain maximum amplification of the color burst
- *Reactance coil:* used in some FET-type control circuits; tuned to 3.58 MHz
- *Varactor control pot:* used in some varactor control circuits for adjusting subcarrier oscillator frequency
- *Oscillator coil:* used to adjust oscillator frequency
- *Oscillator or amplifier output transformer adjustment:* tuned to 3.58 MHz for maximum drive to the demodulators
- *Tint control:* front-panel user control for altering the phase of chroma or oscillator signals relative to the color burst

*Alignment Procedures*

*Note:* An AFPC alignment is called for whenever associated components are replaced or critical circuits disturbed. All adjustments must be performed carefully and critically. Avoid damage to coils and core slugs by using *only* approved adjusting tools.

1. Tune in the best possible color picture, or inject a color bar signal and observe the pattern. Set tint control to midposition and turn up the color control.
2. Kill the burst signal by connecting a jumper between the base and emitter of the burst gate transistor. Similarly, defeat the ACC function. Connect an EVM (on a low dc range) to the ungrounded end of the oscillator phase detector load resistor. A negative or positive reading of 10 to 20 V can be expected. If no dc, the oscillator is probably dead.
3. Adjust the oscillator coil or varactor pot as applicable for a maximum dc reading. A "floating" pix or bar pattern should be observed on the screen. This indicates that the oscillator is working and close to the correct frequency. A drastic frequency error results in many color bars (the barber-pole effect). Two or three color bands indicate that the frequency is nearly correct. For proper crystal control, the free-running frequency must be within $\pm 200$ kHz of 3.58 MHz. If a floating bar display cannot be obtained, either the oscillator has a defect or it is being forced off frequency by an AFC circuit defect or an abnormal dc error voltage from the phase detector.
4. Restore the color burst by removing the jumper from the burst gate transistor. You should get an increased reading on the meter. Adjust the burst transformer for maximum indication. If removal of the jumper fails to produce an increased reading, check for a weak or missing color burst. [*Reminder:* There are two conditions that can upset the color sync: a weak or missing burst (when the oscillator frequency is okay) and an off-frequency oscillator even though the burst is okay.]
5. Kill the dc error voltage by grounding the common junction of the phase detector split-load resistors. The oscillator is now free-running and subject to frequency drift. Adjust the reactance coil or oscillator pot (as applicable) to obtain a floating picture or bar pattern with the color bands nearly vertical.
6. Remove the jumper to restore the dc error voltage. Colors should lock abruptly into sync. Check the lock-in stability by slightly misadjusting the fine tuner. Colors should lock at two or more color bands. If lock-in occurs only when close to the correct frequency as indicated by one or two bars, the sync is not too good. If removing the jumper caused a drastic change in frequency, suspect the phase detector.
7. If the color sync is still poor, check the error voltage produced by the phase detector. It should be zero for a floating picture; if not, there is an imbalance in the two diode circuits. Typical causes of this are leakage in one of the coupling capacitors, a bad diode, or the load resistors are not equal in value. Diodes and resistors should be replaced as a *matched pair*.
8. Where the error voltage seems normal and changes as the fine tuner is adjusted but the color sync is still poor, the varactor or FET control circuit is probably at fault. Check the applied operating voltages compared to the schematic. If the varactor or the FET are suspect, replace them.
9. If there is an adjustable oscillator or amplifier output transformer, connect the meter to one of the demodulators (or some convenient test point isolated from the oscillator) and adjust the coil for maximum indication. Try to increase the reading with a slight touch-up of the oscillator coil or potentiometer.
10. If warranted, and because of circuit interactions, go back and repeat all adjustments at least one more time. Check the range of the tint control. If normal skin tones are not obtained at its midsetting, make a slight touch-up of the burst transformer.
11. Restore the ACC function and check its effectiveness using the ACC defeat switch.

*Reminders:* When a tuned circuit will not adjust properly, there are two possibilities: a circuit defect or a bad coil or slug. Shorted coil turns are common and a clue is where near resonance is obtained with the slug fully entered into the coil. Check for broken or missing core slugs.

## QUESTIONS

1. Briefly explain how color sync is accomplished.
2. What is the effect on a picture when the subcarrier generator is (a) off frequency; (b) out of phase with the color burst. State why in each case.
3. What is the effect on a color picture if the subcarrier signal to one of the demodulators is (a) missing; (b) of the wrong phase?
4. Explain why a subcarrier signal is required.
5. What is the purpose of the oscillator crystal, and what trouble can be expected if it is defective?
6. Explain the purpose and functioning of the burst gate.
7. What are the indications of a dead subcarrier generator, and how would you check it?
8. Explain the purpose and functioning of a color killer.
9. What is a clean color burst?
10. Briefly explain the operation of an ACC circuit.
11. Explain the importance of proper AFPC alignment.
12. Loss of color is commonly caused by either a dead oscillator or a weak or missing color burst. Explain.
13. Name and briefly describe the operation of three types of subcarrier generators and their control functions.
14. Briefly describe how to adjust a killer threshold control.
15. Where a scope shows strong video or noise on the burst signal at the gate output, how would you proceed?
16. What is a barber pole display, and what condition does it indicate?
17. What symptoms can be expected if the killer stage is (a) inoperative; (b) conducting at all times? Explain your answers.
18. Why is a signal generator not required for AFPC alignment?
19. Explain the purpose of horizontal gating pulses and where they originate.
20. What would you suspect when performing AFPC alignment if (a) a floating picture cannot be obtained with the oscillator adjustment; (b) a floating picture is obtained but no color lock-in?
21. Where best skin color is obtained at one extreme setting of the tint control, how would you proceed?

# 17 Working with CRTs

Picture tubes used in the earliest monochrome TV sets employed ES (electrostatic) deflection, similar to that found in an oscilloscope. They were small tubes with round screens ranging from 1 to 7 inches in diameter. These quickly evolved into 10-inch EM (electromagnetic) deflection types, a system that is still in use. From then on it became a new ball game, with the public demanding bigger and bigger screens. Then along came color, and "flatter" rectangular screens to add fresh impetus, and the trend continues. At this time, 35-inch direct-view sets are becoming popular, along with a new generation of projection sets with their life-sized wall screens.

As illustrated and described in Chapter 2, there are three kinds of color CRTs used in TV sets and monitors: the so-called delta or shadow mask type, and two types of in-line tubes, including the Sony Trinitron. The latter types are now used almost exclusively. Then there is another type, the light tubes used in projection sets, which are described in Chapter 19.

Here we are concerned only with the practical aspects of CRTs and their operation, common defects, testing and restoration (rejuvenation), and replacement and setup procedures.

## 17-1 CRT OPERATING CONDITIONS

There are four essential requirements for obtaining a good picture: (1) a CRT that is in perfect condition, (2) proper CRT operating voltages, (3) proper setup adjustments, and (4) the CRT must be driven with proper signal voltages. When there is a problem, a technician must be prepared to check each condition in logical order: first, to obtain a proper raster, then a BW picture, and finally, a color picture.

## 17-2 CRT OPERATING VOLTAGES

To create electron flow in any vacuum tube, you must have a heated cathode and the proper grid bias, screen grid voltage, and plate voltage. Another essential requirement, of course, is a complete, uninterrupted *external* path for the electron flow from the plate back to the cathode. These same conditions apply to a CRT except for slight differences in terminology; plate voltage corresponds with the HV applied to a CRT, and instead of plate current we call it beam current, which amounts to the same thing. In general, most voltages applied to a color CRT are considerably greater than for a BW tube, and the larger the screen size, the greater the voltage requirements.

### Monochrome CRT Operating Voltages

*Heater Voltage.* With the exception of battery-operated portables and a few transformerless tube-type sets of yesteryear, practically all CRT heaters (filaments), including color CRTs, are supplied with 6.3 V ac. With older sets it was obtained from a 6-V winding on a power transformer or a separate filament transformer. For greater efficiency (less power consumption) modern sets heat the filament from SCAN power, a 6-V winding on the flyback transformer. With scan power, the frequency is the horizontal sweep rate.

With solid state, sound comes on at the instant of set turn-on, but you still have to wait a few seconds for the screen to light up. To shorten the time, some early models had an "instant-on" feature, where the CRT was supplied with reduced heater voltage at all times, even with the set turned off. At turn-on, the voltage was increased to normal. The system is no longer used, but modern CRTs are designed for a fairly fast warm-up time.

*Grid Bias.* As with any vacuum tube, this is the negative voltage on the control grid (G1) in reference to the cathode. Low bias, of course, causes an increase in electron flow and increased brightness. High bias retards the current and darkens the screen. Normal operating bias depends mainly on the tube size. Beam *cutoff bias* is the amount that stops current flow and produces a dark screen. Cutoff bias for a small CRT is typically about −40 V; for a large CRT it may be closer to −100 V for each gun.

Since bias is the grid voltage relative to the cathode, it may be obtained by applying a − dc voltage to the grid, a + dc voltage to the cathode, or both methods. Several circuits are shown in Figure 17-1. In circuit (a) the grid is adjustable from zero to −100 V. In circuit (b), bias is the result of positive voltage changes on the cathode. The amount of voltage variation depends on the relative values of the resistors tied to each end of the control. A +10-V cathode, for example, corresponds with a negative grid bias of −10 V. In circuit (c), a + voltage is applied to both grid and cathode. Resistor values must be such that the grid never goes positive. In circuit (d), with the video amplifier directly coupled to the CRT, the bias and brightness of the CRT are varied with variations of transistor bias. Since this is an NPN type, an increase in base voltage causes an increase in collector current, an increase in the *IR* drop across the collector resistor, thereby reducing the collector and the CRT cathode voltage and increasing the CRT beam current. The LDR (light-dependent resistor) provides automatic brightness control for variations in ambient lighting. Circuit (e) is typical of most modern sets, where the brightness control is in some video amplifier stage upstream from the CRT. With direct coupling the dc voltage changes are passed on stage by stage to the CRT. (*Suggestion:* Try to determine whether CW rotation of the control brightens or darkens the screen, and why.)

To check bias voltage on a CRT, measure between grid and cathode, noting minimum and maximum readings as the control is varied to both extremes. If there is a bias problem (too little or too much), the trouble may be with either the grid or the cathode circuit. Check these voltages in reference to ground while comparing with schematic. Where control is in a dc-coupled amplifier stage, refer to troubleshooting procedures later in the chapter.

*Screen Grid Voltage.* Typical voltage for a BW CRT is around +200 V. It is measured in reference to ground.

*Focus Voltage.* For a typical BW tube it is anywhere from +200 to 400 V. Most modern CRTs are of the "fixed focus" type and no control is required.

*HV.* With small-screen CRTs it may be as low as 10 kV; with larger tubes, about twice that amount.

### Color CRT Operating Voltages

Except for small CRTs, voltages are considerably higher than for BW tubes in order to obtain adequate brightness. All adjustments are made as part of the CRT set-up procedures to be described later.

*Heater Voltage.* This is 6.3 V ac as for BW tubes, but because of the three internally connected heaters, and for optimum emission, heater current is considerably higher. Most sets now use scan power for the heaters.

*Grid Bias.* Early-model sets employed the same circuits for developing bias as for BW tubes. Most modern sets apply a fixed amount of + dc to both grids and cathodes, and brightness is controlled from one of the upstream dc-coupled video amplifier stages. For normal brightness, typical grid-to-cathode bias for each of the guns is around −20 V. Beam current cutoff occurs at about 50 V, although it may be adjustable up to 100 V or more (beyond cutoff). Depending on the tube type, each of the three guns are adjusted simultaneously or individually.

*Screen Grid Voltage.* This is slightly higher than for a BW tube. Depending on the CRT, the grids

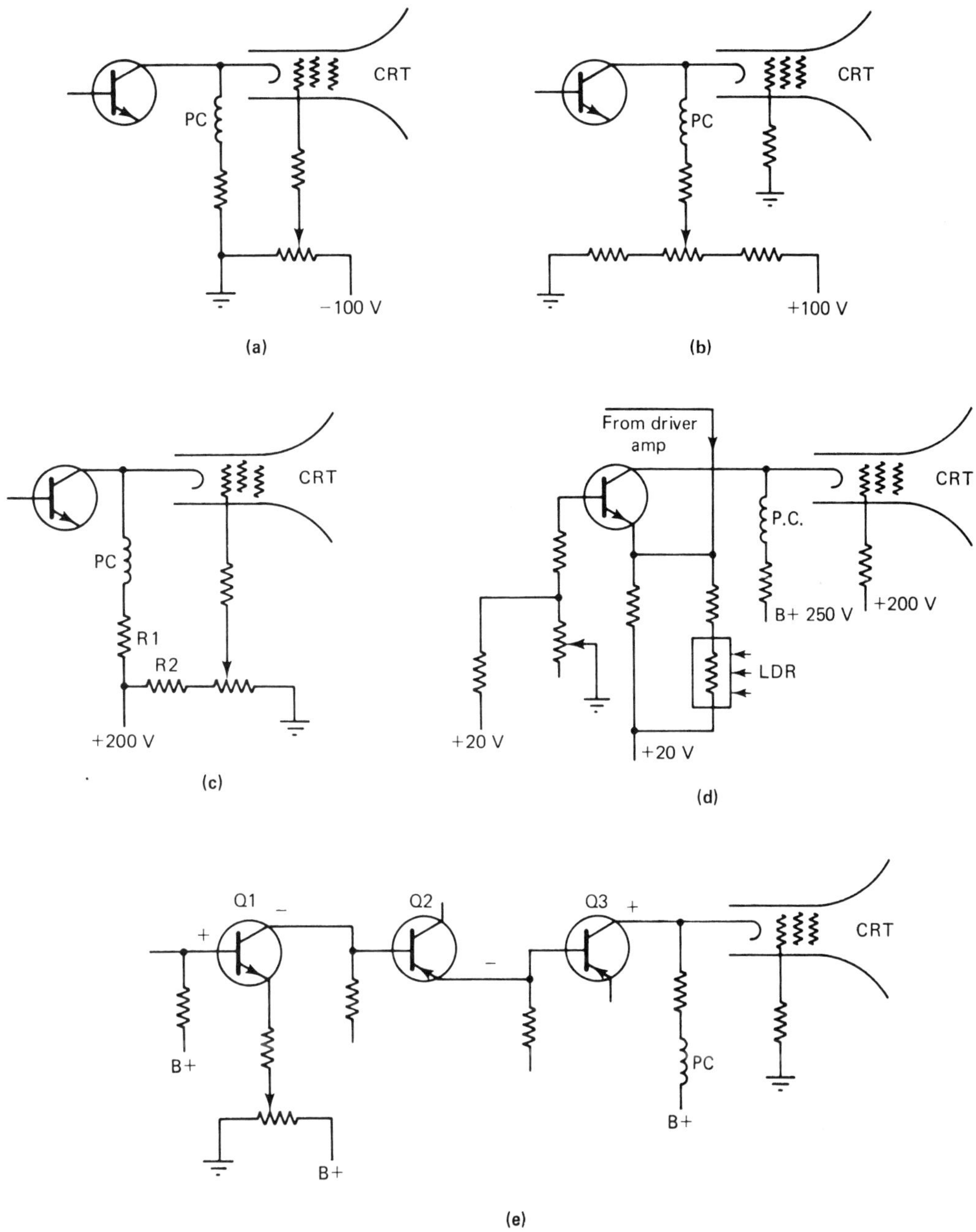


**FIG. 17-1** CRT bias and brightness controls. Bias is the potential difference between the grid and cathode voltages. The higher reading of the two establishes the polarity.

may be supplied separately or together. Most sets individually vary the voltage on each of the three grids.

*Focus Voltage.* This is anywhere from 1500 V to as much as 6 kV, and is adjustable with the focus control. Focus voltage may be obtained from B-boost, a separate rectifier, or what is currently more common, from the HV supply using a suitable voltage-dividing network.

*HV.* For small tubes, this is as low as 10 kV; for some large CRTs, as much as 50 kV. Sounds dangerous and it can be, but the current (as with a car ignition system), is minimal. HV is measured using a special well-insulated probe containing a high-megohm dropping resistor and a grounding wire.

## 17-3 FOLDOUT SCHEMATIC

One side of the CRT heater circuit is ground. With some sets it ties onto some B+ point to reduce the chance of internal arcing. Heater voltage is supplied from the HOT via pin 3. The cathodes get their voltage from the collectors of the three video output transistors, via the base pins 3, 4, and 5. The three control grids have a common ground connection. The three screen grids also have a common connection and are supplied with adjustable B+ from the screen control pot. The common focus grids are supplied with adjustable B+ from the focus control. The screen and focus grids are both supplied from an internal tap on the integrated HOT. As is common practice, each grid and cathode are protected against arc-over with a *spark gap* (SG). The CRT uses 18 kV of HV (with the control set for full brightness). Since regulation is never 100%, the voltage tends to vary somewhat between no load and full load as the brightness control is varied. Two series-connected brightness controls connected to the +12-V bus feed a low adjustable voltage to the video amplifiers via pin 40 of IC501.

With the (G1) grids grounded, signals are applied individually from the video output transistors to the three cathodes. Signal levels are adjusted with the RGB drive controls in the transistors' emitter circuits. Note that this set does not require convergence coils or circuitry; this function is performed by the adjustable ring magnets on the CRT neck (see Figure 17-5).

## 17-4 SERVICE ADJUSTERS AND CONTROLS

User controls are listed in Chapter 2. Service adjusters are listed and described in Table 17-1.

***TABLE 17-1***

Servicing adjusters

| *Control or Adjuster* | *Function* | *Where Used* |
|---|---|---|
| Master brightness (kine bias) | Establishes range of user brightness control | CRT grid/cathode circuit or video amplifier |
| CRT screen grid control(s) | Adjusts screen grid voltage(s) | Screen grid circuits |
| Drive controls | Adjust levels of Y or RGB signals driving the three guns | CRT cathode or control grid circuits |
| Purity ring | Used to obtain pure RGB color fields | On neck of CRT |
| Static convergence adjusters (blue lateral and RGB static convergence adjusters) | For converging beams at center areas of screen | Part of convergence assembly on CRT neck |
| Dynamic convergence controls | For converging beams at edges of screen | On a convergence board or the CRT socket assembly |
| Pincushion adjusters | Align all raster edges with mask opening | Supplied from vertical and horizontal sweep circuits |
| Raster centering | Centers raster vertically and horizontally | Dc current is injected into yoke coils |
| Yoke adjustments | For raster tilt and longitudinal positioning when adjusting purity | Screw-type locking adjustments on yoke support |
| Focus control | Adjusts beam focus | Voltage usually provided by the HV PS |
| HV control | Adjusts for correct amount of HV | In HV circuit; new model sets do not have it |

## 17-5 X-RAY RADIATION HAZARD

Voltages higher than 20 kV produce potentially harmful x-rays under conditions of close and sustained exposure. Certain breakdowns in the horizontal output circuits can cause the HV to increase beyond safe limits. To prevent this, all large-screen sets today incorporate a protective automatic shutdown circuit (Chapter 11). Never defeat its purpose, and when servicing, always check the HV compared to the specified amount. If excessive, take corrective measures. This includes adjusting the HV control if one is provided. A malfunctioning HV regulator (in the primary P.S.) is a common cause of excessive HV.

## 17-6 HV REGULATION

As described in Chapter 6 for LV regulation, poor HV regulation has similar causes, creating raster and pix problems. The two most common symptoms are blooming and poor focus. The *deflection sensitivity* of a CRT depends somewhat on the amount of HV; the lower the HV, the greater the sweep, and vice versa. The amount of HV at the CRT ultor contact tends to vary as the brightness and screen controls are adjusted. With no load on the PS (no beam current and a dark screen) the HV is maximum. At full brightness (maximum load), the beam current develops an internal *IR* voltage drop across the HOT and rectifier(s), reducing the voltage at the CRT by that amount. Up to a 1-kV variation is considered normal in some cases, but more than that causes defocusing and blooming, a condition where the raster grows larger and dimmer as the brightness and color controls are turned up. Modern sets regulate the HV by regulating the amount of B+ applied to the horizontal output transistor.

## 17-7 COLOR CRT SYSTEM OPERATION

There are a number of external components, subsystems, and functions all working together to produce a raster: to be specific, *three* single-color *overlapping* rasters. The components are listed in Chapter 2. They are described further below.

### Deflection Yoke

The deflection yoke is located on the tube neck close against the tube flare, it produces the EM flux to sweep the beam vertically and horizontally.

### Convergence Yoke Assembly

The conversion yoke assembly (for a delta CRT; not used with Trinitron-type CRT) consists of three pairs of coils located on the tube neck, with the coils positioned over internal pole pieces of the corresponding gun elements (Figure 17-2). One of each pair of coils is supplied with a parabolic waveform sampling of the vertical sweep circuit. The other three coils are driven from the horizontal sweep circuit. The EM flux from the coils adds to or subtracts from the flux produced by the deflection yoke to aim the three beams precisely for proper convergence at the outer edges of the screen. This is called *dynamic convergence*. Numerous controls are provided to vary the shape and amplitudes of the parabolic waveforms. Adjustment of these controls, which is extremely critical, is described later.

Included as part of the assembly are three adjustable magnets. These are *static adjusters* for converging the beams at the center areas of the screen. Their adjustment is depicted in Figure 17-5. Note the direction of beam movement with each adjuster. An additional adjuster on the tube neck is called the *blue lateral adjuster*. It moves the blue beam sideways.

Another type of convergence unit is shown in Figure 17-3.

Figure 17-4 shows the type of convergence assembly used with some early-model GE sets using an in-line CRT. Note that only the red and blue beams are affected. Most modern sets now use the system shown in Figure 17-5. There are a number of rotatable ring magnets positioned on the tube neck as shown. Each has a specific function and is adjusted individually. Note the absence of convergence coils. Dynamic convergence is adjusted simply by tilting the yoke slightly with wedges as shown.

The Trinitron tube (Figure 17-6) uses a different system. Static convergence for the horizontal is obtained by varying the dc applied to internal ES convergence plates. Dynamic convergence is accomplished by rotating the twist coil on the tube neck (see Figure 2-9).

### Purity Ring

The purity ring is a two-section ring magnet on the aft end of the tube neck. It is adjusted to obtain a pure, single-color raster during the setup procedures.

### Pincushion Correction

As explained earlier, the raster on a large CRT tends to bow inward or outward creating a distorted image. This is prevented by introducing parabolic vertical and horizontal waveforms into the yoke coils, much the same as for dynamic convergence. Vertical deflection is increased for the middle of each horizontal trace, while the beams are at the top and bottom of the screen. Similarly, for the middle of the vertical sweep, the left and right sides are expanded with an increase in horizontal deflection. Service adjusters are provided but seldom need adjusting.

## 17-8 TROUBLESHOOTING, ADJUSTMENTS, AND REPAIRS

The following paragraphs deal with problems associated with the operation of a CRT: setup adjustment procedures, CRT testing and restoration, proper handling and replacement procedures, and

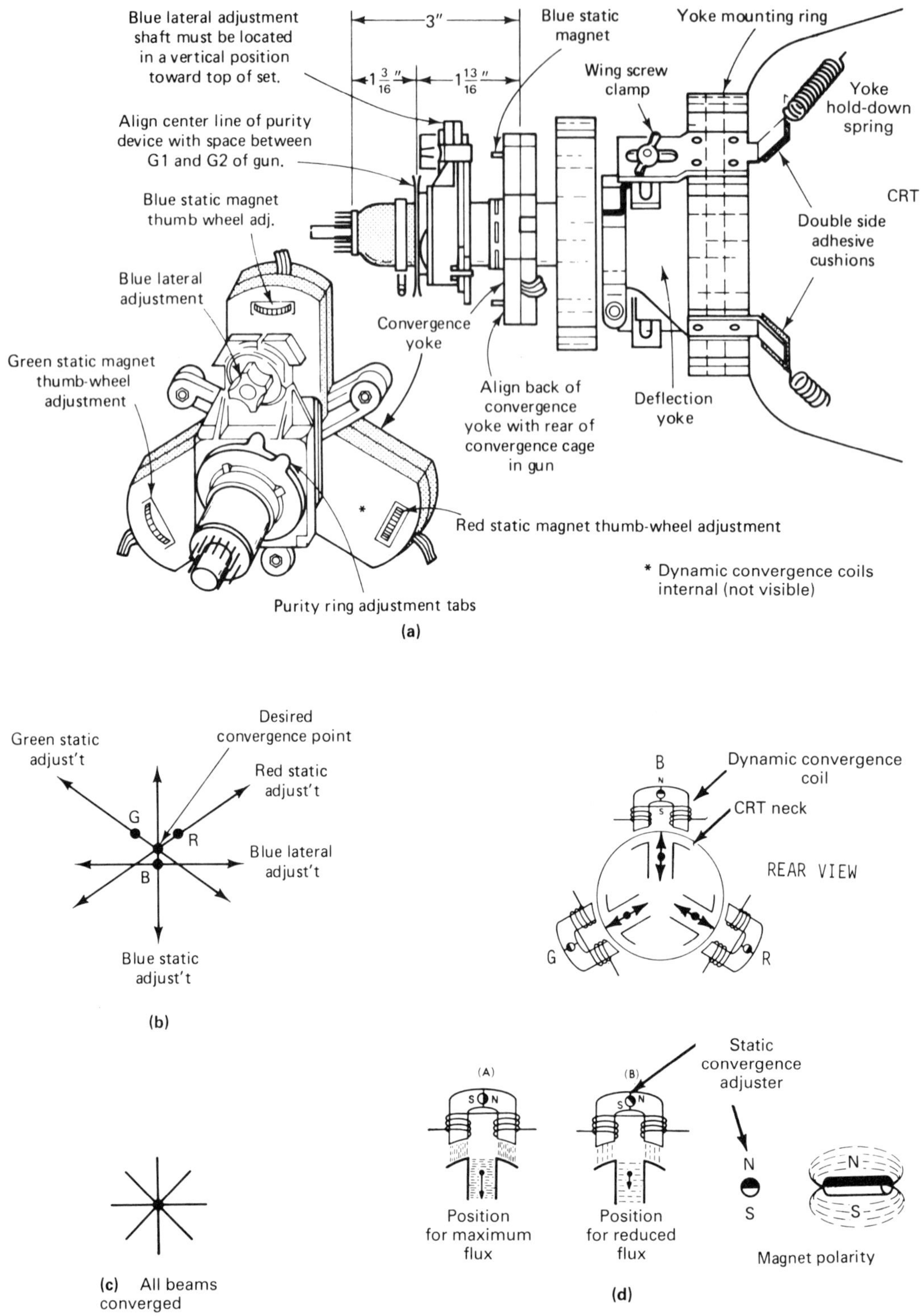


**FIG. 17-2** Delta CRT convergence: (a) delta CRT external component locations (to be effective, all external components must be positioned directly over the corresponding gun elements); (b) three misconverged, dots of generator dot patterns (viewed facing the screen); (c) all beams converged; (d) the convergence magnets are arranged around the neck of the color tube, opposite the internal pole pieces. Rotation of the little round magnet alters the flux of the pole pieces and moves the beam to a new position.

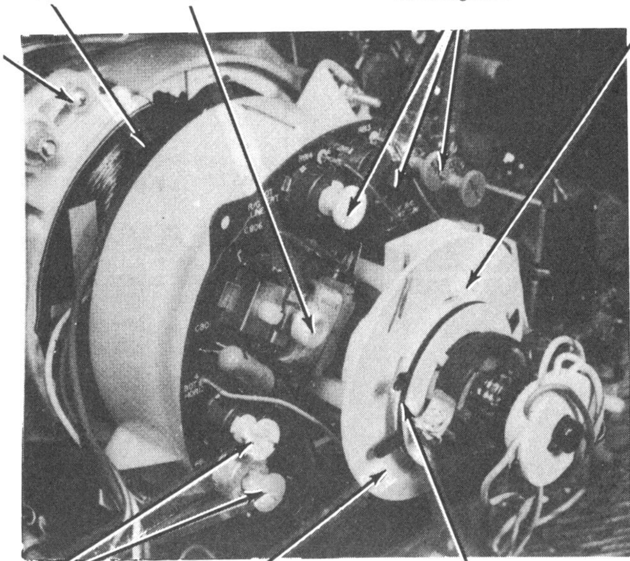


**FIG. 17-3** Typical delta CRT convergence unit. With this configuration, convergence controls are part of the assembly.

finally, typical trouble symptoms resulting from a bad CRT. (*Reminder:* Consider problems in logical order: first those affecting the raster, then the BW picture, and finally, the color picture.)

### Monochrome CRT Setup Procedures

The objective here (and for color CRTs later) is to obtain a raster that is normal in every respect (i.e., a bright, properly proportioned raster with scanning lines uniformly spaced and in *perfect* focus). This entails a number of adjustments that are normally required only after replacing the CRT. When that is accomplished, and only then, we concern ourselves with the applied video signal, the contrast level, and the overall picture quality. The following operations require a large mirror placed in front of the screen for viewing from the rear. Raster adjustments are made when set for an unused channel.

*Yoke Adjustments.* Loosen the wing nuts or other locking device that secures the yoke to its frame. Move the yoke firmly against the flare of the CRT bulb (to prevent neck shadows in the corners). Slowly rotate the yoke for an upright picture with all four edges aligned with the cabinet mask. Secure the yoke, then recheck, making further adjustments if needed.

*Raster Centering.* Rotate the magnetic ring on the tube neck to center the raster vertically and horizontally.

*Raster Height.* Adjust the control for a slight overscan to allow for line voltage variations. Readjust the centering if needed. Check with a picture to be sure that the vertical blanking bars are not visible at the top or bottom or that no images are obscured.

*Focus.* For normal setting of the brightness control, adjust for sharpest focus of scanning lines. Do not proceed until perfect focus is achieved.

*Vertical Linearity.* Adjust for uniform spacing of scanning lines over the entire screen area. Readjust height and centering if needed. Height and linearity adjustments often interact. Tune in a picture and check the image proportions. Watch for flat heads, short or stretched legs, heads or feet cut off, and so on. A crosshatch generator can be useful here.

*Width.* (There is no adjustment provided on many modern sets.) Adjust for slight overscan at the left and right of the screen.

*Horizontal Linearity.* (This adjustment appears on older sets only.) Adjust for uniform spacing

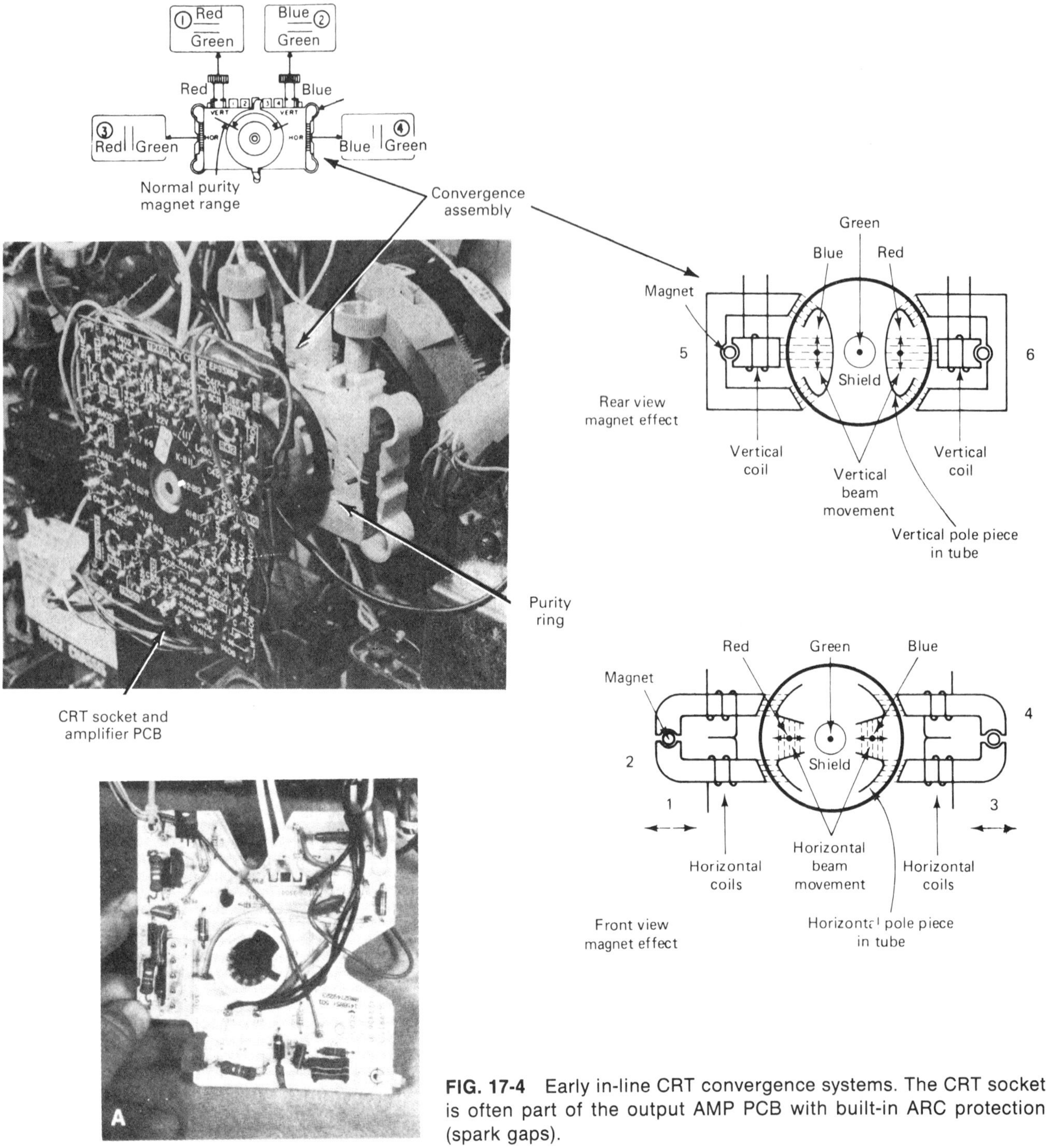


**FIG. 17-4** Early in-line CRT convergence systems. The CRT socket is often part of the output AMP PCB with built-in ARC protection (spark gaps).

of crosshatch generator lines and/or correct picture proportions. For example, a circle should not be oval-shaped.

*Vertical Hold.* While observing a picture, make the picture move slowly downward, then upward, until stable lock-in occurs. With some older sets, a slight readjustment of height and linearity is needed to obtain good vertical sync.

*Horizontal Frequency.* If there is picture tearing or sync instability, set the horizontal hold to midrange and adjust the frequency control (if provided) for pix lock-in.

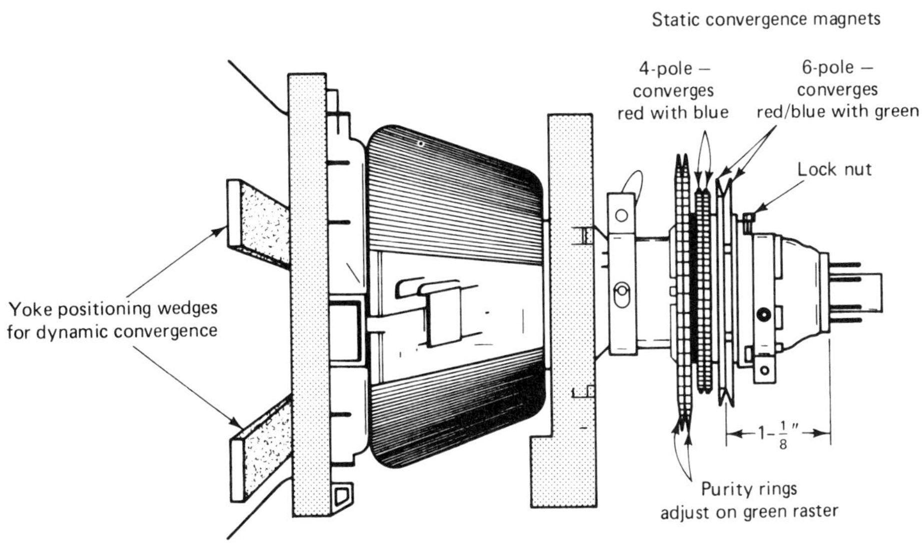


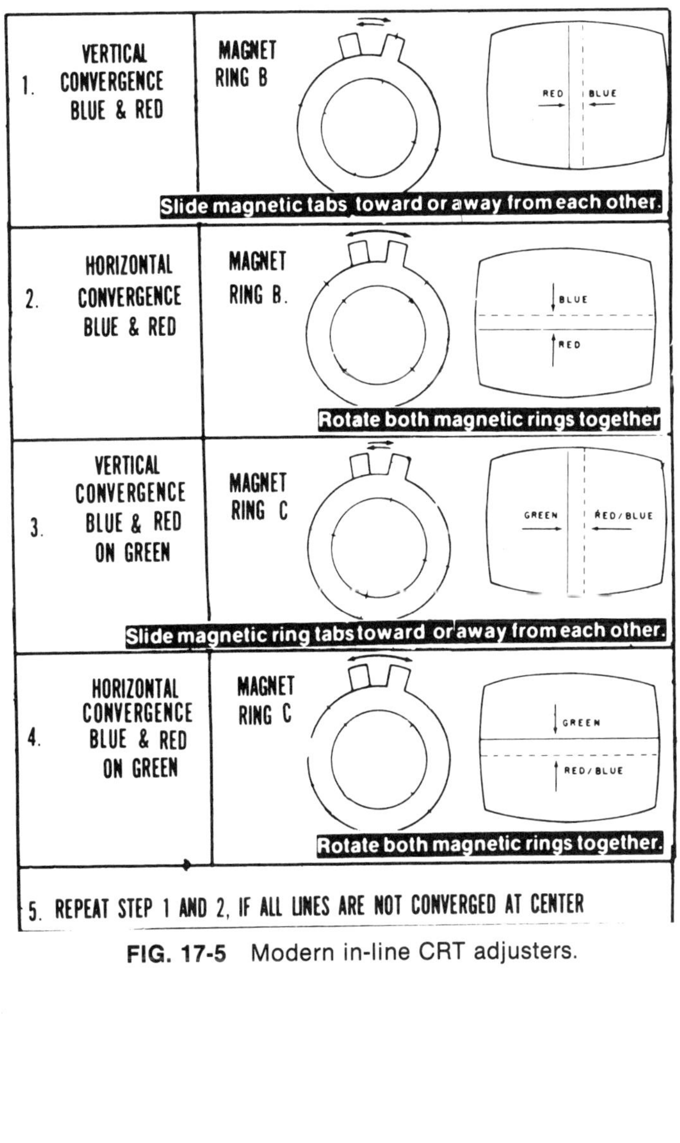


**FIG. 17-5** Modern in-line CRT adjusters.

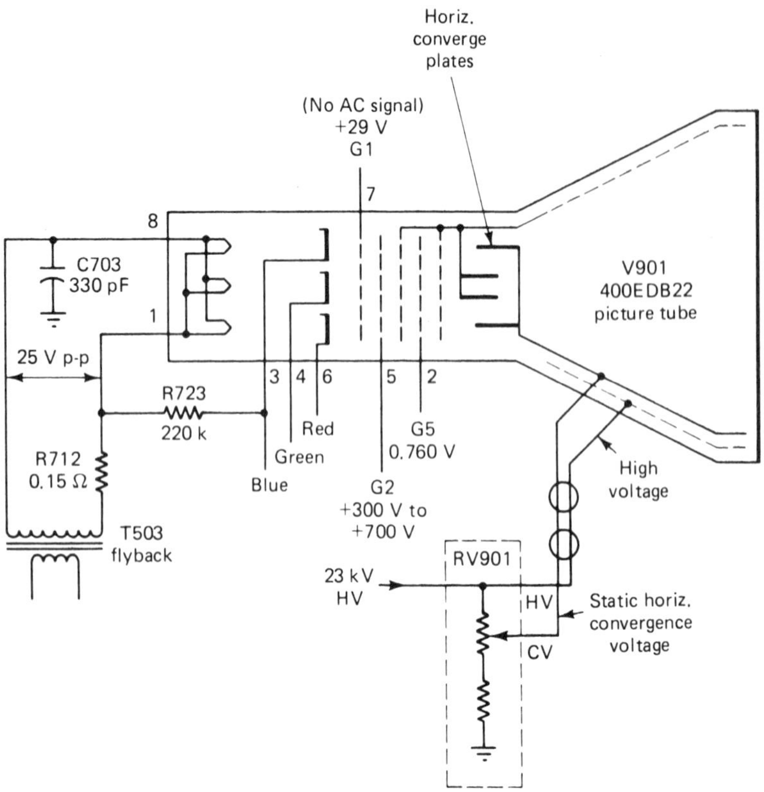


**FIG. 17-6** Trinitron CRT operating conditions.

### Delta CRT Setup Adjustments

After replacing a CRT and ascertaining that there are no circuit malfunctions, make appropriate preliminary adjustments as described for a monochrome receiver. Convergence adjustments are made as follows.

*Degaussing.* With a service-type degaussing coil removed at least 4 feet from the set, energize the coil. Hold the coil flat against the tube face for a few seconds. Slowly move the coil around the screen surface and the cabinet edges. The set may be turned on or off as desired. Slowly back away until the coil is 4 feet or more from the set. Rotate the coil 90° and switch off the power.

*Color Purity Adjustment.* Loosen the yoke locking devices and position the yoke slightly away from the tube flare. Turn down the green and blue screen controls until only a red raster is observed. Without twisting the yoke, slowly move it away from the tube flare until a red blotch is observed near the center of the screen. Adjust the two purity ring washers relative to each other (by rotating the tabs) to obtain the best possible vivid red "fireball" at the center of the screen. Slide the yoke forward to obtain a full-sized red raster without color contaminations or neck shadows at the corners. Check for raster tilt, and if necessary, correct by twisting the yoke slightly. Readjust the purity ring if necessary, then secure the yoke locking devices. With the screen controls, turn the red raster off and the green or blue raster on. Check the color purity and intensity of the green and blue rasters individually. If any color contamination or neck shadows, readjust for a red raster as described. Problems pertaining to the three single-color rasters can be due to one or more weak guns, improper operating voltages, or severe misadjustment of the convergence adjusters.

*Producing a White Raster.* Alternately adjust the RGB screen controls to obtain the mixture that produces white. This will not be possible if the CRT is defective in any way. Adjust the RGB drive controls to obtain the whitest white. If the set has a "service switch," move it to the service position and adjust the red–green–blue levels on a horizontal line. Turn down the brightness to avoid burning the screen. Reexamine the raster. If there is any color contamination, repeat all the purity adjustments as described.

*Gray-Scale Tracking.* Tune in a BW picture. For normal raster brightness, readjust the drive controls if needed for the brightest picture highlights.

Any color fringing on the BW images is due to improper purity or convergence adjustments. With proper tracking and a good CRT, the white level should remain constant over the full range of the brightness control.

*Static Convergence.* This is best performed with a crosshatch or dot generator, although it can be done using only the picture. While observing a BW picture, alternately adjust the red–green–blue static adjusters (on the convergence assembly) to obtain proper beam crossovers for the central areas of the screen. The object is to resolve the three single-color images into one perfectly overlapped image. When this occurs, no colors will be observed around the BW images. In Figure 17-2, note the *direction* of beam movement (and color movement on the screen) for each of the adjusters. To move the blue beam (and blue image) *horizontally,* use the blue lateral adjuster. Alternately adjust all four adjusters as often as necessary to obtain perfect center convergence, while disregarding conditions at the edges of the screen.

*Dynamic Convergence.* For this, a dot/crosshatch generator is essential unless you can work with a picture that is constantly changing. In this procedure we are concerned only with conditions near the screen edges. Obtain a dot or crosshatch pattern as shown in Figure 17-7. Alternately adjust all dynamic convergence adjusters to move the three beams and obtain color-free overlapping dots or lines at the outer areas of the screen. Procedures vary considerably with different sets and are not given here. Refer to the service manual. Picture quality is greatly dependent on proper convergence, and usually, due to interactions, static and dynamic convergence must be performed alternately at least two or three times (or oftener, until you get the hang of it). But a job well done can be very gratifying, to say the least.

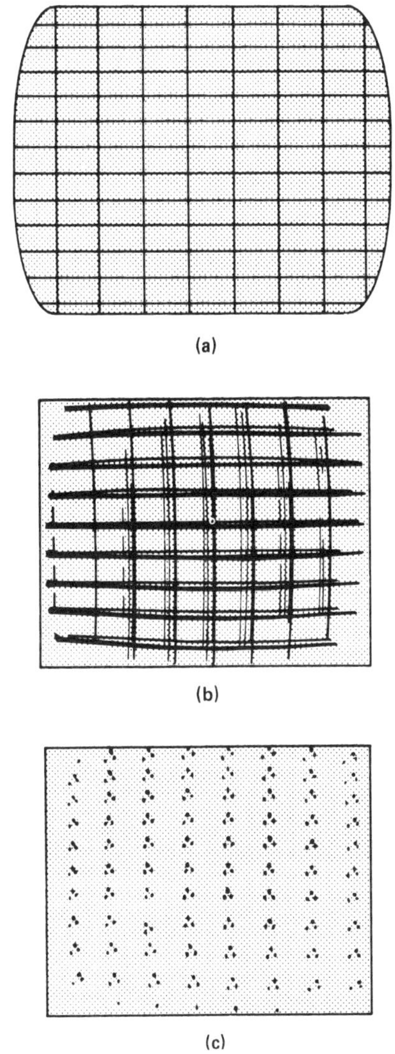

**FIG. 17-7** Normal and abnormal convergence patterns: (a) pattern for a properly converged set; all lines (or dots) appear white, with no colors visible; (b) serious misconvergence using a crosshatch pattern; lines of all three colors are visible; (c) misconverged dot pattern; dots of all three colors are visible. A properly converged CRT contributes greatly to pix quality.

### Setup Adjustments for In-Line CRTs

Good purity and convergence are easier to obtain than with a delta-type CRT. Start with a thorough degaussing and preliminary adjustments, as described for BW and delta tubes.

*Color Purity.* With the red and blue rasters turned off, and the yoke retracked from the tube flare, adjust the ring magnets (Figure 17-5) or if a Trinitron tube, the twist coil, to get a *green* blotch at the center of the screen. (*Note:* We are concerned only with the red and blue beams since the green beam travels in a straight line.) Move the yoke forward to obtain a full-sized green raster without any R or B contamination. Check and compare all three raster colors for purity and brilliance. Secure the yoke locking devices.

*Static Convergence.* Adjust the ring magnets, or static converge pot as applicable to converge the dot/crosshatch lines at the center of the screen. For GE in-line tubes, refer to Figure 17-4.

*Dynamic Convergence.* With some in-line tubes, insert small wooden wedges between the CRT bowl and the yoke (Figure 17-5). By trial and error, adjust the yoke slightly to converge the beams at the four edges of the screen. For a Trinitron tube, adjust the tilt control (if provided), which varies the shape of the parabolic waveform applied to the internal deflection plates.

*Reminders:* Proper setup adjustments cannot be made unless the tube and all associated external components are in perfect condition and operating with the correct applied voltages.

### Picture Tube Testing

Many trouble symptoms can be attributed to a bad CRT; on the other hand, because of false assumptions and misleading test results, a good tube may be replaced when the defect was elsewhere. Verify its condition before considering replacement. The most common defects associated with a CRT are burned-out filament (heater); internal opens, shorts, or leakage between elements; partial loss of vacuum (gassy); loss of some screen phosphors; and more common, loss of emission for one or more guns. Another, but rare condition is a loose or warped shadow mask or grill. All these possibilities must be considered and checked out (Figure 17-8).

If a bad CRT is suspected, one approach is substitution, if there is an identical tube on hand. Simply exchange CRT sockets between the set under test and the one that is operating properly. Similarly, exchange the HV lead from one tube to the other. Ground the two chassis together. Of course, certain controls such as brightness will control conditions on the opposite CRT. With no deflection yoke, only a bright dot is observed so reduce brightness to avoid burning the screen.

A more conventional approach is to use a tube checker. On a color CRT, all three guns must be checked individually, with each providing the same (or close to the same) amounts of emission.

One common tube defect is an intermittent open or short. Typical symptoms are either loss of raster or full brightness that is not controllable with the brightness control. An ohmmeter check or a neon bulb will often show up an internal short or leakage. Other than replacement, there are two possible remedies for shorts. Either place the tube face down and tap the neck with a blunt instrument to dislodge particles that are shorting the elements, or burn out such contaminants by flashing the tube with a fairly high voltage applied *momentarily* across the shorted elements. Most CRT testers can do this.

### CRT Restoration

This is a common expedient that often prolongs the life of a bad CRT. To clear shorts, *momentarily* apply several hundred volts of dc between the two elements that are shorted or intermittently shorting out. Repeat as often as necessary while realizing that the tube can be destroyed in the process. Most

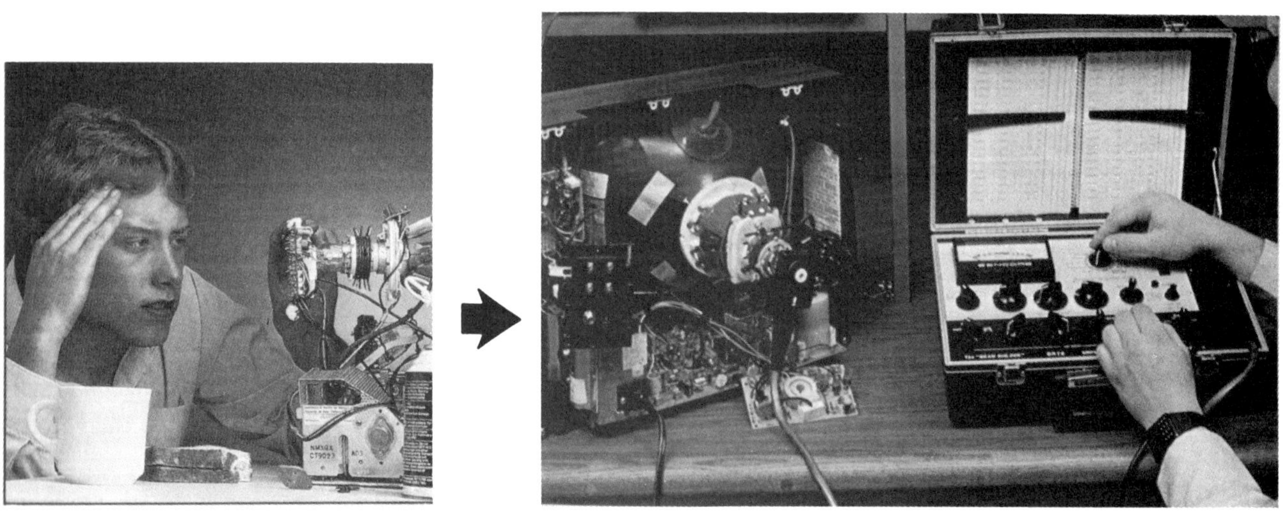

**FIG. 17-8** CRT testing. Checking the CRT before beginning a repair may save you hours of wasted time, wasted efforts, and wasted profits. (Courtesy of *Sencore News.*)

testers provide some protection against such a mishap.

To restore a weak gun (low emission) or to verify the condition, try a filament "booster" to increase the heater voltage by roughly 2 V. If this works, leave it installed permanently. To restore emission, most testers momentarily apply a fairly high positive voltage to the grid(s) with the cathode(s) grounded. This strips away any "crud" buildup on the cathode that is inhibiting emission. As when flashing shorts, the process is repeated several times as necessary until results are improved or until the tube is DOA, whichever comes first.

In the absence of a tester, this can be performed using a dummy socket connecting an external PS to the tube. Some arcing will be observed in the tube neck. To prevent further damage, avoid prolonged application of the positive grid voltage and check results frequently.

### CRT Handling and Replacement

In general, proceed as follows. Ground out any residual charge on the CRT by grounding the ultor contact (the tube can retain its multi-kV charge for long periods). Disconnect the HV lead. Remove the CRT socket and all components on the tube neck. Make note of their respective positions and record it for future reference. Place the set face down and remove the CRT hold-down band or screws securing the CRT to the chassis or front of the cabinet. Prepare a clean padded surface on which to deposit the tube when removed from the cabinet. Once again discharge the CRT at the ultor. Failing to do so can result in a shock, a violent reaction, and dropping the tube.

*Warning:* Improper handling of the CRT can be dangerous, with serious injuries resulting from a violent implosion. Never lift the tube by the neck, and avoid bumping or striking with tools or other metallic objects. It is advisable to wear safety goggles.

Carefully lift the tube clear of the cabinet, being careful not to make contact with the chassis or other parts. Reminder: Never lift a tube by the neck without supporting the heavy bowl. If a large console, remove the tube horizontally after first blocking up the tube to support its weight in a safe manner. With the tube removed, carefully place it face down on the surface, which you have previously prepared.

To install a tube, position the chassis and cabinet ready to receive the new CRT. Install the tube in the same manner and in the reverse order of removal. If it is an older set, clean the CRT faceplate and the inside of the safety glass. Make sure that all rubber pads are in place. If the tube is held with a band, do not overtighten. Install the yoke and other items on the neck at their original locations. Be careful to avoid breakage, as the glass neck is fairly thin. Reconnect the socket, the HV lead, and the means of grounding the outer aquadag coating. Turn the set on and perform setup procedures described earlier.

*CRT Disposal.* Because of the danger of implosion, a tube should never be discarded without first neutralizing the vacuum. A safe procedure is as follows. Place the tube face down in a large carton or other container. Not to expect the worst, but as a precaution, cover the tube with a blanket, leaving only the base exposed. Gain access to the evacuation stem protruding from the end of the neck. With older tubes this means breaking off the keyed covering. With pliers, snap off the glass stem. Air will enter the tube with a slight hissing sound. The tube is now safe for disposal, but keep it away from children. Cuts from glass breakage can be infected by the toxic screen phosphors.

### CRT Trouble Symptoms

Following are the trouble symptoms that could be (but not necessarily) caused by a bad CRT, its operating conditions, or associated components. Other causes of the same symptoms are treated elsewhere. Investigate these other possibilities and verify the suspected CRT defect before contemplating replacement. In particular, check *all* applied voltages, comparing with expected voltages shown on the schematic. A troubleshooting flow drawing is shown in Figure 17-9.

*No Raster.* (sound okay)

***Probable causes:*** Bad CRT; loss of HV or other applied voltages; excessive grid-to-cathode bias.

Test the CRT for opens, shorts, loss of emission, burned-out heater, and so on. Turn up the brightness and screen controls. If the tube is okay, check all applied voltages. If there is no HV, see Chapter 10. (*Reminder:* A shorted HV rectifier provides HV but it is *ac* and will not produce a raster.) If there are no screen or focus grid voltages, check

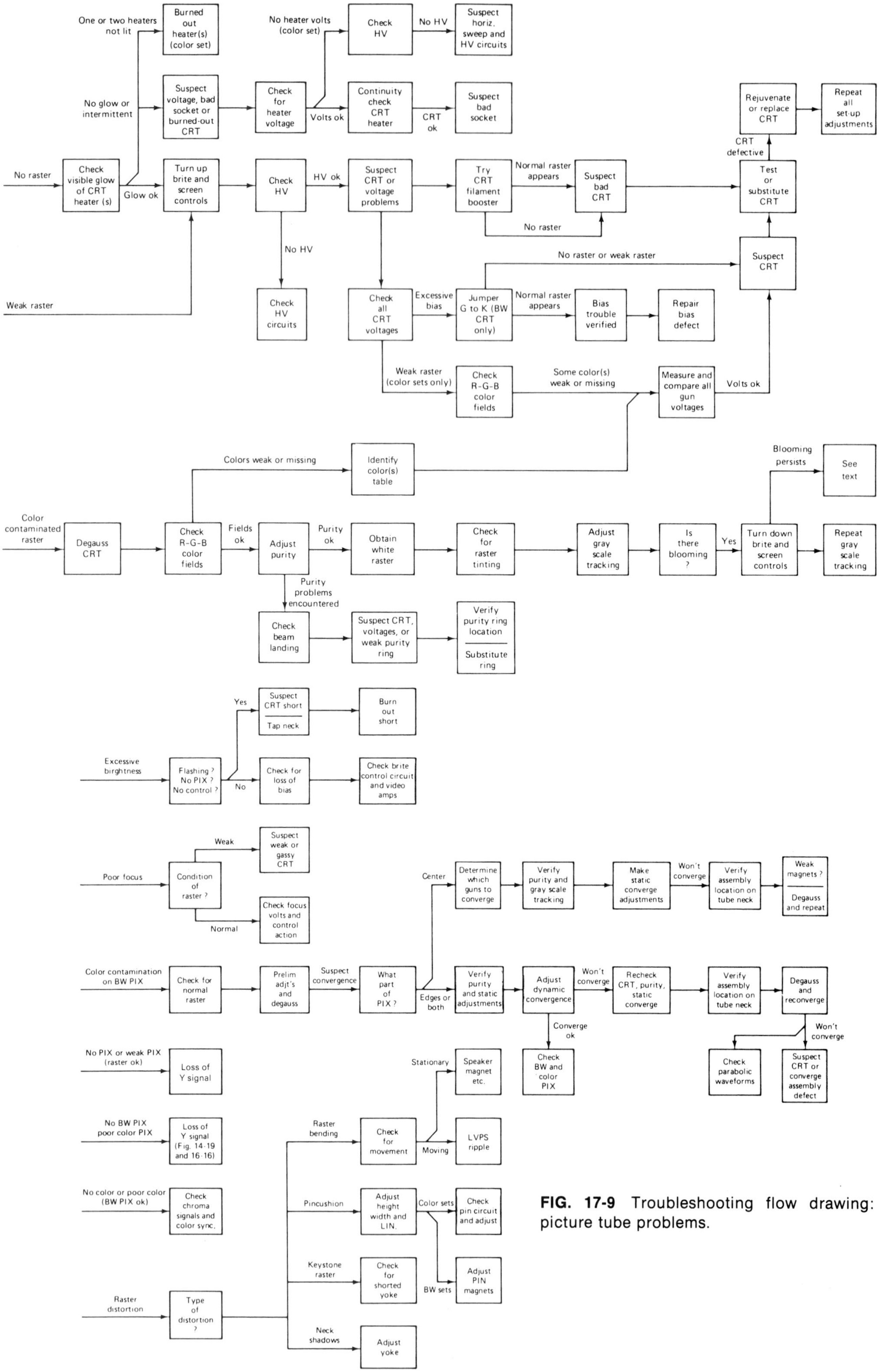


**FIG. 17-9** Troubleshooting flow drawing: picture tube problems.

the source. With the brightness control turned up, check the bias between the control grid and cathode (on each gun if a color tube). If the bias is more than 20 V or so, check the grid and cathode voltages relative to ground. The usual cause is too much + dc on the cathode, although high negative dc on the grid will have the same result. Check against schematic readings and troubleshoot the suspected circuit. If working on a BW set with high bias, try a jumper between the grid and cathode (with zero bias, the beam current should increase). With modern color sets it is usually a defect in the dc-coupled amplifiers between the brightness control and the CRT.

#### Dim Raster

***Probable causes:*** Weak or gassy CRT; low HV, focus, or screen grid voltages; excessive grid bias.

Check the CRT and its applied voltages. Turn up the brightness and screen controls. If excessive bias, proceed as described for no raster. Other symptoms of a weak CRT are a silvery appearance to white images (especially noticeable on faces), and a raster slow to brighten when the set is turned on.

#### Excessive Brightness

***Probable causes:*** Insufficient grid bias or grid to cathode short in CRT.

If the screen cannot be darkened with the brightness control, try tapping the tube neck with the control fully CCW. If there is insufficient CRT bias (with the control turned down), check the grid and cathode voltages and dc-coupled video amplifiers as described for no raster.

#### Intermittent Raster

***Probable cause:*** Intermittent shorts in CRT; bad CRT socket (a common problem).

Tap the CRT neck. If raster comes and goes and the brightness control has no effect, it is a bad tube. Test for shorts and try flashing. Try wiggling the socket and its wires; watch for changes in heater glow. If the socket is suspected, replace it.

#### Poor Focus

***Probable causes:*** Weak or gassy CRT; incorrect focus voltage or bad focus control; poor HV regulation and excessive blooming.

Check the CRT. Check the focus voltage and compare with the schematic. Check for an erratic focus control. If the focus voltage is low, check back to its source. Typical troubles are a bad rectifier and the voltage-dividing network from the HV supply. Check the HV regulation by monitoring the voltage changes as brightness control is varied. Improper operation of the HV regulator is common.

#### Arcing in CRT

***Probable causes:*** Gun elements shorting out; gas or partial loss of vacuum.

A new CRT will often arc inside for a short time but is generally no cause for concern. If it persists, check for shorts and try flashing out particles. If there is no raster, and no visible heater glow but the neck gets warm, look for a crack in the glass, usually near the base.

#### Colored Raster

***Probable causes:*** One or two guns not working; one or two screen controls turned off or without voltage.

Check the CRT. Determine which gun (or guns) are not working, and why. Check for a bad socket or loss of one or more screen voltages. A bad screen control pot is not uncommon.

#### Color-Tinted Raster

***Probable causes:*** Misadjusted purity ring or twist coil; one or more weak CRT guns; misadjusted screen or drive controls.

Check and compare the emission for all three guns; try restoring weak gun(s). Adjust the purity ring or twist coil, and the screen and drive controls.

#### Brownish Blemish on Screen

***Probable cause:*** An indelibly burned screen is usually caused by operating the CRT at full brightness when there is loss of deflection. The moral is obvious, and the only remedy is a new tube.

*Poor Convergence.* (color fringing and visible color on BW images)

***Probable causes:*** Bad CRT or improper setup adjustments; magnetized CRT.

Check CRT and if okay, degauss and perform all setup adjustments.

*Poor Color Picture.* (normal white raster)

***Probable causes:*** Troubles in video or chroma signal stages.

Signal trace suspected stages, including chroma demodulators. Refer to Chapter 15.

## QUESTIONS

1. What are the main differences between a BW and a color CRT?
2. Explain convergence and how it is accomplished.
3. Explain the purpose of a shadow mask or aperture grill.
4. How is it possible to obtain a white raster when there are only color phosphors on the screen?
5. Explain blooming and what causes it.
6. Briefly describe the setup procedures for a color CRT.
7. State the precautions for safe handling of a picture tube.
8. The scanning lines on an in-line CRT appear to be vertical. Explain.
9. State the probable causes where only a blue or green raster is obtained but no white.
10. Why is it difficult to obtain perfect convergence at the edges of the screen?
11. The curvature of the screen creates problems in focusing. Explain.
12. One weak gun can make it difficult or impossible to obtain a white raster and a good BW and color picture. Explain.
13. Explain a procedure for removing shorts from a CRT and increasing the electron emission.
14. What causes a neck shadow, and how is it overcome?
15. State possible causes where the grid bias on a CRT is too high or too low.
16. Explain the function of a purity ring and the result of misadjustment.
17. What is the pincushion effect, and how is it prevented?
18. What is the expected result of operating a CRT at high brilliance when there is loss of deflection?
19. A normal raster is prerequisite to obtaining a good BW picture, and a normal BW picture is needed to obtain a good color picture. Explain why.
20. State probable causes of a poor color picture when there is (a) a normal white raster; (b) a color-tinted raster.
21. Explain the need for degaussing and how it is done.
22. After replacing a CRT the picture is inverted and transposed. State the cause.

# 18 Television sound

Until recently, TV sound has taken a back seat to the picture, which is regrettable, considering that hearing is one of our main sources of sensual pleasure. But no longer is the viewer content to listen to harsh and barely tolerable sound emanating from a tiny speaker tucked away in some obscure corner of the cabinet. Now we demand more—the same that the dedicated audiophile has enjoyed for years, high fidelity and stereo.

Thanks to technological breakthroughs, we can now enjoy the best of two worlds, high-quality pictures and superior sound. By utilizing previously vacant portions of the channel allocations, we now have MTS (multichannel television sound), true and realistic stereo for TV sets, VCRs, and monitors. This chapter deals with two aspects of the same subject: conventional monaural receivers and MTS/stereo.

The human ear is a remarkable biological device, able to translate a wide range of vibrations to a form perceptive to the brain. There are good sounds and bad sounds, sounds that evoke emotion, pleasurable or otherwise—rich and vibrant harmonious sounds that gladden the heart, and harsh discordant sounds that irritate and jangle the nerves—happy sounds and sad sounds, and we wish to hear them all.

Whereas some species communicate in the ultrasonic range (the common grasshopper, for one), we as humans communicate verbally in the low register. The range of the human speaking voice, for example, is roughly from 200 Hz to 2 kHz for males and several octaves higher for females. The range of musical notes is considerably greater: from the deep bass of the viol at 40 Hz or so, and lower frequencies (some of which can be felt rather than heard), to those in the upper register, the piccolo, for example, at 5 kHz, or those emanating from the throat of a coloratura soprano. For some of us with "tin ears," hearing is limited to frequencies of 5 kHz or thereabouts; those more fortunate, persons with "golden ears," go higher, to 10 kHz or better. Then there are the overtones, which go even higher, frequencies we are consciously unaware of, but sounds that contribute much to the appreciation of good music.

To achieve the ultimate in sound reproduction requires a well-designed amplifier and high-quality components, including the speakers. All this will be considered later in the chapter.

## 18-1 AM AND FM FUNDAMENTALS

With AM radio broadcasting the amplitude of the carrier is made to vary in accordance with the strength of the modulating signal (Figure 18-1a). The audio modulation, which originates from a microphone, recording, or whatever, is contained in the sidebands that extend up to 5 kHz on both sides of the carrier. In the modulation process, the different audio frequencies heterodyne with the carrier to produce the AF frequencies contained in the sidebands. Low audio frequencies are close to the carrier; the

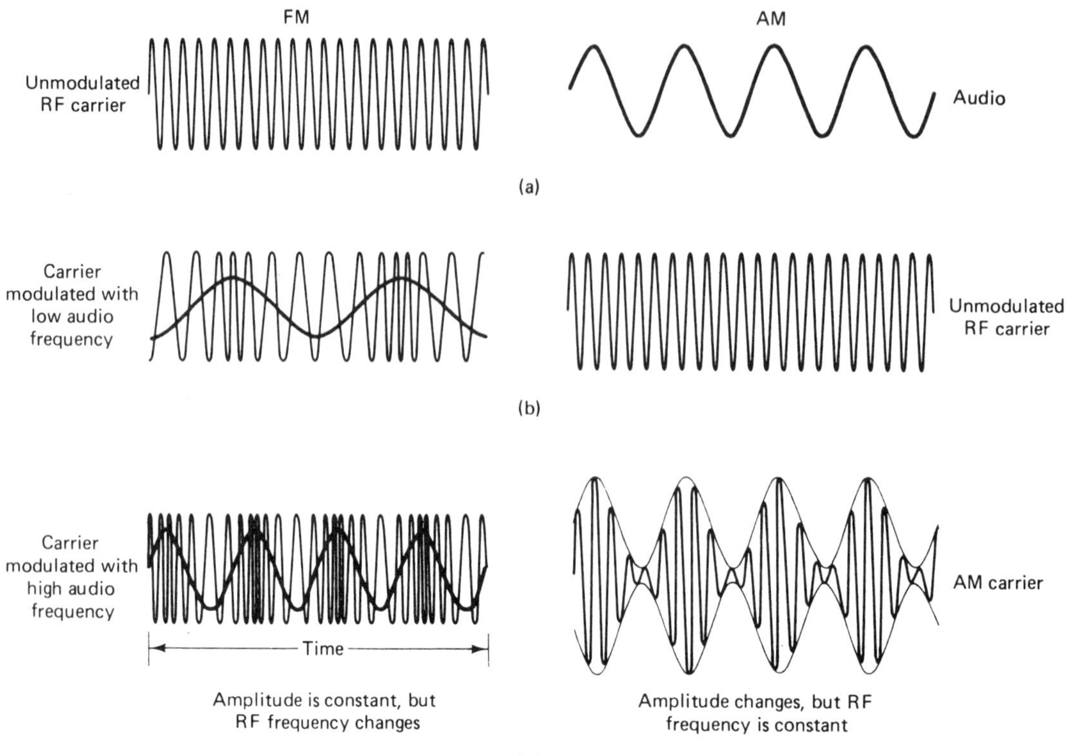


**FIG. 18-1** AM and FM signal comparisons.

higher frequencies extend further out, to a maximum of 5 kHz. In the demodulation process, the audio component is "detected" by rectifying the RF (i.e., getting rid of either the positive or negative half-cycles of the RF). The recovered audio is the envelope that follows the average amplitude variations of the RF as shown in the diagram. The frequency of the RF remains constant at all times, both with and without modulation.

FM is considerably different. Although the *unmodulated* carrier is the same, its frequency is made to vary in accordance with the audio modulation as shown in Figure 18-1b; that is, the carrier frequency is constantly changing from its normal, assigned resting frequency, sweeping up to a maximum of 25 kHz in both directions. With or without modulation, the carrier *amplitude* remains constant. The amount of sweep varies in accordance with the volume (modulation) level. To paraphrase, the *amount* of frequency deviation above and below the carrier is a function of sound level; the greater the frequency shift (deviation), the greater the volume, and vice versa. With a total sweep of 50 kHz, an FM station occupies a greater proportion of the broadcast spectrum than an AM station with its 10-kHz allocation. By the same token, tuned circuits require a correspondingly greater bandpass.

The *rate* at which the changes in RF occur corresponds with the frequency of the audio modulation. Low audio frequencies produce slow changes in the RF frequency; high audio frequencies produce rapid changes. With FM, the audio sweep rate is from 50 Hz to 15 kHz, a significant increase over the allowable 5 kHz for AM. Besides a higher fidelity capability, another advantage of FM over AM is fewer problems with noise and other amplitude interference.

As described in Chapter 1, a TV sound signal is generated and transmitted separate from the video signal, although they are both contained within the same channel allocation. As shown in Figure 1-1, the sound signal is at the high-frequency end, just beyond the limits of the video bandpass, with its sound carrier 4.5 MHz from the video carrier. Note the frequency gap where one leaves off and the other begins. These heretofore unused frequencies are now used for MTS stereo sound, to be described later.

### Preemphasis and Deemphasis

Preemphasis and deemphasis is one method used to reduce the intensity of hiss, static, and other extraneous high-pitched noises. At the station, the high audio frequencies (those in the 2 to 15 kHz range) receive more amplification than the lows. This is called *preemphasis,* an important consideration with FM. At the receiver, the highs are deemphasized to their normal level. In the process, high-pitched noise is reduced by the same proportion. The effect is similar to reducing highs with a tone control, except that the essential treble tones are still retained. MTS/stereo uses another method of noise reduction called DBX, described later.

## 18-2 MONAURAL SOUND SYSTEM

The block diagram of Figure 18-2 shows the various stages in the sound section of a typical monaural TV. As described earlier, the received picture and sound RF carriers heterodyne with a CW oscillator signal in the tuner(s) to produce two *lower* carrier frequencies, the picture and sound *IF carriers,* at 45.75 and 41.25 MHz, respectively. In the video IF strip, both picture and sound IF signals are amplified as one.

For a *monochrome* set, the beat between the picture and sound carriers in the video detector becomes a new and still lower sound IF carrier of 4.5 MHz, the frequency difference between the two carriers. As shown in the diagram, at some point downstream from the video detector (commonly referred to as the *sound takeoff*), the 4.5-MHz sound signal is further amplified by one or more tuned-sound IF amplifier stages, then passed on to the sound detector. In some cases, the detector is preceded by one or more limiter stages, described later. The sound detector recovers the audio from the frequency-modulated carrier. From the detector, the audio signal is boosted by one or more voltage amplifiers. These amplifiers, in turn, drive the power output stage (or stages) to obtain sufficient audio *power* to operate the speaker(s).

With color TV, all stage functions are the same except for one basic difference. As shown in the diagram, the sound takeoff is ahead of the video detector, usually the last IF stage. This is to reduce the possibility of a 920-kHz beat between the 4.5-MHz signal and the color subcarrier of 3.58 MHz. If such interference reaches the CRT, it gives the picture a fine-grained "wormy" appearance.

The 41.25-MHz sound carrier goes from the sound takeoff to a separate sound detector, called a *sound IF detector,* to distinguish it from the FM sound detector described previously. Its function is to produce the new 4.5-MHz sound carrier, as was done in the video detector for the monochrome signal. This 4.5-MHz sound IF signal is then demodulated and amplified by the downstream stages just described for monochrome TV. With most late-model sets, all sound functions are performed by a single IC.

### Sound Takeoff Circuits

Figure 18-3 shows three typical circuits. In circuit (a), a BW set, the 4.5-MHz sound IF signal is extracted from the video detector through a small coupling capacitor. A low value is used to prevent the AM video and sync signals from reaching the sound stages and producing buzz sounds (intercarrier buzz) from the speaker. The 4.5-MHz tuned circuit performs a dual function: selecting the sound IF carrier (for the sound section) and as a trap to reject sound from the video stages. Circuit (b) is similar except for the use of inductive coupling. Circuit (c) is a color set. The 41.25-MHz sound signal is capacitively coupled to the sound IF detector, described next.

### Sound IF Detector

The purpose of this stage is to produce the 4.5-MHz beat that becomes the new sound IF carrier. It is not a demodulator in the true sense, and the FM signal at its output is the same as at the input except for the lower carrier frequency. Some sets use a

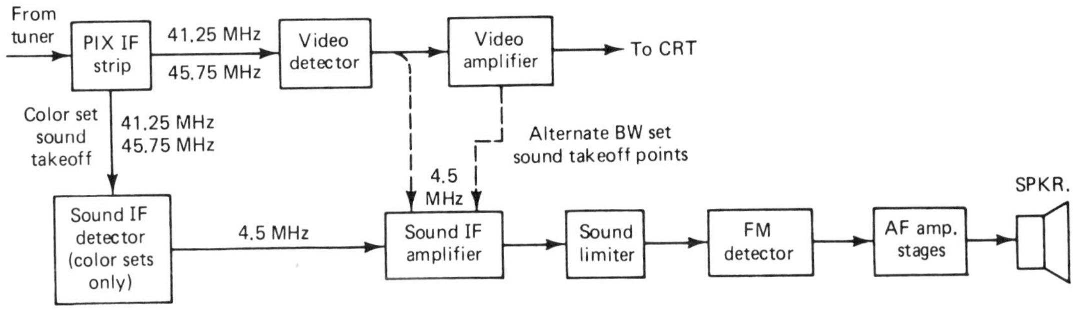


**FIG. 18-2** Monaural sound system.

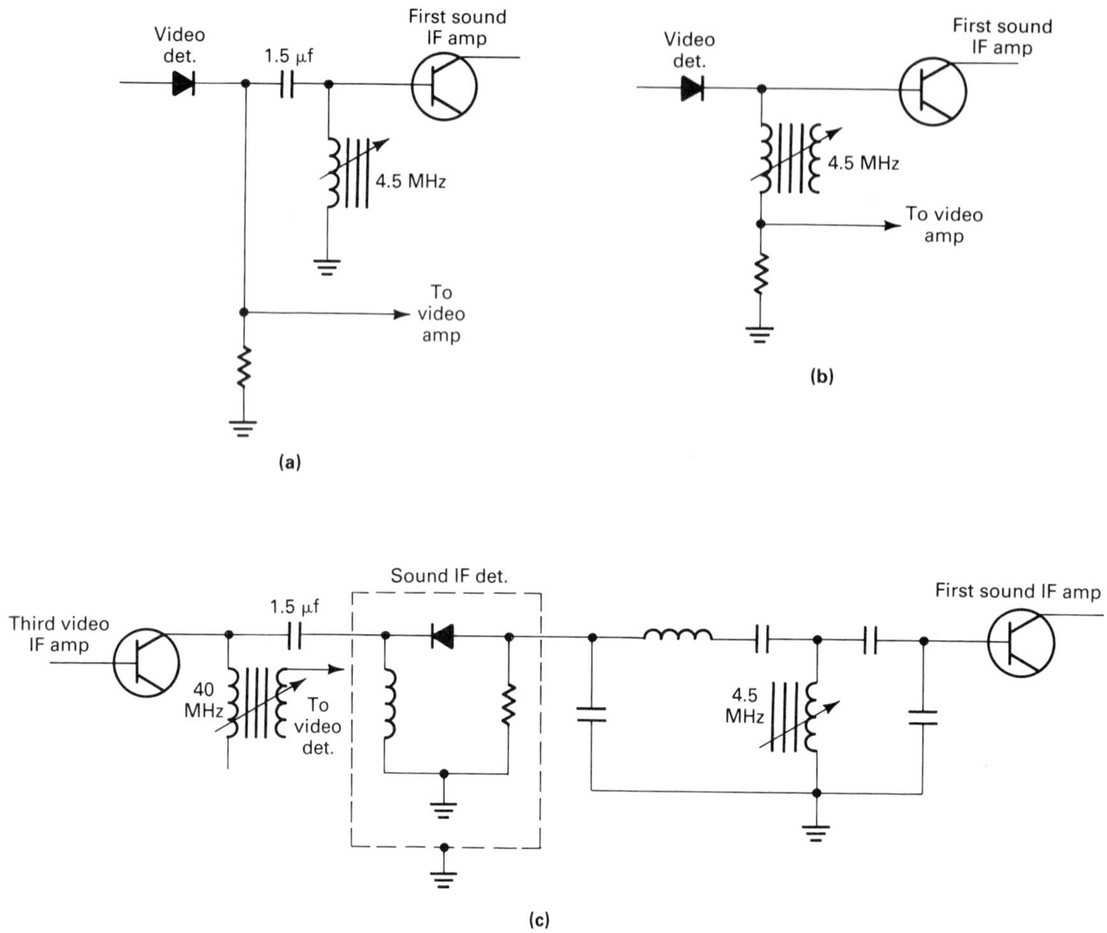


**FIG. 18-3** Sound takeoff circuits.

transistor to increase the signal level, but a diode as shown in Figure 18-3c is more common. As is customary, the detector diode and associated components are shielded to prevent radiation of high-frequency harmonics that if picked up by the tuner creates "tweet" (tunable beat) interference on the picture. Most of the small-value capacitors shown are to keep video and sync out of the sound stages and to prevent 920-kHz interference.

## Sound IF and Limiter Stages

The function of these stages is to amplify the weak 4.5-MHz sound IF signal prior to detection. As compared to the video IF strip, fewer stages are required because of the much narrower bandwidth of the sound signal. A typical BW set has but one stage; a color set (Figure 18-4), two or three stages. They are known by various names: limiter, driver, or just plain IF amp. They are tuned amplifiers, peaked to 4.5 MHz. Although the maximum allowable sweep for FM is only 50 kHz, a somewhat wider bandpass of roughly twice that amount is used to prevent distortion that can occur with tuner oscillator drift, except where AFT is employed. To prevent oscillations, negative feedback and neutralization are sometimes used, along with ferrite beads on critical leads.

A *limiter* stage provides some amplification, but *its* main function is to reject amplitude modulated signals (video and sync) and strong noise impulses. This is accomplished by operating the transistor class C with relatively high bias and low collector voltage so that it will saturate at fairly low signal levels. Signals whose amplitude exceeds that of the FM carrier are thus prevented from getting through.

## FM Detectors

Unlike the sound IF detector, the purpose of this stage is to demodulate the 4.5-MHz sound IF carrier and recover the audio from its sidebands, converting frequency variations into a signal that varies at an audio rate (Figure 18-5). The methods used to demodulate FM are different from those for AM be-

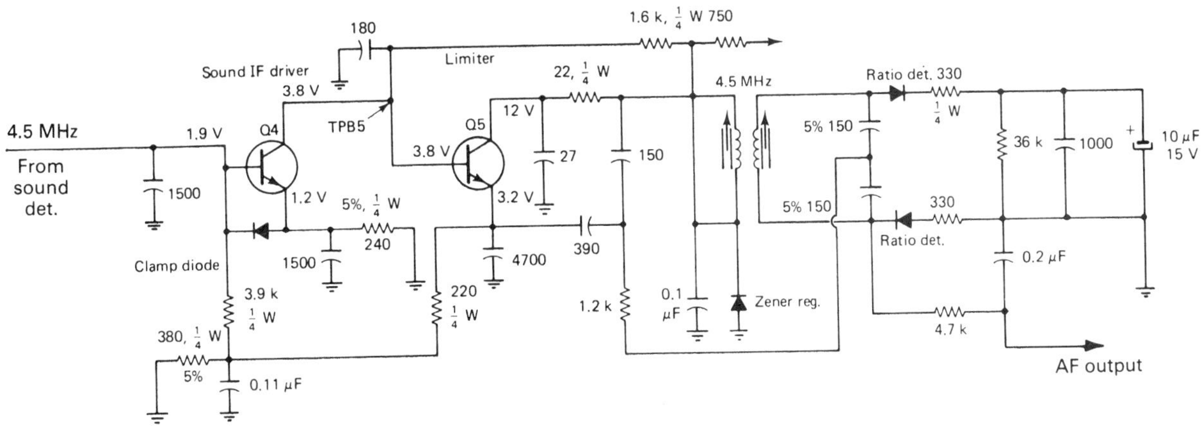


**FIG. 18-4** Color TV sound IF and DET circuits.

cause of the dissimilarity between the two kinds of signals (Figure 18-1).

Five types of detectors in common use are named and described in the following paragraphs. Each performs its function in a different way, although the end result is the same. The first two circuits named use diodes; the more complex circuits employ transistors as a means of achieving some signal gain.

*Ratio Detector (Figure 18-4).* This is one of the earliest FM detectors that is still used to some extent. Circuit operation is described briefly as follows. Two diodes that are connected series-aiding conduct alternately in accordance with the signal applied to each at any given instant. Note the similarity to the AFC circuits described in Chapter 8. The voltage at each diode depends on the ever-changing phase relationship between the voltages applied in two ways: voltages of opposite polarity from the two ends of the transformer which are 180° apart, and an in-phase signal voltage obtained from the preceding stage to the junction of the two 150-pF capacitors. Note the 10-μF electrolytic across the output resistor, which "absorbs" amplitude variations, making the circuit relatively immune to video and sync pulses and impulse noise. In effect, the signal input transformer converts FM to AM, and the amplitude-modulated IF signal is then detected (demodulated) to produce the audio signal which is developed across the load resistor. From here it is passed on to the next downstream stage, the first of several audio amplifiers.

*Discriminator (Figure 18-6a).* This circuit and its operation is similar to that of the ratio detector. One difference is the center-tapped coupling transformer that supplies the diodes with an in-phase

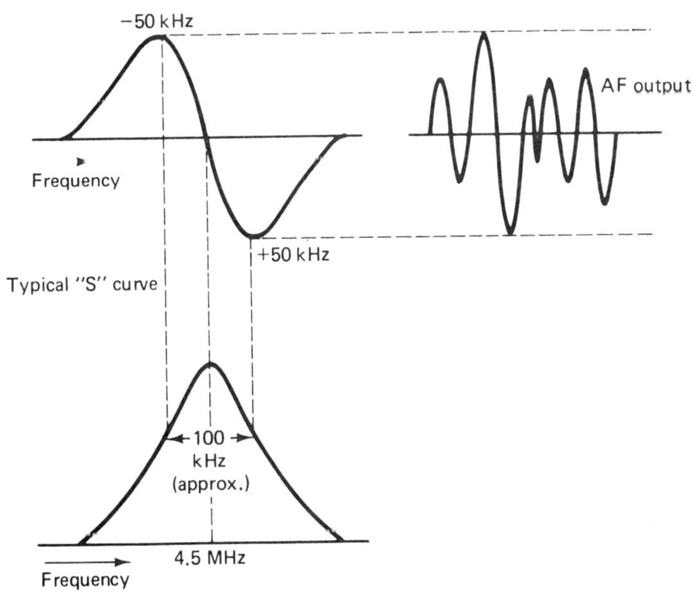


**FIG. 18-5** FM demodulation. An FM detector converts IF frequency variations into amplitude changes at an audio rate.

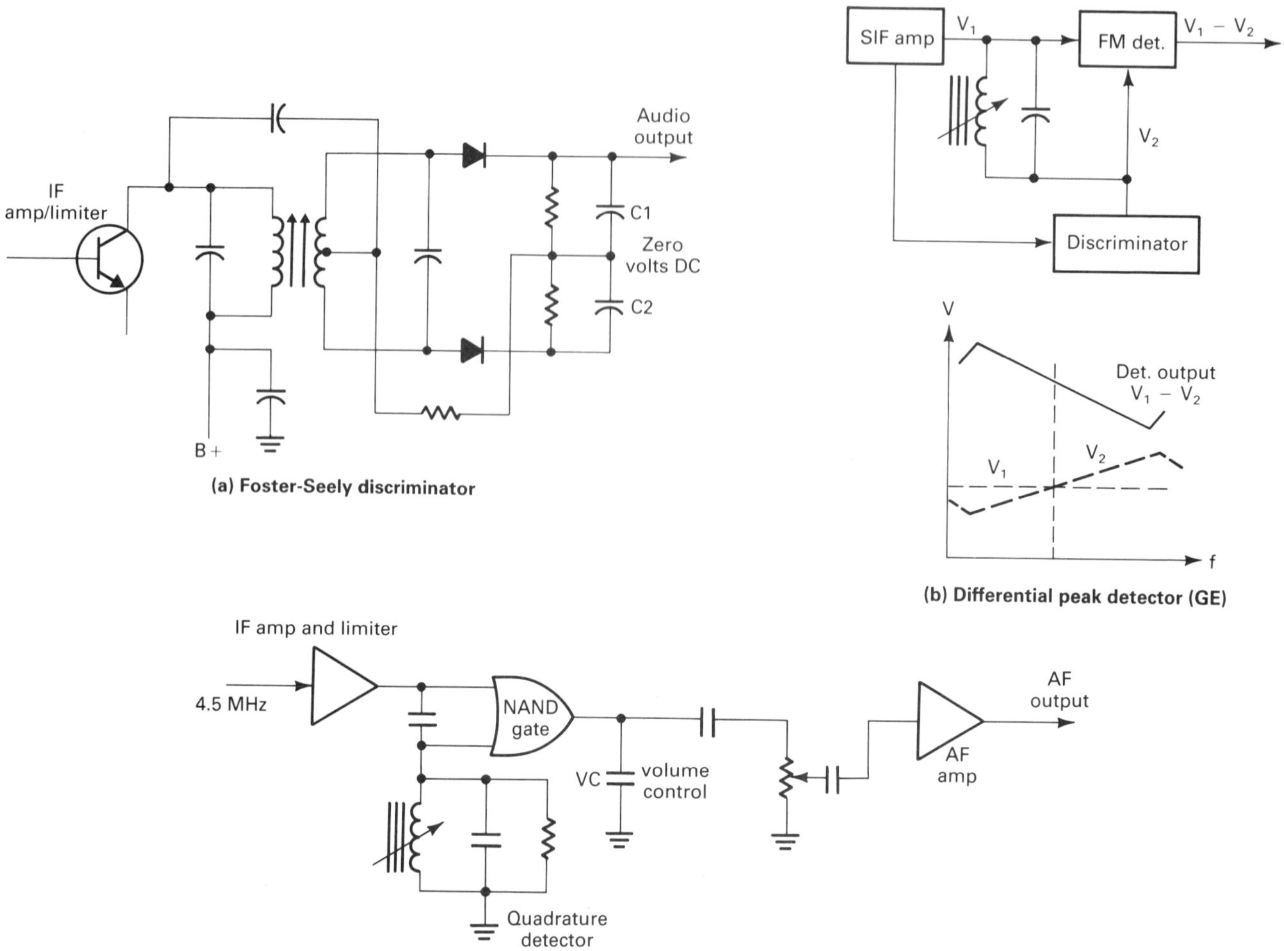


(c)

**FIG. 18-6** FM sound demodulators: (a) Foster-Seely discriminator; (b) differential peak detector; (c) Quadrature detector. (Courtesy of General Electric.)

signal from the preceding stage. Another difference is the split-load resistors that provide a dc return path for the diodes. The diodes conduct alternately in accordance with the polarity and amplitudes of the in-phase and out-of-phase applied signal voltages. As each diode conducts, it develops an *IR* drop across its associated load resistor. This occurs only with modulation, that is, when the FM signal sweeps above or below the carrier frequency. At the carrier "resting" frequency, the diodes conduct equally, producing equal and opposite voltages across the resistors, the condition that equates with zero audio output. This type of detector has a high output, but it does not discriminate against amplitude interference and must be preceded by one or more limiter stages.

*Differential Peak Detector (Figure 18-6b).* This detector uses differential amplifiers and two resonant circuits. One tuned circuit is shown in the diagram. It is resonant to a frequency slightly higher than 4.5 MHz. The other tuned circuit is represented by the stray capacity between point A and ground and is resonant slightly lower than 4.5 MHz. The signal amplitude at point A is greatest at frequencies lower than 4.5 MHz. At the SIF input to the detector, the signal is strongest for frequencies higher than 4.5 MHz. As indicated in the diagram, the signal is demodulated by the two curves, then applied to the differential amplifier. In this manner, IF frequency deviations are converted into audio voltage variations.

*Quadrature Detector (Figure 18-6c).* Here the detector is fed from a limiter stage that removes noise and any amplitude variations from the signal. The relative phase relationships between signals at the ends of the tuned circuit (commonly called a quad coil) are compared by the NAND gate, which functions as a balanced discriminator. The gate is turned on to produce an output when both input signals are either positive or negative. The width of the output signal varies at an audio rate dependent on the FM signal deviations above and below the center frequency.

*Synchronous Detector.* An equivalent circuit is shown in Figure 13-8. The only major difference between a synchronous sound detector and the video detector shown is the frequency. As described in Chapter 13, the generated carrier signal is synchronized with the station signal to produce two out-of-phase signals from the differential amplifiers. These signals are alternately switched on and off by the four switching transistors to produce the demodulated AF output.

### Audio Stages

Several audio stages are needed to boost the low output of the detector to develop enough audio *power* to drive the speaker(s). Besides voltage gain and power, the amplifier must have a good frequency response with negligible distortion and hum. A well-designed high-fidelity amplifier has a linear response that is nearly flat for all frequencies in the AF spectrum, from about 50 Hz to 15 kHz, and preferably higher to do justice to the high overtones that contribute greatly to the quality of the sound. To satisfy individual tastes, some form of tone control or frequency compensation is usually provided. Several factors must be considered in a sound system to reproduce faithfully all frequencies in the AF spectrum.

*Sound Power (Volume).* The average TV produces up to 1 or 2 W of audio power as developed by the AF output stage. The power-handling capability of the speaker(s) is rated accordingly. By comparison, an outdoor sound system may be rated at several hundred watts with a speaker system to match.

*AF Voltage Amplification.* This must be sufficient to drive the output stage to full power without distortion.

*Frequency Response.* This is established in the overall design of the amplifier and the quality of the speakers.

*Distortion.* This is minimized with proper design and the use of good-quality components. Amplifier overload is a common cause of distortion.

*Hum.* Hum is no longer the problem that it once was. Hum pickup from the power line and power circuits in the set is prevented with proper placement of parts and shielding. Good filtering of the primary power supply is essential.

*Power Supply.* This is an important consideration often overlooked. It must have good regulation and be able to supply sudden high current demands of the output stage, particularly at low audio frequencies.

### Audio Voltage Amplifiers

One or two *voltage* amplifiers are generally required because the audio output from the detector (about 1 V p-p) is much too weak to drive the next stage. A typical amplifier operates class A in a common-emitter configuration for maximum gain (about × 10) and minimum distortion. A typical circuit for a BW set is shown in Figure 18-7. All audio functions in modern sets, of course, are performed by ICs. Earlier models using discrete components often used transistors in pairs in a Darlington hookup. Dc coupling is generally used between stages to prevent phase distortion and attenuation of the low bass frequencies. Negative feedback is commonly employed for stability, improved frequency response, and to reduce distortion.

As with any high-gain amplifier, signal input

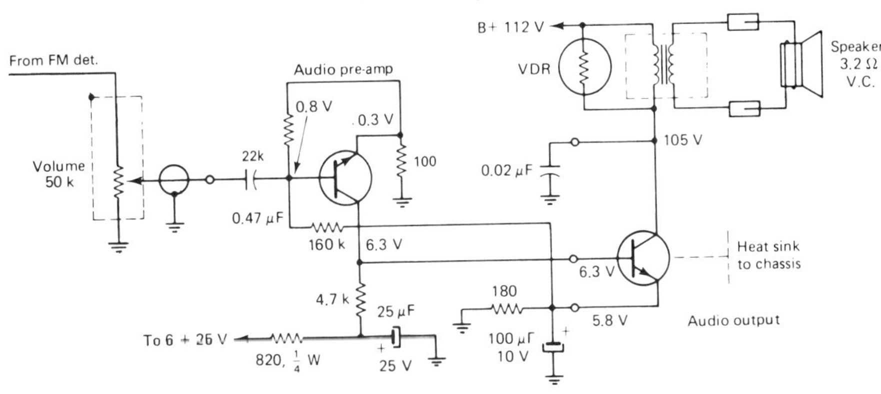


**FIG. 18-7** Typical BW set AF circuit. Note typical component values and dc voltage distribution.

leads must be shielded to prevent hum pickup. The same holds true for the hot wires connecting to front-panel volume and tone controls in older sets. Currently, most controls vary the dc bias of a transistor (or IC amplifier), and with the control at "signal ground" potential, shielding is not necessary.

### 18-3 VOLUME CONTROL

Sound volume is controlled by varying the amplitude of the audio signal in the first AF stage. There are two methods of control. Early-model sets used a potentiometer that functions as a variable (AF) voltage divider (Figure 18-7). To compensate for the nonuniform response of the human ear and other factors, such controls often had one or two taps connecting to capacitors as a means of increasing bass response when the control is turned down. Some controls are linear; others are tapered to provide a more gradual resistance variation and smoother control. With many sets, the volume and power-on switch are combined. Modern sets use dc control as explained previously, and many are slide controls rather than the older rotary type.

### 18-4 TONE CONTROL

A simple but effective tone control consists of a capacitor and a pot, series connected to some hot (high-impedance) point in an AF amplifier (Figure 18-8a). The capacitor shunts some of the treble frequencies (those in the 1 to 15 kHz range) to ground, giving the effect of an increase in bass. It also attenuates undesirable high frequencies such as static and background hiss. The larger the capacitor, the greater the effect as more and more high frequencies are grounded out. The pot provides a convenient way of changing the capacitive reactance of the circuit for a gradual change in tone. With some sets, the switch is on the tone control.

In Figure 18-8b there are two coupling capacitors (CCs) in series, with a pot shunting the smaller value. With the pot arm to the left, the capacitor is shorted out, and the larger CC readily passes the

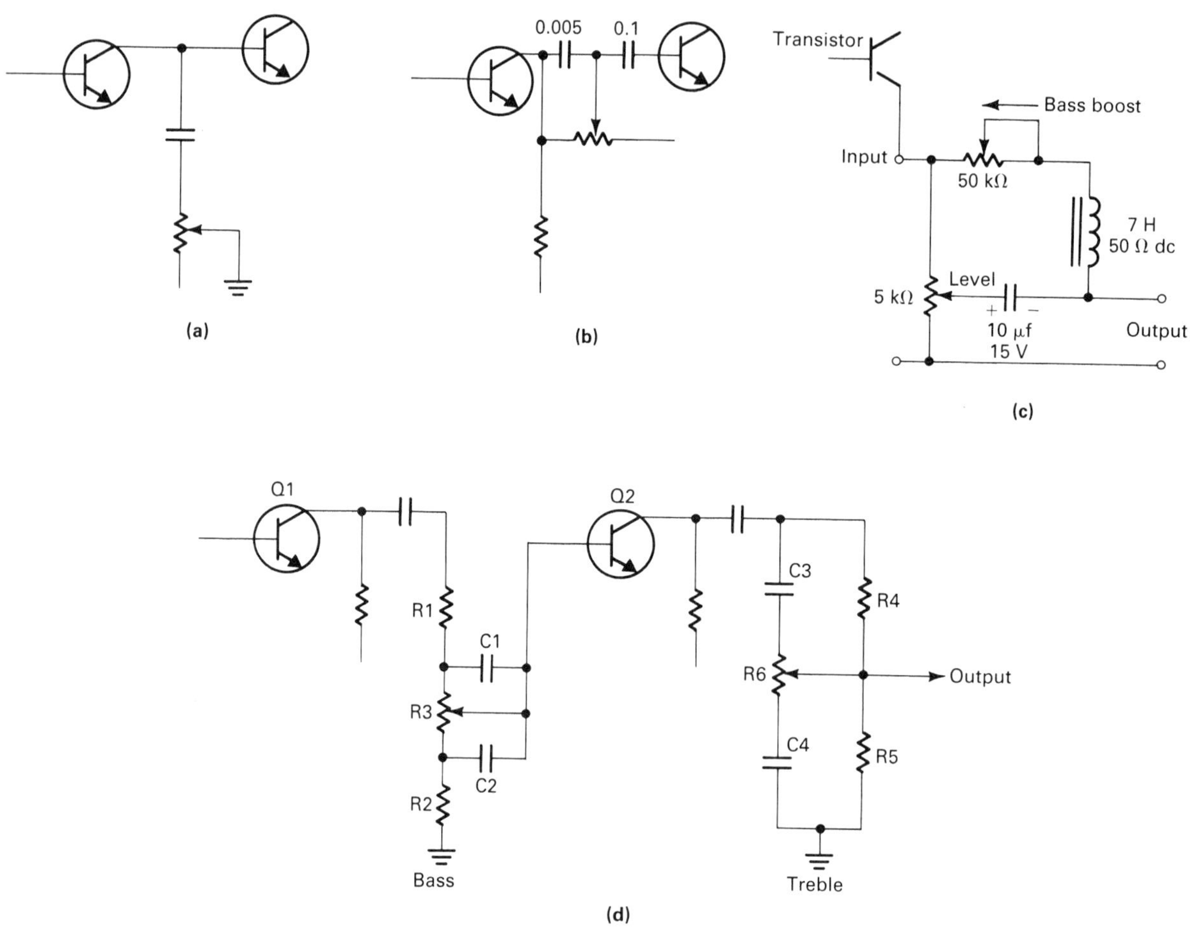


**FIG. 18-8** Tone control circuits.

low frequencies. With the pot arm at the extreme right, the net value of coupling capacitance is somewhat less than the smaller one of the two. With the increase in capacitive reactance only the high frequencies get through.

Figure 18-8c shows a *bass boost* circuit to raise the level of frequencies in the 30 Hz to 1 kHz range. Here the pot and the inductor represent a variable XL circuit shunting the 5 kΩ volume control and the coupling capacitor. Maximum boost occurs when the inductive reactance is highest with the pot shorted out.

Circuit (d) has separate bass and treble boost controls. The bass boost control functions as a variable-frequency voltage divider. With the control arm at the top, C2 bypasses R3, creating low impedance for high frequencies at the Q1 output. For reduced bass (more treble) C1 bypasses R3 to increase the high-frequency output. With the treble control arm at the bottom, the parallel *RC* components attenuate the high frequencies because C4 bypasses the output resistor. The effect is negligible at low frequencies.

### Negative Feedback

This is one method to reduce distortion and improve the quality of sound from an AF amplifier. It is the opposite to positive feedback used to produce oscillations in an oscillator. With negative feedback, some of the signal from the output of an amplifier is fed back via an *RC* network to some upstream point, where the signal is 180° out of phase to partially cancel any distortion on the feedback signal. Of course, the total signal is reduced by the same proportion. The greater the feedback (within practical limits), the lower the distortion and the better the response, but at the expense of amplification. But this is no problem since signal loss is easily compensated for by adding more amplifiers.

The feedback "loop" may encompass either one or several stages to improve their response. In Figure 18-7, for example, feedback is used from the emitter of the output stage, through a 160-kΩ resistor, to the input of the previous stage. Some feedback circuits are frequency selective, a system of tone control. Another use of negative feedback is to improve the stability of an amplifier by offsetting any positive feedback that may be present.

### Audio Driver Amplifiers

As an electromechanical device, a speaker requires audio *power* (in the form of voltage *and current*) for its operation. For moderate sound levels, most small receivers use a "single-ended" output stage operating class A, which can be adequately driven by a *voltage* amplifier (Figure 18-7). Modern sets have a two-transistor output stage operating class B or A-B with a fairly high bias. To overcome the bias and produce an output, such a stage requires a certain amount of drive *power*. This calls for a medium-power driver stage following the AF voltage amplifier. In the example shown, the output stage is driven by a stage called a preamp, which, operating in the emitter-follower configuration, functions as a combined voltage and driver amplifier.

### Power Output Stage

Early-model TV sets had a single-ended output stage, but for efficient operation and high output with minimum distortion, most sets now use two output transistors, operating *push-pull*. This means each transistor is operating on alternate half-cycles and each contributing one-half of the total output power. In the absence of a signal, each transistor is biased at (or close to) current cutoff for class B or A-B operation. With signal applied, the transistors conduct alternately for brief periods corresponding with the peaks of the input signal, with one transistor taking over where the other leaves off. At the output circuit, the audio power produced by the two transistors is combined to drive the speaker(s). As in other power amplifier stages (e.g., the vertical and horizontal sweep outputs), considerable heat is developed by the transistor(s) and a heat sink is required. Sometimes the driver also has a sink.

*Coupling and Impedance Matching.* In any electrical or electronic circuit, a 1:1 impedance match is required for maximum power transfer from the source to the load. With an AF power output stage, both the input and output circuits must be considered, in this case the previous stage being the source, and the speaker, the load. Where the output stage is preceded by a driver, the driver is usually an emitter follower and a good match is obtained from the emitter of the driver to the base of the output transistor. In early model sets, an impedance matching transformer was used here.

There are two ways of coupling the signal from the output stage to the speaker(s): from the low-impedance emitter circuit, or with a "step-down" output transformer to match the low impedance of the speaker voice coil.

*Power Output Circuits.* The earliest push-pull output amplifiers used center-tapped transformers at both input and output. This provided a signal gain and even-harmonic distortion was canceled out by bucking action at the speaker. But high-quality transformers are expensive. Modern sets use some version of the complementary-symmetry amplifier now used in all *vertical sweep* output circuits described in Chapter 7 and shown in Figure 7-12. Except for component values and that the yoke is replaced by the speaker, the theory of operation is essentially the same. Where identical transistors are used, they must be driven with signals of opposite polarity. If one transistor is an NPN and the other a PNP, the same signal polarity drives both. Note that some circuits are supplied from both positive and negative PSs, and some circuits require a large-value coupling capacitor feeding the load. This can be dispensed with where there is zero dc voltage at the junction of the two transistors. A problem with complementary-symmetry circuits is a form of crossover distortion that occurs if the transistors are not balanced or driven by improper amounts of signal voltage.

## 18-5 SPEAKER(s)

As shown in Figure 18-9, a speaker has a paper cone to which is attached a small coil called the voice coil. Connections are made via flexible leads to small eyelets on the cone. An iron yoke surrounds the voice coil with a small gap between it and the center pole piece, which consists of a strong permanant magnet. The cone and voice coil assembly is supported by a flexible inner cone and the flexible outer rim of the cone. This enables the cone and coil to move freely in and out when energized.

A speaker operates using the same principles as an electric motor. Audio signals applied to the voice coil develop magnetic fields that react with the flux of the permanent magnet. By attraction and repulsion the cone is moved in and out in accordance with the signal, the direction of motion reversing with each reversal of the signal. High frequencies create small but rapid excursions of the cone: low bass frequencies create large and slow movements. Audible harmonics are generated by vibrations of the cone surface between the apex and the rim.

The quality of sound emanating from a speaker can be enhanced by enclosing it in a box or cabinet of the proper proportions and volume, based on the time required for sound waves at the front to interact with those coming from the rear. Such an enclosure adds volume and depth to the sound, especially the lows. A good speaker will faithfully reproduce sounds over the entire audible spectrum. For optimum results, separate speakers are often used: a large speaker (called a *woofer*), which favors the low frequencies, and small speakers, called *tweeters,* for the highs. One or more midrange speakers may also be used in an enclosure. Multiple speakers must be *phased*—connected such that their cones move in and out in unison.

Speakers are rated according to their power-handling ability, efficiency, and frequency range. A small speaker from a radio or TV will be destroyed quickly if connected to a high-power sound system. Voice coil impedances vary from about 3 to 32 Ω or so. The resistance of a voice coil as measured with an ohmmeter is considerably less than its impedance.

Where multiple speakers are used, generally they are excited separately via a combination of

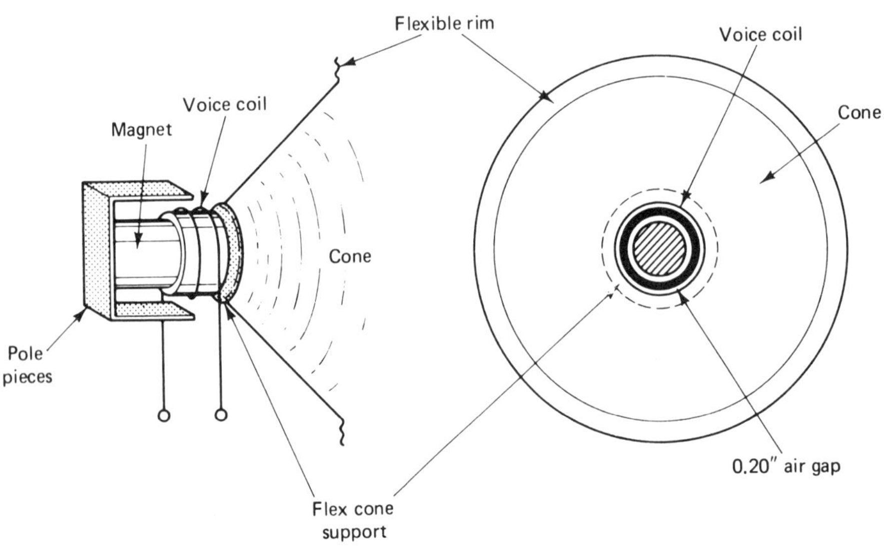


**FIG. 18-9** Typical speaker construction.

LCR components called a crossover network, whose function is to split up the signal, driving each speaker with the range of frequencies for which it was designed.

## 18-6 FOLDOUT SCHEMATIC

Most of the sound processing takes place in IC601. The 4.5-MHz SIF signal from pin 12 of IC101 is applied to pins 1 and 2 of IC601 through C601, C602, and the 4.5-MHz ceramic filter Z601. In the IC the signal is amplified by a limiter, then applied to the differential amplifier type detector which is tuned by L602 and the ceramic filter Z602. The detected signal is applied to the internal AF amplifier via pin 14. The dc volume control varies the gain of a control amplifier from pin 6, prior to deemphasis of the high frequencies. The amplified AF output signal at pin 12 is coupled through C 654 to the power output transistors Q 601, Q 602. From the complementary symmetry output stage the signal goes to the speaker via C 656 and the output transformer.

## 18-7 MTS/STEREO

Two ears enable us to "orient" and determine the direction from which sound is coming. Monaural sound coming from one or more TV speakers is not oriented to any particular images or their positions on the screen. Stereo, on the other hand, adds a sense of realism and directivity to TV sound. Sounds corresponding to the "action" observed on the left side of the screen are most predominantly picked up by our left ear, and sounds relating to the right side of an image are heard mostly by our right ear. A stereo system has two separate "channels"; amplifiers that handle the left-side signals and identical amplifiers for the right-side signals. Each channel drives its corresponding left and right speakers which are spaced some distance apart.

To clear up a common misconception, the terms stereo and HI-Fi are not necessarily synonymous. You can have one without the other; an inferior stereo system having poor separation but good fidelity, or a good stereo system with poor or mediocre sound quality. The ideal of course is both, the best of two worlds.

The long awaited method for producing true stereophonic TV sound that's compatible with monaural receivers became a reality with the first TV stereo broadcasts in 1985. Prior to that, a less practical method called "simulcast" was used for a time where the dual channel sound for a TV station was transmitted on the FM broadcast band. Another system, still in use on some sets is known as "quasi" or "pseudo" stereo," a system that somewhat enhances monaural sound by giving it a simulated stereo effect. Then there are adaptors available for converting a mono set to stereo. In this writer's opinion, they are hardly worth the bother or expense.

Actually, MTS stereo is not too different from the system long used for FM (MPX) stereo radio broadcasting and reception. Compatibility with regular TVs came about by utilizing previously unused portions of each TV channel allocation. (Figure 18-10). When broadcasting stereo, a station simultaneously transmits several different signals, as shown in Figure 18-11. These are processed into one mul-

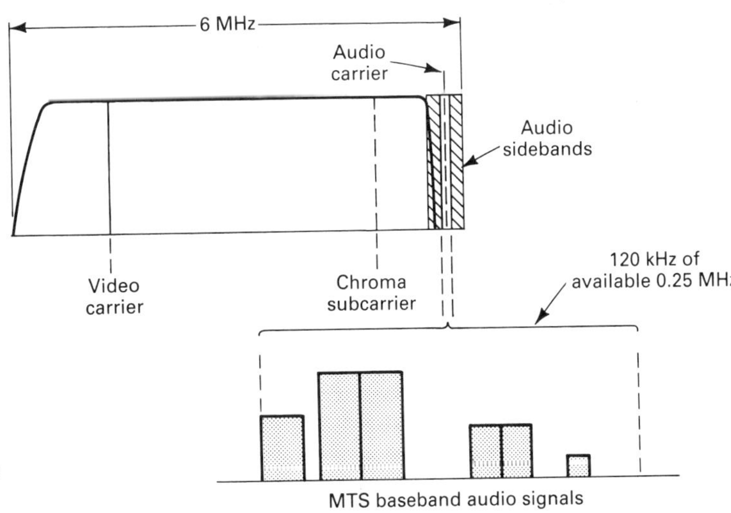


**FIG. 18-10** MTS usage of TV channel allocations.

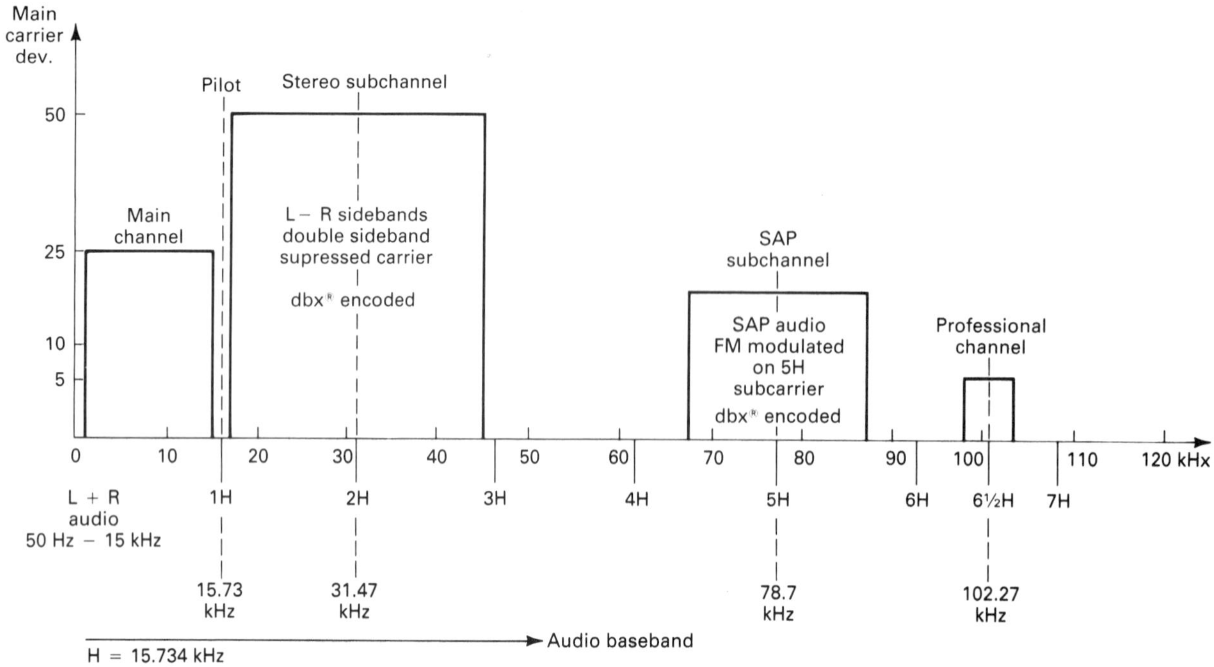


**FIG. 18-11** MTS/stereo baseband signals. Each of the signals making up composite audio occupies a different range of frequencies so that the receiver is able to separate and process each signal individually. (Courtesy of *Sencore News.*)

tiplexed *composite audio signal* prior to transmission. At the receiver, each signal is separately processed, then recombined to produce left and right audio signals to drive the speakers.

## Composite Audio Signal

In the figure, the various signals that comprise the composite signal are shown on an audio *baseband* representing 120 kHz of the assigned audio portion of the RF spectrum. The symbol H corresponds to 15.734 kHz, the horizontal sweep frequency, to which all signals are phase locked. Each of the MTS "signals" exists as a *sideband* to a subcarrier of a specific frequency. Each group of sideband frequencies (as indicated by rectangular blocks) is called a *subchannel.* A stereo receiver separates and processes the subchannel signals individually. The subcarriers of each subchannel are generated at the station and in the receiver. Each subcarrier is a multiple of the H reference frequency.

The "height" of the subchannel blocks is indicative of signal strength, that is, the amplitude of the signals, which for FM is usually expressed as *frequency deviation* (in kilohertz). The greater the deviation, the stronger the signal. From left to right in the drawing, the channels are as follows.

*Main Channel.* This block represents the signals broadcast for both regular monaural reception and stereo. For compatibility, requirements are the same for each. The frequency range is from 50 Hz to 15 kHz, with a deviation of ±25 kHz for 100% modulation. For a stereo broadcast, the sound signals from both the left and right sources (microphones or whatever) are combined in the receiver to produce left and right speaker signals.

*Pilot.* This is a CW signal slightly higher in frequency on the baseband at precisely 15.734 kHz (the frequency of the horizontal sweep). As with the 19-kHz pilot of FM stereo radio, it is used by the receiver as a reference signal for phase locking and synchronizing all other MTS signals and functions. Its presence also tells the MTS circuits that stereo is being broadcast.

*Stereo Subchannel.* This block represents L − R (left minus right) double sidebands of a 31.468-kHz (2H) subcarrier. The carrier is suppressed at the station, then reinserted at the receiver for the purpose of demodulation. Unfortunately, the bandwidth of this subchannel is restricted to 13 kHz, somewhat less than the 15-kHz capability of the main channel. With an amplitude (deviation) of 50 kHz, the transmitted stereo signals are twice as strong as those of the main channel to obtain a high signal-to-noise ratio which is necessary to minimize noise. The signals described thus far are all that are needed for stereo reception.

*Second Audio Program (SAP) Subchannel.* This is a band of frequencies allocated for the optional transmission of special programs, such as a second-language broadcast. It consists of sidebands to a 78.67-kHz (5H) subcarrier that is suppressed at the station and reinserted at the receiver. As noted, the deviation is somewhat less than for the main and stereo subchannels.

*Professional Channel.* At the time of writing, this band of signals is not intended for use by the general public. The subcarrier used is 102.371 kHz ($6\frac{1}{2}$ H), with considerably less amplitude and frequency range than those of the other subchannels.

### TV Station Functions

MTS/stereo theory as applied to a receiver requires some understanding of what takes place at the station where the signals are generated. A block diagram of station functions is shown in Figure 18-12.

*Developing the MTS/Stereo Signals.* The amplified audio signals from the microphones (or other stereo source) are added together in a matrix amplifier. One output from the matrix is the sum of the left and right signals identified as (L + R). The right signal in the matrix is inverted to produce a "difference" signal identified as L − R (L minus R) audio. After going through a preemphasis network, the L + R audio is transmitted for use by mono receivers. For a stereo broadcast it is combined with other signals as shown.

For stereo, the L − R output from the matrix is first processed by a *DBX encoder,* whose function is to reduce noise. The L − R audio signal, which is virtually noise-free, then goes to a balanced AM modulator where the L − R audio modulates a 31.468-kHz subcarrier. (By comparison, the subcarrier used with FM stereo radio is 38 kHz.) The subcarrier itself is suppressed by the modulator. The modulator output consists of amplitude variations of the sideband signals that correspond with the left and right inputs from the microphones. The encoded sideband signals are then combined with L + R audio.

The 15.734-kHz pilot signal, as used by the receiver for synchronizing all signals, is also combined with the L + R and L − R signals as part of the composite audio signal.

The optional SAP and professional channel signals (if used), which also exist as sidebands to subcarriers, are likewise combined with the others. The

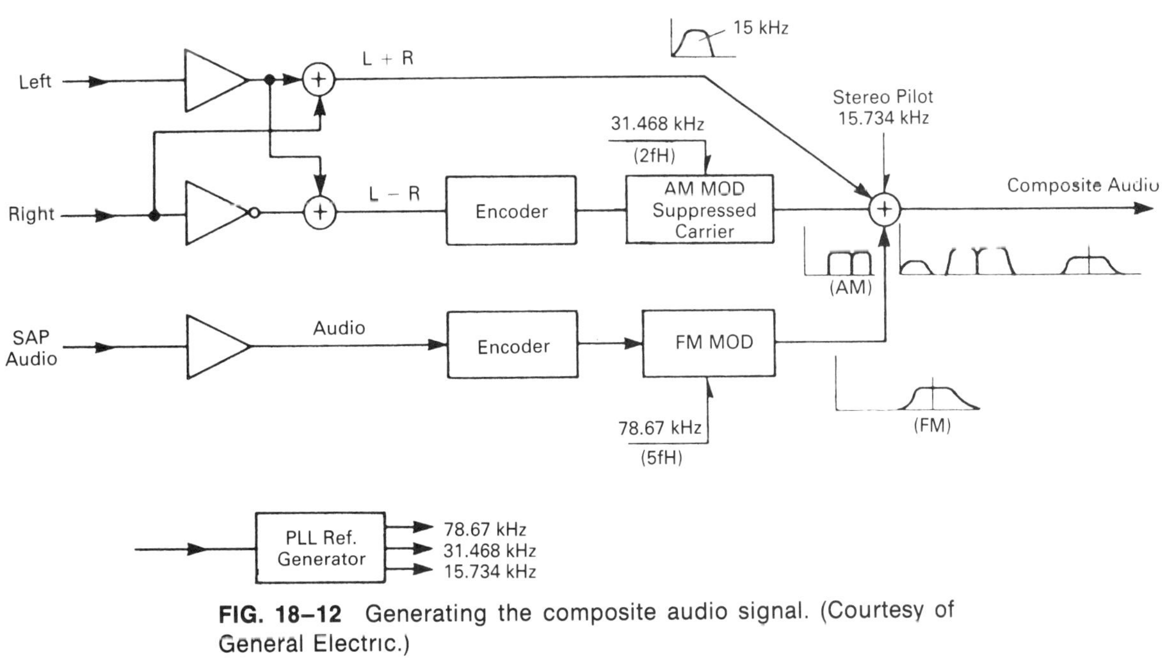


**FIG. 18–12** Generating the composite audio signal. (Courtesy of General Electric.)

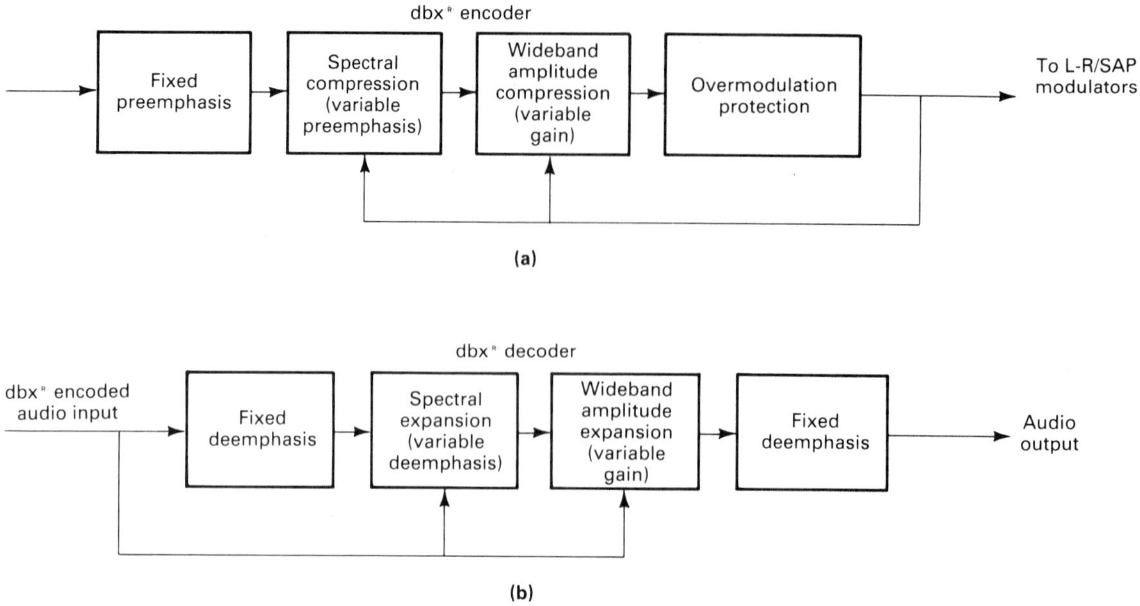


**FIG. 18-13** DBX noise reduction system: (a) the stereo subchannel (L − R) and SAP circuits each use noise encoding to reduce the noise level in the audio signals; (b) the receiver decodes the L − R and SAP Audio to complete the noise reduction process begun at the transmitter (a development of the DBX Corporation).

combined signals (the composite audio signal) are then used to frequency modulate the transmitter.

*DBX Encoder.* Noise reduction is an important consideration with MTS/stereo. High-frequency noise (hiss) is created from various sources, primarily from the use of 2H and 5H subcarriers. Most of the noise is overcome in three ways: using a high modulation level for the L − R signal compared to the main channel L + R signal, with conventional preemphasis and deemphasis, and by "masking" the noise with the DBX system.

The functions performed by the DBX noise reduction system as used by the station and the receivers are shown in Figure 18-13. The high treble frequencies of the signal are first preemphasized with a 390-μs *RC* network. The next stage (sometimes called *spectral compression* or *companding*) is a system of variable preemphasis which monitors the high-frequency content of the signal and adjusts its level accordingly: emphasizing the highs when they are down and attenuating them when they exceed certain limits. The next stage provides *wideband amplitude compression,* which, simply stated, automatically regulates the overall gain. In this respect it can be likened to AGC. The final stage of the DBX encoder as shown is needed to prevent overmodulation of the audio carrier.

## Stereo Receiver

Although the following description is for MTS/stereo TV, in essence, it also applies to some monitors and late-model stereo VCRs. A simplified block diagram is shown in Figure 18-14. Note how each block corresponds with those at the station. Having only a few discrete components, most stereo functions are performed by ICs.

A mono set receiving a stereo broadcast simply disregards the information contained in the stereo subchannels, and for a mono broadcast, only the L + R main channel is transmitted. At the receiver, in the absence of a pilot signal, all stereo-related circuits are disabled. The audio from the FM sound detector goes through a 1H low-pass filter which passes the normal range of audio frequencies, from 50 Hz to 15 kHz. From here, a conventional deemphasis network restores the treble frequencies to their normal level. At the same time, a phase comparer delays the signal to match the phase shift introduced by the DBX circuit in the L − R subchannel when receiving stereo. From here the mono signal is routed via a matrix and an electronic switch to the audio amplifiers and speaker(s).

When receiving stereo, the *composite sound signal,* which contains additional signals, divides, as shown in the diagram. The main channel (L + R

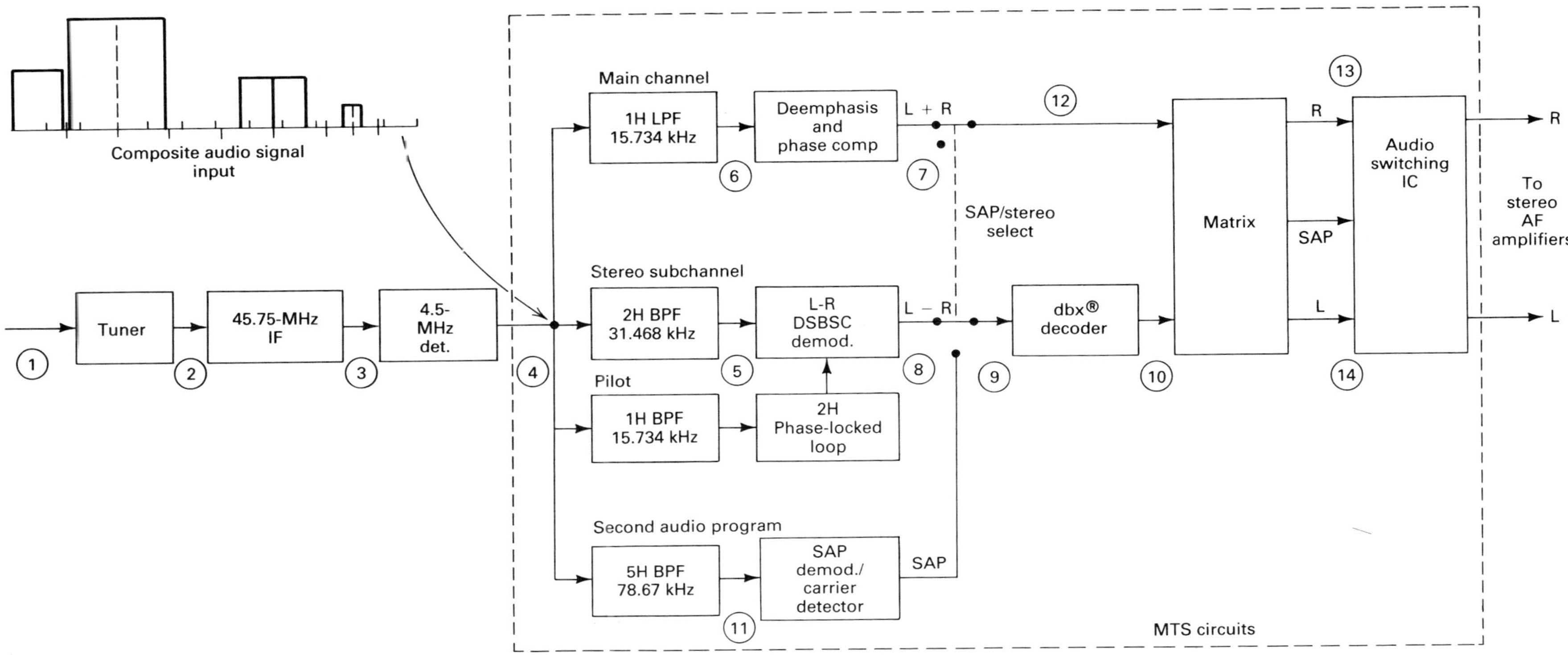


**FIG. 18-14** MTS/Stereo receiver functions. The MTS receiver separates the composite audio signal to process each part of the signal in its own circuit.

mono signal) is routed to the matrix as for mono reception. The L − R signal is amplified in the stereo subchannel, then demodulated to recover the L − R sidebands. Demodulation is accomplished with a balanced demodulator and a locally generated 31.468-kHz subcarrier that is phase locked to the 15.734-kHz pilot signal received. The demodulated stereo signal is routed through a selector switch and processed by a DBX *decoder* (Figure 18-13b), to remove noise generated in the receiver. It is then combined in a matrix with the phase-delayed L + R audio to produce the two original left and right channel signals. These are then routed via an audio switching IC to conventional dual-channel driver and power output stages to drive the speakers.

The stereo pilot is an unmodulated 15.734-kHz carrier signal that first passes through a 1H bandpass filter. Its frequency is then doubled to demodulate the L − R signals. Besides telling the set when a stereo signal is being received, the pilot also operates the panel stereo light.

SAP processing is essentially the same as for an L − R signal. If SAP audio is being received, its 78.67-kHz subcarrier is demodulated and its audio sidebands routed through the stereo/SAP selector switch, processed by the DBX decoder and the matrix, then switched by the audio switching IC in the same manner as the L − R signal. Note that the L + R and L − R signals are disabled when receiving SAP, and vice versa. Sometimes the SAP circuit has its own separate decoder.

*Noise Reduction at the Receiver.* The functions performed by the receiver DBX *decoder* are opposite to those performed at the station (see Figure 18-13b). Here the decoder *expands* the previously compressed L − R and SAP signals. This is accomplished in three steps as shown, with deemphasis to counteract the preemphasis. Deemphasis attenuates the signal to its normal level, reducing the noise by the same proportions.

*Audio Switching.* An analog electronic switch (in a switching IC) is used to switch the left and right outputs of the matrix between SAP and stereo as manually selected by the user. Switching is initiated either manually or automatically when a SAP signal is received. The IC has several inputs but only two outputs, the left and right signals driving the dual-channel AF amplifiers.

### Dual-Channel AF Amplifiers

Stereo, of course, requires two AF amplifiers and at least two speakers physically separated from each other, preferably by at least 10 feet or more, consistent with the position of the listener(s). From the stereo matrix (Figure 18-14), and after going through the electronic switch, the left and right audio signals are amplified by separate voltage and power amplifiers to drive the speakers. The amplifiers are identical, each driving its associated speaker(s) by the same amount, although the gain of each channel can be independently controlled. A balance control is provided to equalize the sound outputs. In some cases the user can also control the amount of separation. Needless to say, hi-fi stereo requires amplifiers with low distortion, excellent frequency response, and adequate sound power for the purpose intended. Equally important are good-quality speakers, which do not come cheap. Reminder: the terms *hi-fi* and *stereo* are not necessarily synonymous, since you can have one without the other, which is often the case.

## 18-8 MONAURAL TV TROUBLESHOOTING

Although sound stages use the same basic circuits and components as in other sections of a set, strangely enough, problems here are relatively few. When they do occur, the usual troubleshooting approach is followed: that is, analyzing the symptoms; familiarizing yourself with the schematic and the chassis; inspection, particularly in the suspected areas; signal tracing or injection to localize the defect; and finally, isolating and replacing bad components. Although always a possibility, alignment of the tuned circuits in the IF strip is seldom required.

A good place to start is midway between the sound takeoff and the speaker, namely, the FM detector. Assuming a picture but no sound, check for the presence of an AF signal at the detector output. If okay, work downstream using a scope or other indicator until a point is reached where the signal becomes lost. An alternative approach is with AF signal substitution. For trouble ahead of the detector, the procedure is the same, working upstream with signal tracing or injection with a modulated RF generator.

Trouble symptoms and procedures for a mono receiver are described first. As a guide, refer to the flow drawings, Figure 18-15. Troubles peculiar to stereo are treated later.

### Symptoms and Procedures

*No Sound. (picture okay)*

***Probable causes:*** Loss of B+ to sound stages; bad speaker; defect in some stage between the sound takeoff and the speaker, which includes the

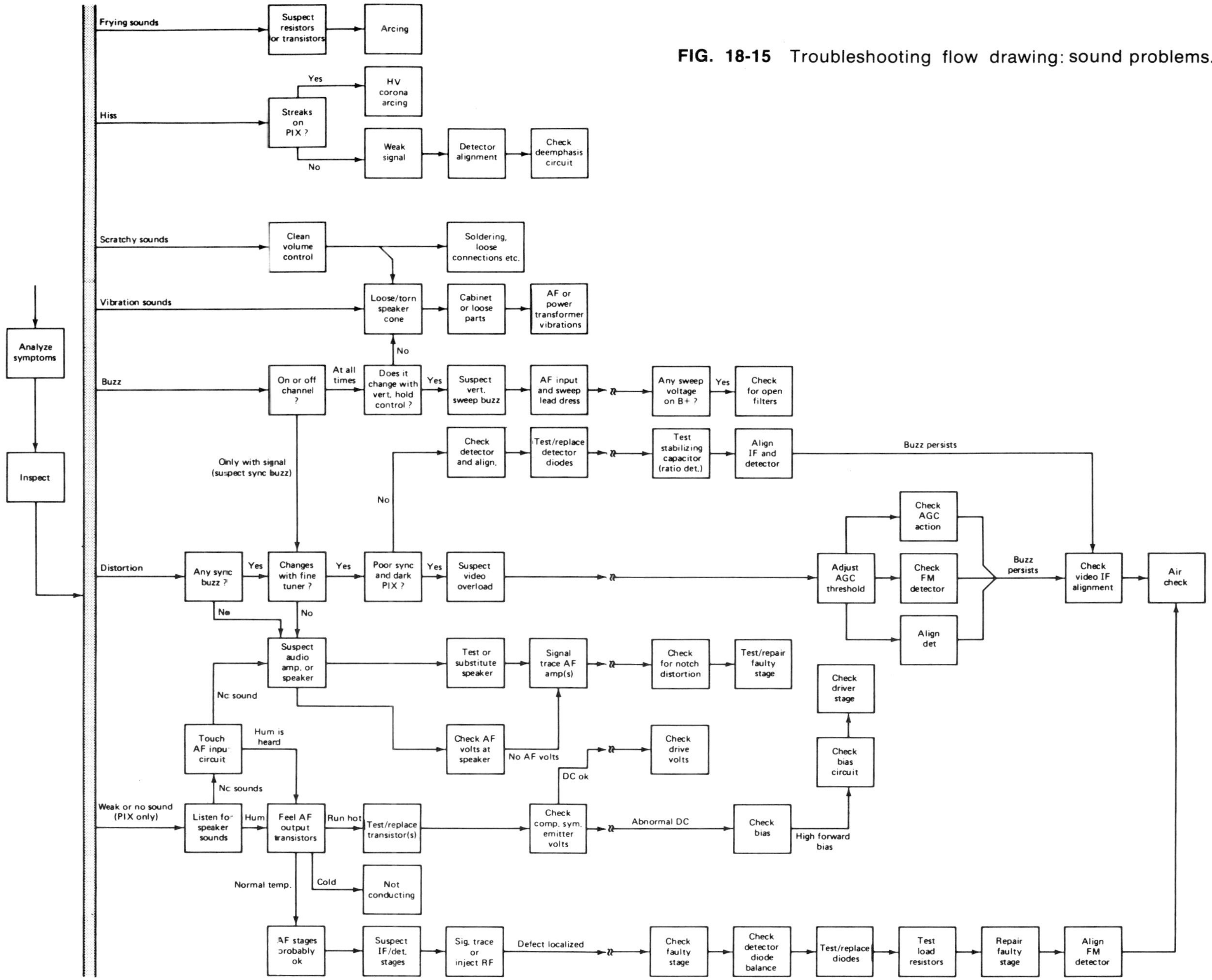


**FIG. 18-15** Troubleshooting flow drawing: sound problems.

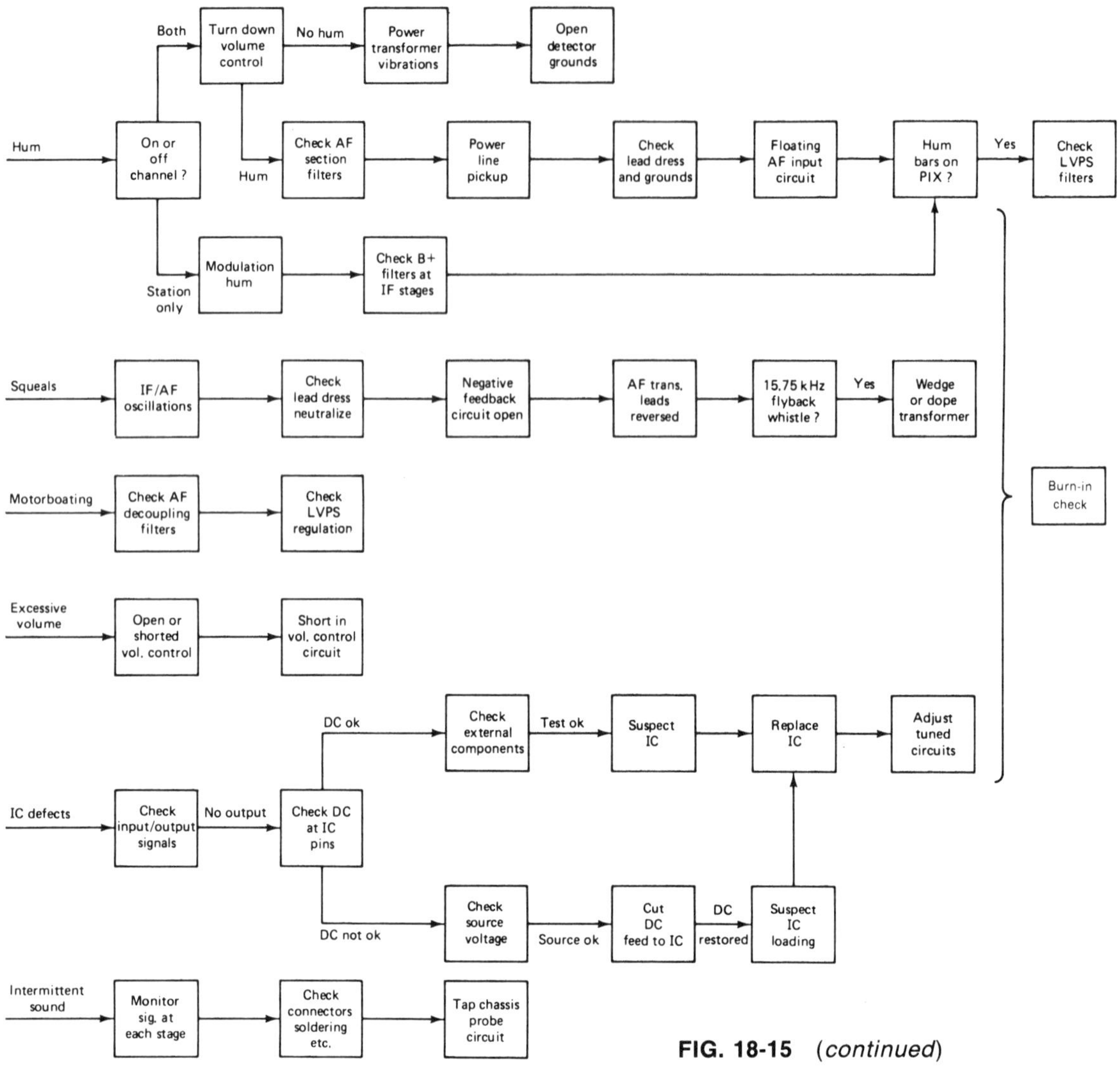


**FIG. 18-15** *(continued)*

sound IF detector if a color set, the sound IF and limiter stages, the FM detector, and the audio amplifiers.

Listen for hum or other background sounds from the speaker. If there is some sound, the AF amplifiers and speaker are probably okay. Contact the input to the first AF stage. Body pickup of the power line field should produce a hum from the speaker. Little or no hum indicates trouble downstream from the point of contact. Check for B+. For AF amplifier problems, localize the defect by injecting an AF signal at the input and output of each stage. As an alternative, signal trace the station or generator signal using a scope, ac meter, or other indicator.

If the defect is ahead of the detector, trace the signal through the IF and limiter stages using a demodulator probe with the scope or other indicator. As an alternative, use signal injection with the generator set for 4.5 MHz. Where IF and AF stages are not the problem, check the detector. Once localized, check applied voltages and all components in the bad stage, starting with the transistor or IC. Replace any that are suspect.

*Weak Sound.* (Picture Okay)

***Probable causes:*** Gain loss in any of the sound stages; Low B+; IF misalignment.

Check B+. Localize the defect by signal tracing or injection, as described for total loss of sound. In this case, look for a weak rather than a dead stage. Misalignment is rare, but if suspected, proceed as described later.

*Distorted (Garbled) Sound.* (not to be confused with buzz, hum, or other background noises)

***Probable causes:*** Bad speaker; AF amplifier defect; FM detector defect or misalignment.

Try a substitute speaker. Monitor the sound at

the input and output of each AF stage. When localized, check the transistor, its operating voltages, and all associated components. Common problems are transistor leakage and improper bias. Notch distortion in the push-pull output stage is usually caused by B/E input circuit defects and defective or unbalanced transistors. Check for thermal runaway. Replace transistors as a matched pair.

The cause of moderate distortion and general poor quality can best be localized by injecting either a sine- or square-wave signal and scope checking for abnormal waveshapes at each stage. Check for different frequencies and signal levels, but avoid overload, particularly in low-level preamp stages. If warranted, run a complete frequency response check for different power output levels, using a resistor instead of the speaker as a load. Where multiple speakers are used, make sure that they are properly phased.

Improper operation of an FM detector will create distortion. Try substituting for the transistor, IC, or other suspect components. If the problem persists, check the detector alignment as described later.

*Background Sounds.* (hum, buzz, squeals or motorboating, hiss or sizzling sounds, static and scratchy noises)

***Probable causes:*** Although all possible causes are too numerous to be described fully at this time, the characteristic sounds are easily recognized and can generally be associated with certain kinds of defects or abnormal operating conditions.

*Hum* is usually caused by poor filtering of the primary PS, improper lead dressing, or inadequate shielding or grounding of AF amplifier input circuits. If hum is present off channel, suspect the AF B+ feed. If it is a tunable hum that is present only when tuned to a station, it is probably poor filtering of the B+ feeding the IF stages. Where open or dried-up electrolytics are suspected, try bridging with a suitable substitute capacitor. Another approach is to measure the ac component at the terminals. An ac reading greater than 1 or 2 V generally indicates a filtering problem.

There are several kinds of *buzz,* each with a different cause: a torn speaker cone, for example, or vibrations due to loose laminations in a power transformer or the vertical or audio output transformer on some older sets. Then there is an intercarrier "sync buzz" resulting from video and vertical sync getting into the sound stages, as caused by video overdrive, IF/detector misalignment, or an improperly operating limiter stage. Interference from the vertical sweep can be identified by a change in pitch as the hold control is varied.

*Squeals and motorboating* sounds are generally caused by positive feedback and oscillations. Check for improper shielding or grounding of critical components in the video and sound stages. Poor grounding of the coax between the tuner and the IF strip input is quite common. Check for open decoupling capacitors in signal stages that are suspect. Another possibility is poor regulation of the PS, or inadequate decoupling.

*Hiss* is a faint high-pitched sound often caused by HV corona arcing (Chapter 10), or problems with the deemphasis network and tone control circuits. A certain amount of background hiss is considered normal when receiving a weak station.

*Scratchy noises* or frying sounds can be caused by bad tuner contacts in older sets, and also by "noisy" volume and tone controls. Cleaning usually takes care of such problems. Other possibilities are poor soldering, defective components, or a speaker voice coil that is rubbing. Look for telltale signs of corrosion around component terminals. Suspect resistors that have been overloaded as indicated by a scorched appearance or obscured color coding. Alternate applications of heat and cold will often show up such conditions. Where an IC is suspect, replace it.

Many of the sounds described and others also show up on the CRT screen, which often provides a clue to the cause: for example, picture streaking due to horizontal oscillator squegging, internal arcing or interference picked up from external sources, the bright sparkles caused by car ignition systems, lightning, or nearby electrical equipment. Use coax for the antenna lead-in. Although not always effective, try installing filters in the power line. Where the problem is persistent and severe, also consider adding a noise-limiting circuit in the sound section.

*Intermittent Sound*

***Probable causes:*** Anything that interrupts the normal sound from the speaker(s): intermittent dc supplying the sound stages, defects at any point between the sound takeoff and the speaker; common troubles include poor soldering, loose or dirty edge connectors on PCBs, hairline cracks in PCB wiring, and intermittent open or short circuits in wiring or components.

Proceed as described in Chapter 5. Monitor the dc feeding the sound stages. Monitor the station signal or an injected generator signal at various key checkpoints. Try to create the condition by tapping, probing, applying heat and cold or whatever it takes until the trouble shows up and can be identified. Test or replace all suspected components.

### Sound IF and Detector Alignment

As with most tuned stages in modern sets, realignment is seldom required unless tampered with, the circuit is disturbed, or a part is replaced. When adjustments *are* called for, generally a slight touch-up will suffice. The procedure is not difficult or time consuming, but the adjustments are *critical,* especially those in the FM detector, where the slightest misalignment results in symptoms of weak distorted sound, sometimes accompanied by buzz. Three alignment methods are described as follows. To avoid damage to coils and core slugs, use the proper nonmetallic alignment tools. A screwdriver is a no-no.

*Alignment by Ear.* No instruments are required. Select any given channel, and switch on the AFT or critically adjust the fine tuner for best picture and sound. Peak all tuned circuits, including the sound takeoff, for maximum undistorted sound. Final step should be a critical adjustment of the FM detector. Where an IC is used, there is usually only one tuned circuit, generally a quad coil. It, too, is adjusted by ear for maximum undistorted sound.

*Alignment with RF Generator and Meter.* To prevent interference pickup and misleading indications, switch to a blank channel and short out the antenna terminals. Avoid damage to the signal generator and receiver components by using a small blocking capacitor between the generator and the set. Connect the generator to some convenient point ahead of the sound takeoff. Set the generator to 4.5 MHz.

Where a ratio detector or discriminator is used, connect an EVM (on a low dc range) across one of the split-load resistors. If there is only one resistor, temporarily bridge it with two 100-kΩ resistors in series and connect meter to the junction. Adjust the generator output to get an indication. Vary generator tuning to make sure that the reading changes with frequency. Restore the generator tuning to 4.5 MHz. With the exception of the secondary coil adjustment of the detector, peak all sound IF and limiter tuned circuits for maximum indication. Connect the meter across the total load or from the "hot" side to ground. With reduced output from the generator, critically adjust the secondary coil to obtain a zero reading on the meter. Remove the resistors if installed. Tune to a station and, if necessary, adjust the fine tuner for best sound. If there is distortion or buzz in the sound, touch up the secondary adjustment by ear.

*Sweep Alignment.* This method, which was described in Chapter 13 for the video IF strip, requires a sweep generator, marker generator, and a scope. Connections are much like that shown in Figure 13-13, except here we are concerned with the sound section. As for the method just described, connect the generators to some point upstream from the sound takeoff. Connect the scope to the detector load resistor. Set the sweep generator for an output of 4.5 MHz and a sweep of about 200 kHz. An S-shaped response curve like that shown in Figure 18-5 will be seen on the scope. Center the curve with the sweep generator tuning dial. Tune the marker generator to 4.5 MHz. A blip should appear at the "crossover point" at or near the center of the curve. Peak the IF coils for maximum amplitude of the curve. Critically adjust the secondary coil of the FM detector until the two curves are alike, with the 4.5-MHz marker at the crossover. The two curve peaks should be of the same amplitude and equidistant from the crossover. Tune in a station and adjust the fine tuner for best sound. If any buzz or distortion, touch up the detector adjustment by ear.

## 18-9 MTS/STEREO TROUBLESHOOTING

Besides a thorough understanding of operational theory, familiarity with the user controls and indicators and their functions, and the service adjusters, is essential for repairing this equipment. Controls and indicators for a typical receiver (Mitsubishi) are listed and described as follows. Following that is a listing of MTS adjusters and their functions.

*Stereo/SAP Switch.* This switch enables the user to select either stereo or SAP when being broadcast.

*Auto/Manual Switch.* This switch determines which signal is routed to the speakers. When switched to Auto, with the stereo/SAP switch at Stereo, the speakers reproduce stereo regardless of which of the two signals is broadcast. With the Auto/Manual switch at Auto and the Stereo/SAP switch at SAP, the AF amplifiers are connected for SAP. If SAP broadcasting is discontinued, the circuits automatically switch to stereo. When the manual mode is selected, with the Stereo/SAP switch at Stereo, the circuits are connected for stereo regardless of which signals are being broadcast. When SAP is selected, the SAP circuits are energized. If there is no SAP transmission, there can be no sound even when stereo is being broadcast.

*Stereo/SAP Indicator Lights.* There are usually two LED-type indicators to show when stereo and SAP signals are being received on the TV channel selected. The indicators may or may not be integral parts of the switches, depending on the set. They are not to be confused with the operating mode indicators.

*Blend Control.* Blend is adjusted by the user to obtain the desired amount of noise reduction but at the expense of decreased separation.

### MTS Service Adjustments

Typical adjusters and their functions are as follows. Some of those listed are not found in all receivers or VCRs. For specific adjusting procedures, refer to the proper service manual. (*Caution:* Do not indiscriminately adjust any control without good reason. The slightest misadjustment of most controls will mask the original trouble and create misleading symptoms to compound the servicing problems.)

*Volume Control.* This is the regular user panel control. It is adjusted periodically in conjunction with the service adjusters, to establish the proper audio level for MTS reception.

*Composite Level Control.* This is an additional control to set the level of composite audio feeding the MTS circuits.

*L − R Gain Control.* The level of the L − R signal feeding the DBX decoder is adjusted using this control.

*Variable Deemphasis or Spectral Control.* (DBX Adjuster). The gain of an op-amp in the L − R DBX IC is adjusted to obtain the desired amount of deemphasis. It is adjusted in conjunction with the user Blend control if one is provided.

*L − R Timing Control.* This adjusts the output level of the generator in the DBX decoder for optimum noise reduction.

*Separation Control.* The relative levels of the L − R and L + R signals feeding the AF stages are established to obtain maximum separation of sound from the R and L speakers.

*PLL Control.* This control manually sets the free-running frequency of the VCO for proper phasing with the pilot signal.

*SAP Level Control.* The amplitudes of the SAP and L − R signals are equalized and the level at which the SAP light comes on is established using this control.

*SAP Timing Control.* This control sets the SAP level for optimum amount of deemphasis when receiving SAP broadcasts.

### Symptoms and Procedures

Most of the sound problems described for monaural sets are also applicable to stereo receivers and VCRs. Troubles *peculiar* to MTS/stereo circuits of TV and VCRs are as follows. As a guide, refer to the MTS troubleshooting flow drawing (Figure 18-16). In this drawing, all testing is done with an MTS/stereo signal generator. Note that the various tests are referenced to numbered test points in Figure 18-14. Most of the functions are performed by IC's.

*No Sound. (picture okay)*

***Probable causes:*** Same as for monaural sound receivers plus defects in the MTS circuits that are common to both L and R channels; improper operation of the audio switching IC.

Check the *main channel* circuits between the FM detector and the speakers. Check that *both* speakers are producing sound. If no sound, inject an AF signal at the input/output of the matrix IC. If no signal through the matrix, check for applied dc and the possibility of external defects. If the IC is still suspect, replace it. If still no audio, suspect the electronic switch. Check for applied dc/logic signals, and if present, replace the switching IC.

If the trouble is upstream, signal trace the main channel circuits, the deemphasis network and the low-pass filter. Check associated external components and replace if suspect.

Assuming that there is monaural sound but no stereo, make sure that all panel switches are properly set. See if the stereo indicator is lit. If it is not lit, the station may not be transmitting stereo. If in doubt, select a channel known to be broadcasting stereo. If the stereo indicator is lit but there is no sound, the trouble is probably in the L − R path

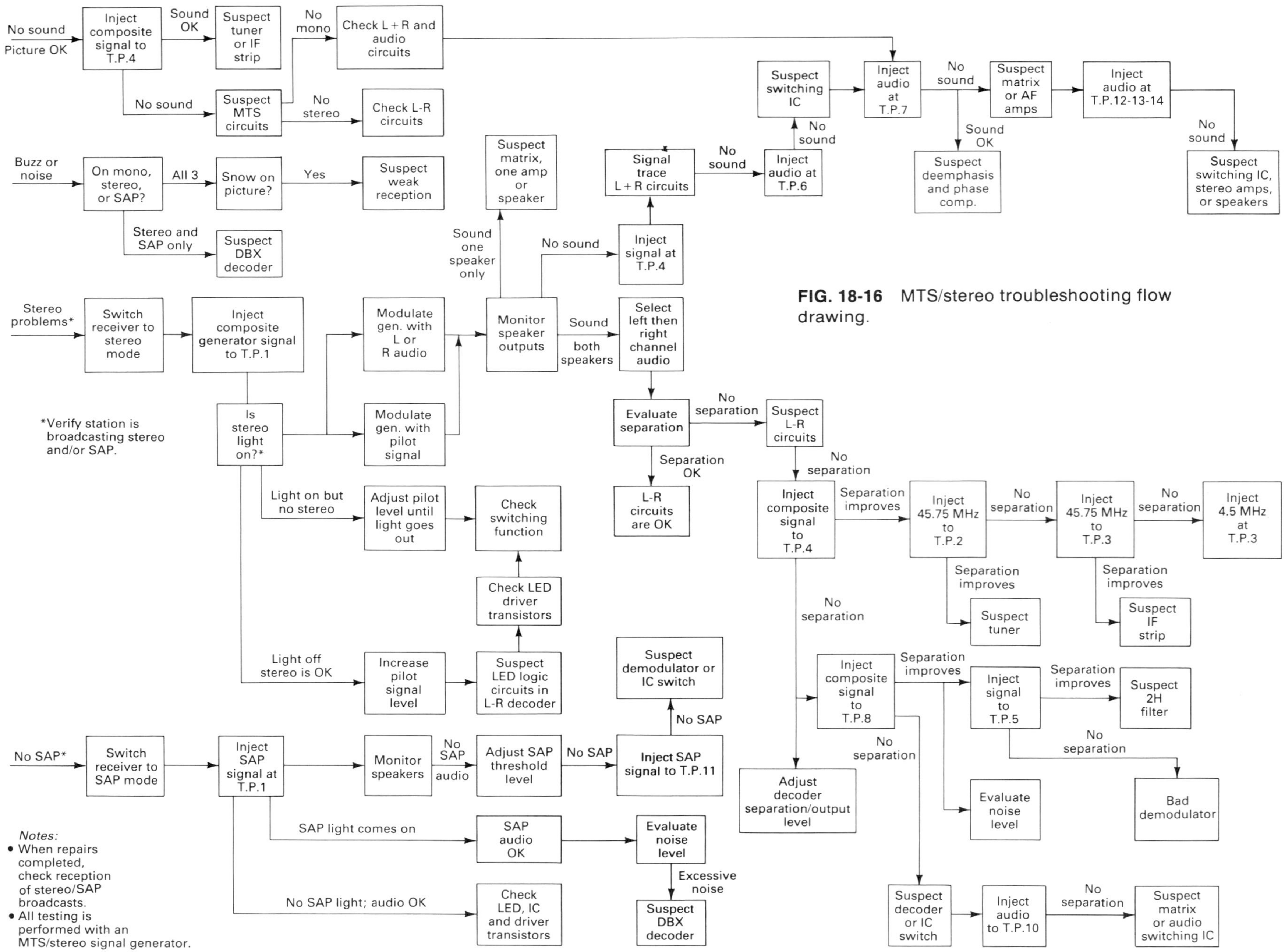


*Verify station is broadcasting stereo and/or SAP.

*Notes:*
- When repairs completed, check reception of stereo/SAP broadcasts.
- All testing is performed with an MTS/stereo signal generator.

**FIG. 18-16** MTS/stereo troubleshooting flow drawing.

shown in Figure 18-14, or the DBX decoder. Inject a composite signal (from a suitable generator) at the MTS input where the FM detector feeds the stereo subchannel stages. If stereo comes on with sound from the speakers, the trouble is ahead of the injection point. If no stereo, concentrate on the L − R circuits. If warranted, adjust the DBX controls per instructions in the service manual.

If there is no output from the L − R demodulator, check for dc applied to the IC. Check for a 2H pilot signal at the demodulator. Reminder: The pilot performs a switching function, and if no pilot, there can be no sound. If weak or missing, check the phase-locked loop, including the discrete components of the 1H bandpass filter. Adjust the pilot threshold level. If there is a good pilot signal at the demodulator input, check all components associated with its operation. If no defects can be found, replace the IC.

Check the switching action of the SAP/Stereo select switch. If there is a normal signal at the DBX decoder input but little or no output to the matrix, suspect input switching problems. If necessary, replace it and the decoder IC—similarly if there is normal L − R input to the matrix but no divided output to the audio switching IC. Where suspect, replace the matrix and/or switching IC.

#### *Stereo or SAP Light Blinks.*

***Probable causes:*** Weak reception (antenna problems, and so on, as described for a mono receiver); MTS circuit defects or misadjustments.

Check for adequate amount of composite audio at the MTS input. If okay, check all circuit functions associated with the stereo or SAP signal, as applicable. *Critically* adjust the corresponding threshold levels.

#### *Little or No L/R Separation.*

***Probable causes:*** Improper adjustment of relative levels of the L + R/L − R signals; defects in the separation control circuitry; speakers too close together.

The two signals are combined in the matrix. If the L − R signal at this point is significantly weaker than the L + R signal, you get poor separation between the L and R channels, with results difficult to distinguish from mono.

Adjust the separation control for maximum separation of sounds from the L and R speakers. It can be done "by ear," by equalizing voltages measured across the two speakers, or preferably adjusting for the proper levels as specified in service literature. Strive for a separation of 50 dB or better. Make sure that there is no "bleeding" between the L and R channels. If necessary, adjust the spectral and L − R level controls.

#### *No SAP Reception.* (mono and stereo okay)

***Probable causes:*** Improper setting of panel switches; no SAP being broadcast; defects in SAP processing circuits.

Verify the setting of all switches. If the SAP indicator comes on it indicates only that SAP has been selected and no indication that SAP is or is not being broadcast. Some sets, however, have an indicator to show when SAP is being received. Start by injecting a composite/SAP signal from a generator at the MTS inputs. If SAP audio is heard from the speakers there are three possibilities: no SAP broadcasting, a switching problem, or a defect ahead of the MTS circuits. If no SAP audio is heard using the injected signal, the trouble is in the SAP stages, the 5H bandpass filter, the SAP demodulator (carrier detector), the SAP selector switch, or the audio switching IC. For the latter, check the switching control logic. Try adjusting the SAP threshold level and other related controls.

#### *Excessive Noise*

***Probable causes:*** Fringe-area reception problems; antenna problems; low signal-to-noise ratio; defects in TV tuner or preamp stages; faulty deemphasis networks in the main channel or stereo subchannel signal path; defective or misadjusted DBX decoder.

If weak noisy reception for monaural operation, troubleshoot as described in Chapters 9, 12, and 13. Replace or overhaul the antenna and lead-in system. Try a subber if the tuners are suspect. Check the AGC voltage and adjust the threshold and AGC delay controls as appropriate. Make a gain check of the IF strip, particularly the preamps. Check the signal level at the MTS input. If there is weak and noisy monaural sound, signal trace each stage in the L + R path, including the deemphasis network, the select switch, and the matrix.

If the monaural sound is normal, concentrate on the MTS stages. Signal trace the 2H BPF and the demodulator. Check for a weak 2H pilot injection to the demod. This is a fairly common cause of weak L − R audio. When receiving stereo (or the equivalent signal from a generator), check and compare amplitudes of the L + R and L − R signals at the matrix input. The L − R should be the stronger of the two. If it is not, check the stereo subchannel amplifiers for low gain. Adjust the gain controls to obtain levels indicated in the service instructions.

Check the inputs and outputs of the L − R decoder IC(s), the most likely cause of excessive noise when receiving stereo or SAP. Try adjusting the PLL and all DBX associated controls per service instructions. If the ICs are suspect, replace them.

If there is normal stereo reception but excessive noise on SAP broadcasts only, check all SAP circuits as described earlier for total loss of SAP audio. Make gain checks using the SAP output from the signal generator. Verify proper operation of the SAP DBX decoder and replace if suspect. Adjust SAP controls per instructions. (*Reminder:* Under weak signal conditions, some noise can be expected, particularly when receiving SAP broadcasts.)

## 18-10 STEREO AF AMPLIFIER TROUBLESHOOTING

Fault finding for these stages is relatively easy considering that identical circuits are used in the left and right AF channels that follow the MTS circuitry. In general, the same procedures are used as described earlier for the AF stages of a monaural set. First determine which channel has the problem by comparing the sound (if any) from the two speakers and by adjusting the balance control. When checking voltages and signal tracing, compare the readings taken at the same points on both channels, and compare with those indicated on the schematic. A dual-trace scope is especially useful here. Make the same comparison when checking suspected components. Most breakdowns occur in the drivers and output stages, although the primary *cause* is often traced to an upstream stage. After several minutes of operation, check and compare the operating temperatures of the four output transistors. A cold or excessively hot transistor is always worth investigating. Thermal runaway is common and provides a good clue and starting point.

## QUESTIONS

1. What are the advantages of FM over AM?
2. Explain frequency deviation as applied to FM.
3. Explain the changes that take place when an RF carrier is frequency modulated. How does this differ from amplitude modulation?
4. Where, and how, in a color receiver are the 41.25-MHz and 4.5-MHz sound IF carriers developed?
5. At what point is the sound separated from the video in (a) a BW set; (b) a color set?
6. How is sound prevented from reaching the CRT and video kept out of the sound stages?
7. Explain the functions of an FM detector in producing audio from a frequency-modulated carrier.
8. Briefly explain the operation of a basic ratio-type FM detector.
9. Briefly explain how an S curve is produced when aligning an FM detector with a scope and sweep generator.
10. Explain how a dc volume control does its job.
11. What is the purpose of a sound limiter, and how does it operate?
12. Explain preemphasis and deemphasis.
13. Explain the need for (a) audio voltage amplifiers; (b) a power output amplifier.
14. The AF signal voltage is first increased, then decreased to drive the speakers. Explain this apparent contradiction.
15. State three ways of coupling a power output stage to a low-impedance speaker.
16. Briefly explain the operation of a typical complementary-symmetry output stage.
17. High-fidelity sound systems use woofers, tweeters, crossover networks, and speaker enclosures. Explain the purpose of each.
18. Explain how negative feedback in an AF amplifier reduces distortion. How and why is stage gain affected?
19. MTS/stereo is a compatible system. What does this mean, and how is it accomplished?
20. What comprises the composite audio signal?
21. Noise is a problem with MTS/stereo. State two ways in which it is overcome.
22. Explain two functions of the pilot signal.
23. Explain the function of (a) the DBX decoder; (b) the matrix; (c) the audio switching IC.
24. Briefly explain how the L and R speaker signals are developed.
25. Speakers must be well separated to get the true stereo effect. Explain.
26. Why is the transmitted stereo subchannel twice as strong as the main "mono" channel?
27. What special items of test equipment are required for servicing and adjusting the MTS/stereo system?

# 19 Digital television, monitors, and picture enhancement

The race is on! Japan, our chief competitor and unchallenged leader in the field, is expected to start broadcasting HDTV sometime in 1989. Are we in the United States going to be left behind and lose out on this unprecedented and potentially lucrative market?. The same thing that happened with the automobile, VCRs, and TVs?

HDTV (high-definition television)—the exciting new concept that promises pictures of unparalleled clarity with more than double the number of scanning lines of the present system, a concept guaranteed to revolutionize the industry with a greatly expanded market for consumer products. Nevertheless, this is a tremendously expensive proposition with almost prohibitive costs of implementation—a new generation of TV sets to design, produce and market, plus a major overhaul and updating of station equipment and all the peripherals. There is the inevitable weighing of costs against anticipated rewards—big bucks in any language.

True, we have what it takes—the expertise, the technology, and the wherewithal—but there's trouble in River City, big and almost insurmountable problems that must be resolved before we can even hope to get involved.

The problem is one of frequencies and the limited expanse of the RF spectrum and the fact that each station with the new system requires a bandwidth some five times wider than now: an unrealistic 30 MHz compared to the present allocations of 6 MHz permitted under the NTSC standards. These frequencies are unavailable, having already been assigned to other services; frequencies inextricably tied in with the number of lines that make up a picture. Unfortunately, increasing those lines does not come easily.

## 19-1 SHORTCOMINGS OF THE NTSC SYSTEM

When the NTSC standards were established in the early 1950s, who could have guessed that there were built-in problems that would begin to surface several decades later? First the problem of compatibility between existing black-and-white and color sets that were just emerging from the drawing boards: the sharing BW and color images within the same bandpass. And now there is another hurdle to overcome, a more formidable one than before: the need for more frequencies and a picture of more than the 525 lines that the present system provides. Until now the NTSC standards have served us well. But what of the future and the new advances and problems that with each passing year become more and more acute?

Other problems peculiar to the NTSC system are line flicker, a poor color signal-to-noise ratio, and an effect called *color crawl,* most noticeable at the edges of large color images.

## 19-2 HIGH-DEFINITION TELEVISION

High-definition television (HDTV) holds great promise for the future if and when it finally comes to pass—all made possible with computer technology. It is ironic that some foreign countries have long enjoyed 900-line TV, despite the need for wider bandwidths. Hopefully, bureaucracy will not prevail in the United States and we too can begin to forge ahead. At the time of writing, there are over a dozen proposals for new standards by individual companies and countries throughout the world, all aimed toward obtaining at least a 1000-line picture. Some of the proposals call for expanding the present allocations to more than 6 MHz. Some of these systems are in the works; some are still in R&D and on the drawing boards.

Instead of conventional broadcasting with its bandpass limitations, some of the systems currently being considered are CATV; DBS (direct broadcast from satellites), where frequency requirements are not so stringent; and fiber optics as a means of transmission. All have capabilities for an expanded bandwidth and are outside the jurisdiction of the FCC. Meanwhile, as we enjoy what we have, R&D continues. At this time few details on the Japanese HDTV system are available except that it is expected to provide over 1200 lines of resolution.

## 19-3 PICTURE QUALITY AND RESOLUTION

Resolution is a measure of how well or how poorly a TV set can resolve images. There are a number of things involved: screen size, number of scanning lines, brightness, contrast, condition of the CRT, and other factors.

The NTSC system ostensibly provides for 525 lines. This sounds fine, but unfortunately, all of the 525 lines are not usable. Some are used up or lost during the vertical retrace intervals. Others are hidden from view beyond the mask opening at the top and bottom, due to overscanning. As a result, horizontal resolution under the most favorable conditions is reduced to about 340 lines more or less. With a reasonably small screen, there is no problem, but with a large screen, the gaps between the picture lines become all too obvious and objectionable, especially at up-close viewing. With older sets, it is the horizontal scanning lines; for later sets, such as the currently popular 35- and 50-inch direct-view models, and particularly the larger projection screens, it's the vertical lines inherent with in-line CRTs, such as Trinitron. It's like comparing a high-quality fine-grained photograph with a newspaper reproduction. All things being equal, the greater the number of scanning lines, the better the resolution.

### High Quality

In the past few years the term *high quality* (HQ) has been hyped and bandied about by overzealous salespersons, a sales gimmick for electronic consumer products, most notably TV sets, monitors, and VCRs. Although not synonymous with or attributed to the digital concept, it does imply certain worthwhile refinements. In the strictest sense, the HQ label means that a set has certain desirable features and capabilities: expanded bandwidth of the RF, IF, and chroma tuned stages; extended response of the video and chroma amplifiers; improvements in CRTs; and the use of that rather innocuous but extremely effective device called a comb filter. Both it and SAW filters are largely responsible for better separation of the luminance and chroma signals and a better color picture.

### Vertical and Horizontal Resolution

Everyone can recognize and appreciate good picture quality, but let's take time out to review some of the things that contribute, both directly and indirectly, to the quality of a viewed image. And there are many.

We might start with two general catagories: raster conditions and signal considerations, equally important. Picture quality is influenced by many things: the CRT and its operating parameters, screen size, brightness, contrast, color purity, and *resolution,* the ability to resolve the finest picture details. With a TV or monitor picture there are two kinds of resolution, vertical and horizontal.

*Vertical Resolution.* Vertical resolution is the ability of a TV set or monitor to resolve *horizontal* lines: with the NTSC system, the 250 or so lines of picture information actually available from the 525-line transmission. With interlaced scanning of odd and even lines, we actually see only one field (roughly half the total picture) at any given instant, although persistence of the screen phosphors gives the illusion of a smooth transition. With a system called *double scanning*, we view twice as much picture in the brief 1/30-s duration of each frame. Less than perfect interlacing of the odd and even lines results in a further reduction in resolution, as does any tendency toward flicker or the beating of the vertical trace with the 60-Hz power-line frequency or other kinds of interference.

*Horizontal Resolution.* Horizontal resolution is the ability to resolve *vertical* lines. It relates to bandwidth and overall frequency response, which involves every stage between the antenna input and the CRT. To reproduce the finest detail adequately, the optimum bandwidth of a color set is 4.2 MHz. With inexpensive sets, this is not always obtainable. By comparison, the bandwidth of a typical medium-sized BW set is only about 3.8 MHz. Considering their size, small screens do not require a wide bandpass.

Bandwidth restrictions apply to both color and monochrome, and any narrowing beyond the norm has a marked impact on both the purity and intensity of the color image. Alignment is another important factor, as are the traps (of which there are three kinds): the 3.58-MHz trap used to remove the color burst; the 920-kHz trap, which prevents beat interference from the heterodyning of the 4.5-MHz audio carrier and the 3.58-MHz color burst; and adjacent channel traps. Each trap removes some color information, particularly if they are misadjusted by the slightest amount.

High-resolution monitors and receivers can provide better than 400 lines of horizontal resolution even within the NTSC framework. The better the resolution, the more vertical lines and picture elements that can be observed horizontally.

Besides the amount of amplification provided by the different stages, several variables influence the strength of the low and high frequencies that drive the CRT. The bandwidth and alignment of the tuner circuits (channel selector) is one determining factor. With a narrowed bandpass the high video frequencies simply cannot get through. Equally important is the frequency response of the video and chroma amplifiers downstream from the demodulators. As described in Chapters 14 and 15, design considerations include the use of peaking coils. Also, proper lead dress must be observed to minimize the capacity shunting effects, which tend to bypass the highs to ground. The opposite extreme of overpeaking will also degrade a picture.

### Raster

Since a normal raster is prerequisite to a good picture, let's review some of the many factors to consider: brightness and contrast, linearity of scanning, conditions of interlace between the odd and even line fields, and focus. Some of the conditions are interdependent on others: for example, the condition of the CRT, beam landing, and the diameter of the beam(s) on impact: also, the correct operating voltages of the CRT and the accuracy of the setup adjustments, which includes raster height and width, sweep linearity, anti-pincushioning, and convergence adjustments. Then there is the possible detrimental influence from external magnetic sources, including the CRT itself.

### Signal Considerations

In the scanning process, the intensity of the CRT beam(s) is constantly changing in acccordance with the amplitude and frequency variations of the video and chroma signals applied to the control grid(s) or cathodes. Low frequencies correspond with slow changes in the signal to produce large objects (on a horizontal plane). High video frequencies create rapid changes to produce small objects, in particular the fine picture detail. Attenuation or loss of low frequencies results in an overall loss of contrast, and symptoms of smearing and unstable sync. Loss of high frequencies (those in the range 3 to 4 MHz) causes loss of picture detail. Once these signals are lost, nothing can be done to regain them or to compensate for their loss. Resolution is a measure of how well or how poorly a TV set can resolve the finest picture details.

Some of the CRT-related things having a detrimental effect on the sharpness of an image are a weak or otherwise defective CRT, a magnetized CRT or external magnetic influences, improper CRT operating voltages, blooming, poor beam focus, poor interlacing of the scanning lines, and improper setup adjustments, particularly color purity, convergence, and gray-scale tracking. (*Reminder:* The smallest picture details are not reproduced in color.)

Interference will also degrade a picture. Such interference may be generated internally or picked up from some external source. A similar picture degradation can be due to ghosting or an impedance mismatch in the antenna system.

Anything that contributes to a weakened or degraded signal (luminance, chroma, or both) will have a bad effect on the picture. Despite a widened bandpass of the RF/IF stages and better separation of the luminance and chroma signals, the high-frequency tuned stages of a set do tend to affect the signals adversely. For this reason, better picture quality can be obtained by circumventing these stages, as when a monitor is used for viewing. More on this later.

## 19-4 DIGITAL TELEVISION

Digital television has at last come of age, with its long-promised improvements in picture quality and numerous ingenious spin-offs (special effects), perhaps some of them not essential, but good selling features and nice to have, like pix-in-pix (PIP) (Figure 19-1). Much progress has been made in recent years in improving both picture and sound, and in the offing, promises of more and unforeseen breakthroughs that push the state of the art to its limits in the near term. Meanwhile, even the most discriminating viewer should be pleased with what is presently available and at reasonable cost. The modern receiver is truly a marvel of hi-tech engineering and a credit to those who brought it about.

So that there is no misunderstanding, however, at least for the present and with certain makes of receivers, picture enhancement and digital are two unrelated functions. The first deals with picture resolution, the latter with special effects that have nothing to do with normal receiver operation. There are exceptions, however, and they are discussed later. Both systems are relatively new and good examples of high technology at its best.

But why digital? Because it promises to be the way of the future—and for good reason. As with computers, a digital system makes it possible to handle and manipulate large quantities of information at incredible speeds.

Digital receivers use memories to store images (in digital form), and have special enhancement circuits that display images at twice the rate of ordinary TV. With digital technology, the analog video and chroma signals are converted to digital, which makes possible many innovations and special effects, such as PIP, in addition to a high-resolution picture of over 1000 lines, for better than twice the vertical and horizontal resolution of ordinary TV and with a picture equal to or surpassing that shown in movie houses. An increased number of scanning lines is particularly desirable for large-screen projection sets.

PIP is now provided by most top-of-the-line sets (Figure 19-1). This feature enables the viewer to monitor one or more small pictures (window images) (from other channels) superimposed on the main picture. A zoom feature is provided in some cases to enlarge portions of the main picture. The small pictures being monitored can be positioned anywhere on the screen. With some sets, the size of the picture being monitored is adjustable, it can be "frozen" (still frame), or it can be stored in memory for later recovery.

Two functional circuits peculiar to all digital TV systems are: an A/D (analog-to-digital) converter and its converse, a D/A (digital-to-analog) converter. These circuits convert the signal from one form to another.

The signal received from the station is an analog signal that is constantly changing in frequency and amplitude. Unfortunately, the number of things you can do with an analog signal is quite limited. Therefore, the signal (after being converted to digital) is stored in memory as a series of binary pulses (digits). A binary digit represents one of two states, true or false, corresponding with a voltage or no-voltage condition. Each picture element (pixel) is represented by a single digit. As digital, the signal can be manipulated to accomplish certain desired tasks. When these are completed, the signal is converted back to its original analog form to produce a picture in the normal manner. Most digital functions, including A/D and D/A conversion, are performed by very large-scale integrated circuits (VLSI), which, incidentally, can be quite expensive.

## Binary Logic Fundamentals

Digital circuits operate with computer logic. One example, described previously, is the PLL tuner (Chapter 12). Whereas a TV analog signal is constantly changing in frequency and amplitude, a digital signal consists of a series of coded "binary" pulses. The presence of a pulse is alternatively referred to as logic 1 or logic high. The absence of a pulse is expressed as logic 0 (zero) or logic low. Each condition represents a particular *state* as explained earlier.

To summarize, the analog signal received is first converted into digital by the A/D converter. In its digital form, each tiny picture element (pixel) is manipulated bit by bit and rearranged where necessary to perform various functions (the special effects). After processing, the signals are reconverted back into analog by the D/A converter, to produce the picture.

In the double-conversion process, each binary digit is constantly monitored and analyzed for anomalies in brightness, contrast, and color intensity. Where imperfections are found, corrections are automatically made before the images are displayed.

Diodes and transistors are used in different circuit configurations using the pulses to perform the various tasks. Data or commands are passed from one device to another in one of two forms: *serial* (on one conductor with bits of information conveyed consecutively), or *parallel,* with all data concurrent. The latter requires a separate line for each data bit. Early equipment used discrete components; with modern equipment all functions are performed by ICs. Some of the terms used with digital circuitry

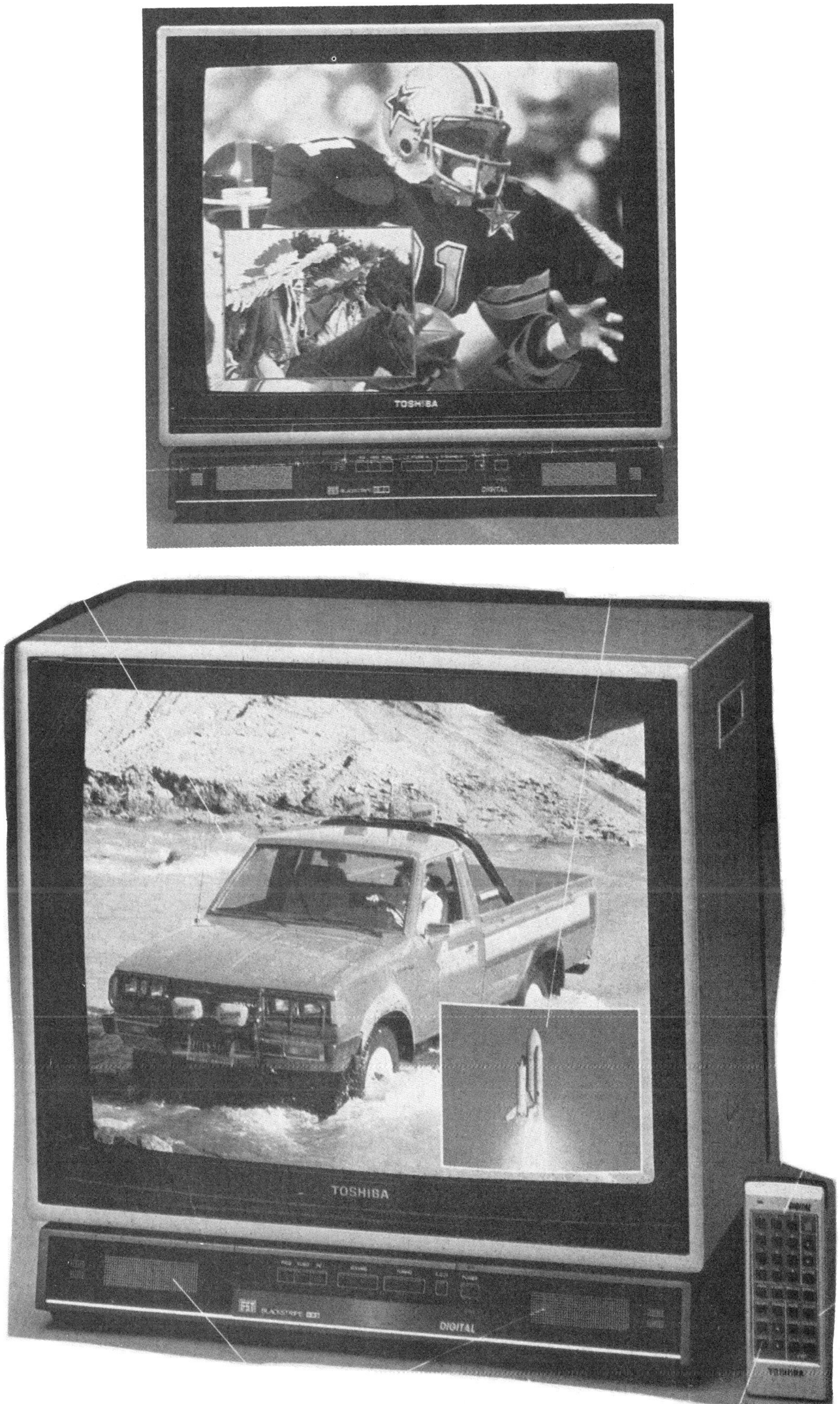


**FIG. 19-1** Typical digital TV. Toshiba's entry in the digital television competition will have 256 kilobytes of random-access memory and an 8-bit microprocessor, making it more sophisticated than many desktop computers. (Courtesy of Toshiba.)

and various *logic devices* are listed and described briefly as follows:

- *Logic circuit:* binary circuits that perform various electronic functions.
- *Logic diagram:* a block diagram or schematic using logic symbols to indicate signal flow and circuit functions.
- *Logic level:* the voltage level of a particular logic signal, which is usually quite low (10 V or less).
- *Binary digit (bit):* a logic 1 or 0, indicating one of two states, on or off, high or low, true or false.
- *Binary-coded decimal (BCD):* binary digits coded to correspond with a specific decimal number or value. There are many applications of BCD: for example, controlling the clock or channel number readout on a TV set or VCR.
- *Truth table:* a table of "weighted" numbers corresponding to a particular decimal number. There are different systems in use, the most popular being the binary table. The simplest is known as the 8-4-2-1 code (Table 19-1) with each of the four digits indicated by a zero or a 1. Each BCD digit is weighted with 8 as the most significant number on the left, then 4, 2, and 1 at the right. Only the ones (true numbers) are counted; the zeros (false numbers) are not counted. With this four-digit code, the 1 digits are additive and you can easily convert from the BCD notation to numeric, or vice versa. For example, BCD 0010 corresponds with the numeral 2 (only the weighted 2 digit is considered true and is counted). BCD 0111 represents the number 7 (4 + 2 + 1). As can be seen from the table, the number of possible combinations and codes is almost unlimited. Some complex functions require as many as 16 or more bits.
- *Logic device:* an arrangement of diodes or transistors to perform one or more logical functions. Each device is identified with a *symbol*. They are used in various combinations in a circuit. Common logic devices are shown in Figure 19-2 and listed and described briefly as follows.
- *Switching logic:* switching of pulses, and so on, by logic signals in or out of logic devices.
- *Amplifier:* the symbol is a triangle with input on the left and output at the right; a signal-inverting amplifier has a small circle added (Figure 19-2).
- *Gate:* logic signals are gated from one device to another in a logical manner. In essence, a gate is a form of controlled switch that can either pass or inhibit the transfer of signals. A typical gate consists of diodes, transistors, or both. The gate may be opened or closed, depending on the circuit configuration and polarity of the applied signal voltages. When "enabled," a gate is said to be closed. A disabled gate blocks a signal. There are several types of gates, as indicated in the drawing. Each may be switched by two or more inputs. The switching function depends on the *amplitude* and *polarity* of the input gating signal(s). Besides the switching function, transistors, when used, provide amplification. Diodes, of course, do not. Gates are used extensively in "comparator" and other logic circuits.
- *AND gate:* an arrangement of diodes or transistors as shown in the diagram. To enable the gate and to produce an output, signals must be applied simultaneously (with the proper amplitude and polarity) to all inputs. With one or more input signals missing, there can be no output. Sometimes called a "coincidence" gate.
- *Gating logic:* enabling or disabling gates by logic control.
- *OR gate:* can be enabled by one *or* more inputs.
- *NOR gate:* neither AND nor OR, a contraction of the two terms. With this gate the output is out of phase with the input signal.
- *NAND gate:* a NOT AND circuit, abbre-

***TABLE 19-1***

8-4-2-1 code

| *Decimal Number* | *BCD* |
|---|---|
| 0 | 0000 |
| 1 | 0001 |
| 2 | 0010 |
| 3 | 0011 |
| 4 | 0100 |
| 5 | 0101 |
| 6 | 0110 |
| 7 | 0111 |
| 8 | 1000 |
| 9 | 1001 |
| 10 | 1010 |

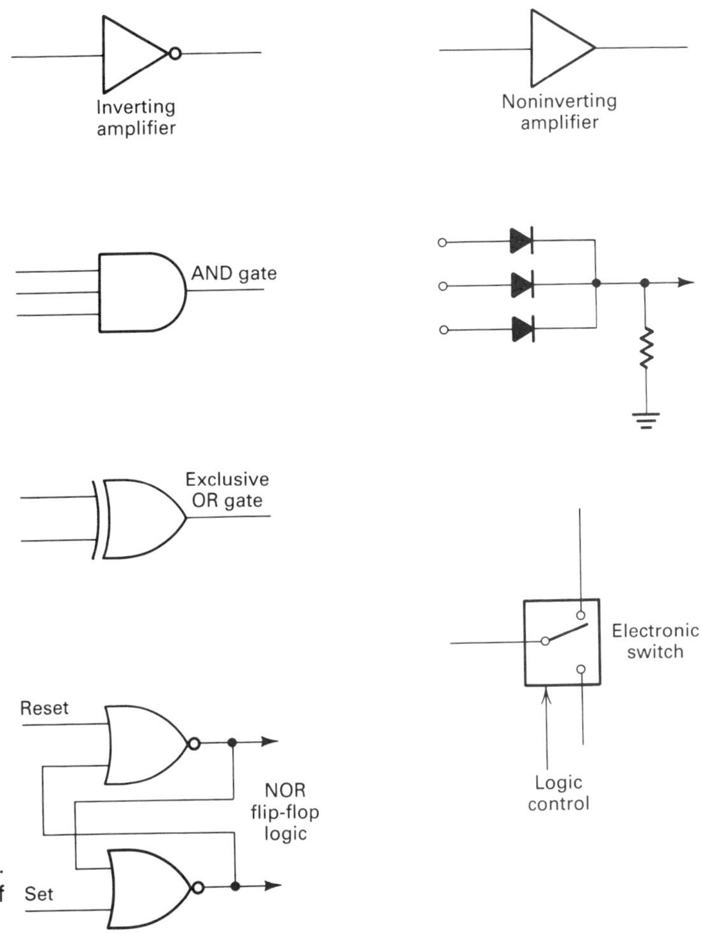


**FIG. 19-2** Typical logic symbols. Logic circuits perform a variety of functions.

viated to NAND. This gate produces a polarity reversal between the input and output.

- *Clock and clocking pulse:* many logical functions are timed or regulated by a digital clock circuit that operates at a precise frequency. It is esentially a crystal-controlled oscillator functioning as a binary "counter." A clocking pulse often serves as an enabling input to a gate.
- *Comparator:* a system of gates or op-amps for comparing one kind of digital information with another. Pulses to be compared may be entered in serial or parallel mode and processed accordingly. Parallel comparisons are made concurrently; serial comparisons (one bit at a time) take longer. An output is produced when the gate input(s) are in coincidence.
- *Flip-flop:* an electronic switch using two transistors operating together to develop a controlled output. The logic "on/off" state" of the two transistors is governed and alternately changed by variations of the amplitude and polarity of applied pulses. The switching function is usually timed and controlled by clock pulses. Electronic switches are used extensively in many late-model consumer products to change from one operating mode to another.
- *Shift register:* one of several types of "memory" registers used for the storage of data. Storage may be temporary, or more or less "permanent" unless the power is removed. Flip-flops are often used for temporary storage of data. Magnetic disks or tapes are examples of permanent storage. The register can be shifted by gating pulses to read or write information to or from the memory. Specific areas of a memory are accessed or addressed with BCD codes. A memory reset is usually provided.
- *Buffer stage:* a buffer amplifier or an in-between memory stage for temporary storage of data.
- *Counter:* a circuit designed to count pulses or the timing of events.

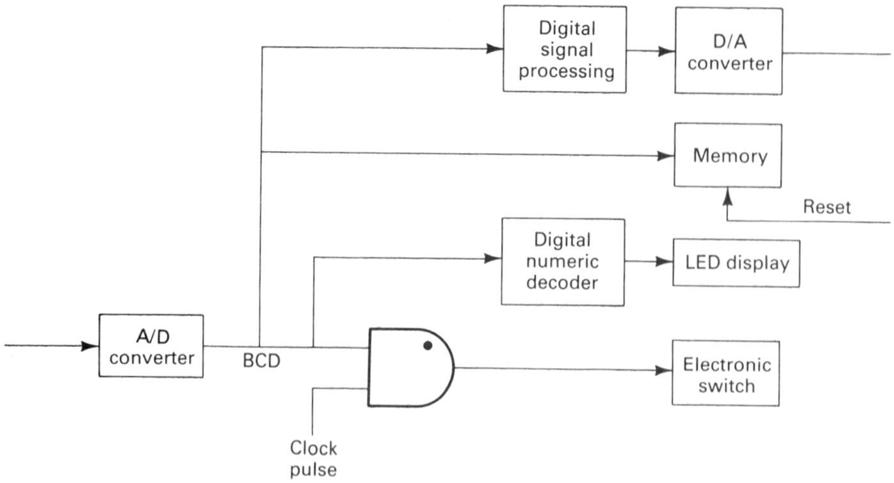


**FIG. 19-3** Typical logic functions.

A hypothetical example of operations performed by a typical, basic logic circuit is shown in Figure 19-3. Here an analog signal is fed to an A/D converter, which produces a BCD output corresponding to the amplitude and polarity of the signal at some given instant. In this case the BCD of 0011 (coincidental with a clock pulse) enables the AND gate (both inputs at logic high), which in turn triggers the electronic switch to change the operating mode of the equipment.

At the same time, the BCD is decoded to a decimal equivalent and displayed on a LED readout. If the BCD code should coincide with the access gates in the memory device, the data are stored for possible retrieval at a later time. If a reset pulse is initiated, either manually or as a result of some function, the memory is reset to 0000. As in digital TV receivers, the digital signal is processed, performs various tasks, then is reconverted back to analog.

## 19-5 IMPROVED-DEFINITION TELEVISION

HDTV may still be a long way off. In the interim, to satisfy public demand, several companies are producing sets using different schemes to enhance the picture while adhering to the NTSC standards. These are generally referred to as ACTV systems (advanced compatible television), or simply improved-definition television (IDTV). At this time the merits of the various systems are still in flux. Here we consider three makes of receivers and their systems: Toshiba, Philips, and Mitsubishi.

### Toshiba System

In 1986, Toshiba became the first company to break loose from the constraints of the time-honored NTSC system, long considered "chiseled in granite," and introduced what they refer to as a *noninterlace double-scanning* concept, designed to improve picture quality. This is a radical departure from the NTSC system of interlaced scanning, with its problems of flicker and a less-than-desirable picture quality. This is one of several IDTV systems presently in-process by different companies, pending the arrival of HDTV, if and when it comes. With the Toshiba method, the picture is double scanned at twice the scanning rate of conventional TV.

Digital technology is employed, with each line of picture information converted from analog to digital and stored in memory (a computer-type digital storage device), and later released to produce the extra lines to fill in the gaps so apparent with conventional TV. This is sometimes called *interpolating*.

One shortcoming of previous double-scanning systems is that the edges of rapidly moving objects in the picture become smeared because the signal is transmitted and received field by field. Toshiba uses a *motion adaptive system,* where the precise location of each pixel makes it possible to determine whether an image is stationary or moving, and in what direction. The digital circuitry then uses the stored line information for the moving image(s). This set provides the same special effects as other modern high-quality receivers: PIP and other screen displays, multichannel monitoring (Figure 19-4), speed search, and so on.

### Basic IDTV System

This method has several advantages over conventional TV: 450 lines of *vertical* resolution (a 50% increase over the current system); scanning lines are virtually invisible and line flicker is minimized. As a further bonus, noise level is reduced by 3 dB.

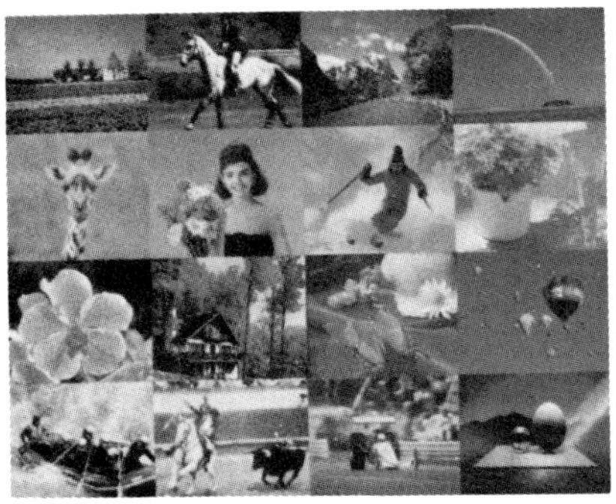

**FIG. 19-4** Multichannel monitoring. PIP, zoom, superb clarity, speed search, and stereo sound—all part of today's technology. (Courtesy of Toshiba.)

Figure 19-5 shows a block diagram of the Toshiba IDTV system. Note the two main functional areas, the stages on the left that convert from analog to digital and those on the right that store, then convert the digital information back to its original form. One block is for storage of line-by-line picture information, the other for the double scanning of stored information.

*Double-Scanning Principles.* Double scanning involves a read/write function with picture information being constantly read into and out of a memory (Figure 19-6). This is accomplished by electronic switching, alternating line by line, at incredible speeds (44,000 times per second). As shown in the drawing, while line 1 video information is being written into the memory (SW1 closed), the information stored for the previous line is being read out (as indicated by the closure of SW2). Concurrently, while line 1 is being read out, information for the next line is being stored. In this manner, each bit of information is reproduced twice in the scanning process. Although each field is scanned twice, the total number of frame lines remains the same since the lines overlap.

Figure 19-7 shows a comparison between the resolution obtained for conventional interlaced scanning with that obtained with double scanning of

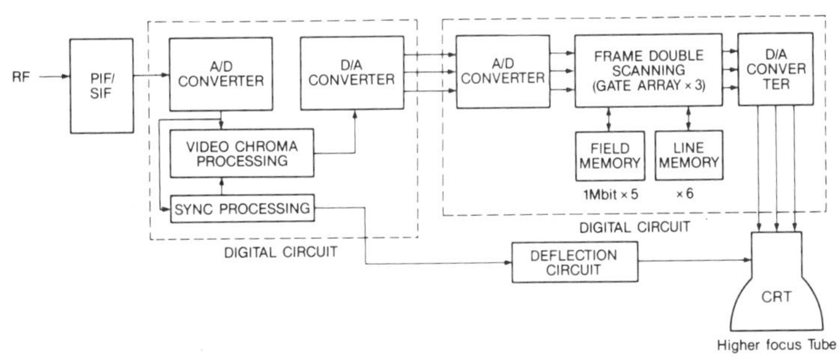


**FIG. 19-5** IDTV system block diagram. A/D and D/A conversions, megabit memories, and manipulations are all fundamental to digital television. (Courtesy of Toshiba.)

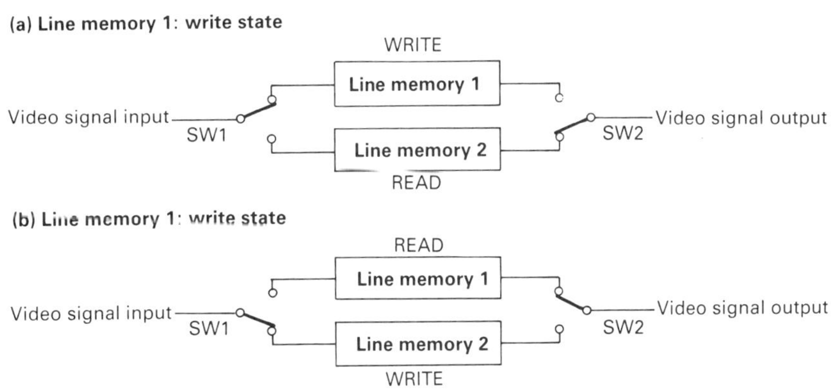


**FIG. 19-6** Double scanning simplified. High resolution and picture enhancement from a simple basic concept.

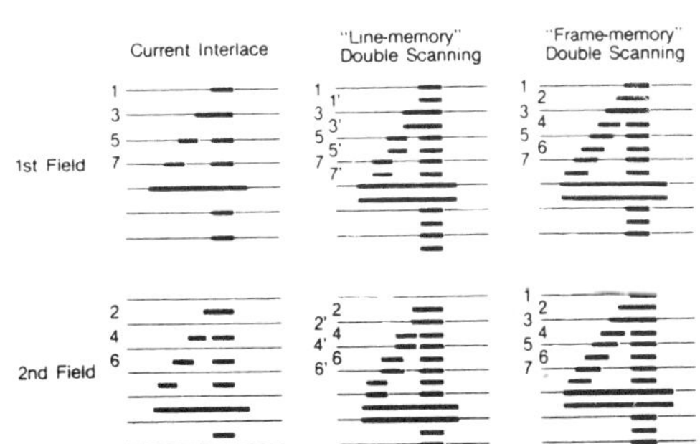


**FIG. 19-7** Comparison of scanning systems. Frame memory scanning produces a superior image. (Courtesy of Toshiba.)

an image. Note how the image (the numeral 4) becomes progressively more distinct with each scanning. In reference to the block diagram, a brief description of the events that take place follows.

Each of the VLSI microchips in the system performs a different task. Starting with the input on the left, the first one samples the incoming signal. Each sampling checks and momentarily stores information (in digital form) on the signal's wavelength, frequency, amplitude, and rate of change for all three parameters. The A/D chip passes the information on and is free to process the next bit of information. At this point the signal is processed by a comb filter that separates the luminance and chroma signals from each other. Both signals are then monitored bit by bit and compared with preprogrammed reference values stored in an 8-bit micro. These values are representative of color brightness and intensity for each pixel that makes up the picture. Such variations can be caused by things like interference and weak reception. Any deviations from the previously established values is instantly corrected for.

After the video has been digitally processed and manipulated, a D/A chip converts the signal back to analog. Another chip in the system is responsible for encoding, processing, and decoding the mono and MTS sound signals.

*A/D Converter.* Numerous methods have been used to convert from analog to digital. A basic system is shown in Figure 19-8a. A problem with this basic circuit is that it requires a number of synchronized operations that are too slow for today's technology. With this circuit, the counter (after being reset), with successive count (which is clocked) is converted from digital to analog and fed to the comparator together with the received signal. When the two voltages differ in amount, the count advances. Where the voltages are alike, the comparator changes state and inhibits the clock and stops the count.

A simpler and faster type of A/D converter, known as a *flash converter,* is shown in Figure 19-8b. It is fast-acting because it processes data simultaneously in parallel. Note that no clock is required. Each tap on the resistive divider furnishes an increasingly greater voltage, which is applied along with the incoming analog signal, to its associated comparator. As the analog signal passes through different voltage levels, it causes the corresponding comparator to change state. Although a 4-bit converter of this type requires only 15 comparators, an 8-bit converter requires over 250, which can be costly.

Another basic system is shown in (c). This system (Mitsubishi) senses 32 levels of the analog signal, representing that many picture shades, from white through gray to black. For simplicity, only three are shown in the diagram. Sensing is done with the three op-amps connected as comparators. Each op-amp is connected to a specific dc reference voltage obtained from a divider network as described previously. In the example, the three reference levels being detector are 1 V, 2 V, and 3 V, respectively. The clocked output from each op-amp at any given instant depends on the analog level for that point in time. Where the analog level is low compared to the reference level, the output will be high, and vice versa. A typical clock frequency is 10 MHz.

The encoder uses the op-amp outputs to generate a 5-bit code. The output of the encoder is stored temporarily in a "latch" type memory where it is updated continuously by changes in the analog level. From the latch, the digital code is stored in a frame memory to be read out at a later time. If the sampling times occur at the same time for each horizontal scanning line, the picture appears to be made up of vertical lines. This is called the *dither effect* (Figures 19-7 and 19-9).

*D/A Converter.* Compared to A/D conversion, conversion in reverse can be relatively simple. A typical circuit uses three converters to feed a switching network and subsequently the CRT. The converters, each represented by a separate IC, are identified with the kind of signal they process: the luminance (Y signal) and the R-Y and B-Y color signals.

### Philips System

As with the Toshiba system, this IDTV system uses noninterlaced scanning but is still compatible with NTSC standards. Although there are still 525 lines scanned every 1/60 s (instead of 262½ lines). With this concept the extra lines are not a repetition of those scanned for the same field. Here the extra lines are digitally generated to fill the "gaps" between the lines, giving the illusion of increased detail. Video information is processed pixel by pixel in accordance with the average values of the preceding three lines. The information for the inserted (interpolated) lines is obtained from line and field data previously read into the memories. This results in an apparent increase in vertical resolution.

In addition to improvements in resolution, this system also employs a two-level, digital noise reduction system, to produce sharper and cleaner

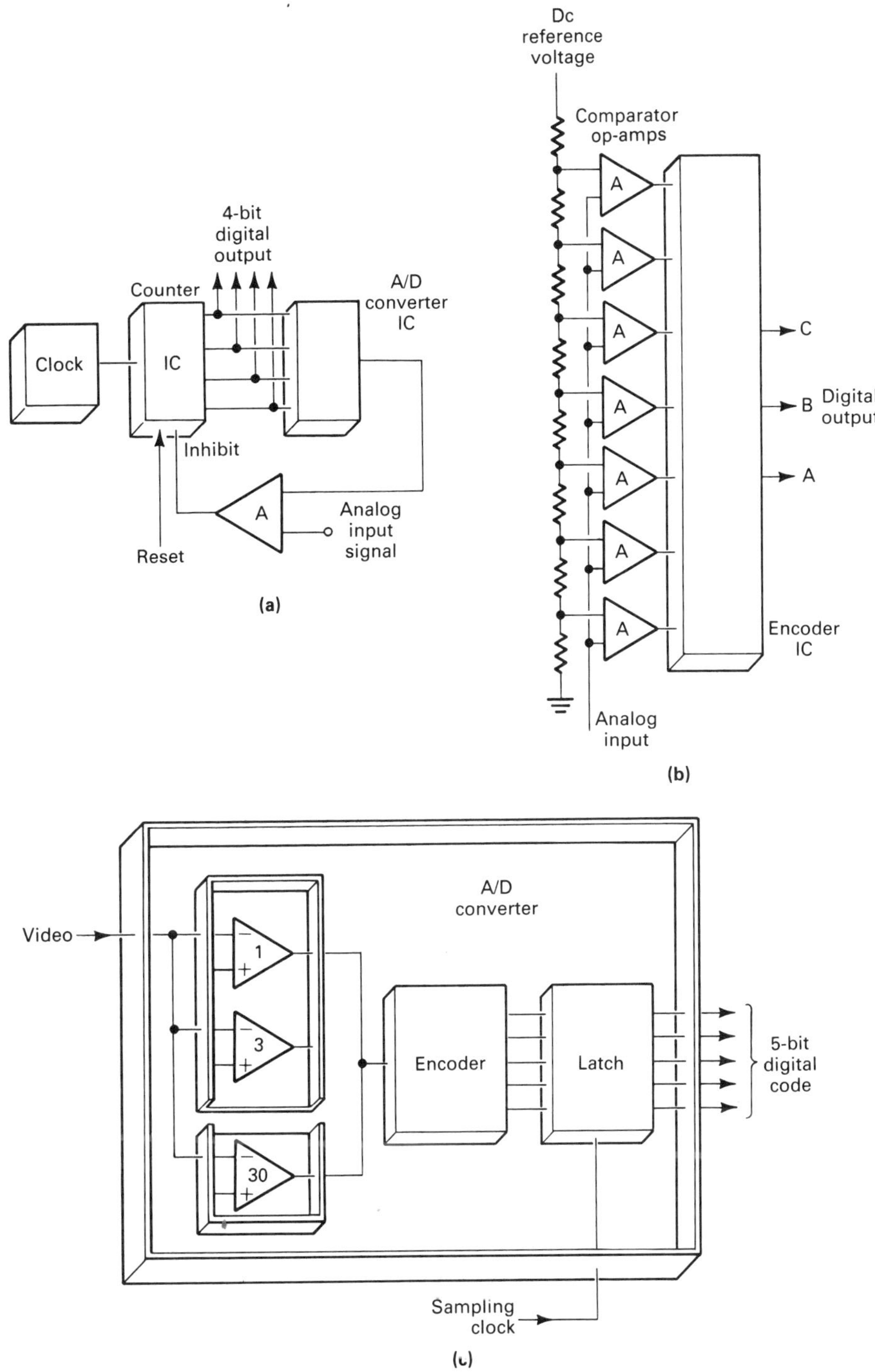


FIG. 19-8 A/D converters. (Courtesy of Mitsubishi.)

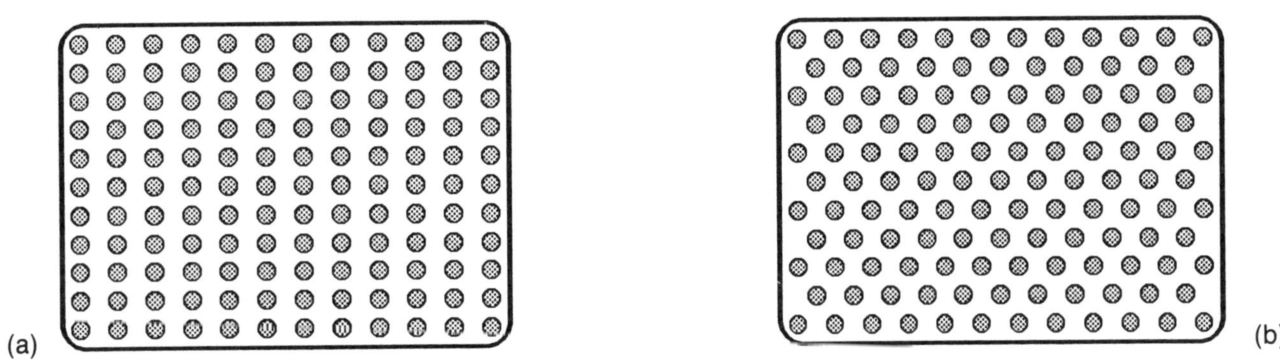


**FIG. 19-9** Dither effect. A straight-line picture (a) abnormal- is the result of sampling at the same time for adjacent scanning lines; (b) normal.

noise-free images with a minimum of smearing. The degree of video noise reduction (as selected by the user) comes from the use of a motion detector and a filter with a delay equal to one field of information. Increases in field differences equates with motion. The detector senses motion by comparing incoming data with the stored field data, to reduce the noise level by cancellation.

The Philips system also features an improved type of comb filter designed to reduce interference such as dot, line, and color crawl, often associated with double-scanning systems. This system provides 480 lines of horizontal resolution when supplied from a good signal source such as S-VHS tapes and videodiscs.

### Mitsubishi System

Besides special effects, this IDTV system has numerous features, including total freedom from dot and line crawl, and a capability for reproducing scenes where there is rapid motion. The latter is accomplished with an 11-megabit memory and micros that control the video processing in accordance with signal content. With a still picture or slow motion, interpolating lines poses no problem. Where there is rapid motion in the scene, however, line-by-line interpolation as used is more effective than the storage of complete fields and their insertion.

At present, Mitsubishi has not gotten onto the double-scanning bandwagon and their digitized circuits are used only for producing special effects. The special effects featured for Mitsubishi sets are described as follows:

- *Freeze frame:* freezes the main picture being viewed. Either field or frame reproduction may be selected by the user.
- *Preview:* displays a still picture of nine channels in sequence.
- *PIP:* inserts a $\frac{1}{9}$ normal-sized picture in one corner, superimposed on the main picture being viewed. The main and insert pictures may be exchanged with a user button.
- *Strobe:* displays eight time-sequenced still pictures simultaneously with the real-time "main" picture in a lower corner.
- *Editing:* allows the user to change the still pictures displayed in the strobe mode.

*Analog and Digital Processing.* A functional block diagram of the Mitsubishi system is shown in Figure 19-10.

*Circuit Descriptions.* The analog signal received is first converted to digital using an A/D converter, as described earlier. The analog signal is sensed at periodic intervals called *sampling times*. The analog value at each sampling time is converted to a digital code and stored in memory, to be retrieved later to create various special effects. The greater the number of sampling times and analog levels sensed, the more accurate the waveform that is developed. For this set, sampling occurs 480 times for each horizontal line, with a clock frequency of 10 MHz. The output of the A/D converter is a 5-bit digital code capable of denoting 32 different analog levels or shades of gray.

If sampling occurs at the same instant for each horizontal scan line, the overall picture would appear to be made up of vertical lines as shown in Figure 19-9 (the *dither effect*). It is prevented by using a sampling frequency where the sampling time is not the same for adjacent lines. After performing their assigned special effects, the data are restored to their original analog form.

*Video/Chroma Signal Flow.* All digital functions are performed by seven or eight LSI ICs mounted on two PCBs, identified as DIG 1 and DIG 2. Figure 19-11 shows the division between "conventional" signals and the digital signals. The signal from the video detector is applied to a video select circuit, which has three additional inputs, EXT 1, EXT 2, and RGB sync. The signal selected is routed to conventional video/chroma signal processing stages, which generate the luminance and the three color difference signals, R - Y, B - Y, and G - Y. These three signals are directed to the digital circuitry and processed into analog.

*Scan Velocity Modulation (SVM).* This is a system used by Mitsubishi to enhance the apparent resolution by adding crispness to a pix. It operates by changing the horizontal scan velocity of the electron beam during the transistion from light to dark picture elements. It is most effective at the edges of the screen but gives the effect of uniform sharpness over the entire screen area. The electronics that does this is contained on a single PCB mounted on the CRT neck as part of the convergence assembly. In operation, the SVM circuit receives a sample of the luminance signal, a parabolic horizontal sweep signal, and several dc voltages (Figure 19-12). Additionally, a control signal from the RGB video circuit disables the SVM when the receiver is in the RGB mode. The luminance signal is amplified and

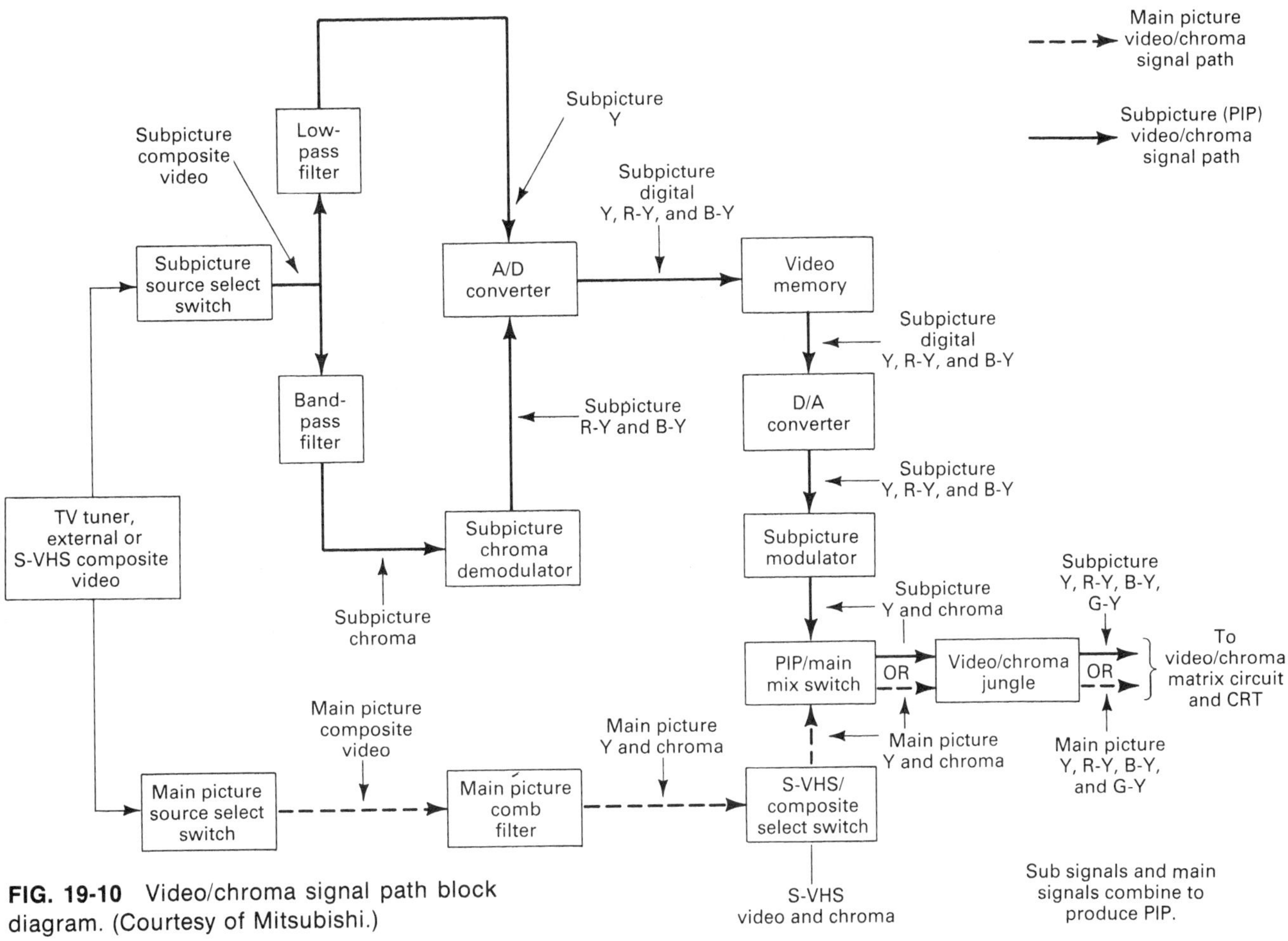


**FIG. 19-10** Video/chroma signal path block diagram. (Courtesy of Mitsubishi.)

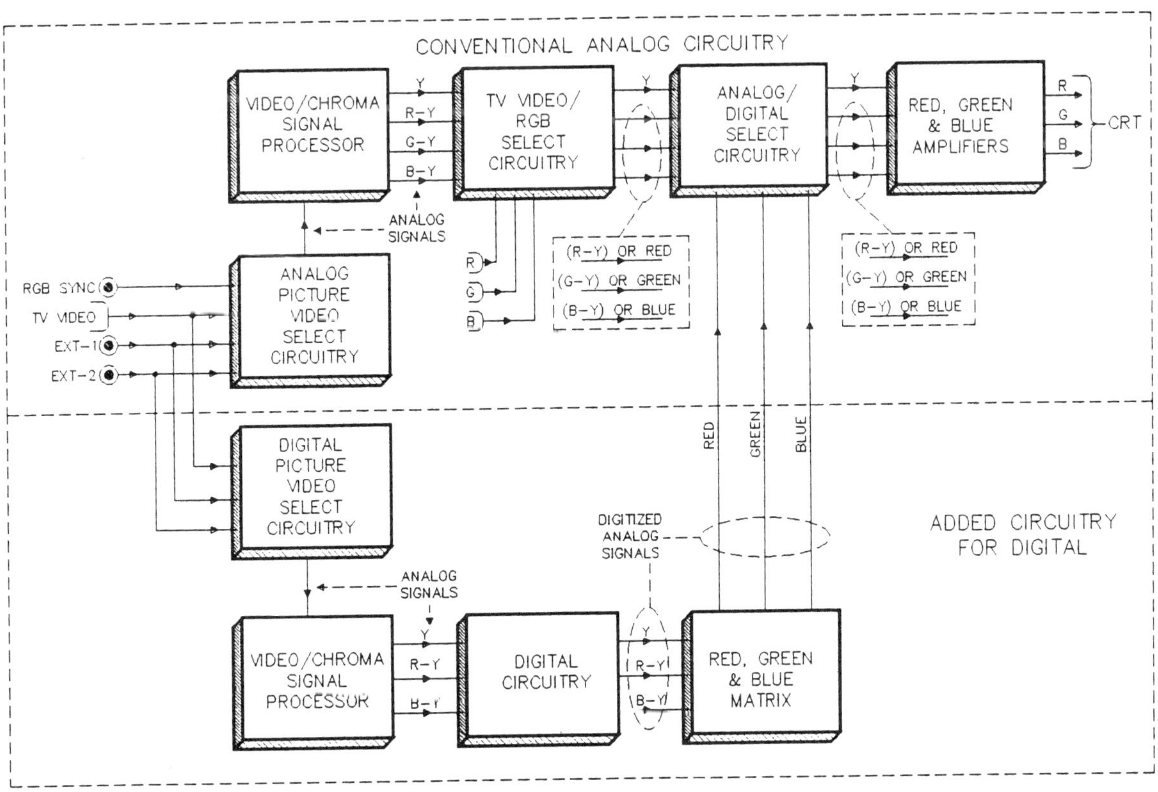


**FIG. 19-11** Analog and digital processing. (Courtesy of Mitsubishi.)

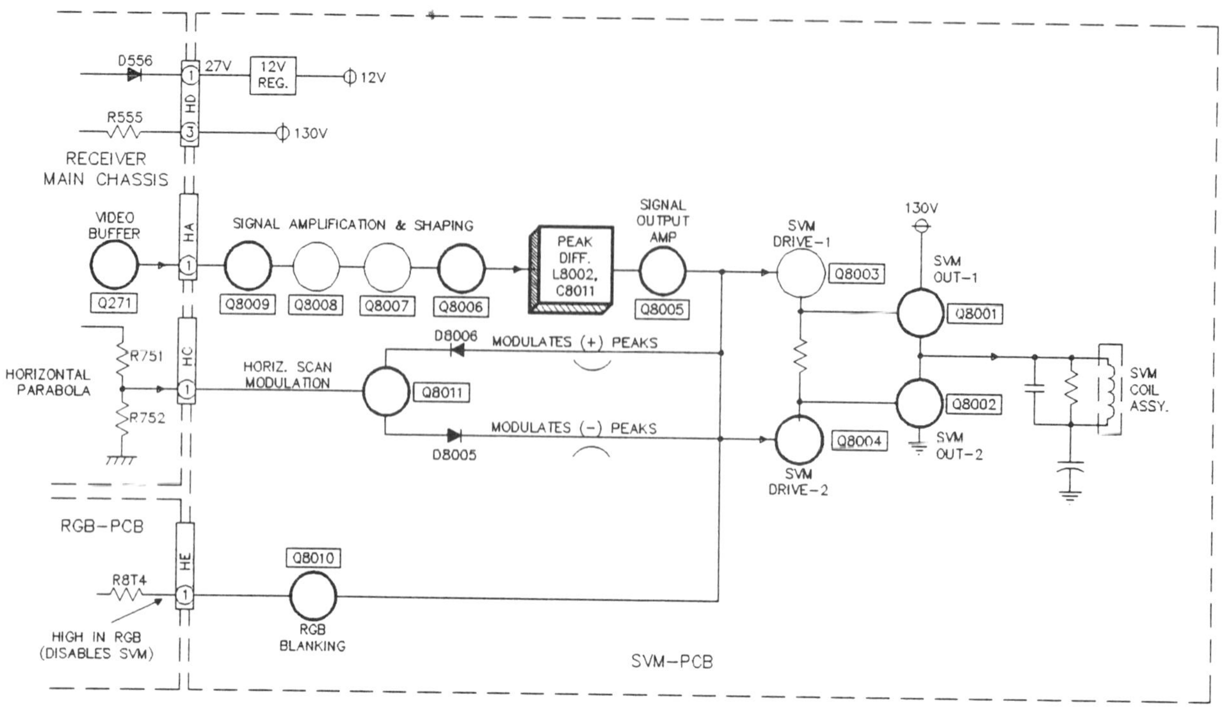


**FIG. 19-12** SVM block diagram. SVM contributes to picture enhancement. (Courtesy of Mitsubishi.)

shaped with all but the level transitions needed by the SVM discarded. The parabolic signal is used to vary the gain of the horizontal driver and sweep output stage. This signal is also applied to a special coil within the convergence assembly, to control the three CRT beams as they exit the guns. The SVM circuitry is relatively simple, much like an audio amplifier.

## 19-6 MONITORS

A typical monitor contains all the stages and circuitry of a TV receiver with the exception of the channel selectors, the IF strip, and detectors. Tuned stages tend to degrade a picture by limiting the high-frequency response, as explained earlier. In this regard, a good-quality monitor provides a better-quality picture than is possible with all but the best TV sets. A typical top of the line monitor has better than 560 lines of horizontal resolution and uses a CRT capable of dividing the image into extremely small pixels.

Video monitors are commonly used as a display device in conjunction with VCRs, camcorders, videodisk players, computers, and in some cases, to obtain maximum resolution in conventional and satellite receivers. A problem with using a monitor with a VCR, however, is the inability to record one program while viewing another.

Although a small screen is often preferable to a large screen with its wider-spaced scanning lines, medium-sized monitors are frequently used as a substitute for the small-screen display terminals used with computers. Except for screen size, they have one thing in common—a high-resolution capability resulting from the absence of RF/IF stages. With computers, particularly for word processing and graphics, sharpness and clarity of an image are paramount. As might be expected, a monochrome monitor (terminal) has better resolution than a color monitor. As a comparison, a medium-priced monochrome terminal (green, amber, or white) will produce a sharper image than that of an expensive three-color terminal.

You get what you pay for. Some so-called monitors are little more than an inexpensive TV without the tuned stages. On the other hand, a well-designed monitor incorporates all the latest circuitry needed to enhance an image. Of particular importance is the use of comb filters, other HQ features described previously, and the use of high-resolution components. To ensure the best quality image, some monitors even provide for manual degaussing in addition to ADG.

In general, as with TV, there are two basic types of monitors: digital and analog RGB. RGB is a relatively new design that provides superior resolution. This design, which is somewhat complex, can be likened to the sandcastle system described in Chapter 14. Unlike a conventional system, an RGB monitor requires up to *six* signals for the CRT to function. These are the regular RGB video signals, a sampling of vertical and horizontal sync pulses, and in some cases, what is called an "intensity" signal. All six must be present for the CRT to develop a picture. This can be a real challenge to the repair technician.

In judging picture quality on a monitor or TV, you should, among other things, check and evaluate the following.

- *Fine detail.* Check the image for sharpness and freedom from smear.
- *Brightness contrast and focus.* Check for adequate brightness and contrast and the range of each control. Perfect focus is essential.
- *Color tracking.* Color tints should be constant and uniform over several scene changes and should not change as the brightness control is adjusted.
- *Color distortion.* Whites should be pure with no color tinting. Black areas and images should be jet black, not grayish.
- *Raster distortion.* There should be no curvature to straight lines, and circles should not appear oval-shaped.
- *Color purity and convergence.* Raster should be near-white and not color tinted. BW images should have no color fringing, especially at the center of the screen.
- Sound quality should also be considered (see Chapter 18).

### MTS Stereo

A monitor with stereo capability employs the same means of separating and decoding the left and right channel signals as described in Chapter 18 for TV. However, some inexpensive models still use the pseudo system of *simulated stereo* mentioned earlier.

### Driving the Monitor

There are two ways to feed signal(s) from a TV set or VCR to a high-quality monitor: converting to RF and feeding the tuner (if there is one) or bypassing the early stages of the monitor and feeding the demodulated signals directly to the video/chroma and sound amplifiers. VCRs and camcorders provide outlets for this purpose, one for sound and one for video.

## 19-7 TROUBLESHOOTING AND REPAIR

High-resolution TV sets and monitors are subject to the same kinds of breakdowns as other electronic devices, calling for the same troubleshooting procedures as described in previous chapters. Alignment is of particular importance and the high-resolution capabilities of such sets can be achieved only by proper setup adjustment, particularly focus, color purity, and convergence. The same procedures are used as described in Chapters 15 and 17—with one possible exception, the RGB monitor. To obtain a picture with this system, it is necessary to inject vertical and horizontal sync and an intensity signal to enable the CRT drive circuits. In this way the monitor can be locked in sync while you localize the defect to the troublesome stage using normal troubleshooting procedures.

For many technicians, digital troubleshooting is a whole new ball game. As an introduction to the subject, we have chosen a late model Mitsubishi receiver which is typical of many. Trouble symptoms, causes and procedures are shown in the troubleshooting flow drawings of Figure 19-13. Although the information applies specifically to Mitsubishi sets, much of it is also applicable to other receivers. Since all functions are performed by ICs, fault finding is only to the PCB level. As stated earlier, the digital processing and control involves two PCB boards, identified as DIG1 and DIG2. These are called out on the flow drawings as likely suspects for specific trouble symptoms. Troubleshooting procedures for "conventional" circuits as used in high-resolution TVs and monitors were covered in earlier chapters. For checking logic in and out of the boards, use a logic probe.

Loss of a memory address signal is a typical problem. The symptom for this is a "digitized picture," as shown in Figure 19-14. The low or high number of a Y signal denotes which address is missing.

For additional treatment of digital troubleshooting, a highly recommended book is *New Digital Troubleshooting Techniques*, by R. Middleton (Prentice-Hall, 1983).

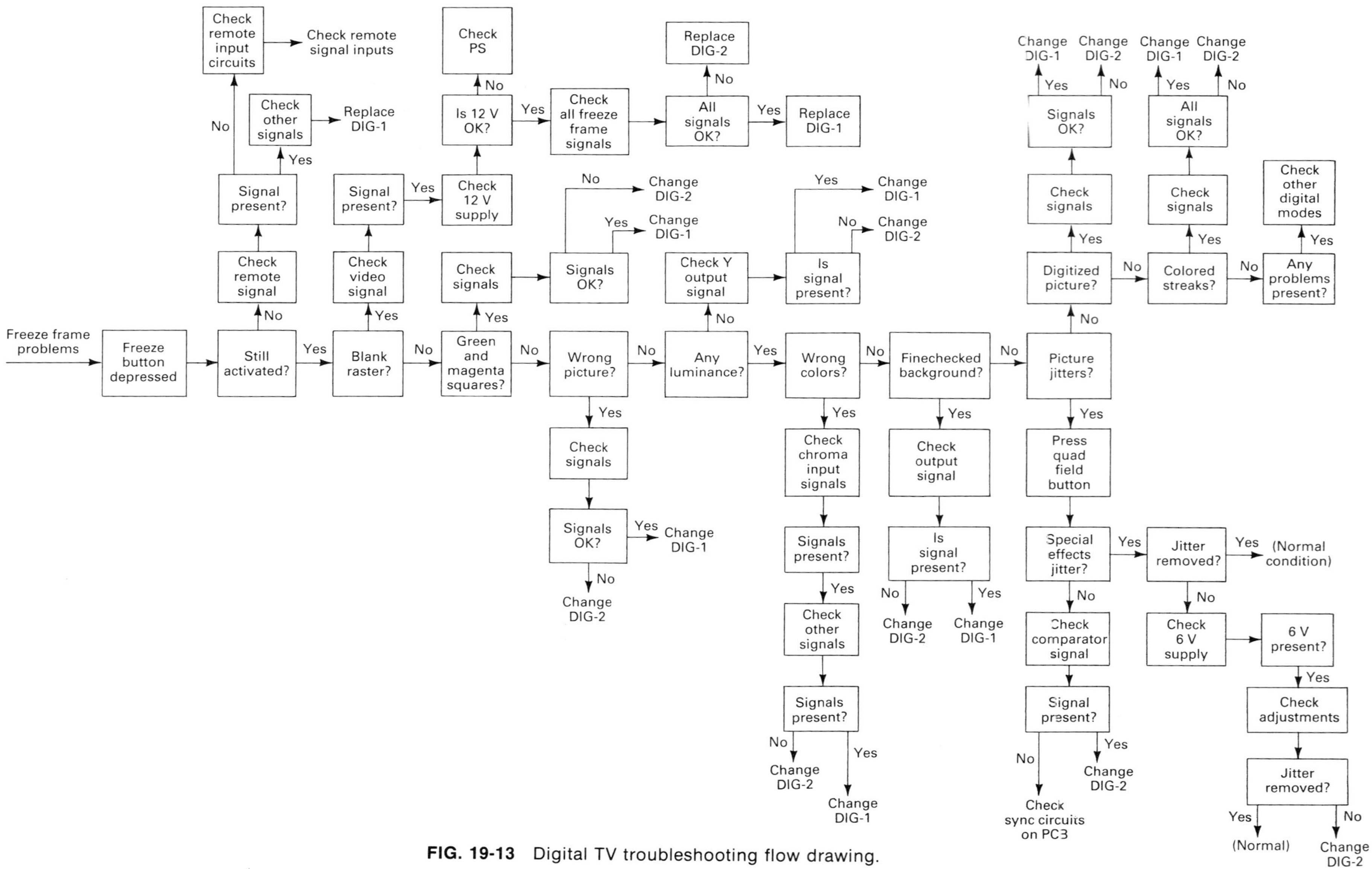


**FIG. 19-13** Digital TV troubleshooting flow drawing.

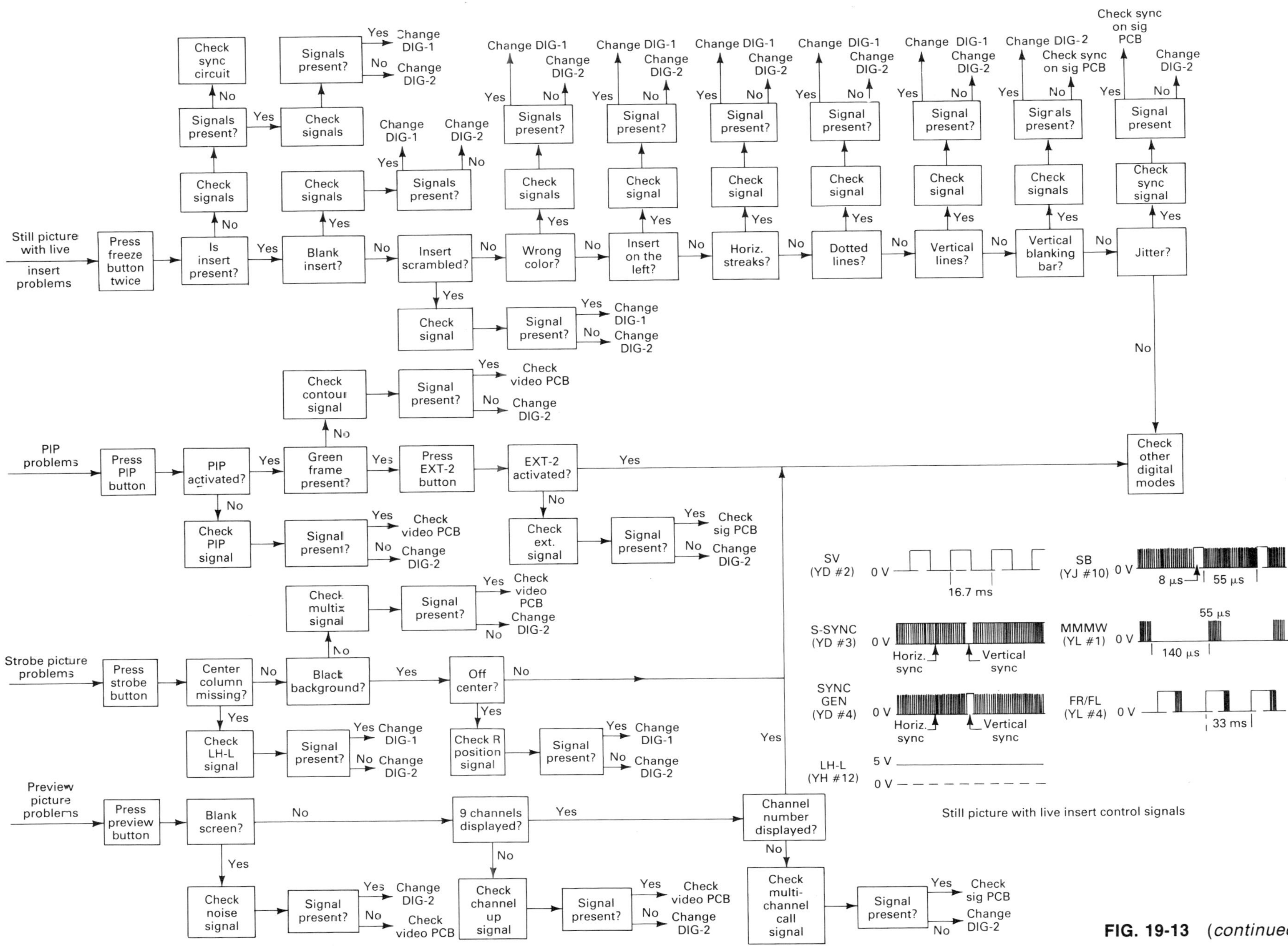


**FIG. 19-13** *(continued)*

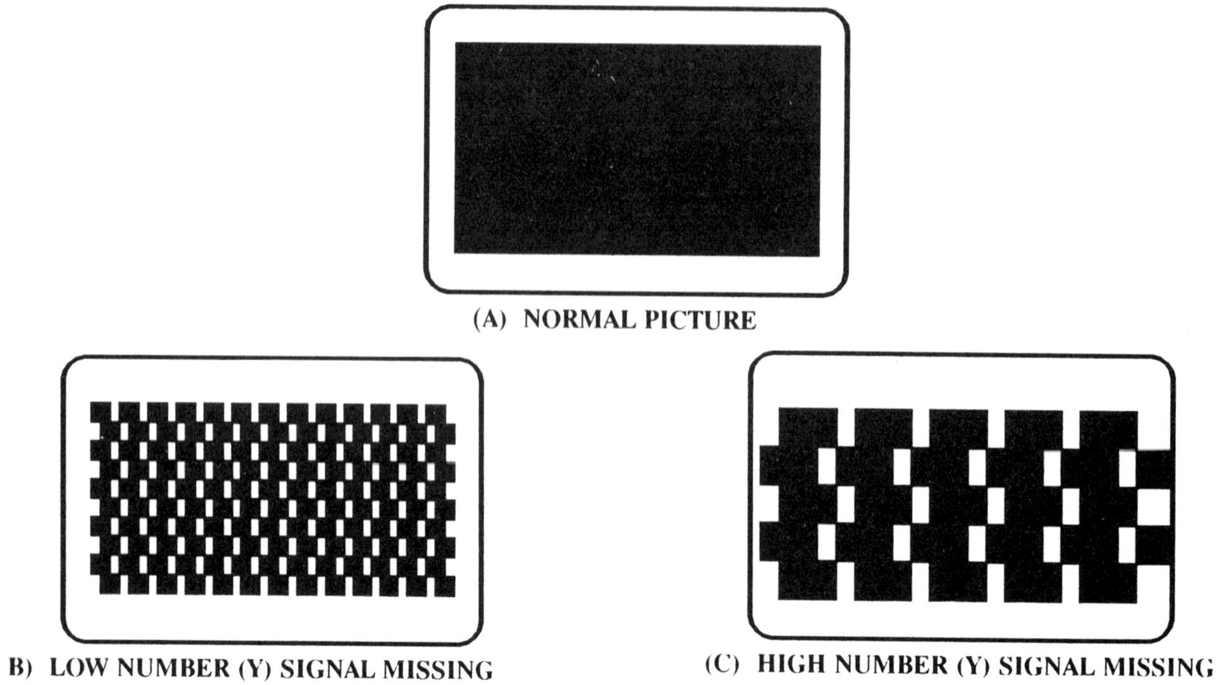


**FIG. 19-14** Digitized picture. The pattern identifies which of two address signals is lost. (Courtesy of Mitsubishi.)

## QUESTIONS

1. Explain why a video monitor provides a sharper image than is possible with most TV sets.
2. State some of the things that impair picture resolution.
3. Explain how a comb filter contributes to good picture quality.
4. Explain why picture resolution is limited by the 6-MHz bandwidth allocation.
5. Why does a monochrome receiver provide sharper details than a color set?
6. Explain why the development of an American HDTV system may be difficult or impossible under the present NTSC standards.
7. Explain double scanning, its purpose, and how it is accomplished.
8. Explain several methods presently used to enhance picture quality.
9. Explain HQ and the factors involved.
10. Explain the difference between vertical and horizontal resolution and how each affects the picture.
11. Explain the relationship between bandpass and the number of scanning lines that makes up a picture.
12. Special effects are dependent on the use of digital technology. Explain.
13. Identify and describe a number of logic devices and their functions.
14. Explain a binary truth table and what it represents.
15. Using computer logic, how is it possible to perform a variety of functions using only ones and zeros?
16. State two other ways of identifying the two logic states.
17. Name at least six special effects provided by most late-model, high-quality TV sets.
18. Explain the need for and functions of A/D and D/A converters in modern TV receivers.
19. Briefly explain signal processing for developing special effects.
20. In the 525-line picture, only about 250 of the lines are "usable" active lines. Explain.

# 20 Videocassette recorders

Not since TV came on the scene has a device for home entertainment and enlightenment achieved such popularity in so short a time. And rightly so, especially when one considers the latest state-of-the-art features and innovations: super VHS with resolution capabilities rivaling that of the most expensive TV sets; HQ circuitry to further enhance picture quality; four-, five-, and six-head machines with freeze frame, slow motion, and digital "special effects"; hi-fi stereo sound with Dolby noise reduction; one-touch recording capability; cable-ready tuners; and of course, remote control for all functions. This is high technology at its best, and to top it off, it is "user friendly."

As a consumer product in the hands of so many, a modern VCR is a most complex and sophisticated device. Unlike a TV set, which it rivals in complexity, it comprises both electronic and electromechanical devices: numerous sensors and interrelated computer-controlled systems and subsystems; motors, reels, pulleys, and gears; intricate mechanisms with incredibly fine tolerances; and computer logic circuitry embracing nearly 100 transistors, diodes, and numerous ICs. There are also some 50 or more adjustments that must be made with precision, a harmonious mix of components and circuitry all working together to perform their assigned functions at the touch of a few buttons. In addition, a VCR contains most of the signal processing circuitry found in television tuners, video and sound IF strips, video and chroma amplifiers, and chroma and color sync stages.

There are two formats, Beta and VHS, the latter by far the most popular. Because of the scope of the subject and space limitations, the former, and the now-obsolete top-loaded machines, are given only cursory treatment at this time. In this chapter we describe typical VHS machines, what they consist of, and what makes them tick. In Chapter 21 we deal with troubleshooting, maintenance, and repair, with emphasis on trouble symptoms, testing, and corrective procedures.

## 20-1 RELATED EQUIPMENT

Although beyond the scope of this book, other consumer products are available that relate to magnetic recordings and should be mentioned at this time. Included in the long list are the following: wireless distribution systems for transmitting signals to and from a VCR to remote receivers in a home or building, thus eliminating the need for unsightly cables; video amplifiers and image enhancers for improving picture quality; satellite system components; CATV accessories, including decoders; bulk erasers for erasing information from a tape quickly and completely; fast rewind devices for rewinding tapes external to a VCR or camcorder; and, of course, the currently popular laser/videodisc (CD player) that plays back images and sound prerecorded on a magnetic disk using a laser beam for pickup with no direct contact with the disk itself.

## 20-2 VCR COMPONENTS

The major components of a typical VCR and their functions are shown in Table 20-1. There are three general categories: mechanical and electromechanical devices, and the electronics that controls and monitors all functions. As an aid to understanding, and when an opportunity presents itself, the novice is advised to inspect the inner workings of a normally operating machine, learn to identify items that are visible and to observe what takes place during all modes of operation. Be careful not to disrupt the normal cycling or tape travel and not to contaminate the tape (by touching) it or any components in its path.

## 20-3 POWER SUPPLY

This is the one common denominator for all VCR functions. Actually, there are several PSs in one, and they are not too different from the switching-type power supply described in Chapter 6. Each has its own voltage regulator. Each PS serves one or more functions. Each voltage is switched on and off by logic commands from the system microprocessor(s).

## 20-4 MAGNETIC RECORDING FUNDAMENTALS

After leaving the supply reel on the cassette, the moving tape first makes contact with an *all-erase head,* where a supersonic bias current rearranges the molecules in the oxide-coated tape and prepares it for a recording. This high-frequency bias reduces hiss and ensures that previous recordings are completely erased. When the tape passes over a record/playback head on the drum (the same heads perform both functions), information to be recorded is applied to the heads to arrange the magnetically polarized tape molecules in definite patterns corresponding with that information. The magnetic flux is concentrated at the head gap, where it contacts the tape. Several tracks of information are recorded on the $\frac{1}{2}$-inch tape, video, monaural sound (including hi-fi stereo if it is a late-model machine), and a control track (Figure 20-1) for use by the servo systems. More on this later.

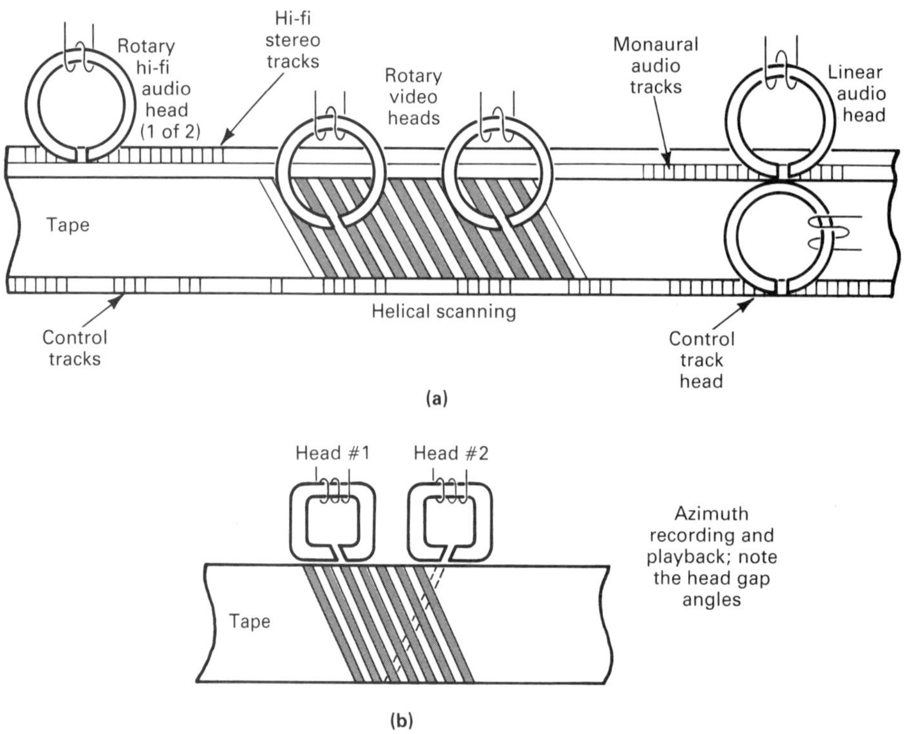


**FIG. 20-1** Recording and playback of tape tricks. During record or playback, the video heads alternate, each recording or playing back from diagonal tracks that correspond to pix fields. One revolution of the drum records or plays back a complete picture from two adjacent tracks. In (b), azimuth recording and playback, note the head gap angles.

***TABLE 20-1***

VCR components

| Component | Description and Functions |
|---|---|
| Control buttons (keys) | Initiate the various operating modes; each button has an LED to indicate the mode selected |
| Cassette | Plastic container for the recording tape; contains two reels, a supply reel and a takeup reel; has a protective hinged door or flap which opens when the cassette is in position, to permit tape loading; reels rotate CW for play and record modes and CCW for rewind; the reels have ratchets and small spring-loaded pawls help to take up slack, prevent snapped leaders, jamming, and tape spills; a small safety tab can be broken off to prevent accidental erasure of an important recording; when covered with tape the recording capability is restored; VHS and Beta cassettes are not interchangeable |
| Magnetic recording tape | Has a polyethylene/Mylar base with an iron oxide coating; when passing in close proximity to the heads during record, the iron molecules are arranged in patterns corresponding with the recording signal; in the playback mode, the recorded signals are recovered as the magnetized molecules induce the original signal currents in the head |
| Cassette loading mechanism | Motor-driven worm-and-gear arrangement; when a cassette is inserted, a sensor activates the motor and the cassette is drawn into the machine and deposited into a basket, then onto a reel table |
| Reel table | Supports the reels when a cassette is loaded and in position; the motor-driven tables have splined hubs to mate with and drive the reels |
| Cassette tray or basket | Receive the cassette during cassette loading operation |
| Heads | A head is a small electromagnetic device and there are several: video record/playback heads, audio record/playback heads, control track record/playback head, an "all-erase" head, and an audio erase head; the audio and control heads are usually stacked together; some heads are on the rotating drum, some are stationary in the tape path; the moving tape lightly contacts the head pole pieces; the erase heads erase information from tape prior to making new recording; the other heads serve a dual function, "writing" information during the record mode and "reading" it during playback; the tilt or azimuth adjustment of a head is extremely critical; heads are very fragile and easily shattered by abuse (e.g., improper cleaning and demagnetizing procedures, and the use of damaged tapes); in time, normal abrasion causes the pole pieces to wear, with predictable results; another problem is contamination, where oxide particles from the tape flake off and lodge in the "gap," creating record and playback problems for picture, sound, and sync |
| Head preamps and switching ICs | Amplify the weak recorded signals picked up by the rotating heads in the drum while in the playback mode; the electronic switches, operating from 30-Hz servo reference pulses, switch from one head to another at the proper times and in sync with the field and frame rate of the TV or monitor |
| Drum or cylinder (Figure 20-1) | A three-section motor-driven drum whose upper section contains the rotary video and hi-fi audio heads, a control pulse pickup coil magnet, and *rotary transformer* coils for conveying information to and from the spinning heads; the drum is tilted from the perpendicular and the moving tape (guided by a machined "ledge"), wraps around the drum in a spiral manner to contact the rotating heads; the drum rotates at 1800 rpm (30 rps, equivalent to the picture frame rate); its speed is constantly monitored and controlled by a "servo" system |
| Rotary transformers | These tiny transformers are built into the drum; there are usually four, one for each video and stereo head; each is in two parts, a coil in the rotating upper section, connected to the head winding, and a matching coil in the stationary lower section to pass information to and from signal processing circuits |
| Tape transport system | The means of transporting tape from the supply reel in the cassette, around the drum, pulleys, and tape guides, past a capstan, pinch roller, and various heads, then back to the cassette and the takeup reel |
| Capstan and pinch roller | They work together to move the tape; the tape is sandwiched between the small-diameter, motor-driven capstan spindle and a spring-loaded, solenoid-actuated rubber roller; as with the drum, the capstan speed is constantly monitored and controlled by a servo system |
| Tape threading ring | Motor-driven mechanism operating on rails to extract tape from the cassette (in the play/ |

**TABLE 20-1**

*(continued)*

| *Component* | *Description and Functions* |
|---|---|
| | record mode), threading it through and around various items in the tape path; after completion of record or playback, the process is reversed and the tape is returned to the cassette |
| Motors | There are several: a drum motor, capstan motor, reel motors, threading ring motor, and cassette load motor; some motors are direct drive, others serve a dual purpose using pulleys and belts; most are dc variable-speed reversible types operated from driver transistors; in some cases the drum motor is a synchronous hysteresis ac motor with a built-in "Hall effect" device |
| Tape guides and rollers | There are typically from 6 to 12 guides to guide the tape around the tape path; rollers and tapered guides at the head drum are tilted to spiral the tape around the drum in a precisely correct manner (helical scanning) for accurate reading and writing by the rotating heads |
| Tape tension and torque devices | Adjustable devices to ensure correct motor torques and tape tension, both of which are extremely critical; one type, called the back-tension band, consists of a fabric band that tightens against the revolving supply reel table to help control rotation and stop the reel |
| Brakes | Two types, solenoid-actuated mechanical brakes, and electromagnetic brakes; the latter makes use of induced eddy currents and opposing magnetic hysteresis forces to slow rotation. They operate in conjunction with servo systems to maintain correct tape tension and capstan and drum speeds. Also for instant stopping of cassette reels in the stop mode |
| Servo systems | For precise control of drum and capstan rotation; each system is comprised of two closed servo loops; in record mode, a *control track* is recorded on the tape; during playback, the servos use pulses from the track and those generated by the drum and capstan to maintain synchronization between a playback and a recording |
| Servo control pulse generators | Small magnets in the rotating drum and capstan motor drive that generate timing pulses in small stationary coils; there are two kinds of pulses: PG (pulse generator) and FG (frequency generator); many modern VCRs use a device called a *Hall effect generator,* which develops *all* the servo control pulses; it is contained in the direct-drive drum motor along with two sensing and switching ICs |
| Sensors (Figure 20-13) | Used to sense events and to monitor the status of the VCR and its operating condition; typical sensor functions: to sense reel rotation, tape tension and torque, end of tape, presence of moisture, and selected operating modes; sensor outputs are evaluated by microprocessor "micros" (computer ICs), which initiate the appropriate action(s); a "stop mode" is commanded at the completion of each function or when troubles develop |
| End-of-tape sensor | The VHS format has a clear segment on the leader at each end of the tape; when light from an LED or incandescent lamp passes through a see-through tunnel in the cassette and the leader, a light sensor initiates the stop mode; the Beta system uses opaque metal foil on the leader with an appropriate sensor |
| Reel rotation detector | A reflective segmented disk at the bottom of the takeup reel; light reflections picked up by a light-sensitive transistor generate a square wave; if no pulses are sensed (no reel rotation), the VCR goes into the stop mode |
| Relays and solenoids | A relay is basically an electromagnetic switch; most VCRs have at least two relays, one for switching heads and another for selecting the signal to be viewed, either directly from antenna or cable, or from the VCR; a solenoid has a coil and an iron core (plunger), which when drawn into the coil initiates a mechanical function, such as actuating the pinch roller or operating the reel brakes |
| Tape speed select switch | For the user to select one of three optional tape speeds: SP (standard play), LP (long play), or SLP (super long play); the recording is made at the speed selected; for playback, the servo system adjusts automatically for that speed |
| Tracking control | User control to remove picture and sound dropouts (bright horizontal streaks) caused by a bad tape or one recorded on another machine that is not 100% compatible |
| Service adjustments | There are many, and most are extremely critical; some are mechanical adjustments, head azimuth and tape tension being two important examples; trimpots are used extensively to establish proper pulse levels in the electronic circuitry and the timing of head switching |

**TABLE 20-1**

*(continued)*

| *Component* | *Description and Functions* |
|---|---|
| Digital readout | Fluorescent or LCD panel display of real-time and timer programmed events, and a counter with arbitrary numeric count to establish the start and finish of recordings and to aid in locating specific places on a tape; the counter range is from 0000 to 9999 |
| Program timer | A provision on most VCRs that enables the user to preset the machine to turn on and off automatically to record one or more programs on selected channels at specific times up to two weeks or so in advance of the scheduled telecasts; the programmed directions are stored in electronic memory ICs and acted upon unless the power is disrupted or the cassette runs out of tape; some VCRs also have a related feature called XPR (express) recording; with this, you can start a recording and program the VCR to shut down after a specified interval |
| RF modulator | A self-contained miniature transmitter that generates a carrier signal corresponding to the frequency of channel 3 or 4, as optionally selected by the user; in the playback mode, the carrier is modulated by the recorded luminance, chroma, and audio signals and fed to the antenna input of a TV set tuned to the same channel |
| Channel adjustments | Preset user adjustments associated with the VHF/UHF tuners; usually located behind a hinged door on the front panel; any programmed channel selected (from cable or antenna system) can be recorded and/or viewed directly on the TV set; most VCR tuners are "cable ready" |
| Remote control | Hand-held transmitter as used for TV and described in Chapter 12 provides for power turn-on and turn-off and all other functions of the front-panel buttons; may be wired, or wireless using digital pulse-modulated infrared; the VCR itself contains the infrared pickup sensor and circuitry |
| Electronics | This includes the following: several switched power supplies, a digital counter with readout, most of the luminance and chrominance "signal stages" found in a modern TV set, including HQ and S-VHS circuitry, SAW and comb filters, and the same PLL cable-ready VHF/UHF tuners; sensor circuitry; a key matrix encoder; electronic flip-flop analog switches; a channel 3 or 4 RF modulator; numerous op-amps, oscillators, counters, and frequency dividers; pulse generators and signal and servo system circuitry; Dolby and DBX decoders for noise reduction; AFM recording and playback circuitry; control microprocessors (the brains of the system); trimpots and the front-panel mode-select buttons; most of the functions are performed by the many ICs contained on a large PCB "mother board" |

VCRs are sometimes rated by the number of heads on the drum (Figure 20-2). The early machines had two heads, which is all that is actually required to record and play back a picture. Most current models have either four or five heads; the two basic video heads, two for hi-fi stereo, and one for special so-called "trick" effects such as freeze frame and slow motion.

After leaving the drum, the tape passes in front of an audio erase head that removes any residual noise or sound recordings. It then comes under the influence of the linear audio heads (sometimes there are two), and finally, the control track head for the recording of control tracks for use by the servo systems during playback. As stated earlier, audio record/playback heads and the control head are usually stacked together.

### Helical Scanning

To record and play back the highest video frequencies representing the finest picture detail requires a very rapid scanning rate relative to tape motion. With the earliest recorders this called for high tape speed, greatly limiting the amount of tape that could be contained on a reasonably sized reel. Helical scanning as used today was a real breakthrough. Instead of a fast tape speed, scanning (by the rotary heads) is speeded up. Some early VCRs shuttled the heads at a rapid rate transversely across the surface of the tape.

Helical scanning accomplishes the same thing in a different manner, by rotating the head drum at high speed and recording in diagonal strips (Figure 20-1). Just as a satellite in polar orbit looks at every

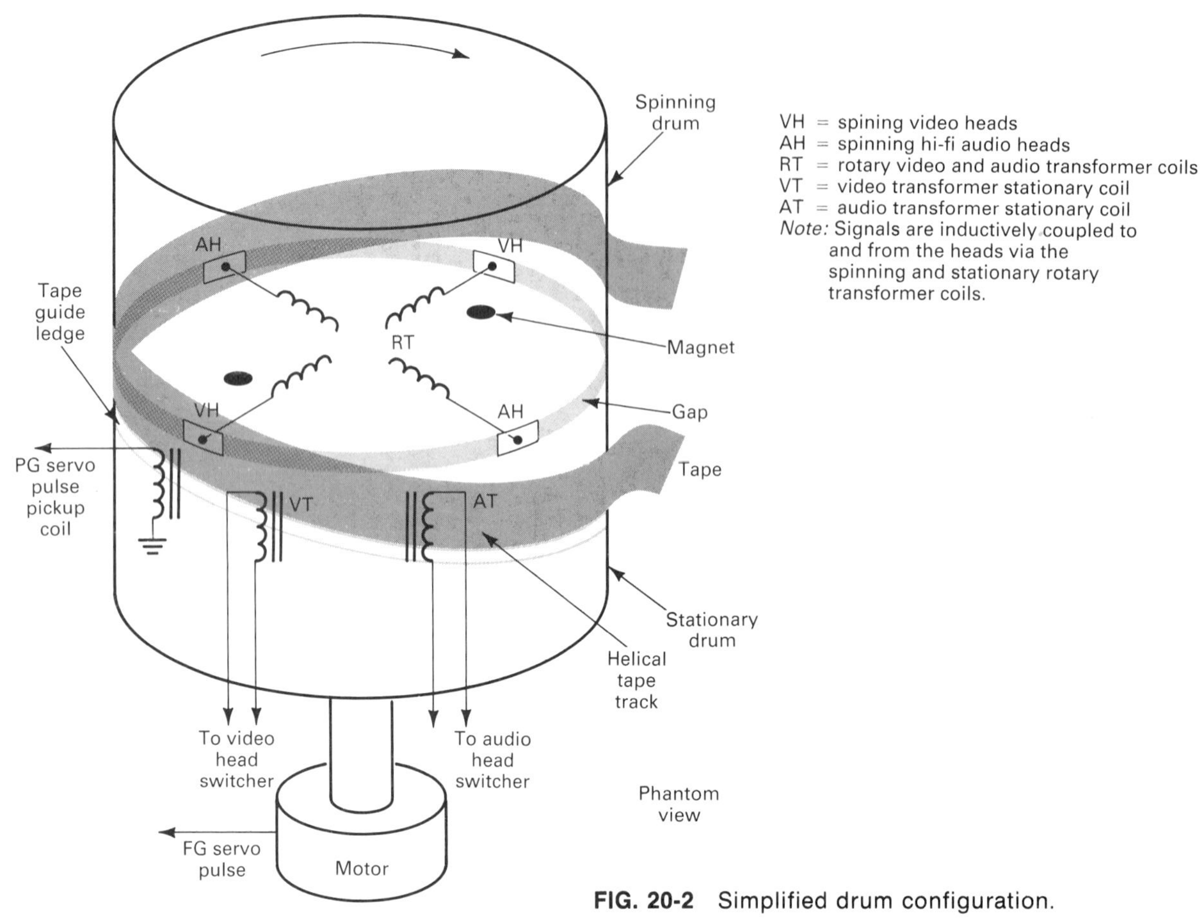


**FIG. 20-2** Simplified drum configuration.

spot on a revolving earth, each head, for every half revolution of the drum, scans the entire surface of the tape. And with two spinning heads, this translates into a high tape speed and fine picture detail, and for hi-fi stereo, good high-frequency audio response.

With the head drum axis tilted slightly from the vertical and the tape spiraled around the drum, the recorded information is laid down in narrow (2-mm) diagonal tracks (Figure 20-1). The tracks may be up to 4 inches in length depending on the format. Each track recorded by one of the heads contains all the monochrome and color information for one 262½-line field reproduced on a TV or monitor screen. This occurs for each half-revolution of the drum, which takes place in 1/60 s. To complete the revolution, the other head lays down another set of tracks interlaced with the first set. Sometimes they are referred to as odd and even line fields. Two adjacent tracks are equivalent to a 525-line frame: a complete interlaced picture that corresponds with TV vertical sync pulses and the vertical scanning of the picture.

To minimize *crosstalk* (the bleeding of signals between the tracks), different systems are in use. One system uses *guard bands* between the tracks so that the heads do not pick up information from adjacent tracks. The guard bands equate with vertical retrace intervals. With another system the tracks overlap. The most popular system is called *azimuth scanning*. Here the two video heads are physically offset from each other (12°) in opposite directions, with the head gaps cut at different angles, as can be seen in the drawing. The azimuth (tilt) of the heads is sometimes adjustable.

Ideally, for maximum signal transfer between the tape and the heads and to obtain a high signal-to-noise ratio and reduce crosstalk, the two heads should traverse the center of the tape tracks. Beyond this point in either direction, the signal drops off, as shown in Figure 20-3. With hi-fi, even a small tracking error creates problems with the audio (a clicking sound) even before it is noticeable on the picture.

## Head/Tape Tracking

Any misadjustment of the two video heads, or deviations of the tape in its path around the drum, has an adverse effect on picture strength and quality (and the signal-to-noise ratio) for both record and

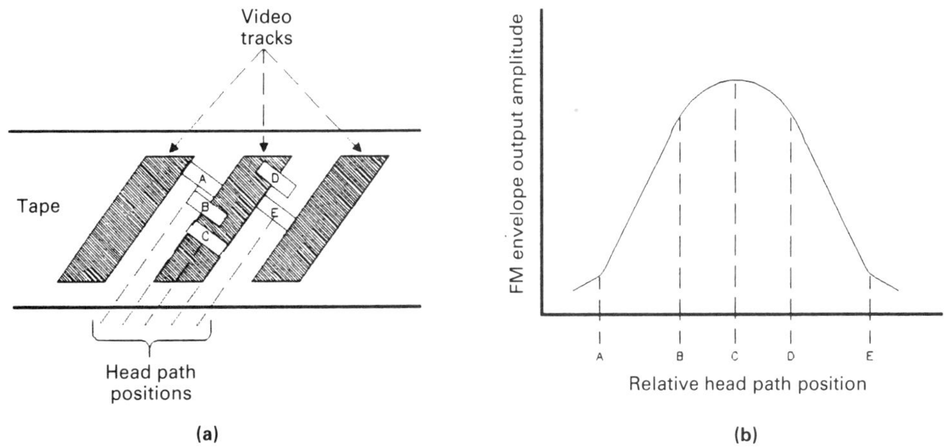


**FIG. 20-3** Helical scanning and tracking consideration: (a) head path location versus video tracks; (b) envelope amplitude versus head path position. A tracking error shows up first on hi-fi, audio, and CTL tracks on the edges of the tape. (Courtesy of Mitsubishi.)

playback. A tracking error also results in streaks and "sparkles" on a picture similar to those produced by a bad tape or a dirty head. This is normally overcome by a critical adjustment of the front-panel tracking control.

For improved results, one late-model VCR (Mitsubishi) features *automatic tracking,* where the optimum tracking point (the center of the tape) is determined and maintained by detecting the amplitude of the FM signal coming from the heads, and making an automatic correction if needed. The user can select either manual or autocontrol, as desired.

### Head Switching

During playback of a recording, the two video heads (and hi-fi audio heads) are alternately switched on and off at the proper times so that each field overlaps the next by approximately six horizontal lines. Switching is accomplished by electronic analog switches controlled by 30-Hz square-wave pulses generated by the servo timing circuits. Each head is switched on when it is in the proper "read" or "write" position relative to drum rotation and tape travel, as shown in Figure 20-4. Hi-fi stereo heads on the drum are switched in the same manner. Rotary transformers transfer the signals to and from the spinning heads. Note the absence of head switching in the record mode.

To summarize, Figure 20-4a shows video and sound being recorded by heads A and C, respectively. One track of video (equivalent to one picture field) is being laid down on the tape. In Figure 20-4b, which is one-half revolution later, another track, corresponding to another field, is laid down by head B. This completes the recording of a frame, a complete picture.

During playback (Figure 20-4c), head (A) is switched on by the switcher and the head picks up the recorded information from where it is processed and routed to the TV or monitor. The same thing occurs for the sound, with its head C in the read position. In Figure 20-4d, one-half revolution later, heads B and D are in position for reading the tape. Monaural sound is recorded and played back using the stationary linear head(s) as shown.

### Picture Resolution and HQ

Because of information lost during vertical retrace, until recently only about 330 of the 525 lines of a picture could actually be observed as described in Chapter 19. As stated earlier, a modern TV set and VCR have better than 400-line resolution. A good monitor has about 450. Pictures of 1200-line resolution are a promise for the near future.

Many of the recent improvements in picture quality are due to HQ and S-VHS, features now found in most modern VCRs. With these, there are many "pluses": greatly enhanced picture quality, an increase in the "white clip" level, low noise from the luminance circuits, reduced interference, sharper fine picture detail, less color streaking, and an overall improvement in color fidelity.

Factors that contribute to recording high frequencies (for optimum fine picture detail) are frequency modulating the luminance signal, using ex-

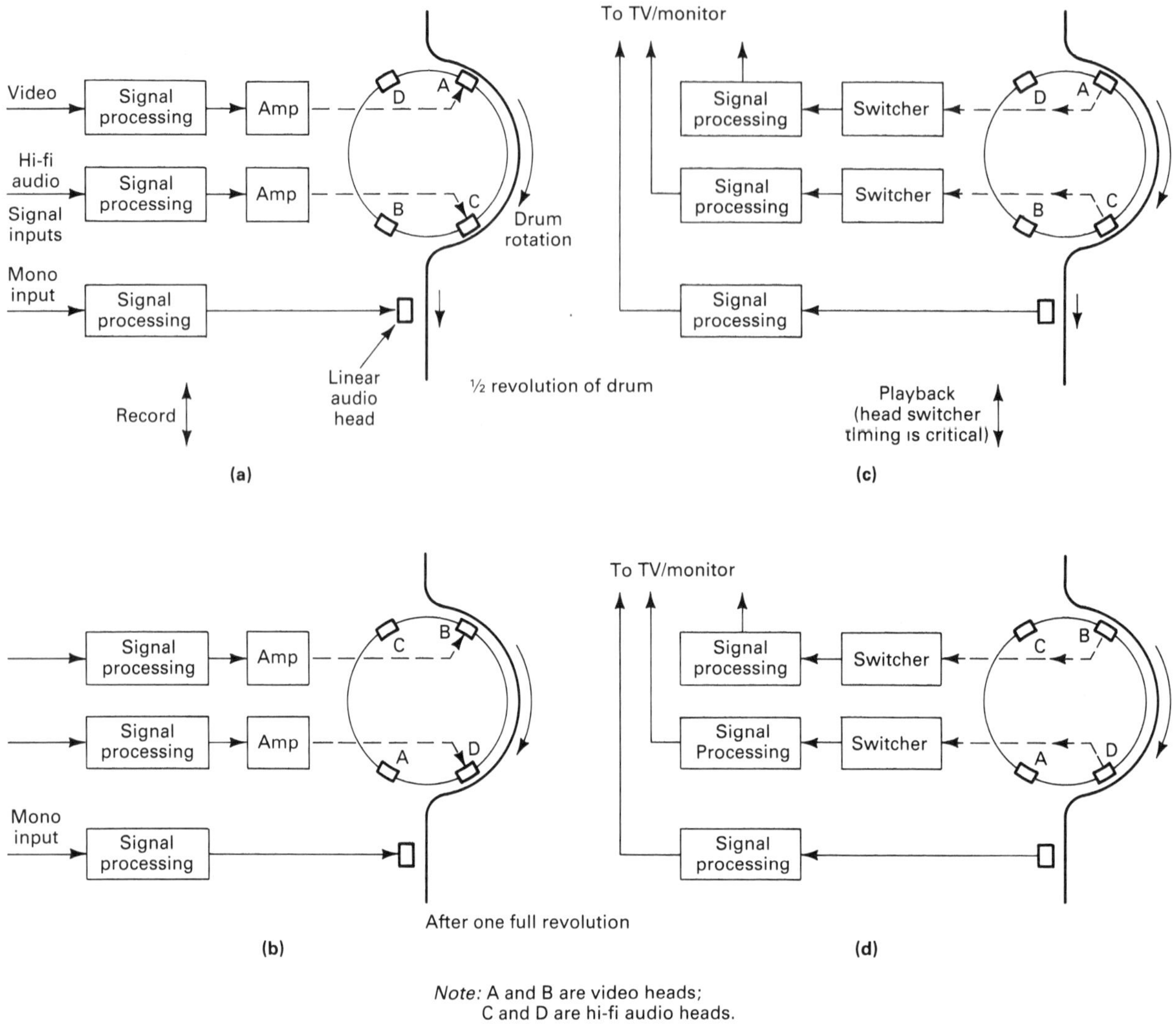


**FIG. 20-4** Record/playback head switching and signal flow.

tremely narrow head gaps, the use of equalization, and the super-VHS format. More on this later.

## Sound Recording

Monaural sound is usually recorded on a narrow track on one edge of the tape. It is made by linear audio record/playback head(s) located in the tape path, as with a conventional sound recorder, in this case downstream (in the direction of tape travel) from the drum. Most modern VCRs provide hi-fi stereo using the MTS system described in Chapter 18. Two additional sound channel tracks are recorded from two revolving heads located in the spinning drum, in the same manner as writing picture information, except that the tracks are usually laid down next to the mono track. With some designs, hi-fi sound is superimposed on the video and recorded alongside the diagonal video tracks. This is equivalent to a high tape speed for recording and playback of the highest audio frequencies. The recording and playback of hi-fi stereo uses a system called AFM (audio frequency modulation), described later.

With the advent of stereo and the limited tape width, it became necessary to reduce the width of each audio track. Unfortunately, this causes a decrease in the signal-to-noise ratio. However, this shortcoming is largely overcome by the use of Dolby and DBX noise reduction circuits, described in Chapter 18.

For hi-fi stereo, an additional head switcher and rotary transformer is used. Audio switching occurs slightly delayed from video switching to compensate for head separations on the drum, using the same 30-Hz switching pulses. Monaural heads are still required for compatibility with nonstereo systems and monaural recordings.

### Control Track

This is a narrow track (Figure 20-1) produced by 30-Hz timing (synchronizing) pulses that originate from a sampling of 60-Hz vertical sync pulses. The servo systems use these pulses to ensure that playback is synchronized precisely with the recording.

In the playback mode, most functions are the reverse of the record functions. The spinning heads read the video information from the tape, one field at a time. The heads are automatically switched between fields with the electronic head switcher as each head makes contact with the tape every half-revolution of the drum. Sound is similarly played back with either the stationary audio head or the hi-fi heads in the drum. An electronic head switcher is used for the latter to provide left and right audio outputs for the speakers. The control track head continuously reads the timing pulses as recorded previously. These pulses, which are locked in phase with vertical sync, are used by the servos to control the speed and phasing of the capstan and drum motors, and for head switching.

## 20-5 VCR OPERATION

When a cassette is inserted in the machine and either the record or play button (key) is pressed, the following scenario takes place (see Figure 20-5). The cassette load motor starts up and with an arrangement of gears, pulls the cassette inside and deposits it in a tray or basket directly above a reel table. The TAPE IN light comes on. The splines of two motor-driven shafts engage with corresponding splines in the cassette reels. A pin pushes upward into the cassette, causing the flap to open, exposing the tape. With loading complete, a sensor starts the drum and tape threading motors. Pins on the threading ring engage the tape; the ring moves back with a rotating motion, pulling the tape out of the cassette and through and around the various items in the tape path (Figure 20-6). Tape guides direct the tape diagonally across the drum surface and over the heads as shown in Figure 20-2. VHS and Beta machines have different threading configurations; the latter is simpler, having fewer tape guides (Figure 20-6).

With tape threading complete, the capstan motor becomes energized, the solenoid-actuated pinch roller squeezes the tape against the capstan spindle, and the tape begins to move, slowly un-

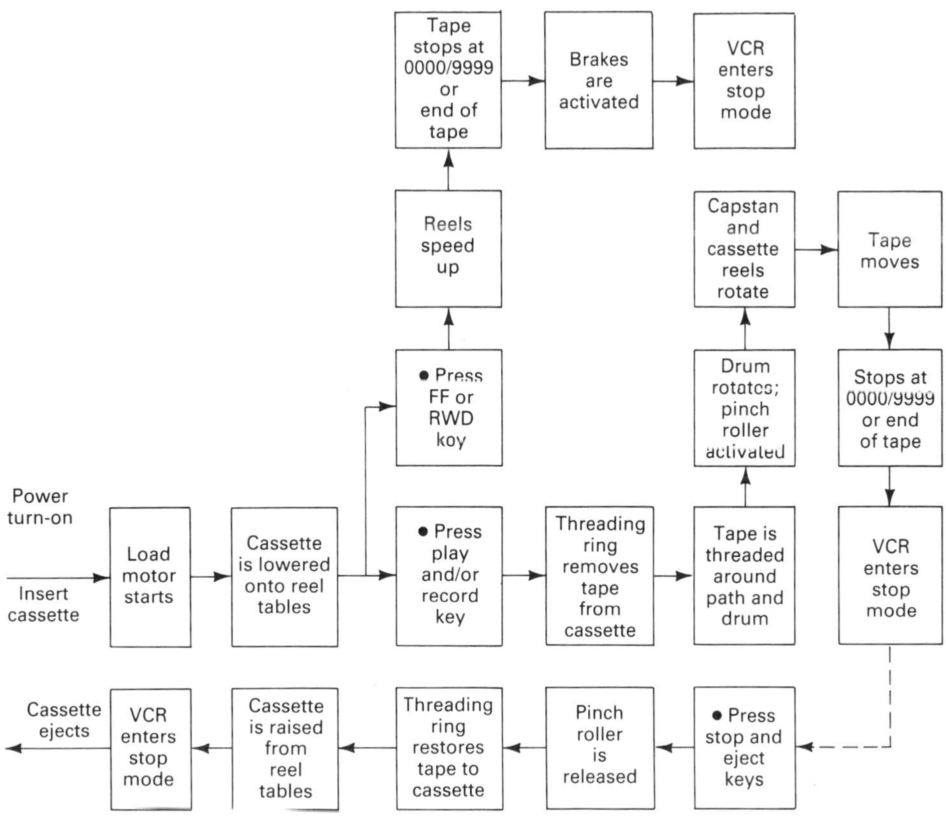


**FIG. 20-5** Cassette/tape loading and eject.

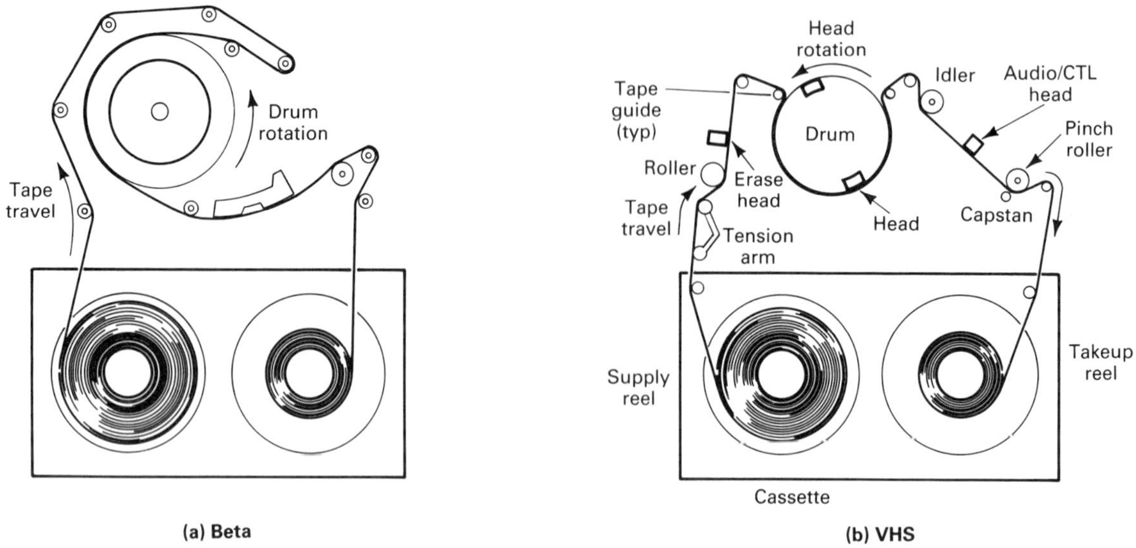


**FIG. 20-6** Typical tape threading configurations: (a) Beta; (b) VHS.

winding from the supply reel, around the tape track, the spinning drum, and onto the takeup reel. With the VCR now fully energized, the various heads begin writing or reading to or from the tape, depending on which mode is selected.

### Recording

To record a program it is necessary to press the play and record buttons simultaneously. With some VCRs this is done with a latching arrangement. The pinch roller is engaged to move the tape at the speed selected. The VCR/TV button is pressed to monitor either the program being recorded or a program from another channel. In the record mode, the erase heads are energized and all previous recordings are being erased prior to recording the new material.

As information is supplied to the heads, video and stereo sound (via the rotary transformers) and mono sound directly, video and sound tracks are laid down, the video as diagonal strips, and the mono and stereo sound on one edge of the tape. Also, a sampling of 60-Hz vertical sync pulses is reduced to 30 Hz (by a 2:1 divider) and recorded onto the control track on the opposite edge of the tape. At the same time, the rotation of both the capstan and drum is maintained constant by the two servo systems.

### Tape Speed Selector

The desired tape speed is established by the user with the manual speed-select control. It is used only for recording a program. The correct speed is *selected automatically* and maintained during playback). Head *selection* (not to be confused with head switching, which uses an IC analog switch) is accomplished by *relay* switches in accordance with the manually selected tape speed.

The higher the tape speed, the better the picture and sound quality but at the expense of tape usage. A T-120 cassette, for example, will record up to 6 hours at the SLP speed, 4 hours at the LP setting, and only 2 hours at the SP speed. Rented tapes are recorded at the highest (SP) speed, and only a discriminating viewer can notice or appreciate the difference in picture quality. At the start of a recording, it is customary to reset the counter to 0000. When the recording is completed, the new readout is noted for future reference.

### Playback

When the cassette is inserted and the PLAY button pressed, the threading ring removes the tape and threads it around the track as in the record mode. The drum starts spinning and the pinch roller is engaged to move the tape. The VCR/TV button is pressed to make the VCR LED light come on. In the playback mode the erase bias is removed.

The various heads start reading information previously recorded; the linear audio head(s) reading from the mono sound track, the spinning stereo heads reading from the stereo tracks, the control head reading from the control track, and the rotating video heads reading alternately from the diagonal video tracks. Video signals exit the drum via rotary transformers, are amplified, and fed to the video switchers. From the switcher(s) the signal is processed by various luminance and chroma circuits, routed to the RF modulator, and then routed to the TV set input.

### Search Mode

In the play mode, pressing either the SEARCH FORWARD or SEARCH REVERSE buttons will speed up the capstan motor to quickly locate some desired spot on the tape. While the tape is being scanned, the image is observed on the TV or monitor screen. This is most easily done with the tape speed set for either LP or SLP. For *SP* (except on a multiple-head machine) the monitored image is barely distinguishable as a picture while searching. In the search modes the audio is muted. Unless the stop button is pressed, the tape will stop when the counter reads either 0000 or 9999.

### Fast Forward and Rewind

For fast forward or rewind, the STOP button is pressed followed by pressing either the FF or RWD buttons. With most VCRs, in the FF or RWD modes the pinch roller is released and the tape is restored to the cassette. For FF, the takeup reel speeds up clockwise. For RW, the supply reel speeds up counterclockwise. When tape runs out, when the counter reaches 0000 or 9999, or when the stop button is pressed, motor power is removed and the brakes instantly stop the tape. Some modern VCRs feature superfast FF and RWD.

### Special Effects

This includes such features as *freeze frame* (which permits viewing of a single frame), *frame advance* (for advancing tape one frame at a time), *slow motion* (to play back a recording at reduced speed), and *search scan* (to view the picture, either forward or reverse, at a faster than-normal speed as an aid in locating a particular place on a recording). Most late-model machines also feature PIP, a digital function where a small picture from another channel is superimposed onto one corner of the screen. This is described in Chapter 19.

For example, when the PAUSE button is pressed during playback, the pinch roller is released, the tape stops moving but the drum continues to spin, reading one section of the tape (two adjacent tracks) to produce a still picture. The sound is muted. Leaving the VCR in the pause mode for more than a minute or so can risk damaging the tape and contaminating the heads. For slow motion, the pinch roller is engaged and capstan motor power is reduced to slow the tape and the action viewed on the screen.

Although two heads are all that is required to produce a picture, and another pair for hi-fi stereo, a five-head machine is best for special effects. With only two heads, a picture tends to be scrambled and unstable in these modes, particularly when the recording was made at the highest (SP) speed.

### Stop Mode

The system enters the stop mode when the stop button is pressed, when exiting other modes, when a sensor detects an unsafe operating condition, or when there is a breakdown. The reels, drum, and capstan motors stop turning, the pinch roller releases the tape, the brakes come on to instantly stop and lock the reel tables, and the threading ring is activated in reverse and restores the tape to the cassette. Unless there is a circuit defect, the electronic functions are still operational but in standby.

### Eject

Pressing the eject button (after VCR enters the stop mode) energizes the cassette load motor in reverse, the basket lifts the cassette off the reel table, the cassette is ejected from the front access portal, the TAPE IN light goes out, and the VCR returns to the stop mode. All motors stop turning, but the electronics are still energized until the power OFF button is pressed and its associated LED indicator is extinguished.

### Automatic and Special Features

At the present, many late-model VCRs incorporate the following innovations and convenience features:

- *Auto-turn-on*. The machine is turned on when the cassette is inserted.
- *Auto-play*. Playback starts when the cassette is inserted. The record mode is entered by pressing only the record button.
- *Auto-rewind*. The tape rewinds at the end of a recording, when tape is used up, or when the counter reaches 0000 or 9999.
- *Auto-replay*. The tape replays after it is rewound.
- *Auto-tracking*. Optimum head/tape tracking is maintained automatically.

- *Indexing*. The VCR automatically searches for an indexing signal recorded at the start of each recording to assist the user in locating program material.
- *Up-down search*. For rapid up-down searching of channels.
- *Speed search*. Tape speed is greatly increased when searching.
- *Fast playback*. This is an alternative to fast search.
- *Super VHS*. Picture quality is enhanced by increasing the number of picture scanning lines and increasing the signal-to-noise ratio.
- *Hi-fi stereo*. As with TV stereo, it provides directivity and realism to the sound coming from dual speakers.
- *Spinning erase head*. An erase head on the drum for diagonal erasure of the tracks facilitates dubbing.
- *PIP*. One or more small pictures from different channels are superimposed on the main picture.

## 20-6 MICROPROCESSORS AND SYSTEM CONTROL

One or more micro ICs perform as a *master control* of practically every mode and function—a big job for such a small and insignificant device. There are usually two or more micros working together and exchanging information on serial and parallel data lines. Note the various inputs and outputs and the signal exchange shown in Figure 20-7. Also note the inputs from the various sensors to initiate appropriate actions at the proper times for different conditions.

A microprocessor is very reliable and unless some abnormal condition develops with interfacing circuit or components, they seldom give trouble. Normally, despite their complexity and the numerous and diversified functions they perform, they are

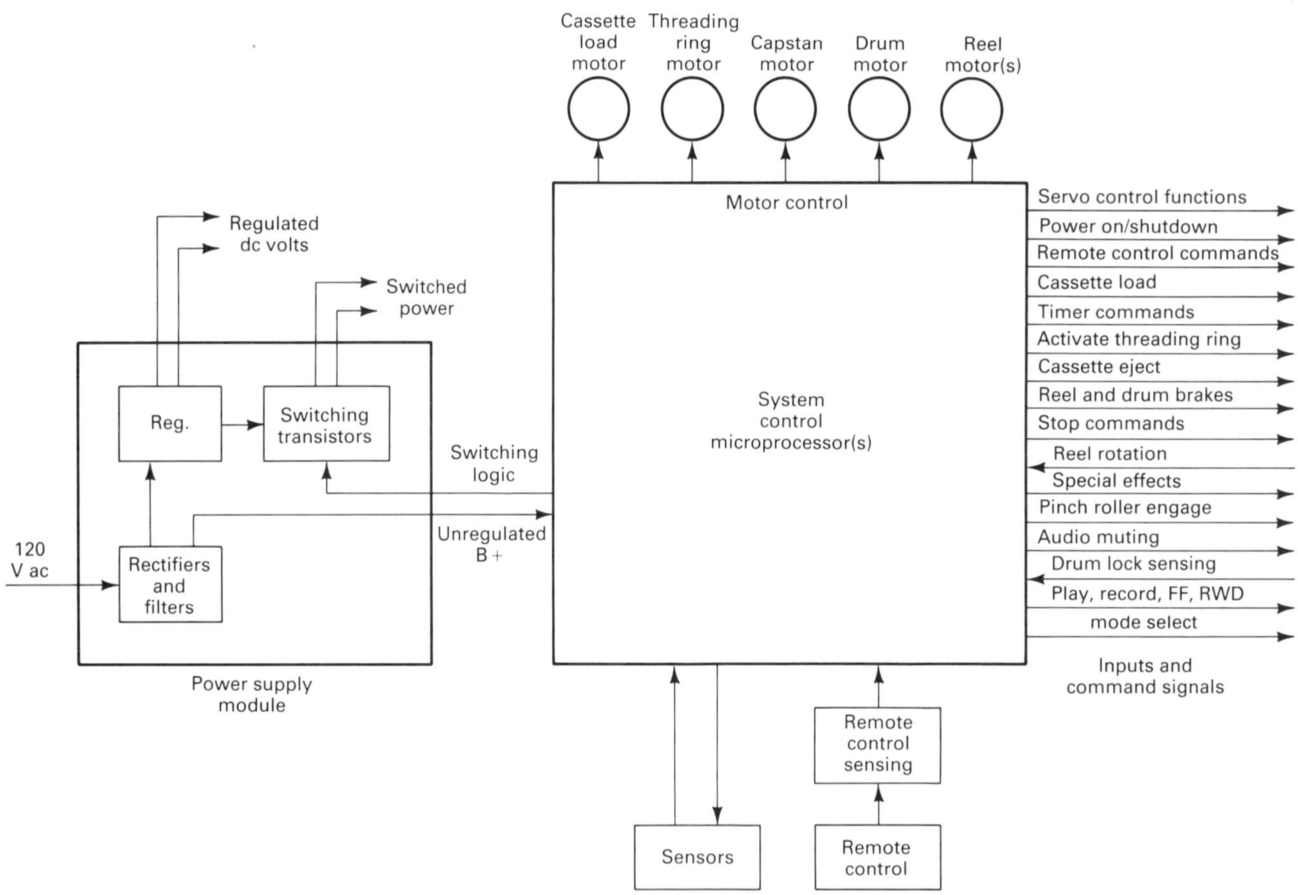


**FIG. 20-7** The micro: master control of all functions.

usually the last thing to suspect or replace. But as might be expected, when they do break down, the result may be strange and confusing symptoms that defy interpretation.

### Key Matrix Encoder

This encoder enables the system control microprocessor to monitor several of the front-panel switch buttons (keys) that share a common input. The micro continuously scans the closure status of all buttons. When a depressed button is sensed, a string of serial pulses is produced that corresponds with that button to feed a comparator (IC201 in Figure 20-8). Note the path taken by the key input/output pulses when one of the buttons is pressed. The comparator has a similar input coming from the infrared receiver when mode selection is made from a remote control unit. The comparator output feeds a micro (IC203) that evaluates the situation and takes whatever action it has been programmed for.

### Servo Control

By definition, servo control is the means of maintaining the proper speed and phase relationships between the capstan and drum rotations for both the record and playback modes (Figure 20-9). In the record mode (Figure 20-10), a sampling of vertical sync pulses (when reduced from 60 to 30 Hz) is used to record the control track on the tape. At the same time, this signal is used as a reference for comparison with the PG and FG pulses generated by the rotating drum and capstan, in order to maintain a drum speed of 1800 rpm and a constant rotation of the capstan, which determines the tape speed. During this time, each of the video heads is recording one field of picture information for each half-revolution of the drum, to coincide with the servo timing.

As shown in the drawing, there are four servo loops, two for drum control and two for capstan control. The FG loops provide coarse control of both motors. The PG loops are for fine (precise) control of motor speeds. Each loop includes a comparator circuit for comparing motor rotation with the 30-Hz reference pulses, which, in turn, correspond with the TV field and frame rates.

During playback (Figure 20-11) the tracking pulses picked up by the control track head are continuously monitored and compared in frequency and phase with the PG and FG pulses generated by the rotating drum and capstan. If either the rotation of the drum or capstan is in error (out of frequency or phase with the recorded tracking pulses), *error voltages* are developed by the comparators and their associated phase detector circuits to speed up or slow down the drum and capstan motors until drum rotation (scanning) and tape travel are in step with the recording.

There are different ways to generate the FG pulses: a toothed magnetic device, one rotating and one fixed; a Hall-effect device; or a small pickup coil external to the motor flywheel. The frequency of the pulses varies with tape speed (720 Hz for SP, 360 Hz for LP, and 240 Hz for SLP). Modern high-quality VCRs use the Hall generator. This device, besides developing all the pulses, is used in conjunction with reel sensors to keep track of the amount of tape used and the amount remaining on the reels. PG and FG pulses are used to maintain constant capstan speed (for both record and playback) by comparing with the divided-down 3.58 MHz- to 30-Hz signal. The amplified error voltages resulting from the comparison are used to drive their respective motors.

Besides their servo function, the 30-Hz PG pulses generated by the drum also control the electronic switches that continuously switch the spinning video heads and hi-fi stereo heads. Each pair of heads is alternately switched on and off twice for each revolution of the drum. This ensures that each segment of the tape is read by one head at precisely the right time where the other head leaves off. Actually, as explained earlier, there is some overlap, the equivalent of about six horizontal lines of each field. Signal exchange between the various servo control units is shown in Figure 20-12.

## 20-7 SENSOR FUNCTIONS

Most sensors operate by applying a small dc voltage to turn on a transistor. From the transistor output, a signal is sent to the micro, commanding it to take appropriate action, consistent with the circumstances.

There are four general categories of VCR sensors (Figure 20-13): resistive, photocoupler, mechanical/electrical, and Hall effect. The first, used as a dew sensor, changes in resistance with moisture. The photocoupler type is used in conjunction with a light source for sensing end-of-tape and reel rotation. The resistance of the device decreases when subjected to light. For monitoring reel rotation, light from an LED shines on a disk under the takeup reel. The disk has alternating dark and reflective surfaces to reflect or absorb the light, to produce pulses corresponding with the rotation.

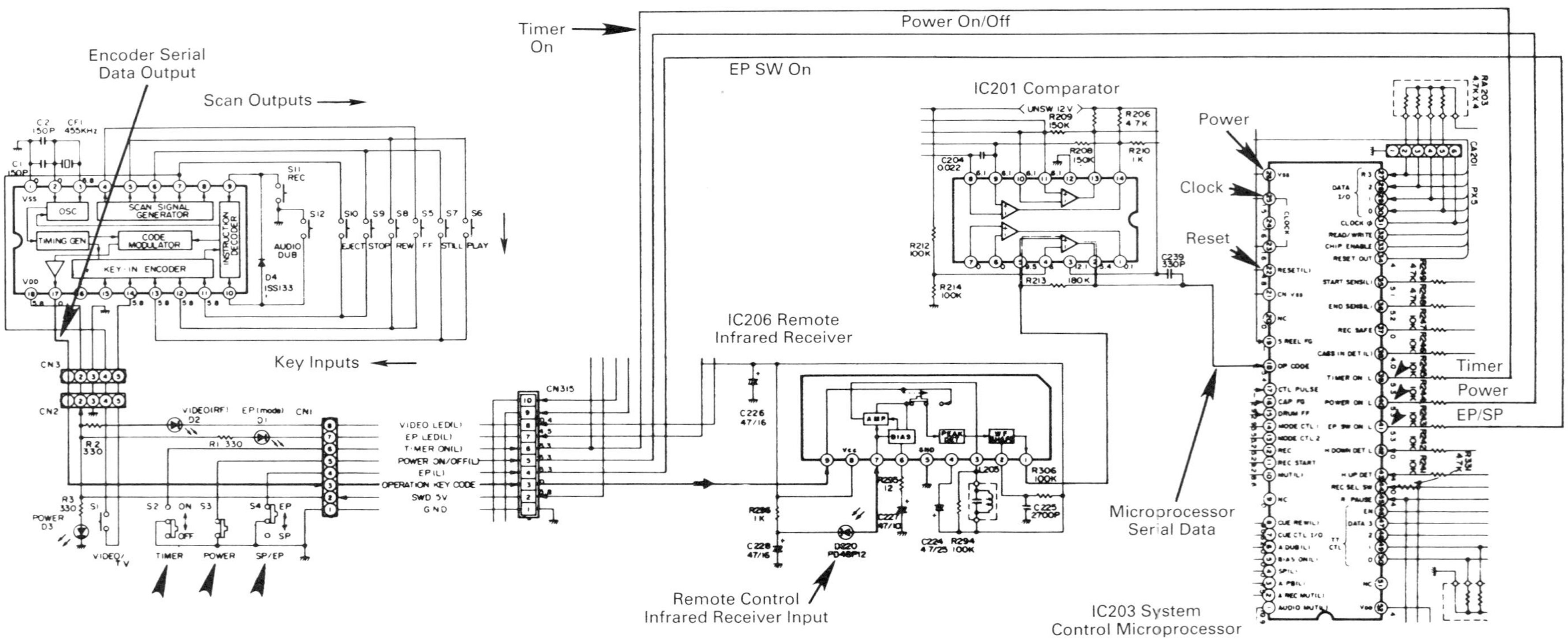


**FIG. 20-8** Mode select signal processing. (Courtesy of *Sencore News*.)

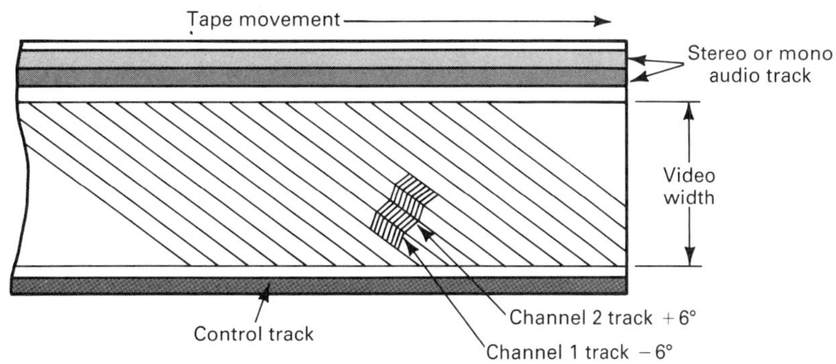


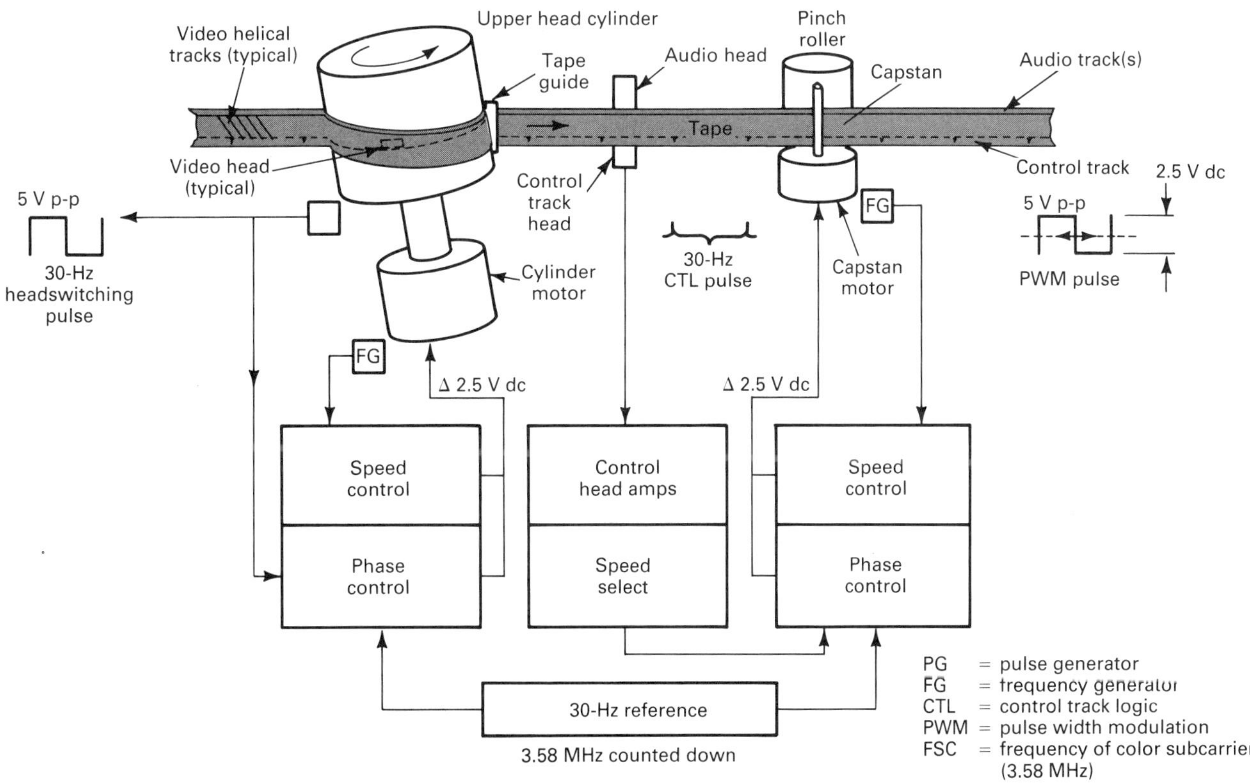


**FIG. 20-9** Basic servo systems. Using control track signals from the tape, the servo system synchronizes the video heads to play back the proper track. Tape movement must be perfectly synchronized with drum rotation and head switching. (Courtesy of *Sencore News*.)

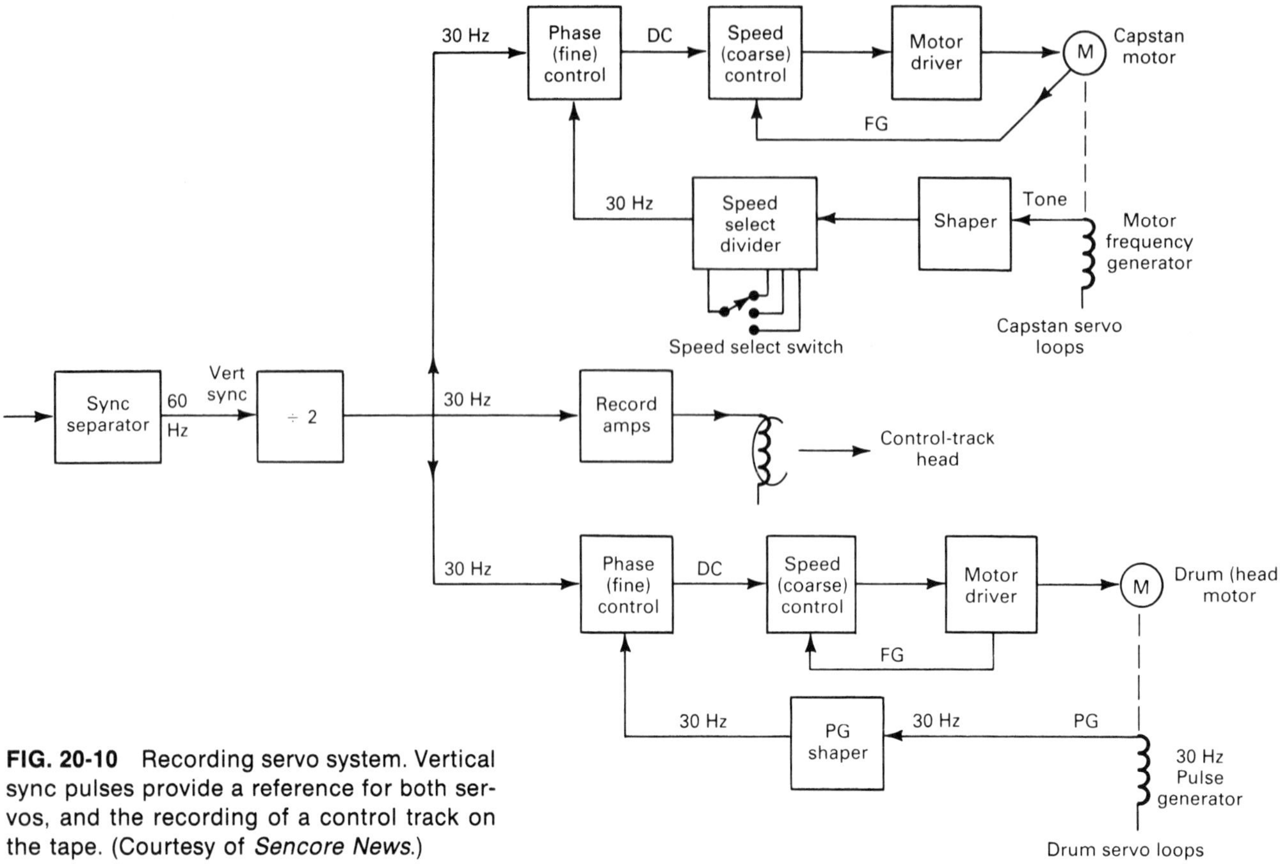


**FIG. 20-10** Recording servo system. Vertical sync pulses provide a reference for both servos, and the recording of a control track on the tape. (Courtesy of *Sencore News*.)

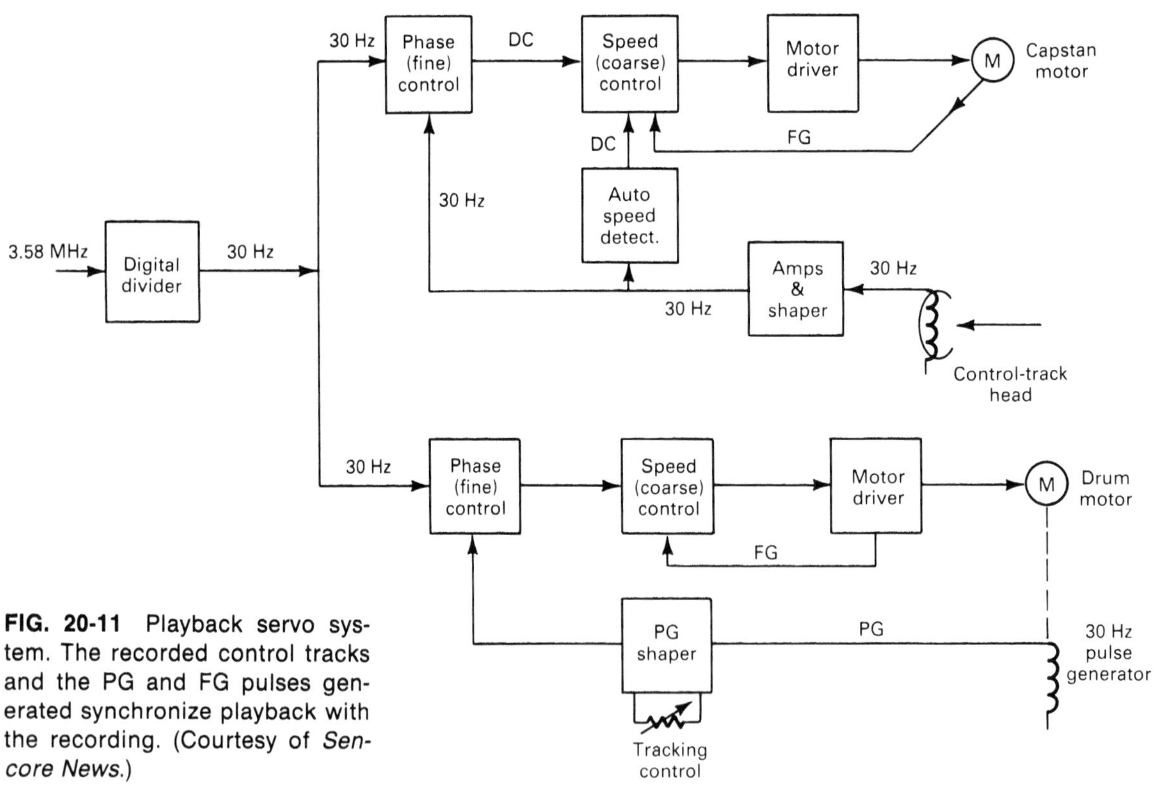


**FIG. 20-11** Playback servo system. The recorded control tracks and the PG and FG pulses generated synchronize playback with the recording. (Courtesy of *Sencore News*.)

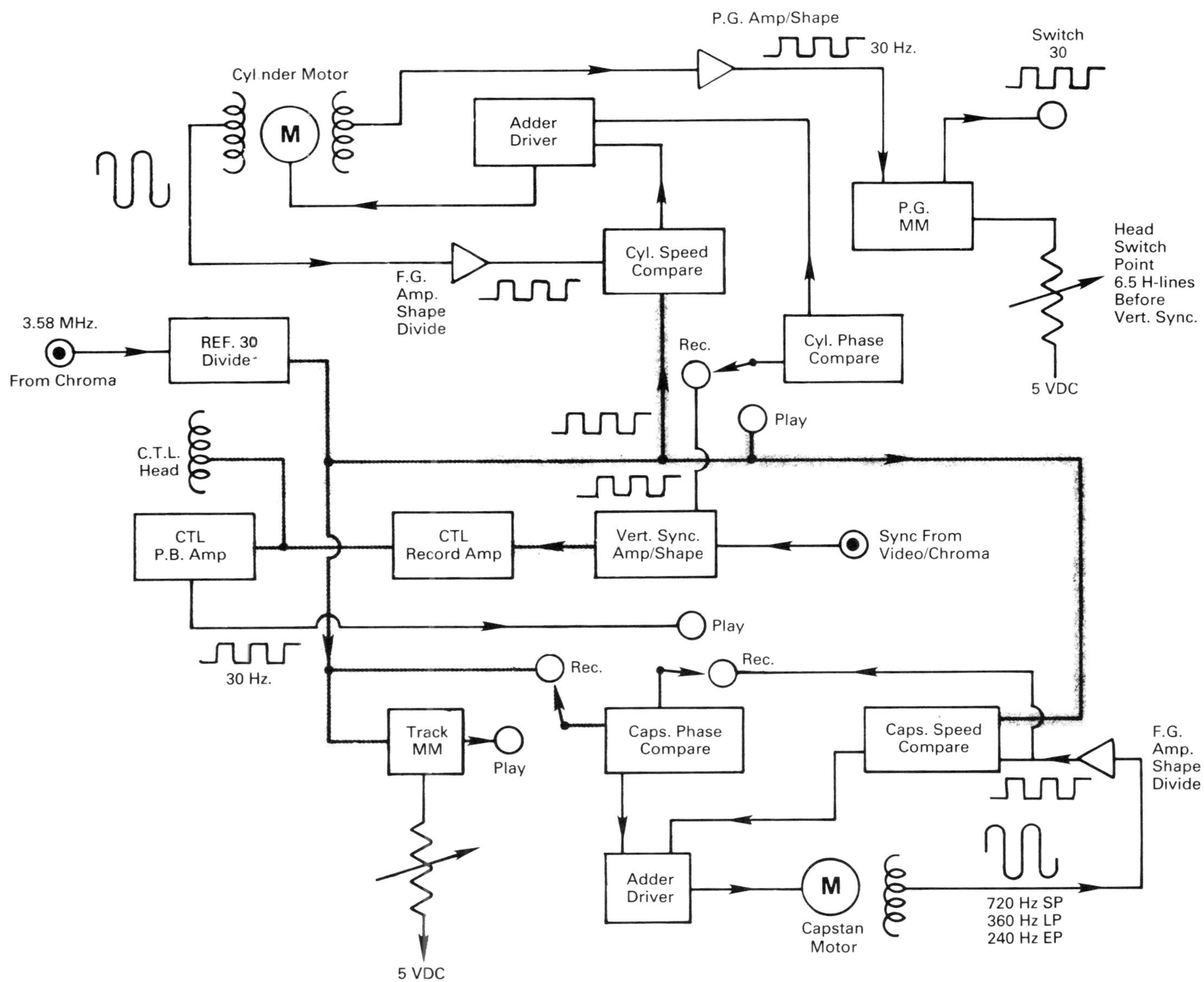


**FIG. 20-12** Servo control signal flow. VCR servo circuits need a stable 30-Hz signal source as a reference. During recording, vertical sync is divided to 30 Hz to feed the control amps and the cylinder phase control. During playback, 3.58 MHz from the color circuits is divided down to 30 Hz. (Courtesy of *Sencore News.*)

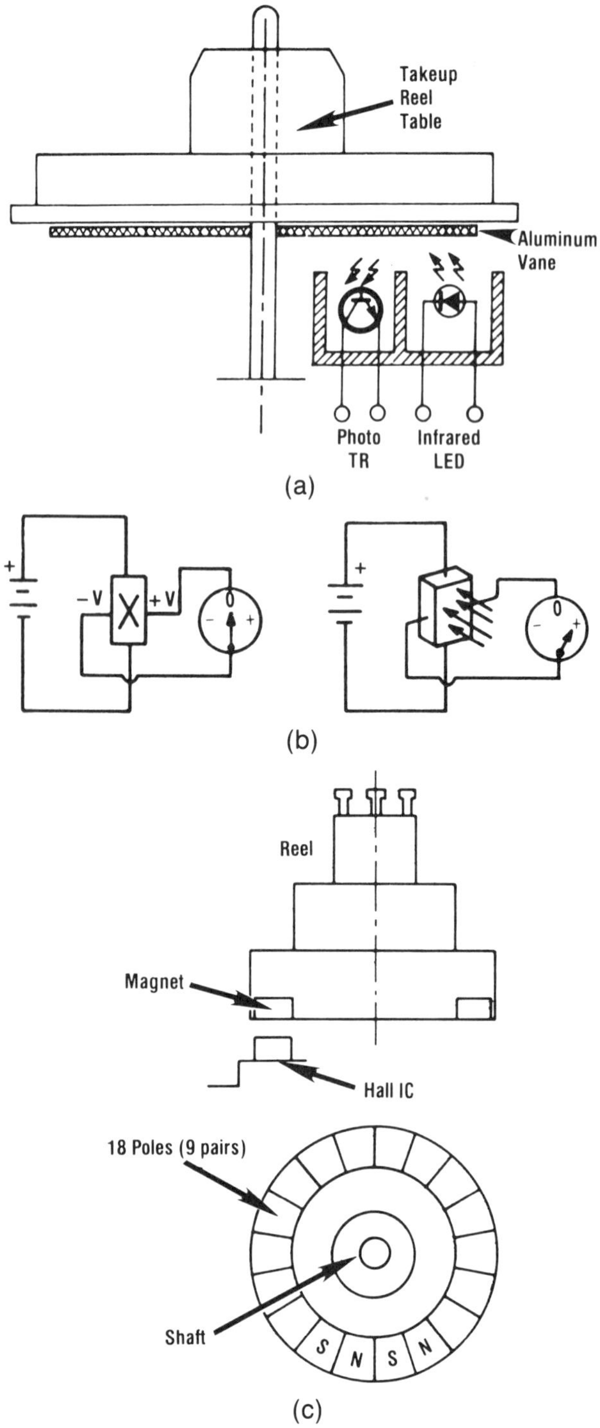


**FIG. 20-13** Basic sensor types: (a) in one type of reel sensor, the light beam from the LED to the phototransistor is alternately cut off as the reel rotates; (b) a Hall-effect sensor produces a voltage when in a magnetic field; (c) the alternate changing of the magnetic poles in this type of reel sensor causes the voltage from the Hall-effect IC to turn on and off as the reel turns. (Courtesy of *Sencore News*.)

A mechanical sensor is a basic micro switch. It is used to sense such things as mode selected (the panel switch keys), cassette UP/DOWN, and cassette IN.

A Hall-effect sensor (not to be confused with the Hall-effect generator used with many drum motors) is used mostly for takeup reel sensing and sometimes in servo circuits. The device consists of a sheet of semiconductor material to which a small dc voltage is applied (Figure 20-13b). A sensing voltage is developed across two attached plates when under the influence of a magnetic field. Used as a rotation sensor, the field is produced by a small magnet mounted on the reel.

### Stop Sensor

Besides the sensors that monitor every mode and issue signals to the system control micros, there are several status sensors whose function is to recognize unsafe conditions that could damage the VCR. An output from any of the following sensors results in a stop command.

### End-of-Tape Sensor

The end-of-tape sensor senses the end of tape on either reel and for either direction of rotation. There are two systems in common use. One system has a incandescent lamp adjacent to the cassette when in the play or record position. The light shines through a tunnel in the cassette housing. The light path is normally blocked (during record, play, and rewind) by the opaque tape. The *leader,* a short section of translucent tape at the start and finish of a reel, passes the light, which is picked up by a photosensor at the opposite side of the cassette to initiate a stop command.

Another system uses an infrared beam that is sensed by an IR sensing diode. To prevent tape stretching or breakage, a system start is inhibited using the same system if a reel is full and the user presses the wrong button. A stop is also initiated by the counter circuit when the count reaches 0000 or 9999 on the front-panel readout. If tape runs out before a recording is completed, the tape will rewind to 0000 (the start of that particular recording) and the VCR will shut down.

### Slack Tape Sensor

One system uses a spring-loaded adjustable arm resting against the tape. Excessive slack is signaled by the closure of a microswitch to command a stop.

## Dew Sensor

Moisture can cause the tape to stick to the drum and other items in the tape path. This can result in tape spill, tape damage, and sometimes damage to the VCR, the heads in particular. A dew sensor is a small, flat semiconductor that changes resistance (from about 100 kΩ to near zero) in accordance with localized moisture conditions. If a stop is initiated, the VCR should be permitted to dry out (with the power on) before a restart is attempted.

## 20-8 SIGNAL PROCESSING

In general, there are two kinds of signals: *received* signals and those generated within the equipment. Admittedly, this can be confusing when the term is used interchangeably. Here we are concerned with the latter, that is, the composite video signal (both luminance and chroma) and the sound signal. Some of the signals are processed as in conventional TV, but there are significant and extensive differences, particularly in the stages downstream from the video detector.

In the following paragraphs, signal processing is described separately for the luminance, chroma, and sound signals in both the record and playback modes.

### Record Mode Signal Processing

A typical VCR contains the same PLL type, cable-ready UHF, and VHF tuners found in modern TV sets (see Chapter 12). The video and sound stages up to and including the detectors are also essentially the same with one possible exception: the video IF strip has a wider bandpass than some of the early sets.

After processing by conventional tuners, IF, and detector, as in television, the demodulated video signal divides. The monochrome video (the luminance signal) is converted to *FM* with a center frequency about 3 MHz and a deviation of ±1 MHz. The chroma signal is *down-converted* from 3.58 MHz to 629 kHz (688 kHz for Beta). The two signals are then recombined in a mixer stage and fed (via a rotary transformer) *as an FM signal* to the two heads (Figure 20-14). A more detailed description of what takes place follows.

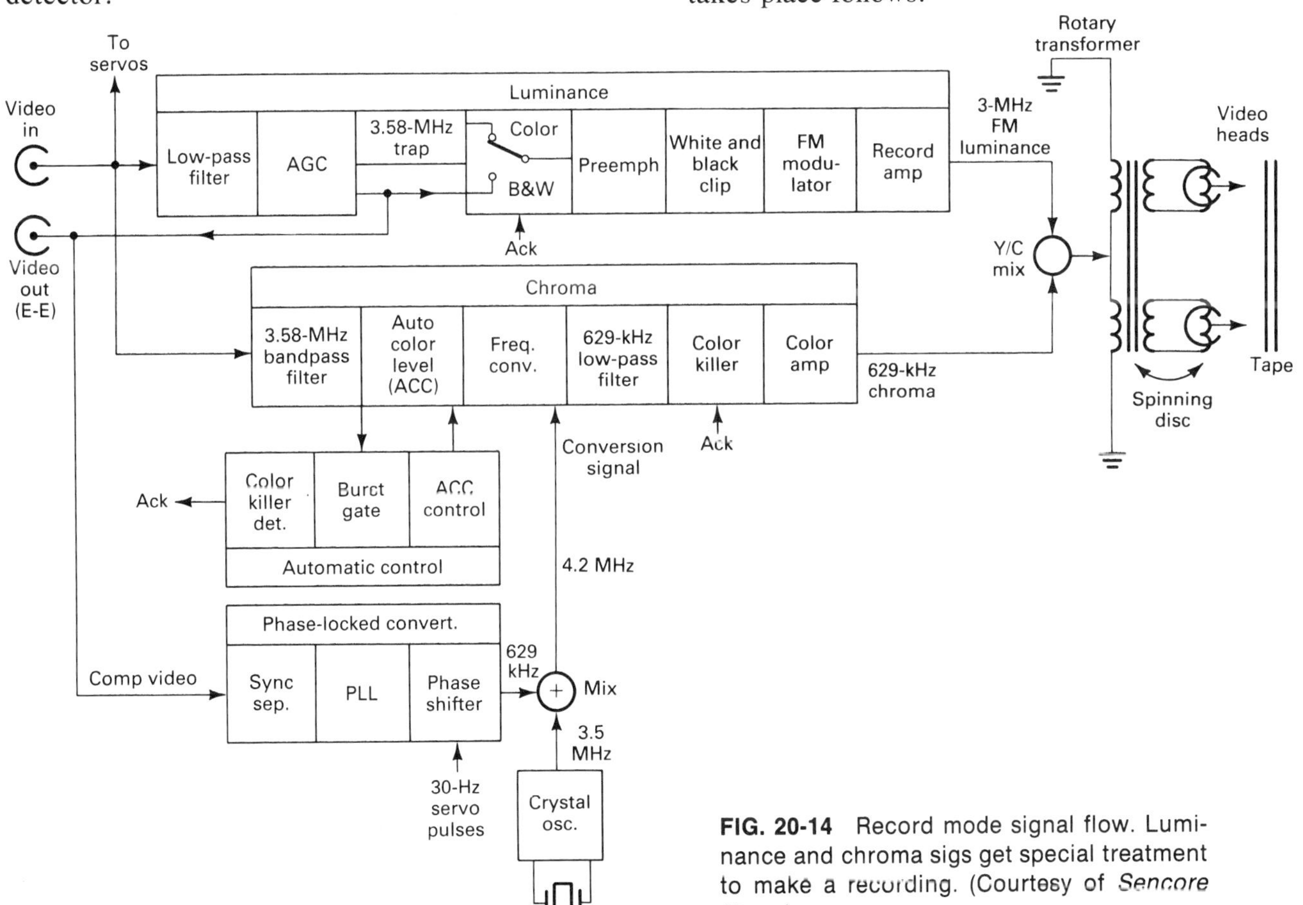


**FIG. 20-14** Record mode signal flow. Luminance and chroma sigs get special treatment to make a recording. (Courtesy of *Sencore News*.)

*Luminance Signal Processing* (Record). In Figure 20-14 note that the demodulated composite video signal first goes to a low-pass filter, which attenuates the 3.58-MHz chroma signal. Leaving the filter, the color signal is further attenuated by a 3.58-MHz trap, and the desired luminance signal is controlled by AGC action. From here the clamped signal goes through a preemphasis network, which improves the signal-to-noise ratio of the highest video frequencies. The white-and-black clip stage that follows is needed to limit the overshoot for white and dark areas of a picture, which would otherwise become blurred. Adjustments are provided to regulate the amount of overshoot. The FM modulator stage which comes next converts the amplitude-modulated video signal to FM with a deviation corresponding to the amplitude of the signal. The term *modulator* can be misleading since it is actually a VCO (voltage-controlled oscillator) operating at 3.4 MHz (3.5 MHz for Beta). The oscillator frequency is controlled by the dc level of the incoming video signal.

From the modulator, the signal goes through several stages of amplification to obtain the power needed to magnetically saturate the tape. Luminance and chroma recording levels are adjustable and either too little or too much record current is undesirable. In the Y/C mixer, the processed luminance and chroma signals are combined, then fed (via rotary transformers) to the two heads. Unlike converter-type mixers, where heterodyning occurs, the Y/C mixer is simply a resistive network.

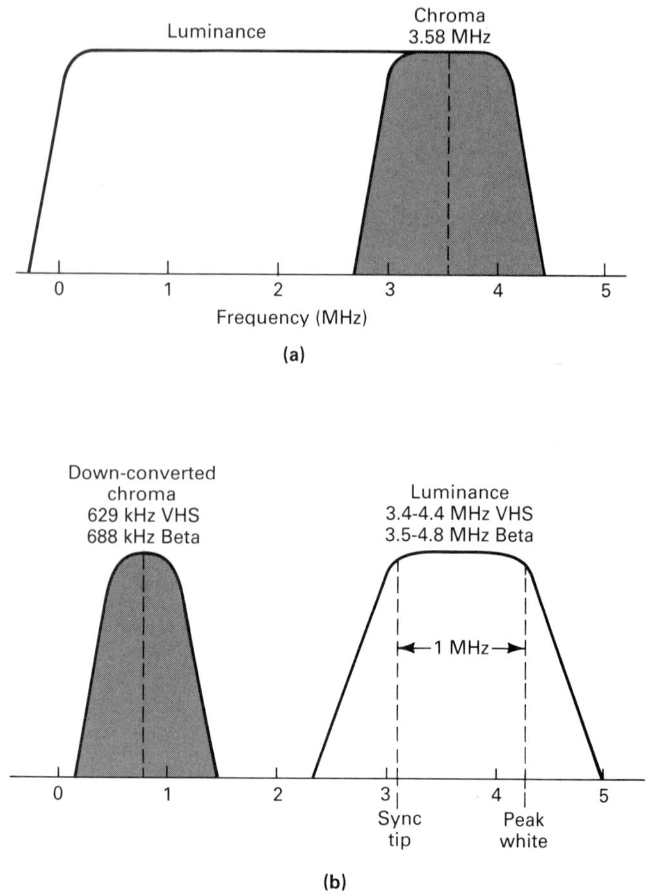


**FIG. 20-15** VCR frequency allocations: (a) chroma and luminance signals overlap in the NTSC format; (b) for videotape, the chroma information is "down-converted" and recorded separate from luminance. (Courtesy of *Sencore News*.)

*Chroma Signal Processing* (Record). In reference to the IF response curve (Figure 13-2 and 20-15a), which is about 4.2 MHz wide, the color carrier is located at 3.58 MHz, within the luminance bandpass. Since videotape frequency response does not permit recording the NTSC signal as is, the luminance signal is FM modulated on a 3.9-MHz carrier. With the proper deviation, the video sync tips are at 3.4 MHz and peak white is at 4.4 MHz (Figure 20-15b). Since luminance and chroma cannot be recorded at the same frequency, chroma information is down-converted to a lower frequency, 629 kHz for VHS and 688 kHz for Beta (Figure 20-15). To understand how this is done, consider how chroma information is recorded onto the tape. As a first step, the chroma is separated from the luminance with a bandpass filter (Figure 20-14). The chroma then goes through a "leveling" process in the ACC block shown in the diagram. The next step is frequency conversion, where the 3.58-MHz signal and the 629-kHz signals are combined to produce a 4.2-MHz signal which feeds the main frequency converter. After conversion, the signal goes to a 600-kHz low-pass filter which permits only the down-converted 629-kHz signal to get through.

The next block represents a color killer (sometimes shortened to ACK, "automatic color killer"), which functions much the same as described for TV. The chroma signal is then amplified by color amplifiers to feed the Y/C mixer, where the FM luminance and the 629-MHz down-converted chroma signals are combined and sent to the video heads. In the diagram note the 3.58-MHz crystal oscillator, whose signal combines with the phase-locked 629-kHz signal in a submixer to develop the 4.2-MHz signal. The 3.58-MHz oscillator may be a conventional crystal-controlled oscillator or a voltage-controlled oscillator (VCO). The 629-kHz signal is produced by a PLL (phase-locked loop) oscillator as shown. The frequency of the 629-kHz signal is precisely controlled with a dc error voltage.

### Playback Mode Signal Processing

In the playback mode (Figure 20-16), the audio erase and "all-erase" heads are disabled and the video signals as picked up by the revolving heads and after being alternately switched field by field are split into two paths. The monochrome signal, which was recorded as FM, is converted back to AM. The chroma signal, which was down-converted to 629 kHz, is restored to 3.58 MHz. The video and chroma are recombined in a mixer stage. The audio and composite video signals are then fed to an *RF modulator* (a miniature transmitter), which develops two new carriers (for VHF channel 3 or 4). The combined signal is fed to the antenna input of a TV receiver or monitor tuned to the corresponding unused channel, an option of the user. A more detailed description follows.

*Luminance Signal Processing* (Playback). The weak signals (less than 1 mV) (luminance and chroma combined) being recovered from the tape by the two heads are boosted to a usable level by two high-gain preamps as shown in Figure 20-16. The preamps are essentially high-$Q$ resonant circuits whose overall frequency response and adjustment are extremely critical. From the preamps they go to the head switcher, which switches alternately from one head to the other in sync with the drum rotation and tape travel. The switcher is activated by 30-Hz pulses generated by the servo system. Usually, the switcher and preamps are combined.

Leaving the switcher, the luminance (Y), and chroma signals divide, each going its separate way. The 3-MHz luminance signal first goes through a high-pass filter, which readily passes all the Y signal while attenuating the color signal. From here the luminance signal goes to the "DOC" stage, which will be described shortly.

The next functional block is an FM detector, whose job is to demodulate the FM signal which was frequency modulated in the recording process. In general, the demodulator does two things: increases the carrier frequency and acts as a pulse density detector. The greater the density of the FM signal, the greater the demodulator output.

From here the signal goes to a deemphasis network, which restores the signal to normal by attenuating the highest frequencies that were overemphasized in the record process. After receiving additional amplification, the recovered luminance signal is combined with the color signal and routed to the RF modulator. Here the combined signals amplitude modulate a 3- or 4-MHz carrier. The combined signal then leaves the VCR to feed the TV/monitor tuner, which is tuned to the same frequency. In the drawing, note the composite video takeoff ahead of the RF modulator. An enhanced picture can be obtained by avoiding the losses inherent with RF circuits and feeding the signal directly to the video input of a monitor.

*Chroma Signal Flow* (Playback). The 629-kHz chroma signal coming from the heads is separated from the luminance signal by a low-pass filter, then fed to an ACC color leveling stage as shown in Figure 20-16. A frequency converter or mixer then reconverts it back into a 3.58-MHz color signal. The next stage, a bandpass filter, permits only the chroma information to get through. Additional filtering is provided by a comb filter. After switching by the color killer, and amplified, the signal combines with the luminance signal in a Y/C mixer, from where it is routed to the RF modulator, then on to the TV or monitor.

Unavoidable frequency variations in the 629-kHz signal coming from the tape can cause *pix jitter*. A mixture of the 629-kHz and 3.58-MHz signals produces a 4.2-MHz signal. A jitter-corrected 629-kHz signal is created with the aid of horizontal sync pulses, by cancellation. The phase correction circuits shown in the diagram eliminate phase errors, which would otherwise result in tint problems, or in some cases, a total loss of color. Combining the jitter-corrected 629-kHz signal and the phase-corrected 3.58-MHz signal in a "conversion signal mixer" results in a stable 4.2-MHz signal, to faithfully recreate a color picture.

To summarize, four signals are required for chroma recording and playback. These are the chroma signal itself, a horizontal sync signal, the 30-Hz switching pulse, and a locally generated 3.58-MHz oscillator signal.

*Crosstalk Prevention.* With the video tracks recorded next to each other in close proximity on the tape, there may be an interchange (crosstalk) between adjacent tracks which shows up as an interference pattern of finely spaced lines, particularly on a color picture. This is prevented in two ways; with a critical azimuth adjustment of the heads to record the tape tracks in opposite directions and by alternately shifting the phase of the 629-kHz signal for each horizontal scanning line that makes up the

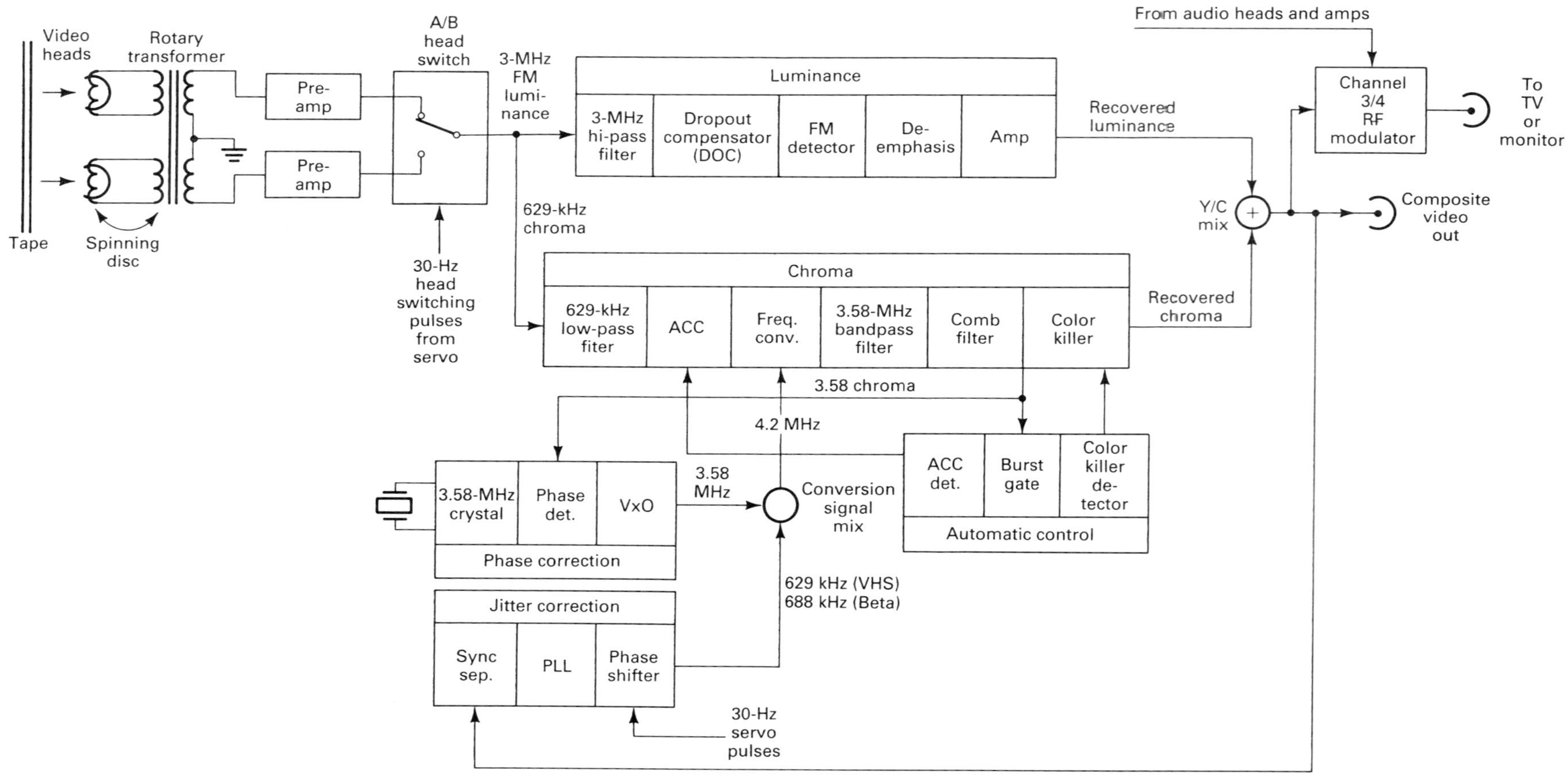


**FIG. 20-16** Playback mode signal flow. Head switching is a critical function in the play mode. (Courtesy of *Sencore News*.)

picture. With VHS the shift is 90°; with Beta it is 180°. In the playback mode, crosstalk is eliminated (by cancellation) by removing the phase shift. Phase shifting makes use of two signals, the 30-Hz head switching pulse and horizontal sync pulses. In this way, during head switching, the sync pulses maintain the proper phase shift for each horizontal line being scanned.

*Dropout Compensation (DOC).* The purpose of this circuit is to eliminate loss of video information if the video head signal is interrupted during playback. Basically it consists of a delay line that delays the signal by one horizontal line. In the event of a dropout, a detector senses the momentary loss of the FM luminance carrier and operates an electronic switch. This switch "toggles" and picks up the signal intended for the preceding line at the delay line output and reinserts it in the "gap." Thus a small bit of the picture is reproduced twice. The duration is usually so short as to be unoticeable to the viewer. Although the effect on the picture may be similar, do not confuse this action with the tracking control which is part of the servo control system.

*Burst Identification (BID).* Sync loss due to a phase shift in the 4.2-MHz converter circuit (Figure 20-16) causes color variations between record and playback and problems with color flicker. Minor phase errors are normally taken care of by the playback AFPC circuits, but additional control is needed to prevent such problems. This is done by comparing the phase of the playback chroma burst to that of the 3.58-MHz crystal oscillator and making the necessary correction if there is a discrepancy.

### Super-VHS

Compared to conventional VHS, S-VHS has the *capability* of playing back almost double the amount of fine picture detail. In addition, there is a great reduction in background noise, herringbone beats, and color crawl. This is accomplished, in part, by increasing the video bandwidth, which in turn increases the number of horizontal lines that make up the pix. Figure 20-17a shows the comparison, 240 lines of resolution for conventional TV, and a capability of 400 lines for S-VHS. The word *capability* is significant, because there are other considerations.

For one thing, the signal being recorded must possess the same high degree of detail. For example, the video response for conventional TV is limited to 4.2 MHz, for a maximum resolution of 330 lines. Second, the TV or monitor used with the VCR must be capable of reproducing a high-resolution picture. Older sets with a 3-MHz bandwidth limit the resolution to 240 lines. Modern sets using comb filters can produce up to 330 lines. The latest models with S-VHS inputs can produce the full 400 lines coming from a VCR with the S-VHS format.

Figure 20-17b shows a comparison of regular and S-VHS signal handling capabilities. Note that the lower-frequency limit of the S-VHS video FM signal has been increased from 3.4 MHz to 5.4 MHz, and the upper limit increased from 4.4 MHz to 7 MHz. The change in the FM video frequencies increases the video bandwidth that can be recorded to 5 MHz.

Besides the frequency increase of the FM signal, the maximum deviation has been increased from 1 MHz for conventional VHS to 1.6 MHz for S-VHS (Figure 20-17b). This alone results in a significant increase in signal-to-noise ratio to reduce background noise.

The video heads are another consideration. To record and play back the higher FM signals, the heads are modified by reducing the gap by $\frac{2}{3}$. Also, special high-density tape must be used for S-VHS. The cassette has a small hole on the bottom side which is used in conjunction with an "identification switch" under the VCR. When such a cassette is inserted, the VCR is prepped for S-VHS; where a conventional cassette is used, the VCR will record and play only in the normal VHS format.

With conventional VHS, the luminance and chroma signals are separated and processed individually. Incomplete separation causes such effects as color crawl and beats in the picture. With S-VHS, the two signals are handled separately, which effectively eliminates these problems.

Because of the difference in the FM frequencies used for VHS and S-VHS, the two formats are not compatible. However, a VCR designed for S-VHS can be used in either format, as selected by the user. A conventional VCR on the other hand will play tapes recorded on an S-VHS machine when regular VHS is selected, but not when recording is made in the S-VHS format.

### Audio Processing

The recording and playback of monaural sound is somewhat different for hi-fi/stereo compared to early-model VCRs without stereo. For example, nonstereo machines have one linear head for record and playback. For compatibility with nonstereo machines, a hi-fi stereo VCR has two stationary linear

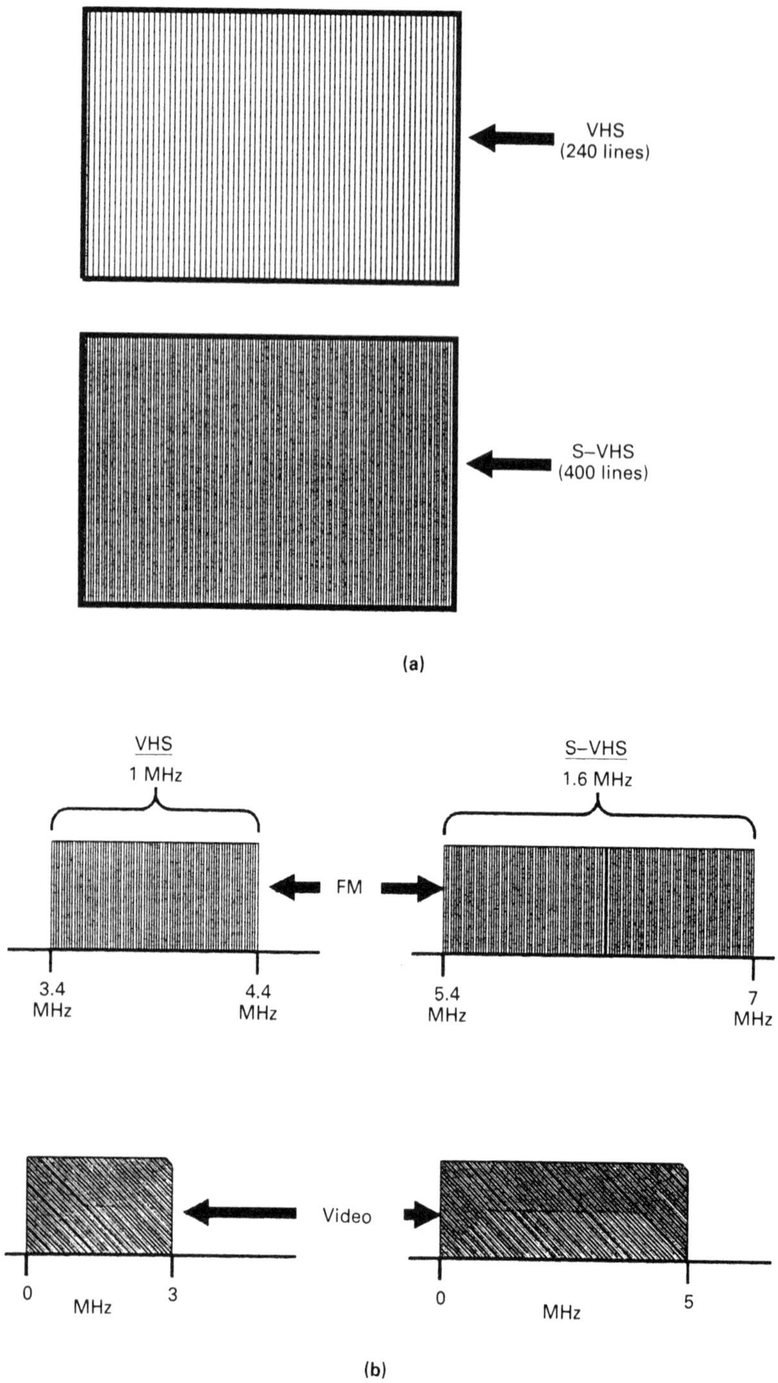


**FIG. 20-17** VHS and S-VHS comparisons. (Courtesy of Mitsubishi.)

heads. A hi-fi program recorded on a nonstereo VCR will of course be reproduced only in mono. A mono broadcast will be handled by both hi-fi channels but without the stereo effect from the speakers.

*Monaural Audio Processing.* For recording monaural sound (on machines not equipped for stereo), the audio signal (after separation from the video) is amplified and fed directly to the stationary (sometimes called linear) audio head downstream in the tape path. For playback, the signals recovered from the tape feed the channel $\frac{3}{4}$ RF modulator for routing to the TV or monitor. Sound quality is somewhat limited by the relatively slow tape speed.

*Hi-Fi/MTS/AFM Stereo Processing.* With a capability for low harmonic distortion and a greatly increased frequency response and dynamic range, MTS stereo far surpasses that of monaural sound. As an added bonus, wow, flutter, and hiss have all but been eliminated. This is due largely to the use of DBX and Dolby noise reduction and a rapid tape scanning rate. It should be remembered, however, that high-fidelity stereo sound is possible only with a good-quality amplifier/speaker system, with widely separated speakers.

With modern VCRs, superior sound quality is obtained by using rotating heads, which simulates a high tape speed. These signals have their own rotary transformer and head switcher. Hi-fi stereo VCRs use the same MTS circuitry for decoding and separating the SAP and L and R channel signals as described in Chapter 18 for stereo TV (Figure 18-14). The separated signals, now called left and right channel audio, are processed further and (like the video) recorded as FM signals by the spinning hi-fi audio heads. The method used is known as AFM (audio frequency modulation).

***AFM/stereo recording:*** In the record mode the signals are processed by identical L and R channel circuitry and fed via the rotary transformers to the rotating audio heads. As shown in Figure 20-18, left and right audio signals (from the MTS circuitry) are fed to two FM modulators, where the AM signals are converted to FM. These signals feed two balanced mixers, along with a 150-kHz CW signal from a crystal-controlled oscillator to produce two FM carriers; a 1.3-MHz carrier corresponding to the left channel audio, and a 1.7-MHz carrier corresponding to the right channel audio. After preemphasis to further enhance the highest treble frequencies and additional amplification, the two signals are routed separately to the two rotary heads. Note the level controls used to adjust the relative amplitudes of the two signals. The BPF (bandpass filter) blocks eliminate undesired frequencies created in the mixing process.

Note the paths taken by the two AFM signals in driving the two heads. Although only one head is in contact with the tape at any given instant, each head is supplied with both signals, to leave their separate imprints on the tape.

***AFM/stereo playback:*** In the playback mode (Figure 20-19) the L and R channel AFM signals picked up by the heads from either the edge tracks or diagonal tracks on the tape are amplified and fed to the audio head switcher, which functions the same as the video switcher (i.e., to turn the heads

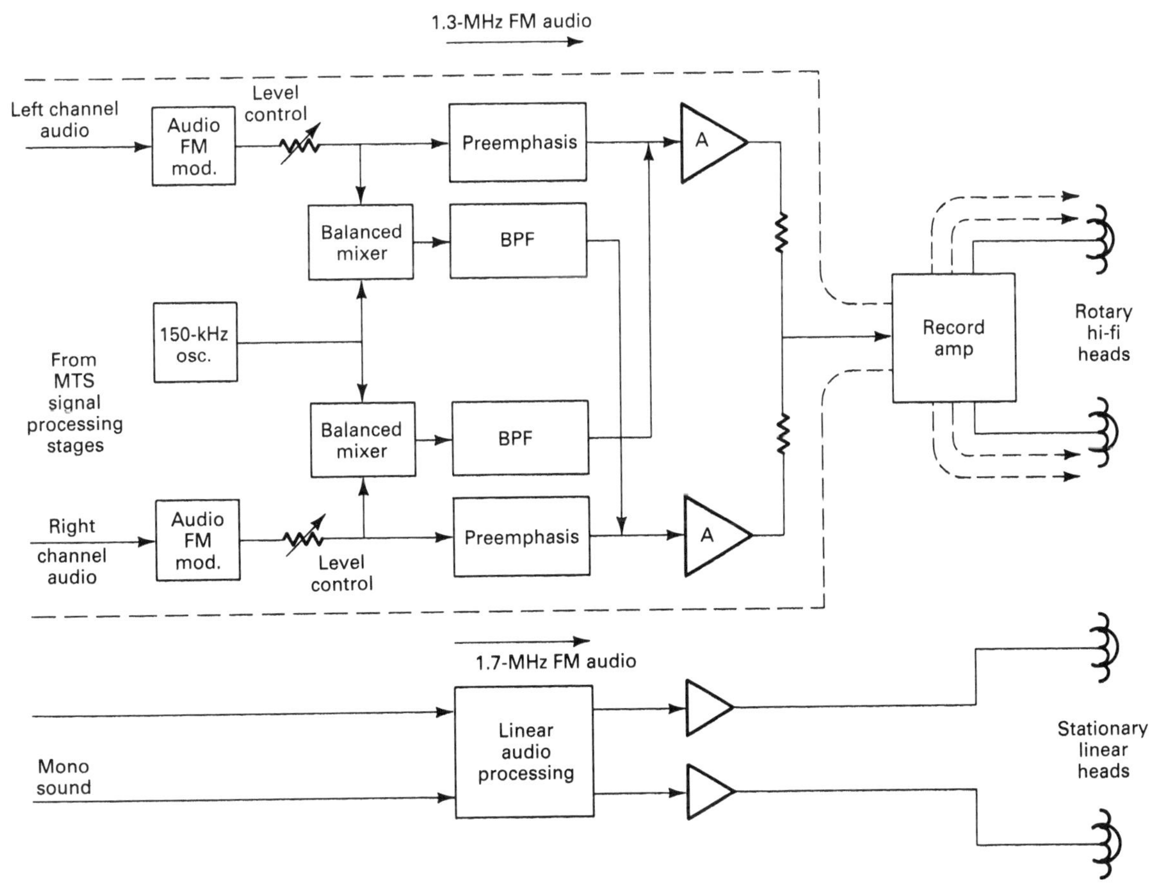


**FIG. 20-18** Hi-fi/AFM recording.

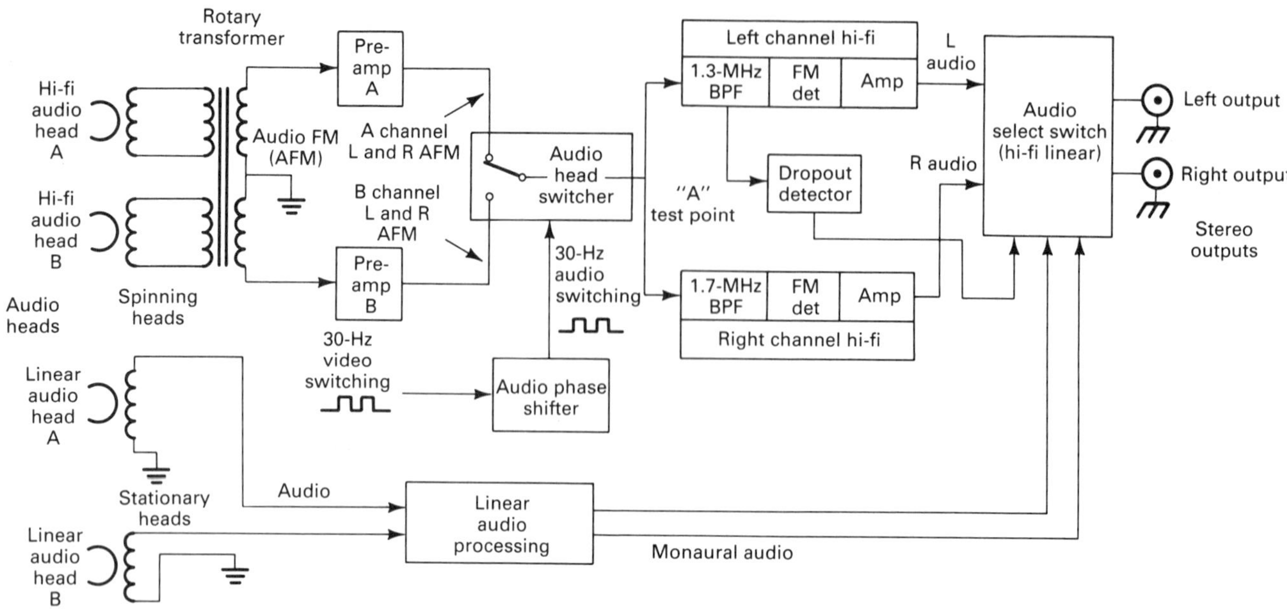


**FIG. 20-19** Audio playback signal flow. Sound is greatly enhanced by the use of rotary heads. (Courtesy of *Sencore News*.)

on and off at the proper times relative to drum rotation, tape movement, and the picture observed on the screen). Leaving the switcher, the left and right signals go through two bandpass filters, to ensure that each channel receives only its designated 1.3-MHz or 1.7-MHz signal, corresponding with left and right audio. The two FM detectors demodulate the FM signals, converting them back to AM. Note the dropout detector. Its function is to monitor one channel. If excessive dropout is detected on the signal, the AFM signals are momentarily rerouted and played back by the linear heads. From here on the signals are amplified and combined with the mono signal and the luminance/chroma signals in the RF modulator, and routed via coax to the TV or monitor.

## 20-9 SERVICE ADJUSTMENTS

A VCR has numerous adjusters to compensate for the slight tolerance variations that normally occur with any precision instrument during fabrication, and to adjust the timing of certain functions. It must be emphasized that none of the adjusters should be tampered with indiscriminately and without proper instruments and know-how. Some of the main adjusters (sometimes known by different names) are listed and described briefly as follows:

*Tape Tensioner.* Proper back tension must be maintained at all times to ensure constant and uniform tape travel and to prevent spills. Tension is monitored by a photosensitive sensor on an adjustable arm near the supply reel. Tension is adjustable by altering the drive of the supply reel motor with a potentiometer.

*Head Azimuth.* Record/playback heads must be mounted and adjusted with a slight tilt to minimize luminance/chroma crosstalk.

*Video Head Position and Height Adjust.* This is a mechanical adjustment for rotary heads.

*Linear Head Alignment.* As with conventional audio recorders, for good quality and optimum sound level, the mono audio head(s) must be precisely positioned and oriented relative to the tape.

*Video Head Switching.* A head switcher adjustment is provided to alter the relative timing between the head square wave and switching action, relative to vertical sync, and so that each track overlaps adjacent tracks by a precise amount. This ensures proper interlaced scanning of the pix. Any inaccuracy results in no picture or a weak, noisy picture.

*Hi-Fi Audio Head Switching.* This adjustment compensates for the offset between the video and audio heads on the drum. As with the video switcher, it alters the timing between audio record and playback relative to the timing pulses.

*Tracking Control Adjustment.* This control adjusts the delay between the 30-Hz switching pulse and a servo-generated pulse to ensure the user that tracking control is operating near the center of its range. As an alternative adjunct, some VCRs provide for automatic tracking.

*Torque.* The torque of the reel tables (in conjunction with the tape tensioner) must be precisely controlled to prevent slack tape, tape spills, and insufficient contact with the heads. Too much tension causes excessive head wear, drum scoring, and stretched tapes. Adjustments are made on the reel brakes using torque and tension measuring instruments.

*Tape Guides.* The angle of the guides where the tape enters and exits the drum is critical. Any slight misalignment upsets the normal tape path around the drum, resulting in improper scanning and reading/writing by the heads.

*Capstan and Drum Servos.* Adjustments are provided to establish the "coarse" free-run speed of these motors, after which servo control is maintained automatically.

*AFM Head Alignment.* When provided, this adjustment operates in conjunction with the regular hi-fi head switcher for more precise control of the signals being played back by the left and right heads.

*Dropout Compensator.* This DOC adjuster in the luminance stages is adjusted to minimize the picture dropouts.

*RF Modulator Adjuster.* This control adjusts the signal level at the input to the modulator.

*Tracking Fix Adjuster.* This is a servo adjustment, used to adjust the 440-$\mu$s delay between two square waves.

*Tuned Circuits Alignment.* This includes circuits such as those found in TV, including traps in the IF strip, the 5 to 10 traps in the luminance/chroma stages, horizontal and color AFPC circuits, the comb filter, 3.58-MHz oscillators, and so on.

*Record Current Adjusters.* The proper amounts of recording currents are established to obtain optimum signal-to-noise ratio and a "clean" picture. Typical signal levels are 25 to 30 mV p-p for chroma and about 100 mV p-p for luminance.

*Timing Adjustments.* This includes the following: head switching position, RF switching phase adjust, and record mode servo lock phasing. All these adjusters are used for the same purpose: to adjust the timing between a square wave and the vertical sync pulse.

## 20-10 USING YOUR VCR

A VCR has many uses. For example, video tapes are a source of education and entertainment for those living in remote areas or in areas of poor TV reception where there is no CATV and TV reception is either poor or nonexistent. Rental tapes are a source of late-release movies and an endless variety of educational material that would otherwise not be available to the average person. A VCR provides the means for recording a program for viewing later at a more convenient time and enables the user to record one program while viewing another when both are telecast at the same time.

As with books and other items, there are many who like to develop and maintain a library of favorite recorded programs. Where two VCRs are available, it is easy to make copies of tapes to exchange with your friends. Home movies, particularly those priceless shots of young children growing up, can best be preserved for posterity by transcribing from movie film onto magnetic tape for the greater convenience of viewing with a VCR setup. This can be arranged from your local camera shop for a nominal charge. But a few words of caution. For best results, record at the highest tape speed (SP), even at the expense of less footage on a cassette. Also, where multiple copies are required, make each directly from the film to avoid the degradation that results from making copies from copies.

### VCR Hookups

Many persons are confused and overwhelmed by the complex and often frightening array of cables, switches, signal splitters, and impedance-matching transformers required for interconnecting a VCR with CATV, satellite, or antenna system, camcorder, and one or more TV sets or monitors. Two common hookups are shown in Figure 20-20. In both examples it is assumed that both the VCR and TV tuners are "cable ready" (with vintage tuners, you can receive only the regular VHF and UHF channels). There are numerous other configurations, some quite elaborate, depending on the equipment and how it is to be used. These are beyond the scope

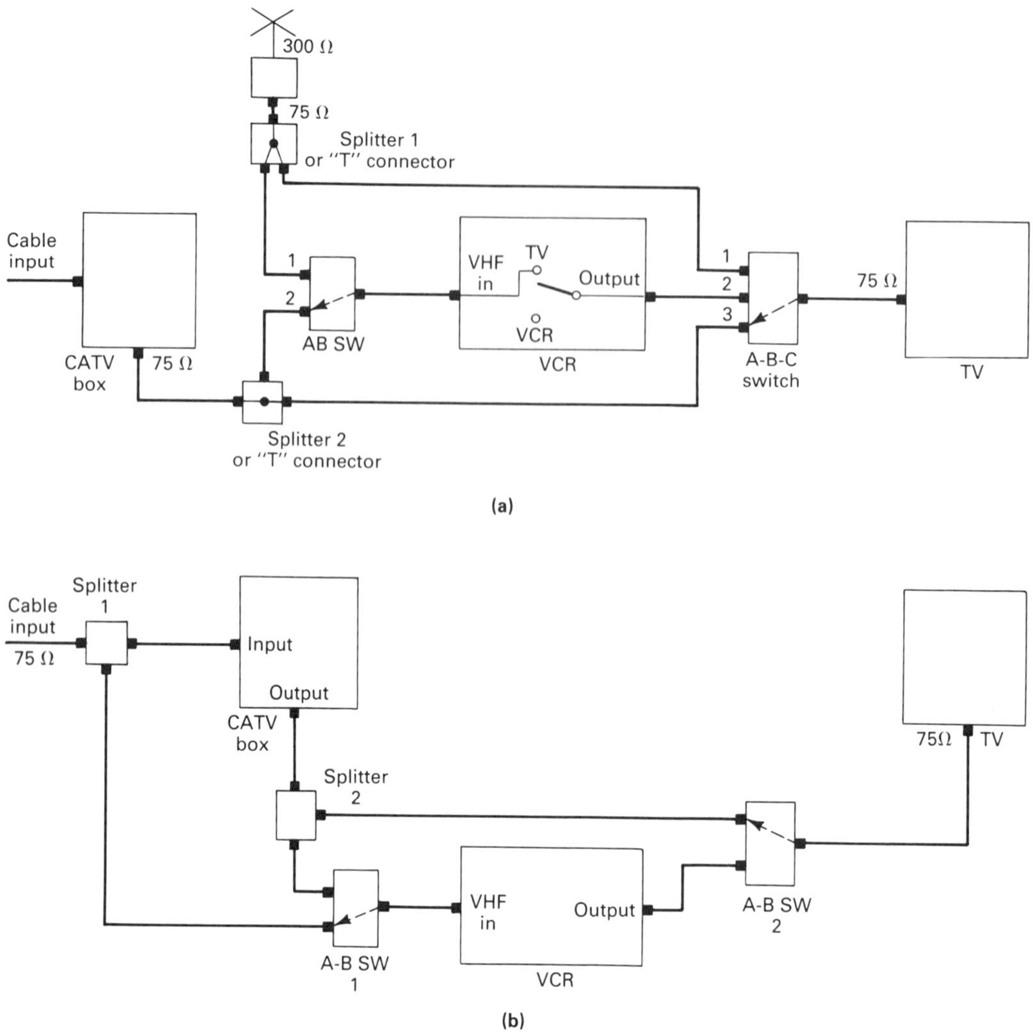


**FIG. 20-20** VCR/CATV/TV hookups. In these examples signal flow is from left to right. The switch positions as shown are arbitrary.

of this book. For such hookups an excellent book is available: *Electronic Connections* by Martin Clifford (Prentice-Hall, 1987).

Coaxial cable is used for the most part to prevent interference pickup and to match the low (75-Ω) inputs and outputs of the different items. The cables terminate with standard F-type connectors. Where the TV has a 300-Ω tuner input and/or 300-Ω flat ribbon line is used with the antenna system, one or more 75/300-Ω impedance-matching transformers must be used to prevent signal attenuation and ghosting problems. A matching transformer can be used either way, to match 75 Ω to a 300-Ω circuit, or vice versa.

Signal splitters need no explanation. They provide a means of dividing the signal between two or more pieces of equipment. Without such connectors it would be necessary to cut cables and do considerable soldering—a messy business to say the least. In any hookup, signal splitters should be kept to a minimum since they do introduce a signal loss. Switching is done with coaxial A-B switches or their equivalent. Such switches maintain the 75-Ω impedance with little or no loss to RF.

For a general understanding of what takes place, note the following. All VHF channel signals are present at the input to the CATV converter box (some CATV systems use two inputs). Whatever channel is selected by the tuner box is converted to the frequency of either channel 3 or 4. To conform, the output switch on the back of the VCR is also switched to the same channel 3 or 4. Therefore, to view a signal from either the VCR or CATV, the TV must also be switched to the same channel, 3 or 4. To record some channel other than 3 or 4 (from an antenna or the converter cable input), the channel desired is selected using the VCR tuner. To record one program while simultaneously viewing another requires two alternate signal sources. In the examples, one source is the cable box input, the other is an antenna. (*Caution:* Avoid connecting the output of the VCR directly to an antenna. The RF modulator in the VCR transmits a signal that can be picked up by nearby receivers.) Now back to the hookups.

In Figure 20-20a, the transformer T matches the 300-Ω antenna to 75 Ω for the rest of the hookup. If the TV has no 75-Ω input, an additional transformer is needed at that point. Two switches and two three-way connectors are used. One switch is an SPDT A-B switch, the other is a three-position A-B-C switch. The A-B switch selects which signal is supplied to the VCR, from CATV or an external antenna. The A-B-C switch selects the signal to be viewed. This switch is somewhat redundant to the VCR-VCR/TV front-panel switch.

With this hookup, an antenna is needed to record one program while viewing another. In the drawing, note the internally connected TV/VCR switch found on most VCRs. It enables the user to select which signal is to be viewed. In the TV position, the received signal (from either CATV or the antenna) goes directly to the TV. The VCR position is for monitoring the VCR recording and for viewing a taped recording. In this position, only the station signal selected on the VCR tuner will be passed on to the TV. Switching for different modes of operation is described as follows:

- *To record and monitor a CATV program (E-E mode):* A-B switch at position 2 and A-B-C switch at position 2 or 3. Both the VCR and the TV are set for channel 3 or 4.
- *For off-the-air recording and monitoring direct broadcasts with an antenna:* A-B switch at position 1 and A-B-C switch at position 1 or 2. The station desired is selected with the VCR tuner. With the A-B-C switch at 2 and the TV set for channel 3 or 4 the VCR output is being monitored. With the switch at position 1, channel selection is made with the TV tuner.
- *To record a CATV program while viewing an off-the-air broadcast:* A-B switch at 2 and A-B-C switch at position 1. The channel to be viewed is selected with the TV tuner.
- *To record a direct broadcast while viewing a CATV program:* A-B switch at 1 and A-B-C switch at 3. The station to be recorded is selected with the VCR tuner. The TV is set for channel 3 or 4.

In the absence of an antenna, the hookup in Figure 20-20b uses the CATV cable input as a signal source for programs other than those provided by the box. For this, the TV must be cable "ready," and the box is not required. Two signal splitters and two A-B switches are used. No impedance-matching transformer is required. With an understanding of the switching for the previous hookup, the switching here needs no further explanation.

For recording and viewing a program picked up from the cable input, the signal flow is through splitter 1, A-B switch 1, the VCR, A-B switch 2, to the TV set, which is tuned to channel 3 or 4. To simultaneously view a channel selected by the converter box, the A-B switch 2 is switched as shown on the diagram. To record from the output of the CATV box, signal flow is via splitter 2 and A-B switch 1.

*Record and Playback with a Camcorder.* The video and sound signals from the camcorder go directly to the video and sound input terminals on the VCR. To record from the camcorder onto a regular cassette, or to play back a recording, operate the play and record buttons in the regular manner.

*Dubbing.* This is the term used in the common practice of making copies of a tape, or when editing a recording. Two VCRs are required, one (the source) set for playback of a prerecorded tape, the other (the target) set for recording onto a blank tape. Either Beta or VHS equipment may be used for recording one onto the other. The cassettes are not interchangeable, of course. Bear in mind that a copy is never as good as the original, and second- and third-generation copies are hardly worth the while. Before beginning, it is a good idea to clean the target tape using a bulk eraser. But do not get it near the VCR or tapes you want to preserve.

There are two alternative hookups. In one case the channel 3 or 4 output of the source VCR is supplied to the tuner input of the target VCR. Somewhat better results are obtained without the RF transfer, that is, by circumventing the target tuner and feeding the video and sound signals (via two separate cables) from the video and audio output jacks of the source VCR directly to the corresponding input jacks on the target VCR. Copying from one *S-VHS* machine to another gives excellent results, especially if you transfer the luminance, chroma, and sound signals separately using the S connector (sometimes called the Y/C connector). Monitor the dubbing operation on the TV set.

To delete unwanted portions of a recording while editing, use the PAUSE control (on the target VCR) to start and stop the tape at the proper times. If your VCR has a rotary erase head, it makes the job that much easier. Editing also enables you to add narration or whatever to an existing recording.

This is particularly useful when working with a camcorder.

*Reminder:* When prerecorded tapes first became available, copying was commonplace, but now it is illegal. Most of the newer rentals now available have built-in features to make them copy protected.

### Satellite TV, CATV, and Signal Scrambling

Many of the signals provided by CATV and satellites are ready to be used, as is, by a receiver; others, so-called premium channels such as HBO and Showtime, are scrambled or encoded, and to view such programs requires a special decoder box other than the one provided by the cable company for basic CATV. Extra charges are made for such services. It is illegal to use unauthorized decoders.

### Programming the VCR Channel Buttons

These are the front-panel tuner buttons that select which channels are fed to the VCR input. Most VCRs have about 12 such buttons. The tuned circuits associated with each button are "fine tuned" to receive the most-used VHF or UHF channels from an antenna system. For a CATV system, one circuit must be adjusted for either channel 3 or 4 to receive any and all channel signals coming from the cable system "black box." Adjustment procedures are as follows:

1. Set the channel 3 or 4 switch on the back of the VCR to whichever of these channels is unused or noise-free in the area. Set the TV tuner for the same channel selected. While viewing a VCR tape or receiving a cable signal, fine tune the TV receiver for best sound and picture.
2. Access the VCR tuning adjustments. Press one of the channel buttons on the VCR, or, depending on design, set the selector switch to VHF, UHF, or a mid or superband channel, as applicable.
3. Set the VCR/TV selector button to VCR. Set the VCR AFT switch to manual. Fine tune the VCR to receive the best picture and sound on the channel selected.
4. Select another channel and tune as described for best picture and sound. Repeat for all channels desired.
5. While receiving a cable signal, fine tune one of the circuits to the channel 3 or 4 that coincides with the cable box output.
6. Switch the VCR tuner back to AFT.

### Programming the Clock and Timer

With limitations on the cheaper models, most VCRs can be programmed to record up to 14 events automatically, in some cases up to a year in advance of the scheduled broadcasts (albeit many things can go wrong in the interim). To accomplish this, it is necessary to program the day or days the recording(s) are to take place, the channel or channels to be recorded, and the times for starting and stopping the recording(s). Unfortunately, because of the complex and sometimes confusing procedures, many users choose to ignore this feature after several futile and abortive attempts. For improved customer relationships, and when called for, the technician should instruct the user in these procedures. Following are a few guidelines and the steps to be taken with a typical VCR. For detailed procedures, which differ somewhat with different machines, refer to the user's instruction booklet.

Make sure that there is sufficient blank tape in the cassette considering the anticipated duration of the recordings and which tape speed is selected: SP, LP, or SLP. Preferably, start with a full cassette that is completely rewound. Make sure that the clock readout is set for the current time of day (A.M. or P.M.). Naturally, any power outage during the programmed interval will reset the timer memory and the recordings will not be made.

1. Turn on the VCR.
2. Select the first channel to be recorded and program it into memory.
3. Select the day, the week, and the time (the hour and minute) when recording is to be made. Enter it into memory.
4. Select the hour and minute when recording is to finish. Enter into memory.
5. For additional programs (considering the amount of tape), repeat all steps as outlined. If desired, the same program can be recorded every day of the week, as can a program each week at the same time and day using the same procedures. Check the accuracy of the programming by pressing the timer SET/CHECK button. The readout should display all programmed events in their proper sequence. To clear a program, use the timer CLEAR or RESET button.
6. When satisfied, press the timer button sometime prior to the first unattended re-

cording time. (*Note:* Since the VCR cannot be used for other purposes when the timer light is on, to use the VCR in the interim, temporarily switch the timer off, remembering to restart it later. Otherwise, no recordings will be made and the effort will be wasted.

### Express Recording

To stop a recording automatically when it is completed when the VCR is unattended, make sure that the clock is set for the current time of day, then start the recording in the normal manner. Press the XPR button. Continue pressing it until the readout shows the anticipated duration of the recording, from 30 minutes to 4 hours. This locks up all control buttons on the VCR. After the programmed time has elapsed, the VCR will shut down automatically. If necessary to regain control during express recording, press the XPR button until the readout indicates 0000. The VCR will enter the stop mode and the programmed instructions are lost.

## QUESTIONS

1. Explain the purpose of the following: (a) head switchers; (b) capstan and pinch roller; (c) control track and head; (d) drum; (e) servo control system; (f) threading ring; (g) rotary transformers; (h) tracking control.
2. Explain briefly how signals are recorded onto tape, then recovered during playback.
3. What makes it possible to record and play back high audio and video frequencies at a low tape speed?
4. Explain dropouts, giving two common causes.
5. Explain how freeze frame and slow motion are accomplished.
6. How is the rotation of the reel tables sensed and controlled?
7. Explain erase bias and why it is used.
8. Explain helical scanning and why it is used.
9. What is the function of the system control microprocessors? Give some examples.
10. Explain the importance of (a) the tape guides; (b) tape tension; (c) motor torque.
11. Briefly explain servo control for both record and playback.
12. Name and explain the purpose of each of the four closed loops in the servo system.
13. What events take place (a) when a cassette is inserted and the play button is pressed; (b) when the stop and eject buttons are pressed?
14. Why are linear audio heads still required on a hi-fi VCR?
15. Where are mechanical and electromechanical braking systems used? Explain their purpose.
16. Explain how and why the luminance signal is converted from AM to FM for recording, then back to AM for playback.
17. Distinguish between cassette loading and tape loading.
18. How is tape tracking maintained as it wraps around the drum?
19. Why is head switching not required in the record mode?
20. State three functions performed by the 30-Hz reference pulse during playback.
21. Why are timing (control) pulses recorded onto the tape?
22. Identify and explain the purpose of several oscillators used in a VCR.
23. What is the advantage of four or more heads over two heads?
24. How does S-VHS produce a sharper picture than the conventional VHS format?
25. Explain "color under" (down-converting) the chroma signal and why it is done.
26. Explain dropout compensation for both picture and sound.
27. How are video and hi-fi sound signals transferred to and from the revolving drum?
28. Briefly explain servo control of (a) the drum; (b) the capstan.
29. Why is the tape spiraled around the drum?
30. Explain head switching, its purpose, and how it is accomplished.
31. Explain the purpose of a Hall-effect generator.
32. How is proper tape tension maintained?
33. How are a still frame and slow motion produced?
34. Name three kinds of erase heads and the function of each.
35. Explain how playback tape speed is adjusted automatically to conform with the selected record speed.
36. Why are the video and sound signals converted to FM (RF) and recorded as such?
37. Explain how and why the video tracks are recorded as straight and parallel diagonal tracks on the tape.
38. What is tape tracking relative to the rotary heads, and how is it maintained?
39. Briefly describe the AFM system for recording/playback of hi-fi sound.

# 21 VCR troubleshooting, maintenance, and repair

Nobody said it would be easy. And they are right. In many respects a VCR is more difficult to service than a TV set. This is because so many circuit problems can create the same symptoms. For example, a noisy or unstable pix can be caused by a defective or contaminated head, a bad rotary transformer, a head amplifier, a servo system defect, and numerous other possibilities. And symptoms are often misleading, especially with servo and head switching problems. Also, problems in one circuit can create problems in another circuit, but this is par for the course with any electronic device. On the other hand, the majority of defects are mechanical or electromechanical in nature and can often be spotted by observation alone. Sometimes the problem is simply a broken belt, a bad tape, or a need for cleaning. For efficiency, and besides having the right tools and test equipment, it is essential to have a properly operating backup VCR, a TV or monitor, and a good cassette recording, for comparison purposes. Without them there is a problem in deciding if it's a record or a playback problem and which is at fault, the VCR, the TV/monitor, or the tape.

Needless to say, servicing these items requires a good understanding of VCR theory and some background working with electronic equipment and intricate mechanisms. It is hoped that some of the information presented in earlier chapters has rubbed off and will be helpful in this regard.

Besides the know-how, a schematic and other service literature are just as important as the proper tools and test equipment. Essential items for VCR servicing are a meter, a good scope, a signal generator and/or analyzer, a frequency counter, and of course a logic probe, an almost indispensable tool for tracing and testing binary logic circuits.

Many breakdowns are caused by dirt and dust. These can usually be prevented by routine preventive maintenance, particularly regular cleaning, as described at the end of the chapter. Components most prone to failure are those that are overworked, stressed, or subjected to normal wear over a long period: power supply diodes and transistors, mechanical switches, pulleys, belts, and the various heads. Because of the high reliability of solid-state components, electronic malfunctions are not too common and are usually the last thing to suspect.

When troubles arise, and after diagnosis and a tentative estimate, the dilemma often faced by the owner is whether to repair the VCR or to discard it and buy a new one. Things to consider are the age of the machine and the relatively low (and still dropping) prices of new ones having state-of-the art features, labor costs (presently around $50 per hour) and the cost of parts, which can be considerable. Heads alone, for example, can cost over $100 and about half that amount for their replacement and adjustment, which can take several hours. Then there are the drum, motors, multifunction ICs, and perhaps a Hall generator, all of which are expensive.

As might be expected, each trouble symptom has many possible causes. To get a handle on the problem, and after trying operating modes and evaluating the performance, try to determine whether the trouble is with the VCR, the taped recording, the TV/monitor, the cable service or satellite system if used, or the interconnecting cables and switches. Even deciding which mode is at fault (record or playback) is not always easy unless you have a properly operating standby VCR and a good prerecorded tape. A poor playback, for example, may turn out to be a record problem.

Follow up with a thorough inspection, first with the power removed, then when powered up. Look for bent levers, arms, and pins; loose or broken parts; foreign objects; and so on. Observe the response when each front-panel button is pressed. Study the sequence of events as they occur. Use the "divide-and-conquer" technique, as a general rule, considering problems of the various systems and subsystems in the following order: system control, servos, luminance, chroma, and finally, the audio. Troubleshoot the playback problems before considering record problems. And do not even think of replacing expensive heads and ICs until other possibilities have been checked out.

Here we will attempt to treat the more common complaints with possible causes and logical procedures. The opening paragraphs deal with general troubles as they relate to major sections of a VCR. A number of "quick-reference" troubleshooting flow drawings are provided for use in conjunction with specific symptoms and causes in the pages that follow. Although there's sometimes an uncertainty as to which is at fault, the cables, switching, VCR, TV, or monitor, for most of the symptoms listed it is assumed that the TV or monitor is operating normally. For IC testing and other general procedures, refer to Chapter 5. In some cases, because of the numerous makes and models and the differences in design, detailed descriptions and procedures cannot be given. For specifics on adjustments, alignment, and so on, refer to SAMS VCRfacts or the manufacturer's literature.

## 21-1 GENERAL TROUBLESHOOTING PROCEDURES

### Disassembly

Certain precautions need to be stressed. Work only in a clean, dust-free area. Start by removing the wall plug (turning off the machine is not enough). Read the removal/installation instructions in the service manual, if available. Note all warnings. During removal, make note of all screws and small parts such as washers—their type, size, and locations—for later reference. The same goes for removing subassemblies or other items. Hours or days later, one tends to forget. Never remove certain items in the tape path, such as tape guides, whose alignment is *critical*. Except under controlled factory conditions, proper readjustment can be difficult or impossible. Exercise great care when working around easily damaged components. Treat delicate mechanisms with finesse and respect. Avoid the use of spray cleaners or lubricants. Probing with a screwdriver with the power on is a "no-no," of course. A momentary short can have disastrous, sometimes catastrophic results.

Procedures for a typical VCR are as follows.

1. Unplug the VCR and remove the top cover. Make a preliminary inspection of the upper section for such things as foreign objects in the tape path, damaged parts, jammed mechanisms, and telltale deposits of rubber dust. Operate the machine in *all* modes while observing the rotation of reels and pulleys, and the tape travel. If necessary, remove the cassette tray for further access. Make a preliminary diagnosis.
2. If necessary to access the lower section, remove the bottom plate. In some cases this requires removing the front panel.
3. With VCR inverted or on its side, remove any screws securing the PCB mother board. Release any hold-down clips provided. In most cases, the large board is hinged in some manner to swing outward. Carefully swing it open to gain access to motors, belts, pulleys, and so on, in the interior as well as the mother board electronics. Secure PCB in the open position, being careful to avoid bending or stressing in any way. Avoid indiscriminate touching of circuit contacts even with the setoff. A sensitive MOSFET or IC can often be damaged by the slightest static charge (see Chapter 5).
4. Make the necessary repairs and take the time to inspect belts and tires for wear. If dry, cracked, or stretched, replace them. (*Reminder:* Unless accomplished during troubleshooting, and depending on circumstances, it may be advisable to do a complete cleaning job at this time. Refer to the maintenance section at the end of the chapter.)
5. When repairs are completed, and after ver-

ifying the proper operation of all functions, reassemble the machine in the reverse order of removal.

6. Before wrapping it up, operate VCR in all modes, and allow at least a brief "burn-in" period.

## Power Supply Troubleshooting

This calls for the same general troubleshooting procedures as described in Chapter 6 for TV, particularly the section dealing with switched-type PSs. Where there is loss of B+ at some circuit point, check the schematic to identify the source and what circuit or unit is being supplied. Check for voltage at various points between the PS and the system micro (see Figure 20-7). Loss of B+ can be a PS defect, a system micro failure, or it is being grounded out by a short in some downstream circuit being supplied. For the latter possibility, try isolating that circuit to see if the B+ is restored. For a low-voltage condition, look for a stage drawing excessive current or a B+ short downstream from the source.

Check for switching logic associated with the particular function, in and out of the micro. If there is loss of input logic, it could be a bad sensor (Figure 21-1). If the input is okay but there is loss of output commands to the PS, the micro is suspect. If there is logic voltage reaching the PS but no B+ for that function, the latter is probably the culprit. Shorted regulator diodes and transistors are very common.

## Super-VHS Troubleshooting

In general, troubleshooting these machines is not too different than for the conventional VHS format. Signal tracing, however, is somewhat more complicated because of the increased number of analog switches and their corresponding control lines. For this, a proper circuit diagram is essential. Most switching voltage pulse levels are critical and *must be* within tolerance.

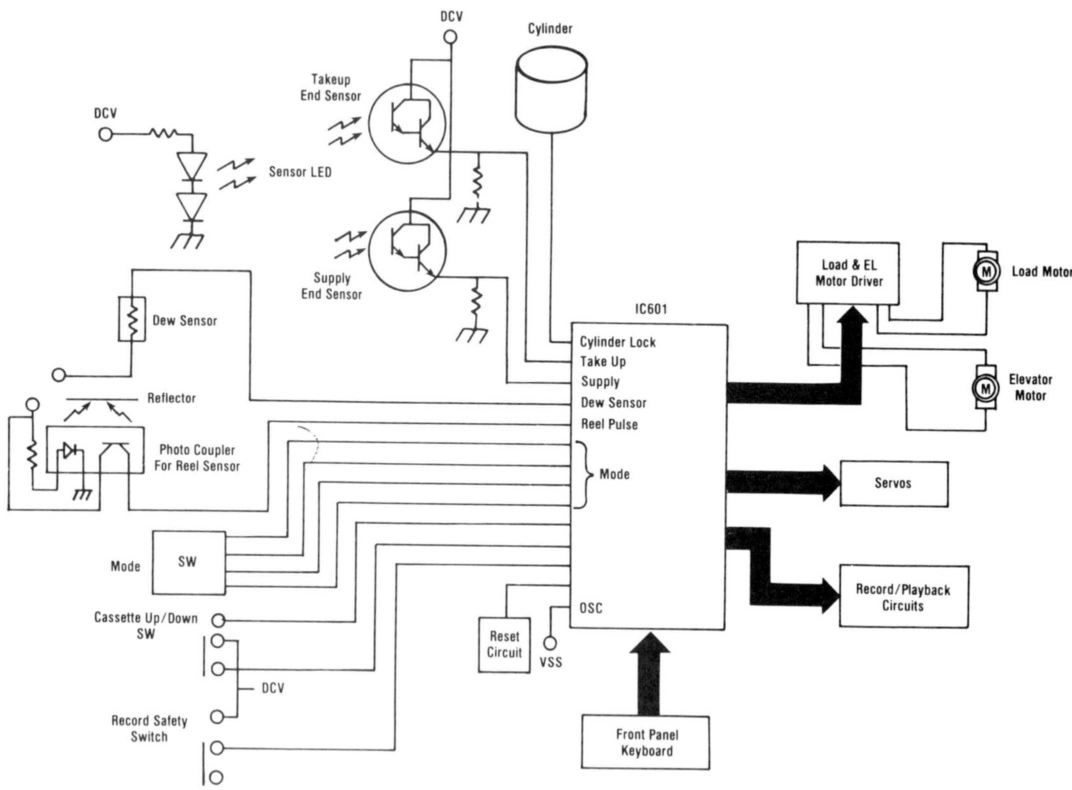


**FIG. 21-1** Sensors and system micro interractions. The system microprocessor takes data from the safety circuits and front-panel controls and the remote transmitter, and uses these data to control the operation of the VCR. (Courtesy of *Sencore News*)

If the picture quality is less than expected for a new installation, the cause could be the VCR; more likely possibilities are that the station is not broadcasting high-definition signals, or the TV/monitor is incapable of reproducing the superior picture quality provided by the VCR.

First make sure that you are using the proper cassette and that the VHS/S-VHS selector switch is in the right position. Try recording and playback in the conventional VHS format. Where the VCR is suspect, check the bandpass of the tuned circuits and the overall response of the video amplifiers. Do nothing that will attenuate the high frequencies. This includes altering the lead dressing, which in some circuits is extremely critical. If there is a problem with crosstalk, check the alignment of the comb filter.

Because of the narrower head gaps, clogging can be a problem with S-VHS. Use only high-quality tape and clean the heads frequently. Treat the heads with respect; they are expensive and easily damaged. All VCR's have essentially the same servo circuits, so for most problems proceed as for conventional VHS. Some models have one difference in tape loading, so do not be upset or suspect trouble where initially the tape only "half loads" around the drum. This is required for certain special effects.

### Mono and Stereo Troubleshooting

Where there is a problem with monaural sound only, check the linear head(s), the audio processing stages, and the audio select switch (see Figure 20-19). Localize the fault by signal injection or by examining waveforms and comparing with the schematic. If there is weak, noisy sound, try a good prerecorded tape and if necessary, clean the heads and tape path. If the record/playback amplifier is suspect, replace it. For other mono sound problems, refer to Chapter 18.

Where monaural sound is normal but there are stereo problems in the record mode, check all hi-fi components and AFM circuits between the inputs from the MTS circuits and the audio drum heads. For playback problems, check everything between the heads and the input to the RF modulator (Figures 20-16, 21-2, and 21-3). Most problems are associated with only one audio channel, and comparing one channel against the other using a dual-trace scope makes troubleshooting relatively easy. For the audio circuits, proceed as described in Chapter 18 by making voltage checks, scope tracing, and signal injection. For the AFM circuits, check the operation of all stages depicted in Figure 20-18. Refer to the VCR schematic for proper voltages and waveforms.

For weak or erratic stereo sound with *noise*, concentrate on the heads, the rotary transformers, the preamps, and the head switcher. All are common sources of trouble, the same as for the corresponding video circuits when there is noise in a picture. A common cause of noise is improper timing of the switcher. Where there is little or no separation between the left and right channels, and the decoder in the MTS circuitry is suspect, replace it.

*Hi-Fi Adjustments.* The timing of hi-fi head switching in the playback mode is *critical*. Switching is performed using the same 30-Hz pulses as those derived from the servo PG pulses, which also control video switching. Unless switching is performed with precision, dropouts occur, you get noise and in some cases, complete loss of hi-fi sound. The correct hi-fi alignment is verified by comparing the 30-Hz video head switching pulse to the 30-Hz audio switching pulse. Adjustments are made as follows:

1. Connect a dual-trace scope to monitor both pulses.
2. Adjust the scope until the rising edges of the two pulses coincide.
3. Determine the time interval between the two pulses.
4. Adjust the audio phase shifter to correct any timing error that is present.
5. To confirm the adjustment, simultaneously observe the square-wave switching pulses (on channel A of the scope) and on channel B, the FM audio information. If necessary, touch-up the phase-shifter adjustment to eliminate the dropout (see Figure 21-11).

### Logic Circuit Troubleshooting

Most VCRs use a combination of TTL (transistor/transistor logic) and CMOS (complementary metal-oxide semiconductor) logic. For proper VCR operation, the logic levels (input/output digital voltages) of solid-state devices, particularly safety sensors, are critical. Note the reliable and unreliable ranges for turn on/turn off shown in Figure 21-4, and comparative voltage levels. In troubleshooting, compare all test readings taken with those shown on the schematic. Voltage falling in the "questionable range" is a common cause of improper operation, especially intermittent problems. Logic probes can greatly facilitate troubleshooting such problems.

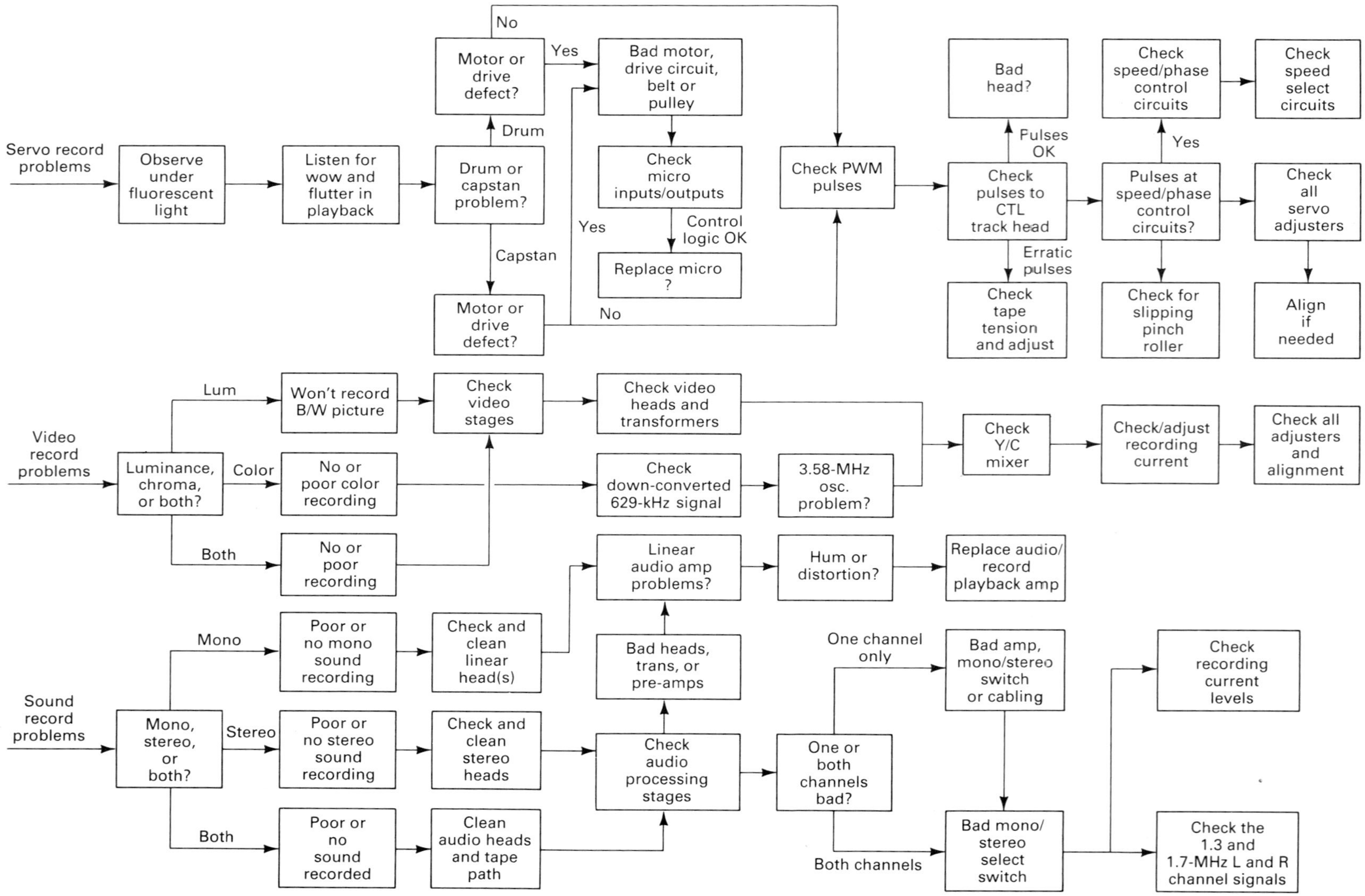


**FIG. 21-2** Record mode troubleshooting.

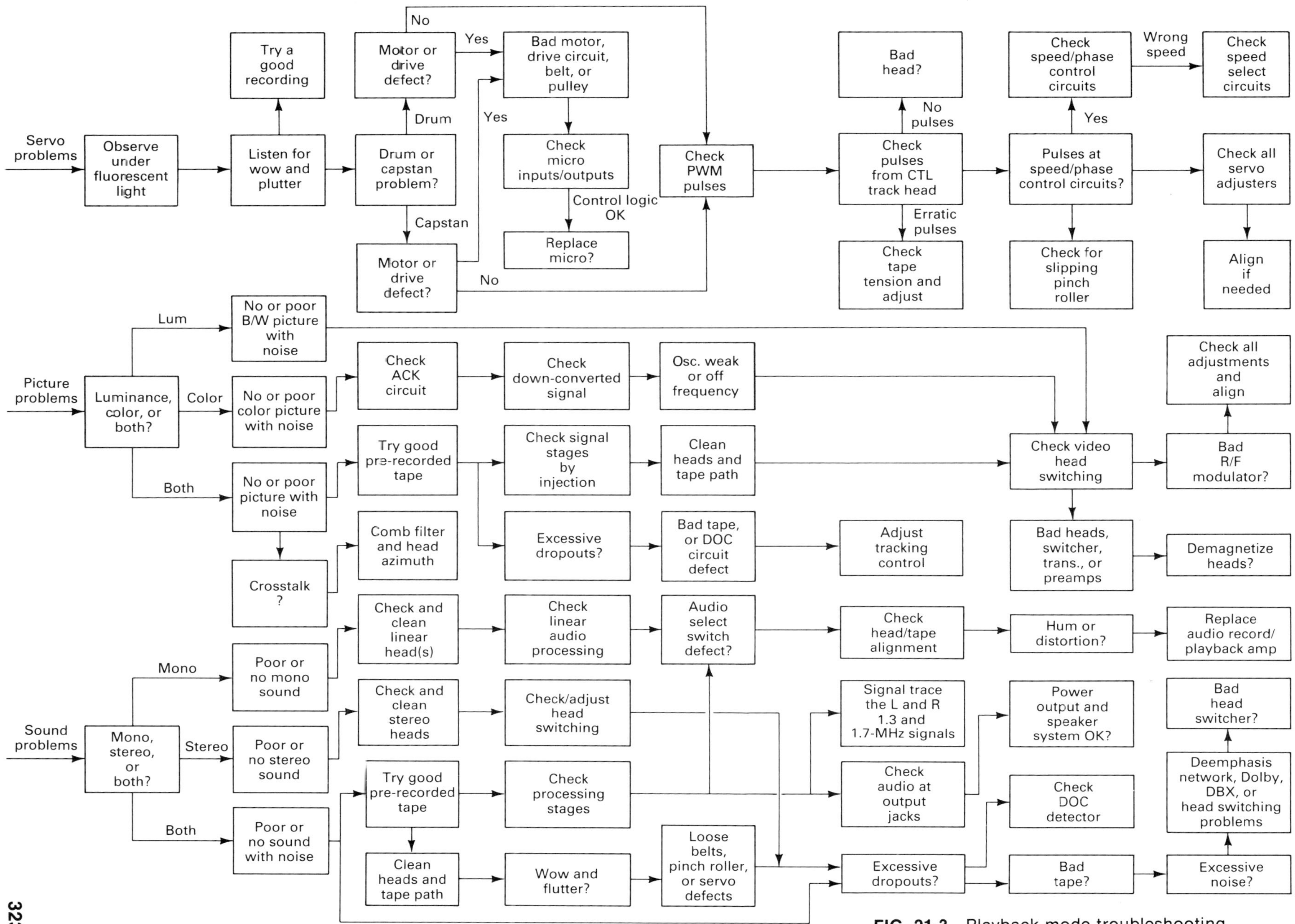


**FIG. 21-3** Playback mode troubleshooting.

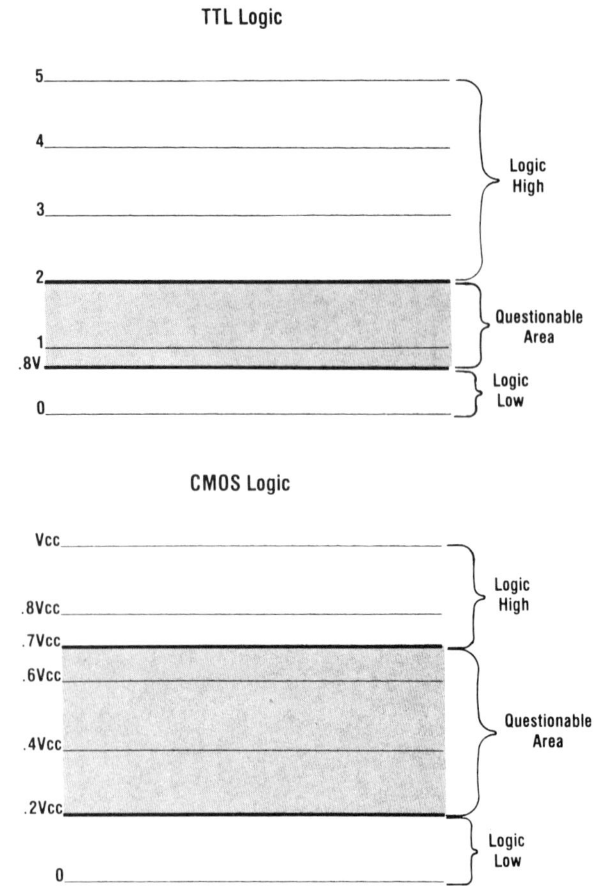


**FIG. 21-4** TTL and CMOS logic levels. Digital circuits operate correctly only when the digital pulses go from logic high levels to logic low levels. Erratic operation occurs if these logic levels fall in the questionable region. (Courtesy of *Sencore News.*)

## Mechanical and Electromechanical Device Troubleshooting

As shown in Table 20-1, there are many mechanical and electromechanical devices: motors, mechanical and electric brakes, gear pulleys and sprockets, threading ring, head drum, pinch roller and capstan, tape guides and rollers, cassette loading mechanism, sensing arms and levers, mechanical adjusters, and reel tables, to name a few. Many problems associated with these items can be spotted by inspection; others show up when troubleshooting specific functional disorders (Figure 21-5). Assuming that there is ac and dc power in the machine, where a motor does not turn or some other device is not activated when a mode button is pressed, make a cursory inspection for broken or slipping belts, a cassette basket that is hung up, a jammed threading ring, and so on. Avoid excessive bending and distorting switch and sensor arms or placing undue stress on delicate parts.

See if there is voltage reaching the troublesome unit. If not, it could be a sensor or a system microprocessor problem. If a device is receiving power but is not activated, the device itself may be bad (e.g., a burned-out motor, an open relay or solenoid coil, etc.).

Bushings and spindles of rotating devices such as motors, rollers, and pulleys tend to dry out with constant usage. This inhibits their turning and in some cases cause them eventually to seize up. Cleaning and lubricating is the solution to this problem.

## Servo Troubleshooting

There are two categories of servo problems, electromechanical and electronic. The former relates to things such as the drum and capstan motors and the drum and capstan/pinch roller. Electronic problems embrace all components and circuitry that control all the servo functions, specifically the rotation and timing of the drum and capstan (Figure 20-9).

Improperly operating servos can produce a great many symptoms. Many of the symptoms, however, can be caused by other things. Common symptoms are a weak or noisy picture, loss of picture, poor color or sync, and a variety of sound problems.

The first step is to determine if there is truly a servo problem, and which mode is involved, record or playback (see Figures 21-2 and 21-3). This is not too difficult. Simply operate the VCR directly under a fluorescent lamp while observing the drum rotation. If the drum appears to be motionless (or nearly so), the servo function is okay. If the heads seem to move or become blurred, it is a servo problem.

Next, determine which is at fault, the drum or the capstan servo. This also is not difficult. If the sound is normal, it means that the tape travel is being controlled okay and that it is a drum servo problem. On the other hand, a capstan servo defect causes improper tape movement and "Donald Duck" sounds, in addition to picture problems.

Assuming that the drum and capstan are turning okay, check the following for amplitude, frequency, and waveform, all of which are crucial: the 30-Hz headswitching pulse and the FG and PG pulses generated by the servo system; and the control track pulses being recorded and recovered from the tape. Weak or missing pulses are a common cause where there is no or weak servo lock.

The next step is to localize the trouble to either the "coarse" or "fine" speed loops of the drum or

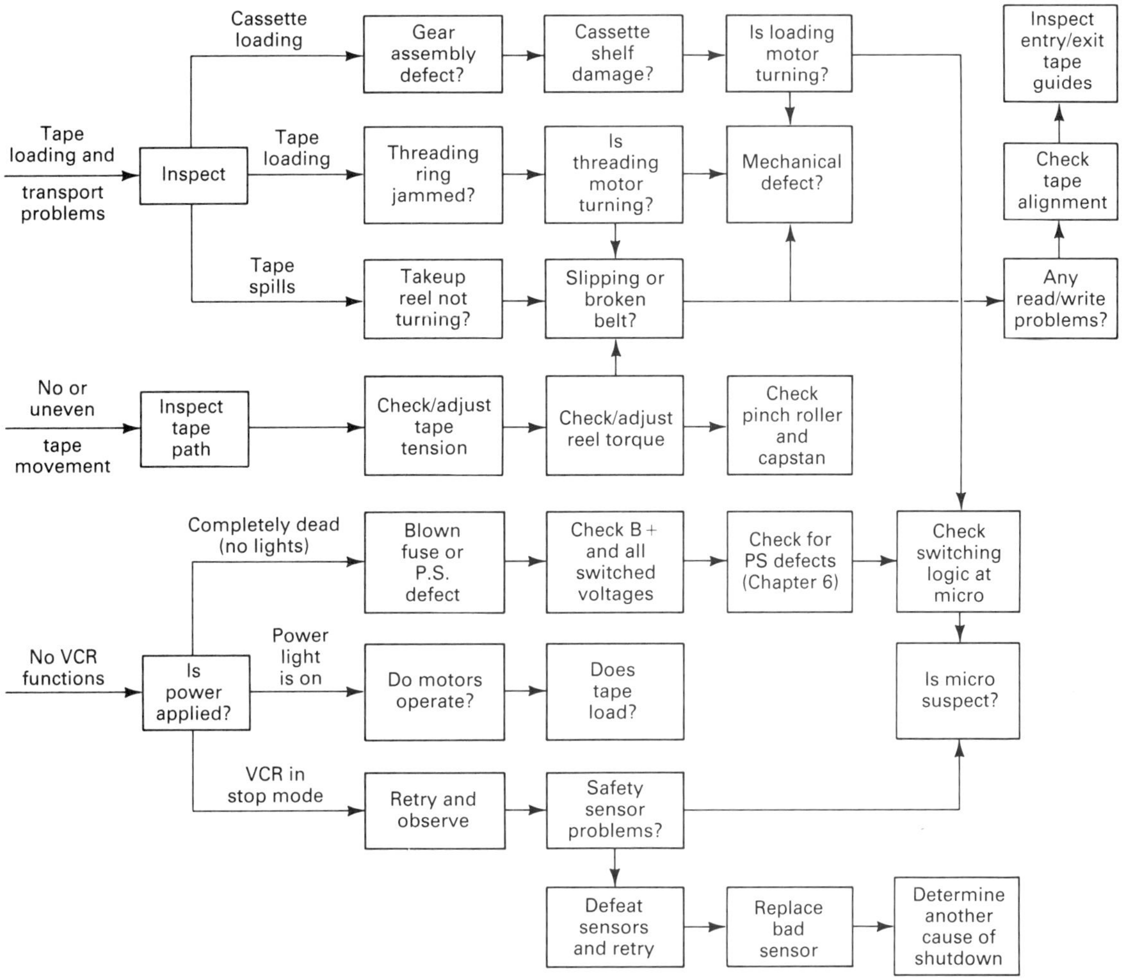


**FIG. 21-5** Troubleshooting electro/mechanical problems. If the VCR inexplicably enters the stop mode, or if there are improper operating conditions or electromechanical malfunctions or other anomalies, check the input/output logic voltages at the microprocessor(s). If weak or missing, check associated sensor(s) or other source. If logic control signals are okay and there are no external defects, replace the micro(s).

capstan, as applicable. This means breaking into the servo loops. Inject a 30-Hz signal in place of the feedback signal. If all downstream circuits now work okay, the symptoms will change. If no change using the substitute signal, the trouble lies between the injection point and the output.

### Sensors and Microcontrol Troubleshooting

From experience one learns that system control problems are those encountered most frequently. As the master control of all systems, the microprocessor(s) are often blamed for troubles created by a breakdown in some sensor circuit or elsewhere, and as stated previously, a micro should be the last thing to suspect, at least until more likely possibilities have been investigated and checked out. Among other things, the micro receives inputs from a number of safety sensors that monitor all operations to initiate a shutdown in the event of trouble. The various sensors and their functions were described in Chapter 20. Interconnections with the micro are shown in Figures 20-7 and 21-1. There are usually seven of them, identified here by way of review: (1) a cylinder lock sensor, which checks the rotation of the drum; (2) cassette switches, which verify the position of the cassette; (3) end sensors, which sense the end of the tape on the supply and takeup reels; (4) reel sensors, which monitor the rotation of the takeup reel; (5) a mode switch, which determines if the tape is properly wound onto the drum; (6) a dew sensor, which checks for moisture; and (7) a record safety switch, which prevents recording onto a protected tape. A malfunction associated with any of these sensors will instruct the micro to initiate a shutdown.

As a starter, with the VCR in the troublesome mode, check the following at the pins of the micro while referring to the schematic: the applied dc voltage(s), the clock pulses for amplitude and frequency, the input/output data, the reset pulse, and the integrity of all ground connections. To expedite the repair, the tests should be made in the order stated. Bear in mind that the high and low logic levels of sensor outputs are critical and any variations from the norm should be investigated before proceeding. Use extreme care to avoid creating a short at the closely spaced IC pins. If all tests prove out, the micro is probably defective, although this is seldom the case.

If the VCR works at all, try all buttons, noting which mode is associated with the problem. Carefully observe the sequence of events as they occur, especially prior to a shutdown. Armed with a good understanding of each function and what *should* take place can go a long way to solving a problem. Consider the following examples.

1. Where the tape loads and threads properly but the VCR shuts down after a few seconds, a good possibility is that the takeup reel is not turning. This results in a tape spill and the reel rotation sensor initiates the stop mode. With a spill, be careful not to crinkle the tape when restoring it to the cassette. Correct the problem before risking another tape. Sometimes it is an intermittent problem, where the VCR may run for minutes or hours before shutting down. In this case, check for a slipping belt or the need for lubrication on a takeup pulley. Where shutdown is almost immediate, look for a broken belt. Another possibility is a shorted or leaky sensor that creates a shutdown when there is no problem. With the reel not turning (stopping it by hand, if necessary), check for sensor output and voltage reaching the micro. These voltages have close tolerances, so compare with the schematic. If no sensing voltage, the sensor may be bad or the voltage is grounded out by a short in the micro.

2. Another example. Where the cassette loads okay but tape does not wrap around the drum, it could be an end sensor problem, some difficulty associated with the threading ring, or the drum is not turning. With logical reasoning and a few tests, the cause should soon become apparent.

3. Where a cassette loads but quickly ejects, make sure that it is not caused by ambient room lighting getting into the cassette light tower and picked up by the end sensor. If this is not the case, it could be a bad sensor (Figure 21-6). Also, the eject button switch could be shorted, which would feed pulses to the micro when there should be none. Check for sensor output with light and without light (with tape covering the sensor). Normal readings are a logic high of about 9 V with light (cassette removed) and close to zero for no light. Either a low reading for the first, or a high reading for the second, will create problems. As a further test, try defeating the sensor by grounding it. If the sensor is suspect, replace it. If the problem persists, check the cassette-IN, the cassette UP-DOWN, and the dew sensors, all of which are operational with the cassette loaded. Where all else fails, look to the micro.

### Key Matrix Encoder Troubleshooting

Troubleshooting for this is not difficult if you understand the functions as described in Chapter 20. For example, if the VCR will not go into the FF mode when the button is pressed, but the other functions are okay, determine which scan line connects to the FF button (Figure 20-8) and scope that line. If pulses are present, check the input line connecting the encoder to the FF switch. If the pulses are okay but there is no FF, the encoder is not doing its job. If the serial data output from the encoder changes when different buttons are pressed, the encoder is working okay. The presence of pulses with no buttons pressed indicates a keyswitch defect. If there are no pulses on the input or output lines, check to see where the pulses are lost and why. The IC may or may not be the cause. Before considering replacement, first check its supply voltage and the clock pulses for amplitude and frequency (455 kHz) and the reset pulse. A normal clock pulse is shown in Figure 21-7 (shown on page 332). If necessary, check all the associated components. If there are data at the encoder output but not at the comparator, the infrared receiver (IC206) is probably the culprit. If okay from this IC but there are no data at the micro input, blame the comparator. For loss of logic at the micro input, it is suspect.

### Luminance Circuit Troubleshooting

For a general procedure, see Figures 21-2 and 21-3. Where the complaint is a *noisy picture,* the logical suspects are the composite video stages, the FM luminance circuits, and the playback head circuits. Besides voltage checking, troubles are localized, then isolated by a combination of signal tracing and signal injection. For the latter method remember that the signal ahead of the detector is a 3.5-MHz FM-modulated signal as compared to TV, where the IF frequency is 45.75 MHz, and *AM*. To locate troubles by signal injection, proceed as follows.

1. Load a standard test tape into the VCR and press the play button. Feed a crosshatch generator signal to various stages between the deemphasis network and the amplifier output (see Figure 20-16). If a normal crosshatch pattern is observed, the stages downstream from the FM detector are okay. If not okay, they are the stages to check further.
2. Feed a 3-MHz FM luminance signal to the input of the high-pass filter. If a normal response, all downstream stages can be considered okay.
3. Inject the same FM signal alternately to both inputs of the head switcher preamp IC. If the result is a noisy picture, you have narrowed the problem to the preamp and switcher IC (they are usually combined). For a normal response the heads and rotary transformers are suspect. Head testing procedures are described later in the section on symptoms and causes.
4. To further isolate the trouble, check the IC B supply, which is typically about 12 V dc. Scope check for a clean waveform. Check the 30-Hz switching pulse. A normal pulse is about 5 V p-p at a frequency of 30 Hz with a good waveform. If everything is within tolerance, check the switcher alignment. If troubles persist, the switcher IC is probably at fault and should be replaced.

### Chroma Record Troubleshooting

For a general approach, see Figures 21-2 and 21-3. As with the luminance circuits, troubles are isolated either by scope tracing, signal injection, or both. [*Reminder:* Unlike TV, VCRs prevent luminance/chroma interference by using a color carrier of 629 kHz (688 kHz for Beta) prior to reconverting back to 3.58 MHz, the original color carrier.]

Where the complaint is weak color, inability to record color, or a normal color recording will not play back, proceed as follows:

1. Verify the integrity of the tuner and IF sections. Certain problems, such as misalignment, can result in loss of chroma signal even when the luminance signal gets through okay.
2. Check for clean dc outputs from the power supply, and verify that the playback function is okay.
3. Check the microprocessor control signal on the record status line. With the record button pressed, compare the dc voltage on this line with that specified on the schematic. If the voltage is incorrect, check the system control circuits.
4. Check the down-converted chroma signal (629 kHz for VHS and 688 kHz for Beta) at the output of the color amplifier and the input of the Y/C mixer (see Figure 20-14).
5. Insert a blank tape in the VCR. Press the record button. Locate the record luminance level control and turn it down fully. When the VCR repairs are completed, readjust the control.
6. Check the 3.58-MHz crystal oscillator frequency with a counter. If the 629-kHz (or 688-kHz) down-converted signals are missing or the wrong frequency, an incorrect *oscillator* frequency may be the cause. In this case the tape may play back okay on the worked-on VCR but not on another machine.
7. Check for a 30-Hz switching pulse at the phase-shifter input. If weak or missing, there may be loss of color or intermittent color bursts when tape is played back on another VCR.
8. Check for a horizontal sync pulse and a normal composite signal at the input of the sync separator.
9. Weak recorded color may be caused by misadjustment of the chroma record current. Adjust to the amount specified. If the color is still weak, verify all inputs to the chroma IC. If all are present, replace the IC.

### Chroma Playback Troubleshooting

As a starter, verify that the problem is truly with the color circuits. Check for normal operation of the servo and luminance circuit. Play a good prerecorded tape. Make sure that the tape speed is correct. Ascertain that the BW picture is okay. A defective or contaminated head will sometimes result in flashes of color along with a noisy BW picture. Correct any luminance problems before proceeding.

Servo problems can be mistaken for color problems, but this is easily determined by scoping the luminance signal. If the BW picture is poor or jittery, suspect a servo defect. Check the tracking control action. Correct all such problems before proceeding.

After validating the servos, video heads, and luminance circuits, check the quality of the color picture, including that from a prerecorded tape. Compare with playback on another machine.

Typical color playback problems include loss of color, weak color, and poor tint. For such symptoms, proceed as follows:

1. Insert a test tape in the VCR and press the play button.
2. Check the power supply to the chroma IC. Compare the voltage with that shown on schematic. Verify that there is no ripple problem or extraneous noise on the PS lines.
3. Check the system control signals as produced by the microprocessor to turn on the record or playback circuits in the chroma IC. Compare with the control voltage shown on the schematic for the play mode. An incorrect voltage here usually indicates trouble with the system control circuits rather than with the chroma circuits.
4. Inject a down-converted chroma signal (629 kHz or 688 kHz for Beta) at the input to the chroma IC, and the output of the A/B head switcher (Figure 20-16). A fairly strong signal is required. With the VCR in the play mode, observe the picture on the TV or monitor. If the signal is weak or noisy, increase the strength of the injected signal. The picture should show some color. If there is poor color lock-in, there may be a problem relating to the 30-Hz servo pulses. If the color is good, the chroma IC and associated circuits are okay. The problem is now isolated to the video heads, rotary transformer, head preamps, or A/B switchers. Problems in these areas, however, generally show up as poor luminance.
5. Where problems persist, check the 3.58-MHz oscillator in the chroma IC, or external in some cases. If the amplitude or frequency is incorrect, check all related oscillator components or replace the IC, as applicable.
6. Check the horizontal sync pulse, which triggers the various burst gates, color killers, and phase-shifting circuits. Also check for video at the IC input. If all the foregoing tests prove out, replace the chroma IC. This also applies where the complaint is weak color or a tint problem.

### Adjustments and Alignment

The most minute misadjustment of certain adjusters can be detrimental to normal VCR operation. Most of the adjustments as described in Chapter 20 are extremely critical and should never be tampered with unless you know what it is all about, and then, cautiously and with precision: for example, the record current levels, where an error of only a few *millivolts* can be crucial; reel torque and tape tension; head switching; head azimuth; and the timing of events as encountered in the drum and capstan servos.

Many adjustments require special equipment and a test/alignment tape, which is quite expensive. Because of possible damage to the tape, most technicians make a working copy and never work with the original. If you are short of funds, ask a technician friend to make you a copy. Adjustment procedures vary with different makes and models, and such procedures are beyond the scope of this book. Refer to the service manual for this information.

## 21-2 SYMPTOMS AND PROCEDURES

Specific problems and procedures are treated in the following paragraphs. Refer to the preceding general information as applicable.

#### *No Power; Indicator Lights are Off*

***Probable causes:*** No ac power at outlet; damaged line cord; blown fuse; bad switch; power supply breakdown.

Troubleshoot per Chapter 6.

*Dead; Blows Fuses.* (there may also be burned odors and smoke)

***Probable causes:*** B+ short in power supply; excessive loading by some circuit, transistor or IC drawing high current; seized motor.

Proceed as in Chapter 6. Check for 120 V ac at the VCR input. In some circumstances try a suitable substitute PS. Try disconnecting suspected circuits to relieve the loading and isolate the defect. If overheating with burned odors, feel all suspected diodes, transistors, and ICs and study the schematic to determine possible causes. An overheating resistor or other component often provides a good clue in isolating a short. Make sure that louvres and ventillation holes are not obstructed.

*No Response to One or More Button Commands.* (loss of some modes or functions)

***Probable causes:*** Stuck key(s); VCR in stop mode; buttons hung up or an open-circuited button microswitch; faulty keymatrix circuit; bad system micro.

Check for stuck buttons and release. Make a continuity check of the suspected microswitch. Operate the switch key several times; it could be intermittent. Check the logic signals at the input and output of the micro. Check the inputs and outputs of associated sensors and the key matrix encoder. If the encoder or micro is suspect, look for external defects, and if none, replace them.

*Reels or Drum Not Turning.* (indicator lights are on)

***Probable causes:*** Bad motors; loss of motor drive voltage; broken belts; slipping belts or pulley tires; won't accept cassette; low or no output from one of the power supplies; bad system control microprocessor; system may be in stop mode.

Inspect for broken or slipping belts or tires. Try cleaning. Apply tire dressing as appropriate. Replace stretched belts. Check for seized motors. Release and lubricate. Check for drive power at the motor terminals. Check the continuity of the motor coils. If there is no switched B+, check the PS or logic commands. Check for an open fuse link. For loss of the start command, suspect a system control microprocessor but replace it only if no other defects are found. If there is no cassette loading, inspect for damage. Try another cassette. Check the loading motor, its drive, and the gears. If hung up, release; inspect for damage, bent arms, foreign objects, and so on. Lubricate with light gear grease. If the VCR is in the stop mode, refer to the section on stop function problems.

*No Tape Movement.* (drum spins and cassette loads ok)

***Probable causes:*** Slipping belts or pulleys; bad cassette or tape; pinch roller not activated, worn, or slipping; capstan not turning; tape or cassette defect; tape not loaded properly; threading ring defects; bad tape loading motor; loss of start signal; reel brakes not released; tape stuck to drum or other transport item; bent or misaligned tape guides; foreign objects in the tape path.

If the pinch roller is not activated, check for loss of play command, a defective actuator (solenoid), or a seized capstan. If slipping, clean the roller or replace if worn. If the capstan is not turning, check the capstan motor and drive power. For loss of drive, suspect a loss of logic command or a bad drive circuit transistor.

Check for tape slippage or hang-up or a bad cassette. Try another. Observe the tape threading operation (the loading ring should rotate when the play button is pressed). Look for such things as misaligned guide pins, bent tension arm, and other defects in the tape path. See if the threading ring is jammed or hung up or its motor not turning. Look for broken or slipping belts. If there is no start signal, suspect the micro. Check the reel brakes. For tape sticking, check for moisture and clean all items in the transport system.

*Tape Spills*

***Probable causes:*** Jammed threading ring; takeup reel not turning or insufficient torque; reel brakes not working; damaged tape or cassette; foreign objects in the tape path; misaligned or bent guide pins; slack tape; misadjusted back tension arm or torque adjustment; tape sticking to drum or other transport item.

Carefully remove tape from VCR to avoid tape damage, such as kinks and creases, especially around sharp corners of cassette access opening and the hinged flap. Once removed from the machine, crank the tape back into the cassette by turning the appropriate reel hub until the tape is taut. It is advisable to use clean cotton gloves to avoid finger contact with the tape. If the tape is crinkled, it can cause head damage. Repair or discard.

Check for the cause of the spill. If there is no apparent cause, make further checks using a tape that is expendable. If the threading ring does not operate, check its motor and drive power. Look for foreign objects that prevent or hinder normal movement. If the takeup reel is not turning, look for a broken or slipping belt or a reel motor defect. Check the operation of the reel braking system; check to see if they are withdrawn; adjust if required. Examine the entry and exit tape guides for defects, but *do not attempt to straighten.* They are mounted at an angle and only appear to be bent.

For tape sticking to the drum, and so on, clean the drum and other items in the tape path. If misadjusted tape tension or motor torque is suspected, adjust as specified in the service manual. Special gauges are needed for these adjustments, which are extremely critical.

*Cassette Will Not Load or Eject.* (panel lights are lit)

***Probable causes:*** Loading motor or worm gear mechanism defect or hung up; damaged or warped cassette; foreign objects; cassette jammed in tracks or basket; bent or damaged rails; loss of loading motor power or logic command; defective load/unload status sensing switch; no eject command logic; bent or distorted arms, rods, levers, and so on; VCR may be in the stop mode.

In testing, defeat the end-of-tape sensor (by covering the sensor, light, or infrared source with a piece of masking tape) to permit operation of reels, without a cassette being in place. Try another cassette. If the cassette is "hung up" midway through the load cycle, and the IN LIGHT is on, try pressing the eject button. If necessary, manually operate the load mechanism, using your fingers to turn the worm gear, until the cassette settles into the basket and the IN LIGHT goes out. Lubricate the gears with light grease. Inspect for foreign objects. Check the loading motor. Check for loss of motor drive power or load command logic. Check for a bad "loading complete" sensor. If no eject and there's a tape spill, check for a threading ring problem, including loss of takeup motor drive. If there is a tape spill, avoid tape damage or contamination when removing it through the hinged door.

The VCR will not enter the play mode if a safety sensor initiated a stop mode. In such cases, determine which one and correct the problem. See the section on stop function problems.

*Tape Tracking Alignment Problems.* (poor recording and playback of picture and stereo sound)

***Probable causes:*** Contamination or moisture on drum surface; worn drum ledge (rabbet); bent or misaligned entry and exit tape guides; improper tape tension.

The tape must track properly and uniformly with the heads as it wraps around the drum. Clean the drum of oxide buildup and check for moisture. Ragged edges on one edge of the tape usually indicate wear or buildup on the rabbet. Check for any roughness on the tape guides or rollers. Make sure that the rollers turn freely. Check the tape tension and adjust if needed. Do not tamper with the entry/exit guides; their position and tilt relative to the drum is *critical*.

*No Tape Loading.* (cassette loading is okay)

***Probable cause:*** Usually a threading ring problem (see the section on no tape movement).

*Tape Stretching or Breakage*

***Probable causes:*** Excessive motor torque or incorrect tension adjustment.

Adjust as specified in the service manual, using the proper gauges. Common symptoms of a stretched tape are wow, audio distortion, and poor sync. Continued use of a stretched tape results in oxide flaking and possible head damage.

*Belt or Tire Slippage*

***Probable causes:*** Misadjusted belt tensioner; stretched or worn belt; oil contamination; worn or defective tire; in some cases, belt slippage causes the servo control to initiate a VCR shutdown.

Inspect. If the belt is stretched or cracked, replace it. If oily, clean it and the pulley. If necessary, adjust the tensioner. If dry, try soaking in glycerin to restore resiliency, then dry thoroughly. If the pulley(s) do not turn freely, lubricate *sparingly*. An emergency remedy for a worn tire is to wet it, carefully remove, and turn it inside out. Dry before using.

*End-of-Tape-Sensing Problems*

***Probable causes:*** Burned-out lamp, bad LED, or loss of voltage; defective photosensor; cassette defect; light or IR beam obstruction; loss of stop command; defective microprocessor.

Observe if the lamp is lit. Check the voltage. Check the positioning of the lamp, LED, and sensor, as applicable. Check the sensor by substitution (Figure 21-6). Try another cassette. Check for the stop command. If weak or absent, the microprocessor may be bad. Check all other possibilities before considering replacement.

*Stop Function Problems.* (two kinds: failure to shutdown; and an unscheduled "premature" shutdown). With the latter, VCR goes into stop mode a few seconds after initiating play or record.

***Probable causes:*** Defective sensor or associated circuitry; defective microprocessor; electromechanical failures; broken or slipping belts.

Identify the stop function: i.e., dew sensing, end of tape, reel rotation, tape tension or whatever. Check the troublesome stop function sensor and its circuit. Check for defects as applicable, such as the presence of moisture, bad tape leader, or other end-

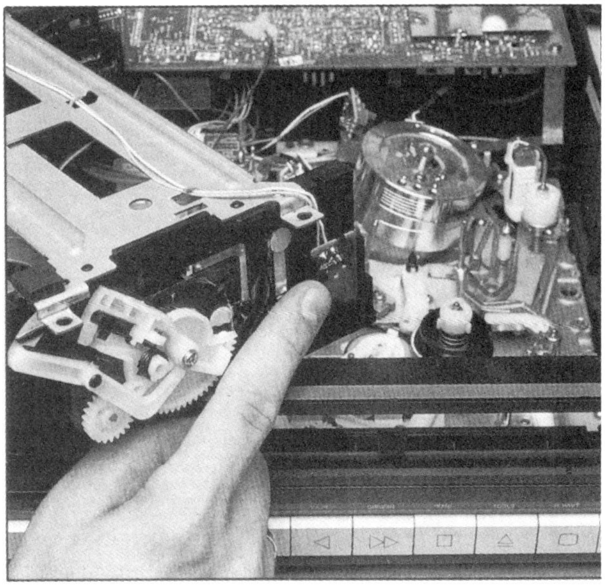

FIG. 21-6 One source of startup/shutdown problems. For end-of-tape sensing problems, the end sensor is a likely suspect. (Courtesy of *Sencore News*.)

of-tape-sensing device described previously, such as misadjusted tape tensioner. Check for electromechanical malfunctions that created the problem. If dew light is on or blinking, allow the VCR *and* cassette plenty of time to dry out with the tape stopped but power on. If a frequent problem, install a packet of silica gel at a suitable location. To isolate the problem to a particular function, check the outputs of suspected stop-mode sensors and try to restore operation by disconnecting them. A typical sensor output is about 0.15 V. If necessary, and as a last resort, replace the system control microprocessor(s). After the repairs are completed, restore any circuit that was disconnected.

If shutdown was due to an accidental liquid spill, it can create serious problems and damage to sensitive components. Mop up to the extent possible. Use a hair dryer (but with caution). With tape stopped but power on, let the VCR sit for several hours in a warm, dry environment before attempting a restart.

Where an *unprogrammed* stop occurs, look for a bad relay or solenoid that is stuck and not tripping. Check for loss of the relay or solenoid energizing power (see if they energize when a stop command is initiated). Other possibilities are slipping belts, a capstan braking system defect, end-of-tape or slack-tape sensing problems, an abnormal or noisy PG pulse, or no takeup reel rotation if there is a tape spill. Assuming no sensor defects, out-of-sequence stopping is sometimes caused by a bad system control microprocessor. Where there's a tape spill and no takeup reel rotation, a stop will occur a few seconds after the play button is pressed. The usual cause is a broken belt.

#### *No (or Sluggish) Fast Forward or Rewind*

***Probable causes:*** Reel is empty; reel brakes defective or hung up; brake release circuit defect; bad reel motor; loss of command logic; bad microprocessor; bad cassette; slipping belts.

In these modes, brakes are released and power to the reel motors is increased. Check the braking action. Check the logic signals (Figure 21-4). If warranted, replace the suspected micro(s). If slow FF or RWD, check for slipping belts or a worn tire. Check for a bad reel motor or low drive voltage (normally about 4 V). Try another cassette.

#### *Drum Not Turning.* (but tape moves)

***Probable causes:*** Bad drum motor; loss of drive power; broken or slipping belt; drum brake defect.

Check the motor, drive power, and brake system. Inspect for a broken or slipping belt unless the drum uses direct drive. If the brake is ineffective, check for mechanical defects or a weak or missing logic command. If necessary, adjust the brake.

#### *Tape stops at 0000 or 9999*

***Probable causes:*** Improper programming of timer; counter logic problem.

Reset the timer and counter. Press the RWD button to proceed. If trouble persists, check the counter logic circuit. If necessary, replace the timer or counter IC.

#### *Clock or Timer Problems.* (time error, or inability to preprogram a recording, or recording doesn't start or stop as programmed)

***Probable causes:*** User error; defective timer memory; power outage; loss of timer B+; defective timer clock or crystal.

If appropriate, instruct the user on correct programming procedure, the need for sufficient tape to complete recording, and caution against pulling the plug. If the clock does not keep correct time or will not reset, check the timer clock pulses for frequency and amplitude. If there is a frequency error, adjust, or replace the timer IC or its crystal. If there is no clock output, check the applied dc operating voltage, and if okay, replace the IC.

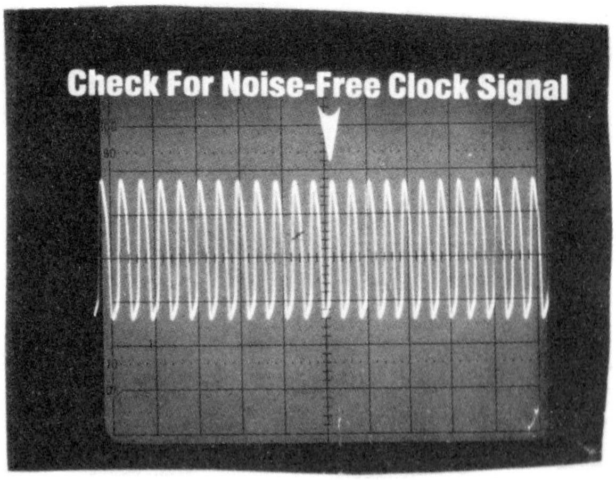


**FIG. 21-7** Key matrix encoder clock pulse. The encoder clock pulse must have good amplitude and waveform and the correct frequency.

*Problem in Locating Start or End of a Recorded Program.*
Instruct the user. At the start of each recording, reset the counter to 0000: make a note of the counter readout when recording is completed. At a future time, if desired, simply subtract the last recorded number from 9999 and rewind until that number comes up. This is not a problem if the VCR has automatic indexing.

*Will Not Record.* (prerecorded playback is okay)

***Probable causes:*** Tab removed from cassette; loss of record logic signal; changeover relay or solenoid stuck or defective; Interconnecting cables or switching problems; loss of input signal (from TV antenna, cable, or camcorder); VCR tuner not set for channel 3 or 4 (cable system only).

Try another cassette, or cover the missing tab with tape. Check for a record start command. Try alternate signal sources. Check the integrity of the external cable switches, interconnecting cables, and connectors. Check for a bad tuner. Check the input and output of the luminance IC, and if suspect, replace it. Try injecting a 1-V p-p signal to the comb filter input and other downstream stages as appropriate. If only a sound recording problem, concentrate on the audio stages only. When recording from a cable system, make sure that the VCR tuner selection matches channel 3 or 4 of the CATV box.

*Weak or Poor Recording.* (prerecorded playback okay)

***Probable causes:*** No or incomplete erasure of previous recording; bad tape; weak, noisy, or distorted signal sources; servo problems; VCR signal stage problems; erase head or drum surface contaminated, defective, or magnetized; loss of supersonic bias.

Use a bulk eraser or try another cassette. Check for loss of the supersonic erase bias at the "full-erase" head. Check for a contaminated or defective erase head. Clean and demagnetize the head. Investigate the strength and quality of signals to be recorded. Check the signal stages between the VCR tuner and the video detector output, as described in the TV chapters. Check the applicable luminance or chroma signal stages between the detector and the head inputs. Make a test recording for comparison. There may have been excessive noise or interference when the recording was made. Press the pause button. If the picture does not remain upright, check for a drum servo problem as described later.

*Tape Erasure.* (unscheduled or inadvertent)

***Probable causes:*** Accidental user mistake; storing or permitting cassettes near strong magnetic fields such as speakers, a head demagnetizing tool, or any electrical appliance or toys; erase head(s) not disabled in playback mode.

Take the necessary precautions.

*No or Incomplete Erasure of Previous Recording*

***Probable causes:*** Defective or incorrectly positioned erase head; dirty or contaminated head; weak or missing erase bias voltage.

Check the head and its azimuth adjustment. Try a bulk eraser and recheck and compare with another cassette. Clean the head (see Section 21-3).

*Head Switching Problems.* (flecks of snow, picture tearing, picture or sound noise, poor picture quality, weak or no picture, weak or no sound, no color or poor color, loss of sync, no stereo effect, part of alternate fields moving vertically through the picture, and so on.

***Probable causes:*** Defective switcher IC or a servo problem; switching pulse weak, missing, improper waveform, or a frequency/phase error; misadjusted phase timing (Figure 21-8).

Determine whether the problem is with the picture, the sound, or both, although causes and procedures are essentially the same for each. Check the video or hi-fi audio head switcher as appropriate. If suspect, replace the corresponding switcher IC. Adjust the servo circuits timing adjustments, which

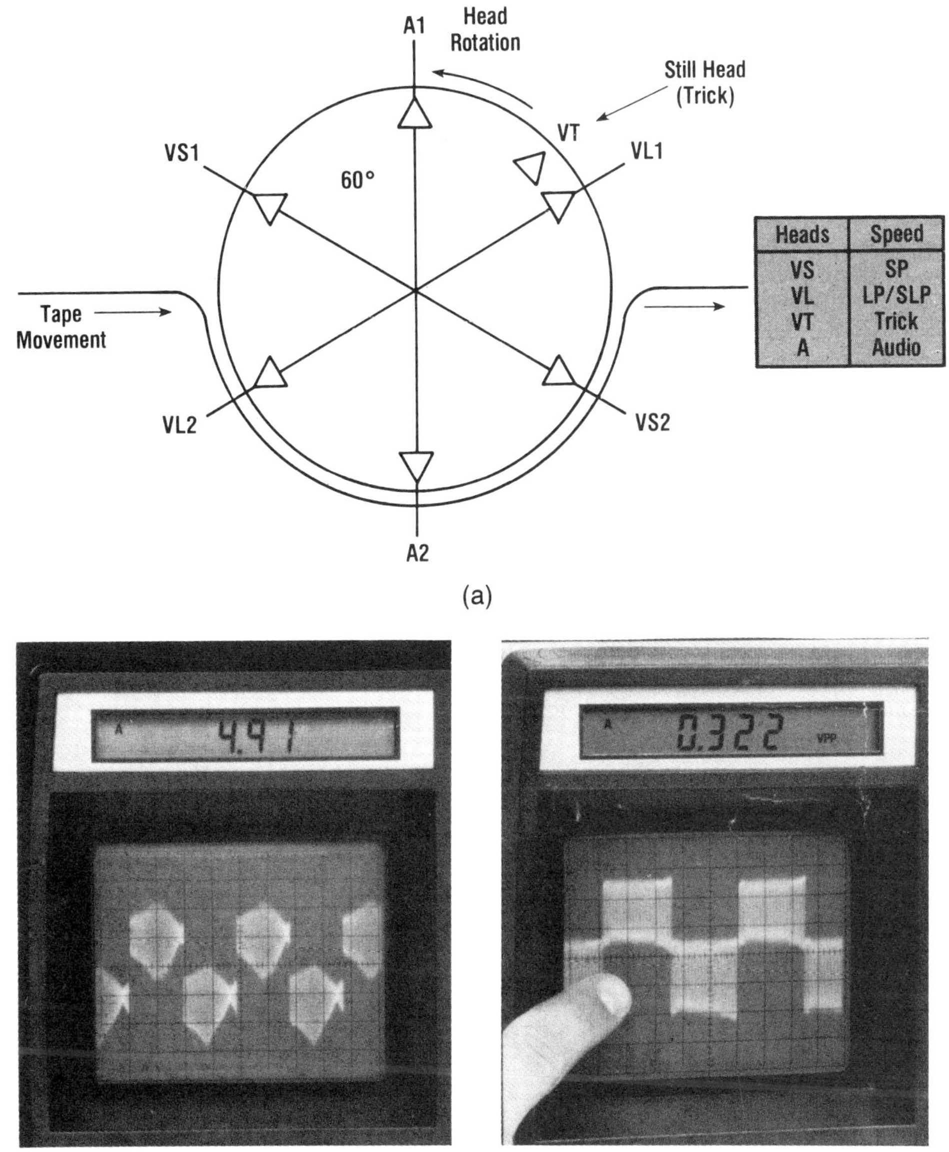


(b) (c)

**FIG. 21-8** Video head switching problems. (a) Note that the hi-fi audio signals come from the rotating cylinder drum (in the same manner as the video). Proper switching prevents dropout. Also note that the video heads are positioned 180° apart and offset from the hi-fi heads. (b) Notice how the video is rounded off at the switching pulse transitions in a VCR with a misaligned tape path. (c) Distinguishing a tape path problem from a servo problem. Notice how the video information is squared off at the switching pulses; this indicates a properly aligned tape path. (Courtesy of *Sencore News*.)

varies the timing of the switching pulse relative to vertical sync. If switching occurs too early or too late, you get tearing at the top or bottom of the picture. If severe, the picture may be wiped out. Check for the switching pulse at the switcher input. If weak, missing, or a poor waveform, trace back to the source, the pickup point on the drum. Switching pulse *waveforms* are critical. An abnormal waveform, for example, can cause confusing symptoms that can be mistaken for servo problems. If necessary, scope trace through the PG amplifiers and switching generator. A shorted switcher IC can weaken or kill the pulses, so isolate to see if there is any loading. Try operating the switcher from a 30-Hz square-wave generator signal before considering replacement.

### Head Testing and Replacement

The symptoms of a bad head can easily be mistaken for other defects, and many heads are replaced unnecessarily. Possible head defects are an open or shorted coil, core damage, excessive wear, and contamination.

Some techs find this an area of uncertainty. A continuity check shows up an open coil but not shorted windings because of the low resistance. Also, the heads are tiny and easily damaged. Core damage and wearing away of the pole piece can sometimes be observed by close scrutiny under a strong magnifying lens. Both these conditions call for replacement. Contamination can usually be corrected by cleaning as described later. Shorted windings are not easily detected. Substitution is one method, but when it does not solve the problem, it can be time consuming and expensive.

An alternative approach is to check with an inductance tester (impedance bridge), if available, comparing with a similar head known to be good. Another method uses the same principles used in flyback/yoke tester (see Chapter 4). Connect the head as the resonant circuit in a suitable oscillator hookup. For video heads use a fairly high frequency in the kilohertz range; for erase, audio, and control track heads, a lower frequency. When compared with a similar head, shorted turns show up as a higher-than-normal frequency. Still another method is to feed the suspected head (or rotary transformer, as appropriate) with a 2-V p-p generator signal while monitoring for excessive loading. Shorted windings in the head or transformer will substantially reduce the voltage. For this test, the generator must have a reserve of power to drive such a low-impedance load. The Sencore VA 62 is one of the few instruments having this capability. Head replacement is always followed by an azimuth adjustment using a frequency counter, meter, scope, and an alignment tape.

It is difficult to gain access to the *rotary* heads and transformers (Figure 21-9), so do not be hasty in considering replacement. One workable method is to play back a blank tape and inductively couple a weak signal to the spinning heads (video or hi-fi heads as applicable), to detect a loading condition due to shorted windings. A Sencore video analyzer simplifies the operation. As an alternative, use a sweep generator tuned to approximately 3 MHz, with a 1-MHz sweep. Use a three- or four-turn loop to couple the signal to the spinning heads (Figure 21-10). If heads and transformer are okay, you should get a good response on the TV/monitor screen in the playback mode, and for the audio heads, sound from the speaker. Heads and transformer are not repairable and must be replaced and aligned. A bad rotary transformer calls for replacement of the entire upper drum assembly. Because of close tolerances, some manufacturers recommend replacement of the entire drum for any problems relating to heads and transformers. [*Caution:* Since this is a time-consuming (3 to 4 hours typically) and expensive job, *verify* the need before proceeding. *Reminder:* Where both heads are defective or badly clogged, you get loss of picture; if only one head is bad or contaminated, you get a noisy picture of poor quality.] Try adjusting the head positioning. Check the tape alignment (look for bent or damaged

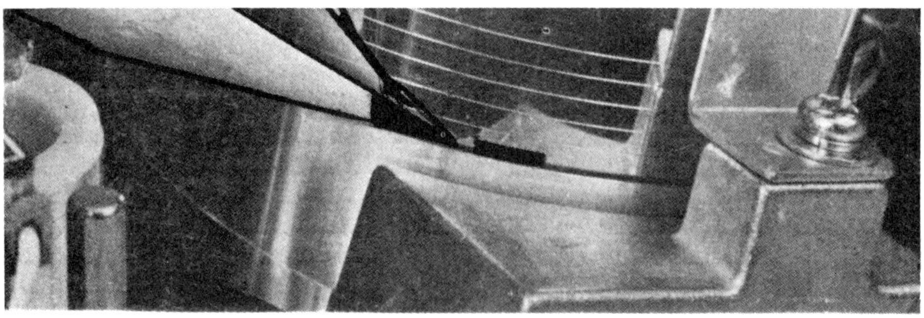

**FIG. 21-9** Drum and video head considerations. Only the head face and gap are visible. The head assembly is contained in the upper drum section and is accessible after removal of the drum. Spacing between the lower (stationary) drum section and the head is very small. Any imperfections here can cause problems. (Courtesy of *Sencore News.*)

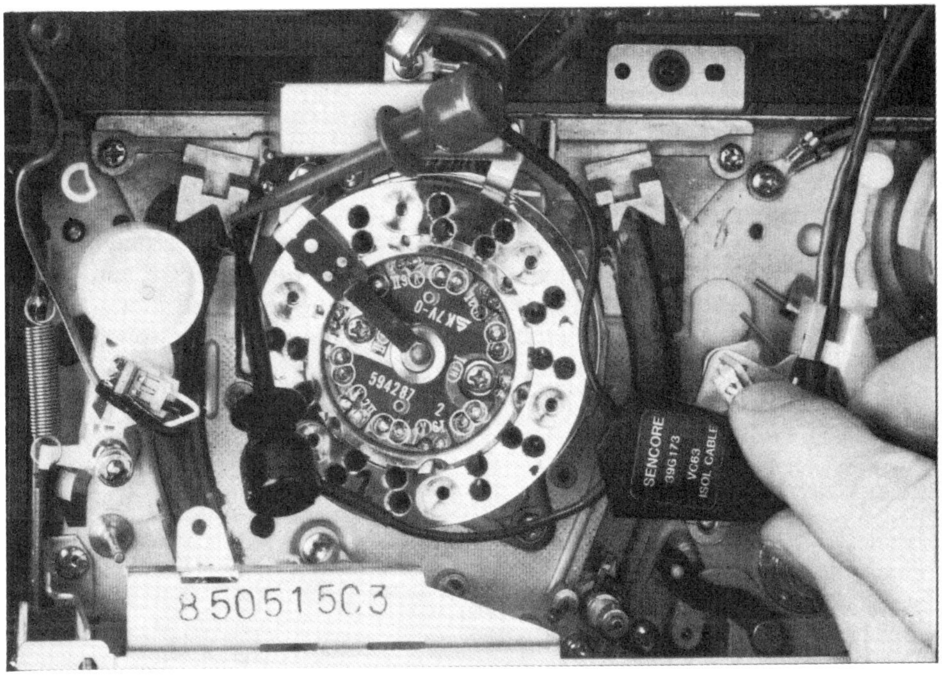


(a)

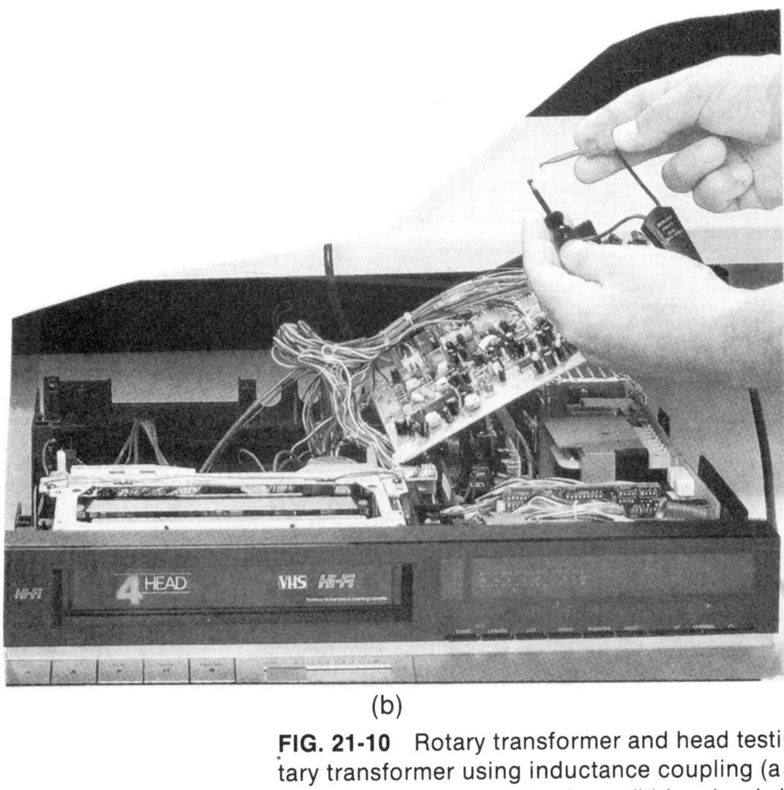


(b)

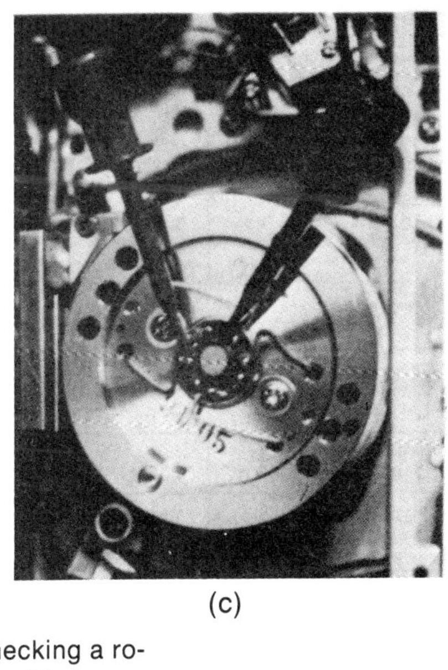

(c)

**FIG. 21-10** Rotary transformer and head testing: (a) checking a rotary transformer using inductance coupling (a snoop loop) between the signal source and the drum; (b) low-level signal injection as substitute for video heads; (c) preparing to inject signal into the PCB. (Courtesy of *Sencore News*.)

tape guides, a ridge worn into the drum, and clogging of the drum grooves). Clean the drum, the heads, and everything in the tape path.

*Need for Frequent Head Replacement.* Normal life expectancy: 1000 to 3000 hours. Besides normal wear, the usual causes of head breakdowns are excessive tape tension; operating the VCR in a dirty/dusty environment; frequent use of rental tapes that may be contaminated; poor-quality tapes (they flake readily); damaged tapes; infrequent or improper cleaning of heads and tape path; and overuse of abrasive head cleaner cassettes (see the section on preventive maintenance).

*No Playback.* (record function is okay)

***Probable causes:*** Defective or contaminated control track head; defective control track amplifier; defective video head switcher or loss of switching pulse; bad tape; loss of playback signal between switcher and channel 3–4 RF modulator (if loss of monaural sound playback only, suspect the AF playback amplifiers; if no stereo playback, suspect the audio head switcher, or loss of the switching pulse); defective modulator; system control problems; switching or cable problems between VCR output and antenna input of TV or monitor. TV or monitor tuner not set to channel 3 or 4 to match the VCR output.

Check and clean the control track head. Check the associated pulse amplifier. Try another tape. Check the head switching function (see the section on head switching problems). Signal trace the playback signal stages between the switcher and the modulator. Signal injection is necessary at the head outputs because the recorded signal is much too weak to observe on a scope. Use the lowest practical signal level. Concentrate on the monaural sound, stereo sound, luminance, or chroma stages as appropriate to the symptoms. Check or substitute a suspected modulator (if the inputs are okay but there is no RF output). Check the input and output play signals at the system microprocessor, and if suspected, replace the IC. Check the integrity of interconnecting cables and switches. Make sure that the TV or monitor tuner setting corresponds with the channel 3 or 4 selected at the VCR.

*Weak, Distorted, or Noisy Video Playback.* (record function okay)

***Probable causes:*** Bad tape; head switcher defect; problems with some signal stage between head switcher and modulator; bad modulator; switch or cable problems between VCR and TV or monitor; TV or monitor not *accurately* tuned to channel 3 or 4; improper adjustment of VCR tracking control; interference during playback. (*Reminder:* A recording problem can be mistaken for a playback problem. Play a good prerecorded tape. If it is okay, there is a record problem. If the playback is bad with a good tape, it is obviously a playback problem.)

Fine tune the VCR and TV tuners. Try another tape, although a bad tape generally means that the recording will also be poor. Check the function of the head switcher and the presence of switching pulses of the proper amplitude and waveshape (see the section on head switching problems). For a weak or noisy signal, check for loose VCR/TV interconnecting cable connectors or a bad switch. Simple ohmmeter checking will usually suffice. If appropriate, circumvent the switching by feeding the VCR directly to the TV input. Make sure that impedance-matching transformers and signal splitters are used properly. Trace all playback signal stages by injection. For a complaint of noise or distortion, scope check the waveforms. If the signal inputs to the modulator are normal but the output is weak or distorted, replace the modulator. *Critically* adjust the TV or monitor tuner to match the VCR channel 3 or 4 output. For dropout streaking, adjust the VCR tracking control. If streaking persists, discard the tape. Try to identify and correct the causes of interference. (*Note:* Symptoms of no picture but normal sound are rare, but *can* be caused by loss of the luminance signal.)

*No or Weak Video Record or Playback.* (drum spins and tape moves okay)

***Probable causes:*** Defective or contaminated heads or drum surface; bad rotary transformer; head switching problems; tape alignment problems; misadjusted tape tension or torque; improper hookup between VCR, cable system, and TV/monitor; loose, defective, or intermittent cable connectors; improper or defective impedance-matching transformer or signal splitter; servo problems; loss of switched B+; misaligned or magnetized heads.

Verify the presence of B+ at play/record circuitry. If not, check for logic control and possible PS defects. If there is no logic control, suspect the system control micro(s). Make sure of proper interconnections with the TV set, and so on. Check the video heads and the rotary transformer. Clean the heads. Check the head switcher and the switching pulse (see the section on head switching problems).

A frequency/speed error of drum or capstan

can also result in no picture. If suspected, check the servo systems for both record and playback (see the section on servo problems). Check particularly the PG and FG pulses for amplitude and waveform. If a Hall generator is used, check its outputs, comparing them with the schematic. Also check for a contaminated or defective control track head if the pulses are weak or otherwise abnormal. Where there is a *gradual* deterioration of picture quality, chances are that a thorough cleaning followed by complete alignment should clear up the problem.

*Picture and/or Sound Dropouts.* (streaks or "sparkles" obliterating strips of the picture; brief sound interruptions, popping sounds)

***Probable causes:*** Bad tape; contaminated heads; misadjusted tracking control; capstan servo phasing error; DOC (dropout compensator) problems. Do not mistake a misadjusted tracking control for a defective or contaminated head.

Play back another cassette for comparison. Adjust the tracking control. If necessary, adjust the tracking centering adjuster (with user thumbwheel control at the center of its range). Check the DOC detector and its associated circuit. (This circuit tries to compensate for tape stretching and the difference between VCRs by "fine tuning" the servo loops.) If unable to reduce or eliminate dropouts with the adjuster, replace the IC. If there are audio dropouts only, try adjusting the head, which can be extremely critical when combined with the control track head. This can also result in complete loss of sound.

Thoroughly clean all heads and the entire tape path. Retry the same tape. Try a new tape. If the tape was bad, discard it. (*Reminder:* Continued use of a bad tape or a dirty machine can result in serious damage.) If trouble persists, suspect a servo problem. Check the amplitude and waveshape of the capstan FG pulses, and associated control circuits, including the Hall generator if used, and the phasing control loop in particular (see the section on servo problems).

*Intermittent Record or Playback*

***Probable causes:*** Loose or corroded connections; hairline crack in PCB wiring; poor soldering, and so on; loose cable connectors.

Check security of all interconnecting cable connectors and antenna wires at tuner input board. Monitor the B+, logic, and signal voltages at all suspected stages, while tapping the chassis, gently probing, and so on. Try exerting gentle pressure to various points on all PCBs in an attempt to localize the problem. If localized, remove the PCB and examine for hairline cracks and resolder as necessary. Look for damaged or dirty PCB edge connectors and clean if needed (salt-spray corrosion is a common problem in seaside areas). Do the same for suspected module connector plugs. For other suggestions, see Chapter 5.

*Won't Record Sound.* (picture and playback function okay)

***Probable causes:*** Loss of audio signal in some stage between the sound takeoff (in the video IF strip) and the audio head(s) (the stationary head if a monaural problem; the audio AFM circuits if a stereo problem).

See if the safety tab is broken off the cassette. Signal trace all sound stages by injection. (The heads and rotary transformers are not suspect because the playback is okay.)

*Weak or Distorted Sound Recording.* (playback function okay)

***Probable causes:*** Defect in an audio stage as for no record function just described; loss of high-frequency erase head bias; magnetized head; head contamination or oxide clogging of grooves in the upper drum.

If stereo, compare the condition in the troublesome left or right channel with the channel that is trouble-free. For MTS/stereo defects, see Chapter 18. Refer to Section 21-1 for AFM troubleshooting procedures. Demagnetize the head(s), if suspected. (*Caution:* Heads may be destroyed if the demagnetizer gets too close or makes contact.) In record mode, check for erase bias at the head(s). If none, troubleshoot the bias generating circuit. If playback of a good tape is okay it could be a CATV problem. Check CATV reception with VCR turned off. Cable boxes often go bad.

*No Sound Playback, or Weak and Distorted.* (record function okay)

***Probable causes:*** Defect in some audio stage between the monaural head (or audio head switcher if hi-fi) and the input to the RF modulator; defective or misadjusted hi-fi head switcher (Figure 21-11); missing or abnormal switching pulses; uneven tape travel (see wow and flutter); defective modulator; TV or monitor slightly mistuned from channel 3 or 4; troubles with the TV or monitor audio or bad speaker(s). The heads are not suspect because the record function is okay.

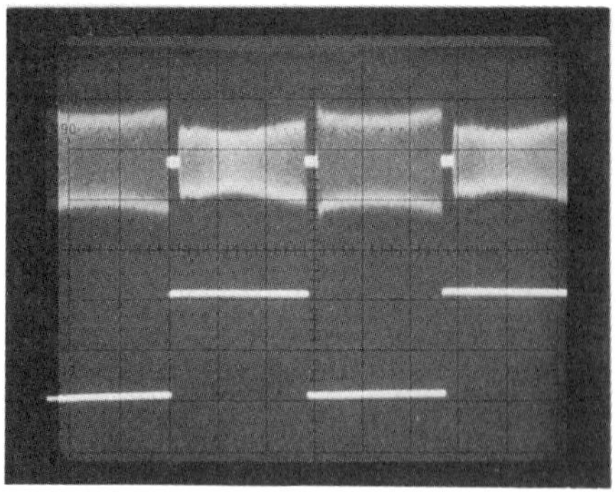

(a)

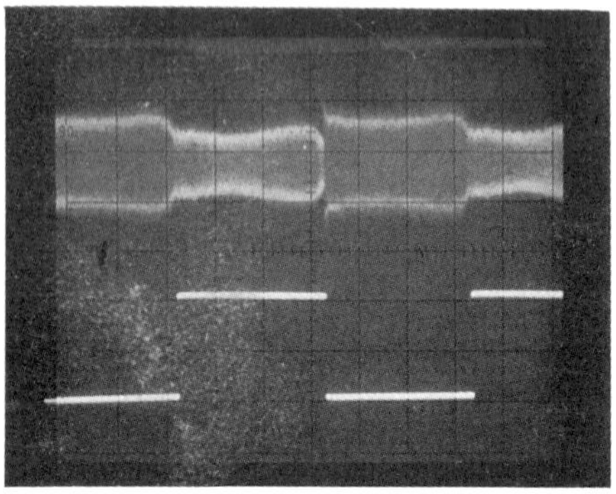

(b)

**FIG. 21-11** Hi-fi head switching waveforms: (a) incorrect audio head switching causes the signal from one head to drop out before the other audio head picks up the signal resulting in no or poor hi-fi audio; (b) when the audio head switching is correct, the AFM envelope is continuous, with no gap between the signal from the A head and the signal from the B head. (Courtesy of *Sencore News*.)

Note whether it is a mono or a hi-fi problem. Try another recording known to be good. Signal trace all suspected stages. If there is distortion, scope check the waveforms of an injected generator signal. If hi-fi stereo, compare the left and right channel circuits (Figure 21-6) for signal amplitudes and waveshapes. Try substituting with a good-quality audio amplifier and speaker system (a high-quality test tape can be useful here). If there is loss of high frequencies (or excessive hiss), check the Dolby/deemphasis/frequency compensator, HQ circuits, and AFM circuits as appropriate. Try switching the Dolby on and off for comparison. Replace these ICs if suspect. For audio dropouts, see the section on picture/sound dropouts. If the audio head switcher is suspected, see the section on head switching problems. If the modulator is suspect, replace it. Repair of this item is not advisable. *Critically* tune the TV or monitor to channel 3 or 4 and switch on the AFC. Verify the integrity of the TV/monitor audio capabilities.

*Wow and Flutter.* (undulating low-pitched sounds or pitch variations of treble frequencies)

***Probable causes:*** Uneven tape travel due to worn or slipping belts or tires that drive the capstan; defective capstan motor bearings; loose flywheel; poor regulation of capstan drive power; capstan imperfections; dry or worn motor or pulley bearings; pinch roller worn or contaminated with oil or dirt; insufficient roller pressure against tape; misadjusted tape tension or hub brake; bad tape slack sensor; bad speed select switch; defective cassette; stretched tape; tape sticking randomly to drum or other transport items due to moisture or oxide buildup; erratic operation of servo systems, although most VCRs mute the sound when the servos are not locked in.

Try another cassette. If the tape is too loose or tightly packed, tap the cassette against a hard flat surface to repack. Fully wind and rewind once or twice, then retry. If contamination is suspected, clean all components in the tape transport loop. Check the capstan motor for torque and smooth, quiet running. Check the tape tension and torque and adjust if required. Inspect the belts and tires, replacing any that are worn or cracked. Check regulation of the capstan drive power. Inspect the capstan for rough or flat spots and oxide buildup. Clean or replace if necessary. Inspect the pinch roller for dryness, cracks, flat spots, and oxide buildup. Clean or replace. Check for adequate spring tension. Check the action of the solenoid actuator. Check the tape tension and reel torque. Adjust the tensioner of the hub brake if needed. Check for a bad tape slack sensor. For dry pulley or roller bearings, apply light oil, sparingly, with a toothpick. Clean up any drips or seepage. If servo problems are suspected, proceed as described next.

*Servo Problems.* (wrong capstan or drum speed; picture streaking, tearing, or blanked out during playback—see Figure 21-12); "Donald Duck" sounds from the speaker)

***Probable causes:*** *There are many.* PWM (pulse-width modulator) problems; weak or missing PG, FG, or CTL (control track logic) pulses; defective or contaminated control track head; capstan or drum electromechanical defects; defective magnetic brake or its control circuit; misadjusted back tension lever (supply reel hub brake); loss of switched B+; servo misadjustments; frequency and phase control

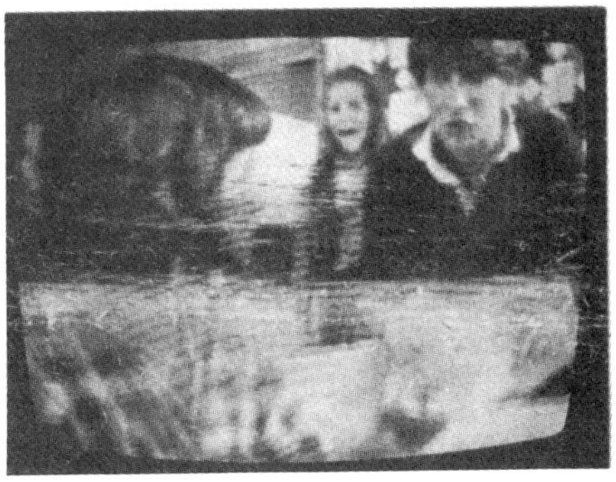

FIG. 21-12 Typical servo trouble symptom. Timing errors in the servo circuits cause increased video noise or tearing in the picture during playback.

circuit problems; phase detector problems and abnormal or missing dc error voltage.

As a first step, determine if it is truly a servo problem. As a rough check on servo operation and its ability to correct for errors, apply light finger pressure to the top of the drum and/or the capstan, to slow rotation. Observe any changes in the FG and PG pulses and the sound. For another check, mark a spot at the top of the drum, and in the record mode, operate the VCR under a fluorescent light. If servos are working, the mark will appear to be stationary (stroboscopic effect). If only a blur, there is a servo problem. Determine whether it is a drum or a capstan problem.

Picture noise and tearing is probably the most common servo problem, and it could be either the drum or capstan loops. Listen to the sound. If the problem involves both picture *and* sound playback (wow, flutter, etc.), suspect the *capstan* servo system. If there are only picture problems, with normal sound, suspect the *drum* servos.

As a first step, check the generated PWM pulses for amplitude and waveform. Check the operation of the phase detector in each loop and the dc error voltage developed. Check the speed control circuit and the motor drive amplifiers. For an incorrect error voltage, try substituting with an external power supply. Try breaking the loops and injecting a generator signal in place of the feedback signal. If the downstream stages now operate, the symptoms will change. If there is no response to the substituted signal, the trouble is between the injection point and the output.

Check for CTL, PG, and FG pulses. If CTL pulses are weak or missing, suspect the control track head or the pulse amplifier. Try cleaning the head, and if necessary, replace it, but only as a last resort. If PG or FG pulses are weak, missing, or have an abnormal waveshape, suspect the drum or capstan pickup coils or Hall effect generator ICs, as applicable, including the associated amplifiers. Try substituting the pulses with a suitable generator to see if normal operation can be resumed. Check the timing and adjust if necessary. For this, a frequency counter is required.

Check for smooth running of the capstan and drum motors. If there are torque variations, lubricate if necessary, but sparingly. Check for slipping, clutch, tires, and belts. Check the magnetic braking and its control circuitry. For a mechanical brake make the necessary adjustments.

*Sync Instability and Picture Noise.* (examples are: jitter, roll, horizontal pulling, and/or horizontal noise bar in picture)

***Probable causes:*** Contaminated heads; weak or abnormal head switching pulse; defective switcher; tracking error; improper tape tension.

Clean the video heads. Check the amplitude and waveshape of the head switcher pulses (see the section on head switching problems). Check and adjust the tape tension. Critically adjust the head azimuth if suspected. If trouble persists, troubleshoot both the drum and capstan servo systems for instability or frequency and phase errors. A quick check is to monitor the dc error voltage produced by the frequency and phase comparators while slowing the capstan motor or the drum with a light touch. Avoid touching the tape path surfaces.

For horizontal pulling (bending of vertical picture objects) make sure that the TV horizontal hold control is critically adjusted.

*Crosstalk on Playback.* (interference from adjacent video tracks, with thin fine lines on the picture)

***Probable causes:*** Improper azimuth adjustment of heads; head switching circuit defect; tape improperly positioned around the drum (tracking).

Adjust the head azimuth. Check the head switching function and switching pulse (see the section on head switching problems).

*Hum Problems.* (hum bar in the picture and/or hum in the sound)

***Probable causes:*** If on a recording, poor filtering of the VCR power supply, the TV/monitor, or the CATV converter box; if only on playback, probably poor filtering in the TV/monitor.

Check for open or dried-up filters or a bad active power filter (see Chapter 6). To isolate the problem to one of the three possible sources, check for hum with and without the VCR connected, and again with and without cable reception. Where hum is experienced only during CATV reception, it is probably coming from the converter box or ac pickup on the CATV lines, possibly from one of the CATV opamps. Although this is the responsibility of the cable company, determine which, by routing the box input cable directly to the TV with its tuner set on some UHF channel. Switch the converter off.

### No Fine Picture Detail (and imperfect color with picture noise)

***Probable causes:*** Bad tape; contaminated video head(s) or head switching defect (may only be playing back alternate fields); misadjusted heads; loss of supersonic erase bias or magnetized or contaminated erase heads if sound is also bad; improper tape tension; weak high video frequencies from signal source; defective video head preamp; problems with one of the luminance signal stages in the VCR; poor high-frequency response of TV or monitor used for playback; problems with S-VHS circuitry.

Determine if there is a problem with record, playback, or both by trying a recording known to be good. Clean and adjust the heads. Check for erase bias and if weak or absent, check the erase generator output. Clean and demagnetize the erase heads. Check the head preamps if suspect. Signal trace the VCR luminance circuits, and if warranted, replace the IC. Try another TV set/monitor for playback. If video head switching is suspect, see the section on head switching problems.

### Interference from Strong Local Channel 3 or 4

***Probable causes:*** Poor adjacent channel selectivity of TV or monitor tuner; pickup from a radiating RF modulator in a nearby VCR.

Switch the VCR and TV/monitor to the optional channel. If a problem with the CATV is suspected, try disconnecting the box while making an off-the-air recording. Reorient the antenna against the interfering station. Avoid the use of unshielded 300-Ω ribbon line.

### Dry, Squeaky Sounds during FF or RWD

***Probable causes:*** Dry pulleys; dry rollers in the tape path; warped cassette; dry reel bearings.

Try to locate the source of the sound with a length of tubing used as a stethoscope. Be careful not to interfere with the tape travel. Lubricate suspected pulleys, rollers, and motor bearings. Use oil sparingly and wipe up any excess *immediately*. See if the tape is scraping against the guides or the drum rabbet. Try another cassette.

### Playback at Wrong Speed

***Possible causes:*** Speed select switch or relay problem; defective or contaminated control track head; loss of control track pulses; no capstan FG pulses; defective capstan FG countdown circuit; faulty sensor.

Check and clean the control track head. Check for control track pulses and if weak or missing, check the pulse amplifier. Check for capstan FG pulses at the source and through the FG circuitry.

### No Color or Poor Color Recorded

***Possible causes:*** Loss of luminance or chroma signal; color killer problems; no color sync (see the section on the barber-pole-effect); defects in the VCR chroma stages that correspond to their counterparts in a TV set (see Chapters 15 and 16); loss of record control voltage; loss of head switching pulse; VCR or TV fine tuner misadjusted.

Check the input and output of the luminance/chroma IC. If suspect, replace it. Check for loss of the color record voltage. If the color killer is suspect, replace the ACK IC. Check the 3.58-MHz subcarrier. If far off frequency, complete loss of the picture can result. Try the adjustment. If suspect, replace the crystal and/or the IC. Check the head switching function (see the section on head switching problems). Fine-tune the TV and VCR for channel 3 or 4.

### No Color or Poor Color on Playback. (BW picture okay; records color okay)

***Possible causes:*** Playback tracking is off; head contamination; improper head switching; bad RF modulator; luminance or chroma circuit defects; servo problems; misadjusted TV fine tuner.

Check for improper phasing of capstan and drum servos on playback. Clean the heads. Check the head switching pulse and switcher function (see the section on head switching problems). Check the input and output of the chroma playback IC. If suspect, replace it. If the chroma is okay at the modulator input and it is suspect, replace it. Fine-tune the TV to channel 3 or 4.

If no color (or poor color with snow) while using TV only, see if the TV/VCR switch is inadvertently set to the VCR position.

### *Barber-pole Effect.* (color bars on the picture)

***Possible causes:*** As for TV (Chapter 16); frequency or phase error with the 3.58-MHz oscillator; AFPC misalignment; weak burst signal; unstable head switching.

Check and adjust the 3.58-MHz oscillator. Replace the crystal and/or the chroma IC if suspect. A serious frequency error usually results in no picture. A phasing error upsets the color tint. If necessary, perform a complete AFPC alignment (see Chapter 16). Check the head switching function (see the section on head switching problems).

### *Interference on Record or Playback.* (RF or electrical)

***Possible causes:*** RF interference (narrow, black, diagonal lines through the picture) from a transmitter or other RF source (e.g., CB or ham station, harmonics of local broadcast station or crosstalk on CATV lines; static sounds and dots or streaks in the picture from power-line transients, electrical equipment, razors, vacuum cleaners, car ignition, fluorescent lights, and so on; and, of course, dirty heads and switching problems.

If there is interference on playback, the cause may have been present during recording or is being picked up by the TV/monitor at the time of playback. Determine which, by trying another recording and monitoring TV reception. For RF interference, try adding a high-pass filter at the antenna input and reorient the antenna. Use a shielded lead-in. If CATV problems suspected, compare reception from an antenna. Check with the cable company. One common cause is the use of inferior, poorly shielded signal splitters or A-B switches. For electrical interference try to locate the source, and if possible, add filters. Try installing a power-line filter at the TV and VCR, and a surge (spike) protector and a good earth ground for line transients. Avoid using the VCR during severe electrical storms, and as an added precaution, ground the antenna.

### *Weak, Noisy Picture and Background Hash*

***Possible causes:*** If only during record, it may be a noisy fringe-area location; poor antenna system; CATV or satellite system problems; misadjusted VCR fine tuner; VCR or TV tuner defects; bad tape; contaminated heads; one head defective or switching problems (only alternate fields are reproduced); tracking problem; weak luminance signal.

Noise and picture tearing are the most common servo problems. If there is a playback problem (with a good prerecording and the record function is okay (as tried on another machine), suspect the playback head circuits, including the rotary transformer, a head preamp, switcher or an abnormal switching pulse, and the FM luminance IC. Replace any that are suspect. A normal switching pulse is about 5 V p-p at 30 Hz. For possible timing errors, adjust the tracking control.

For recording problems, check for a weak antenna or cable input signal. (An indoor antenna should not be used.) Check the VCR and/or TV tuners and fine-tune as appropriate. Try another tape. Clean the heads. Check for imperfect servo phasing, particularly the amplitude and shape of the FG, PG, and control track pulses, their comparison, and resultant error voltage.

### *Special Effects Problems.* (other functions okay)

***Probable causes:*** For pause (freeze frame) problems, suspect the pause control relay (it may be stuck open or closed), its associated control circuits, or a bad system control microprocessor. For slow motion, or forward/reverse speed search problems, suspect a capstan phase error instability, an incorrect capstan motor speed, or reel motor drive problems. An incorrect drum speed is another (but less likely) possibility.

Procedures depend on the kind of problem. For remote control problems, suspect the system control microprocessors. Try another remote transmitter (see Chapter 12). For the others, consider the following, as applicable. Check the pause control relay function. Check the servo timing and adjust if needed. For motor speed problems, check operation of the braking systems and for a sticking solenoid. Adjust if needed. This can be a critical adjustment. Where control logic is questionable for any functions, check the inputs and outputs of the system control microprocessor ICs and replace if suspect.

### *Sudden Mode Changes*

***Possible causes:*** Defective sensors or microprocessors; bent arms or switch levers; end of tape is reached.

Many strange and inexplicable actions can result from a sensor that is not doing its job or a bad system control microprocessor. And these are the things to suspect when the VCR suddenly starts to rewind, goes into the stop mode, or spews out the cassette during a normal record or playback session. Of course, if the dew light is flashing, the reason is obvious.

Before jumping the gun and replacing a micro, however, first make sure that it is not getting wrong inputs from the sensors. Bad sensors and bent arms and levers are common problems. Incorrect programming of the timer or express record can result in an abrupt shift to rewind. Most VCRs will rewind when the counter reaches 0000, 9999, or the end of the tape.

*Digital Display Problems.* (real-time, timer, and counter readout problems)

***Probable causes:*** Defective display unit (generally not repairable), its operating voltages, logic control, or driver circuits; missing or improper inputs from clocks and timer and tape counter as applicable; defective timer microprocessor. (*Reminder:* The reset resets both the timer and the display.) Loss of start/stop of a recording may be caused by a power outage. Another possibility is a user programming error or failure to reset.

If there are no readouts, suspect the display unit or loss of voltage. If only some functions are not working, check for loss of the corresponding inputs. Check for a 4-V p-p 32.8-kHz oscillator signal at the timer IC. If timer IC, its crystal, or the system control microprocessor ICs are suspect, replace them. Check the timer backup battery if provided.

*Remote Control Problems.* Try a new battery or substitute for the transmitter (see Chapter 12). Check the operation of the remote receiver in the VCR. If there is trouble with only one or several functions, concentrate on the related circuits.

*Conditions Worsen after Cleaning or Repairs.*

***Probable causes:*** Improper cleaning procedure that damaged heads or contaminated the tape or transport devices; improper demagnetizing of heads; tape alignment and tension may be disturbed; inadvertent wiring errors or shorts (e.g., solder splashes) created during component replacements, or wrong types or values of components; damage to mechanical parts (bent arms, etc.), PCBs, or sensitive solid-state devices from inadvertent shorts or static charges when troubleshooting (see Chapter 5).

*Electronic Problems (General).* Feel all suspected transistors and ICs. A hot transistor or IC is usually defective, but a bad one does not always run hot. Make voltage and ohmmeter tests at the terminals, comparing readings with the schematic. Check for defects external to a suspected IC, and if none, replace it.

For high B+ voltages, check the line voltage. Check the voltage regulator(s) and the possibility that some circuit is not drawing current. For loss of B voltage, check for shorts, particularly the transistors and ICs. Frequently, such shorts or those created by careless probing of live circuits can result in catastrophic failures where numerous components are destroyed. Although not always required, use an isolation transformer when servicing. (*Reminder:* Frequent electronic breakdowns are often due to high operating temperatures or line surges. Check the ventillation and install a surge protector. For other hints, see Chapter 5.)

## 21-3 PREVENTIVE MAINTENANCE

Most VCR breakdowns can be prevented or forestalled by proper maintenance, both routine and periodic, particularly operating the VCR in a suitable environment and with regular cleaning. For the tapes, a little commonsense TLC with proper handling and storage also pays off in many hours of trouble-free use. Cleaning and other procedures are covered in the following paragraphs.

### VCR Maintenance

Operate the VCR in a warm, dry, dust-free environment. To prevent condensation, avoid extremes in temperature and never insert a cold cassette in a warm machine. Do not operate the VCR under direct sunlight or near other heat sources that can destroy sensitive electronic components. Make sure that the ventillation openings are not obstructed. Clean the outside at least weekly, being careful not to get dust inside. A dust cover is a worthwhile investment. Prevent small children from inserting small objects in the cassette loading door, where insects can also gain access to create problems. Inspect for such things any time the cover is removed. Periodically check the belts for cracks and stretching. Watch that coffee cup and cigarette ash! Liquid spills can be disastrous. Contamination of the heads and other items in the tape path (by dust, dirt, and oxide flakings) is a common problem that calls for frequent cleaning. Less frequent requirements include head demagnetizing and lubrication of moving parts.

Observe antistatic precautions when checking around sensitive ICs. Be careful to avoid shorts while testing live circuits. Remove power when connecting and disconnecting components and test equipment. Failure to heed such warnings can open up a real can of worms! When troubled with power surges, install a "spike" protector at the ac plug-in.

### Tape Maintenance

Use only the best-quality tapes. Inferior brands have a relatively short life and flake readily, resulting in poor recordings and playback, and eventually, damage to the VCR. Stretched tapes create similar problems and should be discarded. After each use, and periodically thereafter, completely rewind the tape to repack the loops and take up any slack. Where problems develop, strike the flat side of the cassette against a hard surface to repack, then wind or rewind once or twice. Avoid opening the cassette flap and touching the tape. Broken or crinkled tape can be spliced but should be avoided since a bad splice can damage the heads. If a tape has creases or is worn out (poor-quality recordings with many dropouts), discard it. Completely rewind the tape after each use and after a lengthy storage period. Wipe the cassette frequently and store upright in a warm, dust-free environment well away from magnetic fields such as speakers motors, and soldering guns in use. Even the flux from a TV degauss coil can weaken or erase a tape during the first few seconds of TV turn-on.

### Head and Tape Path Cleaning

Tiny bits of dust, lint, cigarette ash, or oxide particles can adhere to or lodge in the head. As the buildup increases, the gap between the head and the tape widens, degrading both picture and sound. A badly clogged head can even result in complete loss of picture and/or sound. In time the buildup becomes permanent, necessitating head replacement.

For prevention and to maintain the quality of recordings, the heads and tape path should be cleaned when needed—how frequently is debatable. Some claim that it should be done periodically; others say only when symptoms develop. But the jury is still out.

Periodic cleaning is done using either a wet or dry head cleaning kit, avoiding the more abrasive dry types that cause undue head wear and shorten life. Where rented tapes are used frequently, clean more often. (*Reminder:* Heads are *extremely* fragile and must be treated with respect.)

A more thorough cleaning should be done whenever the VCR cover is removed and after several months, depending on usage. Unplug the VCR. Use only a proper swab (chamois or cellular foam) saturated with Freon, denatured alcohol (*not* isopropol rubbing alcohol), or a fast-evaporating typewriter cleaner. *Never* use cotton swabs on the heads (the lint can entangle and lodge in the pole piece). Using gentle pressure, wipe the pad *sideways* against the head in the direction of tape travel, *never* up and down. Repeat for each of the stationary heads.

To clean the drum heads, hold the fluid-impregnated pad lightly against the head(s) while slowly turning the drum. To prevent contamination, avoid touching the heads or sides of the drum. Clean the drum surface to remove any buildup in the grooves or on the rabbet.

Clean other items in the tape path: the capstan and pinch roller, the tape guides, and the drum surface. Cotton swabs and a lint-free cloth are okay for this operation. Allow time for the cleaner to evaporate before operating the VCR. A hair dryer, used judiciously, can speed it up.

### Lubrication

Whenever required, oil such items as motor bearings, pulleys, and rollers. Apply oil sparingly with a toothpick. Avoid getting oil on belts, tires, and anything that contacts the tape. Clean up spills or seepage immediately. Use light grease on the gears.

### Demagnetizing the Heads

A magnetized head cannot function properly and produces symptoms of poor recordings and playback. The condition is hard to verify, and when suspected, the usual approach is to degauss, needed or not. A special demagnetizing probe is used but never use one designed for audio recorders. They are much too powerful and can destroy the heads. Follow this procedure: Switch off the VCR. Slowly approach the head to be degaussed. When no closer than 3 feet, energize the probe. Slowly approach the head with the probe tip but *never closer than $\frac{1}{2}$ inch.* Strong vibrations and direct contact with the head can shatter it instantly. After a few seconds, slowly back off, and when about 3 feet distant, cut the probe power. Repeat for each head, including those on the drum. An alternative procedure for checking drum heads was described earlier. (*Reminder:* Keep the energized probe far removed from all cassettes.)

## 21-4 FINAL CHECKOUT

After repairs are completed, make a final "burn-in" check. Try all modes, noting anything abnormal. Critically evaluate the picture quality and stability and both mono and stereo sound. Check for excessive noise or dropouts on both picture and sound. Check for cleanliness. If a bad tape is found, discard it. Check timer operation by programming it for a short period. For an intermittent condition, make every effort to locate and correct the problem, even when it appears to clear up. Most such problems reappear later, which can be costly and embarrassing. As a memory peg, refer to a previously prepared burn-in checklist. Keep a maintenance log for future use, recording such things as symptoms, repairs made, and any maintenance performed.

## QUESTIONS

1. A worn-out or damaged tape can damage the VCR. Explain.
2. Explain the need for cleanliness and frequent cleaning of the heads and other items in the tape path.
3. If one video head is defective or contaminated, you get a noisy picture of poor quality. Explain.
4. Give the proper procedure for demagnetizing a head.
5. List several symptoms that can be caused by a servo timing error.
6. What servo system would you suspect (drum or capstan) if the complaint involves (a) both picture and sound; (b) picture only? Explain your reasoning.
7. For VCR troubleshooting you need a properly operating TV set or monitor and a good-quality prerecorded tape. Explain why.
8. What is crosstalk, and how is it prevented?
9. Explain dropouts and how you would proceed.
10. What tests would you make before considering head replacement?
11. Give several symptoms that *might* indicate a defective or contaminated head.
12. How would you proceed where the trouble symptoms are: picture rolling or tearing and pulsating sound?
13. List several possible causes for (a) loss of picture; (b) BW picture but no color.
14. State the possibilities where mono sound is okay but there is no stereo during playback.
15. Explain head contamination: the causes, probable results, and remedies.
16. Symptom: Audio distortion when the VCR/TV switch is on VCR but okay at the TV position. State the possible cause and how you would proceed.

# 22 Projection television

## 22-1 PROJECTION TV FUNDAMENTALS

Projection TV sets, with their large screens, are fast becoming popular with the viewing public. Besides being a status symbol, they are particularly suited to large living rooms and viewing by large audiences, as in bars and conference halls. Such sets have been around for many years but until recently never enjoyed wide acceptance for a number of reasons: lack of brightness and picture contrast, poor focus, faded and fuzzy colors, a restricted viewing angle, and severe picture degradation unless viewed straight on. Modern sets, although still not as bright as direct-view receivers, have largely overcome these shortcomings as well as incorporating most state-of-the art features: for example, increased brightness and color intensity; uniform focus over the entire screen surface; all the latest refinements resulting from technological breakthroughs; enhanced video, increasing the scanning lines to well over 500, an essential ingredient for good resolution on life-sized images; innovations based on digital wizardry as described in Chapter 19; PIP; still-frame images; channel search; and so on; and, of course, MTS/stereo.

There are two basic kinds of projection receivers: front and rear projection. Early models used a single CRT whose limited light output was greatly reduced by the necessary optics. Modern sets have *three* CRTs, resulting in greatly improved brightness and picture quality and a wide viewing angle. A rear projection receiver is the preference of most home viewers.

### Front Projection

With this system (Figure 22-1), the three CRTs with their attached lens assemblies are mounted in a cabinet which is critically positioned (at a precise focal distance) in front of an opaque aluminized screen onto which the image is projected. Some sets have a large plane mirror that reflects the images from the three CRTs onto the screen.

### Rear Projection

A rear projection set is completely self-contained, and with a system of lenses and mirrors the image is projected internally from behind the screen and viewed from the front (see Figure 22-1). Except for the difference in optics and the means of projection, both front and rear projection receivers are basically alike.

Much of the information contained in the following paragraphs applies to a late-model front-view receiver (Mitsubishi model VS-464 R), which reflects the current state of the art. In general, the functions and circuit descriptions also apply to other high-performance sets presently available. Some of the features of this set are noted briefly as follows. They are described in more detail later.

- *Power supply(s)*. Besides the primary PS, there are numerous secondary PSs. Most of them are regulated and protected with fuses.

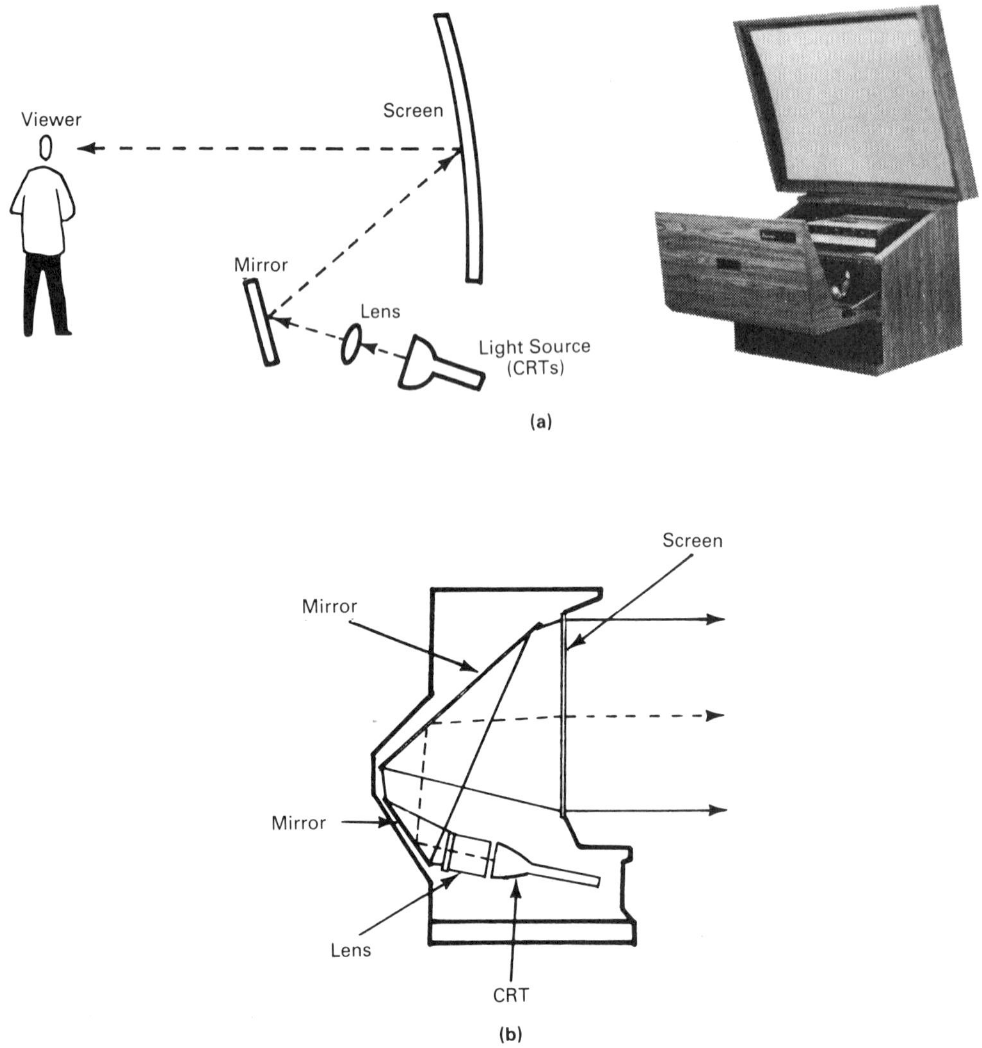


**FIG. 22-1** (a) Front and (b) rear projection systems. (Courtesy of Mitsubishi.)

- *X-ray protection*. As for all sets where voltages exceed 16 kV, special circuits are used to sense hazardous conditions and to shut down the receiver.
- *Extensive use of ICs*. This particular set has about 35 ICs, most of them multifunction types.
- *Comb and SAW filters*. These are used for optimum separation of the luminance and chroma signals to obtain a high-quality picture.
- *Parabolic generators and keystone amplifiers*. With projection sets, such circuits are essential to obtain a linear rectangular raster.
- *MTS/stereo and audio expansion*. These provide state-of-the-art stereo separation and high-quality sound. Audio muting is also provided.
- *Video displays*. Channel number and time of day are displayed on the screen.
- *Channel selector*. A cable-ready, frequency-synthesized tuning system is provided.
- *Remote control*. This is a typical all-function IR type of system, including up-down search, sap and mono/stereo select, menu display, and so on.

## 22-2 SYSTEM COMPONENTS

The main components (other than those found in a conventional direct-view TV) are identified and described in Table 22–1.

**TABLE 22-1**

Projection television components

| Component | Description and Function |
|---|---|
| Picture tubes (light tubes) (see Figure 22-2) | Three 5-inch high-intensity magnetically focused, liquid-cooled single-gun CRTs mounted side by side as an assembly; the screen of each CRT is coated with either a red, green, or blue phosphor, corresponding to one of the three primary colors; each CRT produces a single-color image which is projected with a series of lenses and a mirror onto the rear of the viewing screen; as with conventional TV, white and the various complementary colors are a mix of the three primaries |
| Liquid coolant (coupling) | The coolant (Figure 22-2) is an integral part of each CRT assembly; the coolant (ethylene glycol) is contained in the space between the CRT screen and a lens; its purpose is to prevent overheating and damage to the screen coating by the high-intensity electron beam |
| CRT gun assemblies | Mounted on the neck of each tube is a conventional deflection yoke, centering ring, focus coil, and a focus alignment magnet; a convergence yoke is part of the deflection yoke |
| Optical lens assembly | Each of three lens assemblies is comprised of several lenses positioned in front of each CRT; their purpose is to magnify and focus an image onto a plane mirror; each assembly has its own optical adjustment (not to be confused with *electron beam* focusing by ES/EM focus adjusters on each CRT neck) |
| Mirror (one or two, depending on type of set) | Flat (plane) mirrors mounted at an angle in front of the CRTs; the combined images of the three CRTs are reflected from the mirror(s) onto the rear of the viewing screen (see Figure 22-1); a mirror "tilt" adjustment is provided to obtain a distortion-free raster at the screen surface |
| Viewing screen | The screen is comprised of two components: a Fresnel lens, which receives the image from the mirror, and a lenticular screen, which directs the image to the viewer; a Fresnel lens consists of a number of concentric grooves (prismatic rings) which greatly increase its light-gathering properties and help to reduce reflections from ambient lighting (see Figure 22-3); the lenticular screen has embossed vertical grooves to distribute the light into horizontal bands with little or no vertical spread; the lens and the screen are sandwiched together |
| The electronics | Except for some added features peculiar to projection sets, circuit functions are essentially the same as for a conventional direct-view receiver |

## 22-3 RECEIVER OPERATION

Except for the three separate CRTs and the optical system, operation is not too different than for a conventional set. Each CRT is individually controlled and has its own external gun components, which must be individually adjusted (Figure 22-4). The cathode of each CRT is driven from a separate RGB output amplifier, as for the three guns in a tricolor tube. Because of the high beam intensity, the CRTs can be damaged if there is a loss of deflection. A protective circuit disables the set if deflection is lost for any reason on any of the CRTs. As with conventional sets, x-ray protection is provided with a shutdown circuit.

There are other similarities and differences. With conventional TV, the single-color images from the three guns in the CRT converge at the phosphor-coated screen to produce white and a mixture of colors. With projection TV, three separate tubes are used, each producing one of the three primary colors. You can think of each projection CRT as a single gun in a tricolor CRT. The single-color images combine at a mirror, to be reflected or projected onto a large screen.

With conventional TV the deflection angles of the three images from the three CRT beams is constantly changing and must be compensated for. With projection TV the problem is much the same—directing three images from three separate CRTs so that they overlap precisely and converge into one, for perfect registry at the screen surface. With direct-view receivers, this is accomplished by controlling the three beams within the CRT. With projection sets it is done with lenses and mirrors. The green CRT projects its image to the center of the screen; the red and blue tubes project from the sides. Unlike a conventional TV set, this creates problems of raster distortion [keystoning (pie-shaped) and pincushion or bowing] which must be corrected for. A sampling of several circuits with brief descriptions is contained in the following paragraphs.

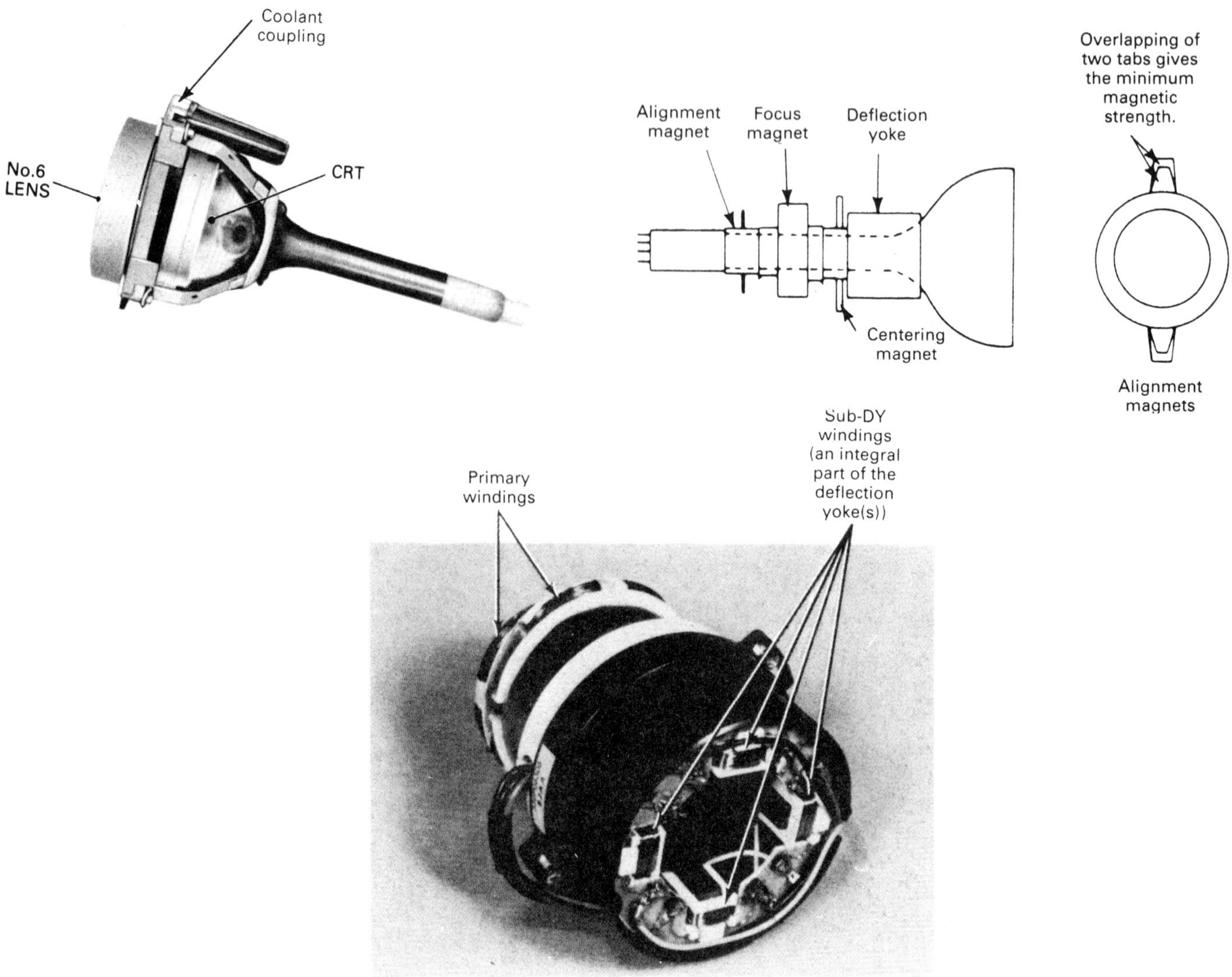


**FIG. 22-2** Typical light tube and associated components. (Courtesy of Mitsubishi.)

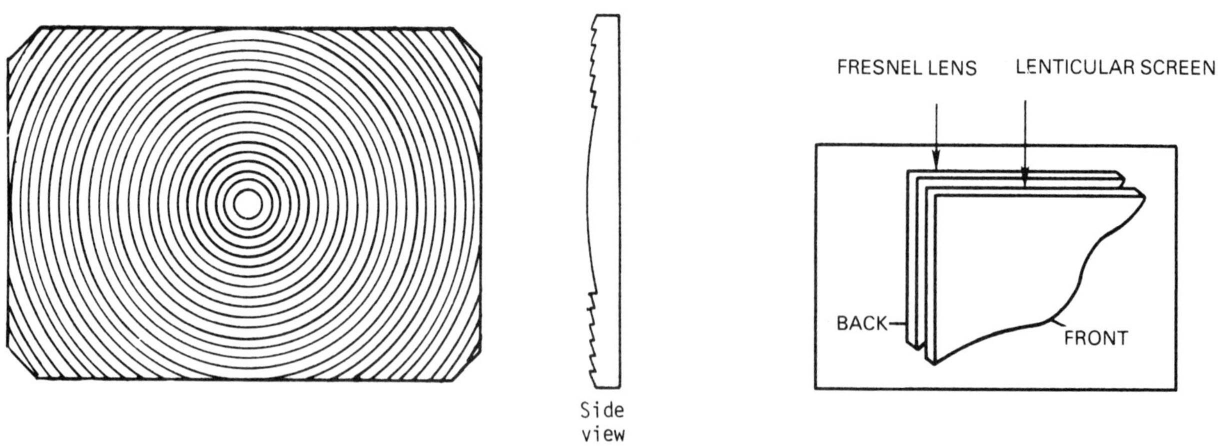


**FIG. 22-3** Rear projection viewing screen.

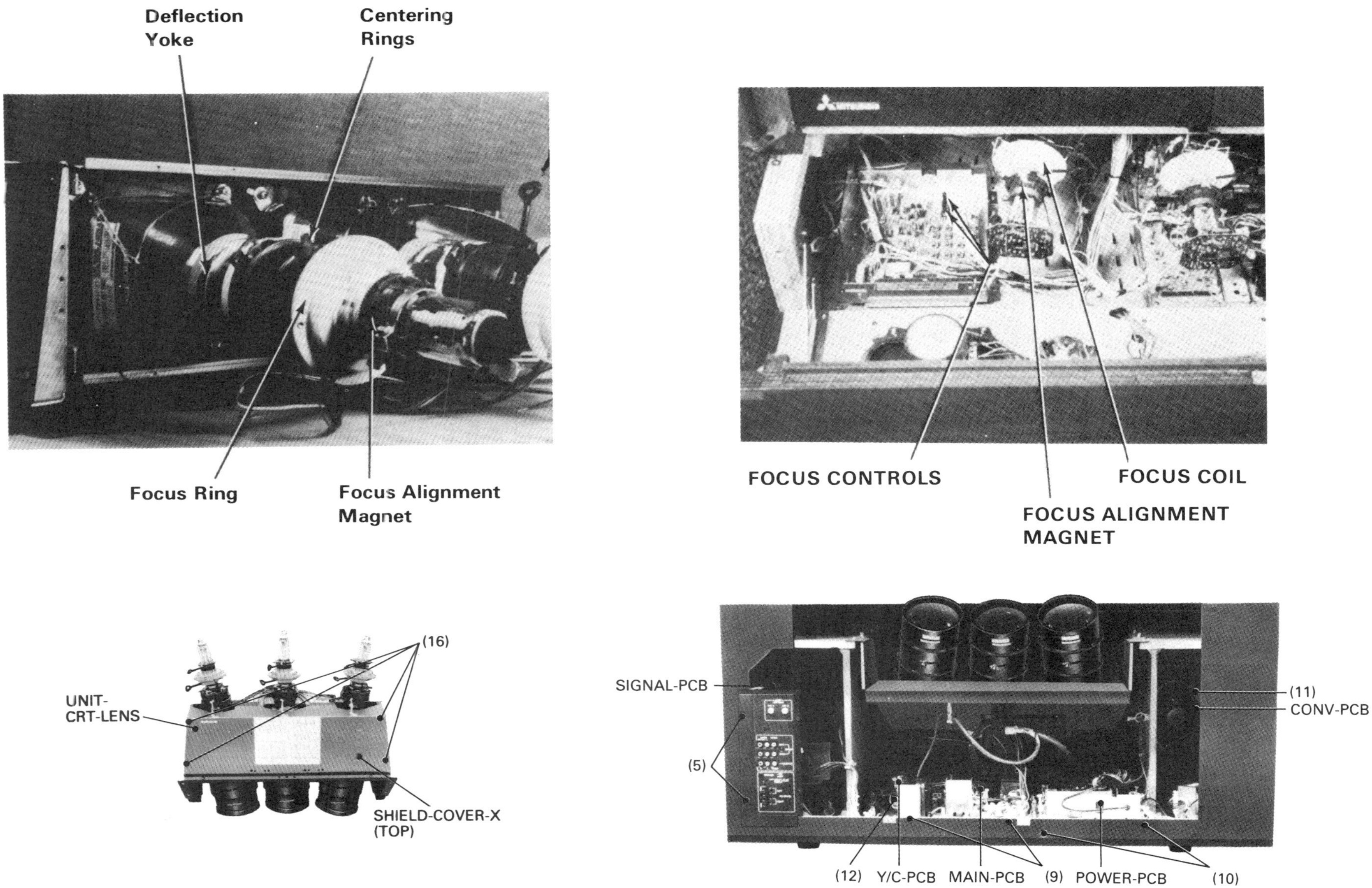


**FIG. 22-4** CRTs and adjusters (Courtesy of Mitsubishi.)

## 22-4 POWER SUPPLY

A typical projection set has several primary power supplies plus a number of scan PSs. The CRT heaters are supplied with scan power. The HV for all three CRTs come from a common source. This is also true for the vertical and horizontal sweep circuits. Most of the dc outputs are regulated using either discrete components or regulator ICs. Fusible resistors are used extensively as protection against overloads. Blooming can be a serious problem with this type of set because of the high beam currents, which go as high as 1 mA or more. This in turn makes it difficult to obtain good focus, convergence, and white highlights in a picture—hence the need for good low- and high-voltage regulation.

The sample set PS schematic is shown in Figure 22-5. Except for the 110-V dc supplying the horizontal output stage, most of the voltages are in the range 12 to 50 V and are obtained from bridge rectifiers. Note that power turn-on is via a power relay at the ac input.

## 22-5 HV REGULATION

With projection sets in particular, blooming and focus problems are common where the HV regulation is even marginally poor, especially noticeable on large white images and at high brightness levels. To prevent such problems, the sample set uses the circuit shown in Figure 22-6.

As with most sets, HV regulation is achieved by controlling the B+ applied to the collector of the horizontal output transistor. With this circuit, T591 functions as a *saturable reactor* with primary current flow established by the conduction of transistor Q509. The degree of saturation and therefore the amount of effective inductance of the reactor is dependent on the amount of primary current. The reactor transformer secondary is an integral part of the resonant collector circuit of the horizontal output transistor Q591. Variations of primary current produce changes in inductance which alter the frequency, which in turn increases or decreases the HV. The controlling factor is the conductance of Q509, which responds to control voltages developed by the preceding network of transistors. These, in turn, operate from a sensing voltage developed across the HV voltage divider at the left of the diagram.

### HV Safety Circuit

Excessive HV can produce dangerous x-radiation and damage or destroy components. One protective circuit in use is shown in Figure 22-7. Here the HV is monitored and sampled from a voltage divider, which in turn triggers the thyristor Q410 into conduction and effectively shorts out the B supply to the horizontal oscillator. A disabled oscillator kills the HV and the set shuts down. Startup/shutdown circuits are described in Chapter 11.

## 22-6 TYPICAL IC

Figure 22-8 shows the largest (42 pins) of the many multifunction ICs used in the sample set, along with portions of the related circuitry and discrete components. The functions performed are shown in circuit (b) with arrows indicating signal flow. As is customary, normal voltages are indicated for each pin connection. Measuring all voltages and comparing with the schematic are standard practice before contemplating replacement of a suspected IC.

## 22-7 TYPICAL CRT AND DRIVER CIRCUIT

The circuit shown in Figure 22-9 is essentially the same for each of the three CRTs and their driver amplifiers, and not too different from that of a conventional color set. For a functional description, see Chapters 15 and 17.

## 22-8 REMOTE CONTROL

The IR system used is the same as that found in most modern sets. Figure 22-10 shows a typical transmitter unit where all functions are performed by a single discrete transistor and an IC. Note the variety of functions initiated from the numerous buttons. The IR pickup and recognition circuits contained in the receiver proper are conventional, as described in Chapter 12.

## 22-9 CONVERGENCE

Static convergence (for center portion of the screen) is accomplished with front-panel convergence controls and raster centering magnets. For convergence at the edges of the screen, special dynamic convergence coils are incorporated within the deflection yoke. These coils are energized by parabolic waveforms generated by keystone and pincushion/bowing circuits. Convergence adjustments are provided and used in conjunction with mirror adjusters to ob-

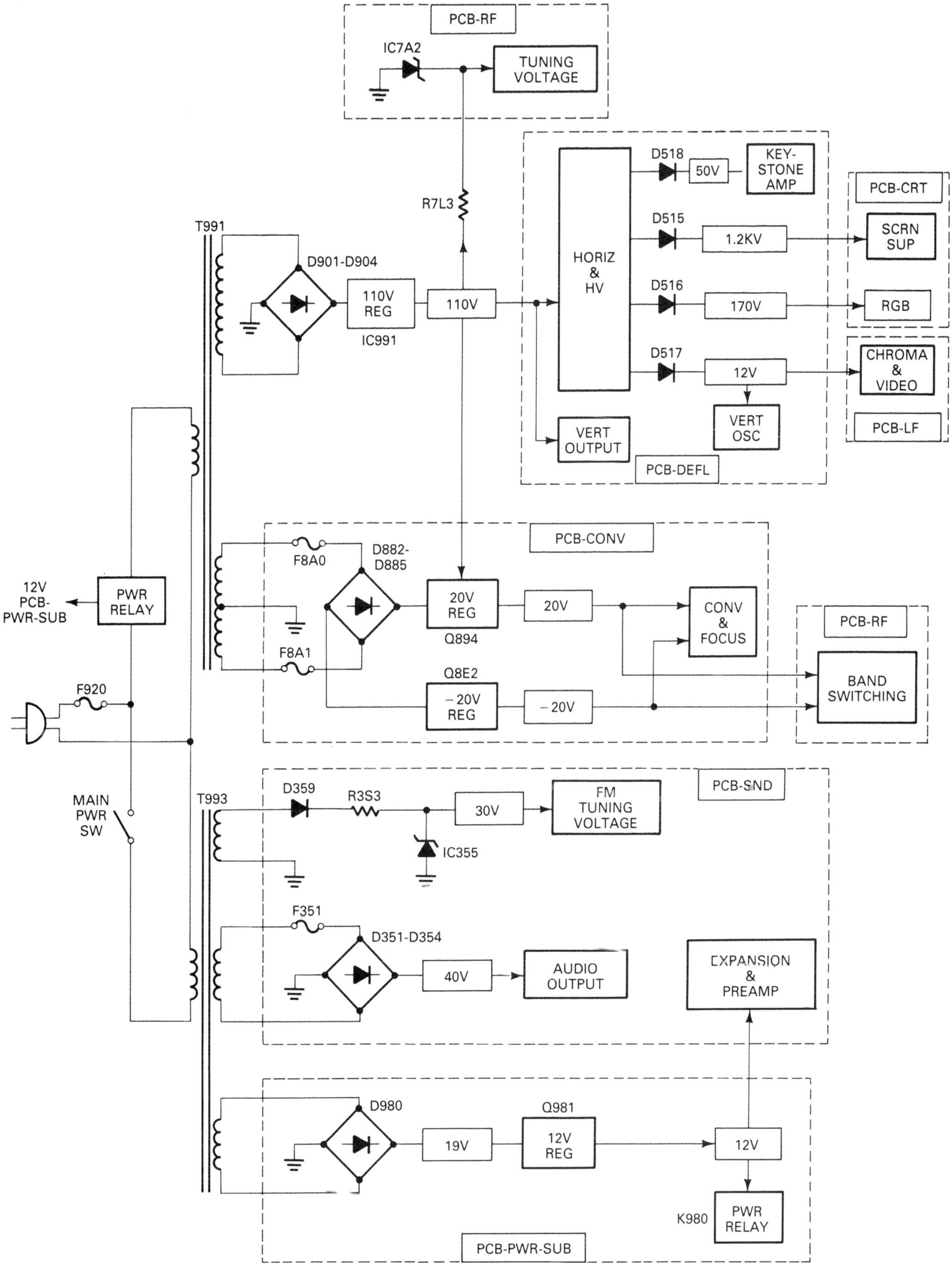


**FIG. 22-5** Power supplies and voltage distribution: the common denominator of all stage functions. (Courtesy of Mitsubishi.)

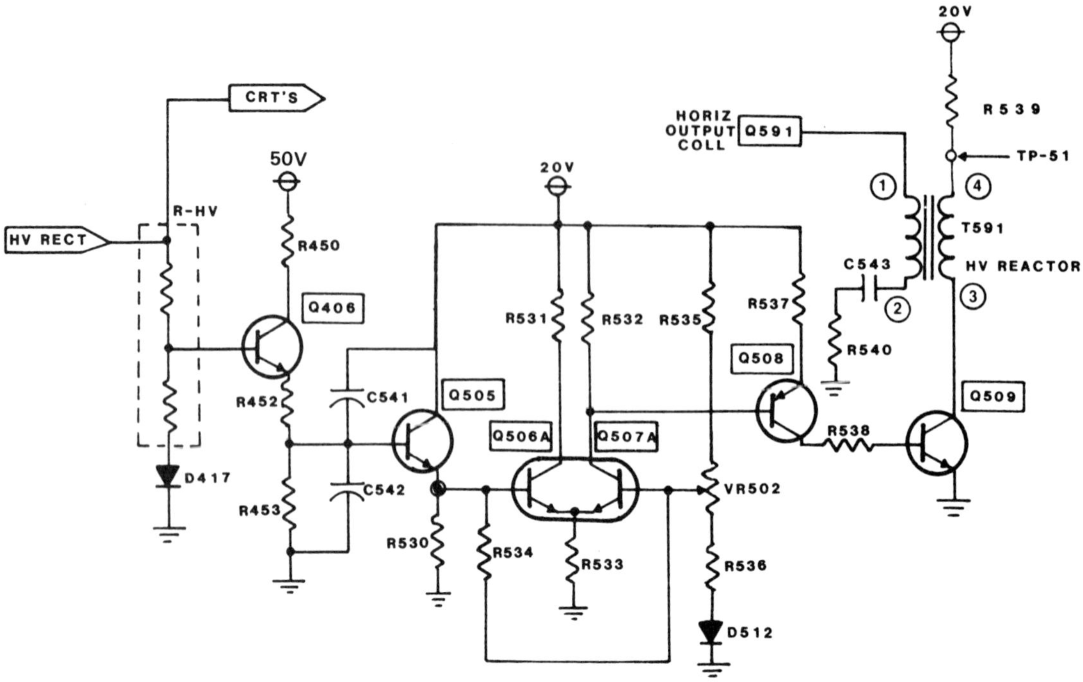


**FIG. 22-6** HV regulator. Near-perfect regulation is especially important to the operation of projection receivers. (Courtesy of Mitsubishi.)

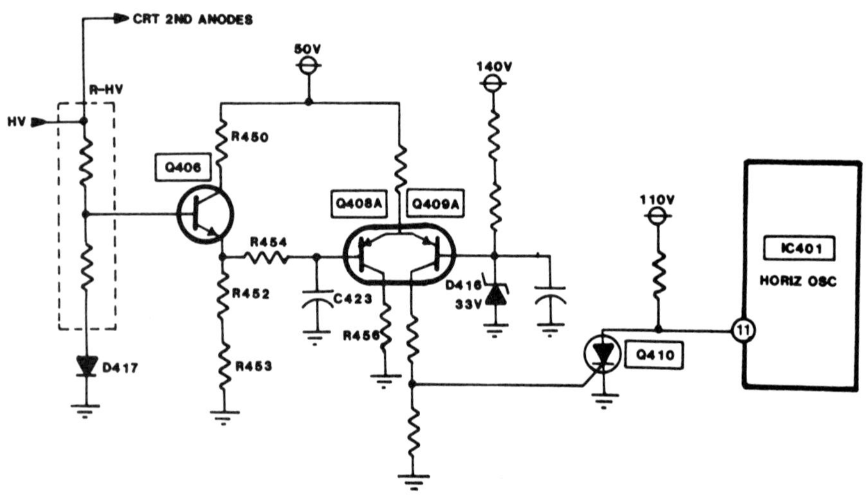


**FIG. 22-7** HV protect circuit. Such circuits protect against x-radiation and damage to the set and expensive CRTs. (Courtesy of Mitsubishi.)

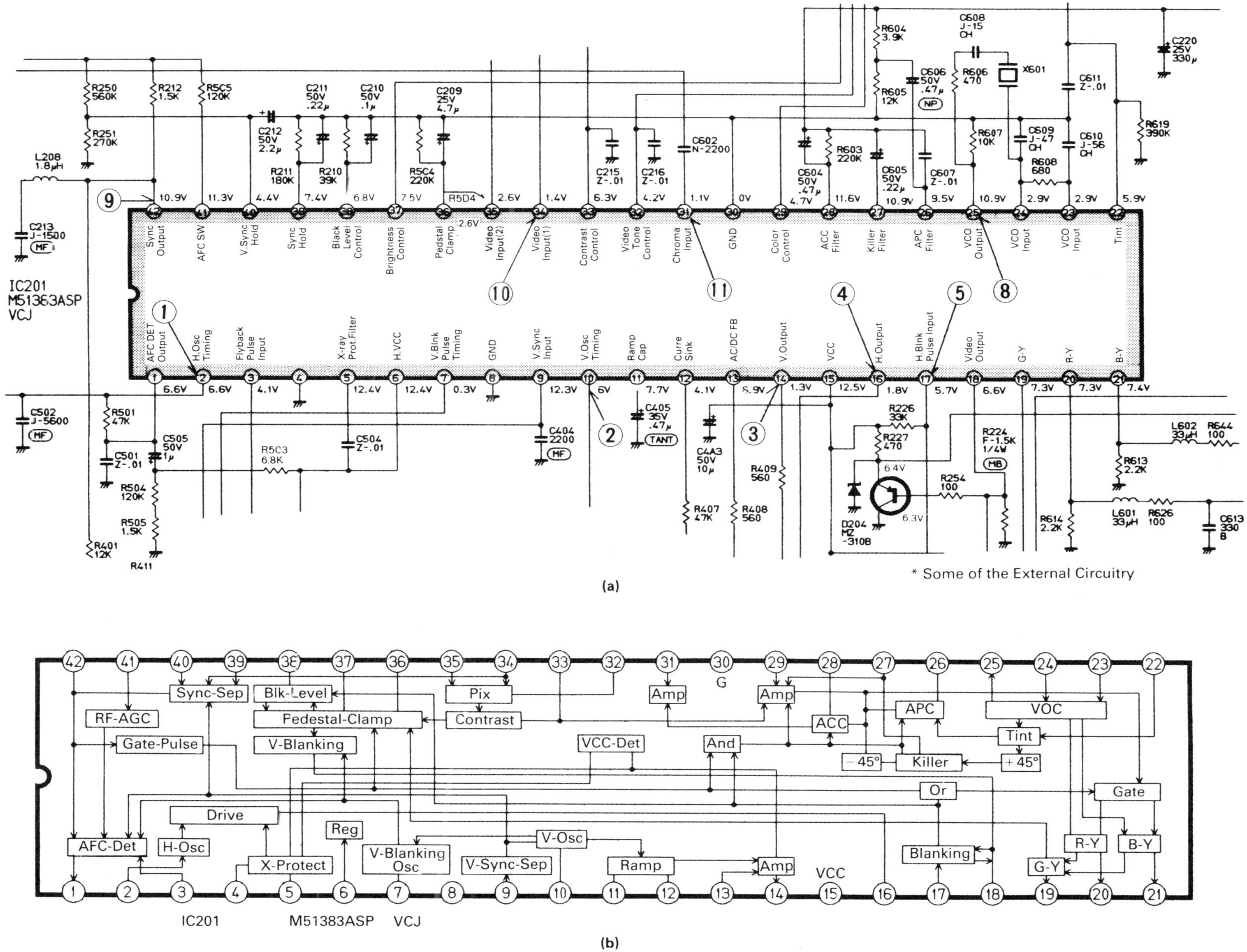


**FIG. 22-8** Typical multifunction IC: a good example of modern technology. (Courtesy of Mitsubishi.)

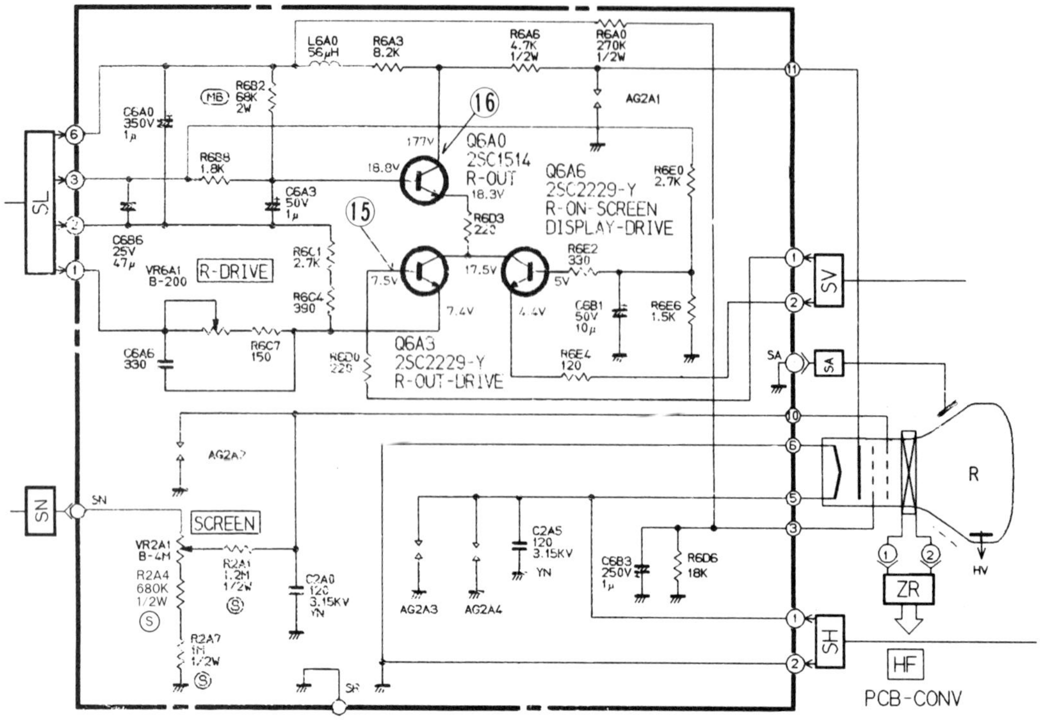


**FIG. 22-9** Typical CRT and driver circuit. This is but one of the three CRTs and output amplifiers. The green and blue circuits are similar. (Courtesy of Mitsubishi.)

tain a properly shaped raster that is free of distortion. When this is achieved, the three overlapping images on the screen will be in registry (converged).

## 22-10 TROUBLESHOOTING, ADJUSTMENTS, AND MAINTENANCE

### Troubleshooting

Troubleshooting the electronic functions is essentially the same as for a conventional direct-view TV. Refer to other chapters as applicable. The main difference is problems involving the three CRTs and the optical system adjustments. Typical problems in these areas with appropriate procedures are shown in the flow drawing of Figure 22-11. These are general procedures and are not necessarily applicable to all makes and models. For specifics on replacing certain items, such as the CRTs, refer to the service manual. (*Caution:* Do not attempt to measure HV at a CRT outlet. The lead is bonded to the glass, and breaking the seal will result in arcing and damage to the tube.)

### Adjustments

There are three categories: *raster* adjustments (height, width, linearity, etc.), *convergence,* and *focus.* All are critical and important to obtaining a good picture. Each is considered in the following paragraphs.

Focus is a major concern with projection sets, and special procedures are required for setting up and adjusting the three CRTs and their optical systems. As with conventional TV, good focus is impossible if there are problems other than misadjustment: for example, incorrect CRT operating voltages, one or more weak or magnetized CRTs, blooming, and poor LV and HV regulation. Such conditions must be corrected *before* any adjustments are attempted. As with a weak gun in a tricolor CRT, reduced emission in one or more CRTs can make it difficult or impossible to get good white highlights on a picture and proper color tones. Adjustments can compensate to some extent but not always. Replacing one weak tube only serves to compound the problem because the strong color overwhelms the others, resulting in a color-tinted raster, poor tracking, faded white objects, and loss of some secondary colors.

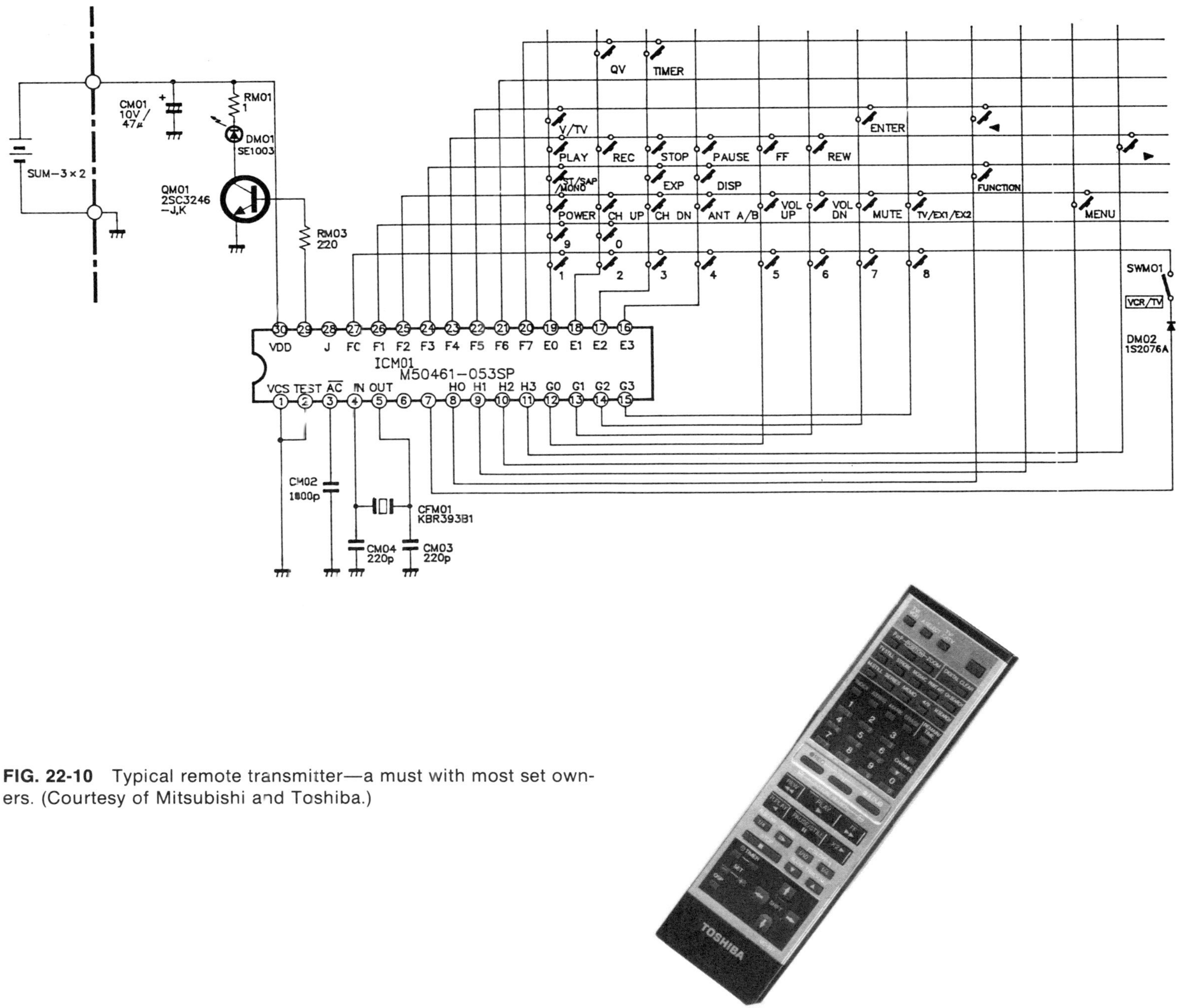


**FIG. 22-10** Typical remote transmitter—a must with most set owners. (Courtesy of Mitsubishi and Toshiba.)

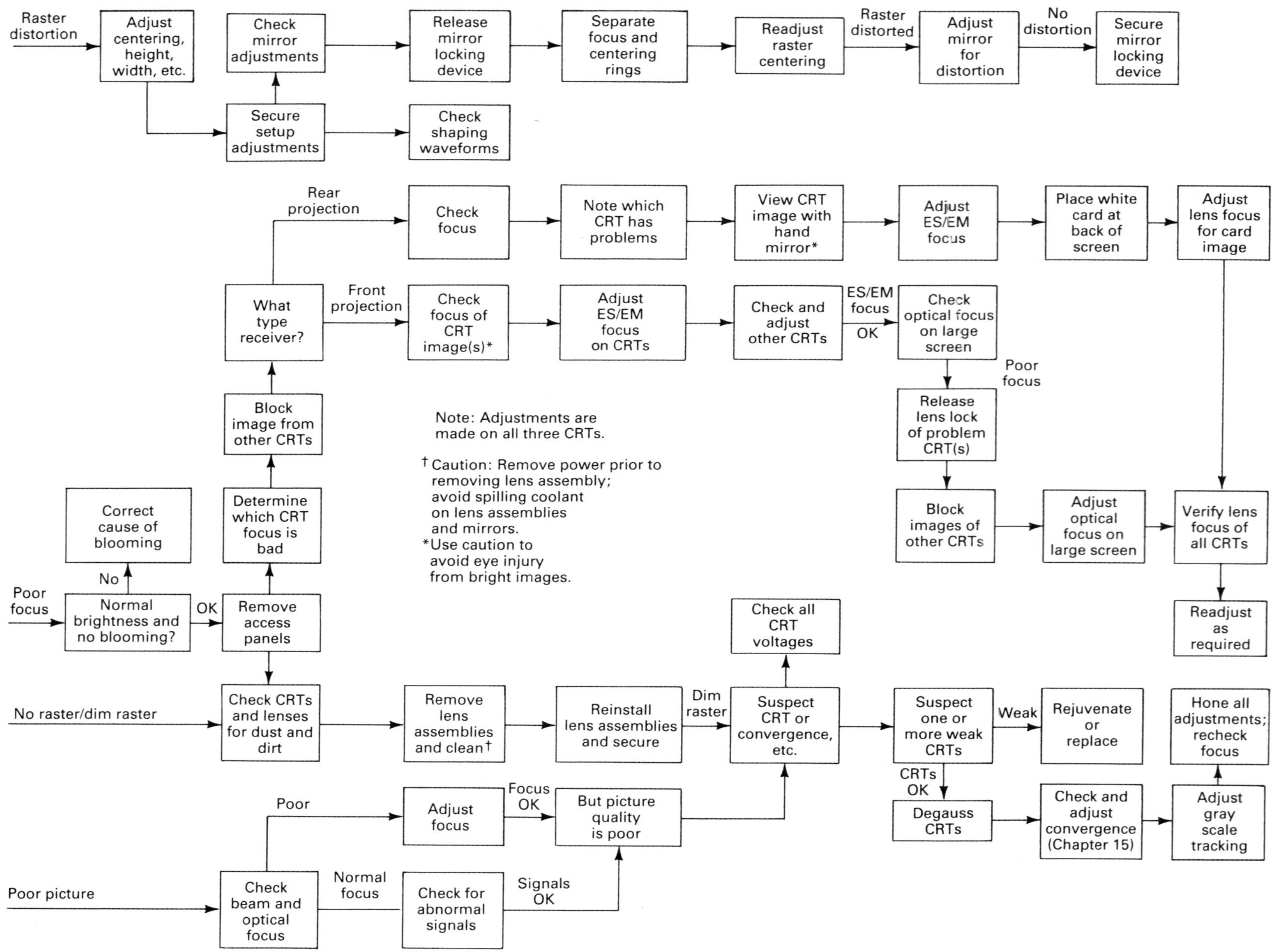


**FIG. 22-11** Projection receivers: troubleshooting and adjustments.

There are two kinds of focus, beam focus and optical focus, and each must be done separately and in the proper order for each of the CRTs individually. Early-model sets used ES (electrostatic) focus; modern sets use a combination of ES and EM (electromagnetic) focus (Figure 22-4); the latter is obtained by adjusting the amount of current in the focus coils. Focusing of each CRT is done while blocking off the image from the two CRTs not being worked on. It is a two-step procedure: first the beam focus while observing (with caution) the face of the CRT, followed by optical (lens) focusing while observing the reflected or projected image on the large screen.

Except for the three CRTs (instead of three beams in one tube), convergence (the precise overlapping of the three single-color images) is much the same as for conventional TV. The setup and adjustments are performed in the following sequence. For specifics, refer to the receiver service manual.

*Preliminary Adjustments.* With all components on the neck of each CRT in their proper relative positions, and after performing any necessary cleaning, the following adjustments are made *for each CRT:* raster centering, tilt, height, width, and vertical and horizontal linearity. Try to correct any raster distortion, particularly keystoning and pincushion/bowing (Figure 22-12). A fine correction is made by adjusting the tilt angle of the assembly holding the three CRTs. When completed, tighten and secure all locking devices.

*Adjusting for White Balance* (Gray-Scale Tracking). When tuned to a BW program, the RGB screen grid, brightness, and drive controls are adjusted for the brightest whites in the picture with no color contamination on the raster.

*CRT Beam Focus.* This is done by observing focus conditions *on the face of each CRT.* **Warning:** To prevent eye damage from the high-intensity light, prolonged viewing of the bright image must be avoided. Proper focus is achieved by rotating the focus magnet on each CRT (to obtain sharply defined scanning lines on the face of each CRT). This is followed by the adjustment of the alignment magnets on rear of each CRT gun.

*Optical Focus.* Generally, this is only required after replacing a CRT or its lens. While viewing a BW program *on the screen,* the lens of each CRT is adjusted individually while covering the face of the other two to obtain a single-color raster. Concentrate only on the raster(s) that are out of focus. To facilitate the adjustment, the image can be viewed on a large white card held directly behind the screen.

*Raster Centering.* The three color rasters are centered on the screen using the centering magnets on each CRT individually, while preserving proper registry.

*Raster Tilt.* Each CRT yoke is turned to obtain proper tilt with raster edges parallel to the screen edges.

*Static Convergence.* After degaussing each CRT and adjusting vertical linearity (with a cross-

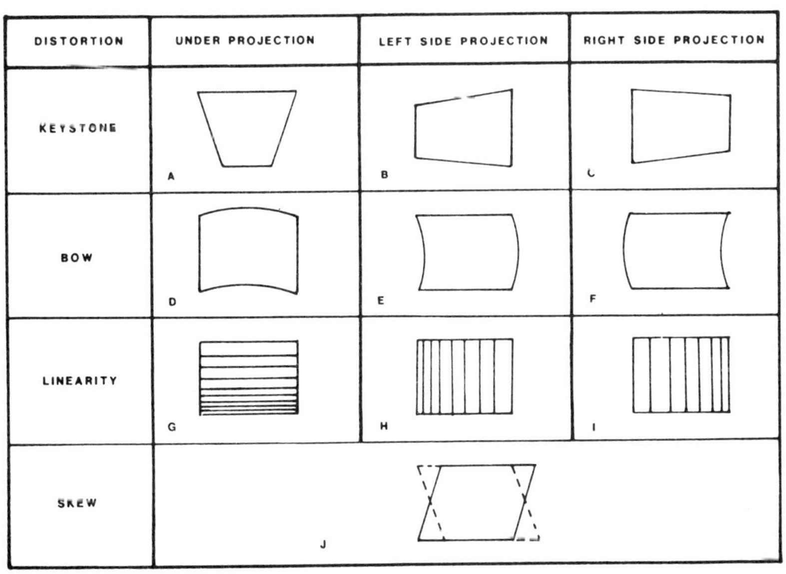


**FIG. 22-12** Examples of raster distortion. (Courtesy of Mitsubishi.)

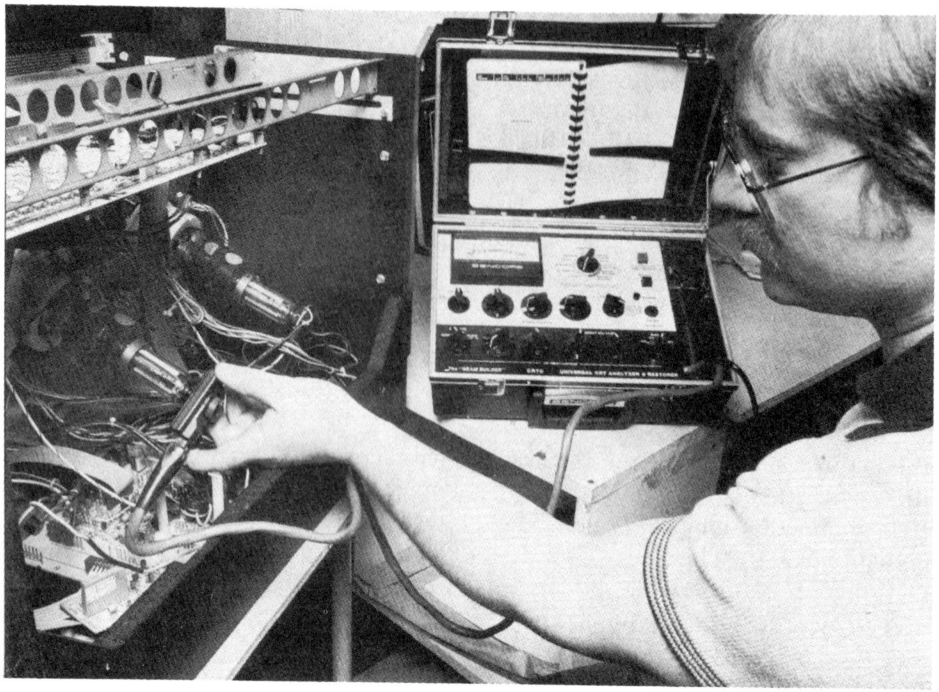

**FIG. 22-13** Testing and restoring CRTs. With one weak light tube it is impossible to obtain a good picture. (Courtesy of *Sencore News*.)

hatch generator), convergence of the three beams is accomplished with the front-panel converge controls and the RGB centering magnets. Unless *each* of the three CRTs has good emission, it is impossible to obtain pure white and true colors. The CRTs are expensive, so instead of replacing one weak tube, try rejuvenation (Figure 22-13).

*Dynamic Convergence.* Convergence adjustments are made (by converging two colored images at a time) using the RGB controls provided. Because of interactions, this must be done several times in conjunction with other adjustments just described.

*Gray Scale (White Balance Adjustments).* Cutoff bias of the CRTs is determined by the screen control adjustments. White balance is adjusted on a BW picture using the drive controls as with conventional TV. The white balance observed varies with the viewing angle.

### Tuned Circuit Alignment

Tuned circuit adjustments of a modern set are few in number and seldom get out of whack unless indiscriminately tampered with or after replacing an associated component. To obtain good picture resolution with an enhanced-type receiver, the bandpass of the luminance and chroma stages is of particular importance, as is the adjustment of certain traps. Where alignment is needed, refer to the general procedures outlined in previous chapters, and more specifically, those presented in PHOTOFACTS or the manufacturer's literature. Figure 22-14 shows the equipment necessary and the hookup to obtain a proper response.

### Cleaning

With projection sets, cleanliness is a must. When magnified, dust particles, lint or hairs, and fingerprints really show up on a large screen. To maintain a bright image, the exposed surface of each lens, the mirrors, and the large screen should be cleaned every time the set (or light box) is opened up for repairs. *Before* working on the set, remove dust accumulations with a vacuum cleaner, being careful not to strike or disturb any of the optical components. Carefully remove dust from the optics with a soft brush or a lint-free cloth. For smudges and blemishes, use soap and water or a liquid glass cleaner. Never use abrasive soap powders. If a lens assembly is removed from its CRT for any reason, clean both items before reassembling. Be careful to avoid spilling the coolant, which can damage certain parts. If any seeps into the lens holder, it can cloud and blur the image.

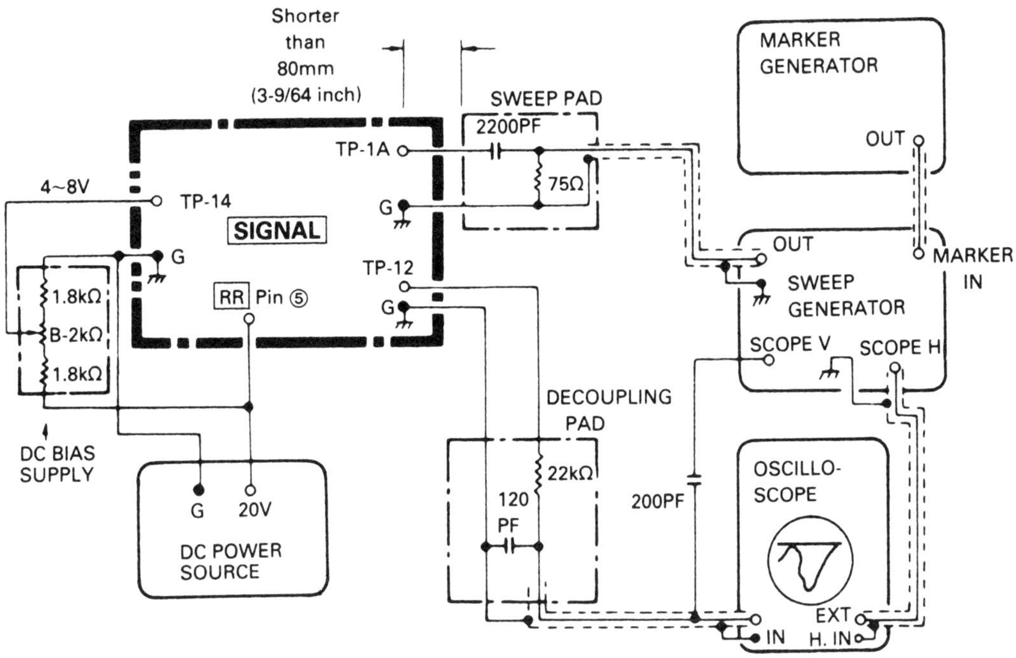


**FIG. 22-14** Tuned circuit alignment hookups. Tuned circuit alignment requires extensive know-how and special test equipment. (Courtesy of Mitsubishi.)

## QUESTIONS

1. What two kinds of focus adjustments are made for each CRT in a projection set?
2. Why do modern projection sets use three tubes instead of one?
3. What adjustments correct for raster distortion, particularly keystoning and bowing?
4. Explain the similarities and differences in converging projection and conventional TV sets.
5. Explain the coolant coupling device used with each light tube.
6. It is not possible to get a good picture if only one weak CRT is replaced. Explain.
7. What is the purpose in covering two CRT lenses when adjusting the third lens?
8. Why do projection sets use single-gun CRTs?
9. What precautions are taken in receiver design to prevent screen burning by the high-intensity beams?
10. Tricolor conventional CRTs have only one deflection and convergence yoke. A projection set has three of each. Explain.
11. Why is the viewing screen made in two parts?
12. Explain the purpose of (a) the lens assembly; (b) plane mirrors.
13. A projection set should be used and serviced in a clean, dust-free environment. Explain.
14. Briefly explain the step-by-step procedures for setup and adjustment of a projection set.
15. What components make it possible to obtain a blown-up image from the relatively small CRTs?
16. Briefly explain color mixing and how and where all secondary colors are derived from the three primary colors.
17. Explain the term *picture registry* and how the single-color images from the three CRTs are made to converge at the screen surface.
18. Give several possible causes where good convergence cannot be obtained.

# Glossary of terms

**AC** Alternating current. Standard 120-V 60-cycle (Hz) U.S. household current. Also called line voltage. VTRs and cameras often use the 60 Hz as a horizontal sync reference.

**ACC** Automatic color control.

**ACK** Automatic color killer.

**AFC** Automatic frequency control.

**AFM** Audio frequency modulation.

**AGC** *See* Automatic gain control.

**ALC** Automatic level control (same as AGC).

**Alignment tape** Special manufacturer's tape containing picture and sound reference signals to use in aligning a VCR.

**Analog** A signal that varies in frequency and amplitude.

**APC** Automatic phase control.

**Aperture grill** Screen-like feature of Sony Trinitron and other TV sets which controls the amount of electrons that hit the phosphor coating of the TV screen.

**Aspect ratio** Numerical ratio of picture width to height.

**Attenuate** Reduction of sound or picture levels.

**Audio** Sound portion.

**Audio dub** Recording of sound only, without disturbing the picture.

**Audio head** Magnetic recording head that records or plays back sound.

**Audio in** Audio input jack.

**Audio mixer** Device that allows the simultaneous combining and blending of several sound inputs into one or two outputs.

**Audio out** Audio output jack.

**Audio track** Portion of the videotape that stores the sound.

**Automatic gain control** Automatic circuit that controls the audio or video intensity during recording.

**Azimuth** Angle of a particular recording head.

**Back porch** That portion of the composite picture signal which lies between the trailing edge of the horizontal sync pulse and the trailing edge of the corresponding blanking pulse.

**Bandwidth** Number of cycles per second expressing the difference between the limiting frequencies of a frequency band. For example, the 2.0–3.0-MHz band has a width of 1 MHz.

**Beam** Flow of electrons in the camera or TV tube.

**Blacker-than-black** Amplitude region of the composite video signal below the reference black level in the direction of the synchronizing pulses.

**Black level** Bottom portion of the video waveform, which contains the sync, blanking, and control signals.

**Blanking (picture)** Portion of the composite video signal whose instantaneous amplitude makes the vertical and horizontal retrace invisible.

**Blanking level** Level of the front and back porches of the composite video signal.

**Blooming** Defocusing of regions of the picture where the brightness is at an excessive level, due to enlargement of spot size and halation of the fluorescent screen of the cathode ray picture tube.

**BPF** Bandpass filter.

**Bulk eraser** A device for quickly erasing a taped recording.

**Burst** Color burst. High-frequency pulses (3.58 MHz) that determine the phase of the color signal.

**BW** Black and white.

**Cable TV** Television signals transmitted primarily by cable instead of antennas.

**Capacitance** Electronic circuit that stores a charge.

**Capstan** Roller and rotating shaft in the VCR that is motor-driven and determines the speed at which the tape is moved through the VCR.

**Capstan servo** Speed control system.

**Carrier** RF/IF unmodulated (cw) wave.

**Cathode-ray tube** Electron tube assembly containing an electron gun arranged to direct a beam onto a fluorescent screen. Scanning by the beam can produce light at all points in the scanned raster.

**CATV** Cable TV.

**Chroma (chrominance)** Hue or saturation (intensity) of color.

**Clamper** Device that functions during the horizontal blanking or sync interval to fix the level of the picture signal at a predetermined reference level at the beginning of each scanning line.

**Clamping** Process that established a fixed level for the picture signal at the beginning of each scanning line.

**Clipping** Shearing off of the peaks of a signal. For a picture signal this may affect either the positive (white) or negative (black) peaks. For a composite video signal, the sync signal may be affected. Also, a circuit that eliminates excessive variations in the video signal.

**Coaxial cable (coax)** Standard single-ground, single-conductor cable which is used for most video connections. Technically referred to as 75-Ω type RG-59U cable.

**Color bars** Series of colored bars of calibrated signal that is used as a reference for brightness, contrast, color intensity, and correct color balance. Usually generated electronically.

**Color difference signals** Resultant R-Y, G-Y, B-Y signals after subtracting the (Y) luminance signal.

**Color lock** Circuit that stabilizes the color hues during playback.

**Color phase** Timing relationship of the color signal. The correct color phase will produce the correct color hues.

**Color subcarrier** The 3.58-MHz carrier frequency that contains the color signal information.

**Color sync** Complete reference and control signal necessary to record and reproduce color—3.58 MHz (contains the color subcarrier also).

**Comb filter** circuit used to separate the chroma and luminance signals.

**Comparator** Circuit for comparing frequency and phase of two signals.

**Compatibility** Ability of one piece of equipment to interface with another (interchangeability).

**Composite sync** Complete sync containing both horizontal and vertical sync signals.

**Confetti** Multi-colored snow on a TV picture.

**Contrast** Range of light and dark values in a picture, or the ratio between the maximum and minimum brightness values. For example, in a high-contrast picture there would be intense blacks and white, whereas a low-contrast picture would contain only various shades of gray.

**Control track** Portion of the tape containing the speed control pulses.

**Control track head** Head that records or plays back the control track pulses.

**Control track pulses** Speed control pulses created by the VCR.

**Crosstalk** Undesired signal interfering with the desired signal.

**CRT** Cathode ray tube. Vacuum tube used in all TV sets.

**CTL** Control track logic.

**Cut-off frequency** That frequency beyond which no appreciable energy is transmitted. It may refer to either an upper or a lower limit of a frequency band.

**CW** Continuous wave (unmodulated).

**Damped oscillation** Oscillation which, because the driving force has been removed, gradually dies out, each swing being smaller than the preceding in smooth regular decay.

**dB** *See* Decibel.

**DC** Direct current. Electrical current that maintains a steady flow and does not alternate.

**DC restoration** Circuit in a camera or VCR which restores the dc signal elements to the picture, resulting in good blacks.

**Decibel** Subjective measure of sound volume or strength.

**Decoder** Device for decoding a coded signal.

**Definition** Degree of detail or sharpness in a TV picture.

**Delay line** Device used to delay video (Y) signal in a color set.

**Demodulator** Converts RF/IF to audio or video.

**Detail** Refers to the most minute elements in a picture which are distinct and recognizable. Similar to definition or resolution.

**Dichroic mirror** Mirror that reflects only certain wavelengths or colors and allows others to pass through.

**Distortion** Departure, during transmission or amplification, of the signal waveform received from that of the original waveform transmitted.

**Dropout** Loss of picture signal during tape playback—displays as a black or white streak in the monitor.

**Dropout compensator (DOC)** Electronic circuit that replaces a missing line of video information (dropout).

**Dubbing** Duplication of a videotape or the addition of new audio information to the tape.

**Echo (or reflection)** Wave that has been reflected at one or more points in the transmission medium, with sufficient magnitude and time difference to be perceived in some manner as a wave distinct from that of the main or primary transmission. Echoes may be either leading or lagging the primary wave and appear in the picture monitor as reflections or "ghosts."

**E-E** Electric-to-electric. Monitoring a signal being recorded.

**Electron gun** Assembly inside the TV or camera tube which fires electrons at the face of the tube and performs the scanning process.

**Electrostatic focus** Newer type of camera tube that is able to focus the electron beam without using heavy deflection coils.

**EM** Electromagnetic. Magnetic flux created by current through a coil.

**Encoding** Combining of electronic elements.

**Equalizing pulses** Pulses of one-half the width of the horizontal sync pulses which are transmitted at twice the rate of the horizontal sync pulses during the blanking intervals immediately preceding and following the vertical sync pulses. The action of these pulses causes the vertical deflection to start at the same time in each interval, and also serves to keep the horizontal sweep circuits in step during the vertical blanking intervals immediately preceding and following the vertical sync pulse.

**Erase head** Magnetic head that erases electronic information on the tape.

**ES** Electrostatic. Influenced by voltages only.

**E to E** Electronics to electronics. Method of analyzing the output of a VCR relative to its input.

**Expansion** Undesired increase in amplitude of a portion of the composite video signal relative to that of another portion. Also, a greater than proportional change in the output of a circuit for a change in input level. For example, expansion of the sync pulse means an increase in the percentage of sync during transmission.

**Ferrite** Brittle, high-frequency response material that is used to make video heads, coil slugs, transformer coils and "beads," etc.

**FG** Frequency generator, for developing an AC voltage that corresponds with VCR drum and capstan rotation.

**Field** One half of a complete TV scanning cycle, or 262½ scanning lines; one half of a 525-line TV frame.

**Field frequency** Rate at which a complete field is scanned, nominally 60 times a second.

**Fly-back** *See* Horizontal retrace.

**Flying erase head** Extra video head that erases video information during the editing process.

**Focus coil** Electromagnetic coil that surrounds the camera tube and focuses the electron beam.

**Following (or trailing) blacks** Term used to describe a picture condition in which the edge following a white object is overshaded toward black. The object appears to have a trailing black border. Also called "trailing reversal."

**Format** Limited grouping of similar VTRs, such as ½-inch and ¾-inch or small-format and large-format.

**Frame** Complete TV picture of 525 horizontal lines which is composed of 2 scanned fields of 262½ lines each. One complete TV frame is scanned in 1/30 of a second.

**Frame rate** Speed at which the frames are scanned—30 frames a second for video.

**Frequency** Number of times a signal vibrates per second.

**Frequency response** Ability of an electronic device to reproduce a wide range of frequencies.

**Freznel lens** Circular grooved lens used on projection sets.

**Front porch** That portion of the composite picture signal which lies between the leading edge of the horizontal blanking pulse, and the leading edge of the corresponding sync pulse.

**Gain** Level of signal amplification.

**Gate** Device consisting of diodes or transistors for "gating" logic signals.

**Ghost** Shadowy or weak image in the received picture, offset either to the left or right of the primary image, the result of transmission conditions which create secondary signals that are received earlier or later than the main or primary signal. A ghost displaced to the left of the primary image is designated as "following" (lagging). When the tonal variations of the ghost are the same as the primary image, it is designated as "positive" and when it is the reverse, it is designated as "negative."

**Glitch** Form of low-frequency interference appearing as a narrow horizontal bar moving vertically through the picture. This is also observed on an oscilloscope at field or frame rate as an extraneous voltage pip moving along the signal at approximately reference black level. Also, any picture distortion.

**Gray scale** Various shades of gray in a TV picture which correspond to color.

**Guard bands** Separations between the video tracks on the tape.

**HDTV** High-definition television.

**Head** Electromagnetic device that records or retrieves information from magnetic tape.

**Head switcher** Electronic analog switch for alternately switching rotating video and high-fi sound heads.

**Height** Size of the picture in a vertical direction.

**Helical scan** Helix-like method of recording video information on tape in which the signal is recorded diagonally in adjacent strips. Also called "slant track" recording.

**Hertz (Hz)** Cycles per second.

**High-frequency distortion** Distortion effects that occur at high frequency. Generally considered as any frequency above the 15.75-kHz line frequency.

**High-frequency interference** Interference effects that occur at high frequency. Generally considered as any frequency above the 15.75-kHz line frequency.

**High impedance (HI-Z)** 800–10,000 Ω. *See* Impedance.

**High lights** Maximum brightness of the picture, which occurs in regions of highest illumination.

**Horizontal (hum) bars** Relatively broad horizontal bars, alternately black and white, which extend over the entire picture. They may be stationary, or may move up or down. Sometimes referred to as a "venetian blind" effect. Caused by approximate 60-Hz interfering frequency or one of its harmonic frequencies.

**Horizontal blanking** Blanking signal at the end of each scanning line.

**Horizontal resolution** Number of vertical lines that can be perceived by a video camera in a horizontal direction on a test chart.

**Horizontal retrace** Return of the electron beam from the right to the left side of the raster after the scanning of one line.

**Horizontal sync** Sync pulses that control the horizontal scanning of the electron beam—generally, 15.73 kHz.

**IC** Integrated circuit, solid state IC "chip."

**Iconoscope** Camera tube in which a high-velocity electron beam scans a photo-emissive mosaic that has electrical storage capability.

**IDTV** Improved-definition TV.

**Impedance** Resistance of a component to the flow of electrons—rated in ohms (Ω). Generally expressed as high impedance (high-$Z$) or low impedance (low-$Z$).

**Interference** In a signal transmission path, extraneous energy which tends to interfere with the reception of the desired signals.

**Interlace** Process of scanning whereby the alternate lines of both scanned fields fall evenly between each other.

**Interlaced scanning (interlace)** Scanning process in which each adjacent line belongs to the alternate field.

**Ion** Charged atom, usually an atom of residual gas in an electron tube.

**Ion spot or blemish** Spot on the fluorescent surface of a cathode ray tube, which is somewhat darker than the surrounding area because of bombardment by negative ions, which reduce the sensitivity.

**Ion trap** Arrangement of magnetic fields and apertures that will allow an electron beam to pass through but will obstruct the passage of ions.

**IPS** Inches per second. Tape speed or writing speed.

**Jitter** Tendency toward lack of synchronization of the picture. It may refer to individual lines in the picture or to the entire field of view.

**Kilohertz (kHz)** Thousand cycles (hertz).

**Kinescope ("Kine")** Process of recording a TV picture by photographing a TV set with a film camera.

**Leading blacks** Term used to describe a picture condition in which the edge preceding a white object is overshaded toward black. The object appears to have a preceding or leading black border.

**Leading white** Term used to describe a picture condition in which the edge preceding a black object is shaded toward white. The object appears to have a preceding or leading white border.

**LED** Light emitting diode.

**Level** Average intensity of an audio or video source.

**Limiter** Electronic circuit that adjusts or limits the audio or video intensity to a preset level.

**Line frequency** Number of horizontal lines scanned in one second—15,750 lines or 15.7 kHz.

**Low-frequency distortion** Distortion effects that occur at low frequency. Generally considered as any frequency below the 15.75-kHz line frequency.

**Low impedance** 30 to 600 Ω. *See* Impedance.

**Luminance** Photometric brightness or radiance of a light source.

**Magnetic brake** Utilizing magnetic flux to slow down a motor or other rotating device.

**Magnetic focus-magnetic deflection** Tube-focusing design that requires external focusing coils.

**Matching transformer** Device that changes the impedance of the audio or TV signal.

**Matrix** Electronic circuit that is used to combine several electronic signals.

**Megahertz (MHz)** 1 million hertz.

**Microphonics** In video transmission, refers to the mechanical vibration of the elements of an electron tube resulting in a spurious modulation of the normal signal. This usually results in erratically spaced horizontal bars in the picture.

**Microsecond** One millionth of a second.

**Mil** Unit of measurement used for denoting videotape width, 1 mil = 0.001 inch.

**Mistracking** Picture distortion caused by improper tape-to-head or tape-path contact. Also related to tuners.

**Mixer** Device that combines and blends two or more audio or video sources.

**Modulation** Process of adding video and audio signals to a predetermined carrier frequency.

**Modulator** Circuit that superimposes audio or video on an RF/IF carrier.

**Moire** Herringbone interference patterns in a TV picture.

**Monitor** TV set without receiving circuitry that is used primarily to display video signals.

**Monitor/receiver** Dual-function standard TV receiver and monitor.

**Monochrome** Black and white.

**MTS** Multi-channel TV sound (stereo).

**Multiple blanking lines** Evidenced by a thickening of the blanking line trace or by several distinct blanking lines as viewed on an oscilloscope. May be caused by hum.

**Multiplexer** System of optics that allows simultaneous use of slide and film projectors as inputs for a video camera.

**Negative image** Refers to a picture signal having a polarity which is opposite to normal polarity and which results in a picture in which the white areas appear as black and vice versa.

**Noise** The word "noise" is a carryover from audio practice. Refers to random spurts of electrical energy or interference. May produce a "salt-and-pepper" pattern over the picture. Heavy noise sometimes is called "snow."

**Non-composite video signal** Video signal that contains picture and blanking information only, no sync.

**NTSC** National TV System Committee. U.S. color TV standard.

**One line delay** *See* Dropout compensator.

**Oscilloscope** Electronic test device that measures electronic signals. It is used for alignment of video equipment.

**Overshoot** Excessive response to an undirectional signal

change. Sharp overshoots are sometimes referred to as "spikes."

**Oxide** Magnetic particles that are bonded on recording tape.

**Pairing** Partial or complete failure of interlace in which the scanning lines of alternate fields do not fall exactly between one another but tend to fall (in pairs) one on top of the other.

**PCB** Printed circuit board.

**Peak** Highest level of signal strength.

**Peak to peak** Amplitude (voltage) difference between the most positive and the most negative excursions (peaks) of an electrical signal.

**Pedestal** Part of the composite video signal that corresponds with the blackest portions of the picture.

**PG** Pulse generator for servo control. *See* FG.

**Phase** Relative timing of one signal to another, as measured in degrees.

**Photoemissive** Emitting or capable of emitting electrons upon exposure to radiation in and near the visible region of the spectrum.

**Picture monitor** This refers to a cathode ray tube and its associated circuits, arranged to view a television picture.

**Picture signal** That portion of the composite video signal which lies above the blanking level and contains the picture information.

**Picture tube** Cathode ray tube used to produce an image by variation of the intensity of a scanning beam.

**Polarity** Positive and negative orientation of a signal.

**Preamplifier** Electronic circuit that raises the signals high enough to be fed into an amplifier.

**Preemphasis (predistortion)** Change in level of some frequency components of the signal with respect to the other frequency components at the input to the transmission system. The high-frequency portion of the band is usually transmitted at a higher level than the low-frequency portion of the band.

**PWM** Pulse width modulation.

**Random interlace** Unstable type of sync which allows the two scanning fields to fall randomly on top of each other.

**Raster** Scanned or illuminated area of the TV picture tube.

**RBG** Red, blue and green or chrominance signal.

**Reference black level** Level corresponding to the specified maximum excursion of the luminance signal in the white direction.

**Reference white level** Level corresponding to the specified maximum excursion of the luminance signal in the white direction.

**Registration** Precise overlapping of the red, blue, and green signals to form a correctly colored image.

**Remote control** Hand-held device for controling TV or VCR.

**Resolution (horizontal)** Amount of resolvable detail in the horizontal direction in a picture. It is usually expressed as the number of distinct vertical lines, alternately black and white, which can be seen in three-quarters of the width of the picture. This information usually is derived by observation of the vertical wedge of a test pattern. A picture which is sharp and clear and shows small details has a good, or high, resolution. If the picture is soft and blurred and small details are indistinct it has poor, or low, resolution. Horizontal resolution depends on the high-frequency amplitude and phase response of the pickup equipment, the transmission medium and the picture monitor, as well as the size of the scanning spots.

**Resolution (vertical)** Amount of resolvable detail in the vertical direction in a picture. It is usually expressed as the number of distinct horizontal lines, alternately black and white, which can be seen in a test pattern. Vertical resolution is primarily fixed by the number of horizontal scanning lines per frame. Beyond this, vertical resolution depends on the size and shape of the scanning spots of the pickup equipment and picture monitor and does not depend upon the high-frequency response or bandwidth of the transmission medium or picture monitor.

**Retrace (return trace)** *See* Horizontal retrace; Vertical retrace.

**RF amplifier** Amplifier used for amplifying RF signals.

**R-F pattern** Term sometimes applied to describe a fine herringbone pattern in a picture. May also cause a slight horizontal displacement of scanning lines resulting in a rough or ragged vertical edge of the picture. Caused by high-frequency interference.

**Ringing** Oscillatory transient occurring in the output of a system as a result of a sudden change in input. Results in close-spaced multiple reflections, particularly noticeable when observing test patterns, equivalent square waves, or any fixed objects whose reproduction requires frequency components approximating the cutoff of the system.

**Roll** Lack of vertical synchronization which causes the picture as observed on the picture monitor to move upward or downward.

**Roll-off** Gradual attenuation of gain-frequency response at either or both ends of the transmission pass band.

**Rotary erase head** *See* Flying erase head.

**Rotary transformer** Brushless method of transferring video signals from the rotating video heads to the VCR electronics.

**RPM** Revolutions per minute.

**Saturation** Intensity of the color.

**SAW filter** Sharp cutoff filter for separating video and chroma signals.

**Scanner** Video head drum.

**Scanning** Process of breaking down an image into a series of elements or groups of elements representing light values and transmitting this information in time sequence.

**Scanning line** Single continuous narrow strip of the picture area containing high lights, shadows, and half-tones, determined by the process of scanning.

**Serrated pulses** Series of equally spaced pulses within a pulse signal. For example, the vertical sync pulse is serrated in order to keep the horizontal sweep circuits in step during the vertical sync pulse interval.

**Serrations** Term used to describe a picture condition in which vertical or nearly vertical lines have a sawtooth appearance. The result of scanning lines starting at relatively different points during the horizontal scan.

**Servo** Feedback circuit for controlling and synchronizing drum and capstan to a reference signal.

**Shadow mask** Large screen containing half a million holes which helps focus the color electron beams inside a color TV set.

**Signal** Information transposed into electrical impulses.

**Signal-to-noise ratio** Amount of visible "snow or noise" in a given picture relative to the actual picture signal. The higher the signal-to-noise ratio, the better the picture.

**Skew** Tape tension.

**Slant track** *See* Helical scan.

**Smear** Term used to describe a picture condition in which objects appear to be extended horizontally beyond their normal boundaries in a blurred or "smeared" manner.

**Snow** Heavy random noise.

**Solenoid** Electromagnetic circuit control device.

**Solid state** Electronic circuitry that contains no vacuum tubes.

**Spike** *See* Overshoot.

**Startup/shutdown** TV system used as protection against x-rays and set damage.

**Streaking** Term used to describe a picture condition in which objects appear to be extended horizontally beyond their normal boundaries and, in extreme cases of low-frequency distortion, can extend over a whole line interval.

**Subcarrier** A subcarrier of a main carrier, e.g., the 3.58-MHz color subcarrier.

**Switcher** Video switching and mixing device.

**Sync** Abbreviation for the words "synchronization," "synchronizing," and so on. Applies to the synchronization signals, or timing pulses, which lock the electron beam of the picture monitors in step, both horizontally and vertically, with the electron beam of the pickup tube.

**Synchronization** Maintenance of one operation in step with another.

**Sync level** Level of the tips of the synchronizing pulses.

**Tape path** Path of the videotape past the heads.

**Target** Image-forming area of the camera tube.

**Tearing** Picture condition when the image is displaced horizontally, usually caused by horizontal sync problems.

**Termination** Resistance or load that must occur at the end of a video signal—usually 75 Ω.

**Tracking** Position of the video head over the recorded signal on the videotape.

**Transients** Signals that endure for a brief time prior to the attainment of a steady-state condition. These may include overshoots, damped sinusoidal waves, and so on, and therefore, additional qualifying information is necessary.

**2:1 interlace** Method of scanning whereby both scanned fields are evenly spaced together.

**UHF** Ultrahigh frequency. TV frequencies, 470–812 MHz.

**VCO** Voltage-controlled oscillator.

**VCR** Videocassette recorder.

**Vertical blanking** Refers to the blanking signals that occur at the end of each field.

**Vertical frequency** Number of vertical fields scanned every second—60.

**Vertical interval** Time during which the VTR switches from one head to another and the picture is blanked out.

**Vertical retrace** Return of the electron beam from the bottom to the top of the raster after completion of each field.

**Vertical sync** Sync pulses that control the vertical scanning of the TV picture—59.94 Hz.

**Vestigial sideband transmission** System of transmission wherein the sideband on one side of the carrier is transmitted only in part.

**VHF** Very high frequency.

**Video** Term pertaining to the bandwidth and spectrum position of the signal which results from television scanning and which is used to reproduce a picture; picture information.

**Video band** Frequency band utilized to transmit a composite video signal.

**Videocassette** One reel of videotape and one empty reel in a closed plastic container.

**Video switcher** *See* Switcher.

**Watt** Unit of electrical power.

**Writing speed** Resultant difference between the speed of the video heads and the speed of the videotape.

**Xtal** Oscillating crystal for controlling frequency.

**Y** Symbol for the luminance portion of a color signal.

# Index

## A



## B

## C

## D

## E



## F



## G



## H

## I



## J



## K



## L



## M

## Y



## Z